P9-EDJ-454

God's Generals

God's Generals

Why They Succeeded
and Why Some Failed

Roberts Liardon

ALBURY PUBLISHING
Tulsa, Oklahoma

Unless otherwise indicated, all Scripture quotations are taken from the *King James Version* of the Bible.

7th Printing

God's Generals
Why They Succeeded
and Why Some Failed

ISBN 1-88008-947-5

Copyright © 1996 by
Roberts Liardon
P. O. Box 30710
Laguna Hills, California 92654

Published by ALBURY PUBLISHING
P. O. Box 470406
Tulsa, Oklahoma 74147-0406

All possible efforts were made by ALBURY PUBLISHING to secure permission and insure proper credit was given for every entry within this book.

Endorsements

The strength and power of the body of Christ today did not come by accident. True, it is a work of the Holy Spirit, but the Holy Spirit anoints faithful and humble servants to bring about His purposes. In this book, Roberts Liardon has done a masterful job of opening new windows of insight upon the lives of some of the greatest heroes of the faith. *God's Generals* will encourage you and strengthen you to succeed in whatever purpose God has for you in His kingdom.

Dr. C. Peter Wagner
Author and Professor of Church Growth, Fuller Theological Seminary
Pasadena, California

A project which combines the stories of great twentieth century Pentecostal preachers into one book has been much needed, and I am sure this publication will be greatly appreciated. I am glad my mother, Aimee Semple McPherson, has been included among God's other Generals, for she served wholeheartedly as a pioneer in the front line trenches for the greatest of all Generals, her Lord Jesus Christ. I appreciate the tribute this book has given her.

Rolf K. McPherson
President, International Church of the Foursquare Gospel
Los Angeles, California

Until Roberts Liardon came along, very few people here had heard of John Alexander Dowie, Maria Woodworth-Etter, Jack Coe, and the likes. His teachings have impacted the young churches of Asia in a very profound way. The lessons we can learn from the great revivalists of the twentieth century — what attributed to their successes and failures — are absolutely vital to propel an emerging generation to greater spiritual heights as we enter a brand new millennium.

Hee Kong
Pastor, City Harvest Church; President, City Harvest Bible Training Centre
Singapore

I've known Roberts Liardon since he was a teenager. I met him when he was searching for information about my father, Jack Coe Sr., who is one of the twelve Generals studied in this book. I was impressed with Roberts' diligence then, and am happy to see the fruit that has been born from his life and ministry today. I recommend this book for not only its historical value, but for the insight into what it takes to carry the very power of God.

Jack Coe Jr.
International Evangelist; President, Christian Fellowship
Dallas, Texas

Roberts Liardon is one of America's leading experts on the dynamic healing ministries of the nineteenth and twentieth centuries. Having spent almost two decades researching and studying the most significant spiritual leaders whose lives have been characterized by signs, wonders, and miracles, Liardon presents a powerful and inspirational panorama of their ministries. This is the first comprehensive volume to bring together a thorough survey of these giants of the faith. It is church history at its best.

Paul G. Chappell, Ph.D.
Dean of Graduate School of Theology, Oral Roberts University
Tulsa, Oklahoma

God's pioneers are controversial figures. They often get things wrong, perhaps, because few if any have been this way before. Roberts Liardon has done an excellent job in providing well researched material on God's Generals, the pioneers of Pentecostal and Charismatic history. Through reading this book your faith will be inspired, and you shall learn a few lessons along the way.

Gerald Coates
Pioneer International

We need to rediscover our Pentecostal heritage. As we seek to tap into the pure stream of Pentecost that stretches from the pages of the New Testament to the revivals of this century — we will see God take us to our full potential in Him. Roberts Liardon has recognized the importance of honoring those who have gone before us, learning from their mistakes, and drawing inspiration from their testimonies. I know from hearing Pastor Roberts' presentation on the material in this book, that the years he has spent studying the lives of these great men and women of God have resulted in a resource that will encourage, exhort, and teach many in this generation. I give it my highest recommendation knowing that it will change lives and re-introduce to us an element of Pentecostal living with which many are unfamiliar.

Colin Dye B. D.
Pastor, Kensington Temple
London, England

Dedications

I want to dedicate this book to three groups of people:

To my Associate Pastors, Larry and Kathy Burden, and to my congregation at Embassy Christian Center in Irvine, California. I want to especially thank you for all of your faithfulness, your loyalty, and your trustworthiness. I want you to know that I recognize you as one of the best gifts I have in the call of God.

To Pastors Hee and Sun Kong and the congregation in City Harvest Church in Singapore, I want to especially thank you for the encouragement and the very special friendship that we share together. Your fellowship is a very important part of my life. It's great to be an official member of your church, even though I am thousands of miles away!

To Pastors Richard and Gail Perinchief and their congregation at Spirit Life Christian Center in Florida, I want to especially thank you for your loyal friendship through the years. And I want to thank you for the uniqueness that we seem to have in our heavenly call – we always seem to end up preaching together in the same nation, at the same time! It's wonderful to minister throughout the nations with you, as well as being counted as your friend.

My friends, we must never quit in our pursuit to reach the high call of God!

Contents

Foreword

I want to commend my dear friend and fellow minister, Roberts Liardon, for this contribution to making known the history of the great moving of God through the ministry of His true Generals. This book will show you their strengths and their weaknesses.

It is clear that this is not the work of a man, but of the Holy Spirit of the living God. It will show you that it is not what we are, or what we possess in ourselves that God is depending on, but what He can make of us!

As you read this most inspiring book, you will be stirred to remember that the God of Elijah is your God — just as He was the God of His other past Generals. So take your Bible now and read Hebrews 11:1-12:2 before you embark on this historic journey, and you will see that "all truth is parallel."

God has always had His Generals — "For many are called, but few are chosen" (Matthew 22:14). God would not have us to forget this as we see many new Generals emerging on the battlefields today. So always let us look to "Jesus the author and finisher of our faith" (Hebrews 12:2).

This literary work is destined to be a spiritual classic. It will show you that even the smallest, seemingly insignificant person can be used by God. Roberts' commentary is powerful and practical, and will leave you with great hope to succeed.

God's Generals were diamonds in the rough — mostly unsophisticated, uneducated by man's standards — yet vessels God recognized who possessed the unique characteristics that He could use if they would surrender their call.

Will you?

Dr. Morris Cerullo, President
Morris Cerullo World Evangelism
San Diego, California

11

Preface

Roberts has always had a hunger to understand the calls of great men and women of God. As his mother, I saw his spiritual hunger develop in two ways.

First, as a very young boy, Roberts' interest grew because my mother told him so many stories about great ministers and their camp meetings, of which she had been a part. Her descriptions were lively and vivid, and with almost every story, she would have a lesson to preach.

Second, when Roberts was twelve years old, the Lord appeared to him and instructed him to study the lives of the great men and women of God. The Lord told Roberts that this intensive study would be an important part of his training for the ministry.

Immediately after that visitation from the Lord, Roberts began to study. In our house there was already an atmosphere conducive to study. I spent many years pursuing my education while the children were growing up, and I myself had a well-developed library. The combination of my mother's influence and my diligence to study seemed to impart into Roberts what he needed for that hour. I remember many nights when each of us would sit around the table, pouring over and highlighting books.

Roberts began to dig into every book he could find that had to do with a move of God. If he came upon a name in the book, he would research everything he could about that person. If in his research he discovered that the person had died, he searched until he found the closest living relative or friend. God's favor on Roberts' life was so evident. He would always be granted interviews with these people and inevitably was able to develop personal relationships with them. These people seemed to give Roberts whatever he asked for, whether it was artifacts, pictures, or books.

There never seemed to be any fear or inhibitions about Roberts' pursuits. I remember one particular incident when he was in junior high school. I had come home from work to find that somehow, Roberts had made contact with someone overseas who was eager to help him do research on the revivalists and reformers like Evan Roberts and John Wesley. The more he studied, the more the doors would open to him. He was obeying God, so the doors had to open. When other people who were pursuing the same end as Roberts would hear of the success that he had in obtaining materials they would ask, "How did you get these things?" He would answer simply, "I just asked."

I was a student and staff member at Oral Roberts University during the years Roberts was researching the lives of the Generals. Roberts spent a great

13

deal of time there studying the research materials at the Holy Spirit Research Center. In fact, he worked there for two summers, volunteering as they needed him. When the ORU staff discovered all the memorabilia that Roberts himself had obtained, they were very surprised. They offered to buy it. He actually considered the offer, but I put my foot down. Today, those materials are in the Reformers and Revivalists Library at his Bible college.

Roberts' desire to know and understand the lives of these men and women was as pure as it was diligent. I distinctly remember that when Roberts first stepped into the pulpit at age sixteen, his research was complete. He had fulfilled his assignment for that hour. He had no formal training, no connections, and no expertise. He just obeyed God. He was faithful to what was put before him, and that faithfulness matured into an international call. To me that is such a testimony of someone who not only understood the season of his life, but also completed it.

Roberts will probably always continue to research the lives of God's Generals. It is still part of his call. Now, the ministry has a research department responsible for continuing on with the research where Roberts left off when he stepped into his call to help prepare the nations for the return of the Lord.

Carol M. Liardon, B.S., M.L.S.
Executive Vice President, Roberts Liardon Ministries
Irvine, California

Acknowledgments

I want to personally thank two people:

My Editor, Denyse Cummings, and my Research Director, Laurel McDonald. As a team, we waded through endless research, interviews, writings, and edits, to put this book together and make it work. You two have helped me to fulfill a vital part of my call in the earth. Thank you, my friends.

Introduction

When I was almost twelve years old, the Lord appeared to me in a vision. In this vision, He told me to study the lives of the great preachers, to learn of their successes, and of their failures. From that day on, I gave a large portion of my life to the study of church history.

When prominent people in the secular world die, people begin to look at their natural accomplishments. But when leaders in the body of Christ die, I believe Jesus would have us look at not only what was accomplished in the natural world through their lives, but at what they also accomplished within the body of Christ. The purpose of their remembrance is not to praise or criticize the leaders, but to see him or her as an example for our own lives.

The "Generals" that are written of in this book were human. Their stories represent a collaboration of the way life is. I have not made anyone out to be superhuman or bionic. I have told of their tears, their laughter, their successes, and their failures. They were all persecuted, lied to, betrayed, slandered, as well as honored, adored, and supported.

But most importantly, I have attempted to reveal the secrets of the power in their individual calls to the ministry – how they operated, what they believed, and what motivated them to CHANGE each of their generations for God.

The failures that took place in the lives of these great men and women will attempt to take place again. But their successes also challenge us, and are waiting to be grasped again. There is nothing new under the sun. If there is something new to you, it is because you are new under the sun.

It takes more than a desire to fulfill the will of God. It takes spiritual strength. As you read these chapters, allow the Spirit of God to take you on a journey that points out the areas in your life which need to be focused or subdued. Then, determine that your life and ministry will be a spiritual success in this generation that will bless the nations of the earth to the glory of God.

Roberts Liardon

John Alexander Dowie

"The Healing Apostle"

"THE HEALING APOSTLE"

'**6 6 6** Will he dare pray for rain?...If he does and no rain comes, then he's not Elijah. If he doesn't, then he's afraid to — and that's almost worse.'

"At last the preacher dropped on his knees behind the pulpit. Never before had an audience followed his prayers with more strained attention. '...God, our Father, we have seen the distress of this land...look upon it now in Thy mercy and send rain....'

"Suddenly the General Overseer stopped...then said, 'Get to your homes quickly, for there is sound of abundance of rain.' But he was too late. Just as the multitude turned to go, rain descended in torrents."[1]

Few in our generation today know of the fascinating and dramatic ministry of John Alexander Dowie. Undoubtedly, this man succeeded in shaking the world at the turn of the century. He brought to the forefront of society, the visible Church of the living God – primarily in the area of divine healing and repentance. Whether one agreed with Dr. Dowie or not, the fact remains that his incredible story is one of unflinching faith and powerful vision. John Alexander Dowie's recorded converts numbered in untold millions. Although the end of his ministry is a tragic one, rarely has there been a mission containing more strength and vitality. His apostolic ministry was world-changing. From coast to coast it single-handedly challenged and triumphed over the great apostasy and lethargy of his time, demonstrating soundly that Jesus Christ is the same yesterday, today, and forever.

Against hypocritical, opposing clergy, fierce and slanderous tabloids, murderous mobs, and relentless city officials, Dr. Dowie wore his apostolic calling as a crown from God, and his persecution as a badge of honor.

Against hypocritical, opposing clergy, fierce and slanderous tabloids, murderous mobs, and relentless city officials, Dr. Dowie wore his apostolic calling as a crown from God, and his persecution as a badge of honor.

MORE THAN ORDINARY

John Alexander Dowie was born May 25, 1847, in Edinburgh, Scotland. His Christian parents, Mr. and Mrs. John Murray Dowie, named him what they hoped he would grow up to be: "John," meaning "by the grace of God;" and "Alexander," "a helper of men."

Born in poverty, one would have to see through the eyes of faith to ever believe what was to come in the future for this small child. Although his school attendance was irregular due to frequent illness, young Dowie portrayed brilliance and enthusiasm. His parents trained and helped him because they had hope for his call. Young Dowie was an active part of their prayer meetings and Bible studies. They never left him out of the ministry, and loved him dearly. This parental security produced a key element in his early foundation.

At the mere age of six, young Dowie read the Bible through from cover to cover. Deeply convicted by what he had read, he developed an intense hatred for the use of alcoholic beverages. A Temperance Movement was on the rise in Scotland at the time, and without even realizing the hand of God upon him, he campaigned against alcohol abuse and signed a petition to never partake of it.

Dowie continued to read the Bible and accompany his father as much as possible on "preaching journeys." On one such journey, he came upon a humble street preacher by the name of Henry Wright. As young Dowie listened to the details of the Gospel, he gave his heart to Jesus Christ.

...God continually spoke to him. His heart was constantly tugged toward full-time ministry. He realized there were many truths in the Bible that had been neglected by the clergy of that day.

At the tender age of seven, Dowie received his call to the ministry. But he didn't yet know how to answer.

At the age of thirteen, John and his parents left Scotland for a six-month journey to Australia. Once situated in this new country, John began to earn his living by working for his uncle in the shoe business. He soon left his uncle and began working at various other places, always in menial positions. And even then, his peers noticed that he was a "more than ordinary" young businessman. Dowie soon became the assistant to a firm's partner in a business that grossed more than $2 million a year.

Through these years of "climbing the occupational ladder," God continually spoke to him. His heart was constantly tugged toward full-time ministry. He realized there were many truths in the Bible that had been neglected by the clergy of that day. One such teaching – divine healing – had been realized at his own expense. Dowie had been a sickly child. And he suffered from "chronic dyspepsia," a severe indigestion problem that plagued him in his teen years. But, after reading the will of God concerning healing, Dowie petitioned the Lord and was "completely delivered of the affliction."[2] And this divine manifestation was only a token of the revelation that was to come in his life.

Finally, at the age of twenty-one, Dowie made an absolute decision to answer the call of God. He would take the money he had saved from his occupation and begin studying under a private tutor to prepare for the ministry. Fifteen months later, he left Australia to enroll in Edinburgh University, to study in the Free Church School. Majoring in theology and political science, he was not regarded as a model student because of his disagreements with the professors and their doctrine. He challenged their lethargic interpretations brilliantly. John Dowie had an incredible hunger and thirst for the Word of God. He read constantly, and had a photographic memory. This established him far beyond his superiors in substance and accuracy.

While in Edinburgh, Dowie became the "honorary chaplain" of the Edinburgh Infirmary. It was there that he had the unique opportunity to sit under the famous surgeons of his day, comparing their diagnoses with the Word of God. But as patients lay helplessly under chloroform, Dowie heard these surgeons lecture on their medical inadequacies. It was then that he realized these surgeons could not heal, and that they could only resort to removing the diseased organs, hoping for a cure. He watched many surgeries end with deadly results. As he heard from the lips of these medical professors the confession that they were only guessing in the dark, and witnessed their experiments, Dowie developed a strong antipathy to surgery and medicine.[3]

Many today still accuse Dowie of condemning the medical field. But I want to point out that in his time, the medical practice was very primitive. And he was one of the privileged few who saw behind the scenes. He witnessed how the physicians of his day offered great hope to patients, but confessed in private that they knew nothing. He saw poor victims paying untold amounts of money in the hope for a cure, while receiving the worst of results. He despised falsehood, so, he searched for an answer. And when he began to publicly come against their deceiving methods, his accusations proved true.

While studying at Edinburgh University, Dowie received a cablegram from his father in Australia. In response, he made a hasty return home to free himself from any inheritance in the family business because of his love for the ministry.

Because he dropped everything and returned home so quickly, he was under a tremendous financial strain. But, he resolved that this setback would not hinder him and vowed that he would fulfill the mission of his life. He would be an ambassador for God in full-time ministry.

Soon Dowie accepted an invitation to pastor the Congregational Church in Alma, Australia. His duties were divided among several churches. And as was to be expected, his bold preaching sent uneasy rifts throughout the church. Persecution quickly arose against him and resentment was openly voiced because of his penetrating method of ministry. Dowie was a visionary, but despite his repeated endeavors, he was unable to arouse the people from their lethargy. Although he needed the church financially, he chose to resign the pastorate because he felt it a waste of time to continue with them.

John Alexander Dowie was a reformer and a revivalist. This kind of calling *has to see results* because of the passion for God that burns so strongly within them. He loved people, but his commitment to the truth caused him to focus only on groups that would respond.

Soon after his resignation, he was asked to pastor the Congregational Church in Manly Beach. He was warmly received. But, once again, he was distraught over their lack of repentance and sensitivity to the Word of God. Still, Dowie remained with this pastorate. His congregation was small and it gave him the time to pursue his studies and gain direction.

He knew he was a man on a mission, but he had no idea of where or how his mission would be accomplished.

As time passed, Dowie continued to have a tossing restlessness in his spirit. He knew he was a man on a mission, but he had no idea of where or how his mission would be accomplished.

He began to long for larger congregations, and an opportunity soon opened to pastor a larger group in Newton, a suburb of Sydney. So in 1875, Dowie moved again. Unknown to him at the time, this move would take him into the revelation that would launch his ministry into worldwide acclaim.

"OH, COME AT ONCE! MARY IS DYING...."

While pastoring in Newton, a death-wreaking plague swept through the region, particularly in the outskirts of Sydney. People were dying at such a high rate that the population was totally paralyzed with fear and dread. Within a few short weeks at his new appointment, Dowie had presided over forty funerals. Sickness and death seemed to be waiting at every corner. The tragedy of it all struck the heart of Dowie to such an extreme, that he sought for immediate answers. And he knew those answers were available in God's Word. Listen to the sense of tragedy the young pastor wrote in his own words:

> "I sat in my study in the parsonage of the Congregational Church, at Newton, a suburb of Sydney, Australia. My heart was very heavy, for I had been visiting the sick and dying beds of more than thirty in my flock, and I had cast the dust to its kindred dust into more than forty graves within a few weeks. Where, oh where, was He Who used to heal His suffering children? No prayer for healing seemed to reach His ear, and yet I knew His hand had not been shortened.... It seemed sometimes as if I could almost hear the triumphant mockery of fiends ringing in my ear whilst I spoke to the bereaved ones the words of Christian hope and consolation. Disease, the foul offspring of its father, Satan, and its mother, Sin, was defiling and destroying ...and there was no deliverer.

> "And there I sat with sorrow-bowed head for my afflicted people, until the bitter tears came to relieve my burning heart. Then I prayed for some message.... Then the words of the Holy Ghost inspired in Acts 10:38, stood before me all radiant with light, revealing Satan as the Defiler, and Christ as the Healer. My tears were wiped away, my heart was strong, I saw the way of healing...I said, 'God help me now to preach the Word to all the dying around, and tell them how 'tis Satan still defiles, and Jesus still delivers, for He is just the same today.'

> "A loud ring and several loud raps at the outer door...two panting messengers who said, 'Oh, come at once, Mary is dying; come and pray.' ...I rushed from my house and ran hatless down the street, and entered the room of the dying maiden. There she lay, groaning, grinding her teeth in the agony of the conflict with the destroyer...I looked at her and then my anger burned....

> "In a strange way it came to pass...the sword I needed was still in my hands...and never will I lay it down. The

doctor, a good Christian man, was quietly walking up and down the room.... Presently, he stood at my side and said, 'Sir, are not God's ways mysterious?' 'God's way!...No sir, that is the devil's work and it is time we called on Him Who came to "destroy the work of the devil."'[4]

Offended by the words of Dowie, the doctor left the room. Dowie turned to Mary's mother and asked why she had sent for him. Learning that she wanted the prayer of faith, Dowie bowed by the girl's bed and cried out to God. Instantly the girl lay still. The mother asked if her daughter was dead, but Dowie replied, **"No...she will live. The fever is gone."**[5]

Soon, the young girl was sitting up in bed and eating. She apologized for sleeping so long and exclaimed how well she felt. And as the small group thanked the Lord, Dowie went into the room of her brother and sister, prayed for them, and they were instantly healed.[6]

From that moment on, the plague was stayed as far as Dowie's congregation was concerned. Not another member of his flock died of the epidemic. And as a result of this revelation, the great healing ministry of John Alexander Dowie was launched.

From right to left: John, Gladstone, Jeanie, and Esther Dowie

WEDDING BELLS

Soon after his remarkable revelation of divine healing, Dowie began to think about a possible mate. When he did, he found he was in love with his first cousin, Jeanie, and that he could not be happy without her. After many controversial discussions with family members, it was agreed that the two should marry. So at the age of twenty-nine, on May 26, 1876, John Dowie married Jeanie and the two began their incredible mission together.

Their first son, Gladstone, was born in 1877. But Dowie had misjudged certain persons in financial matters and found himself in great financial hardship. So Jeanie and Gladstone were sent to live with her parents until the situation could be worked out. Needless to say, such a decision caused an even greater turmoil, due to the in-laws' mistrust of their son-in-law. However, even through these shaky hardships, Dowie remained a man of divine vision. In the midst of the chaos, he held fast to the work before them and wrote this to his beloved wife: **"...I can see that future far more clearly than I can solve the mysteries of the immediate present."**[7]

Every ministry has a future. But we must believe in that future or we will never take the first step. Like Dowie, we must determine to hold fast to the Word of God and fight for what is ours in the earth. Setbacks are always present, but we determine if the problem is to remain permanent. Even though we are called, we still have to war against spiritual evils that are sent to destroy our vision and to discourage us. God's angels can help, but the war for our destiny is a personal responsibility that we must win.

NO MORE RELIGION!

During this trying time, Dowie made an unprecedented decision to leave the denomination he was a part of. He couldn't understand or operate with the cold, lethargic state of their leadership. And he burned with a passion to proclaim the message of divine healing throughout the city. His congregations had grown to over twice the size of the others. But his success spoke to deaf ears, and he was constantly fighting through the politics and "letter of the law" theology that threatened to dampen his faith.

Because of the hostility presented by denominational leaders, he found himself constantly on the defensive. In a letter to his wife proclaiming his decision to begin an independent ministry, Dowie wrote that the political system of his denominational church:

> **"...killed initiative and individual energy, made men denominational tools, or worse, caused them to become worldly-minded, and left them high and dry and useless for the most part – good ships, but badly steered and terribly overladen with worldliness and apathy."**[8]

Dowie had come to realize that revival was possible if the church could be awakened. He considered the vast opportunities that lay ahead of him. He studied the lethargic side of the church, then he studied the unchurched. He made the decision that reaching the vast number of the unchurched would result in a greater fervor for Jesus Christ. And he decided to stop his laborings among the cynical. So he determined that his mission would reach the uncared for and perishing masses of the city with the revelation that Christ was the same yesterday, today, and forever.

In 1878, Dowie broke free from his denomination and secured the Royal Theatre in Sydney to begin an independent ministry. Hundreds flooded the theatre to hear his powerful messages. But, once again, a lack of funds halted his work. Though the crowds were large, many had no financial income. The only answer Dowie could see was to sell his home and furnishings, put the money into the work, and move to a smaller residence. After Dowie did this, the work flourished. In a message describing his decision, he said:

> *...he determined that his mission would reach the uncared for and perishing masses of the city with the revelation that Christ was the same yesterday, today, and forever.*

"My beautiful furniture and pictures were gone, but there came in place of them men and women that were brought to the feet of Jesus by the sale of my earthly goods."[9]

In Dowie's passion, he had no thought for the strong opposition that arose against him. He vehemently denounced the evils of the day and formed a group to distribute literature city-wide. Violent persecution, mostly from local pastors, arose from these pamphlets. Still Dowie was merciless in dealing with the lethargic clergy. He didn't mince his words, responding that he **"did not recognize their right to request any information of his actions, nor did he have any respect for their judgment."** He answered one minister:

> **"I consider your judgment to be as feeble and incapable as your ministry.... I wish I knew who distributed these 'obnoxious tracts' among your flock; I would certainly commend his choice of a field...."[10]**

Part of Dowie's call was to deal with moral evils. A strong stance on morals usually goes with a strong healing ministry. (Sin causes much of the sickness and disease.) But Dowie paralyzed his critics with such astute sharpness, that it led them to consort and plan in private to destroy him. And so the stage was set for the seemingly invincible John Alexander Dowie.

MISREADING THE CALL

Dowie was an apostle who didn't have the complete understanding of that office. The anointing he carried pierced the religious theocracies of his day, but there were few who understood him, including himself. As a result, he misunderstood several administrations that came with the passion of his office. One passion was in the area of politics.

Dowie's leadership was gaining a strong national influence. So seeing his potential and knowing his stand, the Temperance Society asked him to run for Parliament. At first, he opposed the idea. But he later changed his mind, thinking he could possibly influence more in the political arena and decided to enter the race.

But Dowie suffered a sound defeat in the elections. The local newspapers that had been so damaged by his ministry, waged an all-out attack against him. The politicians and alcoholic beverage industry paid untold amounts of money to see him slandered and defeated. After the election, Dowie had wounded his church, and disgraced his ministry.

Dowie was moved by such strong spiritual yearnings that he sought to fulfill them in the natural. I can only speculate why he made this move. It could have been because the church world wasn't grasping the truth fast enough to satisfy him. Whatever his reason, he misread the timing and plan of God for his ministry.

We need to understand that God has a central point from which every aspect of our lives operate, whether individually or corporately. That area is called "timing." From the operation of that one word, lives can move forward with God or be hindered. Nations can advance spiritually, or regress. Life in the spirit realm has a timing to it just as life in the natural. Therefore, it is vitally important for us to follow the leading of our spirit. We must learn that it's not always right to move into action because it seems like the thing to do. This kind of obedience only comes from seasons of prayer and intercession.

Politicians and the political arena have never changed the world, church-wise or government-wise. Only a people whose hearts are changed by the Gospel can transform civil laws and regulations. Politics are meant for compromise to please people as a whole. The apostolic office presents the Word of the Lord, then it is up to the people to conform to and follow it. The apostolic and political don't mix. Dowie with his calling, should have never resorted to a political lifestyle.

While campaigning for office, Dowie also neglected his commandment to preach divine healing. He simply steered away from his calling to pursue a personal goal, thinking he could reach a greater mass of people. And as a result, the rest of his time in Australia was spent in darkness and futility.

PEOPLE CAME FROM EVERYWHERE

Dowie finally repented and in 1880 returned to the message of divine healing, with great physical and spiritual blessings coming to him as a result. The gifts of the Spirit began to manifest in his life and revelation abounded like never before. Because of his spiritual obedience, thousands were healed under his ministry. Persecution abounded, even to the point that his enemies in organized crime once schemed to plant a bomb under his desk. The bomb was set to explode during the late hours Dowie kept, but he heard a voice that said "Arise, go!" The third time he heard it, he grabbed his coat and went home to finish his work. Within minutes after arriving safely home, the bomb exploded under his desk, several blocks away.

> *The gifts of the Spirit began to manifest in his life and revelation abounded like never before. Because of his spiritual obedience, thousands were healed under his ministry.*

In 1888, Dowie sensed the unction to come to America, then possibly on to England. His unction became reality in June of that year as he passed under the Golden Gate Bridge in San Francisco. Newspapers carried the story that Dowie was heading for America, and that people were coming from all parts of California to be healed. From morning until evening, halls would overflow with people waiting for an audience with Dowie, and he would pray for only one person.

The reformer had a unique way of praying for the sick. He fervently believed no one could come for healing unless they were born again and had repented of any lifestyle contrary to the Gospel. He was usually indignant if he sensed worldliness on someone who came for healing. As a result, he prayed for very few people early in his ministry – but the ones he did pray for were instantly healed.

FORSAKING THE DIVINE

Soon Dowie began healing crusades up and down the coast of California. It was during this time that he met Maria Woodworth-Etter, the great woman healing evangelist. But there arose a conflict between them, and Dowie denounced her method of ministry. I believe this was a tragic mistake on his part.

In our lives, we have many relationships, casual and sometimes intimate. But the most significant ones to the kingdom of God are "divine relationships." In every call, whether secular or ministerial, God sends divine relationships to help strengthen your walk with Him. We may have many casual relationships, but divine relationships are very few. They can usually be counted on one hand.

I believe Dowie and his family missed a tremendous opportunity to have a divine relationship with Maria Woodworth-Etter. But for some reason, possibly a "manly-ministerial" pride, Dowie crucified Etter every chance he got. Once he attended her meeting, took the stage, and proclaimed her to be of God. But he forsook that leading of the Spirit, and later renounced her.

Etter's method of ministry made Dowie uneasy, because he didn't understand it. But he never took the time to speak with her privately about it, heart to heart. His ministry "preference," or favorite style of ministry, caused him to cut Maria off. Etter also had a revelation of divine healing, but she was more experienced in cooperating with the Spirit. And she had the spiritual strength to speak into Dowie's life. She could have instructed him on how to live out of his spirit while resting his body at the same time. Dowie had a problem in this area. He sometimes worked forty-three hours straight in his passion. Through Maria, he could have befriended others of like faith and call, furthering his own ministry. But he didn't.

As a result, Dowie experienced only casual relationships with certain followers, rather than the kind of divine relationship he could have had with other fellow leaders.

I think it's interesting to note that Dowie interviewed the great impostor of his day, Jacob Schweinfurth, who claimed to be Jesus Christ.[11] He also challenged the famous atheist, Robert Ingersoll, to a confrontation.[12] But he never gave Sister Etter the courtesy of a conversation.

Don't miss your divine relationships in life. There will always be fellow laborers, but divine relationships are few and far between.

FINALLY, A HOME

Persecution from envious ministers began to rise feverishly against Dowie. But by this time, he had become a veteran in the art of facing opposition. Persecution brought out his brilliance and strength and he never gave those bringing it thought *unless* they were in the immediate way of his mission.

Dowie toured the regions of America and eventually chose to settle in Evanston, Illinois, outside of Chicago. The Chicago newspapers bitterly attacked him, calling him a false prophet and impostor. They boldly declared that he was not wanted in Chicago. But none of their attacks caused Dowie to flinch. He remained where he had chosen, and ministered wherever he felt led to go.

Once while speaking at a divine healing convention in Chicago, he was summoned to pray for a lady dying from a fibroid tumor. At the time, Chicago was the second largest city in America. There were strong, evil spiritual influences ruling Chicago, and Dowie was very interested in establishing his headquarters there. So he took this woman's request for healing as a test as to whether or not he should begin a work in the city. The woman's tumor was reportedly the size of a coconut that had grown into various parts of her body. When Dowie prayed for her, she was instantly healed. In fact, the healing was so remarkable that several Chicago newspapers ran the story. Now he was convinced, and Dowie made his worldwide headquarters within the city. His enemies didn't like it, but Dowie didn't care.

The World's Fair was to open within a matter of months, so Dowie built a small wooden "hut" outside its gates. From the top of the hut named, "Zion Tabernacle," hung a flag with the words, "Christ is All." Services went on day and night. Though the beginning was small, the crowds grew steadily, and soon people had to stand outside in the snow to get a glimpse of the miraculous healings taking place inside.

> *...Dowie built a small wooden "hut" outside its gates. From the top of it hung a flag..., "Christ is All."*

As was true in Australia, Dowie had opened the doors to the city of Chicago by way of divine healing. Never before or since has one man so captured a city. Still, Dowie experienced the fight of his life in those early years. He demonstrated God's Word in power, and by so doing, the medical profession and the religious churches suffered financially. So the newspapers frantically formed a list of allies, including ministers, to pull out all the stops to paralyze his ministry. But none could tarnish his work. To their dismay, the constant articles and unrelenting slander only caused his work to increase.

ANOTHER HOME — JAIL!

By now, hundreds of people flooded the city of Chicago to attend Dowie's services. As a result, lodging was difficult to come by, so Dowie opened several large rooming houses called "Healing Homes." Here, the sick who had come for healing could find shelter and rest between the services held at Zion Tabernacle. Once there, they were able to receive constant ministry from the Word until their faith mounted to the place of complete manifestation. But the newspapers, mainly the *Chicago Dispatch*, were merciless, calling the homes "Lunatic Asylums" and continued to print every lie imaginable.[13]

Because of these healing homes, Dowie's enemies thought they had found a vulnerable spot. So early in 1895, they arrested him on the charge of "practicing medicine without a license." Obviously untrue, Dowie would have been the last person to allow medicine into his homes. He hired a brilliant attorney, but he only kept Dowie advised of the legal matters. So Dowie chose to represent himself in court because no one else could articulate his call as accurately as himself.

Dowie's superior intellect was not enough to overrule the evil jurisdiction of the court. Despite his profound arguments, the court fined him. But they never dreamed he would take the case to a higher court, costing much more money than the fines they had issued. When he did, the higher court denounced the evil of the lower court, and reversed the decision.

The city hoped Dowie would get discouraged if they continued to arrest and fine him. So before the year was over, he had been arrested one hundred times. Although severely persecuted, he was never discouraged. Persecution brought out great resiliency in his character. He actually thrived on his persecutor's affliction and interrogation.

Evil will always try to persecute the power of God. But Dowie was supernaturally secure and anchored in his godly authority. The supernatural never bows to the natural.

LEAVES OF HEALING

Having foiled the legal system, his enemies then plotted to take away his mailing privileges. By 1894, Dowie's newsletter, *Leaves of Healing*, had a weekly worldwide circulation. It was filled with teachings and healing testimonies. Needless to say, the newsletter was very dear to his heart. Dowie fondly spoke of it as the "Little White Dove."

True to his form, Dowie never minced words in his writings. He fervently denounced sin and exposed evil industries. And those who were the most hurt by the publication saw it as another opportunity to end his ministry. *Leaves of Healing* also warned its readers of lethargic and controlling denominations.

People loved Dowie's dramatics and straightforward talk. Many wanted to say the same thing themselves, so they looked to him as their voice. Even those who despised him read the newsletter to see what he had to say. As a result, circulation increased rapidly. Much of his support and ministry was attributed to this publication.

The Postmaster General of Chicago was a devout Catholic. So to take his mailing privileges, Dowie's enemies gave one of his sermons that renounced the infallibility of the Pope to this man. The Postmaster was instantly offended and revoked his second-class mailing privileges, forcing Dowie to pay fourteen times the usual cost!

But Dowie could not be outdone. He paid the increase and solicited his readers to write Washington, D.C., to tell of this injustice. His supporters came out in full force, and he was granted an immediate audience with the Postmaster General in Washington. Once Dowie shared his story and showed the malicious lies printed in the Chicago newspaper, both the editor and the paper were denounced by the U.S. government. In fact, by 1896, this particular editor, one of Dowie's greatest persecutors, was put in prison on a separate charge and was made a public spectacle, forever ruined.

While in Washington, Dowie was also granted an audience with President William McKinley. He assured the president of his prayers while in office and the president warmly thanked him. While leaving the White House, Dowie commented to his staff that he feared for McKinley's life. He later asked his followers to pray for the safety of the president because he was not properly guarded.[14] But in spite of Dowie's prophetic warnings, President McKinley was shot in Buffalo, New York, on September 6, 1901. He died eight days later, being the third U.S. president to be killed by an assassin.

"ZION HAS COME"

By the end of 1896, Dowie had gained great influence over the city of Chicago. His enemies were either dead, in prison, or silent. The local police, who had once arrested him a hundred times, were now his friends and protected him at a moment's notice. The political officials, including the mayor, had all been voted in by Dowie's people. Divine healing was preached on every street corner. Dowie had sectioned off the districts of the city, and sent teams called "The Seventies" proclaiming the Gospel into each area.

Soon, there was scarcely a person in Chicago who had not heard the Gospel message.

Soon, there was scarcely a person in Chicago who had not heard the Gospel message. Now Dowie was praying for thousands every week to receive divine healing. Sadie Cody, niece of Buffalo Bill Cody, was miraculously healed, having first read a copy of *Leaves of Healing*. Among other notable healings were Amanda Hicks, cousin of Abraham Lincoln; Dr. Lillian Yeomans; Rev. F. A. Graves; John G. Lake's wife; and the wife of a U.S. congressman.

34

Through his apostolic mantle, John Alexander Dowie literally ruled the city of Chicago for Jesus Christ. He leased the largest auditorium in Chicago for six months, and moved the great Zion Tabernacle into the building, filling its six thousand seats at every service.

Now Dowie was finally able to pursue the dream he had long held in his heart – to organize a church on apostolic principles. It had been his lifelong desire to bring back the teachings and foundation of the early church found in the book of Acts. So, in January, he held his first conference and laid the groundwork. The work was named "Christian Catholic Work," with the name "Catholic" meaning "universal," and was by no means connected to the Roman Catholic Church.

He would never allow this church to be known as a "new thing." He looked at it as a "restoration" of the principles that had been lost to the body of Christ. His theology was good in that he warned if something was "new," then it was "false." Within a few years, Dowie's Christian Catholic Church had multiplied into tens of thousands.

I believe without a doubt, that all of the five-fold ministries listed in Ephesians 4 are alive and well today (see verses 11-13). The apostolic office was not done away with when the original twelve died. Nor did God allow His plan for the Church to die when the apostles' flesh did. His new covenant principles were to continue until His return. They aren't bound by men's ideas or theology, nor do His promises end when men get nervous. There have been many more than the original twelve apostles, and men today are still called to that office.

Ephesians 2:20 says the foundations of the Church are built upon the apostles and prophets, with Jesus Himself being the chief cornerstone. Great authority comes with the office of an apostle, and I believe God sovereignly chooses and equips those He wants to stand there. But there has always been a lack of knowledge concerning the administration of that office. I believe Dowie was sovereignly called and equipped as an apostle. And I don't believe his ministry failed because he accepted the apostolic office. But I do believe that because of his lack of knowledge and understanding, that he misread the spiritual operations of his office. And I believe that this in itself was the main spiritual deficiency that caused him to misuse his authority.

During the time in which Dowie's church was being instituted, some very interesting events transpired. This period has been called, "The Golden Years" of Zion.[15] The next three years were quiet, prosperous, and influential. It was then that Dowie made his secret plans for his special city.

Dowie and wife, Jeanie, seated in front of trophy wall at Christian Catholic Church

Dowie preaching in Australia

Last photo of Dowie before his death

Knowing that such an effort would produce curiosity, Dowie diverted the attention of the multitudes by declaring a "Holy War," and announced a coming message entitled "Doctors, Drugs, and Devils." Advertising the message for weeks, the title caused no small stir. Then while his enemies were distracted by it all, Dowie secretly hired proprietors to survey land forty miles north of Chicago to build a city. After they found sixty-six hundred acres on Lake Michigan, Dowie dressed himself up as a tramp so as not to be recognized, then toured the site. And before his enemies could discover what was happening, the land had been purchased, and decisive plans were made for building the city of Zion, Illinois.

Dowie unveiled the architectural plans for Zion at the New Year's Eve Watch Night service on January 1, 1900. His business ability was praised by his people and the secular world, for starting the Zion Land Investment Association. Subdivisions were allotted, and home-building began. The land was not to be sold, instead it was to be leased for a period of some eleven hundred years. The terms of the lease strictly forbade the possession or use of tobacco, liquor, and swine's flesh anywhere within the limits of the city.[16] And in two years' time, houses had been erected and the city was taking shape.

THE ELIJAH COMPLEX

Though his "moral utopia" seemed to abound, those closest to Dowie noticed a change. Trouble was brewing in Zion. There was no longer any time for divine healing to be preached because all of Dowie's efforts were focused on running the city. He deemed himself as Zion's General Overseer. The rule of the city was to be absolutely in his hands. And problem after problem arose to cleverly divert him from his original ministry command.

Eventually Dowie had so sadly diverted from God's plan for his life that he embraced the suggestion and proclaimed it as truth. He believed he was Elijah.

It was during this season that some ministers came to Dowie and proclaimed him to be the Elijah foretold in the Bible. At first, Dowie soundly denounced them. But their words kept "ringing in his ears." Then after awhile Dowie himself said a voice seemed to say, "Elijah must come, and who but you is doing the work of Elijah?"[17]

Eventually Dowie had so sadly diverted from God's plan for his life that he embraced the suggestion and proclaimed it as truth. He believed he was Elijah. He even went on to believe that by establishing other cities like Zion outside of every major city in America, that he could eventually have the money to build outside of Jerusalem. His plan was to buy out the Turks, the Muslims, and the Jews to take over Jerusalem for Jesus so He could establish His city during the millennial reign. Dowie was thoroughly deluded. Soon his preaching had deteriorated into the mere denouncing of his enemies. He also gave "lectures" on political views while he exhorted his hearers to invest more heavily into the work of the city.[18] He took counsel from no one, except in minor matters. And he removed all restraints that could have kept him in check or hindered his plans.

THE MADISON SQUARE KNOCKOUT

What was once a persecution battle against the Word of God had now become a personal war to maintain Dowie's own level of influence. It was godly persecution that activated the mantle of his apostolic office, but now he was fighting to maintain his own personal influence and success. And it destroyed him.

A vividly sad example of Dowie's vanity in this area happened at what was deemed, the "New York Visitation." The bishop of the Methodist church and the editor of its denominational newspaper, Dr. Buckley, asked for an interview with Dowie. So Dowie granted them audience and thought that he had fully persuaded them to believe his acclamations. But he hadn't. According to Buckley's newspaper article, Dowie was "in the moonlit border land of insanity where large movements of limited duration have sometimes originated." Buckley also added, "If he believes it or not, he is but another impostor."[19] Enraged, Dowie rented the Madison Square Garden, and though financially strained, arranged for eight trains to take thousands of his followers to New York City. Once there, he planned to make an open show of the two men to demonstrate the power he still held. What was once inspired by God's divine direction, was now reduced to

John Alexander Dowie, General Overseer of Zion in his high priest robe.

Dowie's own self-appointment. It was totally in the flesh. He reacted out of a hurt and emotional wound and now he was determined to display his vengeance.

The event failed miserably. Though thousands went with Dowie, thousands more came who had another plan. They filled the Garden, but as Dowie took the platform to speak, they began to exit by the droves. The scene confused Dowie terribly and kept him from speaking as he had originally planned. As a whole, the city of New York was virtually unaware that anything had transpired at this meeting. It was as if God silenced the newspapers and had mercy on His servant.

THE FATEFUL END

By now, the city of Zion was broken financially. So Dowie sought to escape by taking an expensive trip around the world where he found himself unwelcome in many cities. It was on this trip that his train pulled into Pomona, California. There had been a severe drought in the land, and no rain had fallen for eight months. So the reporters chided Dowie, reminding him that Elijah prayed for rain during drought in Israel and rain came. And that if he was Elijah, surely he would do the same for California. Dowie did indeed pray for rain at the end of his service, and before the crowd was dismissed, rain was falling in torrents.

Upon leaving California, Dowie planned a venture into Mexico to establish "Zion Plantation." He was hoping this new venture could pay for the debts of the old. But his followers, now broken financially and disillusioned, had left him in heart. They couldn't help but notice how poor they had become – while Dowie lived in extremes, hosted lavish parties, and left for a world tour.

Some say Dowie built his own city because he was tired of the persecution. But in my personal opinion, that doesn't seem true. Although greatly anointed and sent by God, it seemed that Dowie had a weakness for power and success. He said of himself:

"In becoming an apostle, it is not a question of rising high, it is a question of becoming low enough.... I do not think that I have reached a deep enough depth of true humility...of true abasement and self-effacement, for the high office of an apostle...."[20]

Jesus never commanded us to build communes. Jesus commanded us to "Go!" not "Huddle." The book of Acts "commune" didn't work for long either

(Acts 2:44-47; 5:1-10). Persecution hit the group, and they were scattered to the uttermost regions of the earth. (Acts 8:1.) Why? So the Great Commission in Matthew 28:19-20 could be fulfilled. We are to be lights in the world and penetrate Satan's darkness. Huddling together won't accomplish that feat.

The greatest test of a leader is not in the area of persecution, though many fall there. I think one of the greatest snares comes in the form of power and success. We must never think we've "made it" and begin to dictate our personal power as a result of God-given success. Success brings a multitude of avenues and ventures. If we get caught up in the vast selections that come from success and *fail to develop our spiritual tenacity*, we can fall victim to the "whirlwind." We can't find peace with our past by using the power of the present. With each new height, we must build a new tenacity. That's why some churches grow to a certain level, then become comfortable, or fall. The leadership become too busy with the "avenues" and lose the time and energy to develop both themselves *and* their members for higher levels in God.

Whenever we obey God, success should come. So never be afraid of success! But to properly administrate success, we must hold ourselves in the strength of the Spirit, listening for His direction – *not our own*. It is only through the strength of the Spirit and a hunger for God, that we are able to continue in what God has spoken, pioneering into the next level.

> *We must never think we've "made it" and begin to dictate our personal power as a result of God-given success. Success brings a multitude of avenues and ventures. If we get caught up in the vast selections that come from success and fail to develop our spiritual tenacity, we can fall victim to the "whirlwind."*

Dowie soon proclaimed himself as the First Apostle of a renewed, end-time Church, denounced his last name, and signed his documents as "John Alexander, First Apostle."[21] But not long after his "self appointment," Dowie suffered a stroke on the platform from which he delivered his last sermon. Then while he was out of the country to recover, the city of Zion held an organized meeting to vote Dowie out.

Dowie fought this decision to the last ounce of his strength but never succeeded in regaining his position. He was allowed to live his last days inside of Shiloh House, his home for many years, and slipped into eternity on March 9, 1907. His death was documented with these words by Judge V. V. Barnes:

"...the last night John Alexander spent on earth, he was again in spirit upon this platform talking to the assembled multitudes of his people. He preached during that night and thought he was preaching the principles of the Gospel to the assembled thousands. As he taught the same old truths...he lapsed again into slumber, awaking from time to time and continuing the dispensation of the old gospel message. The last song he ever sang as the morning light began to appear was, 'I Am a Soldier of the Cross.' Then they listened for his last sentence, and he said, 'The millennium has come; I will be back for a thousand years.' These were the last words that he spoke; the last sentence he uttered."[22]

How could such a great life end in such sadness? Are there any answers? Again, I believe the answer lies in a basic misunderstanding of spiritual principles.

Dowie was spiritually assigned by God to the city of Chicago – and he conquered it. While living within that city, and carrying out his divine appointment, principalities and powers couldn't touch him. But Dowie seemed to move out of Chicago through his own desire for power and gave the devil freedom to destroy his life. When he left the city of his calling, the enemy killed his worldwide influence through deception, killed a member of his family, destroyed his marriage, and destroyed Dowie himself with "every form of disease" fastening to his body.[23]

We must remain with the original, anointed plan of God for our lives and allow Him to open the avenues to administrate it. Maybe Dowie should have built *churches* and *Bible schools* instead of a *city*. That avenue would have sent thousands into the ministry from his godly influence.

Dowie did go on in peace to be with the Lord. Those who were with him at the end said he had returned to his faith of the early years. Many even testified that he had become a gentle, loving man who acted as if a tremendous burden had been lifted. And the city of Zion, Illinois, remains today, but the leadership is divided among many brethren, "...as no single person could completely fill Dr. Dowie's shoes."[24]

A GREAT OBJECT LESSON

Gordon Lindsay, John Alexander Dowie's official biographer and founder of Christ for the Nations in Dallas, Texas, described Dowie's ministry as "the greatest object lesson in the history of the church."[25] Pertaining to ministry, his life was filled with vivid, instructional detail. The lessons we can learn are never meant to degrade or criticize this great man of God. His personal problems should be held separate from the call of God.

John Alexander Dowie went down in history as an impostor, yet he was a genius called of God. Even in the midst of his error, he prophesied the coming of radio and television to our generation. He had his failures, but from his influence came many great men of God. His ministry produced John G. Lake, the great apostle to South Africa; F. F. Bosworth, and his brother B. B. Bosworth, whose healing campaigns touched untold millions; Gordon Lindsay, whose life and ministry resulted in the great interdenominational college, Christ for the Nations, in Dallas, Texas; Raymond T. Richey, healing crusader; and Charles Parham, "The Father of Pentecost," whose Bible school in Topeka, Kansas, ushered in another move of the Holy Spirit. Many more had large radio ministries and powerful mission works.

> *John Alexander Dowie went down in history as an impostor, yet he was a genius called of God.*

Without a doubt, John Alexander Dowie succeeded in making the Bible alive to untold millions. He was an instrument used of God to restore the keys of divine healing and the revelation of repentance to a lukewarm, lethargic generation. If there is a moral to the message of the failure in his life, that message is this: Never sway from what God has commanded you to do in the earth. No matter what your age, your generation has not passed until you exit the earth and enter heaven. So if God has commanded you to fulfill a commission, make *it* your utmost priority as long as you live.

CHAPTER ONE, JOHN ALEXANDER DOWIE
References

[1] Gordon Lindsay, *John Alexander Dowie: A Life Story of Trials, Tragedies and Triumphs* (Dallas, TX: Christ for the Nations, 1986), 228-229.

[2] Ibid., 15.

[3] Ibid.

[4] Ibid., 22-24.

[5] Ibid., 25.

[6] Ibid.

[7] Ibid., 43.

[8] Ibid., 44-45.

[9] Ibid., 46.

[10] Ibid., 49.

[11] Ibid., 95.

[12] Ibid., 151.

[13] Ibid., 107-109.

[14] Ibid., 133-135.

[15] Ibid., 161.

[16] Ibid., 173.

[17] Ibid., 188.

[18] Ibid., 199.

[19] Ibid., 221.

[20] Ibid., 155-156.

[21] Ibid., 235.

[22] Ibid., 260-261.

[23] Ibid., 251.

[24] *This We Believe*, Handbook of the Christian Catholic Church, 7.

[25] Lindsay, *John Alexander Dowie, A Life Story*, Introduction.

CHAPTER TWO

Maria Woodworth-Etter

"Demonstrator of the Spirit"

"DEMONSTRATOR OF THE SPIRIT"

66"The Lord has given me a special mission to bring about a spirit of unity and love.... God is raising up people in every land who are reaching out after more of God and saying, 'Come and help us. We want the spirit of love. We want the signs and wonders.'"[1]

There hasn't been a greater demonstrator of God's Spirit since the book of Acts in Pentecostal history than Maria Woodworth-Etter. She was an incredible woman of vision and spiritual strength who stood in the face of fierce opposition, lifted her tiny hand, and allowed the Holy Spirit to spread His fire. Sister Etter lived in the realm of the spirit as a powerful vessel of God's divine leading and His supernatural manifestations. She was a faithful friend of heaven, choosing to lose her earthly reputation to gain a spiritual one.

Maria (pronounced "Ma-ri-ah," not "Ma-ree-ah") was born in 1844 on a Lisbon, Ohio, farm. She was born again at the beginning of the Third Great Awakening at the age of thirteen. The preacher who led her to the Lord prayed that her life "might be a shining light."[2] But little did he realize that this little girl he had just prayed for would become the grandmother of the Pentecostal Movement that would spread throughout the world.

Maria immediately heard the call of God and dedicated her life to the Lord. Of her calling she would later write, "I heard the voice of Jesus calling me to go out in the highways and hedges and gather in the lost sheep."[3] But one thing stopped her – she was a woman – and at that time, women were not allowed to preach. In the mid-nineteenth century, women couldn't even vote in a national election, so to be a woman preacher

> "I heard the voice of Jesus calling me to go out in the highways and hedges and gather in the lost sheep."

was definitely frowned upon. And to be a *single* woman in the ministry was out of the question. Therefore, Maria pondered the things the Lord told her, and decided she would have to marry a missionary to fulfill her call. So she planned to continue her education, then enter a formal college to make herself ready.

★★★★★

But tragedy struck her close-knit family. Her father was killed while working in the fields of their farm and she immediately returned home to help support her family. Now her hopes of a formal education were shattered, so she settled into what she thought was a normal Christian lifestyle.

"ANGELS CAME INTO MY ROOM...."

During the Civil War, Maria met P. H. Woodworth, who had returned home from the conflict after being discharged with a head injury. She had a whirlwind courtship with the former soldier and soon married him. They took up farming, but nothing ever came of their labors. It seemed as if everything was failing.

Over the years, Maria became the mother of six children. So she tried to settle into a normal family home life while the Lord continued to call her. But Maria, exasperated in her role as a wife and mother, couldn't answer the call. She was married to a man with no desire for ministry, she had six children to raise, and she was sickly herself. Then real tragedy struck their home. The Woodworths lost five of their six children to disease. Maria was able to pull herself together after this horrible episode, but her husband never recovered from the loss. She did her best to help him while raising their only surviving daughter. Through all these situations she never grew bitter against God, nor did she harden her heart as a result of the loss.

> *Angels came into her room. They took her to the West, over prairies, lakes, forests, and rivers where she saw a long, wide field of waving golden grain. As the view unfolded she began to preach and saw the grains begin to fall like sheaves.*

But Maria needed answers for the nagging heartache that oppressed her because of the calamity that struck her family. Refusing to give up, she began to search the Word of God. And as she read, she saw how women were repeatedly used by God throughout the Bible. She read Joel's prophecy predicting that the Spirit of God would be poured out upon men AND women. But Maria would look to heaven and say, **"Lord, I can't preach. I don't know what to say and I don't have any education."** Still, she continued to read and find truth in the Word of God while she struggled with her call. She would later write, **"The more I investigated, the more I found to condemn me."**[4]

Then Maria had a great vision. Angels came into her room. They took her to the West, over prairies, lakes, forests, and rivers where she saw a long, wide field of waving golden grain. As the view unfolded she began to preach and saw the grains begin to fall like sheaves. Then Jesus told her that, "just as the grain fell, so people would fall" as she preached.[5] Finally Maria realized that she would never be happy until she yielded to the call. In response to this great vision from God, she humbly answered **"yes"** to His call upon her life and asked Him to anoint her with great power.

"W-O-M-A-N" DOES NOT SPELL "W-E-A-K"

Many women reading this book are called of God to preach. You have had visions and unctions from God's Spirit to go and set people free. God has spoken to you in the area of divine healing, deliverance, and freedom of the Spirit. So never allow a religious spirit to silence what the Lord has spoken to you. Religion likes to suppress women and their ministries, especially young ones. You need to learn to obey God without question. If Maria had answered from her youth, possibly her children wouldn't have died. I'm not saying that God killed her children. But I am saying that when we directly disobey God, our actions open the door to the works of the devil. His work is to destroy. God's work is to bring life. So learn to obey God with boldness. Boldness brings the power of God and will leave your accusers speechless in your presence. Also find some strong women with solid ministries from whom you can learn. And allow these words of Sister Etter to stir you in your heart:

> **"My dear sister in Christ, as you hear these words may the Spirit of Christ come upon you, and make you willing to do the work the Lord has assigned to you. It is high time for women to let their lights shine; to bring out their talents that have been hidden away rusting; and use them for the glory of God, and do with their might what their hands find to do, trusting God for strength, Who has said, 'I will never leave you.' Let us not plead weakness; God will use the weak things of the world to confound the wise. We are sons and daughters of the Most High God. Should we not honor our high calling and do all we can to save those who sit in the valley and shadow of death? Did He not send Moses, Aaron — *Miriam* to be your leaders? Barak dared not meet the enemy unless Deborah led the van. The Lord raised up men, women, and children of His own choosing — Hannah, Hulda, Anna, Phoebe, Narcissus, Tryphena, Persis, Julia, the Marys and the sisters who co-labored with**

Paul. Is it less becoming for women to labor in Christ's kingdom and vineyard now than it was then?"[6]

Seek the Spirit of God for yourself. If you are called, you will have to answer for it. Obey God without question. He will handle the details.

THEY WEPT THROUGHOUT THE HOUSE

Maria first launched her ministry into her own community. She had no idea of what she would say, but God told her to go and that He would put the words in her mouth.[7] And God fulfilled His Word. As Maria stood before her first crowd, most of them relatives, she opened her mouth, and the crowd began to weep and fall to the floor. Some got up and ran out in tears. After this Maria was highly sought throughout her community. Several churches asked her to come and revive their congregations. Soon she expanded her ministry westward and had held nine revivals, preached two hundred sermons, and started two churches with Sunday school memberships of over a hundred people. God honored Maria and made up for her lost years in a short amount of time.

One particular meeting was held in a town called Devils Den. No minister had ever been successful there, and people came to mock her. They were looking to see the female evangelist who would soon run out of town shattered and defeated. But they received the surprise of their lives! Sister Etter might have been a woman, but she was not one to be taken lightly. She knew the key to spiritual warfare, and the fervency of prayer that unlocked heaven.

For three days Maria preached and sang. No one moved. Finally, on the fourth day, she exercised her spiritual authority through intercession and tore down the demonic principality that ruled over Devils Den. She prayed that God would show a great display of His power to break the people's stiff formality. That night, people throughout the meeting cried and repented to God. It was the greatest manifestation of the presence of God the town had ever witnessed.

THE DEMOLITION DERBY FORCE

We are not called to give up. We are called to obey God at whatever cost and to let success answer our critics. If it seems you have hit a hard place in your life or ministry, don't whine and complain. Don't offer your reasons for it. Pray! Explanations and excuses rob us of strength and power. Don't shake your head and run. Use the authority that has been given you through Jesus and overthrow the demonic powers that blind the people. Through prayer, take authority and make a clear path for the Spirit of God to minister to the hearts of the people. Sister Etter groomed her spirit through prayer producing invincible strength. She was known as a revivalist who could break towns open.

THEY CAME SCREAMING FOR MERCY

Sister Etter pioneered the way for the Pentecostal manifestations that are so common in the movement today. It was not until she preached at a church in western Ohio that had lost God's power, that the meaning of her vision about the sheaves of wheat became clear.[8] It was at this church where the people fell into "trances." This was the one spiritual manifestation that marked her ministry highly, but brought fierce persecution.

Up to this point, this manifestation had not been known in the Church the way it is known today. In her own account she wrote:

"Fifteen came to the altar scream- ing for mercy. Men and women fell and lay like dead. I had never seen anything like this. I felt it was the work of God, but did not know how to explain it, or what to say."[9]

After laying on the floor for some time, these people sprang to their feet with shining faces while shouting the praises of God. Sister Etter said that she had never seen such bright conversions. The ministers and elder saints wept and praised the Lord for His "Pentecost Power." And from that meeting on, Sister Etter's ministry would be marked by this particular manifestation that always followed her preaching with hundreds coming to Christ.

> *Sister Etter pioneered the way for the Pentecostal manifestations that are so common in the movement today.*

"TRANCE" TALK

The trances became the talk of the day. Hundreds flocked to taste of this outpouring, while others went to observe or ridicule. At one meeting, fifteen doctors came from different cities to investigate the trances. One of the doctors was a world-class leader in his field. Sister Etter wrote of it this way:

"He did not want to admit the power was of God. He would have been glad if they could prove it was something else. He came to investigate...but was called to another part of the house. He went, expecting to find something new. To his surprise he found his son at the altar and wanted his father to pray for him. He could not pray. God showed him what he was, and what he was doing. He began to pray for

On the road

**himself. While praying he fell into a trance, and saw the
horrors of hell. He was falling in. After a terrible struggle
God saved him. He went to work to win souls for Christ."[10]**

Sister Etter also wrote of a party that several young women attended at
which they thought they would have fun and act out a trance. But they were
immediately gripped by the power of God, and their mocking turned into loud
cries to God for mercy.[11]

Once an elderly man who had traveled the world was visiting an area where
Maria was ministering. He was a religious man, so he decided to attend one of
her meetings out of curiosity. As he witnessed the meeting, he made some joking remark to his friends concerning the display of power. Filled with pride,
the man boldly headed for the platform to investigate. But before he reached
the pulpit, he was "struck to the floor by the power of God" and laid there for
over two hours. While in this state, God showed him a vision of heaven and
hell. Realizing he had to choose, he immediately chose God and was born
again. Then he came to, praising God.

The only thing this man could say once he came out of the trance was that
he regretted having spent sixty years lost in religion, never knowing Jesus

Christ personally.[12] Still, newspapers and unbelieving ministers warned others to stay away from the meetings. They said they "would make a person insane." Nevertheless, thousands were saved, many being "struck down, laying as dead men" even on their way home. It is said that many people also fell under the power in their homes, miles away from the meetings.

What are "trances"? They are one of the four ways God manifests in a vision. The first type of vision is an "inner vision." The picture you see in your inner man, or spirit man, will benefit you greatly if you heed it. Secondly, there is the "open vision." This vision comes when your eyes are wide open. It's like watching a movie screen open up in front of you as it displays a scene God wants to show you. Thirdly, is the night vision. This is when God gives a dream to make you aware of a certain thing. The last type of vision is the "trance vision." In this vision, natural abilities are frozen so God can minister whatever is needed. When people came up from a trance vision in Sister Etter's meetings, they told of seeing both heaven and hell.

Sister Etter's style was, to say the least, "different" from the ministers of her day. She never prohibited the audience from participating. Unlike the stoic church order of the late 1800s, Maria believed in shouting, dancing, singing, and preaching. She believed that emotional displays were important, as long as they were in order. And she believed that a lack of physical manifestation was a sign of apostasy.

Unlike the stoic church order of the late 1800s, Maria believed in shouting, dancing, singing, and preaching. She believed that emotional displays were important, as long as they were in order. And she believed that a lack of physical manifestation was a sign of apostasy.

FRENZY OR FULFILLMENT?

I believe God is upset with some of the churches today because they refuse to allow the people to openly and freely express themselves to Him. If people can't express themselves to God, then God can't move upon them. Some people are afraid of emotions in the church. They have no problem with them at home, or at a sporting event. But for some religious reason, they think the church should be quiet and serene. But let me tell you something, heaven isn't quiet and serene! Some people are in for a rude awakening when they die and go to heaven. They are going to have to learn how to rejoice along with the rest of us – because heaven is full of life and energy! We have a lot to shout about – both here *and* there!

Our churches *must* have a fresh move of God. And like it or not, *a move of God affects the emotions.* "Well, Roberts, I just don't believe God is in all that shouting and dancing." The shouting and dancing isn't God. It is simply an unconstrained response *to His power.* Listen, have you ever put your finger in a light socket and remained still? How much more when you touch God! When God touches you, you will react! If you say, "Well, what about the extremes?" I say, "Why are we so concerned about the ditch when we should be looking at the highway?"

Focus on the true, and the false will fade away. When the power of God comes upon you, you will enjoy it! And when you enjoy something, you show it. So learn the truth of what God loves in His worshippers, then do it.

Now you say, "Well, people will talk about us." I say, "So what?" The truth outlives a lie. What people don't understand, they persecute. They lied about Jesus, but He still lives today. When those people experience the true touch of God, they will change their minds.

"What if we lose money?" Well, is money your god? Let me remind you that monetary currency can't save souls. The Spirit of God is what draws mankind to Jesus. By obeying the Spirit, we lift up Jesus. There are no payoffs or short-cuts. If you are a church leader, you are commanded by God to obey the Holy Spirit and learn His ways. The Bible says it is those who are led by the Spirit that are the sons of God. (Romans 8:14.) So let Him lead!

If you are led by the Spirit, visions will increase in the Church. We must be spiritually mature to deal with any problems or evil spirits. New Age religions have dug so deeply into the wrong spirit realm that they've made the Church afraid to pursue the true manifestations of God's Spirit. The realm of the spirit holds both God and the demonic, and if the Holy Spirit is not your Guide when you enter, you are subject to the demonic. But New Agers don't enter the spirit realm with Jesus Christ. They come of their own will. And this is one place where they are deceived. We are nothing without the blood of Jesus. Some are afraid that if they pursue God supernaturally, they will be accused of being involved with the New Age. If you are following God's Spirit, He will keep you pure.

So open your church to the move of God, and learn from those who have gone on before you. Where the Spirit of God is, there is liberty, and yes, *order.* But I'm not talking about the fearful restraints of control or denominational suppression. People are hungry to see God and to be free. Some will travel across the continent to hear someone who truly knows God and the manifestations of His Spirit.

"SHE KNOCKS 'EM SILLY"

By the time Sister Etter reached age forty, she was a national phenomena. Various denominations recognized her ability to stir dead churches, bring in the unconverted, and cheer on a deeper spiritual walk with God. Doctors, lawyers, drunkards, and adulterers – people from all walks of life – were gloriously saved and filled with the Holy Spirit in her meetings. Because of one of her meetings in 1885, the police said they had never seen such a change in their city. The city had been so cleaned up that they had nothing to do![13]

One newspaper reporter wrote of Sister Etter:

"She goes at it like a foot pad tackles his prey. By some supernatural power she just knocks 'em silly when they are not looking for it, and while they are down she applies the hydraulic pressure and pumps the grace of God into them by the bucketful."[14]

She studied the Word and began preaching His divine will in healing. It didn't take long to see that evangelism and healing went hand in hand as thousands were won to Christ as a result of seeing others healed.

Eventually the Lord led Maria to begin praying for the sick. At first, she was reluctant, feeling it would take away from her evangelistic call. But God continued to make His will clear, and she agreed. She studied the Word and began preaching His divine will in healing. It didn't take long to see that evangelism and healing went hand in hand as thousands were won to Christ as a result of seeing others healed.

Maria preached that the strong manifestations of the Spirit were **"nothing new; they were just something the Church had lost."**[15] And she refused to get caught up in the pet doctrines of the day, desiring only for the Holy Spirit to do His works.

Once in a meeting, a crowd rushed to the platform and cried out, "What shall we do?" Maria finishes the story:

"They went down by the mighty wind power of the Holy Ghost. He sat upon the children of God till their faces shone like Stephen's when his enemies said he looked like an angel. Many received gifts; some for ministry, some as

Church built by Etter in Indiana known as the Etter Tabernacle

Sioux City, Iowa

Evangelist Mrs. M. B. Woodworth-Etter. In the last years of her ministry Etter always wore white when she ministered.

Etter in state

evangelists, some of healing, and hundreds of sinners received the gift of eternal life."[16]

In another meeting, over twenty-five thousand people crowded in to hear Sister Etter. And remember, in those days, there were no public address systems! Maria wrote that before she even finished preaching, the power of God fell on the multitude and took control of about five hundred as they fell to the ground.[17]

THE WILD, WILD WEST

Of course, Sister Etter's life was marked with great persecution. There were problems around every corner, not to mention the pressures that came from leading such huge masses of people who were experiencing their first manifestations of the Spirit. In addition to all of this, she was a woman in ministry who was married to an unfaithful man.

While ministering in her controversial crusade in Oakland, California, P. H. Woodworth's infidelity was revealed. Sister Etter stayed in separate quarters, choosing to leave him. Finally, after twenty-six stormy years of marriage, in January of 1891, they were divorced. Then, in less than a year and a half, P. H. Woodworth remarried and publicly slandered Maria's character and ministry. He died not long after on June 21, 1892, of typhoid fever.

Despite her stormy relationship with this man, Maria took time from her ministry schedule to travel to his funeral. It is said that she not only attended the funeral, but also took part in the memorial service.

Etter's greatest trials came while on the West Coast. She believed the West could be won to God, just as it occurred in the Midwest. So in 1889, she arrived in Oakland and purchased an eight-thousand seat tent. And soon, the tent was jammed with onlookers coming to see the trances, hear of the visions, and watch all the other manifestations of the Holy Spirit.

But heavy persecution also visited Maria on the West Coast. Hoodlums, or gangs as we call them today, started harassing her meetings. Several times these men hid explosives in the wood stoves – and miraculously – no one was ever injured. Once a windstorm even ripped the canvas of the tent apart during a meeting. Death threats were sent to her weekly, newspapers slandered her relentlessly, and ministers divided against her. Mischievous people would bring the mentally disturbed to her meetings, knowing they would cause a great emotional scene. This was done so many times, that many naive people thought it was Maria's meetings that drove these people to insanity! And because many misunderstood her theology, the citizens called for the authorities daily to shut her meetings down. Nevertheless, Maria refused to leave Oakland until she felt God was finished.

When it seemed the gangs began to get the upper hand in her meetings, the Oakland Police Department deputized "bouncers" to protect the services. But this got out of hand because the bouncers were inexperienced both in character and common sense.

Then there was the wild prophecy that came from Maria saying disaster would hit the coast and destroy it. After she spoke this, the newspapers terrorized Sister Etter and made her out to be a common criminal. They misquoted and hyped up the prophecy to such a degree that it was not accurately known what was actually said. Then as could be expected, other men and women operating in the counterfeits to the gifts of the Spirit jumped on the prophecy bandwagon. Deceived by the enemy, these people prophesied more doom and gloom for the West Coast, causing great controversy.

When it seemed the gangs began to get the upper hand in her meetings, the Oakland Police Department deputized "bouncers" to protect the services.

Sister Etter had a slew of prominent ministers both for and against her. One was John Alexander Dowie. While she was on the West Coast, he joined her critics and publicly blasted her "trance evangelism," calling it a great delusion.[18] No other minister but Etter matched his own ministry in the area of healing and publicity, so he often referred to her when he spoke of the abuses. Only once did Sister Etter even publicly defend herself against Dowie. She did so with these words:

> **"After stating in our meeting before thousands, that he never saw such power of God, and so wonderfully manifested, and after advising all his people to stand by me, he went up and down the coast preaching against me and the meetings, until he broke up all his missions. His only objection was that some were struck down by the power of God in our meetings.**
>
> **"He lectured against me two or three times in San Francisco, and said I was in line with Satan. Many went to hear him...but his talk was such that many people left in disgust**

while he was talking. I told the people that I had been his friend and had treated him like a brother, and that he was not fighting me, but the Lord and His Word. I always told the people that I would leave him in the hands of God and that I would go right on with the Master.

"I told them to watch and see how we would come out, and they would see that he would go down in disgrace, and that I would be living when he was dead."[19]

Sister Etter outlived John Alexander Dowie by seventeen years.

It can be said that Sister Etter did make some mistakes in her Oakland Crusade. And it isn't any wonder with all the attacks that were plotted against her. However, it should be remembered that in 1906, San Francisco did experience the most devastating earthquake in American history, and Sister Etter's prophecy came forth in 1890.

Sister Etter also made several good friends while there, one being Carrie Judd Montgomery. Montgomery had come from the East Coast to conduct meetings in California. The two met and developed a lifelong friendship. Carrie and her husband, George, were instrumental in the Pentecostal Movement and founded the *Home of Peace* in Oakland. The couple remained strong supporters of Sister Etter throughout their ministry.

"GIFT FROM GOD"

During this phase of Sister Etter's life, there were also some refreshing highlights. Besides the friendships she made, God didn't want her to carry the ministry mantle alone. It took some time, but ten years after her divorce, Maria met a wonderful man from Hot Springs, Arkansas, named Samuel Etter. God sent her the perfect mate. The two were married in 1902. Sister Etter had great respect for this gentleman and often referred to him as her "gift from God." Later she would write of him:

"He stood bravely with me in the hottest battle, and since the day we were married has never shrank. He will defend the Word and all the gifts, and operations of the Holy Ghost, but does not want any fanaticism, or foolishness. It makes no difference what I call on him to do. He will pray, and preach, and sing, and is very good around the altar. The Lord knew what I needed, and it was all

brought about by the Lord, through His love and care for me and the work."[20]

Three years after her marriage to Samuel Etter, Maria disappeared from public ministry and remained silent for the next seven years. No reason has ever been given for this long silence. But when she emerged seven years later, she was just as powerful as before, and now had the loving support of a wonderful husband. Samuel Etter faithfully loved and cared for Maria. He managed her meetings inside and out, and took care of all of her writings and book distribution. In fact, Sister Etter's ministry published several books:

1. *Life, Work, and Experience of Maria Beula Woodworth, Evangelist.*
2. *Marvels and Miracles God Wrought in the Ministry of Mrs. M. B. Woodworth-Etter for Forty Years.*
3. *Signs and Wonders God Wrought in the Ministry of Mrs. M. B. Woodworth-Etter for Forty Years.*
4. *Song Books.*
5. *Questions and Answers on Divine Healing.*
6. *Acts of the Holy Ghost (later published as "A Diary of Signs and Wonders").*

Some of Sister Etter's books were reprinted into several editions, and some were translated into foreign languages. Although we have a large selection of Christian books on the market today, Sister Etter's books are still very rare. I have personally been offered thousands of dollars for my private collection, which I have refused. In my opinion, no amount of money could buy what Sister Etter has written.

So, Samuel Etter – the husband, friend, editor, manager, and minister of helps – "gift from God" – found peace in his position as a support in his wife's ministry. His ability showed a rare and notable character as a man. As a result, he was a vital part of her ministry in almost every capacity until his death twelve years later.

PERSECUTION, PROBLEMS, AND JAIL TRIALS

Maria was the only leading evangelist of the Holiness Movement who embraced the Pentecostal experience of speaking in tongues. Today, we would have called her a "Pentecostal Holiness" preacher. She embraced the Holiness doctrine as well as the Pentecostal doctrine of speaking in tongues. Many ministers didn't understand the manifestations of the Holy Spirit, nor did they understand her doctrine about it. And Maria so rarely defended herself in public, that it was highly noted whenever she did. She would usually tell the people that she was not called to defend herself, but that she was called to lead others to Jesus Christ.

Sister Etter showed an invincible strength to carry on in the face of opposition. When harassed with life-threatening situations, she would refuse to leave a town until she was finished. And she was never afraid of unknown perils because she knew the Lord would fight for her. Many times, rowdy men would find their way into her meetings to disrupt them because of being paid to do so. Others came on their own volition. She once wrote:

Maria was the only leading evangelist of the Holiness Movement who embraced the Pentecostal experience of speaking in tongues.

"I have been in great dangers; many times not knowing when I would be shot down, either in the pulpit, or going to and from meetings...But I said I would never run, nor compromise. The Lord would always put His mighty power on me, so that He took all fear away, and made me like a giant...If in any way they had tried to shoot, or kill me, He would have struck them dead, and I sometimes told them so."[21]

One such man came to her meeting determined to break it up. He marched within ten feet of the platform and let out a stream of vulgarity and cursing. Then suddenly, his tongue refused to obey him as a "strange power seemed to grip his vocal chords." Totally protected by the Spirit of God, Maria seemed oblivious to the man's presence! Questioned later about the experience by two major newspapers, the shaken man replied, "Go up yourself and find out."[22]

Maria was arrested four times during her ministry, but three of the citations never made it to court. New England was the only place where she was arrested and actually taken to court. Her trial in Framingham, Massachusetts, was based on charges that she practiced medicine without a license and hypnotized people with trances. It was a grand spectacle for the cause of Christ. Many people testified on her behalf, retelling their personal testimonies that could be likened to stories in the book of Acts. The great author and founder of Bethel Bible School, E. W. Kenyon, was among those who testified. Kenyon would go on to later have a great healing and teaching ministry. He was a prolific author. Many of his books are used in Bible schools throughout the world.

The love Maria had for different cultures also caused racial persecution. She loved the African American and Native American communities just as she loved white people. She preached many times for the black churches, helped their preachers, and supported their revivals. She also went to an Indian reservation, staying for weeks at her own expense. All social classes were welcome in her home – rich and poor alike. Sister Etter loved them all.

"NOTHING SHORT OF A CIRCUS"

There is no one volume book that can describe all the acts in the ministry of Maria Woodworth-Etter. She was a humble, spiritual powerhouse who looked "just like your grandmother, but exercised tremendous spiritual authority over sin, disease, and demons."[23] Sister Etter couldn't answer all the invitations she received to minister. And the ones she did accept created a national stir that has never been silenced.

One such meeting was planned by the then young pastor, F. F. Bosworth in Dallas, Texas. His writings of the spectacular meeting that lasted from July through December, shook the world. As a result, Dallas became a hub of the Pentecostal revival.

One night three very dignified ministers walked into the meeting. Since there was no place left to sit, the platform preachers gave up their seats for the men. Reluctantly, the "dignified" took their seats. The service got well underway, with the power of God as strong as usual. Then suddenly, one of the starchy preachers tumbled off his chair and fell into the sawdust, motionless. The other two tried to ignore their friend on the ground. But in just a few minutes, the second minister joined his friend, falling helplessly into the sawdust. Then the third fell off the platform and laid motionless with them. The three laid under the power of God for more than three hours. Then finally, one by one, each got up, brushed himself off, and walked in a daze to the exit![24]

Thousands came to Dallas, some from over two thousand miles away, bringing the sick and afflicted for healing. One man had three broken ribs from a fall. He could hardly stand because of the pain. Sister Etter laid her hands on him and offered the prayer of faith, and instantly, the bones that were turned inward came into place. At first, he flinched when she touched him, but he ended up pounding his ribs realizing the pain and swelling were gone. Another man was brought in on a cot, suffering from tuberculosis. His condition was hopeless, being also plagued with a fistula, an open sore that had left a deep hole in his body. But when Maria prayed, the power of God hit the man. He jumped off his cot and ran up and down in front of the crowd. Then he rode home sitting up with the others and gained four pounds a day from that day on.

Cancer had eaten the entire side of one man's face and neck. The cancer was so painful, he had to be taken from the first meeting. But when Sister Etter laid hands on him and prayed, the power of God hit him. The pain, stiffness, and burning left immediately. He was suddenly able to turn his neck from side to side, then he got up on the altar and preached to the people.

> *The pain, stiffness, and burning left immediately. He was suddenly able to turn his neck from side to side, then he got up on the altar and preached to the people.*

One night, three people that had been deaf and dumb, all strangers to one another, stood at the altar, weeping, hugging and shouting because God had opened their ears and given them their speech. Many others looked on and wept, making their way to the altar to know God and be saved. One of the three formerly deaf and dumb went on to testify:

"When Sister Etter put her finger in my mouth at the root of my tongue and then in my ears, commanding a 'deaf and dumb' spirit to come out, God instantly opened my ears and gave me my voice."[25]

One woman had a double affliction of cancer and tuberculosis. She was like a living skeleton. All the best physicians of Dallas had given up on her. She was brought in on a cot, and many thought she would die before Sister Etter got to her. When prayed for, she was instantly healed and jumped up from the cot shouting! Then she came to the rest of the meetings every night and sat with the others. Though she was still very thin, all who knew the woman said that she was gaining weight and improving daily.

The great healing evangelist and pastor, F. F. Bosworth, wrote of the Dallas meetings:

"Night after night, as soon as the invitation was given, all the available space around the fifty-foot altar would be filled with so many suffering with diseases and afflictions and others seeking salvation and the baptism in the Holy Ghost, that it was difficult to get in and out among the seekers."[26]

At every meeting she held there was a demonstration of the power of the Spirit as never seen in our generation. One reporter from Indiana wrote, "Vehicles of all sorts began pouring into the city at an early hour...nothing short of a circus or a political rally ever before brought in so large a crowd."[27] Another wrote that it was the first time that his Iowa community could remember a religious gathering that had "driven out a good show." He wrote that members booked at the opera house went over to the camp meeting to see what had taken their crowds."[28]

THE SPLITTING ISSUE

A well-established Christian businessman from Los Angeles, Mr. R. J. Scott, visited Dallas during these meetings. He and his wife had been baptized in the Holy Spirit at the Azusa Street revival. But by this time, most of the Azusa revivalists had scattered. Scott was searching for a way to bring a unified, supernatural work back into Los Angeles. He had heard of the miraculous healings and had come to see if they were true and if Maria's doctrine matched his own. Elated by what he experienced, he determined to ask Maria to come to Los Angeles and hold what he thought would be a "dream camp meeting." He felt she had the power that Los Angeles needed. So Sister Etter agreed to come.

As could be imagined, thousands poured into the Los Angeles area for the camp meeting. The meetings ran all day and most of the night, and thousands came from all sections of North America. Tents were erected and people stayed on the grounds. In fact, there were so many tents, that tentative "streets" were established with names such as "Praise Avenue," "Hallelujah Lane," and "Glory Avenue." This made the location of someone's tent much easier to find!

Although the results of the meeting were phenomenal, this 1913 Los Angeles Worldwide Camp Meeting (Azusa/Arroyo Seco Meeting) was also known to birth the issue that split the early Pentecostal Movement. It produced the debate surrounding the "Jesus Only," "Oneness," or "New Issue" doctrine. The teaching originated from John G. Scheppe, a man who had spent a night in prayer during the meetings. Scheppe believed he had seen something new about using the name of Jesus and ran through the camp sharing it with others. As a result, people on the West Coast began to baptize in "Jesus' Name" only, and were told if they were baptized in the Trinity they would have to be re-baptized. The teaching split the Pentecostal Movement. R. J. Scott's "dream camp meeting" was designed to promote unity within the body of Christ. Instead, it produced one of the greatest divisions known in this generation.[29]

Soon the Pentecostal Movement broke into a number of other groups that emphasized a variety of doctrines. Sister Etter did her best to stay clear of these issues. She believed the most important issue was to warn sinners that Jesus was coming soon through the preaching of His Word with signs and wonders.

She said it best in a sermon entitled, *Neglect Not the Gift That Is Within Thee*. In this message she said:

> *Years later she called the "Oneness" position "the biggest delusion the devil ever invented."*

"His ambassadors must stop all the contention, all hair-splitting theories must be dropped; this hobby and that hobby with continual harping on finished work or sanctification that antagonizes the saints must be put away. Paul says preaching has to be with demonstration of the Spirit and of power.... Let the Word go forth in demonstration and power so people can see what God has for them."[30]

Sister Etter soon developed a policy of preaching in meetings at which no "hair-splitting" doctrines were spoken of. Years later she called the "Oneness" position **"the biggest delusion the devil ever invented."**[31]

"ELECTRIFIED US ALL"

Understandably, Sister Etter had mixed emotions regarding the Los Angeles meeting. She was advertised as the main speaker, and thousands drove from all parts of America to be in her meetings. But because of the political controversy, the male ministers took control, and Sister Etter was forced to minister only in the mornings. The men took over the afternoons and evenings to primarily expound on the new "Oneness" doctrine. She was pressured to cut her meetings short so the afternoon speaker could begin. And in spite of it all, hundreds were miraculously healed. It was reported that when her scheduled time would come to a close, Sister Etter would just raise her hands toward heaven as she was leaving the tent, and at that moment, many were healed. A young boy remembered, "She raised her small hands and the power of the Holy Spirit electrified us all."[32]

Invalids walked from their sick beds, the deaf heard, the blind saw, arthritis was instantly healed, tumors destroyed, dropsy eliminated. In short, every manner of sickness and disease that dared to show itself at Sister Etter's meetings, bowed its knee to Jesus Christ and was disintegrated by the fire of the Spirit. And all of this in spite of the doctrinal divisions.

Elizabeth Waters remembered these meetings like this:

> "I remember like yesterday, my girlfriend and I rolled my mother in a wheelchair about six or seven long blocks.... Two big men carried the wheelchair in front of the round pulpit as it was already lined up with wheelchairs. It was so hot, my mother begged to be taken home, but I insisted on staying. Praise the Lord, she was pointed out to be put up on the pulpit, where that beautiful little lady I won't ever forget, spoke to my mother. I saw her reply by shaking her head and then she [Sister Etter] hit her on the chest (it looked hard to me). It was like a bolt of lightning struck her, she leaped to her feet and flew around, jumping for joy. All the people yelled and screamed, I doubt if they had ever seen anything like it before. Many more miracles were seen. We almost had to tie my mother in the chair coming home. She wanted to walk, but she was weak as she had been bedfast for two years. When we got

Etter and ministry associates in Indiana, 1924

home, my grandmother and more neighbors were waiting for us. My mother stepped out of the wheelchair and walked up the stairs. They all yelled and cried. From that day on my mother was completely healed, healthy, fat, and loved the Lord."[33]

Because of her Dallas and Los Angeles meetings, Sister Etter would remain a leading evangelist for the rest of her life. And though she loved the itinerant lifestyle, God had yet another plan for her. He wasn't finished writing the pages of history.

TABERNACLE TALES

After forty-five years of ministry and preaching thousands of sermons from coast to coast, God spoke to Maria about building a tabernacle in west Indianapolis. Many had asked her to build a permanent location where they could come at any time to receive from her ministry. All parts of America had offered their region, but she chose Indiana because of its central location. True to the style of Sister Etter, the Tabernacle was a model for the Pentecostal churches of today. She built the church next door to her home, and ministered there for the last six years of her life.

At the time, there were few large churches. So in 1918, when Sister Etter raised the five-hundred seat building, it was no small task. Throughout her ministry, Maria never put pressure on the people to give financially. But in building this Tabernacle, she sent out letters for financial help. The money came in and the building went up. It was dedicated on May 19, 1918, and to date, only one other woman has ever surpassed her "church-building" ability. That woman was the female evangelist who emulated much of Etter's style, Aimee Semple McPherson.

"People would move toward the altar and fall on the floor before they got there."

Sister Etter used the Tabernacle as her home base. She had a special insight for choosing associates who would contribute to the revival. As a result, the church remains today – though in a different location – affiliated with the Assemblies of God. People flocked from around America to be in her church, and many remained as faithful members. One man remembered that "people would move toward the altar and fall on the floor before they got there." He said he never saw pre-suggestions or people ever being pushed over – "It was God. Nothing phony about Sister Etter."[34]

One incredible Tabernacle story involved a Romanian family. Their daughter suffered from tuberculosis and two Pentecostal women had come to their house to pray for her. Discovering that their daughter had been healed after the prayer, the family searched for a Pentecostal church and found the Tabernacle. During their first service, a lady who had been miraculously healed from cancer, stood and delivered a message in tongues for twenty-eight minutes. Some wondered why Sister Etter allowed her to continue so freely in the Spirit for such a length of time. But their questions were answered the next Sunday when it was learned that this woman was speaking Romanian, a language she had never heard nor learned.

This little Romanian family heard a message from God in their own language as they sat listening, completely overwhelmed. The father was the only one who could speak English. It has been said that Maria and the Tabernacle members "learned to expect such experiences as much as some congregations expect to sing the doxology at the end of their services."[35]

Another Tabernacle tale involved the healing of a young boy. He had tuberculosis and developed a tumor the size of a fist. When his mother took him to Maria she said, **"We'll just cut it out with the Sword of the Spirit."** With that, Sister Etter took her Bible and "whacked" him on the neck, and the boy was healed.[36]

GREAT MEETS GREAT

One of my favorite Tabernacle stories is the one that tells about the meeting of Maria Woodworth-Etter and Aimee Semple McPherson. At that time, Aimee was still a traveling evangelist. She truly loved Sister Etter, and eagerly desired to meet with Maria and sit in one of her meetings. In my personal opinion, I believe Aimee devoured all she could read about Sister Etter, and strengthened her own calling from the courage Maria showed.

There had been an influenza ban on the city of Indianapolis until Aimee's "Gospel Car" pulled in. The ban was finally lifted the night she arrived, and Aimee attributed it to an act of God. She writes from her diary, dated October 31, 1918:

> "For years I have been longing to meet Sister Etter, and have been talking more about it in recent months. I have longed to hear her preach and be in her meetings.... Tomorrow Mrs. Etter's tabernacle will be open and I will have the desire of my heart. Glory!"

Following their meeting Aimee wrote:

"We rejoiced and praised the Lord together. The power of God fell...showering His blessings upon us."[37]

Sister McPherson left Indianapolis the next day, no doubt rejoicing on the way to her own divine destination – California. We can only imagine the memories she cherished from meeting with Maria.

While there is no public statement from Sister Etter on what she thought of Aimee, her traveling companion Bertha Schneider, did make a comment. On one occasion, Sister Etter and Aimee were in the same city. It was their night off, so Sister Etter's group attended one of Aimee's services. But Maria chose not to go. The reason Mrs. Schneider gave for this was, "Sister Etter expressed concern over the direction Aimee's ministry was going – theatrical performances and other popular attractions."[38] I personally feel with Sister Etter being from the Holiness background, that her concern was genuine, not critical.

Many great speakers of the day visited the Tabernacle. Though it was never recorded that Sister Etter met the legendary British evangelist, Smith Wigglesworth, many feel he was a disciple of her ministry. It is believed that Wigglesworth picked up several of his mottos from Sister Etter.[39] And Wigglesworth did conduct a series of meetings in the Tabernacle after her death in 1925.

To some of you, these stories may be intimidating. Understand that God is restoring the supernatural to the Church today. Some of you reading this book are afraid of it. God has told some of you to pray for the sick in your churches, and you haven't done it. Maybe you don't know much about God's will for healing. Maybe you feel confused. It is God's will for man to be free. He came to destroy the works of the devil, not to tolerate or live through them. The Church today must learn to deal with the destroyer and bring life to the people.

Too many of us remain inside the confines of a "comfortable" doctrine or a "pick and choose" theology. God wants the whole counsel of His Word to be preached and demonstrated to the people. That's why Jesus gave us His blood. Begin to read the book of Acts and you will learn of the demonstrators of His Spirit and the opposition they aroused. Like the apostles, Sister Etter remained true to the whole counsel of God all the days of her life – despite the pressure and persecution – and we must do the same. She is one who has passed the torch, and we must be faithful to carry it.

THE TRAILBLAZER

The summer of 1924 was difficult for Maria. At the age of eighty, with failing health from gastritis and dropsy, she received heart-breaking news. Her only daughter, Lizzie, age sixty, was killed in a streetcar accident. Now all of

Maria's immediate family had gone to be with the Lord. And though her health was frail, she was still able to summon enough strength to stand in the pulpit to conduct the funeral. When she did, she exhorted the people to have faith in God and look to the heavens – not into the grave.[40]

During that year, there were times when Sister Etter was so weak she could not walk. But it didn't stop her from preaching. If she couldn't walk, she appointed someone to carry her in and place her behind the pulpit. Eventually, the Tabernacle presented a large wooden chair as a gift to Maria. Then when she seemed too weak to walk, a few strong men would carry the wooden chair from the church to her house, place her in it, and carry her back. The minute her feet hit the platform, the Spirit of God would quicken her and she would walk up and down the platform, preaching and ministering in the supernatural power of God. Hundreds witnessed how weak she seemed, then how incredibly strong she became. At the end of the service, the men would put her back in the chair and carry her home.

> *Sister Etter's faith caused her to continue, when many others would have given up.*

Sister Etter's faith caused her to continue, when many others would have given up. Remember, by now Sister Etter had reached her eighties. There were no airplanes and very few luxuries in her time. There was no air conditioning or modern conveniences. She had traveled across the nation in buggies and trains, many times sleeping in a tent when money was scarce, or no room was provided. But it didn't matter to Etter.

Three weeks before she died, the Lord revealed to Maria that, "It was only a matter of days before she would leave" to go to her reward. During this time, a lady brought her flowers to which Sister Etter replied, **"I will soon be where the flowers will bloom forever."**[41] A number of times she would even preach sermons to those who visited her at home.

Of her death, an associate, August Feich, wrote:

> "A few days before she passed away, she called me to her side and took my hand and said, 'Brother Feich, do you realize that I am going the way of all flesh?' The answer came, 'I do, mother,' to which she replied, 'You have been very faithful in your ministry with me for these many years. Now I trust that God's blessing may continue to rest upon you; soon you will have me no more to help you.'"

Maria Woodworth-Etter's end came without a struggle as she sank away slowly into a deep sleep:

> "Her eyesight was good for a person of her age. Her mental powers were keen to the very end. There was not a single moment during all her sickness but what she could freely converse with you on any topic that came up. The saints around her came in freely at all times to see her and have council with her. Some came as they were led by the Spirit to pray for her; others again to be prayed for by her. She laid hands on the sick and prayed for those who were in need. This she did 'til the very end. She did this while at the same time she knew that her own strength was rapidly slipping away. She has repeatedly said during her ministry that *she would sooner wear out for Jesus than rust out.*"[42]

Before Sister Etter went home to be with the Lord at age eighty, she had buried all six of her children and two husbands; preached thousands of sermons from coast to coast; remained the victor over hoodlums and vicious ministers; blazed the trail for women in ministry; and unflinchingly displayed the power of the Holy Spirit with mighty signs and wonders following.

She wasn't well educated. She didn't care about seminary classes and didn't take the time to explain how God worked. She preached a very simple Gospel, offered herself completely to Him, and believed for signs and wonders. Maria's one passion was for the Gospel to come alive and for people to be led by the Spirit. She preached many times with tears streaming down her face, begging those who heard to come to Christ. Her meetings and teachings paved the way for the founding of many Pentecostal denominations, including the Assemblies of God, Foursquare, and other similar denominations.

ETTER'S FAMILY TODAY

Etter's immediate heritage was not heard from again until 1977. Her great-great-great grandson, Tom Slevin, had an interest in researching his family tree. Surprisingly to him, he discovered that an immediate relative of his was a "little pioneer-preacher" named Maria Woodworth-Etter, otherwise known as Grandma Etter. She had been a famous evangelist and founder of a church not far from his home. He inquired of her to his mother, Mary; but she could tell him little, as much information had been lost. Mr. Slevin refused to give up. He researched the Etter books and sermons, reading them continuously.

Soon, his own life was influenced by this woman's sermons, some preached over 80 years ago.

Slevin said, "When I first read her books, I thought they might have been blown out of proportion with all the tremendous miracles. So I went to other towns and researched through the microfilms. I read the old newspapers and discovered a wonderful thing. I found the stories in her books were absolutely true and it was the newspapers that had left a lot of miracles out!"

Slevin and his mother became so curious about the life of Etter, that they went to hear an evangelist who had sat under Sister Etter's ministry as a young boy. This evangelist, Roscoe Russell, had been the boy who, when "whacked" in the neck with a Bible by Sister Etter, was miraculously healed. When Slevin's mother went forth for prayer, the evangelist said to her, "The same God that answered the prayers of your grandmother is here today. He will answer your prayers just the same." Afterwards, Slevin's mother was baptized in the church affiliated with Etter's ministry.

Slevin likes to compare his grandmother Etter's ministry to that of Smith Wigglesworth's. He feels their relationship with God was very similiar, especially in the areas of faith. Though he has many favorite stories, Slevin pointed out that John G. Lake met Etter in 1913. After that meeting, it is said that Lake told his people to, "Pray like Mother Etter."

From his research, Slevin gained an insight into the character of his grandmother. "The thing that impressed me the most," he remembered, "was how completely her life was sold out to God. She was unlike so many today. She went wherever God told her to go; whether they had 20 people or a thousand people. Her time belonged to God. She was never "too busy" to do what He said. Everyone was important to her, because they were important to God. That is why she knew God so well. That is why she could 'punch someone in the stomach' or 'whack them on the neck'. She knew God and she knew He would heal them."[43] It is no doubt that through the Slevin family, the spiritual heritage of Sister Etter will continue.

A PERSONAL VIEW

In my own personal observations, the ministry that Sister Etter carried has passed down and is still in the earth today. Every ministry should have signs and wonders following it. If not, the ministers are just playing with the ministry. If your ministry is following the commands of Jesus, then signs and wonders will follow you.

Styles of ministry and methods of ministry will vary from person to person. No one person will operate in the same way, because we are all individuals and there are different generations to reach.

But when a ministry operates in the same magnitude as one that has gone on before it, I sometimes refer to that operation as the "mantle" that has been passed down. A mantle is a spiritual term that can be described in the natural, like a coat or a shawl. When we "wear" the mantle, we operate similar to the ministry we received it from.

> *If your ministry is following the commands of Jesus, then signs and wonders will follow you.*

From this personal point of view, it seems that Aimee Semple McPherson carried on where Etter left off, through great signs, wonders, and exploits. I believe she received Maria's mantle. From McPherson, a similar mantle seemed to pass on to Kathryn Kuhlman. Kuhlman was also known for the great magnitude of miracles in her ministry and for her hunger for fellowship with the Holy Spirit. Today, in the 1990s, it seems to me that a similar healing mantle has passed from Kuhlman to Benny Hinn, though Hinn doesn't like for that to be said of him. Hinn feels he has his own mantle from God, not someone else's. He is the great pastor and healing evangelist from Orlando, Florida.

DON'T RUST OUT

Maria Woodworth-Etter reached untold thousands from around America with the liberating message of Jesus Christ. These words were written of her:

> "Glory to God and the Lord Jesus for calling her, enduing her with power, keeping her, and making her a 'Mother in Israel' to us. The same love that watched over her is ours today. Amen."[44]

Mighty signs and wonders are in the earth again. So cultivate the godly treasures within you by experience and the Word, then bring them to the surface by prayer and obedience. Believe God for signs and wonders to come through you. Determine to be used in this hour and press on to the fullness that God has for you. Don't allow setbacks to frustrate or hinder you. Call for the Spirit of might and finish your course in complete victory. Adopt these words of Sister Etter:

"It's better to wear out for Jesus Christ than to rust out."

Then don't stop until you are finished. The world is searching for the answer within you.

CHAPTER TWO, MARIA WOODWORTH-ETTER
References

1 Wayne E. Warner, "Neglect Not the Gift That Is in Thee," Etter Sermon from *The Woman Evangelist* (Metuchen, NJ and London: The Scarecrow Press, Inc., 1986), 307, Appendix C.

2 Ibid., 6.

3 Ibid., 7.

4 Ibid., 8.

5 Ibid., 10.

6 Maria Woodworth-Etter, "A Sermon for Women," *A Diary of Signs & Wonders* (Tulsa, OK: Harrison House, Reprinted from 1916 ed.), 215-216, 30-31.

7 Warner, *The Woman Evangelist*, 14.

8 Ibid., 21.

9 Ibid., 22.

10 Woodworth-Etter, *A Diary of Signs and Wonders* (Tulsa, OK: Harrison House, reprinted from 1916 ed.), 67-68.

11 Warner, *The Woman Evangelist*, 41.

12 Woodworth-Etter, *A Diary of Signs*, 111.

13 Warner, *The Woman Evangelist*, 42.

14 Ibid.

15 Ibid., 148.

16 Ibid., 146.

17 Ibid.

18 Ibid., 81, Footnote 18, John Alexander Dowie, "Trance Evangelism," *Leaves of Healing* (March 8, 1895), 382. Reprinted from *Leaves of Healing* (old issue), 98.

19 Maria Woodworth-Etter, *Life & Testimony of Mrs. M. B. Woodworth-Etter*, 12.

20 Woodworth-Etter, *A Diary of Signs*, 151.

21 Ibid., 184.

22 Warner, *The Woman Evangelist*, 41.

23 Ibid., 213.

24 Ibid., 167.

25 Woodworth-Etter, *A Diary of Signs*, 166.

26 Ibid., 173.

27 Warner, *The Woman Evangelist,* 201.

28 Ibid., 202-203.

29 Ibid., 172.

30 Article from *The Latter Rain Evangel* (August, 1913).

31 Warner, *The Woman Evangelist,* 188, Footnote 42 taken from Maria Woodworth-Etter's *Spirit-Filled Sermons.*

32 Ibid., 169 from A. C. Valdez's *Fire on Azusa Street.*

33 Personal letter from Elizabeth Waters to Thomas Slevin, great-great-great grandson of Sister Etter.

34 Warner, *The Woman Evangelist,* 268, Footnote 21.

35 Ibid., 256-257, 267, Footnote 13.

36 Ibid., 256.

37 Aimee Semple McPherson, *This is That,* (Los Angeles, CA: Echo Park Evangelistic Assoc., Inc., 1923), 149-150.

38 Warner, *The Woman Evangelist,* 294, Footnote 11.

39 Ibid., 287.

40 Ibid., 290.

41 Woodworth-Etter, *Life & Testimony of Mrs. M. B. Woodworth-Etter*, 123.

42 Ibid., 124.

43 Personal interview with Tom Slevin, great-great-great grandson of Sister Etter.

44 Woodworth-Etter, *Life & Testimony of Mrs. M. B. Woodworth-Etter*, 138.

Evan Roberts

"Welsh Revivalist"

"WELSH REVIVALIST"

I n my opinion, the story of the young revivalist from Wales, Evan Roberts, is the saddest study I have conducted on the Generals. This young boy-preacher from the coal mines of southern Wales had an unmistakable dispensation of worldwide revival allotted to him. But because of inexperience, limited revelation, and demonic control, his incredible ministry was cut short long before its time. Before we explore his life, let it be clearly understood that the truths presented here are not intended as criticism. The lessons I will bring to light are constructively inserted so that our generation can learn to guard their hearts, carry the anointing, and prevail successfully in the heat of revival fire.

COAL-COVERED TRUTH

Evan John Roberts was born June 8, 1878, into the staunch Calvinist-Methodist home of Henry and Hannah Roberts. I believe a "revivalist spirit" was built immediately within him. Evan's parents had a strong influence in cultivating that spirit and nature within him. His nature was one of excellency and sensitivity. The family was known for their love of God's Word and hard work. Each family member, no matter how young, had his own well-worn Bible.

I want to make a point here: Parents, allow your children to be involved with the move of God. I can't stress how vitally important it is to teach and train your children in the things of God. They need to know how to pray, how to study the Word of God, and how to sit under the anointing. Teach them to worship God with you, and show them how to do it. Revival fires die because parents stick their children in the nursery instead of setting them in the move of God. The nursery is a blessing for taking care of infants and toddlers. But there comes a time when they are able to understand proper behavior and can be included in the revival service.

His nature was one of excellency and sensitivity.

How can revival continue without passing it on? Many past revivals and some revivalists didn't take their next generation into account. As a result, God had to search for another generation to rekindle the fire that should have never gone out. Revivals don't have to end. Revivals are meant to continue. The fire of God must be passed on with each new generation. Children are pliable and sensitive, wanting to learn. They are like little sponges eager to draw in everything you share with them. So be their teachers. If you have children, that godly responsibility of passing the fire of God onto them rests in your hands. And it is evident the family of Evan Roberts took that responsibility seriously.

Evan's strong character was the result of his family's training. While still very young, Evan's father was injured in a mining accident. So his father took Evan out of school to help him in the coal mines. Evan never complained.

Soon, Evan had developed the family's habit of memorizing Scripture. He was never seen without his Bible. It has been said that he would even hide his Bible in the clefts of the mine while he worked. One day, a huge fire burned through everything in its path – except young Evan's Bible. Only the pages were scorched, so he continued to carry it every day and memorize Scriptures from it. Each morning, Evan stood at the opening of the mine to give a particular Scripture to each of the passing workers for their workday meditation. Then when young Evan saw them in the evening, he would ask, "What truth did you find in that text?"[1] As these hard-working men passed by the coal-covered boy, they had no idea of how God would use him to change their nation.

"WHAT WOULD JESUS DO?"

Evan was dramatically different from the rest of the boys his age. He never took part in sports, amusements, or coarse joking. He worked in the mines every day, then came home and walked a mile to his church, Moriah Chapel. At thirteen years of age, Evan experienced his first encounter with God. It was then that Evan vowed to commit himself even further to the work of the Lord. One simple yet profound phrase spoken from the pulpit of Moriah Chapel changed Evan's life. The phrase, "What would Jesus do?" became his obsession. He repeatedly asked himself, **"What have I done for Jesus?"** as he further dedicated himself to the work of the Lord.

> *While others of his age group became interested in dating, Evan was more likely to be inside the church discussing Scripture with other men.*

Evan was so intense on giving his life to God that he read everything he could pertaining to Him. He used his earnings to purchase instruments that he later learned to play. In fact, he was able to succeed at most everything he put his hand to because he put his whole heart into it. He excelled in any business apprenticeship offered to him, and he excelled in personal character. He was also a prolific writer, having several of his poems and essays published in local newspapers.

While others of his age group became interested in dating, Evan was more likely to be inside the church discussing Scripture with other men. Soon, the elders of the church gave him the responsibility of starting a weekly debate group for young men like himself. But these happy times ended abruptly when the mine Evan worked in suffered an explosion. The single men were the first to be relieved of their duties. So in 1898, Evan began work in Mountain Ash, a town north of where he lived. He left home not realizing the spiritual preparation he had gained.

"I AM BURNING, WAITING FOR A SIGN"

At that time few people understood the power of prayer. Most attended church as a moral commitment, instead of a spiritual one. But not Evan. Because of his unique desire for the Lord, Evan gave himself to fervent prayer and intercession. So much so, that by the time he was twenty years old, he was known by some as a "mystical lunatic."[2] Stories about him circulated widely. There were whispers about seeing him standing "trance-like" beside the road while uttering deep sighs as his lips moved without the sound of words.[3] It was also said that he meditated in the Word so long that he often missed the evening meal. Sometimes he would stay up half the night discussing and praying with a friend about revival.

Several concerned ministers approached Evan regarding his unusual behavior. He simply answered them, **But the Spirit moved me.** During this time, friends also introduced him to an American specialist, Dr. Hughes. The doctor told Evan's friends he was suffering from "religious mania." One Christian man said of Evan:

> "We usually had a reading and prayer together before we put
> out the lamp. Then I could hear Evan calling and groaning in the
> Spirit. I couldn't understand what was his message to God again,
> and some holy fear kept me from asking."[4]

Though people didn't understand Evan's methods, the spiritual power he portrayed was unmistakable. On one occasion, he traveled to Builith Wells for a prayer meeting at which he was called on to pray. The people's hearts were melted within them at the power exhibited in Evan's prayer. After the service, the minister approached Evan and advised him to consider full-time ministry.

Evan considered it and answered the call. Through his church, he was required to preach twice at all twelve affiliate churches, and his sermons were met with great approval. He confided to a friend that his heavenly secret was,

"**Ask and it shall be given unto you. Practice entire, definite faith in God's promise of the Spirit.**"[5]

During this period, Evan wrote to a friend and said, "**I have prayed that the Lord will baptize you and me with the Holy Spirit.**"[6] Soon afterward, he got so caught up in the Lord, that his bed shook. Then after that, he was awakened every night at 1:00 A.M. to be "**taken up into divine fellowship.**" He would pray for four hours, fall back to sleep at 5:00 A.M. for another four hours, then pray from 9:00 A.M. until 12 noon.[7]

In December of 1903, Evan knew in his heart that God had planned a great revival for the Welsh community. While preaching at Moriah he said, "**I have reached out my hand and touched the flame. I am burning and waiting for a sign.**"[8]

Let me make a point here. Revival must be in your heart before it comes into the earth. Each revival has nothing to do with the last one, but it has everything to do with the individual who brings it.

During this time, every denomination in Wales was praying for revival. Moriah Chapel had a strong Calvinistic doctrine, so Evan was well-trained in the doctrine of "man, sin, and salvation." The young ministry students were

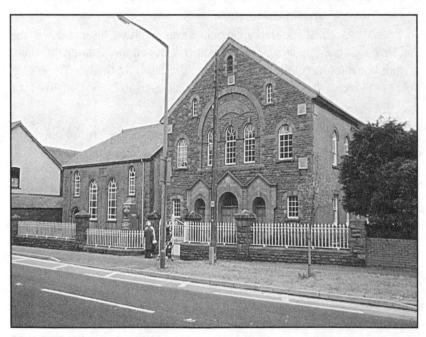

Moriah Chapel

required to listen to great men of their denomination and pattern their preaching styles after them. But Evan was an exception. Though he had been accepted into the Bible college, he couldn't complete his studies because of his burning desire to preach and pray.

"BEND US! BEND US!"

For Evan Roberts, 1904 was a year of great struggle. He was torn between doing what everyone expected and following what he felt the Spirit of God wanted him to do.

His closest friend, Sidney Evans, attended a prayer meeting and came back very excited. He told Evan of how he had fully surrendered his life to the work of the Lord. But Evan reacted strangely. Fearing he wouldn't be able to receive the fullness of the Spirit of God, he went into a deep depression – a pattern he became known for throughout his ministry. He was so consumed with this thought that no one could soothe him.

Then in September, Evan's friends persuaded him to go with them to hear the rugged evangelist, Seth Joshua. Unknown to Evan, Rev. Joshua had prayed for years that God would raise up another "Elisha" from an ordinary person and "mantle him with power."[9] And Joshua got exactly what he prayed for. When mighty revival came through the leadership of Evan Roberts, the great, dignified preachers of England and Wales were forced to sit at the feet of crude, hard-working miners to see the wonderful works of God.

Evan remained silent throughout Joshua's service. But when the minister began to pray, "Bend us! Bend us!" Evan's soul stirred within him. After the meeting, the group went to Joshua's house for breakfast, but Evan refused to eat. He was extremely tense and solemn. He was afraid the Holy Spirit would come to him and that he wouldn't accept Him. So once again, Evan put himself in a state of depression.

When mighty revival came through the leadership of Evan Roberts, the great, dignified preachers of England and Wales were forced to sit at the feet of crude, hard-working miners to see the wonderful works of God.

In my opinion, this showed young Evan's misunderstanding of the ways of the Holy Spirit. This intense, unnatural pressure he put upon himself only led to error later down the road. The Holy Spirit will never force Himself upon anyone. He will never offer you something you can't receive or ask you to perform anything you can't do. The Holy Spirit isn't out to torture your soul, drive you, or pressure you into isolation. He has come to empower you for His service. He came to impart boldness, sensitivity, and strength. All we have to say is, "Come, Holy Spirit." If our lives need adjustment, He will reveal those areas along with His plan to mature them. The kingdom of heaven is righteousness, peace, and joy. Anything else will throw you off balance.

Evan left the company of his friends and went back to the chapel where Rev. Joshua held his meeting. While there, he began to respond to Joshua's earlier prayer by crying out to the Lord, **"Bend me! Bend me!"** In this prayer of total submission, he received a revelation of the love of God. Evan surrendered to the will of God that day and allowed His compassion to fill him. Of the experience he later said, **"It was God commending His love that bent me.... After I was 'bended,' a wave of peace and joy filled my bosom."**[10] Now Evan felt ready to be God's messenger.

Though many times it seemed Evan Roberts was unnaturally driven toward the things of God, it can also be said that he carried a great love for the Holy Spirit and His move in the earth.

AN ARM OUTSTRETCHED FROM THE MOON

Evan wasn't one normally given to visions. He had his first vision in October of 1904.

While strolling in a garden with Sidney Evans, Evan noticed that Sidney was in a daze, staring at the moon. So Evan looked into the sky and inquired, **"What are you looking at? What do you see?"** Then suddenly, Evan saw it too. He saw an arm seemed to be outstretched from the moon, reaching down into Wales.

Evan had been fervently praying for one hundred thousand souls to be added to the kingdom of God, and he received this rare vision as a direct answer to his prayers. Now he was even more determined to launch his ministry. He was ready to give all his time and money to the work before him. His statement, **"We can do nothing without the Holy Spirit,"**[11] set the precedence for the rest of Evan's ministry. Sometimes it was effective while at other times it was extreme.

Fervent for the Holy Spirit, Evan seemed to take up a personal defense for Him at times. Once while sitting in a service, he jumped to his feet, disrupted the sermon, and accused those in the congregation of not being sincere and earnest.[12] His friends were concerned while others labeled him as a lunatic. As quickly as Evan turned extreme, he would often become level-headed and instruct those around him how to obtain peace with God.

THE LOST KEYS

Evan finally obtained approval to begin a small series of meetings. What began on October 31 as a small church meeting quickly grew into a major revival and lasted for two weeks!

The group began with a few consecrated believers who listened intently to Evan's message. Instead of standing behind the pulpit, the young revivalist walked up and down the aisles, preaching and asking questions to those sitting in the pews. This was unheard of in his day. The goal of those first meetings was to dedicate and train intercessors for the coming revival. Evan succeeded in his goal. He believed that revival would come through knowledge of the Holy Spirit and that one must "co-work" with the Spirit in order to operate in power. Even the children were trained to pray morning and night for God to "send the Spirit to Moriah for Jesus Christ's sake!"

Instead of standing behind the pulpit, the young revivalist walked up and down the aisles, preaching and asking questions to those sitting in the pews.

Soon, the services grew to a fervor, and Evan sent word to the Bible college to request more workers. Strong moves of intercession flooded the room during each service, and many times the services would go past midnight. Once, Evan prayed all night with a congregation and didn't return home until the next morning. This small group of intercessors led by the young evangelist transformed the entire community. Some meetings lasted until 4:00 A.M. with crowds gathering outside for 6:00 A.M. prayer. In two years, all of Wales would know the name of Evan Roberts.

During this whirlwind of revival, Evan refused to be recognized as its leader. He denounced anyone who sought him as such and even refused to be photographed. It is said that he once even hid behind the pulpit when a

February, 1905

newspaper photographer came into a meeting with a camera. As a result, the only photographs we have of Evan are family possessions.

Evan's services were marked with laughing, crying, dancing, joy, and brokenness.[13] Soon, the newspapers began covering them, and the revival became a national story. Some of the reporters themselves were converted at the meetings. The revival spread with great fervor throughout Wales. Soon bars and movie houses closed. Former prostitutes started holding Bible studies. People began to pay their longstanding debts. And those who once selfishly wasted their money on alcohol suddenly became a great joy and support to their families.

The Wales revival meetings had no choirs or special ceremonies. There were no offerings, no hymnbooks, no committees, no song leaders, and no paid advertising. Leaders from denominations who were hungry for God attended the meetings. It is said that in one city, all the ministers exchanged pulpits for a day in an effort to break down denominational walls and establish unity. Even the women were welcome to participate. Up until that time, the women of Wales had been banned from any public role in church life, but now could be seen praying and praising openly. Eventually Evan even encouraged national and racial barriers to be broken.

The Wales revival was founded on these four points: (1) Confess all known sin. (2) Search out all secret and doubtful things. (3) Confess the Lord Jesus openly. (4) Pledge your word that you will fully obey the Spirit.

Evan Roberts had discovered the keys to revival. And if those keys were important then, they are certainly important now. I believe "repentance" is a word that is somewhat tarnished today. It has lost much of its meaning due to social issues and wrong attitudes. Some people are so carried away with God's law of grace and mercy that they overlook the rest of His laws. Grace and mercy don't give us license to live however we want to. We don't live under cheap grace and mercy. The righteousness we enjoy as believers was purchased by the blood of Jesus – a price too great for words. If we don't obey, we won't receive. Repentance brought us into the kingdom of God, and repentance will keep us moving with His cloud.

Also, we must love God more than we love anything else. When I was a young boy, I felt impressed to quit playing basketball. There's nothing wrong with basketball. But at the time, I knew what God had called me to do, and it seemed I loved basketball more than I loved to pray. So I quit playing basketball. God had set the plan for my life. I agreed to it, and prayer became my life-giving force. It's fine to enjoy life. Just make sure you don't love life more than God.

"GOD HAS MADE ME STRONG AND MANLY"

Roberts' revival meetings were unlike any Wales had ever seen. One such service began with two girls standing in the pulpit. One pleaded and prayed for the people to surrender to the Holy Spirit. Then the other gave her testimony in song before bursting into tears. They called this, "warming the atmosphere."[14] If the congregation wondered why Evan Roberts didn't take the platform after the two girls finished, they only needed to look at him. He was on his knees, weeping and pleading with God. Many said it was not the eloquence of Evan Roberts that broke men – it was his tears. In his book, *Azusa Street*, Frank Bartleman quotes an eyewitness as saying, "Roberts in the intensity of his agony would fall in the pulpit, while many in the crowd fainted."

It was common in Evan's meetings for members in the congregation to suddenly fall on their knees and pray aloud. Waves of joy and sorrow would flood the congregation. Women fell to their knees and men laid in the aisles weeping, laughing, and praying. All the while, there was no Bible reading or instrument playing. A few were inspired to stand and sing hymns. It was even said the congregation was so caught up in God that they would forget to go home for Sunday dinner. This was unheard of in southern Wales in those days. As the day progressed, the evening service would become a continual prayer meeting. Evan could be seen walking up and down the aisles swinging his arms, clapping his hands, and jumping up and down.

If Evan didn't sense the unction to preach, he remained quiet.

Though his success had become the talk of the nation, many still didn't know what to think of Evan Roberts. They were used to the fiery eyes of the old-time preachers, and Evan never raised his voice. Sometimes he was called the "silent preacher." If Evan didn't sense the unction to preach, he remained quiet. On one occasion, Evan sat on the front row for three or four hours, then rose up to preach for only fifteen minutes.

Also in that day, most people were accustomed to the preachers with stern, dignified faces. But Evan was the opposite. His face constantly beamed. Once when a minister read from a list of thirty-three converts, Evan threw his arms around him and exclaimed, **"Is this not glorious?"**

As a result of the revival, local stores couldn't keep Bibles in stock. The Welsh coal mining industry also took on a new look. Their workhorses had previously been trained to respond to instructions that included profanity. But with the coal mining crew now born again, they found that their horses had to be re-trained because the animals didn't know how to follow a normal command without a curse word in it.

Of course, there was the usual concern. People were murmuring because there seemed to be no order in the services. And Evan was operating around the clock without rest. When asked about it once, he replied:

> **"Tired? Not once. God has made me strong and manly. I can face thousands. My body is full of electricity day and night and I have no sleep before I am back in meetings again."**[15]

It is a documented fact that Evan Roberts slept and ate very little during the first two months of this great revival. In fact, he only slept two or three hours a night.

HEAR THIS: REST

In order to continually walk in the Spirit, we must obey the universal laws instituted by God. One of those laws is to take care of your physical body. While it is true that the Spirit is greater than the flesh, if we don't take care of that flesh while on earth, the body will break down, or even die. If the body dies, the spirit must depart. God established a universal law that says our bodies need proper rest and nourishment. God Himself rested on the seventh day after the work of creation, establishing the principle for us.

When I am in the anointing, it affects every part of me. My body feels energized, and my mind is submitted to the will of God. Why? Because the anointing brings life. However, the physical demands of my body continue, anointing or not. My blood still needs oxygen and nutrients, and my mind still needs rest. We are not in our glorified bodies yet. So mature revivalists *must* learn to care for their physical bodies. You *can* live out of your spirit, operate in the anointing, and get the rest you need. If you don't, disaster is pending. The Holy Spirit will never drive you – He leads you. You can't follow God and hear Him accurately if your body is exhausted and driven. *Pressure and need abound when revival hits* because mankind is made aware of his spiritual condition. A revivalist must know how to *lead* and *rest* in order to remain a vital instrument of God. I believe *one* of the main reasons Evan Roberts' ministry was cut short was because he didn't learn this principle.

Evan was soon showing many signs of emotional strain. But despite the overload, he continued to go from town to town and pleaded with residents to think of the lost. Whenever friends would encourage him to rest, he reacted strongly against them. Though his body was rapidly wearing down, the power of God continued to feed the hunger of the people. One newspaper reported that while some were shouting with conviction, others were literally shaking.[16]

DEMONSTRATING THE DIVINE

It was a supernatural experience to be in an Evan Roberts meeting. He carried the ability to usher in the presence of the Holy Spirit as almost a tangible force. He made the common church-goer aware of the spirit world, especially in the area of purity and holiness toward God. Since he rarely preached, Evan allowed three female singers — Annie Davies, Maggie Davies, and S. A. Jones — to travel with him. Many times, they sang an inspired message from God to the congregation. Evan would rebuke anyone who tried to hush the singing. He believed the Holy Spirit should be given the primary role and that no one had the right to interrupt Him. He felt that so doing invited the wrong kind of authority and control.

To Evan, the Holy Spirit wasn't some unseen force, but a Divine Person who must be praised and adored in His own right and totally obeyed. It even came to the point that when one or two people in the congregation wouldn't participate, Evan would stand up and say, **"The Spirit can't be with us now."**[17] Then, many times he would leave the service.

Residents from local towns and surrounding communities would often pour into the buildings for Evan's meetings. In a town with a population of three thousand people, over one thousand would attend the meetings. If they didn't arrive early enough to get a seat, the people remained outside just to catch a glimpse. Amazed, newspaper reporters noted that communities had never seen so many visitors as when Evan Roberts came to town.

Amazed, newspaper reporters noted that communities had never seen so many visitors as when Evan Roberts came to town.

Soon, word of this revival spread to other nations. The people of South Africa, Russia, India, Ireland, Norway, Canada, and Holland rushed to Wales. One group of Americans came just to say, "I was there when the miracles happened."[18] Many came to carry a portion of this revival back to their own nations. It is said that during this time, the California evangelist and journalist, Frank Bartleman, wrote to Evan and asked how to bring revival to America. Evan corresponded several times with Bartleman, each time listing principles for revival while encouraging him to pursue it, and assuring him of

O! Ysbryd Sanctaidd, tyr'd i lawr
I ogoneddu Iesu mawr:
Plyg yr eglwysi wrth Ei draed.
A golch y byd mewn dwyfol waed.

*Mrs. Roberts, Evan Roberts Home Loughor, Mr. Roberts,
Mr. Evan Roberts, Miss Roberts, and Mr. Dan Roberts*

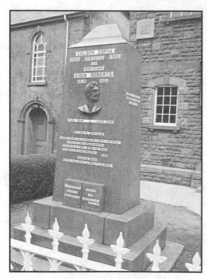

Roberts Monument

Welsh Revivalist

Roberts and his singing ladies

Roberts reading the Word

Evan Roberts in back seat of car with friends

On fire for God

the prayers from Wales. Bartleman would later become instrumental in recording the events of the Azusa Street Revival that originated in Southern California in 1906. There is no doubt that the revival in Wales started a worldwide hunger for God.

CONFUSION AND COLLAPSE

In 1905, Evan Roberts' mind became confused. He often said that he wanted to enter into the **"sufferings of the Master."** Sometimes, he would start a service in gentleness and joy, then suddenly jump up, wave his arms, and sharply rebuke those who weren't pure in heart. Then he would threaten to leave the service. He commented to his friend, Sidney Evans, that he was afraid of speaking words that weren't of God. He heard many voices, and sometimes he wasn't sure which was God's and which was his.[19] He was also constantly examining himself for any unconfessed sin. His number one fear was that people would exalt him instead of God.

As the revival continued and specific needs became apparent, Evan began to operate in the gifts of the Spirit. Out of ignorance, the people labeled Evan telepathic, since they didn't understand how he could be so spiritually accurate. But instead of stopping to teach the people concerning the gifts of the Spirit, Evan simply continued to operate in them.

At times, Evan would be preaching, then suddenly would stop. He would look up into the balcony and exclaim that someone there needed salvation. Within seconds, a person would fall to his knees and cry out in repentance to God. This happened often in his services.

Sometimes Evan would name a specific sin that was present and call for immediate repentance. Other times, he would know of a person outside the building agonizing before God. Evan would abruptly leave the building, head out into the street, and find that person on his knees crying to God.

The voices Evan was hearing began to trouble him greatly. But instead of receiving counsel from mature leaders, he chose to continue following the signs and to ignore the uneasiness within. It was at this time that Evan Roberts suffered his first emotional collapse. He was forced to remain in the home of a friend and cancel his meetings.

"OBSTACLES ARRIVING...AND DEPARTING"

When the people heard of his cancellation, they were outraged and offended. Though still severely fatigued, Evan was swayed by their pressure and rescheduled the meeting.

But as to be expected, at the meeting he was hazy in mind and rebuked the crowd sharply. He even began to point out "**obstacles arriving**" and "**obstacles departing.**" The people became more concerned with the conflict he was pointing out than with their hunger for God. After this, complaints and criticism abounded against Evan from every corner of Wales. They labeled him a "hypnotist," "exhibitionist," and "occultist." In retaliation, Evan began to condemn entire congregations for the cold hearts of one or two who would show up at his meetings. He once even condemned a man's "soul" forbidding anyone to pray for him.

Accusation and criticism spread like wildfire. Every day produced new, bitter charges in the newspapers and letters. And each new meeting was filled with challenging agnostics who called him a "bearer of false fire" or "profaner." Friends tried to justify his actions, saying he was a young, inexperienced minister and subject to making "a young man's mistake."

Soon, Evan Roberts suffered another physical and emotional breakdown. Much to his critics' delight, Evan canceled all his meetings. He was branded as unbalanced, and revival converts began to wonder if they had been deceived by Satan. In response to the outburst, a psychologist who examined Evan published this remark: "Our organisms can't support such pitiless tensions and violent repeated shocks, shaking the nerves and exhausting the brain and body."[20] With this, Evan went into silence for a season.

GREAT GLORY, GREAT STRAIN

Not to be outdone by critics, the supporting public flooded Evan's secretary with requests for him to minister. After a short season of rest, he agreed to accept the invitations, and he published an itinerary of the meetings in the newspapers.

On the day of his first meeting, the streets were packed. Hundreds arrived early to get a seat. As it was about to begin, his secretary took the platform and read a note from Evan: "**Tell the people I shall not come to the service. The Spirit prevents my coming and I can't speak.**"[21] There were great cries of disappointment and anger. Even Evan's friends couldn't support this "leading of the Spirit." The best they could say of him was that he was under great strain.

Evan locked himself away to spend time in the Word and prayer. Then after another short season of rest, he returned to public ministry. This time the results looked like the days of the early revival. Evan saw himself as "the Lord's special messenger who would arouse the churches for their task of saving the nation."[22]

Again sharp criticism arose. Evan, no longer known for his gentleness, openly rebuked public leaders and announced of one particular church he was ministering in that it was not "founded upon the Rock." One devastating blow came at a men's meeting in this same church when Evan filled in for the absent pastor, facing hundreds of disturbed men. When he arrived, he wouldn't step up to the platform, choosing instead to sit silent in his chair for two hours. As criticism was openly voiced by the ministers there, Evan got up and left the chapel. When the pastor returned, he vowed the meetings would continue in peace and begged the ministers to conduct themselves peacefully. When Evan took the platform that night, he smiled and exhorted them to study the true Shepherd in Ezekiel 34.[23]

> *...now he saw himself as "the Lord's special messenger who would arouse the churches for their task of saving the nation."*

Because of his failing condition, Evan's emotional wounds became more difficult to heal. He became greatly disturbed at small things. He took it personally when he heard of converts "barking after the devil," or "following healers and prophetesses." As a result, he remained depressed most of the time.

The critical point of Evan Roberts' downfall came when he returned to northern Wales in the summer of 1906. He was asked to participate in a Keswick-type Easter convention for ministers and church leaders. It was there that Evan spoke on what he called his "new burden," which was the identification with Christ through suffering.[24] Soon afterwards, he became tremendously overstrained and broke down again.

ENTER JEZEBEL

At the Keswick meeting, Mrs. Jessie Penn-Lewis introduced herself to Evan. Mrs. Penn-Lewis was a socially influential and wealthy woman from England. She was also a minister, but her ministry had been scorned by the Welsh due to serious doctrinal conflicts. They rejected her "suffering" teachings and abolished her ministry in their nation.

When Mrs. Penn-Lewis heard Evan's message on the cross, she aligned herself with him to gain his acceptance. And she confided to friends that she felt Evan "had too been shattered and would need some type of getaway."[25] Then she convinced Evan of her position while pointing out his excellent teaching

Mr. and Mrs. Penn-Lewis

and the abuses he was suffering because of it. In his weakened condition, Evan succumbed to her influence. Less than a month after being constantly paired with Penn-Lewis, Evan suffered his fourth and most serious nervous breakdown.

Newly discovered letters show that Penn-Lewis had ulterior motives with Evan Roberts. She used his name repeatedly while exonerating her own methods and beliefs. She also told the ministers of Wales that she was so hurt by their opinion of her and her doctrine that she wouldn't return to their nation. And she added that it was best for Evan to stay away from Wales because he, like her, was "too shattered to do anything."[26]

After this announcement by Penn-Lewis, Roberts was transported quickly and quietly by train from his beloved homeland and place of his call. Penn-Lewis and her husband retired Evan to their estate in England called, Woodlands. Then they built their new home around Evan Roberts' needs. They built him a bedroom, a prayer room, and his own private stairway. It was here that the great evangelist was confined to bed.

> *From this point on, Evan determined from Mrs. Penn-Lewis' counsel that he would no longer trust any moving of the supernatural.*

FIRST KINGS 21?

While at Woodlands, Penn-Lewis visited Evan daily. Evan listened respectfully as she told him of the mistakes and wrong judgments she felt he made while in the ministry. But Evan wasn't able to discern that everything the woman said was based entirely on her opinions.

As Penn-Lewis sat by Evan's bedside, she questioned him about the supernatural gifts that operated through him. She determined that Evan's depression was caused from this spiritual operation. Denouncing these gifts given to Evan, Penn-Lewis lectured that unless he was totally crucified to self, he was deceived. Filled with condemnation, Evan finally agreed that all the supernatural operations he had experienced couldn't have been of God. Besides confounding the multitudes, Evan concluded that he too, had been deceived by the supernatural operations.

From this point on, Evan determined from Mrs. Penn-Lewis' counsel that he would no longer trust any moving of the supernatural. And he concluded that in order for the Holy Spirit to move through any believer, he or she would have to have a far greater wisdom and experience than that which he possessed. The depressed revivalist's condition was extremely frail and was further frustrated by the repeated prodding and drilling of Penn-Lewis.

I wonder if Evan ever considered the thousands that turned to God and became born again because of those gifts. Could he remember the multitudes that came from other nations to receive from his ministry and carry it to their countries? No doubt he heard of their glowing reports in their own nations.

I wonder if he thought of the multitudes, hungry for a touch, who stood in the streets because he had been so transparent for the Holy Spirit to use. Did he ever once consider that his lack of rest – not a lack of consecration – caused his confusion? Did he think the mistakes he made from exhaustion summed the total fruit of his ministry?

If Evan Roberts ever did consider these things, the thought never turned to action. Thus, the spiritual equipment that came as a result of his call was severely damaged for any future manifestation.

PULPIT MINISTRY? NEVER AGAIN

Faced with much criticism for her actions with Evan, Mrs. Penn-Lewis wrote to a respected revivalist. In the letter she stated how Evan Roberts needed to be "safe-guarded" and that he was maturing at a "great rate, seeing how he had been misled." She later wrote the same minister, this time stating how Evan had grown spiritually and that she could see how the two of them were being "specially trained for a special work."[27]

In my opinion, it seems that Mrs. Penn-Lewis was using the strength and call of Evan Roberts to promote herself. From past record, she didn't have the strength, character, or call to make it on her own. Therefore, I believe she needed something that would prove her spiritual validity. And that "something" was Evan Roberts. If she could gain his partnership, then she could share his platform.

Though Evan remained isolated at the home of Penn-Lewis, a minister and a friend were allowed to visit him. As they counseled and prayed with him, they greatly influenced his recovery. Their love helped to encourage Evan spiritually, but it was still another year before the emotionally shattered revivalist was able to physically stand or walk.

After a year, medical advisors told Evan to never undertake pulpit ministry again. He would be able to do informal counseling, but he was advised to never preach again. Obviously, for more reasons than health, Penn-Lewis agreed.

Unaware of his physical condition, the Welsh revival converts were very hurt. They felt deserted by their leader. A year or so after Evan's move to Woodlands, concerned friends made accusations that Penn-Lewis was guilty of misleading Evan and that she had been far too secretive concerning their relationship. Evan answered their criticism by saying that he remained at her estate of his own free will. He also said Penn-Lewis was "one sent by God" and that her work could only be understood by "the faithful ones of God whose eyes are opened of God."[28] But sadly, with eyes wide open, it was Evan who refused to see.

SEVERING THE BLOOD TIE

Shortly thereafter, Evan began to refuse visits from his closest relatives. When his mother became seriously ill, the news wasn't passed on to him because of his nervous condition. It seems the decision was made by Penn-Lewis. But once when Evan's father came to see him, it was not Penn-Lewis, but Evan himself who refused to speak with him. The reason given for not seeing his father was that **he had been set apart for a highly spiritual task and had thus been obliged to forget ties of blood."**[29]

Don't ever cut your family off. Whether or not you see "eye to eye" with them is irrelevant.

There is an important point I want to make here. *Don't ever cut your family off.* Whether or not you see "eye to eye" with them is irrelevant. Many of you are where you are today because of the prayers of your family. The old saying, "Blood is thicker than water," is true. When all of hell turns against you, you can usually count on your family to love and care for you, especially if you were raised in a Christian home. By cutting off your blood ties, you cut off part of your own heritage. For some reason, it seems revivalists can be misled in this area, especially if they feel their family isn't spiritual enough for them. John Alexander Dowie went through the same thing. He even forsook his last name for a season. You can never become so spiritual that you forsake the Word of God that commands: "Honour thy father and mother; which is the first commandment with promise; That it may be well with thee, and thou mayest live long on the earth" (Ephesians 6:2,3).

According to the Word, if you dishonor your family, you will not be at peace and your life could be shortened. If you feel too spiritual for your family, then love them to your level. Never forsake them.

WAR ON THE RANKS

During these isolated years, Penn-Lewis relied on the anointing of Evan Roberts and wrote a number of books. The first one, *War on the Saints*, was published in 1913. Mrs. Penn-Lewis stated the book was birthed from six years of prayer and testing of the truth. It is believed the two authored the book together, but she received the credit. And rightfully so. Intended to be a complete answer manual to spiritual problems, it was instead, a compiled work of spiritual confusion.

Within a year after the book was published, Roberts denounced it. He told friends it had been a **"failed weapon which had confused and divided the Lord's people."**

Though his opinion eventually changed, during the years of writing *War on the Saints*, Evan seemed mesmerized by Penn-Lewis, saying, **"I know of none equal to her in understanding of spiritual things, she is a veteran in heavenly things."**[30] At this stage of Evan's recovery, Penn-Lewis convinced him that his sufferings were a divine plan of God to equip him to do battle against satanic powers and to train others for battle. As a result, she persuaded him to translate into Welsh *her* revelations on warfare and to compose booklets of it into English.

It is amazing to see how a national revivalist, once so strong and invincible from the power of the Holy Spirit, could now become so harnessed, subdued, and deceived. The biblical stories of Elijah and Jezebel, or of Samson and Delilah, continue to repeat themselves throughout history.

SERMONS IN THE SHADOWS

The newly-formed team of Roberts and Penn-Lewis also published a magazine entitled, *The Overcomer*. This was a Penn-Lewis idea in which Evan wrote an essay and she wrote the remainder of the issue. From my personal view, the magazine was just another tool of Penn-Lewis' continued need to bring validity and popularity to her work. It attacked early Pentecostal groups and listed their practices as satanic. But with a mailing list of approximately five thousand people, circulation went throughout Britain, Europe, North America, South Africa, Korea, and China.

Penn-Lewis fell ill in late 1913. In her absence, Evan wrote most of the magazine. Then several months after her health returned, she announced she was closing the magazine. She decided to hold what she called, "Christian Workers' Conferences" where she would preach. During these conferences, Evan was to stay in the prayer room, and at times, he would be allowed to counsel groups of people. This was justified by the fact that his medical advisors had told him to never again stand behind the pulpit. So Evan submitted and used his gifts in counseling. One person who sat under his group counsel said, "What strikes me most is Evan Roberts' accuracy of insight, for he is rarely at fault in his diagnosis and his spiritual discernment."[31]

How could one, who once seemed so invincible from the might of the Holy Spirit, and who balked at anyone who suggested otherwise, now be contained to only counseling sessions?

Penn-Lewis' conferences eventually became less popular over the years. When they did subside, Evan found his outlet through The School of Prayer. The school came out of "The Prayer Watch" that was instituted during the Swansea Convention of 1908. In The School of Prayer, Evan taught how to intercede for families, ministers, and churches. And he wrote essays on various aspects and degrees of prayer. Several ministers commented that everything they knew about prayer came from Evan's teachings.

"I would like to reach a state of prayer where my life would be nought but one prayer from morn to night."

Evan came alive when he spoke of prayer. The school sparked a new flame inside him. Eventually he detached himself from The Prayer Watch and turned privately toward his own prayer life.

For awhile, several met with him in his prayer room within the Penn-Lewis home. Then he pulled himself away from the group and chose to intercede privately before the Lord. Evan once commented to a friend, "I would like to reach a state of prayer where my life would be nought but one prayer from morn to night."[32]

Evan seemed thrilled to be called to a life of intercession. His prayer ministry focused on Christian leaders and believers around the world. When a group of French Salvation Army officers asked him about aggressive warfare, he answered:

"In Luke it does not say, 'preach and faint not,' but 'pray and faint not.' It is not difficult to preach. But while you pray, you are alone in some solitary place, fighting in a prayer-battle against the powers of darkness. And you will know the secret of victory."[33]

I believe this statement supported Evan's choice to leave public ministry. In fact, he became so detached from humanity that he could no longer relate to people. Penn-Lewis wrote this of his behavior:

"Those who are around him can't get into conversation with him – even if present in the same house."[34]

Evan Roberts remained inside the walls of the Penn-Lewis home for eight years.

The life of Evan Roberts was complex. I find it interesting that even though Penn-Lewis used Evan's ministry influence for her own ulterior motives, Evan obviously allowed it. In the beginning, he probably had little choice because of his invalid-like condition. However, the young revivalist remained in her household for *eight years*. And this leaves me with a multitude of questions. Was the Penn-Lewis home a comfort zone for him? Did he lose all confidence in his public image? Why didn't he go home? Did his emotional breakdowns cause him to feel secure with someone else in control? The only thing we can conclude for sure is that Evan Roberts made a choice to leave the public forefront. And the Penn-Lewis home is where he wanted to be.

"SHALL WE HAVE REVIVAL AGAIN?"

It is not exactly clear how or why Penn-Lewis and Evan Roberts separated. First, it was noticed in 1920 that he was no longer contributing to any of her writings. When asked about his absence, she responded, "It is remarkable that Mr. Roberts has never been able to take part in the work again, but his work has been carried on by others."[35]

Then sometime between 1919 and 1921, Evan moved to Brighton, in Sussex. He had purchased a typewriter and began to write several booklets. But they were unorganized and much of the Scripture was out of context. The booklets were never a success.

Evan had written to several friends in his homeland to tell them how he had never forgotten their love and support. England and Wales were bitterly divided at this time. Returning to his homeland wouldn't be easy without the support and the permission from the citizens of Wales. Besides the fact that Evan had left, the converts of the Welsh Revival were shocked and outraged at what they had read in *War on the Saints*. It seemed to them their leader was now contradicting everything he once stood for. The Welsh didn't know what to think of the young revivalist now. They thought they had known his heart, but they couldn't explain his actions.

Evan wrote to his denomination and congratulated a minister who received a new position in it. The minister was elated to receive the letter and asked if he could publish it to break Evan's ten-year silence. Evan consented, and was invited to return to Wales at his convenience. Evan did just that.

In 1926, Evan's father fell ill. When Evan returned home for a visit, the family was receptive. All the members were happy to see him and assured him that all was forgiven. And while he was there, some members of a particular chapel asked him to hold a service. Obviously forgetting the medical advisor's warning, Evan took the pulpit. While the congregation was surprised at his middle-aged appearance, they recognized the power of the Holy Spirit that still rung through Evan's voice. The people became so excited that it was murmured throughout northern Wales, "Shall we have revival again?"

"Something like electricity went through us. One felt that if he had gone on there would have been another revival then and there."

Mrs. Penn-Lewis died of lung disease in 1927. Evan had been longing for his homeland of Wales for some time. After her death in 1927, Evan returned home permanently. It is interesting to note that though he began to *visit* Wales, he never *moved* there from England until Penn-Lewis died.

"THE ROOM FLOODED WITH LIGHT"

Evan's father died in 1928, and at the funeral service, Evan did something unusual. As his father was being somberly eulogized, he suddenly interrupted the ritual and said, **"This is not a death but a resurrection. Let us bear witness to this truth."** Of that day, one person remarked, "Something like electricity went through us. One felt that if he had gone on there would have been another revival then and there."[36]

Indeed, there was a short revival. The deacons of Moriah asked Evan to take part in a special service. When he decided to speak, the exciting news traveled throughout Wales. Visitors poured into northern Wales, and locals rushed to the chapel after work. Two hours before the service began, the chapel was full. Outside in the streets, another large crowd had assembled. Young people were eager to hear the man their parents spoke of. Evan calmly addressed the crowd. Then he went outside to address the overflow of people.

During this brief period, he visited various chapels and warned against the choking materialism that had crept into the church. Once, two parents brought their child to Evan in his prayer room. As he prayed for the child, "the room was flooded with light and with a sense of the Spirit of God." The parents began to praise and worship God at the top of their voice. Soon, nearby workers heard them and left their jobs to join the group. Shoppers in the same district also heard the celebration and ran to take part. In a matter of time, there was such a large crowd gathered in the streets that wagons couldn't get through the streets. According to an eyewitness, Evan prayed for healings and deliverances and operated in the gift of prophecy. But he is said to have openly rebuked someone who tried to speak in tongues. Nevertheless, some thought Evan Roberts had become Pentecostal.[37] Healings, conversions, and answered prayers were the most talked about results of this small revival. A year later, Evan Roberts totally disappeared from public life.

A SHADOW OF SUCCESS

By 1931, Evan was almost a forgotten man. He stayed in a room provided by Mrs. Oswald Williams. She wanted nothing from Evan but to ensure his peace of mind. He spent the last years of his life writing poetry and letters to ministers. He kept a daily journal and enjoyed watching sports and theater. In May, 1949, Evan had to stay in bed all day for the first time. One word was written in the September, 1950, portion of his journal. It was the word, **"ill."**

Evan Roberts was buried on January 29, 1951, at the age of seventy-two. He was buried in the family plot behind Moriah Chapel in northern Wales. Some years later, a memorial column was raised in front of Moriah commemorating his efforts to stir revival.

The funeral service itself turned into a memorial. Hundreds who loved Evan Roberts but had lost sight of him through the years, attended and sang his favorite hymns.

Of the many tributes to him, the memorial in *The Western Mail* eulogized him best. It read:

> "He was a man who had experienced strange things. In his youth, he had seemed to hold the nation in the palms of his hands. He endured strains and underwent great changes of opinion and outlook but his religious convictions remained firm to the end."

Indeed, Evan Roberts was a great revivalist who held the keys of spiritual awakening. He pioneered a tremendous move of the Spirit of God in Wales. However, forty years later, not a trace of this revival could be found in his homeland. It would remain as only a memory in the hearts of those who experienced it.

If a move of God fades away, it is partly because the people never continued in what they received. So we are in error if we solely blame the leader.

But, why just "a memory"?

Because one man can't carry the weight of revival alone. He can *lead* a move of God, but the people also have their part to play. If a move of God fades away, it is partly because the people never continued in what they received. So we are in error if we solely blame the leader.

There are a multitude of unanswered questions circling Evan Roberts' life. Some believe Evan was ordained by God for a two-year public ministry, then was called to spend the rest of his life in worldwide prayer and intercession. If this were totally true, I believe he would have died a happy man. But dark and depressing poetry was found written in his journals. In his sixties, he wondered if there was any purpose left in his life. His reaction was a mixture of "personal loss, loneliness, and failure."[38] It seemed he continually searched for the part he was to play.

I believe Evan Roberts carried the spiritual truths that would shake the world, but those truths were only in his heart. It seemed he could never find the keys to emotional strength. Evan wanted his personality to fade into the shadows and he said repeatedly, **"I do not want to be seen."** Yet, in my opinion, the weakness of his emotional disposition caused him to be seen more than if he had taken his place in the authoritative leadership that comes in the move of God.

To carry the weight that comes with leading a revival – especially for a nation – all three parts of the human being – spirit, soul, and body – must be made strong. So as we can see from his life, there is more to revival than spiritual revelation. Spiritual hunger and revelation are always where it *begins*. But we are more than spiritual beings. The human body and emotions must be strong through the Word of God in order to maintain revival in the earth.

Your work for God doesn't have to fail or be cut short. Strengthen your body, season your soul, and yield your spirit to the plan of God. You *can* have revival in your nation and run with it successfully!

CHAPTER THREE, EVAN ROBERTS
References

1 Brynmor Pierce Jones, *An Instrument of Revival: The Complete Life of Evan Roberts 1878-1951,* (South Plainfield, NJ: Bridge Publishing, 1995), 4.
2 Ibid., 10-12.
3 Ibid., 10.
4 Ibid., 10-12, 19.
5 Ibid., 14.
6 Ibid.
7 Ibid., 14-15.
8 Ibid., 15.
9 Ibid., 23.
10 Ibid., 24.
11 Ibid., 26.
12 Ibid., 28.
13 Ibid., 37.
14 Ibid., 44.
15 Ibid., 41.
16 Ibid., 53.
17 Ibid., 58-59.
18 Ibid., 76.
19 Ibid., 77, 105.
20 Ibid., 92-98.
21 Ibid., 109.
22 Ibid., 145.
23 Ibid., 130.
24 Ibid., 158.
25 Ibid., 161.
26 Ibid., 165.
27 Ibid., 165-166.
28 Ibid., 168.
29 Ibid., 170.
30 Ibid., 169-170.
31 Ibid., 183.
32 Ibid., 190.
33 Ibid., 192.
34 Ibid., 198.
35 Ibid., 204.
36 Ibid., 217.
37 Ibid., 220-221.
38 Ibid., 240.

Charles F. Parham

"The Father of Pentecost"

"THE FATHER OF PENTECOST"

" At Christ's Second Coming the Church will be found with the same power that the Apostles and the early Church possessed. The power of Pentecost is manifest in us. The Christian religion must be demonstrated. The world wants to be shown. Then let God's power be manifest through us."[1]

Charles Fox Parham gave his life to restore the revolutionary truths of healing and the baptism of the Holy Spirit to the Church. *(Note: whenever the "Baptism of the Holy Spirit" is referred to in this chapter, it is inferred that the experience is always accompanied with the "evidence of speaking in tongues.")* The first forty years of the twentieth century were powerfully visited by this man's Pentecostal message that changed the lives of thousands around the world.

The miracles that occurred in Charles Parham's ministry are too numerous to record. Multiplied thousands found salvation, healing, deliverance, and the baptism of the Holy Spirit. When he proclaimed to the world in 1901 that, **"Speaking in tongues was the evidence of the baptism of the Holy Spirit,"** the Pentecostal truths of the early church were wonderfully restored. But the evangelist paid a price for it. The relentless backlash of persecution and slander Parham endured throughout his life would have destroyed others of lesser character. But for Parham, it only served to strengthen his hardened determination and purposeful faith.

> *When he proclaimed to the world in 1901 that, "Speaking in tongues was the evidence of the baptism of the Holy Spirit," the Pentecostal truths of the early church were wonderfully restored.*

PREACH 'TIL THE COWS COME HOME

Charles F. Parham was born on June 4, 1873. After his birth in Muscatine, Iowa, his parents, William and Ann Maria Parham, moved south to Cheney, Kansas. They truly lived as and considered themselves American pioneers.

Aside from the rugged pioneer life, early childhood was not easy for young Parham. At six months of age, he was stricken with a fever that left him bedridden. For the first five years of his life, he was plagued with dramatic spasms, and his forehead swelled making his head abnormally large. Then, at the tender age of seven, his mother died.

Though Parham had four other brothers, he felt an overwhelming sense of grief and loneliness when his beloved mother died. His memories left him melancholy and despondent, as he thought of his mother's loving attention during his illness. As his mother said her last good-byes before dying, she looked at young Parham and said, "Charlie, be good." There, in the presence of God and his dying mother, he vowed to meet her in heaven.[2] Those simple words made a deep impression on him. It has been said that they were influential in his later decision to give his life to God. Parham's father would later remarry a young woman, Harriett Miller, who was greatly loved and needed by the entire family.

When Parham was nine he contracted inflammatory rheumatism. The condition left his body tied in knots. When the affliction finally lifted, his skin was completely transparent. The boy then developed a tapeworm which required such strong medications that the lining of his stomach was eaten away and destroyed. His many trials progressed as the medications stunted his growth for three years.[3]

It was also at the tender age of nine that Parham was called to the ministry. Because he and his brothers had been taken to Sunday school during their first years of life, Parham enjoyed an early awareness of God. Even before he was converted, the boy's constant thoughts were, **"Woe is me, if I preach not the Gospel."**[4]

So he began to prepare himself for God's calling by pursuing literature. Though Kansas was not yet modernized, and libraries weren't readily available, he managed to collect a few history books along with his Bible. And he found other ways to prepare himself for the ministry by doing his chores and helping his brothers. While working with the family livestock, Parham was often known to give the cattle rousing sermons on various subjects ranging from heaven to hell.

"LIGHTNING" THAT PENETRATED

Parham never regretted that he had to do so much studying on his own. It actually worked to his advantage. There were so few churches and preachers on the prairie, and with no one to teach him otherwise, Parham studied God's

Word and took it literally. There were no inferences of man-made theology in his doctrine, and there were no traditions to break through. From an early age, up to the age of thirteen, Parham had only heard the sermons of two preachers. It was during one of these meetings that Parham was converted.

Parham believed that deep repentance must take place within a convert's heart, yet he felt void of such an emotional experience. So when he sought to be saved at the meeting, on the walk home, he began to question his conversion. He was so weighed down with a heavy heart that he was unable to pray. He found himself humming the song, *"I Am Coming to the Cross,"* and upon reaching the third verse, Parham immediately became assured of his conversion. Of the experience he later said, **"There flashed from the heavens a light above the brightness of the sun, like a stroke of lightning it penetrated, thrilling every fiber of my being."**[5] From that moment forward, Parham was never swayed from the "Anchor" of his salvation.

"WILL YOU PREACH?"

After his dramatic conversion, Parham served as a Sunday school teacher and worker. He held his first public meeting at the age of fifteen, with marked results. He preached for a short time, then entered Southwestern Kansas College at the age of sixteen.

When he entered college, Parham had every intention of entering the ministry, but he began to notice the disrespect and general disgust that the secular world held toward ministers. And he began to hear about the conditions of poverty that accompanied ministry. Discouraged by these stories, he looked upon other professions with great interest. Soon, Parham denied his calling and began to backslide.

When he entered college, Parham had every intention of entering the ministry, but he began to notice the disrespect and general disgust that the secular world held toward ministers.

In remembering his traumatic childhood illnesses, Parham reasoned that the medical field would be a good pursuit. So he began studying to be a physician. But he was constantly tormented in remembering his promise to become a missionary, and soon contracted rheumatic fever.

After suffering for months from the flames of the fever, a physician visited his bedside and pronounced Parham near death. But those bedridden months had prompted Parham to remember the words that had once rung in his ears, "Will you preach? WILL YOU PREACH?" Again he hungered to answer his call, but he didn't want to live in the impoverished conditions that seemed unavoidable for ministers of his day. So he cried out to God: **"If You will let me go somewhere, someplace, where I wouldn't have to take collections or beg for a living, I will preach."**

Parham was so sedated with morphine in his condition that he was unable to think of more words to pray. So he began reciting The Lord's Prayer. When he came to words "...thy will be done in earth as it is in heaven," his mind cleared and he envisioned God's majesty. He caught a slight glimpse of how God's will was manifested through every ounce of creation and realized that it was God's will to heal. So he cried out to God, praying, **"If Thy will is done in me, I shall be whole."** As he said this prayer, every joint in his body loosened and every organ was healed. Only his ankles remained weak. But his lungs were clear and his body recovered.

Following his recovery, Parham was quickly asked to hold an evangelistic meeting. So he renewed his promise to God, and vowed to quit college to enter the ministry if God would heal his ankles. Crawling under a tree, Parham began to pray and God immediately sent a "mighty electric current" through his ankles making them whole.[6]

A "BUMPKIN" WITH POWER

Parham held his first evangelistic meeting at the age of eighteen, in the Pleasant Valley School House, near Tonganoxie, Kansas. He was a stranger to the country community when he asked permission to hold a revival at their school. So when they gave their approval, Parham went up on a hillside, stretched his hand out over the valley and prayed that the entire community be taken for God.[7]

The first night of the meeting, the attendance was good, but most of the people weren't used to active participation. He received few responses at first, but before the evening was over, there were many conversions.

The Thistlewaites attended this meeting and wrote of it to their daughter. Their daughter, Sarah, had grown up in the community and was in Kansas City attending school. When she returned home, the meeting had closed, but the community had arranged for Parham to come back the next Sunday.

At the meeting, the refined Sarah Thistlewaite was surprised by what she saw. Parham looked much different from the wealthy, cultured preachers she had been used to in Kansas City. And when he took the pulpit, he didn't have his sermon written out like the preachers she had seen. In fact, Parham never wrote down what he was going to say. He relied on the Holy Spirit to give him inspiration. Then as Sarah listened to the young evangelist preach, she realized her lack of devotion to the faith. She knew she was following Jesus from "far off," and made the decision to consecrate her life totally to the Lord. She also began to cultivate her friendship with Charles Parham and soon, what began as a simple interest, turned into a union of purpose and destiny.

DENOMINATIONS? NO MORE!

When Parham was nineteen years old he was asked to pastor the Methodist church in Eudora, Kansas. This he did faithfully, while also pastoring in Linwood on Sunday afternoons. Sarah and her family attended his services regularly.

The congregation grew steadily and a new building was built to hold the people. The denomination's leadership saw a great future for Parham, and they would have given him most any pastorate or assignment if he would have submitted to their authority. But all was not well between Parham and the Methodist denomination. Parham had vowed to follow the leading of the Holy Spirit, despite what other men asked him to do. In advising new converts, he would exhort them to find any church home, even if it wasn't the Methodist church. He explained that joining a denomination was not a prerequisite for heaven, and that denominations spent more time preaching on their particular church and its leaders than they did on Jesus Christ and His covenant. This caused many conflicts within his denominational ranks. Speaking of these conflicts, Parham said:

Many slanderous accusations had been leveled against him, and he was concerned that the rising persecution would forever ruin his work. Then one day while deep in prayer, he heard these words, "I made Myself of no reputation."

> **"Finding the confines of a pastorate, and feeling the narrowness of sectarian churchism, I was often in conflict with the higher authorities, which eventually resulted in open rupture; and I left denominationalism forever, though suffering bitter persecution at the hands of the church.... Oh, the narrowness of many who call themselves the Lord's own!"[8]**

Parham's parents were greatly disappointed in their son, since they were strong supporters of the church. So when Parham resigned, he sought rest in the home of friends, who welcomed him as their own son.

Parham began to pray for direction. Many slanderous accusations had been leveled against him, and he was concerned that the rising persecution would forever ruin his work. Then one day while deep in prayer, he heard these words, "I made Myself of no reputation." Immediately, Parham was strengthened and encouraged. As the Spirit of God continued to give him Scripture, he set his course. He would enter the evangelistic field, unassociated with any form of denomination. He would hold his meetings in schools, halls, churches, tabernacles – wherever he could – and believe for the Holy Spirit to manifest Himself in a mighty way.

While holding a meeting in western Kansas, Parham wrote to Sarah Thistlewaite and proposed marriage. He warned Sarah that his life was totally dedicated to the Lord and that his future was unclear, but if she could trust God with him, they should marry. Charles and Sarah were married six months later, on December 31, 1896, in her grandfather's home.

HEAL YOURSELF!

As the young couple started traveling, they were received with great approval. September of 1897 saw the birth of their first son, Claude. But the joy of the event was short-lived when Charles fell ill with heart disease. No amount of medicine seemed to work as he grew weaker. Then, without warning, tiny Claude was stricken with a high fever. The Parham's walked the floor praying for the baby, but to no avail. The physician couldn't diagnose Claude's fever, and therefore, had no cure.

Parham was called to pray for another man who was ill, so in his own weakened state, he left for the man's home. While praying for the man, the Scripture, "Physician, heal thyself," exploded inside of Parham and while he was praying, the power of God had touched Parham. He was healed instantly.

Parham eagerly rushed home after the visit, grabbed Sarah, and told her of his experience, then prayed for his baby. He then threw away all of his medicines, vowing to never again trust anything but the Word of God. The fever left Claude's body, and he grew to be a healthy child.

I want to say something here. Parham's healing ministry was always controversial to those who misunderstood it. He lived in a time when physicians, as a whole, stood contrary to the Gospel. It was Parham's *personal faith* that inspired him to throw away his medicine. He believed that to trust totally in medicine was to deny the blood of Jesus and the price Christ paid on the cross. When true revelation comes, it is invincible. It will always produce the success it illustrates. Parham's deep revelation was transferred to his family and medicine was forbidden in his home. But he left the final decision regarding their use of medication to anyone else. There will always be those who follow the inspiration of another, without any revelation themselves. Because of this we have seen entire sections of the body of Christ refuse to use medication and call those who do "sinners." Parham never taught this so it would be a mistake to blame him, as so many have, for the errors some believers have made about divine healing.

THE "LIVE OR DIE" VOW

Not long after Parham and his son were healed, he received some heart-breaking news. Within the time frame of a week, two of his closest friends had died. Consumed with grief, Parham hurried to their graves. It was a day that marked the rest of his ministry:

> **"As I knelt between the graves of my two loved friends, who might have lived if I had but told them of the power of Christ to heal, I made a vow that 'Live or Die' I would preach this Gospel of healing."[9]**

Parham moved his family to Ottawa, Kansas, where he held his first divine healing meeting. During the meeting, he boldly proclaimed the truths of God's Word. A woman with dropsy, given three days to live, was instantly healed. Another young invalid lady, blind and ill with the consumption, felt a tearing sensation through her chest and was completely healed. God also instantly restored her eyesight, and she spent the rest of her life sewing for a living.

The truths of divine healing were rare in the Church during these years.

The truths of divine healing were rare in the Church during these years. Dowie and Etter had great success, but these truths were virtually unknown in the Prairie. Though results couldn't be denied, many claimed the power that manifested through Parham was of the devil. The accusations drove Parham to shut himself in a room to establish himself in the truth. As he prayed and searched the Scriptures, Parham found that everywhere he looked in the Bible, healing was present. He realized that healing, just as salvation, came through the atoning work of Jesus' blood, and from that point on, persecution and slander never slighted him. Then a revolutionary idea had come to him: he would provide a refuge home for those seeking healing. Parham was filled with joy!

A FAITH HOME "ALL THE WAY"

A daughter was born to the Parhams in November of 1898 on Thanksgiving Day. They named her Esther Marie. Not long after, Parham opened his divine healing home in Topeka, Kansas, which he and Sarah named "Bethel." The purpose was to provide a home-like atmosphere for those who trusted God for healing. The ground floor had a chapel, a reading room, and a printing office. The top floor had fourteen rooms with large windows. The Parhams kept the windows filled with fresh flowers, making the atmosphere of the home peaceful and beautiful. Chapel services were held daily, where the Word of God was powerfully taught. And prayer was offered individually, several times throughout the day and night.

Bethel also offered special classes for ministers and evangelists which prepared and trained them for the ministry. This place of refuge also found Christian homes for orphans, and jobs for the unemployed.

One guest at Bethel wrote:

> "Who can think of a sweeter name than 'Bethel'? Surely it is the House of God. Everything moves in love and harmony. On entering the rooms one is impressed with the divine influence shed abroad here.... It is a Faith Home all the way through."[10]

Parham's newsletter, *The Apostolic Faith*, published bi-weekly, had a subscription price at first. But Parham quickly changed this by asking readers to study Isaiah 55:1, then give to the paper as they felt led. The newsletter published wonderful testimonies of healing and many of the sermons that were taught at Bethel.

Parham always believed that God would provide the financial support for Bethel. Once, after a hard day of ministry, he realized the rent was due the next morning and he didn't have the money to meet it. Tired and weary, he looked to the sky and told the Lord that he must have rest and that he knew God wouldn't fail him. The next morning, a man showed up at Bethel, saying, "I was suddenly awakened with the thought of you and your work; no sleep came to me until I promised to bring you this." It was the exact sum for the rent.

Another time, Parham only had a partial sum to pay on a bill that was due. So he set out to the bank to pay what he had and while on the way, he passed an acquaintance who handed Parham some money. When Parham got to the bank, he found the money was the exact amount he needed to pay the bill in full.[11] And there are many other incredible stories of financial provision surrounding Parham's ministry.

The Parham family was blessed with another son in March of 1900. They named him, Charles, after his father. Now his family seemed to be outgrowing the Bethel Home, so a parsonage was built. Along with his growing family, Parham's spiritual hunger was growing so he felt he should leave Bethel and visit different ministries. Leaving two Holiness ministers in charge, Parham set out to visit the ministries of several different godly men in Chicago, New York, and Maine. He returned home, refreshed and renewed with an even deeper hunger:

"I returned home fully convinced that while many had obtained real experience in sanctification and the anointing that abideth, there still remained a great outpouring of power for the Christians who were to close this age."[12]

These words contained the seeds of the truths Parham would later unveil.

SURROUNDED BY A HALO

Because of his tremendous success at Bethel, many began to urge Parham to open a Bible school. So again, Parham shut himself away to fast and pray. Then in October of 1900, he obtained a beautiful structure in Topeka, Kansas, for the purpose of beginning a Bible school, and called it, "Stone's Folly."

The building was patterned after an English castle. But the builder ran out of money before the structure could be completed in style. The staircase that joined the first and second floor was carved with finished woodwork of cedar, cherrywood, maple, and pine. The third floor was finished in common wood and paint.

The outside of Stone's Folly was laid in red brick and white stone, with a winding stairway leading to an observatory. Another doorway led from there to a small room known as the Prayer Tower. Students took turns to pray three hours each day in this special tower.

The outside of Stone's Folly was laid in red brick and white stone, with a winding stairway leading to an observatory. Another doorway led from there to a small room known as the Prayer Tower. Students took turns to pray three hours each day in this special tower.

When Stone's Folly was dedicated, a man looked out from the Prayer Tower and saw a vision above Stone's Folly of a "vast lake of fresh water about to over-flow, containing enough to satisfy every thirsty need."[13] It would prove to be a sign of things to come.

Parham's Bible school was open to every Christian minister and believer, who was willing to "forsake all." They were to arrive willing to study the Word deeply and believe God for all their personal needs. The student's faith was their only tuition; everyone was to believe that God would supply their needs.

Examinations were given that December on the subjects of repentance, conversion, consecration, sanctification, healing, and the future coming of the Lord. When the book of Acts was included for the study of these subjects, Parham gave his students a historical assignment. They were to diligently study the Bible's evidence of the baptism in the Holy Spirit and report on their find-ings in three days. After assigning this homework, Parham left his students for a meeting in Kansas City. Then he returned to Stone's Folly for the annual Watch Night Service.

Stone's Folly, Topeka, Kansas

On the morning that the assignments were due, Parham listened to the reports of forty students, and was astonished by what he heard. While different manifestations of the Spirit occurred during the outpouring of Pentecost in Acts, every student had arrived at the same general conclusion: *Every recipient baptized by the Holy Spirit spoke in other tongues!*

Now there was a great excitement and new interest at Stone's Folly surrounding the book of Acts. Anticipation filled the atmosphere as seventy-five people crowded around one another at the school for the evening Watch Night Service.

During the service, a spiritual freshness seemed to blanket the meeting. Then a student, Agnes Ozman, approached Parham and asked him to lay his hands on her so she would receive the baptism of the Holy Spirit. Ozman believed she was called to the mission field and wanted to be equipped with spiritual power. At first Parham hesitated, telling her that he himself didn't speak in other tongues. But she persisted, and Parham humbly laid his hands upon her head. Parham would later write of the incident, explaining it like this:

"I had scarcely repeated three dozen sentences when a glory fell upon her, a halo seemed to surround her head and face, and she began speaking in the Chinese language, and was unable to speak English for three days."[14]

Ozman later testified that she had already received a few of these same words while in the Prayer Tower. But after Parham laid hands on her, she completely overflowed with the supernatural power of God.

THE TONGUES OF FIRE

After witnessing this incredible outpouring of the Holy Spirit, the students moved their beds from the upper dormitory and turned it into a prayer room. For two nights and three days, the school waited upon the Lord.

They were sitting, kneeling, and standing with hands raised, and they were all speaking in other tongues. Some were trembling under the power of God.

In January of 1901, Parham preached at a church in Topeka, telling the people of the wonderful experiences that were happening at Stone's Folly. And he told them that he believed he would soon speak in other tongues. That night after returning home from the meeting, he was met by one of the students who led him into the Prayer Room. When he stepped inside, he was amazed at the sight of twelve denominational ministers. They were sitting, kneeling, and standing with hands raised, and they were all speaking in other tongues. Some were trembling under the power of God. An elderly lady approached Parham, to relate how moments before he had entered the room, "tongues of fire" sat upon their heads.

Overcome by what he saw, Parham fell to his knees behind a table praising God. Then he asked God for the same blessing, and when he did, Parham distinctly heard God's calling to stand up in the world. He was to reveal the truth of this mighty outpouring everywhere he would go. The enlightened minister was also made aware of the severe persecutions that would accompany his stand. But he counted the cost and decided to obey; just as he had obeyed in proclaiming divine healing. It was then that Charles Parham himself was filled with the Holy Spirit, and spoke in other tongues.

"Right then and there came a slight twist in my throat, a glory fell over me and I began to worship God in a Swedish tongue, which later changed to other languages and continued...."[15]

Soon the news of what God was doing had Stone's Folly beseiged by newspaper reporters, language professors, and government interpreters. They sat in on the services to tell the whole world of this incredible phenomenon. They had come to the consensus that Stone's Folly's students were speaking in the languages of the world. And their newspapers screamed with the headlines "Pentecost! Pentecost!" Newsboys shouted, "Read about the Pentecost!"

On January 21, 1901, Parham preached the first sermon dedicated to the sole experience of the baptism of the Holy Spirit with the evidence of speaking in other tongues.

DOORWAY TO THE SUPERNATURAL

Some say today that "tongues have passed away." But my friend, when miracles pass away, when signs and wonders pass away, when the manifestations of the Holy Spirit pass away, tongues will pass away too. Then we will have no need for other tongues. But as long as we are on planet earth, these things shall remain. The book of Acts continues to be lived out in the life of the Church today. The only thing that has passed away is the sacrificing of lambs, because

Jesus fulfilled the sacrifice system of shedding of blood and removed the veil separating God and man.

Praying in other tongues will birth the will of God in your spirit. You will no longer depend on your intellect or the direction of others. You will "know" for yourself what the will of the Father is for your life. Sometimes we are limited in our prayer life by our national language, and don't always know how to pray for a situation. The Word tells us that "praying in the spirit," or in tongues, enables us to pray the perfect will of God into every situation because praying in tongues moves us into the realm of the Spirit. You can go to heaven without the baptism of the Holy Spirit, but it is not God's highest desire for you.

There are several different operations of tongues spoken of in the Bible. First, tongues can manifest in a supernatural language that other nationalities can understand (see Acts 2:8-11). Secondly, the gift of tongues can be spoken out by one person in a public setting and then followed with the interpretation of that language, which brings edification to the people gathered there (see 1 Corinthians 14:27-28). And there is the prayerful language of tongues, that will edify and build your faith. Finally, praying in the spirit will bring boldness, strength, direction, and guidance into a believer's life. Praying in tongues is also one of the most powerful forms of spiritual intercession (see 1 Corinthians 14:4; Jude 20; Romans 8:26-27; Ephesians 6:18).

If you haven't experienced the baptism of the Holy Spirit with the evidence of other tongues, then earnestly seek God for this. Speaking in other tongues is not just "for some." It is for *everyone,* just like salvation. When you choose to enter into this measure of God's fullness, your life will never be the same.

> *"I am healed of my infidelity; I have heard in my own tongue the 23rd Psalm that I learned at my mother's knee."*

SPIRITUAL FATHERHOOD

At this stage of Parham's life, there had never been such "refined glory" and peace in his household. Parham went throughout the country, preaching the truths of the baptism of the Holy Spirit in wonderful demonstration. Once in a service, he began to speak in other tongues, then when he had finished, a man in the congregation stood up and said, "I am healed of my infidelity; I have heard in my own tongue the 23rd Psalm that I learned at my mother's knee."[16] This was only one of the countless testimonies regarding the gift of other tongues that came out of Parham's ministry. Soon, hundreds upon hundreds began to receive this manifestation. But along with this mighty outpouring came a slanderous persecution of those who despised it.

Then, tragedy struck the Parham household again. Their youngest child, Charles, died on March 16, 1901. The family was grief-stricken. Their sorrow was compounded even further when those who stood against the Parhams persecuted them for contributing to the death of their son. Then many who loved the family, but didn't believe in divine healing, added to the sadness by encouraging the Parhams to forsake their belief in this area. But through it all, the Parhams showed tremendous character by choosing to keep their hearts tender toward the Lord and win this test of faith. As a result Parham would continue in an even greater fervency in the preaching of Christ's *miraculous* Gospel – around the world.

In the fall of 1901, the Bible school in Topeka was unexpectedly sold out from under Parham, for the purposes of secular use. Parham warned the new buyers if they used the school for secular reasons, the building would be destroyed. But they ignored his prophetic warning, and by the end of December news had reached Parham that the building had been totally destroyed by a fire.

After Stone's Folly sold, the Parhams moved into a rented home in Kansas City. It was then that Parham began to hold meetings around the country. Hundreds of people, from every denomination, received the baptism of the Holy Spirit and divine healing. As is true with every pioneering revivalist, Parham was either greatly loved or hated by the public, but his colorful personality and warm heart were recognized by all. One Kansas newspaper wrote: "Whatever may be said about him, he has attracted more attention to religion than any other religious worker in years."[17]

In 1901 Parham published his first book, *A Voice Crying in the Wilderness*. The book was filled with sermons on salvation, healing, and sanctification. Many ministers throughout the world studied and taught from it.

Another son, Philip Arlington, was born to the Parhams in June of 1902. By now Charles had become a father of the Pentecostal outpouring, and was continually watching over his spiritual children to help them grow in the truth. Parham had his first experience with fanaticism in 1903. He preached at a church where wild and fleshly manifestations took place. The experience would add a new dimension to his teaching. Though he never allowed himself to be called the leader in this Pentecostal Movement, Parham felt personally responsible in seeing that the baptism of the Holy Spirit was manifested according to the Word. So he endeavored to learn the personality of the Holy Spirit, and spoke strongly against anything contrary to what he had learned.

Perhaps it was this personal passion that caused him to speak out against the manifestations at Azusa in later years.

"HE PREACHES IN BIG CHUNKS"

In the fall of 1903, the Parhams moved to Galena, Kansas, and erected a large tent. The tent could hold two thousand people, but it was still too small to accommodate the crowds. So a building was located as winter set in. But even then, the doors had to be left open during services so those outside could participate. Huge numbers poured into Galena from surrounding towns when strong manifestations of the Spirit occurred, and hundreds were miraculously healed and saved.

> *"Many...came to scoff but remained to pray."*

In those days, cards were handed to people who came for healing. The common procedure was to write numbers on the cards and hand the cards to those who were seeking prayer. Then during the service, the numbers were randomly called out and prayer was offered for those holding the card number called. So with this practice everyone was given an equal chance. But Parham shunned the practice and chose to pray for all who came, despite the length of time that it took.

Two newspapers, the *Joplin Herald* and the *Cincinnati Inquirer*, declared Parham's Galena meetings to be the greatest demonstration of power and miracles since the time of the Apostles, writing, "Many...came to scoff but remained to pray."[18]

On March 16, 1904, Wilfred Charles was born to the Parhams. One month later, Charles moved the family to Baxter Springs, Kansas, then continued to hold tremendous meetings around the state.

Parham always warned the crowds to never call him "healer," reminding them that he no more had the power to heal than he had the power to save. One observer said, "Brother Parham surely preached God's Holy Word straight from the shoulder; in chunks big, pure, and hard enough to knock the scales from our eyes."[19]

The revivalist's meetings were always very interesting. Parham was known to have a great love for the Holy Land, and always implemented its beliefs in his teachings. So besides the many miracles, he would often display a great array of garments from the Holy Land that he had collected over a period of time. The newspapers always highlighted this aspect of his ministry favorably.

Stone's Folly Students, 1905

Crusade Team, Houston, Texas, 1905

In 1905, Parham traveled to Orchard, Texas. He did so in response to certain believers who had attended his Kansas meetings and had fervently prayed for him to come to their part of the country. When ministering in Orchard, there was such a great outpouring of the Spirit, that Parham was inspired to begin holding his "Rally Days." These were a series of meetings that were strategically planned and held throughout America. Many workers volunteered to assist in the outreach once Parham returned to Kansas.

EVERYTHING'S BIG IN TEXAS!

The first Rally Day was planned for Houston, Texas. Parham and twenty-five workers held this meeting in a place called Bryn Hall, where they were advertised as non-denominational and invited anyone who wanted to experience more of the power of God. The newspapers loved the novelty of Parham's Holy Land array, and favorably wrote of all the miracles that happened.

After these meetings, Parham and his group held large parades, marching down the streets of Houston in their Holy Land garments. The parades helped to spark the interest of many who attended the evening services. When the Rally Days were over, Parham's group returned to Kansas, rejoicing in the Lord.

Due to high public demand, the team returned to Houston once more, but this time, heavy persecution came their way. Several of Parham's workers were poisoned during one meeting making them very ill, with severe pain. But Parham prayed for each of them immediately, and they recovered completely.

Parham's schools were never meant to be theological seminaries.

Parham's own life was threatened several times, but he always escaped. Once, after taking a drink of water on the platform, Parham was doubled over with tremendous pain. But he began to pray and the pain left instantly. Later when the water from his glass was examined chemically, it was found to contain enough poison to kill a dozen men.[20]

Undaunted by the persecution, Parham announced the opening of a new Bible school in Houston, then moved his headquarters there in the winter of 1905. The school was supported like the one in Topeka, through freewill offerings. There was no tuition and each student had to believe for their own means. It was said that a military style of order was practiced at the school and that each person understood how to work in harmony.[21]

Parham's schools were never meant to be theological seminaries. They were training centers where the truths of God were taught in the most practical manner – with prayer as a key ingredient. Many ministers left his schools to serve God throughout the world.

It was in Houston that Parham met William J. Seymour. Up to this time, the Jim Crow Laws forbid blacks and whites from attending school together. And Parham's meetings were segregated, but it was because blacks didn't ask to attend the schools, that is until Seymour. Seymour's humility and hunger for the Word so moved Parham that he decided to ignore the racist rules of the day. Seymour was given a place in the school where he experienced revolutionary truths on the baptism of the Holy Spirit. William Seymour would later become the leader of the Azusa Street Mission in Los Angeles, California.

After Parham's historical Houston school came to a close, he moved his family back to Kansas, and on June 1, 1906, Robert (their last child) was born.

Parham continued to hold meetings throughout the country and was in great demand. It was at this time that he received letters from Seymour, asking him to come to the Mission in Los Angeles at Azusa Street. It was said that Seymour wrote "urgent letters appealing for help, as spiritualistic manifestations, hypnotic forces and fleshly contortions...had broken loose in the meeting. He wanted Mr. Parham to come quickly and help him discern between that which was real and that which was false."[22] In spite of the plea, Parham felt led by God to hold a rally in Zion City, Illinois, instead.

WALKING ON THE WATER AT ZION

When Parham arrived in Zion, he found the community in great distress. Dowie had been discredited in his ministry there, and others were in the process of taking control of the city. There was a strong oppression hanging over the town, because people from all nations and all walks of life had invested their future in the hands of Dowie. Discouraged and broken, these people had lost hope. Parham saw this as a wonderful opportunity to bring the baptism of the Holy Spirit to Zion. He could think of no greater blessing or joy, than to introduce the fullness of the Spirit to these people.

When Parham arrived in Zion, he met with great opposition, and was unable to secure a building for the meetings. So all doors of opportunity seemed to close. Finally, at the invitation of a hotel manager, he was able to set up a meeting in a private room. The next night, two rooms and the hallway were crowded and attendance grew steadily from there.

Soon Parham began cottage meetings in the best homes of the city. One of these homes belonged to the great healing evangelist and author, F. F.

Bosworth. Bosworth's home was literally turned into a meeting house during Parham's stay. Every night, Parham led five different meetings in five different homes, all beginning at 7:00 P.M. When his workers would arrive, he would go preaching from meeting to meeting, driving rapidly to make sure he reached each one. As a result, hundreds of ministers and evangelists went out from Zion filled with the power of the Spirit to preach God's Word with signs.

Though Zion was a Christian community, it seemed the persecution against Parham was the greatest ever there. Secular newspapers had a media blitz, citing the "Prophet Parham" as taking the ground of the "Prophet Dowie."[23] Dowie himself went on public record to criticize Parham's message and actions. The new Overseer of Zion, Wilbur Voliva, was eager to see Parham leave the city. Voliva wrote Parham to ask how long he intended staying in Zion. Parham replied, **"As long as the Lord wants me here."**[24]

In October of 1906, Parham felt released from Zion and hurried to Los Angeles to answer Seymour's call.

SHAKE, RATTLE, AND ROLL: THE L. A. STORY

It was told to Parham that Seymour had gone to Los Angeles with a humble spirit. Those from Texas who moved to Los Angeles with Seymour were impressed with his ability. It was clear that God was doing a wonderful work in Seymour's life. But it was also clear that Satan was trying to "tear it to pieces."[25] Because Seymour had been a student at Parham's school, Parham felt responsible for what was happening.

Parham was exiled from the meetings, and the door to the mission was padlocked so he couldn't return.

Parham's experiences at Azusa added to his understanding of fanaticism. According to Parham, there were many genuine experiences of receiving the true baptism, but there were also many false manifestations. Parham held two or three services at Azusa, but was unable to convince Seymour to change his ways. The door to the mission was padlocked so Parham couldn't return. But instead of leaving Los Angeles, Parham rented a large building and held great services that ministered deliverance from evil spirits to the crowds who had previously attended the meetings.

Parham regarded the Seymour conflict as an example of spiritual pride. He wrote about it in his newsletter and noted that fanaticism always produces an unteachable spirit in those given over to it. He explained that those under the influence of these false spirits:

"...feel exalted, thinking they have a greater experience than anyone else, not needing instruction or advice...placing them out of reach from those who can help."

He ended his newsletter "deposition" by saying:

"...although many forms of fanaticism have crept in, I believe every true child of God will come out of this mist and shadow stronger and better equipped against all extremes that are liable to present themselves at any time in meetings of this kind."[26]

"PART HAM"

Parham returned to Zion from Los Angeles in December of 1906. Unable to obtain a building, he pitched a large tent in a vacant lot. Parham's tent meetings were well attended by some two thousand people. On New Year's Eve, he preached for two hours on the baptism in the Holy Spirit, and produced such an intense excitement that several men approached Parham with the idea of beginning a "movement" and a large church.

But Parham was against the idea. He told the men that he was not there for personal gain and that his idea of coming to Zion was to bring the peace of God to replace its oppression. Parham believed America had enough churches and said that what Zion needed was more spirituality in the churches they already had. Parham felt that if his message had value, then the people would support it without an organization. He was concerned that groups who gathered around the truth of the "baptism of the Holy Spirit" would eventually develop a worldly, secular objective.

After confronting these issues, Parham officially resigned as the "projector" of the Apostolic Faith Movement. Many controversies over leadership had already developed in other states that adopted the movement. He wrote in his newsletter:

"Now that they [apostolic faith tenets] are generally accepted, I simply take my place among my brethren to push this Gospel of the kingdom as a witness to all nations."[27]

Parham's position created many new enemies at Zion and when his meetings closed, he traveled alone to Canada and New England to preach.

His family remained in Zion and were greatly persecuted. Each day at school brought new persecutions to the Parham children. Pork was forbidden in the city, and therefore, children began to call the Parhams, "Part Ham," so the children came home from school very often in tears. The Parham family believed they were persecuted mainly because they wouldn't organize a movement. Later, Charles would write:

"If I differ at all from Zion with respect to any of these truths, it is only as individuals in Zion differ among themselves."[78]

Then one day, Mrs. Parham received a disturbing letter from a Zion citizen that threatened her husband in a scandalous manner. She denounced the letter as a lie, but conditions and persecutions grew so bad that she decided to take her children back to Kansas.

FLAMES FROM HELL: THE SCANDAL

It is here that we come to the greatest controversy in the life of Charles Parham. Clearly, Parham had many enemies in prominent Christian organizations. But his main antagonist was Wilbur Voliva, the General Overseer of Zion. After Parham's public resignation as "projector" of the Apostolic Faith Movement, various rumors were circulated throughout Pentecostal circles that Parham had been arrested for sexual immorality. The *Waukegan Daily Sun* suggested that Parham's sudden departure from Zion had been prompted by "mysterious men, said to be detectives, ready to arrest him on some equally mysterious charge." The paper later admitted that its report was based on rumor and that the Zion police department knew nothing of the incident.[29] But much damage had been done.

Parham had many enemies in prominent Christian organizations.

In the summer of 1907, Parham was preaching in a former Zion mission located in San Antonio when a story reported in the *San Antonio Light* made national news. Its headline read: "Evangelist Is Arrested. C. F. Parham, Who Has Been Prominent in Meeting Here, Taken Into Custody."[30] The story said Parham had been charged with sodomy, a felony under Texas law. And that he had been arrested with his supposed companion, J. J. Jourdan who, along with him was allegedly released after making a payment of one thousand dollars.

Parham immediately fought back with rage. He secured a lawyer, C. A. Davis, and announced that he had been "elaborately framed" by his old nemesis, Wilbur Voliva. Parham was certain that Voliva was furious over a Zion city church that Parham had preached in. It had once belonged to Zion, but left the Zion association and joined the Apostolic Faith Movement.

Parham pledged to clear his name and indignantly refused to leave town. But Mrs. Parham, having previously read the rumors in a letter in Zion, left Kansas for San Antonio. The case never made it to court and Parham's name disappeared from the headlines of secular newspapers as quickly as it appeared. No formal indictment was ever filed, and to date there is no record of the incident at the Bexar County Courthouse.[31]

But the religious newspapers weren't as kind to Parham as the secular. Their press seemed to locate even more details about "his affairs." Two newspapers that took liberty with the story were the *Burning Bush*, and the *Zion Herald* (the official newspaper of Wilbur Voliva's church in Zion). These newspapers were said to have quoted the *San Antonio Light*, along with an eyewitness account of Parham's alleged improprieties, including a written confession. But when researched, it was found the articles "quoted" in the *Herald* and *Bush* *never appeared* in the San Antonio paper. It was also learned that the scandal was only publicized in certain areas – every source of which could be traced to the *Zion Herald*. If the rumor went nationwide, it traveled by the grapevine.[32]

Without a doubt, it seemed that Voliva was making the best of the scandal, "leaving no stone unturned." Though no one could actually pinpoint Voliva as the instigator of the accusations, he had been known to spread rumors frequently about immorality against his chief rivals. In addition to Parham, Voliva had launched many verbal attacks on his associates in Zion, calling them "adulterers," and "immoral." Parham's associates attempted legal action with the U. S. postal authorities for "unlawful defamation," but they refused to act on the matter.[33]

Mrs. Parham felt their enemies must have had great faith in Parham's beliefs because, if this kind of onslaught had befallen a secular person, court action would have surely followed. But Parham never discussed the incident in public. He left the matter to the discretion of his followers, believing that those who were faithful would never believe the charges.[34] On his fortieth birthday Parham wrote:

> **"I think the greatest sorrow of my life is the thought that my enemies, in seeking my destruction, have ruined and destroyed so many precious souls."**[35]

But sorrow and destruction make no difference to those who oppose the ministry of God. When Parham returned to preach in Zion nine years later, the Voliva followers fabricated posters and fliers that showed a signed confession of guilt in the crime of sodomy.[36]

LIVING IN THE LONG-AWAITED DREAM

During the years that followed the scandal, Parham continued to evangelize throughout the nation. Many said his sermons were critical of Pentecostal Christians, others said he was never able to recover from Voliva's accusations. In 1913, he was met by a mob in Wichita who were armed with clubs and pitchforks. But a friend rescued Parham by secreting him away by a different route, and the meeting continued as scheduled. Hundreds were said to have repented in Wichita, and many were healed.

Though wounded by those he thought were his friends, Parham never backed away from the cities to which God had led him. He even returned to Los Angeles and held a tremendous meeting, in which thousands were converted, baptized in the Holy Spirit, healed and delivered. In the winter of 1924, Parham held meetings in Oregon and Washington. It was at one of these that Gordon Lindsay found salvation. Lindsay went on to do a great work for God, establishing the international Bible college, Christ For The Nations, located in Dallas, Texas.

> *"I am living on the edge of the Glory Land these days and it's all so real on the other side of the curtain that I feel mightily tempted to cross over."*

Finally, in 1927, the lifetime dream of Charles F. Parham came true. Funds were collected by friends and Parham was able to visit Jerusalem. The trip was a great joy to Parham. He was thrilled as he walked through Galilee, Samaria, and Nazareth. It was here that Parham encountered his favorite passage of Scripture, Psalm 23. In Palestine the reality of the Shepherd and His sheep came alive to Parham, bringing great peace and comfort. When he returned to New York Harbor in April of 1928, he carried with him the slides of the land he loved. From then on, Parham's meetings consisted of the showing these slides that he called "The 23rd Psalm."

"PEACE, PEACE LIKE A RIVER"

By August of 1928, Parham had grown tired and worn. He told friends that his work was nearly over. To one he wrote:

"I am living on the edge of the Glory Land these days and it's all so real on the other side of the curtain that I feel mightily tempted to cross over."[37]

After spending Christmas of 1929 with his family, Parham was scheduled to preach and show his Holy Land slides in Temple, Texas. His family was concerned with his departure because his health had deteriorated, but Parham was determined to go. Several days later, the family received word that Parham had collapsed during a meeting while showing his Holy Land slides. It is said that while on the floor, Parham regained consciousness and only spoke of wanting to continue the slideshow.

The Parham family set out for Temple to assess his condition. Once they arrived, a decision was made to cancel the meetings and bring Charles home to Kansas by train. Parham, so weak from a heart condition that he could barely speak, waited for his son Wilfred to return from ministry in California. While waiting for him, Parham refused all medication, saying that to do so "would fail his belief." He asked only for prayer.

His youngest son, Robert, quit his job with a department store to come home to fast and pray in the house where his father lay. After several days, he came to Parham's bedside to tell him he had also "surrendered his life to the call of ministry." Thrilled in the knowledge that two of his sons would carry on the work of the Gospel, Parham gained enough strength to say:

Though several men sought to destroy him, they couldn't touch the pillar of strength that was built within his spirit.

"I can't boast of any good works I have done when I meet my Master face to face, but I can say, I have been faithful to the message He gave me, and lived a pure, clean life."

Sarah said she would never forget her beloved's face, knowing "with a joy and a look of peaceful satisfaction that his prayer for many years was answered."[38]

His last day on earth, Charles Fox Parham was heard quoting, **"Peace, peace, like a river. That is what I have been thinking all day."** During the night, he sang part of the song, "Power in the Blood," then asked his family to finish the song for him. When they had finished, he asked them to, **"Sing it again."**[39]

The next day, on January 29, 1929, at fifty-six years of age, Charles F. Parham went to be with the Lord.

His funeral was attended by over twenty-five hundred people, who visited his grave in the newly fallen snow. A choir of fifty occupied the stage, along with a number of ministers from different parts of the nation. Offerings poured in from all over the country, enabling the family to purchase a granite pulpit for a grave memorial. On the memorial was carved "John 15:13," the last passage of Scripture that Parham had read as he had held his final meeting on this earth: "Greater love hath no man than this, that a man lay down his life for his friends."

THE TRULY FAITHFUL

Before Charles Parham died, his ministry contributed to over two million conversions, both directly and indirectly. His crowds often exceeded seven thousand people. And though some spoke in tongues long before Topeka, Kansas, it was Parham who pioneered the truth of tongues as the evidence of the baptism of the Holy Spirit.

> *I challenge you today to take account of your life, to count the cost, and to analyze where you stand in the area of faithfulness.*

His life exemplifies the harsh reality of the persecution and conflict that accompany God's revivalists. Though several men sought to destroy him, they couldn't touch the pillar of strength that was built within his spirit. He was never moved from his calling because of the slander waged against him. And when he left earth, he did so because he *willed* it. Although some will not accept Parham's ministry because of his support for the Ku Klux Klan,[40] most remember Parham for his sacrificial love, and primarily, for his faithfulness. The utmost cry of God is that we be found faithful to His plan. And for Charles Fox Parham, he could live no other plan than what God had prescribed. Faithfulness will always endure the conflict that comes to challenge it.

God has called us to an area of service. Whether we stand before the masses or before the few in our families, we, like Charles Parham, must prove our faithfulness too. But in our fast-paced, "feel good" generation, faithfulness seems to have been compromised. Still, no matter what generation we speak of, God's Word remains the same. First Corinthians 4:2 states that faithfulness is a *requirement* for believers.

Believing the Word of God and *trusting* God to fulfill His promises to you, in spite of life's conflicts, produce faithfulness. How wonderful it will be to hear the Lord say, "Well done, my good and *faithful* servant!" instead of Him saying only, "Well...?"

I challenge you today to take account of your life, to count the cost, and to analyze where you stand in the area of faithfulness. I challenge you to know what you believe in, and what you are against, then to stand true to those convictions. Demonstrate the "cutting edge" of truth to the nations of the earth and never allow yourself to be counted among the persecutors, the despisers or the envious. Whatever your call in life may be, always stand true on God's side. Be faithful.

CHAPTER FOUR, CHARLES F. PARHAM
References

1 Mrs. Charles Parham, *The Life of Charles F. Parham*, (Birmingham, AL: Commercial Printing Company, 1930), 59, 74.

2 Ibid., 1.

3 Ibid., 2.

4 Ibid.

5 Ibid., 5.

6 Ibid., 6-9.

7 Ibid., 11.

8 Ibid., 23.

9 Ibid., 33.

10 Ibid., 42.

11 Ibid., 46-47.

12 Ibid., 48.

13 Ibid., 57.

14 Ibid., 52-53.

15 Ibid., 54.

16 Ibid., 62.

17 Ibid., 76.

18 Ibid., 95-97.

19 Ibid., 100.

20 Ibid., 134.

21 Ibid., 136.

22 Ibid., 155-156.

23 Ibid., 158-159.

24 Ibid., 159.

25 Ibid., 161-162.

26 Ibid., 163-164, 168.

27 Ibid., 176.

28 Ibid., 182.

29 James R. Goff Jr., *Fields White Unto Harvest*, (Fayetteville and London: The University of Arkansas Press, 1988), 136, 223, Footnote 32.

30 Ibid., 136.

31 Ibid., 136-137, 224, Footnote 39.

[32] Ibid., 138-139, 224-225, Footnote 41.

[33] Ibid., 225-226, Footnote 44 & 45.

[34] Ibid., 141.

[35] Parham, *The Life of Charles F. Parham*, 201.

[36] Ibid., 260-261 and Goff, middle section, photos of posters.

[37] Parham, *The Life of Charles F. Parham*, 406.

[38] Ibid., 200, 410.

[39] Ibid., 413.

[40] Goff, *Fields White Unto Harvest*, 157.

CHAPTER FIVE

William J. Seymour

"The Catalyst of Pentecost"

"The Catalyst of Pentecost"

66 As she looked at me through her gold-handled lorgnette, she said, 'Reverend, I believe in the baptism of the Holy Ghost and fire...but I don't appreciate the noise, the shouting.'

"'Sister, you are just like I am, I responded. There are many manifestations that I see among God's people that I don't appreciate myself, but, do you know, when the Spirit of the Lord comes upon me, I enjoy it.'

"Her small mouth pursed in mild disagreement, but I continued:

"'...Now, my little sister, if you want to go into the prayer room and pray to be baptized in the Holy Spirit, please go ahead. And when it happens, don't shout unless you feel like it. Just be yourself.'

"She nodded vigorously, 'Oh, indeed I will.'

"'...I was busy in an office about seventy-five feet away and soon forgot that she was there. Suddenly,...I heard a penetrating outcry.

"Quickly I jerked open the door to look through the church and there came the little lady out of the prayer room as if she had been shot from a cannon. She began jumping, dancing, and shouting in the Lord. It was something to see this reserved, refined lady with the gold-handled lorgnette, dancing and swaying...crying out and singing intermittently in tongues and in English.

"I went out to meet her and smiling on the inside, commented, 'Sister, what you are doing doesn't appeal to me.'

"She made an undignified jump into the air and shouted, 'Maybe not, but it sure appeals to me!'"[1]

Serving as the "catalyst" of the "Pentecostal Movement" in the twentieth century, William J. Seymour turned a tiny Los Angeles horse stable on Azusa

Street into an international center of revival. Because the baptism of the Holy Spirit with the evidence of speaking in tongues was a major part of the meetings held there, Seymour became the leader of the first organized movement that promoted this experience. At Azusa, blacks, whites, Hispanics, and Europeans all met and worshiped together, crossing formerly impossible cultural lines. Although the success of the revival was short-lived, we still enjoy its fruits. Today, Azusa remains a common word within God's household.

> *At Azusa, blacks, whites, Hispanics, and Europeans all met and worshiped together, crossing formerly impossible cultural lines.*

The Azusa Street Mission produced some wild stories. Time was of little concern to these Pentecostal pioneers who would often pray all night for another's deliverance. They believed the Word of God and waited for its manifestation.

In every situation that arose, the seekers made a demand on the Word's authority. If insects tried to destroy someone's crops, believers at Azusa marched out to the field and declared the Word of God over their crops and the insects! In every recorded account, the insects stayed where they were told and didn't cross field borders. If they were destroying a neighbor's crops, they remained about twenty yards away from the believer's crops.

In another story a large group of firemen came rushing into the Azusa Street Mission during a service carrying fire hoses to extinguish a fire. But they never found one! Neighbors of the mission had seen a light that led them to believe the building was engulfed in flames, so they called the fire department. However, what they had actually seen, was the glory of God.

EYE OF THE TIGER

Centerville, Louisiana, is a southern bayou town only a few miles from the Gulf of Mexico. On May 2 of 1870, a son was born in Centerville to Simon and Phyllis Seymour. They had only been freed from slavery a few years earlier, so William was born into a world of horrible racial violence. The Ku Klux Klan had been on the rampage for years. The Jim Crow Law had been established to prohibit all blacks from any social justices. And segregation was prevalent, even in the Church.

Once freed from slavery, Seymour's parents continued working on the plantation. As Seymour grew, he followed in their footsteps. Undaunted by the lack of formal education, he, like many others, taught himself primarily through reading the Bible.

Seymour found his identity in Jesus Christ, believing that the Lord was the only liberator of mankind. He was a sensitive, high-spirited youth, and hungry for the truth of God's Word. It is said he experienced divine visions, and that early in life began to look for the return of Jesus Christ.[2]

At the age of twenty-five, Seymour finally broke through the mental bondage of his inferiority complex. Then doing what few black men dared, he left the homelands of southern Louisiana and headed north to Indianapolis, Indiana.

According to the U.S. census of 1900, only 10 percent of the black race had ever left the South. But Seymour was determined, so he left. He was determined that man-made shackles would never hold him.

SAINTS AND SMALLPOX

Unlike the rural South, Indianapolis was a thriving city that offered many opportunities. But many businesses still closed their doors to the black population, so Seymour could only find work as a hotel waiter.

Not long after his arrival, Seymour joined the Simpson Chapel Methodist Episcopal Church. This branch of Northern Methodists had a strong evangelistic outreach to all classes that appealed to Seymour. The church's example helped Seymour to further formulate his beliefs. To him it was becoming ever more evident that there was no class or color line in the redemption of Jesus Christ.

However, it wasn't long before the racial lines hardened in Indianapolis. So Seymour moved to Cincinnati, Ohio. There he continued to attend a Methodist church, but soon noticed that their doctrine was hardening as well. He was an avid follower of John Wesley. Wesley believed in strong prayer, holiness, divine healing, and that there should be no discrimination in Jesus Christ. But it seemed the Methodists were moving away from their original roots.

Seymour wrestled with his calling and was fearful to answer.

In his search for a church, Seymour stumbled upon the Evening Light Saints, which would later become known as the Church of God Reformation Movement. The group didn't use musical instruments. They didn't wear rings or make-up. And they didn't dance or play cards. Even though it seemed like a religion of "nos," the group was extremely happy. They found joy in their faith in difficult times as well as good.[3]

Seymour was warmly received by the Saints. It was in this setting that he received the call to ministry. Seymour wrestled with his calling and was fearful to answer. In the midst of his struggle, he contracted smallpox, which was usually fatal in that era. He survived three weeks of horrible suffering, but was left with blindness in his left eye and severe facial scarring.

Seymour felt his contraction of the disease was a result of refusing the call of God. So he immediately submitted to the plan of God and was ordained through the Evening Light Saints. Soon he began traveling as an itinerant evangelist and provided his own financial support. In those days, few ministers asked for offerings. And Seymour, like many in his circle, believed that God was his provider. He believed that if God called him, then God would support him.

SPEAKING IN TONGUES...TODAY?

Seymour left Cincinnati and traveled to Texas, evangelizing along the way. When he arrived in Houston, he found family there, so he decided to make Houston his ministry base.

In the summer of 1905, Evangelist Charles F. Parham was holding crusades in Bryn Hall, which was located in downtown Houston. Each evening after the traffic had cleared, Parham and his helpers would march downtown in spectacular Holy Land clothing carrying their "Apostolic Faith Movement" banner. Newspapers wrote positively about Parham's meetings often giving them headlines.[4]

Houston was a city of cultural variety, so all races were drawn to Parham's meetings. A woman friend of Seymour's, Mrs. Lucy Farrow, attended Parham's meetings regularly, and had developed a pleasant relationship with the revivalist's family. Parham offered her the position of governess with his family if she would accompany them to Kansas where they lived. Farrow was the pastor of a small Holiness church, but her love for Parham's family and her spiritual hunger motivated her to go. Upon her acceptance, she asked Seymour if he would pastor the church in her absence. He agreed to do so until she returned two months later with the Parham family.

When Mrs. Farrow returned to Houston, she told Seymour about her wonderful spiritual encounters in the Parham home – including her experience of speaking in tongues. Seymour was very moved by her experience, but he questioned the doctrine. He would eventually accept it, though Seymour wouldn't speak in tongues for some time himself.[5] The Evening Light Saints didn't approve of Seymour's new theology. So, he left the group, still never having spoken in tongues. Then Charles Parham announced the opening of his Bible school in Houston that December and Mrs. Farrow vehemently insisted that Seymour attend. Moved by her fervency and his own growing interest, Seymour enrolled.

Parham's school in Houston was set up much like the one in Topeka, Kansas. It was a communal-type living arrangement in one house, where the students and their instructor spent days and nights together praying and studying the Word in an informal fashion. The students were not required to pay tuition, but did have to believe God for their own needs. Due to the culturally-accepted practice of the day, it is questionable if Seymour was allowed to stay overnight. Parham was moved by Seymour's hunger for the Word. And it is my belief, though very welcomed by Parham, Seymour was only a daytime student. Though Seymour did not embrace every doctrine that Parham taught, he did embrace the truth of Parham's doctrine concerning Pentecost. He soon developed his own theology from it.

IN THE BEGINNING

After completing his studies at Parham's school, the events that led Seymour to Los Angeles started to quickly take place. In early 1906, Seymour began making plans to start a new Pentecostal church in which he could preach his new-found doctrine. Then he unexpectedly received a letter from Miss Neely Terry. Terry, who had been visiting relatives in Houston, had attended the church where Seymour pastored in place of Lucy Farrow. When Terry returned to California, she didn't forget Seymour's gentle and secure leadership. In the letter, Miss Terry asked Seymour to come to Los Angeles and pastor a congregation that had broken away from a Nazarene church. Believing the letter revealed his destiny, Seymour packed his bags and left for California in late January. Later he would write:

> **"It was the divine call that brought me from Houston, Texas, to Los Angeles. The Lord put it on the heart of one of the saints in Los Angeles to write me that she felt the Lord would have me come there, and I felt it was the leading of the Lord. The Lord provided the means and I came to take charge of a mission on Santa Fe Street."[6]**

THE SPIRITUAL CONDITION OF THE CITY

In Los Angeles a spiritual hunger was stirring. There was a deep desire and longing for something to happen.

There was evidence of a spiritual revival even before Seymour arrived. Turn of the century evangelists had spread the fire of God throughout Southern California and many groups of people were praying and witnessing throughout the city door to door. In fact, the entire city was on the verge of a great spiritual happening as many Los Angeles congregations of Christians were earnestly seeking God.

In 1906, Los Angeles was a miniature picture of the world. Racial discrimination was rarely practiced, because every culture, from the Chinese to the Hispanic, flocked to the city.

One particular group, the First Baptist Church of Los Angeles, was waiting for the return of their pastor, Rev. Joseph Smale. He had been on a three-week trip to Wales to sit under the great Welsh evangelist, Evan Roberts. Smale was on fire for God and was hoping to bring the same revival that had visited Wales, home with him to Los Angeles.

Another evangelist and journalist, Frank Bartleman, shared a similar vision and joined with his church in prayer. Bartleman wrote Roberts for revival instructions. One response from Evan ended this way: "I pray God to hear your prayer, to keep your faith strong, and to save California." From these letters, Bartleman said he received the gift of faith for the revival to come. And he went on to believe that the prayers from Wales had much to do with God's outpouring in California, later saying that "The present worldwide revival was rocked in the cradle of little Wales."[7]

In Los Angeles, there was a small black group hungry for more of God, who had formed to worship. The leader of this new group was Sister Julia Hutchinson. She taught sanctification in a way that wasn't in agreement with her church's doctrine. Consequently, the pastor expelled the families involved with her teaching – who would eventually form a group with Seymour as pastor.

The group wasn't discouraged. They quickly banded together in the home of Mr. and Mrs. Richard Asbery, then grew so large that they were forced to rent a small mission hall on Santa Fe Street. Along with this growth came the desire for a change in leadership. The group felt a stranger to the Los Angeles area could be more effective, believing that he would command more respect among them. And Miss Terry, the Asbery's cousin, believed there could be only one man for the job. After praying about it, they all agreed to extend Seymour the invitation.

BREAKING THE MESSAGE IN

Seymour arrived in Los Angeles where there was already a revival climate, citywide. It seemed to validate his sense of destiny. The large group assembled, eager to hear Seymour's first sermon as he expounded powerfully on the gospel of divine healing and the soon return of Christ. He then began his message from Acts 2:4 on speaking in other tongues. He taught that a person is not baptized in the Holy Spirit unless he or she speaks with other tongues. And he admitted that he had not yet received this manifestation. Nevertheless, he proclaimed it as God's Word.

Seymour was met with mixed reactions. While some agreed with him favorably, others denounced him fervently. A family by the name of Lee, invited him home for Sunday dinner. When returning with him to the mission that evening, they found that Sister Hutchinson had padlocked the doors. She was outraged and declared that she wouldn't permit such extreme teaching in her little mission on Santa Fe Street. And Seymour was denied access to his mission sleeping room.[8]

Now Seymour found himself with little money and no place to stay. So the Lees felt obligated to take him home, though they did have reservations. While staying with the Lees, Seymour remained behind the closed doors of his room in prayer and fasting. Then after many days, he invited the Lees to pray with him. They accepted his invitation, and began to feel different toward him. Soon other members of the mission began to hear of the prayer meetings at the Lee household. They began gathering with them and Seymour became known as a man of prayer.[9]

When returning with him to the mission that evening, they found that Sister Hutchinson had padlocked the doors. She was outraged and declared that she wouldn't permit such extreme teaching in her little mission on Santa Fe Street.

Soon Sister Hutchinson learned of those who were joining Seymour. So she arranged a meeting between Seymour and the Holiness clergy to determine the origin of the error. Seymour faced a large, difficult audience of Holiness preachers in his inquisition, but he clung to the Word. He read again from Acts 2:4 and explained that unless the Holiness preachers had the experience that took place in the Upper Room, they weren't baptized in the Holy Spirit. According to Seymour, their problem was with the Word of God, not with him.

One minister who had been against Seymour would later say: "The contention was all on our part. I have never met a man who had such control over his spirit. No amount of confusion and accusation seemed to disturb him. He would sit behind that packing case and smile at us until we were all condemned by our own activities."[10]

214 NORTH BONNIE BRAE STREET

The calming leadership of William Seymour was noticed by all. Following his investigation, the Asberys asked him to move into their home on North Bonnie Brae Street and to begin holding regular meetings there. Seymour accepted, and the small group began to meet in late February of 1906. Their meetings consisted of hours of prayer as they sought for the baptism of the Holy Spirit.

As the meetings grew Seymour asked for the assistance of his long-standing friend, Lucy Farrow. He explained to the group that Farrow had an extraordinary ability to present the baptism of the Holy Spirit, and so money was collected to bring her from Houston.

When Sister Farrow arrived, Seymour announced that the group would enter into a ten-day fast until they received the divine blessing of the baptism of the Holy Spirit. The group fasted and prayed through the weekend. Then on Monday, Mr. Lee called Seymour to his home to ask for the prayer of healing. Seymour anointed Lee with oil, prayed for him, and Lee was healed instantly. Then Lee asked Seymour to lay hands on him and pray for the baptism of the Holy Spirit. So Seymour laid hands on him again, and this time Lee broke out speaking loudly in other tongues! The two rejoiced ecstatically for the rest of the day, then walked together to the evening prayer meeting.

When they arrived at the Asbery home on Bonnie Brae Street, every room was packed with people. Many were already praying. Seymour took charge of the meeting, leading the group in songs, testimonies, and more prayer. Then, he began to tell the story of Mr. Lee's healing and his infilling of the Holy Spirit. As soon as Seymour finished, Lee raised his hands and began to speak in other tongues. The entire group dropped to their knees as they worshiped God and cried out for the baptism. Then, six or seven people lifted their voices and began to speak in another tongue. Jennie Evans Moore, who would later marry Seymour, fell to her knees from the piano bench as one of the first to speak in tongues.

Some people rushed outside to the front porch, prophesying and preaching. Others, while speaking in tongues, ran into the streets for all the neighborhood to hear. The Asbery's young daughter rushed into the living room to see what was happening, only to meet her frightened brother running the other way! Then Jennie Evans Moore returned to the piano and began singing with her beautiful voice – in up to six languages – all with interpretation. The meeting lasted until well past 10:00 P.M. when everyone left in great joy and thankfulness.[11]

For three days, they celebrated what they dubbed, "early Pentecost restored." The news spread quickly bringing crowds that filled the Asbery's yard and surrounded their home. Groups from every culture began to find their way to 214 North Bonnie Brae Street. Some would stand outside the windows hoping to hear someone pray in tongues. At times they heard great shouting. At times it was intensely quiet. Many fell "under the power" and lay on the floor – some for three to five hours.[12]

Unusual healings also took place. One person said:

> "The noise of the great outpouring of the Spirit drew me. I had been nothing but a 'walking drug store' all my life, with weak lungs and cancer. As they looked at me, they said, 'Child, God will heal you.' In those days of the great outpouring, when they said God would heal you, you were healed. For thirty-three years, I have never gone back to the doctors, thank God, nor any of that old medicine! The Lord saved me, baptized me with the Holy Ghost, healed me, and sent me on my way rejoicing."[13]

It is said that the Asbery's "front porch became the pulpit and the street the pews" as Seymour would address the people from this home. Eventually, the front porch collapsed because of the weight of the crowd, but it was quickly reinforced so the meetings could continue.

It was during the third night of these meetings that Seymour finally experienced his own encounter with the Holy Spirit. It was late on the night of April 12, 1906, after many had left the meeting, when Seymour himself was filled and began to speak in other tongues. He was kneeling beside a man who was helping him pray for a breakthrough, when at last he received. The long-awaited gift of the Holy Spirit had finally come to the man whose preaching had brought His freedom to so many others.

312 AZUSA STREET

Everyone knew another meeting place had to be found quickly. The Asbery home could no longer accommodate the crowds. So on April 14, 1906, Seymour and his elders set out to find the perfect place. They wandered around the city near their area, until they came upon a dead-end street that was about a half a mile long. It was there, in the industrial business section of Los Angeles, that Seymour found what had once been an old Methodist church. After its use by the Methodists, the building had been remodeled for a different purpose. It had been divided in half – the top section of which had been turned into apartments. But a fire had destroyed the floor, and the cathedral-shaped roof had been flattened and covered with tar.

The top floor was being used for storage. The bottom floor had been converted into a horse stable. The windows were broken and bare electric light bulbs hung from the ceiling. Seymour was offered the building for eight dollars a month.

When Seymour acquired the building, the top floor was being used for storage. The bottom floor had been converted into a horse stable. The windows were broken and bare electric light bulbs hung from the ceiling. Seymour was offered the building for eight dollars a month.[14]

As the word got out, people came from everywhere to help restore the building. A. G. Osterburg, the pastor of the local Full Gospel Church, paid several men to help renovate the building. Volunteers swept the floors and whitewashed the walls. J. V. McNeil, a devout Catholic and owner of the largest lumber company in Los Angeles, donated lumber for the cause. Sawdust was placed on the floor, and planks were nailed to wooden barrels for use as pews. Two empty crates were nailed on top of each other to act as Seymour's pulpit.

It was in this humble, skid row-like setting that the new tenants of 312 Azusa Street prepared themselves for international revival.

BEGINNING STAGES

April 18, 1906 marked the day in U.S. history of the great San Francisco earthquake. The next day, a lesser shock was felt in Los Angeles, causing many out of fear to repent of their sins. Hundreds of them fled to Azusa to hear the Gospel message and to experience the baptism in the Holy Spirit with the evidence of speaking in other tongues. Even the very wealthy came to this lower-class area to hear of God's power.

The seating arrangement at Azusa was very unique. Because there was no platform, Seymour sat on the same level with the rest of the congregation. And the benches were arranged so the participants faced one another. The meetings were spontaneous, so no one ever knew what would happen or who the speaker would be.

In the beginning stages of Azusa, all of the music was impromptu without the use of instruments or hymn books. The meetings began with someone singing a song or giving a testimony. Because there was no program, someone would finally arise, anointed to bring forth the message. The speaker could be any race, age, or gender. And everyone felt that God was responsible for the altar calls which could take place at any point of the meetings.

At Azusa Street, sermons were inspired in English or in tongues with interpretation. Sometimes the services ran continuously for ten to twelve hours. Sometimes they ran for several days and nights! Many said the congregation never tired because they were so energized by the Holy Spirit. Many could be seen after the services ended in the early morning hours congregating under the street lights talking about the Lord.

At Azusa, the services were so anointed that if anyone got up to speak from their intellectual understanding, the Spirit-filled believers would break out in wailing sobs. This has been illustrated well in a story about a woman called Mother Jones. One man arose to speak, apparently not being led by the Spirit. As he stood and preached, Mother Jones is said to have quietly hurried up to the platform, where she sat at the foot of the pulpit, then stared up at the fellow with

William J. Seymour; 312 Azusa Street

icy, foreboding eyes. Finally she said, "Can't you see that you aren't anointed to preach?" Because of this incident, Mother Jones quickly earned a reputation that discouraged any unanointed preacher from standing at the pulpit. It is said that all she had to do was stand up, and the unanointed preacher would run from the pulpit!

Soon, all classes of people began attending the Azusa Street meetings. In his book, *Azusa Street*, Frank Bartleman wrote:

> "Many were curious and unbelieving, but others were hungry for God. Outside persecution never hurt the work. We had to fear from the working of evil spirits within. Even spiritualists and hypnotists came to investigate, and to try their influence. Then all the religious sore-heads and crooks came, seeking a place in the work. But this is always the danger to every new work. They have no place elsewhere. This condition cast a fear over many which was hard to overcome. It hindered the Spirit much. Many were afraid to seek God, for fear the devil might get them."[15]

Bartleman also wrote:

> "We found early in the 'Azusa' work that when we attempted to steady the Ark, the Lord stopped working. We dared not call the attention of the people too much to the working of the evil. Fear would follow. We could only pray. Then God gave the victory. There was a presence of God with us, through prayer, we could depend on. The leaders had limited experience, and the wonder is the work survived at all against its powerful adversaries."[16]

I believe this statement of Bartleman may be one of the main reasons that Seymour has been severely criticized as a leader. God was looking for a willing vessel – and He found it in Seymour. God is not looking for those who brag of their status and experience. However, in spiritual terms, Seymour's *limited* experience may have been the cause of his difficulties. I agree that leadership should expound strongly on the truth instead of focusing on that which is false. Deceit can't stand against the authority, strength, and wisdom of prayerful, godly leadership. I'm glad they depended on prayer. Prayer will see you through. But God also gives His leadership a voice. That voice, by the strength of the Holy Spirit, will know how to separate that which is of value from the counterfeit that will tarnish. Strong, godly leadership can separate the gold from the brass.

But despite some spiritual confusion, Azusa began operating day and night. The entire building had been organized for full use. Great emphasis had been placed on the blood of Jesus, inspiring the group to a higher standard of living. And divine love began to manifest, allowing no unkind words to be spoken of another. The people were careful to make sure that the Spirit of God wouldn't be grieved. Both the rich, educated people and the poor, unlearned people sat as one in the sawdust and makeshift barrel pews.

PACKING THE STREETS, FALLING LIKE TREES

One man at Azusa said, "I would have rather lived six months at that time than fifty years of ordinary life. I have stopped more than once within two blocks of the place and prayed for strength before I dared go on. The presence of the Lord was so real."[17]

It was said that the power of God could be felt at Azusa, even outside of the building. Scores of people were seen dropping into a prostrate position in the streets before they ever reached the mission. Then many would rise, speaking in tongues without any assistance from those inside.[18]

> *It was said that the power of God could be felt at Azusa, even outside of the building. Scores of people were seen dropping into a prostrate position in the streets before they ever reached the mission.*

By summer, crowds had reached staggering numbers, often into the thousands. The scene had become an international gathering. One account states that, "Every day trains unloaded numbers of visitors who came from all over the continent. News accounts of the meeting spread over the nation in both the secular and religious press."[19]

Inexperience may have been prevalent at the beginning, but seasoned veterans of ministry were now arriving to help support Seymour's work. Most came from the Holiness ranks, or were missionaries returning from the nations. The result of this seasoned mixture of people was a wonderful new host of missionaries who were dispatched around the world. Many, newly baptized in the Holy Spirit, would feel a call to a certain nation. So men and women were now departing for Scandinavia, China, India, Egypt, Ireland, and various other nations. Even Sister Hutchinson, who initially locked Seymour out of her mission, came to Azusa, received the baptism of the Holy Spirit, and left for Africa.[20]

Owen Adams of California traveled to Canada from Azusa where he met Robert Semple, Aimee Semple McPherson's first husband. When Adams met

William J. Seymour and wife, Jennie Evans Seymour

William J. Seymour

Seymour with F. F. Bosworth (middle), and John G. Lake (bottom right)

Daddy Seymour

Apostolic Faith Mission, 312 Azusa Street, Los Angeles, California

Semple, he told him of the miraculous events at Azusa and of his experience of speaking in tongues. Semple then excitedly told his new bride, Aimee, before they went on to China, where Robert Semple would die. But Adam's news had birthed a burning curiosity in the heart of young Aimee. When she returned to America, she would make Los Angeles her ministry base from where her phenomenal ministry would rise.[21]

Though there was much excitement swirling around about the baptism of the Holy Spirit at Azusa, many misunderstood the ultimate purpose of speaking in other tongues. Many felt it was only a divine language for the nation to which they were sent.[22]

At this time, everyone seemed to love William Seymour. When the Spirit moved, he was known to keep his head inside of the top box-crate that sat in front of him, bowed in prayer. He never asked for a salary, so he would very often be seen "walking through the crowds with five and ten dollar bills sticking out of his hip pockets which people had crammed there unnoticed by him."[23]

John G. Lake visited the Azusa street meetings. In his book, *Adventures With God*, he would later write of Seymour: "He had the funniest vocabulary. **But I want to tell you, there were doctors, lawyers, and professors, listening to the marvelous things coming from his lips. It was not what he said in words, it was what he said from his spirit to my heart that showed me he had more of God in his life than any man I had ever met up to that time. It was God in him that attracted the people."[24]**

Missionaries were called from their nations, to come and witness the spiritual phenomena in Los Angeles. Many came, then carried Azusa Street's Pentecostal message around the world. No one could possibly record all the miracles that occurred there.

The members of Azusa all carried tiny bottles of oil wherever they went. They would knock on doors to witness and pray for the sick throughout Los Angeles. They stood on street corners, singing and preaching, and worked as volunteers to clothe the poor and feed the hungry. It was exciting and incredible.

In September of 1906, due to popular demand, Seymour began a publication entitled, *The Apostolic Faith*. Within a few months, the mailing list grew to over twenty thousand names. By the next year, it had more than doubled. In this publication, Seymour announced his intention to restore "the faith once delivered" by old-time preaching, camp meetings, revivals, missions, street, and prison work.[25]

In the first publication, Seymour wrote, **"...multitudes have come. God makes no difference in nationality."[26]**

Then, a few months later, he wrote:

> **"The meeting has been a melting time. The people are all melted together...made one lump, one bread, all one body in Christ Jesus. There is no Jew or Gentile, bond or free, in the Azusa Mission. No instrument that God can use is rejected on account of color or dress or lack of education. This is why God has built up the work.... The sweetest thing is the loving harmony."[27]**

Obviously, these were revolutionary words in a time of such racial division.

BEGINNINGS OF DECLINE

Persecution outside of Azusa was expected, but it finally began within. Early one autumn morning, some members arrived at the mission to see the words, "Apostolic Faith Mission" written across the top of the building, and started accusing the mission of evolving into just another denomination. This was the name of Seymour's early mentor's movement so the Azusa Mission was now being perceived as a loose offshoot of Charles Parham's ministry. And many feared the mission was becoming just another in Parham's network of churches and Bible schools. One who was there wrote, "From that time, the trouble and division began. It was no longer a free Spirit for all as it had been. The work had become one more rival party and body, along with the other churches and sects of the city...the church is an organism, not a human organization."[28]

By now, Azusa outreach centers had been planted in Seattle and Portland under the direction of a woman by the name of Florence Crawford. And the Los Angeles headquarters was attempting to draw the entire West Coast revival outlets into their organization, but failed. So the revival itself was slowly setting itself up for ultimate failure.

Up to this point, it had primarily been taught that tongues were for foreign missions. They believed that if a person were to go to the mission field, they would be gifted to preach in the nation's language. Many Azusa missionaries were greatly disappointed when they discovered this was not the rule.

"TARRYING" AND TONGUES

The new body of believers also had a misconception of the "tarrying" concept. They would simply wait for hours for the Spirit to come, and restlessness began to surface when they felt many were abusing this time. What they didn't realize was that the Holy Spirit had already come. He was there!

Then there was the confusion surrounding their understanding of speaking in other tongues. Up to this point, it had primarily been taught that tongues were for foreign missions. They believed that if a person were to go to the mission field, they would be gifted to preach in the nation's language. Many Azusa missionaries were greatly disappointed when they discovered this was not the rule. Though it is a biblical and historical fact that tongues will manifest for that purpose, this is not their only use! It would be later, during the growth of the Pentecostal Movement, that tongues would be understood as a prayer language as well. But at Azusa Street, the experience of speaking in tongues was in its "first diaper"!

Azusa members also believed that a person only needed to speak in tongues once to be filled with the Holy Spirit. To the early Azusa members, speaking in other tongues was a sovereign move of God that meant waiting for God to come upon them.

Along with these misunderstandings, accusations of fleshly manifestations that people called the moving of the Holy Spirit began circulating. With this spiritual understanding being so new, can you imagine how it must have been to lead it? It was here that Seymour wrote to Charles Parham, and asked him to come to Azusa to hold a general revival.

FANATICS, FAKES, AND FRACTION

Though Seymour didn't fully agree with all of Parham's theology, I believe he respected and trusted Parham's leadership experience. Perhaps he felt Parham could present another view and ignite a fresh move of God.

It is said that many others had written letters to Parham begging him to come and determine which manifestations at Azusa were counterfeit and which were real. While there is not documentation of these letters, Mrs. Pauline Parham has claimed that some are in her collections.[29] We do have one letter written by Seymour to Parham that states, **"...we are expecting a general one [revival] to start again when you come, that these little revivals will all come together and make one great union revival."**[30]

It is true that there were many divisions within the Los Angeles revival. But by previous examples of Seymour's character, I believe he wanted Parham to unite the city instead of discipline it. And it is certain that Parham wouldn't have come to Azusa without an invitation.

When Parham arrived, Seymour introduced him as the "Father in this Gospel of the kingdom.[31]" I believe Seymour was sincere. He needed a spiritual father to help him lead this great movement. But whatever he had expected from Parham, things didn't go as Seymour had planned. After Parham's sermons and private exhortations, Seymour padlocked the mission's door to keep Parham out.

What did Parham say to Seymour? What could have caused him to lock Parham out of Azusa? While it is true that Parham's background in education, leadership, and experience differed from Seymour, their views on the baptism of the Holy Spirit seemed to be the same. Or were they?

Parham sat in the service while looking on in horror at the manifestations around him. In Parham's services, a certain liberality was allowed, but nothing that bordered on fanaticism. Some of Parham's own Bible school students even felt he was too strict in his definition of "fanaticism." And at Azusa, besides the shouting and dancing, the people jerked and shook. It was a highly emotional atmosphere, and there were many genuine, Spirit-filled expressions along with the false. Because of the many cultures represented, Seymour believed that each person should allow their own emotional experience, based on how each individual understood the moving of the Spirit, whether it was right or wrong.

Seymour's theology was to allow the Holy Spirit to do whatever he wanted. But only a few knew enough about the movings of the Spirit to lead the people in it. Seymour felt that if a culture was forced into a certain mode or expression, the Holy Spirit wouldn't manifest Himself among them. I believe Seymour was spiritually sensitive in his leadership, and followed this to the best of his ability. There is a fine line between wounding the human spirit and offending the Holy Spirit.

There is no known written account from Seymour regarding certain hypnotism accounts. But there are from Parham. Here is his account:

> "I hurried to Los Angeles, and to my utter surprise and astonishment I found conditions even worse than I had anticipated...manifestations of the flesh, spiritualistic controls, saw people practicing hypnotism at the altar over candidates seeking baptism, though many were receiving the real baptism of the Holy Ghost.
>
> "After preaching two or three times, I was informed by two of the elders that I was not wanted in that place. With workers from Texas, we opened a great revival in the W.C.T.U. Building in Los Angeles. Great numbers were saved, marvelous healings took place,

and between two and three hundred who had been possessed of awful fits and spasms and controls in the Azusa Street work were delivered, and received the real Pentecost teachings and spake with other tongues.

"In speaking of different phases of fanaticism that have been obtained here, that I do so with all lovingkindness and at the same time with all fairness and firmness. Let me speak plainly with regard to the work as I have found it here. I found hypnotic influences, familiar-spirit influences, spiritualistic influences, mesomeric influences, and all kinds of spells, spasms, falling in trances, etc.

"A word about the baptism of the Holy Ghost. The speaking in tongues is never brought about by any of the above practices/influences. No such thing is known among our workers as the suggestion of certain words and sounds, the working of the chin, or the massage of the throat. There are many in Los Angeles who sing, pray and talk wonderfully in other tongues, as the Spirit gives utterance, and there is jabbering here that is not tongues at all. The Holy Ghost does nothing that is unnatural or unseemingly, and any strained exertion of body, mind or voice is not the work of the Holy Spirit, but of some familiar spirit, or other influence. The Holy Ghost never leads us beyond the point of self-control or the control of others, while familiar spirits or fanaticism lead us both beyond self-control and the power to help others."[32]

Perhaps Parham's perception was right, still, the results may have been different if Parham had been more fatherly than dictatorial. Seymour never changed his theology and neither did Parham. Seymour wouldn't mention the rivalry for some two months. And even when he finally did, his account was discreet, avoiding any direct criticism. Seymour wrote:

> **"Some are asking if Dr. Charles F. Parham is the leader of this movement. We can answer, no, he is not the leader of this movement of Azusa Mission. We thought of having him to be our leader and so stated in our paper, before waiting on the Lord. We can be rather hasty, especially when we are very young in the power of the Holy Spirit. We are just like a baby — full of love — and were willing to accept anyone that had the baptism with the Holy Spirit as**

our leader. But the Lord commenced settling us down, and we saw that the Lord should be our leader. So we honor Jesus as the Great Shepherd of the sheep. He is our model."[33]

So in attempting to uphold his doctrine of unity, Seymour remained true to his teachings by not allowing an unkind word to be spoken against any of his accusers.

THE SANCTIFICATION SLUR

Though Seymour followed John Wesley, he didn't follow his teachings on sanctification. Seymour believed one could lose their salvation if they reacted in the flesh. He taught that sanctification, or sinless perfection, was a separate work of grace aside from salvation. Once you were sanctified, Seymour believed, you acted sanctified all the time. But if you sinned, you lost it.

Can you imagine the trouble and accusations that kind of teaching caused within Azusa? Many overzealous believers got caught up in pointing fingers and judging one another. Their self-righteous behavior resulted in clashes, splits, and controversies. In fact, this is one of the main reasons Seymour never reacted in the flesh to any persecution that came against him. According to his theology, this was necessary to keep his salvation. He said:

> "If you get angry, or speak evil, or backbite, I care not how many tongues you may have, you have not the baptism with the Holy Spirit. You have lost your salvation."[34]

Seymour believed one could lose their salvation if they reacted in the flesh. He taught that sanctification, or sinless perfection, was a separate work of grace aside from salvation. Once you were sanctified, Seymour believed, you acted sanctified all the time. But if you sinned, you lost it.

Seymour would padlock an opposing minister, but he would never speak out against him!

LOVE AND BETRAYAL

In spite of the many accusations, mistakes, and persecutions, Seymour remained faithful in his purpose for revival. It seemed he trusted and believed the best of almost everyone. True to his gentle, almost naive nature, he would later write:

> **"You cannot win people by preaching against their church or pastor...if you get to preaching against churches, you will find that sweet Spirit of Christ...is lacking and a harsh judging spirit takes place. The churches are not to be blamed for divisions. People were hunting for light. They built up denominations because they did not know a better way. When people run out of the love of God, they get to preaching dress, and meats, and doctrines of men and preaching against churches. All these denominations are our brethren.... So let us seek peace and not confusion.... The moment we feel we have all the truth or more than anyone else, we will drop."**[35]

The next spring, Seymour had to decide whether he would purchase Azusa or move to another location. So he presented the option to the congregation and they agreed to make an immediate payment of $4,000 toward the $15,000 needed. Within a year, the remaining balance was paid, far ahead of schedule. By this time, reports of miracles and newly-founded missions poured into Los Angeles from all over the world. Encouraged, Seymour commented, **"We are on the verge of the greatest miracle the world has ever seen."**[36]

During this time, Seymour's thoughts turned to marriage. Jennie Evans Moore, a faithful member of his ministry in Los Angeles, became his wife. She was known for her beauty, musical talents, and spiritual sensitivity. She was a very gentle woman, and was always faithful to stand beside Seymour. It was Jennie who felt the Lord would have them marry, and Seymour agreed. So the couple married on May 13, 1908. After the ceremony, William and Jennie moved into a modest apartment upstairs in the Azusa Mission.

But the news of their marriage angered a small, yet very influential group at the Mission. One of the main antagonists was Clara Lum, the mission's secretary responsible for the newspaper's publication. After learning of Seymour's marriage, she abruptly decided that it was time to leave the mission.

A few believers at Azusa had some very odd ideas about marriage. Lum's group believed marriage in the last days to be a disgrace because of the soon return of Christ and severely denounced Seymour for his decision.

It may have been that Clara Lum was secretly in love with Seymour, and left because of her jealousy. Whatever the reason, she relocated to Portland, Oregon, to join the mission headed by a former Azusa associate, Florence Crawford. And when she did, she took the entire national and international mailing lists with her.

This unthinkable action crippled Seymour's worldwide publication outreach. His entire national and international lists of over fifty thousand names had been stolen, leaving him with only their Los Angeles list. Then when the May, 1908, *Apostolic Faith* was sent out, the cover looked the same, but inside was a column announcing its new address in Portland for contributions and mail. The thousands who eagerly read and sent contributions to the newspaper now started sending them to Portland without questioning the change. By the June issue, no article by Seymour appeared at all. Finally, by midsummer of 1908, all references to Los Angeles were omitted entirely. When it became clear that Lum wouldn't be returning, the Seymours traveled to Portland to confront Lum and ask for the lists. But the lists were never returned. Without this vital information, it was impossible for Seymour to continue the publication, and ended a dramatic era of Azusa.

THE LAST DIVISION: MAN OR GOD?

Throughout 1909 and 1910, Seymour continued his ministry at Azusa, though the number of people decreased dramatically due to lack of influence and funds. So he left two young men in charge at the mission and departed for Chicago on a cross-country preaching tour. In early 1911 William H. Durham held meetings at Azusa in his place.

Durham's dramatic preaching caused hundreds to flock again to the mission. Many of the old Azusa workers, from various parts of the world, even returned to the mission. They called it "the second shower of the Latter Rain," as the fire began to fall at Azusa once again. In one service, over five hundred people had to be turned away. So between the services, the people wouldn't leave their seats for fear of losing them.[37]

The last conflict at Azusa took place between Seymour and Durham. The two differed greatly in their theology. Durham preached adamantly, and soundly, that people couldn't lose their salvation even if they sinned in the flesh. Salvation was by faith with works involved, not by works alone. Durham preached the needed balance between law and grace that the Pentecostal Movement desperately needed, because the "works" doctrine had led to many divisions.[38] His teaching felt like a cool rain on those who heard. It literally brought the people in droves!

Alarmed by Durham's large following and doctrinal differences, the elders of Azusa contacted Seymour. He returned immediately to Los Angeles for a conference. But Seymour and Durham couldn't come to an agreement in their doctrine. So in May, Seymour used the padlock again, locking Durham out of the mission![39]

Unshaken by this action, Durham and his workers secured a large, two-story building that seated more than one thousand people. The upstairs served as a prayer room, which was open day and night. The crowds from Azusa followed Durham. Thousands were saved, baptized, and healed while the old Azusa Mission became virtually deserted.

> *The crowds from Azusa followed Durham. Thousands were saved, baptized, and healed while the old Azusa Mission became virtually deserted.*

"TIRED AND WORN"

But the old Azusa Mission remained open to anyone who would come. Seymour remained its leader and kept his doctrine the same, though no one seemed interested in attending. He changed Azusa's meeting schedule to one all-day service to be held on Sunday. And he regularly attempted to increase the meetings, but the interest was not there. In the end, only twenty people remained. And they were mainly those from the original Azusa group. At times, visitors came from the previous "glory days," and of course Seymour was elated in welcoming them. But he spent more and more time reading and reflecting.

In 1921, William Seymour made his last ministry campaign across America. When he returned to Los Angeles in 1922, people began to notice that he looked very weary. He attended many ministry conventions, but was never publicly recognized from the platform.

Finally on September 28, 1922, while at the mission, Seymour suffered a sudden attack of severe pain in his chest. One of the workers ran for the doctor who was only blocks away. Upon examination, Seymour was told to rest. Then at 5:00 P.M. that same afternoon, while dictating a letter, another chest pain clinched him. He struggled for breath, then went to be with the Lord at the age of fifty-two. The cause of his death was officially cited as heart failure.

The revivalist was buried in a simple redwood casket at Evergreen Cemetery in Los Angeles. He was appropriately laid to rest amid the graves of others from many nations and continents. The words on his tombstone simply read, "Our Pastor." Sadly, only two hundred people attended William Seymour's funeral, but they gave many testimonies of God's greatness through this front-line General's ministry.

SHADOWS AND WOLVES

Following the years after Seymour's death, Mrs. Seymour carried on as pastor of the Azusa Street Mission. Everything continued smoothly for eight years. Then more problems arose in 1931. Through a series of legal battles waged by someone trying to take over the Mission, city officials became annoyed with the group and declared the property a fire hazard. Later that year it was demolished, but not before it was offered to a Pentecostal denomination who replied, "We are not interested in relics."[40] Today only a street sign stands over the property which is now nothing more than a vacant lot.

Five years later, Mrs. Seymour was admitted to the county hospital for terminal care. Jennie died of heart failure and joined her husband in heaven on July 2, 1936.

THE LEGACY OF POWER

Though the legacy and ministry of William J. Seymour seems heartbreaking, the results of his efforts between 1906 and 1909 produced and exploded the Pentecostal Movement around the world. Today, many denominations attribute their founding to the participants of Azusa. Most of the early Assembly of God leaders came out of Azusa. Demos Shakarian, founder of the Full Gospel Businessmen's Fellowship, said his grandfather was an original Azusa member. The evangelistic efforts of the Valdez family, the Garr family, Dr. Charles Price, and countless others are also linked to this revival.

William Seymour's Pentecostal ministry increased public awareness to such a degree that it not only turned around a major U.S. city, it also spread throughout the world at an incredible pace.

Probably everyone in the Pentecostal Movement today can attribute their roots, in some way, to Azusa. Regardless of all the controversy and Azusa's peculiar doctrines, whenever Azusa is mentioned, most immediately think of the power of the Holy Spirit that was poured on their ranks.

GOD IS NOT A RACIST

Some have tried to make the Azusa Street Revival and the ministry of Seymour a racial issue. Unfortunately, sometimes a pure move of God gets hidden under racial overtones. Perhaps this is one of the main reasons Azusa lasted for only three short years. God won't allow His glory to fall prey to the arguments of men. If that should happen, He leaves – end of discussion.

Some who seem racially influenced get upset that Seymour is called the "catalyst" of Pentecost instead of the "father" of it. According to Webster's Dictionary, a "catalyst" is something that "precipitates a process or event, and increases the rate at which a reaction takes place." That is exactly what Seymour did. William Seymour's Pentecostal ministry increased public awareness to such a degree that it not only turned around a major U.S. city, it also spread throughout the world at an incredible pace. It seems that every continent was touched in some way by the revival at Azusa.

As was mentioned earlier, racial issues were only a small part of the *many* interferences that visited Azusa. I believe a great error is made when this revival is looked upon as primarily a black and white issue. No particular race can claim the patent on a move of God. God has *never* worked according to the color of man; He operates through the heart of man.

As we continue to explore the great Generals of our past and determine to learn from their successes, don't allow yourself to be counted among their failures. Refuse to listen to the voices of yesterday and today who only see appearances. Rather, follow those who press into God's Spirit. Let us go on to maturity and fight for the prize rather than personal glory.

Only eternity will fully reveal the fruit of William J. Seymour's ministry. One thing is clear, he was an able stick of dynamite who God could use to send the explosions of Pentecostal revival around the world. And he did.

CHAPTER FIVE , WILLIAM J. SEYMOUR
References

[1] A. C. Valdez Sr., *Fire on Azusa Street* (Costa Mesa, CA: Gift Publications, 1980), 87-89.

[2] Emma Cotton, *Personal Reminiscences* (Los Angeles, CA: West Coast Publishers, 1930), 2, quoted in "Inside Story of the Outpouring of the Holy Spirit, Azusa Street, April 1906," published in *Message of the Apostolic Faith*, April 1939, Vol. 1, 1-3.

[3] James S. Tinney, *In The Tradition of William J. Seymour* 13, quoted from "Father of Modern-Day Pentecostalism," in *Journal of the Interdenominational Theological Center*, 4 (Fall 1976), 34-44, and taken from Dr. Duane Miller, *Autobiography*.

[4] Mrs. Charles Parham, *The Life of Charles F. Parham* (Birmingham: Commercial Printing Co., 1930), 112-123.

[5] Ibid., Tinney, *In The Tradition of William J. Seymour*, 14.

[6] Ibid., 15

[7] Frank Bartleman, *Azusa Street* (Plainfield, NJ: Logos International, 1980), 33, 90.

[8] C. W. Shumway, "A Critical Study of the Gift of Tongues," A. B. dissertation, University of California, July 1914, 173, and "A Critical History of Glossolalia," Ph.D. thesis, Boston University, 1919.

[9] Cotton, *Personal Reminiscences*, 2.

[10] C. M. McGowan, *Another Echo From Azusa* (Covina, CA: Oak View Christian Home), 3.

[11] Thomas Nickel, *Azusa Street Outpouring* (Hanford, CA: Great Commission International, 1956, 1979, 1986), 5, and Shumway, *A Critical Study Of The Gift Of Tongues*, 175.

[12] Shumway, *A Critical Study of the Gift of Tongues*, 175-176, and Cotton, *Personal Reminiscences*, 2.

[13] Cotton, *Personal Reminiscences*, 3.

[14] Shumway, *A Critical Study of the Gift of Tongues*, 175-176.

[15] Bartleman, *Azusa Street*, 48.

[16] Ibid.

[17] Ibid., 59-60.

[18] Tinney, *In the Tradition of William J. Seymour*, 17.

[19] Ibid.

[20] Nickel, *Azusa Street Outpouring*, 18.

[21] Ibid.

[22] Shumway, *A Critical Study of the Gift of Tongues*, 44-45

[22] Tinney, *In the Tradition of William J. Seymour*, 18.

[24] John G. Lake, *Adventures in God*, (Tulsa, OK: Harrison House, Inc., 1981), 18-19.

[25] Ibid., 18.

[26] *Apostolic Faith,* September 1906.

[27] Ibid., November and December 1906.

[28] Bartleman, *Azusa Street*, 68-69.

[29] Interview with Mrs. Pauline Parham.

[30] Parham, *The Life of Charles F. Parham*, 154.

[31] Ibid., 163.

[32] Ibid., 163-170.

[33] *Apostolic Faith*, December 1906.

[34] Ibid., June 1907.

[35] Ibid., January 1907.

[36] Ibid., October 1907 - January 1908.

[37] Bartleman, *Azusa Street*, 150.

[38] Ibid., 150-151, and Valdez, *Fire on Azusa,* 26.

[39] Bartleman, *Azusa Street*, 151.

[40] Tinney, *In the Tradition of William J. Seymour*, 19.

CHAPTER SIX

John G. Lake

"A Man of Healing"

"A MAN OF HEALING"

"I said to them [scientists], 'Gentlemen, I want you to see one more thing. Go down in your hospital and bring back a man who has inflammation in the bone. Take your instrument and attach it to his leg. Leave enough space to get my hand on his leg. You can attach it to both sides.'

"When the instrument was ready, I put my hand on the man's shin and prayed like Mother Etter prays: no strange prayer, but the cry of my heart to God. I said, 'God, kill the devilish disease by Your power. Let the Spirit move in him; let it live in him.'

"Then I asked, 'Gentlemen, what is taking place?'

"They replied, 'Every cell is responding.' "[1]

If there was ever a man who walked in the revelation of "God in man," it was John G. Lake. A man of purpose, vision, strength, and character, his one goal in life was to bring the fullness of God to every person.

He often said that the secret of heaven's power was not in the *doing*, but in the *being*. He believed that Spirit-filled Christians should *enjoy the same type of ministry Jesus did* while living on earth, and that this reality could only be accomplished by seeing themselves as God saw them.

THE SHADOW OF DEATH

John Graham Lake lived his life and fulfilled his ministry in the earth with this type of spiritual understanding.

He was born March 18, 1870, in Ontario, Canada. One of sixteen children, he moved with his family to Sault Sainte Marie, Michigan, while still a young boy.

Lake first heard the Gospel preached at a Salvation Army meeting when he was sixteen, and soon after, surrendered his life to the Lord. Though he had lived a morally pure life, his heart was in turmoil until he asked the Lord to save him. Speaking of his encounter Lake would later write:

"I made my surrender to Him. The light of heaven broke into my soul, and I arose from my knees a son of God, and I knew it."[2]

Lake's parents were strong, vigorous people who were blessed with wonderful health. But a spirit of infirmity and death had gripped the rest of their

family. Eight family members – four brothers and four sisters – died from illness. **"For 32 years some member of our famiy was an invalid,"** Lake wrote. **"During this period our home was never without the shadow of sickness."** His boyhood was filled with memories of **"sickness, doctors, nurses, hospitals, hearses, funerals, graveyards and tombstones; a sorrowing household; a broken-hearted mother and a grief-stricken father, struggling to forget the sorrows of the past in order to assist the living members of the family who needed their love and care."**[3]

WRONG "SCIENCE" – RIGHT ATTITUDE

As a youth, Lake was very interested in the art of science and physics. He enjoyed chemistry and loved to experiment with scientific instruments and equipment. He even took a course in medicine, but later dropped his medical pursuit.

Lake was meticulous in his research both in science and in spiritual matters. He tirelessly investigated the Bible with an eye to not only understand it, but to also prove its accuracy in everyday life. As a result, Lake walked, talked, and breathed in the flow of God's resurrection life.

"My boyhood was filled with memories of sickness, doctors, nurses, hospitals, hearses, funerals, graveyards and tombstones...."

In 1890 when Lake was twenty years old, a Christian farmer taught him about sanctification. The revelation pierced his heart and was solemnly regarded as the crowning work of God in his life. Of this new revelation, Lake said:

"I shall never cease to praise God that He revealed to me the depth...of the power of the blood of Jesus. A beautiful anointing of the Spirit was on my life."[4]

One year later, in 1891, Lake moved to Chicago, and was admitted to the Methodist school of ministry. In October of that year he was appointed to a church in Peshtigo, Wisconsin, but he declined the pastorate. He also decided to leave the Methodist school and moved to Harvey, Illinois, where he founded *The Harvey Citizen*, a local newspaper. While living in Harvey, he would meet his future wife, Jennie Stevens of Newberry, Michigan.

THE GIFT OF "JENNIE"

Jennie was perfect for John Lake. She possessed a wonderful sense of humor, keen judgment, a strong faith in God, and a deep spiritual sensitivity.

The two loved one another dearly and were married February 5, 1893, in Millington, Illinois. God blessed the couple with a marvelous unity in the Spirit, and seven children.

One of Jennie's most important ministries to her husband was prayer and intercession. There were many times throughout the course of their marriage that either of them would be spiritually prompted when the other was experiencing trouble. Lake valued dearly the advice and support of his wife.

But two short years into the Lake's wonderful marriage, sickness and disease crept into their home. Jennie was diagnosed with tuberculosis and heart disease. Her irregular heartbeat would cause her to lapse into unconsciousness, and sometimes Lake would find her unconscious on the floor, or lying in bed.

Now Lake was faced with the crises of his life. Where was God's power now? His entire family had been afflicted with illness.

To combat this she was given increasingly stronger doses of stimulants in an effort to control her heart rhythm, and was eventually forced to use nitroglycerine tablets. For all practical purposes, all of this made her a virtual invalid.

Finally, upon doctors' recommendations, Lake moved his young family back to Sault Saint Marie, Michigan, where he entered into the real estate business. But Jennie's condition continued to worsen until 1898 when the doctors told him there was nothing more that could be done for her.

LET'S GET RADICAL!

Now Lake was faced with the crises of his life. Where was God's power now? His entire family had been afflicted with illness. His brother had been an invalid due to internal bleeding for twenty-two years. His thirty-four-year-old sister had breast cancer. Another sister was once dying from blood disease. And now the person closest to his heart, Jennie, was close to death.

But Lake had experienced God's healing power before. He had been afflicted with rheumatism in younger years. When the leg distorting pain of his malady finally brought him to a breaking point, he traveled to John Alexander Dowie's Healing Home in Chicago. While there, an older man laid hands on him, the power of God came upon him, and his legs straightened out instantly.

The rest of Lake's terminally afflicted family members had been healed at Dowie's home as well. Following his own healing, Lake brought his invalid brother to Dowie's home where he was healed. When they laid hands on him, his blood disease disappeared and he jumped off his death bed.

Then he took his sister who was dying with breast cancer, to Chicago. When they arrived she had some initial doubts, but once she heard the Word of God preached with such great power, her faith grew – and she was healed. Her pain left instantly, and the large core of cancer fell out within a few days. Then the smaller cancers just disappeared and God restored her mutilated breast.

DIE? "I WILL NOT HAVE IT!"

Another one of his sisters had remained very ill even after much prayer. He was planning on taking her to the Healing Home too, but before he could, he received a telephone call from his mother. She told him his sister was dying, and that if he wanted to see her, he would have to hurry. When Lake arrived, his sister was unconscious without a pulse and the room was full of mourners. Moved by it all, he looked at his sister's baby lying in the crib and thought, **"She must not die! I will not have it!"** Of this deep compassion he later wrote:

John, upper left, with the surviving Lake family members. Eight of his original sixteen brothers and sisters died from disease.

"No words of mine can convey to another soul the cry that was in my heart and the flame of hatred for death and sickness that the Spirit of God had stirred within me. The very wrath of God seemed to possess my soul!"

Lake paced the room as his heart cried out for someone with faith to help them. He could only think of one man who had this kind of faith – Dowie. So he telegraphed him the following words:

"My sister has apparently died, but my spirit will not let her go. I believe if you will pray, God will heal her."

Dowie's answer came back:

"Hold on to God. I am praying. She will live."

Upon reading these words, Lake waged a tremendously furious spiritual attack on the power of death, rebuking it fervently in Jesus' name. In less than an hour, his sister revived totally. Five days later, she joined the family for Christmas dinner![5]

But that was then, and now his dear wife was suffering, and her condition was growing worse.

THE DEVIL REVEALED

On April 28, 1898, when Jennie's final hours seemed to be ticking away, a fellow minister encouraged Lake to resolve himself to God's will and to accept Jennie's death. His words weighed heavy, and Lake stiffened in resistance. Still, the reality of death seemed imminent.

In utter hopelessness, Lake threw his Bible against the fireplace mantle and it fell to the floor opened to Acts chapter 10. As he walked over to pick it up, his eyes drifted to verse 38: *"...God anointed Jesus of Nazareth with the Holy Ghost and with power: who went about doing good, and healing all that were oppressed of the DEVIL; for God was with him."*

Those powerful words ripped through his thoughts. "OPPRESSED OF THE DEVIL!" That meant that God wasn't the author of Jennie's sickness, or *any* sickness! And if Lake was a son of God through Jesus Christ, then God was *with him,* just as He was with Jesus! Now he was convinced it was the *devil* who had caused Jennie's illness. It was the *devil* who was stealing the mother of his children. It was the *devil* who was destroying his life!

9:30 A.M.

Then Lake turned to Luke 13:16 and read: *"ought not this woman...whom SATAN HATH BOUND, lo, these eighteen years, be loosed from this bond...?"* Now the realization hit him that not only was Satan the author of sickness and death, but that Jesus Christ – through Lake – could bring healing and deliverance to the afflicted! Through using him, Jesus Christ could conquer the throes of death! There was no doubt in his mind that Jesus died for the healing of his wife, just as He died for her sins. And he determined that absolutely nothing could rob Jennie of that gift.

> *Through using him, Jesus Christ could conquer the throes of death! There was no doubt in his mind that Jesus died for the healing of his wife, just as He died for her sins.*

In a boldness that only the Holy Spirit could have produced, Lake decided to let God, not Satan, have the last say. He marched into the bedroom and declared to the seen and unseen that his wife would be healed at exactly 9:30 A.M.!

Then he contacted Dowie to inform him of what God was about to do at the appointed time. When 9:30 arrived, Lake knelt at his precious wife Jennie's side and called on the living God. When he did, the power of God came upon Jennie and permeated her body from head to foot. Her paralysis left, her heartbeat became normal, her cough ceased, her breathing regulated, and her temperature returned to normal – immediately!

At first Lake heard a faint sound escaping from Jennie's lips. Then she cried out, "Praise God, I'm healed!" totally startling him, because he hadn't heard such strength in her voice for years. Then, Jennie threw back the covers from her bed – and stood up – healed![6] The joyous praise that followed was indescribable as both she and John worshipped God!

THE LIGHTNINGS OF JESUS

Soon, the story of Jennie's healing became national news inspiring many to travel great distances to visit the Lake home. The newspapers had provoked the nation's curiosity and the Lake's were instantly thrust into a highly sought after ministry. People arrived at their home daily to see God's miracle, and to be prayed for. Many others sent in prayer requests.

One day after praying for a man who suffered from a ten-inch fever sore, Lake received a telegram that read, "Lake, the most unusual thing has happened. An hour after you left, the whole print of your hand was burned into that growth that was a quarter of an inch deep."

Lake would later refer to such power in his sermons as the lightnings of Jesus:

> **"You talk about the voltage from heaven and the power of God! Why there is lightning in the soul of Jesus! The lightnings of Jesus heal men by their flash! Sin dissolves and disease flees when the power of God approaches!"[7]**

Lake would also compare the anointing of God's Spirit to the power of electricity. Just as men had learned the laws of electricity, Lake had discovered the laws of the Spirit. And, as God's *"lightning rod,"* he would rise within God's calling to *electrify* the powers of darkness and *solidify* the body of Christ.

EXERCISING SPIRITUAL STRENGTH

In 1901, Lake moved to Zion, Illinois, to study divine healing under John Alexander Dowie. Before long he was preaching at night, studying when he could, and working as Dowie's building manager full time during the day.

But in 1904 when Dowie's increasing financial problems began to surface, Lake decided to distance himself and relocated to Chicago. He had invested in Zion's properties while living in the city, but his holdings depreciated leaving him in near financial ruin following Dowie's death in 1907. So he bought a seat on the Chicago Board of Trade. Over the next year he was able to accumulate over $130,000 in the bank, and real estate worth $90,000.

Recognizing his gifts, certain business executives quickly asked Lake to form a trust of the nation's three largest insurance companies for a guaranteed salary of $50,000 a year. He was now a top business consultant to top business executives, and was making hundreds of dollars through commissions as well.

By turn-of-the-century standards, John G. Lake was now making a fortune. But the call of God inside of him continued to grow. For awhile he was able to juggle his great secular success and grow in God. He had learned to walk in the Spirit, in a way he described like this:

> **"It became easy for me to detach myself from the course of life, so that while my hands and mind were engaged in the common affairs of every day, my spirit maintained its attitude of communion with God."[8]**

Some people think that if you are called to the ministry, you must leave your secular job *immediately*. But as was true with Lake, this is not the case. By learning to commune with God from within his spirit, Lake continued to progress toward the perfect timing for his ministry. He didn't venture out ahead of God or cause his family to suffer. Then when the time was right, he was able to sell everything, because he had learned great faith from his years of walking with God as a businessman.

Lake learned early in his ministry training that *"being"* precedes *"doing."* He had learned to follow the divine timing of heaven.

TONGUES AND THE TIMING OF HEAVEN

While still living in Zion, Lake attended a cottage meeting at the home of his friend, Fred F. Bosworth. Tom Hezmalhalch was preaching, and at the end of the meeting he told Lake, "As I was preaching, Jesus told me that you and I are going to preach together." Lake laughed at Hezmalhalch's proclamation then, but soon surrendered himself to the perfect will of God.[9]

Lake learned early in his ministry training that "being" precedes "doing."

Not long after, in 1906, Lake began to pray for the baptism of the Holy Spirit. He sought the Lord for nine months then quit, thinking it was "not for him." Then one day he went with Tom Hezmalhalch, who was now a close friend, to pray for an afflicted lady. As Lake sat by her bedside he trembled in an unusual yearning for God.

But Hezmalhalch was oblivious to what was happening, and asked Lake to lay hands on the woman. As he did, the lightning of God knocked Hezmolahlach to the ground. "Praise the Lord, John!" he said while picking himself up, "Jesus has baptized you in the Holy Ghost!"[10]

Lake would write later of this:

"When the phenomena had passed, the glory of it remained in my soul. I found that my life began to manifest a varied range of the gifts of the Spirit. And I spoke in tongues by the power of God, and God flowed through me with a new force. Healings were more of a powerful order."

Lake spoke in other tongues often and believed that a lesser degree of infilling could not qualify as the baptism of the Holy Spirit:

"Tongues have been to me," said Lake, "the making of my ministry. It is that peculiar communication with God...[that] reveals to my soul the truth I utter to you day by day in the ministry."[11]

Again, waiting for God's right timing is very important. Our call from God was established before we were born. As we grow in life, we are invited to become aware of it. But just being "aware" of God's calling doesn't mean it is "the time" for that call to be launched into the earth. Divine timing must come before full-time ministry can begin. So don't be discouraged during your time of preparation. And don't compare your call with the call of others. Each call has its own timing and plan. Your faithfulness to the Word of God, along with fervent spiritual preparation determines the timing.

Lake spoke in other tongues often and believed that a lesser degree of infilling could not qualify as the baptism of the Holy Spirit.

AFRICA IS CALLING

After his baptism of the Holy Spirit, Lake's desire to enter full-time ministry increased. So his boss agreed to allow him to take three months off and preach. But he also warned him that, "at the end of three months, $50,000 a year will look like a lot to you, and you will have little desire to sacrifice it for the dreams of religious possibilities." Lake thanked his boss for all he had done for him and left his job. Then once the three months had passed he would boldly declare, **"I am through forever with everything in life but the proclamation and demonstration of the Gospel of Jesus Christ."**[12] He would never return to his job.

In 1907, John and Jennie disposed of their estate, their wealth, and their possessions. In a great move of faith, they determined to be entirely dependent upon God. Now it was time to preach.

While ministering in a northern part of Illinois, the Spirit of God told Lake to, "Go to Indianapolis. Prepare for a winter campaign and get a large hall. Then in the spring, you will go to Africa." When he returned home to tell Jennie, she was already aware of the plan because the Lord had told her as well.

Lake had developed a great interest in Africa when reading about the explorations of Stanley and Livingstone when he was still a boy. As he grew into a young man, he began to experience spiritual visions that seemed to place him more often in Africa than in America. Through the Holy Spirit, Lake was given insight into the geography and people of a land he had never been to. And now that dream was becoming a reality. God said he would go to Africa in the spring!

So Lake moved his family to Indianapolis and joined his old friend, Tom Hezmalhalch. They would stay there for six months as the two formed a powerful ministry team leading several hundred people into the baptism of the Holy Spirit.

Then one morning, Lake felt led to begin a fast. As he sought the Lord over a period of six days He was told that from that point on he would start casting out demons. A special knowing to discern and cast out evil spirits quickly followed, and within a short time, Lake began moving in this area with great precision.

WALKING ON THE WATER

In January of 1908, Lake began to pray for the needed finances to take the Africa trip. Tom joined with him, and they determined the trip would cost $2,000. They had been praying for a while when Tom got up and slapped Lake on the back, saying, "Don't pray anymore, John. Jesus told me just now that He will send us that $2000, and that it will be here in four days."

Exactly four days later, Tom returned from the post office and threw four $500 drafts on the table. "John, here is the answer!" Tom shouted. "Jesus has sent it. We are going to Africa!"

Just as the Lord proclaimed, in April of 1908, the group left for Africa. The team was made up of Lake, Jennie, their seven children, Tom, and three of his companions. One of Tom's companions had lived in Africa for five years, could speak Zulu, and would serve as interpreter. They bought their tickets, but had no extra money for the expenses of the trip. Now God's one-time millionaire would learn how to fully trust Him. He had only $1.50 in his hand.

And as Lake obeyed, the Lord miraculously provided for the team. The immigration laws of South Africa required each family that arrived to have at least $125, or they wouldn't be permitted to leave the ship. And as they pulled into the port, Lake had no money. So Jennie looked at him and said, "What are you going to do?"

Lake responded, **"I am going to line up with the rest. We have obeyed God this far. It is now up to the Lord."**

As he stood in line, ready to explain his dilemma, a fellow passenger tapped him on the shoulder and called him to the side. He asked Lake a few questions, then handed him two money orders, totaling $200.

"I feel led to give you this to help your work," the stranger said. If you've heard from God, then step out in bold, aggressive faith. He'll be there to meet you every time.

HOME AWAY FROM HOME

The Lake family had been praying diligently for a home when they reached Johannesburg. As faith missionaries, they had no support from church boards, and no denomination waiting to accept them at their arrival. All they had was their faith in God.

When they arrived in Johannesburg in May of 1908, they noticed a little woman running around the dock area looking at everyone. She was American. Running up to Tom, she said, "You are an American missionary party?" to which Tom replied, "Yes." "How many are in your party?" the lady went on. "Four," Tom answered back. But she shook her head and said, "No, you aren't the family. Is there another?"

Then Tom directed her to Lake. "How many are in your family?" the lady asked. **"My wife, myself, and my seven children,"** Lake said. The lady suddenly looked ecstatic and shrilled, "You are the family!" Then she went on to explain how God had directed her to meet their boat and that on it would be an American missionary family consisting of two adults and seven children. And that she was to give them a home.[13]

That same afternoon, the Lake's were settled into a furnished home in Johannesburg. God had provided it, just as they had asked. The American lady, Mrs. C. L. Goodenough, remained a faithful friend throughout their ministry.

A SPIRITUAL CYCLONE

Days after Lake arrived, his first ministry door was opened. A South African pastor took a leave of absence for a few weeks and asked Lake to fill his pulpit. He immediately accepted the offer.

Over five hundred Zulus were in attendance his first Sunday in the pulpit. As a result, a great revival broke out among them, and within weeks multitudes from Johannesburg and the surrounding area were saved, healed, and baptized in the Holy Spirit.

The success astounded Lake. Of it, he later wrote:

> **"From the very start it was as though a spiritual cyclone had struck."**[14]

The meetings would often last until 4 A.M.

One of the main features of these miraculous meetings were the powerful demonstrations of answered prayer. The prayer of faith would be spoken for someone in another part of Africa with instant results. News of this spread far and wide, and hundreds packed into Johannesburg to be prayed for. After the meetings ended, the natives would follow the preachers to their homes and continue to ask questions to learn about God. Many times, as dawn broke over the African horizon, the group would still be discussing the power of God. Then all through the following day, people could be seen with Bibles in their hands, witnessing about the power of God that was displayed the night before.

> *Wounded, sick, and weak, the people would line up on one side of the platform and would leave the building after they were prayed for, shouting, "God has healed me!"*

There were also many great manifestations of healing. Wounded, sick, and weak, the people would line up on one side of the platform and would leave the building after they were prayed for, shouting, "God has healed me!" The crowd inside the building shouted wildly and cheered as they witnessed the miracles of God.

JOHN & JENNIE: THE TEAM

If the African people couldn't make it to Lake's meetings, they would travel to "the preacher's" home. At times the throng was so great that Jennie didn't even have time to prepare the family meals. She would usher the people through the front door to be prayed for, then show them through the back door so the room would have space for the others coming in.

Jennie was also John's ministry partner. Lake believed his wife "possessed the spirit of discernment in a more marked degree" than he did. She would often receive a word of knowledge concerning those who were unable to receive healing because of personal difficulty or sin in their life.

The Lakes had a simple way of operating in their healing ministry. As the people passed before John in his office, he laid hands upon them. Those who were instantly healed, were dismissed. But those who continued to suffer, or received a partial healing, were sent into another room. Then when Lake finished with the multitude, he would bring Jennie into the room who would, by the Spirit, personally reveal to each one of them the hindrances of their healing. Upon hearing the inner secrets of their hearts, many would confess and ask God for forgiveness. Then John and Jennie would pray again, and God would heal those who repented. Those who refused to repent, even after acknowledging the truth of what Mrs. Lake had told them, went home suffering in their affliction.

WHAT WAS HE LIKE?

Lake was a man of action. Once after an inspired altar invitation, the entire congregation ran to the front. In the group was a man who fell to the floor in front of the platform in an epileptic seizure. Immediately, Lake jumped off the platform and was at his side, rebuking the demon in the name of Jesus. After the man was delivered, Lake quietly returned to the platform.

The Spirit of God powerfully rested on Lake during these years. As he shook hands with those entering the services, they would often fall to the ground under the power of God. At other times, people would fall prostrate when they came within six feet of him!

Lake demonstrated his deep compassion by never turning away a cry for help. He never refused to answer the call of a sick person, and was even known to pray for dying animals when called upon. There were times when he needed rest, but the people would find him, then bring him their sick. Lake prayed for them night and day and refused to turn anyone away.

The ministry team was always in great need of food and finances. And true to the practices of that day, Lake never took offerings. But He would often find baskets of food or small pouches of money discreetly left on the family's doorstep.

Perhaps one of the most difficult challenges that Jennie experienced in Africa was adapting to the ministry habits of her husband. It was John's task to bring home the groceries needed for their large family. But if he would happen to meet a widow lady on the way home who had hungry children, he would give everything he had to the widow's family. Also, Jennie never knew whether or not John may be bringing home company for dinner, so she would have to stretch any meal to feed a large crowd. Food always seemed to be in short supply.

TAG TEAM

From Lake's first meetings held in the pastor's church building, he moved into rented halls. Then when the crowds outgrew them, the ministry team resorted to cottage meetings. Lake and Hezmalhalch were now "team" preachers. Each would speak five or six times during a meeting, and no one could tell where one's message finished and the other's started. It was all harmonized by the Spirit of God.

Lake established the Apostolic Tabernacle in Johannesburg, and in less than a year he had started one hundred churches. The work of overseeing these churches spread throughout Africa and kept him more frequently away from home.

GOODBYE, JENNIE

> *Lake had become so absorbed in ministering to others that he wasn't aware of what was happening to his own wife.*

Lake was stunned with the most devastating news he had ever encountered on December 22, 1908. While ministering in the Kalahari Desert, his beloved Jennie died. When he returned home twelve hours later, she had already gone to heaven.

Most accounts of Jennie Lake's death attribute it to malnutrition and physical exhaustion. When John was away, scores of sick people would wait on his lawn until he returned. So Jennie would feed them while they waited with what little food she could spare. And she tried to make their stay as comfortable as possible until Lake returned. But in doing so, she physically neglected herself.

Lake had become so absorbed in ministering to others that he wasn't aware of what was happening to his own wife.

One point often ignored in the ministry is that there will always be a "need" to be fulfilled. One ministry can't meet all the needs that will appear, no matter how powerful or anointed that ministry seems to be. So common sense is invaluable to Christian ministry. The natural body and the natural family need attention, and the family unit should always be the core of any ministry.

Understandably, Lake was devastated when he arrived home to find his wife had died. It was a very dark time for him and the agonizing pain stayed with him for many years.

The next year, in 1909, Lake returned to America to gather support for his African ministry and to recruit new workers. And again, God supernaturally supplied the money with one contribution. He was given $3,000 for he and his workers to return.

THE PLAGUE

As the team landed on African soil in January of 1910, a plague was raging over portions of the nation. In less than a month, one quarter of the entire population had died. In fact, the plague was so contagious that the government was offering $1,000 to any nurse who would care for the sick. Lake and his assistants went to help, free of charge. He and one assistant would go into the houses, bring out the dead, and bury them. But no symptom of the plague ever touched him.

At the height of this horrible plague, a doctor sent for Lake and asked him:

> "What have you been doing to protect yourself? You must have a secret!"

To this Lake responded:

> **"Brother, it is the law of the Spirit of Life in Christ Jesus. I believe that just as long as I keep my soul in contact with the living God so that His Spirit is flowing into my soul and body, that no germ will ever attach itself to me, for the Spirit of God will kill it."**

Lake then invited the doctor to experiment with him. He asked the doctor to take the foam from the lungs of a dead plague victim and put it under a microscope. The doctor did so, and found masses of living germs. Then Lake astounded the people in the room as he told the doctor to spread the deadly foam on his hands and announced that germs would die.

The doctor did so and found that the germs died instantly in Lake's hand. Those who witnessed the experiment stood in amazement as Lake continued to give glory to God, explaining the phenomenon like this:

> **"You can fill my hand with them and I will keep it under the microscope, and instead of these germs remaining alive, they will die instantly."**[15]

This same power constantly flowed through Lake's hands into the bodies of the afflicted bringing healing to the masses. The "lightnings of God" blasted all disease and infirmity.

When the Queen of Holland requested Lake to pray for her problems with conception so she could carry a child to full term, he sent the Queen word that her prayer had been answered. Less than a year later, the Queen, who had miscarried six previous times, gave birth to her first full-term child, Queen Juliana of Holland.[16]

MINISTRY OF THE SPIRIT

In December of 1910, Tom Hezmalhalch left Lake's ministry. This was a very difficult time for Lake. He had recently lost his dear wife, and now he was

losing his best friend and partner. But he drew strength from knowing that he was fulfilling the will of God. And he received much comfort from his American supporters. Encouraging letters came pouring in from many reassuring him of their confidence in his ministry.

Lake spent the rest of 1910-1912 ministering healing as he prayed for the sick. Great miracles were performed that still affect Africa today. And he started two main churches: The Apostolic Faith Mission/Apostolic Tabernacle (not related to the Apostolic Faith Church) and the Zion Christian Church.

Lake and his congregation regularly published a newsletter that was mailed to thousands of people. Before they were mailed, church members would lay hands on them and pray that the pieces of literature would be filled with God's Spirit. They believed the power of God would anoint the newsletter's paper, just as it occurred with the handkerchiefs of Paul. As a result, thousands of letters would pour in from all parts of the world, stating how the Spirit of God came upon the recipients as they opened the paper. One lady said that when she held the newsletter, "she vibrated" in such a way that she could hardly sit in her chair. She was then baptized in the Holy Spirit and spoke in other tongues. Lake simply explained this manifestation by saying:

They believed the power of God would anoint the newsletter's paper, just as it occurred with the handkerchiefs of Paul.

"The ministry of Christianity is the ministry of the Spirit."[17]

Lake understood how to carry his entire congregation into the presence of the Lord. He trained and matured them out of his spiritual overflow, and as a result, they were able to accelerate with him in the supernatural. In 1912, the congregation was asked to pray for a man's cousin in a Welsh insane asylum that was located some seven thousand miles away. When the spirit of fervent prayer fell on the people, a great consciousness of God came upon Lake. It seemed as if shafts of light were beaming toward him from the intercessors. Then suddenly, he found himself traveling in the spirit at lightning-like speed. Arriving in a place that he had never seen before, he realized it had to be Wales. Then he walked inside the room of this man's cousin who was tied to a cot with her head bouncing back and forth. He laid hands on her and cast the devil out of her. Then, suddenly, he was back in Johannesburg kneeling on the platform. Three weeks later, the report of this woman's compete deliverance had arrived. She had been immediately discharged when physicians found her "suddenly" healthy and whole.

THE ANOINTED ROVER

By the time John G. Lake would leave Africa to finally return to America, his ministry efforts had produced 1,250 preachers, 625 congregations, and 100,000 converts. The exact number of miracles that occurred in his ministry could never be counted on earth.[18] These statistics are the results of five years of ministry!

Lake returned to America in 1912. The family's first year home was filled with travel and needed relaxation. Then in 1913, John met and married Florence Switzer of Milwaukee, Wisconsin. In the years following they became the parents of five children. Florence was an excellent stenographer and was responsible for recording and preserving many of Lake's sermons.

In the summer of 1914, Lake met with his former railroad financier and friend, Jim Hill. The two had become close when Lake worked in Chicago. Hill was delighted to see Lake and offered his family free railway passes that were good for anywhere his trains traveled.

THE HEALING ROOMS OF SPOKANE

Lake took advantage of his good friend's offer and began to travel the nation. First, he went to Spokane, Washington, where he would stay and set up "healing rooms" in an old office building. It is estimated that some one hundred thousand healings occurred in those rooms.[19]

The Spokane newspapers consistently published the many healing testimonies of the people. In fact, the results were so unbelievable that the Better Business Bureau decided to verify the authenticity of the healings. So they contacted leaders at the healing rooms for an investigation.

To satisfy the bureau's inquiry, Lake called on the people whose testimonies had appeared in print. All eighteen of them gave testimony to the power of the Lord in front of the bureau. Then Lake gave the investigators the names of those who had been healed throughout the city so they could question them. And after that, he offered to sponsor a meeting the following Sunday at which one hundred people would give their healing testimonies. He asked the bureau to formulate a panel of physicians, lawyers, judges, and educators who could render a verdict.

John and Jennie Lake and family before leaving for South Africa, 1907

Lake and campaign workers

Mobilizing the message, Lake on the road

Lake and healing home workers in Spokane, Washington, 1915-1920

Boy healed at Lake's Spokane Healing Home

But Lake received a letter from the bureau the Friday before the proposed meeting informing him that their investigations were very positive, and that the Sunday meeting wouldn't be necessary. They also praised him for the work he was doing in their city. Two committee members even visited him privately to tell him, "You didn't tell the half of it."

> *It is said the boy's head was shaped like a yacht, "upside down." Physicians announced there was nothing that could be done for him until he was twelve years old.*

Those interviewed by the bureau included a woman who no longer had her female organs, yet through healing, was able to procreate. She showed her miraculous baby to those investigating the ministry.

Another woman shared about the miraculous healing of her severely broken kneecap. After she received prayer, the bone popped back into place, without pain, in less than an hour. Still another woman afflicted with incurable cancer was totally healed after prayer. And another was instantly healed of rheumatoid arthritis as her bones reshaped and returned to normal. This same woman was also healed of a prolapsed stomach, and the earlobe she was born without miraculously grew into place.

But the most remarkable case at Spokane's Healing Home was that of a small boy. It is said the boy's head was shaped like a yacht, "upside down." Physicians announced there was nothing that could be done for him until he was twelve years old, and then the surgery would be very dangerous. But after prayer, the boy's bones softened, his head expanded, and his skull was restored to normal. His paralysis also miraculously left and he was able to speak like other children.

How did Lake explain these incredible healings? Many times, he liked to use Sister Etter in his illustrations because of her great spiritual influence on his life.

"When you see those holy flashes of heavenly flame once in a while in a person's life, as we observe in our Sister Etter; when someone is healed, it is because her consciousness and Christ are one. She is fused into God. I saw a dying, strangling woman healed in thirty seconds as Mrs. Etter cast out the demon. The flame of God, the fire of His Spirit, ten seconds of connection with the Almighty Christ at the Throne of God, that is the secret of it."[20]

"STRIVE FOR PENTECOST"

According to government statistics, between the years of 1915-1920, Spokane, Washington, was the "healthiest city in the world," because of the ministry of John G. Lake. The mayor of Spokane held a public commemoration to honor his efforts.

An excellent businessman, Lake made sure his records were always accurate. They showed that up to two hundred persons a day were being ministered to and healed in Spokane's Healing Homes, and that most of them were non-church members.

Lake also founded The Apostolic Church in Spokane that drew thousands from around the world for ministry and healing. He held services six nights a week, twice on Sundays, and made house calls throughout the week.

In May of 1920, Lake left Spokane and moved to Portland, Oregon, where he traveled as an apostle and pastored for a time. Soon, he began another Apostolic Church and healing ministry similar to the one in Spokane.

During Lake's time in Portland, he had a vision in which an angel appeared. The angel opened the Bible to the book of Acts, pointing to the outpouring of the Spirit on the Day of Pentecost. The angel also called Lake's attention to other spiritual manifestations and revelations in the book and said:

"This is Pentecost as God gave it through the heart of Jesus. Strive for this. Contend for this. Teach the people to pray for this. For this, and this alone, will meet the necessity of the human heart, and this alone will have the power to overcome the forces of darkness."[21]

From that day on, Lake strived to fulfill the Word of the Lord with even greater intensity. He traveled around America for the next eleven years, duplicating his work everywhere he went.

LAKE'S MISTAKE

In his later years, John G. Lake enjoyed a wonderful balance of the supernatural and natural. But his understanding came at a very heavy price. The price was his family.

Lake's children from his first marriage suffered greatly because of his constant absence. Even when he was present in a room, he would drift away in meditation, being constantly mindful of the ministry and the Lord. Because of this, his children felt greatly neglected.

Remember, it was these same children who saw their mother starve and work to death in Africa. As a result, each of them had developed very hardened attitudes, and they left home very early, between the ages of fifteen and sixteen, to live in Canada. As they grew into adulthood, their lives were characterized by hardened bitterness. However, two of his sons commented while on their deathbeds, "I wish dad were here to pray for me."

His children borne by Florence had a different attitude toward him. They remembered him as a man who loved to laugh and enjoy his friends.

Lake grieved over his lack of attention given the children. And he would later write in a letter that the many miracles wrought at his hands were personally unfulfilling and not worth the loss of his family.

THE REDEEMING FACTOR

But Lake learned from his experiences, and finally found the key to being a good husband, involved father, and powerful minister. His children borne by Florence had a different attitude toward him. They remembered him as a man who loved to laugh and enjoy his friends.

In his later years, Lake was not "so heavenly minded that he was of no earthly good." He didn't keep his head in the clouds, and people no longer fell into silence when entering his presence because he would lovingly interact with them. Lake had finally learned to enjoy the natural and the supernatural to the fullest extent. The atmosphere in his home was no longer rigid and stiff! He loved to have fun at the dinner table when the family was together. His hearty laugh could be heard echoing down the halls. And he enjoyed symphonic and opera music, so every Sunday evening, he would listen to his favorite radio programs.

Lake also enjoyed a wonderful sense of humor. He loved to read Will Roger's newspaper column, and would later be thought of himself as "a great entertainer." He liked to keep the atmosphere around him light with laughter.

THE MAGNET OF GOD

At the height of his ministry, the outside world had become so drawn to Lake's understanding of God that they constantly flocked to him. It was his understanding of righteousness that allowed him to take dominion over every situation. He despised the Christian songs that spoke of mankind as a "worm."

When he heard them he would wrinkle his nose and twist his mouth, calling them "lower concept" songs. He felt they were a disgrace to the blood of Jesus. Lake's daughter once described her father as having "a very great consciousness of being a king and priest before God, showing a bearing and demeanor of that nobility." This is how he also encouraged others to be viewed. Lake always directed his family to treat all believers as kings and priests.[22]

Lake was the strongest advocate of his day for the supernatural. He often spoke with disgust of educational, medical, and scientific forums that made reference to the weakness of Christianity. One day he would preach, the tables would be turned, and men would flock from everywhere to the – "School of the Spirit" – where they would learn to cooperate and become one with the power of God.

Lake was truly concerned about the world's infatuation with mere psychological power. He tells of once witnessing a man in India who had been buried alive for three days, then came up from the grave well and whole. And of another man who had suspended his body between two chairs in mid-air and had a huge stone smashed on his chest until it broke in two.

He would publicly refute the validity of such manifestations by saying:

> **"These are only on the psychological plane. Beyond that is the spirit plane and the amazing wonder of the Holy Spirit of God, and if God got hold of my spirit for ten minutes, He could do something ten thousand times greater than that."[23]**

> **"Christianity is one hundred percent supernatural,"** he often said. **"'All Power' language is Christianity vocabulary only."[24]**

He possessed a remarkable ability to encourage faith and revelation in the hearts of others who listened to him. The ministers who sat under his teaching soon found their own ministries of faith which resulted in startling healings.

Lake stated:

> **"If he [a Christian] has not the Spirit to minister in the real high sense, he has nothing to minister. Other men have intellectuality, but the Christian is supposed to be the possessor of the Spirit. There should never be any misunderstanding along these lines."[25]**

To further the supernatural goals, Lake called every believer to the power of Pentecost. Once in doing so he spoke this prophecy:

"I can see as my spirit discerns the future and reaches out to touch the heart of mankind and the desire of God, that there is coming from heaven a new manifestation of the Holy Spirit in power, and that new manifestation will be in sweetness, in love, in tenderness, and in the power of the Spirit, beyond anything your heart or mine ever saw. The very lightning of God will flash through men's souls. The sons of God will meet the sons of darkness and prevail."[26]

> *By the end of the talk, his vision was completely restored, and remained that way for the rest of his life.*

LEGACY OF THE MIRACULOUS

By 1924, Lake was known throughout America as a leading healing evangelist. He had established forty churches throughout the United States and Canada in which there had been so many healings that his congregations nicknamed him, "Dr." Lake.

In December, another significant event took place through his ministry. Gordon Lindsay, founder of Christ For the Nations in Dallas, Texas, was converted while hearing Lake preach in Portland. Lindsay attended his services nearly every night of the week and considered Lake to be his mentor. When Lindsay later contracted deadly, ptomaine poisoning, he was totally healed once he was able to get to Lake's home.

In 1931, Lake returned to Spokane at the age of sixty-one. He was now weak with fatigue, and almost blind. So he decided to have a "talk" with the Lord. He reminded Him of how shameful it would be if he were to go blind after over one hundred thousand people were healed in his ministry in America alone. By the end of the talk, his vision was completely restored, and remained that way for the rest of his life.

REIGNING IN THE HEAVENLIES

Labor Day came on a hot, humid Sunday in 1935. The Lakes had attended a Sunday school picnic and John returned home from it totally exhausted. So he laid down to rest. Florence encouraged him to stay home while she attended church that night, and when she returned home, she found Lake had suffered a stroke. He remained in poor condition for two weeks, unconscious most of the time. Then on September 16, 1935, John G. Lake went home to be with the Lord. He was sixty-five years old.

During the memorial service honoring Lake's life, many words of praise were spoken about him. But they are best summed up in this eulogy excerpt taken from one of Lake's many Spokane converts:

> "Dr. Lake came to Spokane. He found us in sin. He found us in sickness. He found us in poverty of spirit. He found us in despair, but he revealed to us such a Christ as we had never dreamed of knowing this side of heaven. We thought the victory was over there, but Dr. Lake revealed to us that victory was here."[27]

If we would just grasp the reality of our position through Jesus Christ, as Lake did, every nation would ring with the praises of God.

As we close this chapter, I want to challenge you to walk in the revelation of your righteousness in Christ. Righteousness is a *lifestyle* that produces victory in every situation. If we would just grasp the reality of our position through Jesus Christ, as Lake did, every nation would ring with the praises of God. And every demonic regime would crumble under that authority.

John G. Lake proved to us that this lifestyle can be lived and enjoyed by those who pursue it. So don't stop short of what God has given us through Jesus Christ. Allow the Holy Spirit to reveal your heavenly position to you, then take your place and change the nations for God.

CHAPTER SIX, JOHN G. LAKE
References

[1] John G. Lake, *Adventures in God* (Tulsa, OK: Harrison House, 1981), 30.

[2] Wilford Reidt, *John G. Lake: A Man Without Compromise* (Tulsa: Harrison House, 1989), 13.

[3] Lake, *Adventures in God*, 73-74.

[4] Reidt, *John G. Lake: A Man Without Compromise*, 21.

[5] Gordon Lindsay, ed., *John G. Lake: Apostle to Africa* (Dallas, TX: Christ for the Nations, Inc., Reprinted 1979), 12-13, Lake, *Adventures in God*, 77.

[6] Lake, *Adventures in God*, 78-80.

[7] Ibid., 35-36.

[8] Lindsay, *John G. Lake: Apostle to Africa*, 16.

[9] Gordon Lindsay, ed., *Astounding Diary of John G. Lake* (Dallas, TX: Christ for the Nations, 1987), 13-14.

[10] Lindsay, *Apostle to Africa*, 18-19.

[11] Reidt, *John G. Lake: A Man Without Compromise*, 27.

[12] Lindsay, *John G. Lake: Apostle to Africa*, 20.

[13] Lake, *Adventures in God*, 59-69.

[14] Lindsay, *John G. Lake: Apostle to Africa*, 25.

[15] Gordon Lindsay, ed., *John G. Lake Sermons on Dominion Over Demons, Disease & Death* (Dallas, TX: Christ for the Nations, Inc., 1949, Reprinted 1988), 108.

[16] Lindsay, *John G. Lake: Apostle to Africa*, 36.

[17] Lake, *Adventures in God*, 106-107.

[18] Lindsay, *John G. Lake: Apostle to Africa*, 53.

[19] Ibid.

[20] Kenneth Copeland Publications, *John G. Lake: His Life, His Sermons, His Boldness of Faith*, (Fort Worth, TX: Kenneth Copeland Publications, 1994), 442.

[21] Reidt, *A Man Without Compromise*, 95.

[22] Ibid., 60.

[23] Kenneth Copeland Publications, *John G. Lake*, 443.

[24] Ibid., 432.

[25] Ibid., 27.

[26] Lindsay, *New John G. Lake Sermons* (Dallas, TX: Christ for the Nations, Inc., 1976), 19-20.

[27] Lindsay, *John G. Lake: Apostle to Africa*, 9.

Smith Wigglesworth

"Apostle of Faith"

"APOSTLE OF FAITH"

"My friend said, 'She is dead.' He was scared. I have never seen a man so frightened in my life. 'What shall I do?' he asked. You may think that what I did was absurd, but I reached over into the bed and pulled her out. I carried her across the room, stood her against the wall and held her up, as she was absolutely dead. I looked into her face and said, 'In the name of Jesus, I rebuke this death.' From the crown of her head to the soles of her feet her whole body began to tremble. 'In the name of Jesus, I command you to walk,' I said. I repeated, 'In the name of Jesus, in the name of Jesus, walk!' and she walked."[1]

Raising the dead was only one amazing facet of the ministry of Smith Wigglesworth. This great apostle of faith walked in such an astounding measure of God's anointing that the miraculous following his ministry was only secondary to it. In his lifetime, this onetime plumber would give new meaning to the word "adventure." Adventure's only requirement? – *"Only believe!"*

To Wigglesworth, simple obedience to what one believed was not an extraordinary feat – it was simply the fruit of it. His own faith was said to be unflinching and sometimes ruthless. But he was also said to possess an unusual teaching anointing and a keen sense of compassion – the fruit of which produced countless salvations and miracles in his ministry every day.

> *To Wigglesworth, simple obedience to what one believed was not an extraordinary feat — it was simply the fruit of it.*

THE LITTLE TURNIP PULLER

Smith was born June 8, 1859, to John and Martha Wigglesworth in the small village of Menston, Yorkshire, England. At the time of his birth in 1859 it was already a historic year. The Third Great Awakening had been underway in America for two years, William Booth had distanced himself from organized religion, forming the Salvation Army, and the Church in Wales was praying for revival.[2] That Smith would be counted among the other great Christian leaders such as Booth in John and Martha's day, was the furthest thing from their minds that spring of 1859. But he would. Their son would put God's fire back into a church that had been smoldering for hundreds of years.

Smith's family was poor. His father worked long hours to support his wife, a daughter, and three sons. So the boy began work at the age of six, pulling turnips in a local field. The work was hard. His tiny hands were sore and swollen from pulling turnips morning until night. But it gave Smith his father's solid work ethic of laboring long and hard for reward.

When Smith turned seven he went to work with his father and another at the local wool mill. From then on, life seemed easier for the Wigglesworth family. Their income increased and food became plentiful.

Smith's father was a great lover of birds. At one time he had sixteen song-birds living in their home. So the boy adopted his father's love for nature and often searched for nests. He sometimes caught and sold songbirds at the local market to help sustain his family.

WHAT'S THE DIFFERENCE BETWEEN US?

Though his parents weren't Christians, there was never a time young Smith didn't long for God. He wasn't taught to pray at home, but he was always seeking on his own. Many times, Smith would ask God to show him where to find a nest of birds. Almost instantly he knew where to look.

His grandmother was an old-time Wesleyan who believed in the power of God. She always made sure Smith attended the meetings with her. As a young boy, he would sit and watch the "old-timers" clap their hands, dance to the Lord, and sing about the "blood." When Smith was eight years old, he got to join in the singing at church. As he began to sing, "a clear knowledge of the new birth" came to him. He realized what Jesus Christ had done for him through His death and resurrection. In later years, Wigglesworth would write of that day:

"I saw that God wants us so badly that He has made the condition as simple as He possibly could — *'Only Believe.'*"[3]

And he never doubted his salvation.

Young Wigglesworth immediatcly became a soulwinner. The first person he won to Christ was his own mother. When his father discovered the Christian "experience" had come to his family, he started taking the family to the Episco-pal church. Smith's father wasn't born again himself, but he enjoyed the parson, as they visited the same pub and drank beer together.

Soon Smith consented to join the church choir with his brother, but because he had to work at such a young age, he was robbed of an education. He was almost ten years old when he was "confirmed." When the bishop waved his hands over the young boy, a powerful awareness of God's presence filled Smith that would remain with him for days. Nothing like that seemed to occur with the others, as Smith would later write:

"After the confirmation service all the other boys were swearing and quarreling, and I wondered what had made the difference between them and me."[4]

THERE'S SOMETHING DIFFERENT ABOUT YOU

When Smith was thirteen, his family moved from Menston to Bradford where he became deeply involved in the Wesleyan Methodist Church. His spiritual life took on a new meaning, and he longed for the Spirit of God. Though he couldn't read well, he never left his house without the New Testament in his pocket.

...he joined the Salvationists when they arrived and would very soon learn about the power of fasting and prayer.

Later, the Methodists were planning a special preaching meeting, and seven boys were chosen to participate, including Smith. With three weeks to prepare, the teenager "lived in prayer." When the day arrived, he took the platform to preach for fifteen minutes, and afterward had no memory of what he had said. All he could remember was the incredible zeal that clothed him along with hearing the hearty shouts and cheers of the people.

Smith began to witness the Gospel to everyone he met, but he couldn't understand why so many seemed uninterested. Then, in 1875, the Salvation Army started a work in Bradford. Smith was ecstatic when he heard the news. Finally, he could be with a group of people who shared his desire for the lost! So he joined the Salvationists when they arrived and would very soon learn about the power of fasting and prayer.

The Salvation Army had more results than anyone else at the time, especially in the area of soulwinning. Many times, they would have all-night prayer meetings, lying prostrate before the Lord. The early Salvationists had great spiritual authority and it was manifested in each of their services. At the weekly meetings, the group would join together and claim at least fifty to a hundred people for God, knowing they would reach that number and more. Scores of people found Jesus as their Savior through the branch at Bradford.

When he was seventeen, Smith met a godly man at the mill who taught him the plumbing business. As they worked together, this man explained to Smith the meaning and importance of water baptism.

Eager to fulfill the commandments in the Word, Smith gladly obeyed and was baptized in water shortly afterwards. During this time, he also learned of the message of the second coming of Christ, and believing strongly that Jesus would come by the turn-of-the-century. He was determined to "change the course" of everyone he met.

Believing that the Lord would help him in everything, Smith set out to minister. In 1877, he went to a plumber's home to ask for a job. The plumber advised Smith that he had no need for anyone. So Smith thanked him, apologized for using his time, and turned to walk away. Suddenly the man called him back saying, "There is something about you that is different. I just cannot let you go."[5] And he was hired.

Smith did such excellent work that the plumber couldn't keep him employed – he worked too fast! So he decided to move to Liverpool, taking his plumbing experience with him. With the power of God resting heavily upon him, he began to minister to the children of the city. Longing to help them, he preached the Gospel to them. Hundreds came to the dock shed where Smith ministered. Ragged and hungry, the girls and boys came, and Smith took care of them all. Though he had a good income, he never spent it on himself, using it instead to clothe and feed these children.

Besides his ministry to the children, Smith and a friend would visit the hospitals and ships, witnessing for Jesus Christ. He would fast and pray all day on Sunday, never seeing less than fifty people saved each time he ministered. The Salvation Army constantly invited Smith to preach at their services, and while preaching, he always stood broken as he wept before the people. Though he wished for the eloquence of Charles Spurgeon and other fine preachers, it was his brokenness that caused hundreds to come to the altar longing to know God.

"WHO ARE THESE SILLY PEOPLE?"

One of the greatest attributes in the life of Smith Wigglesworth was his wife, Mary Jane "Polly" Featherstone. In the lives of many great ministry couples, it seems that when one partner is strong, the other must take a lesser role in order to keep conflict at a minimum. But this wasn't the case with the Wigglesworths! Polly remained equally as strong, if not stronger at certain times, than her husband. She never refused to take a back seat, and Wigglesworth was in agreement with this. He said of her, **"All that I am today I owe, under God, to my precious wife. Oh, she was lovely!"**[6]

Polly Featherstone came from a good Methodist family. Even though her father lectured in the Temperance Movement, he became heir to a large inheritance made through the sale of liquor. However, holding fast to his inner convictions, he refused to touch a "penny" of the tainted inheritance. She watched the lifestyle of her father and echoed his strong character and beliefs of holiness. She was also a woman who said what she thought.

Later, Polly left her socially-affluent surroundings and headed for "fame and fortune" in the city of Bradford. Once there, she accepted service in a large family.

One day, while she was in town, she heard trumpets and shouting. Finding her way to the "noise," she was intrigued by what she saw – an open air meeting! The Salvation Army was a new organization at this time, and she thought, *Who are these silly people?* Curious, she followed the group to a large, dilapidated building. As the Salvationists marched inside, Polly remained on the corner, hoping no one saw her. Finally, overcome with curiosity, she slipped inside and took a seat in the top of the galley.

The Wigglesworth family. Top: Alice, Seth, and Harold. Bottom: Ernest, Smith, Mary Jane (Polly), and George

"HALLELUJAH! IT'S DONE!"

Gypsy Tillie Smith, sister of the famous evangelist, Gypsy Rodney Smith, was preaching. Hurling her fiery message toward the people, she proclaimed salvation through the blood of Jesus. Polly was deeply moved. Realizing her lost condition, she left the galley and made her way to the altar rail, falling to her knees. She refused any prayer from the workers, until finally, Tillie Smith made her way over to pray with her. With the light of Christ warming her heart, Polly jumped to her feet, threw her gloves in the air, and shouted, "Hallelujah! It is done!"[7] Sitting in the audience, not far from her, a young man watched her intently. That man was her future husband and partner in destiny – Smith Wigglesworth.

> *With the light of Christ warming her heart, Polly jumped to her feet, threw her gloves in the air, and shouted, "Hallelujah! It's done!"*

"It seemed as if the inspiration of God was upon her from the very first," Smith said.[8] The next night, as Polly gave her testimony, Smith felt she "belonged to him." Being allowed to forego the customary period of training, she was eventually given a commission as an officer in the Salvation Army by General Booth himself.

Polly went on to serve the Salvation Army in Scotland for a season, then returned to Bradford. She would eventually leave the army because of conflict surrounding her relationship with Wigglesworth. She was an "officer" and he was a mere "soldier." Though Smith never officially joined the army, the rules were strict regarding any intimate relationship between the two ranks.

After she left, Polly joined the Blue Ribbon Army, but she always remained a true friend to the Salvationists. At this time, Methodist ministers called her to evangelize their churches, and hundreds were converted through her ministry. The power of God rested heavily upon her.

"SMITH, YOU'RE NOT MY MASTER"

Polly became "Mrs. Wigglesworth" in 1882, at age twenty-two. Smith was one year older than his new wife, and encouraged her to continue her evangelistic ministry, while he was content in the plumbing business. However, he did have a "burden" for an area in Bradford that had no church. So the couple rented a small building and opened it for meetings, calling it the "Bradford Street Mission."

In their thirty years of marriage, the Wigglesworths had one daughter, Alice, and four sons, Seth, Harold, Ernest, and George (who later died in 1915). But before each child was born, the Wigglesworths prayed over them that they would serve God. After their birth, Smith took care of them during church while his wife preached. Following the message, Smith was always at the altar, praying to bring people to Christ. Not at all intimidated by his wife's ministry role, Smith said, **"Her work was to put down the net; mine was to land the fish. This latter is just as important as the former."**[9] He knew the power of a servant's heart.

The winter of 1884 was a severe one for Bradford, and as a result, the plumbers were in high demand. Not only did Smith spend the entire winter working, but remained busy repairing the damage as a result of the elements for two more years.

During those days of heavy work and great prosperity, Smith's attendance in church declined rapidly and his heart grew cold toward the Lord. But as his fire grew dimmer, Polly's grew brighter, and her zeal for God and her prayer life never wavered. Her consistency and diligence in the things of God made Smith's laxity all the more apparent, and he became irritated by her very presence.

> *Polly Wigglesworth beautifully illustrated the principle of "stability."*

One night, she came home from church a little later than usual. When she entered the house, Smith remarked, **"I am the master of this house, and I am not going to have you coming home at so late an hour as this!"** Polly quietly replied, "I know that you are my husband, but Christ is my Master."[10] Greatly annoyed, Smith opened the back door and forced her out of the house, locking the door behind her. But in his great annoyance he had forgotten to lock the front door. So Polly walked around to the front of the house and came in through the front door – laughing! In fact, she laughed so much that Smith finally surrendered and laughed with her. In his laughter, a revelation came into his heart and mind, so he decided to spend ten days in prayer and fasting to seek the Lord. In desperate and sincere repentance, he found his way to the road of restoration.

WHERE DO YOU RATE ON THE RICHTER SCALE?

"The woman is the thermometer of the household," is a true saying. For example, if your wife is in a bad mood, the rest of the members will end up having a negative attitude. On the other hand, if your wife is cheerful, regardless of how bad you feel, everything seems more upbeat.

Polly Wigglesworth beautifully illustrated the principle of "stability." I am sure that her fidelity and joy were severely tested while her husband was backslidden. She was a very popular speaker, holding evangelistic services throughout the city, seeing hundreds come to Christ – while her husband worked or sat at home. No doubt, there were whispers of Smith's spiritual condition, as Polly's ministry was publicly scrutinized, but she never "missed a step." Obviously, the one thing that caused her to triumph was – *her security in Jesus Christ.*

In many cases, when a husband is backslidden, the wife nags and complains thinking she is pushing him into action and repentance, but a repentant heart is a result of the work of the Holy Spirit. The fire of God kept a joyful heart within Polly. As a result, Smith saw his mistake and was drawn back to Jesus. His wife's attitude was directly responsible for his repentance, and eventually, their world-shaking ministry. This is the highest goal of a "help mate," to help (the mate) meet his or her call, whatever it may be. God knows the heart of your mate and what it will take to move him or her to the place he or she belongs. Just keep your own heart right and leave others to God and the Holy Spirit. That way, you will never lose.

THE FIRST HEALING

In the late 1800s, Smith traveled to Leeds to purchase supplies for his plumbing business. While in Leeds, he attended a church service where divine healing was being ministered. Smith sat in the meeting observing the marvelous healings that took place. His heart was moved and he began to search for the sick in Bradford, paying their expenses to go to the healing meetings in Leeds, never daring to tell his wife what he was doing. He was concerned she would join the other scoffers of that day in labeling divine healing as "fanaticism." But when she found out the truth, she listened intently to his description of the meetings, and, needing healing herself, she accompanied him to Leeds. The prayer of faith was offered for her, and she received an instant manifestation. From that day forward, the Wigglesworths were passionate for the truths in divine healing.

As a result, their church in Bradford grew. So they sought for a larger place and obtained a building on Bowland Street and called the new work, "Bowland Street Mission." They had a huge scroll painted on the wall behind the pulpit that read: "I Am the Lord That Healeth Thee."

Smith's first personal experience with healing came in the early 1900s. A hemorrhoid condition had plagued him since childhood, so a visiting minister prayed and agreed in faith with Smith that this condition would be divinely healed. Up to this point, Smith had used "salts" every day, but being fully persuaded in the will of God, he eventually stopped using them, and found that he was fully healed, remaining so for the rest of his life.

By now, Smith was totally dedicated to the ministry of healing. Being in business for himself, he had the time to take groups of people to the Leeds Healing Home, always paying their expenses. He was known for his great compassion toward the sick and needy. The workers at Leeds would see Smith coming with groups of people and laugh among themselves, because he didn't seem to understand that God could heal the sick in Bradford, just as He did in Leeds.

"PUSHED" INTO THE PULPIT!

Realizing that Smith needed some "prodding" to get his public ministry going, the leaders of the Leeds Healing Home made a decision.

Knowing they were going to the Keswick Convention, they asked Smith to fill the pulpit in their absence. Smith was hesitant at first, but the ministers assured him that he could do it. So he comforted himself by thinking he would just take charge, and there were any number of people who would agree to preach. When the day came to minister, Smith was in charge, but no one would preach. They all agreed that Smith should do it. Hesitantly, he began to minister and at the close of his message, fifteen people came forward for healing. One man hobbled up on a pair of crutches, and when Smith prayed for him, the man jumped all over the place, without his crutches, instantly healed. There was no one as surprised as Smith!

From this meeting, doors began to open for Smith to minister, and he soon announced he would hold a healing meeting in Bradford. On the first night twelve people came for healing, and each one was healed. One lady had a large tumor that was constantly draining. After the prayer of faith, she went home and reported the next day that only a scar was left.

PLEASE...SHUT UP!

All too soon, Smith received his first challenge. It was a life or death situation. The wife of a devoted friend was so ill that the doctors expected her to die during the night. Smith's friend said he couldn't believe for his wife, because he didn't know how. Compassion rose up in Smith's heart and he determined to help that family. So he went to a minister who was opening a small church in Bradford, and asked if he would go to pray for the woman. But the minister refused. Smith then went to a friend, who was known for his eloquent prayers. The friend agreed to go with him and the two set out for the woman's home.

> *"Suddenly, the Lord Jesus appeared. I had my eyes open gazing at Him. He gave me one of those gentle smiles.... I have never lost that vision, the vision of that beautiful, soft smile."*

Smith felt encouraged to have someone with him. He exhorted his friend to begin praying as soon as they entered the home, and upon seeing the weakened condition of the woman, the friend took Smith's advice. He began praying – but not as Smith had hoped. This man prayed for "the family that would be left behind" and continued in a rambling, negative tone until Smith cried out for him to stop. Thinking the worst was behind him, he then asked the woman's husband to pray. But he cried out in just as pathetic a fashion. Finally, when Smith could stand it no longer, he cried out so loudly that he could be heard in the street – **"Lord, stop him!"** The husband stopped.

Smith then pulled a bottle of oil out of his pocket and poured the entire bottle over the body of the woman, in the name of Jesus. Then standing at the head of her bed, Smith experienced his first vision. He said, **"Suddenly, the Lord Jesus appeared. I had my eyes open gazing at Him. He gave me one of those gentle smiles.... I have never lost that vision, the vision of that beautiful, soft smile."**[11] And a few moments after the vision vanished, the woman sat up in bed filled with new life. She lived to raise a number of children and outlived her husband.

"...all he needed to know was in the Word of God..."

"COME OUT, DEVIL!"

As Smith's hunger for the Word of God grew, he never allowed any publications in his home, secular or Christian, except the Bible. He felt that all he needed to know was in the Word of God. Smith said of his wife, **"She saw**

**how ignorant I was, and immediately began to teach me to read prop-
erly and write; unfortunately, she never succeeded in teaching me to
spell."**[12]

Smith's next experience with a life or death situation came in his own life.
One day he was suddenly struck with severe pain and was confined to his bed.
Having agreed previously with his wife that no medications would be in his
house, he left his healing in the hands of God.

The family prayed all night for some kind of relief, but none came. Smith
grew weaker by the hour, and finally, he said to his wife, **"It seems to me
that this is my home-call. To protect yourself, you should now call a
physician."** Brokenhearted, Polly set out for a physician, believing the end
had come for her husband.

When the physician came, he shook his head and told the family that it was
appendicitis and that the condition had been deteriorating for the past six
months. He went on to say that Smith's organs were so damaged that there was
no hope, not even with surgery. As the physician was leaving, an elderly
woman and a young man came into Smith's room. This woman believed in
praying the prayer of faith, and she believed that all sickness came from the
devil. While she prayed, the young man got on the bed, laid both hands on
Smith and cried, "Come out, devil, in the name of Jesus!"

To Smith's great surprise, the "devil came out" and the pain was completely
gone. For good measure, the couple prayed for Smith again, after which he got
up, got dressed, and went downstairs. He said to his wife, **"I am healed. Any
work in?"** As Polly heard his story, she, still in total awe, handed him his job
request. He then set out immediately to remedy the plumbing problem and
was never again plagued by appendicitis.[13]

"THEY'RE RECEIVING DEVILS"

In 1907 another turning point came in the life of Smith Wigglesworth. He
had heard that a group of people in Sunderland were "baptized in the Holy
Spirit" and "speaking in other tongues." So he determined to see this phenomenon for himself.

Until this time, Smith believed he was already baptized in the Holy Spirit.
He, along with his wife, followed the popular belief of the day that sanctification was the baptism of the Holy Spirit. Smith then recalled an earlier situation
that caused him to repent and begin a ten-day fast. During this fast, Smith had
found his way back to God, and in fact, had experienced a definite change in

his life. It is said that as he prayed and wept before the Lord, he consecrated himself to be wholly sanctified. When the fast was over, he was free from his temper and moodiness to such a degree that some often commented that they wanted the spirit that Smith had. As a result, Smith thought he had been baptized in the Spirit or sanctified.

In writing to his friends in Sunderland regarding the subject of tongues, he was warned to stay away because **"those people were receiving devils."** However, when Smith arrived and prayed with his friends about the matter, they looked at him and said, **"Obey your own leadings."**[14]

He was disappointed as he sat in the meetings at Sunderland, under the leadership of Vicar Alexander Boddy. In Bradford, there seemed to be a mighty move of God. But here, it seemed spiritually dry, with no manifestations. In his frustration, he continually disrupted the meetings, saying, **"I have come from Bradford, and I want this experience of speaking in tongues like they had on the day of Pentecost. But I do not understand why our meetings seem to be on fire, but yours do not seem to be so."**[15]

Smith disrupted the meeting so many times in his desperate search that he was disciplined outside the building.

> *"I have come from Bradford, and I want this experience of speaking in tongues like they had on the day of Pentecost. I do not understand why our meetings seem to be on fire, but yours do not seem to be so."*

BATHED IN POWER & GLORY

Seeking God with all his heart to experience this "baptism in the Holy Spirit," Smith went to a local Salvation Army building to pray. Three times he was struck to the floor by the power of God. The Salvationists warned him against speaking in tongues, but Smith was determined to know God in this realm. Four days he sought the Lord expecting to speak in other tongues, but to no avail. Finally, discouraged in his spirit, he felt it was time to return to Bradford. But before his departure, he went to the parsonage to tell the vicar's wife, Mrs. Boddy, good-bye. He told her that he had to go home and didn't get to speak in tongues. She answered, "It is not the tongues you need, but the baptism."[16] Smith asked her to lay hands on him before he left. She prayed a simple but powerful prayer, and then left the room. It was then that the fire fell. Bathed in the power and glory of the Lord, Smith saw a vision of the empty cross with Jesus exalted at the right hand of the Father. Filled with worship and praise, Smith opened his mouth and began to speak in other tongues, finally realizing that even though he had received an anointing earlier, he was now baptized in the Holy Spirit as on the day of Pentecost.

Instead of going home, Smith went straight to the church where Rev. Boddy was conducting the service. Interrupting, he begged to speak for a moment. When he finished his "sermon," fifty people were gloriously baptized in the Holy Spirit and spoke with other tongues. The local newspaper, the *Sunderland Daily Echo*, headlined the meeting, giving detailed accounts of Smith's experience, including the tongues and the healings. He telegraphed his home, telling them of the great news.

HOLY LAUGHTER

On returning to Bradford, Smith felt he would have a challenge to face concerning his newfound joy, and he was right. As he came through the door, Polly stated firmly, "I want you to understand that I am as much baptized in the Holy Spirit as you are and I don't speak in tongues.... Sunday, you will preach for yourself, and I will see what there is in it."[17]

She kept her word, and when Sunday came, Polly sat in the very back of the church. As Smith walked up to the pulpit, the Lord gave him the passage in Isaiah 61:1-3. He preached with great power and assurance while Polly squirmed around in the bench saying to herself, *That's not my Smith, Lord. That's not my Smith!*[18]

At the end of the service, a worker stood and said that he wanted the same experience that Smith had. As he sat down, he missed his chair and fell onto the floor! Smith's oldest son stood to say the same and he also missed his chair and fell onto the floor! In a very short while, eleven people were on the floor laughing in the Spirit. The entire congregation became consumed in holy laughter as God poured out His Spirit upon them. This was the beginning of the great outpouring in Bradford, where hundreds received the baptism of the Holy Spirit and spoke in other tongues.

Soon after Polly was baptized in the Holy Spirit, the couple went throughout the country, answering the calls for ministry. Wherever they went, conviction seemed to settle on the people. Once, when Smith entered a grocery store to shop, three people fell to their knees in repentance. Another time, two ladies were working in a field, and when Smith passed by, he called out to them, **"Are you saved?"** Right after he said it they dropped their buckets and cried out for God.[19]

GOD'S FINANCIAL COVENANT

During the coming days, Smith developed the habit of prayer and fasting. Soon letters from all over the country poured into the Wigglesworth household, begging him to come and pray for their sick. He answered every request he could, and sometimes after a train ride to a city, he would find a bicycle and peddle another ten miles in order to reach the afflicted one.

With such an incredible flood of ministry work, Smith soon saw his personal plumbing business decline. He was called out of town so often that his customers would have to call on another plumber. Each time he returned to Bradford there was less business.

> *With such an incredible flood of ministry work, Smith soon saw his personal plumbing business decline.*

Returning early from a convention, Smith found that most of his customers had called other plumbers to do the work. There was one widow who couldn't find help, so he went directly to her home and did the repair work, as well as the damaged ceiling. When she asked what she owed, Smith replied, **"I won't receive any pay from you. I'll make this an offering to the Lord as my last plumbing job."**[20]

So with that declaration, he paid his accounts, closed his business, and began his full-time ministry. He believed, in spite of the stories of poverty he had heard, that God would abundantly provide as he served Him faithfully. Confident in his partnership with God, he laid down a condition:

> **"My shoe heels must never be a disgrace, and I must never have to wear trousers with the knees out. I said to the Lord, 'If either of these things take place, I'll go back to plumbing.'"**[21]

God never failed to supply all his needs, and he never returned to plumbing.

"LET HER GO"

One of the greatest sorrows of Wigglesworth's life was soon to follow. While waiting in the train station to leave for Scotland, Smith received devastating news: Polly had collapsed with a heart attack while returning from the Bowland Street Mission.

Rushing to her bedside, he found that her spirit had already departed to be with the Lord. Not settling for this, Smith immediately rebuked the death and her spirit came back, but only for just a short while. Then the Lord spoke: "This is the time that I want to take her home to Myself." So with a breaking heart, Smith released his partner, the one he had loved for so many years, to be with the Lord. Polly Wigglesworth served the Lord until the very last moment of her life, January 1, 1913.[22] It is said by some that after her death, Smith asked for a double portion of the Spirit.[23] From that moment on, his ministry carried an even greater power.

HERE'S THE SECRET...

Smith immediately started ministering throughout the country traveling with his daughter and son-in-law. It was extremely unusual for the British press to carry stories on religious news. Yet the *Daily Mirror* dedicated their front page to his dynamic ministry featuring four photographs of Wigglesworth in action.[24] Because this newspaper was the most widely circulated paper in the nation, hundreds sought out his ministry. Smith had an incredible revelation on the subject of faith and his teaching on this subject attracted the masses. Wigglesworth didn't settle for hoping that prayer would work. His revelation on faith was concrete, melting the most hardened sinner to the love of Jesus Christ.

Smith's theory on faith was simple: Only believe. He didn't believe that God had favorites. One of his primary examples of this principle came from the New Testament, where John was noted as the apostle whom Jesus "greatly loved." According to Wigglesworth, John's "leaning against Jesus' bosom" didn't make him a favorite. The factor that called attention to John was his relationship and dependence upon Jesus. Smith constantly proclaimed:

"There is something about believing God, that makes God willing to pass over a million people just to anoint you."[25]

Many books have been written attempting to find the secret of Wigglesworth's power, but the answer is very simple. His great faith came from his relationship with Jesus Christ. From that relationship came Smith's every answer to every situation he ever faced. God has no favorites – He works through those who believe Him.

"I'M NEVER TOO LATE"

Frequently Smith's methods were misunderstood and criticized. He was never moved by the criticism, but he did have compassion on his critics. Instead of retaliation, he would answer, **"I am not moved by what I see or hear; I am moved by what I believe."[26]**

Preaching the Word

Ministering "in" the Spirit

God's student

Later years

Four Generations

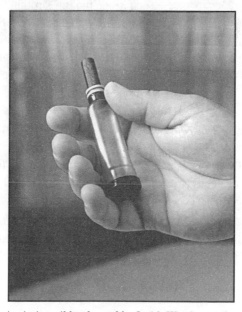

Anointing oil bottle used by Smith Wigglesworth

The Holy Spirit began teaching Smith the varying degrees of faith. He first taught that *faith could be created* in others.

An example of this concept was a young boy who was seriously ill. The family had sent for Smith, but when Smith arrived, the mother met him at the door, saying, "You are too late. There is nothing that can be done for him." Smith replied, **"God has never sent me anywhere too late."**[27] The boy's condition was so bad, that if he were to be moved, his heart would stop and he would die. Needless to say, the family had no faith and the boy was too sick to believe for himself. Before he could pray for the boy, Smith had to leave for an engagement at a local chapel. But before he left their home, he told the family he would return. He then instructed them to lay out the boy's clothes because the Lord was going to raise him up. When Smith returned, the family had not done what he asked, and when they saw his faith, they were embarrassed and immediately set out the boy's clothes. Smith asked them to put only socks on his feet. Then inside the boy's room, Smith closed the door and told the lifeless boy that something would happen different from anything he had experienced before. **"When I place my hands on you the glory of the Lord will fill the place till I shall not be able to stand. I shall be helpless on the floor."**[28] The moment Smith touched the boy, the power of God filled the room and was so strong that Smith fell to the floor. Suddenly, the boy began to yell, "This is for Your Glory, Lord!" Smith was still on the floor when the boy arose and dressed himself. Opening the door, the boy yelled, "Dad! God has healed me! I am healed!"[29]

> *The moment Smith touched the boy the power of God filled the room and was so strong that Smith fell to the floor. Suddenly, the boy began to yell, "This is for Your Glory, Lord!"*

Such glory filled the house that the mother and father fell to the floor also. His sister, who had been released from an asylum, was instantly restored in her mind. The entire village was moved and revival began throughout their city.

On that miraculous day, Smith learned how to *transfer faith* by the laying on of hands. His ministry would never be the same, for he had learned a new degree of faith. *Faith could be created and transferred into the life of another!*

"RUN, WOMAN, RUN!"

As his faith began to increase, the Lord showed him another principle of faith: *Faith should be acted upon.*

Until then, the average believer seemed to think that God moved only in a sovereign way. They felt they had no part in it. The ministry of Smith Wigglesworth brought a new light to this dark area. Through his deep relationship with the Lord, Smith began to notice in the Bible that the people who received from God had *acted* upon His Word to produce results. Thus, his ministry began to adopt this operation of faith in every service. At the beginning of his altar calls he would say: **"If you move forward only a foot, you will be blessed; if you move forward a yard, you will get more. If you come up to the platform, we will pray for you, and God will meet your needs with His supply."**[30]

This was the central truth behind his healing ministry regarding faith. A truth that many called, "ruthless." Smith Wigglesworth's actions were a result of strong compassion and a rock-solid faith in God. A Christian must *act* upon what he believes in order to receive the manifestation, and sometimes, Smith had to *initiate* the action for a few individuals. He called this type of ministry **"retail healing,"** mainly because his faith contributed largely to their individual action.

For example, during a meeting in Arizona, a young lady responded to his call for healing. She was greatly distressed with tuberculosis, but as she stepped into the aisle, he said to her, **"Now, I am going to pray for you and then you will run around this building."** He prayed, then shouted, **"Run, woman. Run!"** The woman said, "But I cannot run. I can scarcely stand." **"Don't talk back to me,"** Smith shouted, **"do as I have said."** She was reluctant, so Smith jumped down from the platform, grabbed her, and began running. She clung to him until she gathered speed, then galloped around the auditorium without any effort. [31]

There was another woman in the same meeting. Her legs were locked with sciatica. Smith told her to *"Run!"* She was so reluctant that he pushed her! Then he ran around the building with the woman clinging to him. Finally, the power of God met her action, and she was completely delivered. She walked to the rest of the meetings, refusing the street car, delighted to have the full use of her limbs again.

"PAPA! IT'S GOING ALL OVER ME!"

Sometimes in his ministry Smith would use another approach to *acting* on faith. He would read portions of Scripture, then act on it himself. Often he held banquets to feed the lame and hungry, with the members of the Bowland Street Mission serving the sumptuous food. He also arranged for healing testimonies to be their entertainment, moving these poor people to tears.

At the first banquet, Smith set a precedent for the other banquets that followed. At the close of the first meeting, Smith announced:

> **"We have entertained you tonight. But next Saturday we are going to have another meeting. You who are bound today and have come in wheelchairs...you who have spent all you have on doctors and are none better, are going to entertain us by the stories of freedom that you have received today by the name of Jesus."** Then he said, *"Who wants to be healed?"*[32]

Of course, everyone did. A woman in a wheelchair walked home, and an epileptic of eighteen years was instantly delivered and was working within two weeks. A young boy encased in an iron brace was instantly healed when the power of God touched him as he cried, "Papa, Papa, Papa. It's going all over me!"[33]

Week after week, the healing miracles of the previous services went out among the sick and afflicted, bringing them to the banquet service. What a tremendous revival began among them – simply from acting upon the Word of God.

Smith knew how to draw the Spirit of God. It all stemmed from faith, not arrogance.

"I'LL MOVE THE SPIRIT"

Smith Wigglesworth took Hebrews 11:6 very seriously. He personally believed it was impossible to please God without faith. As a result, he incorporated that faith into every segment of his spiritual life, including the workings of the Holy Spirit. When the slightest breath of the Spirit came upon Smith, he would go off into a room to be alone with God. In developing this relationship, he understood the action of faith as he cooperated with the Holy Spirit.

Once in a meeting, someone commented on how quickly Smith was moved by the Spirit. When they asked him his secret he replied, **"Well, you see, it is like this. If the Spirit does not move me, I move the Spirit."**[34] Those who didn't understand the principles of faith thought his remark was arrogant and disrespectful. But in reality, *Smith knew how to draw the Spirit of God.* It all stemmed from *faith*, not arrogance. If the Holy Spirit wasn't moving as a service began, then Smith would begin the meeting in the natural state. By his faith, he would focus the hearers to the Word and power of God and increase their expectancy. As a result, the Holy Spirit would manifest Himself in direct response to their faith. Smith took the initiative and stirred up the gifts within himself by faith. He didn't wait for something to come upon him and spiritually overtake him. To him, every action, every operation, and every manifestation stemmed from one thing – *absolute faith. True faith confronts, and it is ignited by initiative.*

Then Smith Wigglesworth began teaching the body of Christ that they could speak in tongues by *initiative*. To him, faith was the main substance that stirred the human spirit, not sovereignty. J. E. Stiles, a great Assemblies of God minister and author, learned this important principle from Smith Wigglesworth and carried it throughout his ministry.

In a large meeting in California, Smith gave the call for those people who had not received the baptism of the Holy Spirit to stand. Then he asked for all those to stand who had received, but had not spoken in tongues for six months. **"Now, I'm going to pray a simple prayer,"** Smith began, **"and when I'm finished, I'll say 'Go,' and you will all speak with tongues."** Smith prayed. Then he yelled, **"Go!"** The sound filled the auditorium like that of many waters as everyone prayed in other tongues. Then, he told them to do the same thing again, only when he said, **"Go,"** everyone would sing in tongues, by faith. He prayed. Then he yelled, **"Go! Sing!"** The sound was like a vast and glorious choir.

That day, Rev. Stiles said he learned that the Holy Spirit operates by faith. Shortly after this revelation, he launched his international ministry.[35]

ANOTHER SECRET

Smith Wigglesworth was a man greatly moved by compassion. As he received prayer requests from all over the world he would cry out to God and weep on their behalf. Many times, as he ministered to the afflicted, tears ran down his cheeks. He was also very tender with children and the elderly. In his services, when the heat became stifling, he felt great compassion and would call for the babies and the elderly to be prayed for first.

Demonstrating the truths in Acts 19:11-12, thousands upon thousands were healed as Smith prayed and sent handkerchiefs to those he couldn't visit. An intimate friend spoke of the sincerity and compassion portrayed by Smith, saying, "When...the time for the opening of the letters came, we all had to stop whatever we were doing and get under the burden. There was nothing rushed or slipshod about his methods.... Everybody in the house must join in the prayers and lay hands on the handkerchiefs sent out to the suffering ones. They were treated as though the writers were present in person."[36]

DOG THE DEVIL!

Realizing that the source of all the miracles of Christ stemmed from His compassion, Smith became positively aggressive in undoing the works of evil. His one goal was to heal all those who were oppressed and to teach the body of Christ to deal ruthlessly with the devil.

> *He had little patience with demons, especially when they dared to interrupt his meetings.*

Once, while he waited for a bus, he observed how a woman was encouraging her dog to return home, but after several "sweet" attempts, the dog remained. When she saw the bus approaching, she stomped her foot on the ground and shouted, "Go home at once!" and the dog ran with its tail tucked. **"That's how you have to treat the devil,"** Smith responded, loud enough for all to hear. [37]

He had little patience with demons, especially when they dared to interrupt his meetings. Once, he was conducting a meeting and couldn't "get free" to preach, so he began to shout. Nothing happened. He took off his coat, and still nothing happened. Smith asked the Lord what was wrong, and after doing so, the Lord showed him a line of people sitting together on a bench holding hands. Smith knew at once they were spiritualists bent on destroying his meeting.

As he began to preach, he walked off the platform and over to where they were sitting. Then, he took hold of the bench and commanded the devil to leave. The group slid into a heap on the floor, then scrambled to leave the building!

When casting out demons, Smith Wigglesworth was totally confident and secure in his faith. Prayers didn't have to be long; if the prayer carried faith, the answer was sure.

INTERNATIONAL AUTHORITY

Smith's international ministry, begun in 1914, was in full swing by 1920. Though the persecution against him was strong, it never seemed to be a major issue in his ministry. Unlike some ministries, there is more written about his great strength and miracles than of his troubles and persecution. Perhaps this is due to his extraordinary faith. He brushed off the criticism like dust off his coat, never allowing it a moment of pleasure.

In Sweden in 1920, the medical profession and local authorities thought they would "harness" the ministry of Wigglesworth, prohibiting him from laying hands on the people. But he wasn't concerned. He knew God would answer *faith*, not *method*. After he conducted the meeting, he instructed over twenty thousand people to **"lay their hands on themselves"** and believe for healing as he prayed. Multitudes received instant manifestation. Smith labeled this type of grand-scale healing as **"wholesale healing."**

In the same year, Smith was arrested twice in Switzerland. The warrants were issued for practicing medicine without a license. On a third occasion, the officers came to the house of a Pentecostal minister with another warrant for Wigglesworth's arrest. The minister said, "Mr. Wigglesworth is away now, but before you arrest him, I want to show you the result of his ministry in this place." The minister then escorted the policemen to the lower part of town to the home of a woman they had arrested many times. Upon seeing the manifestation of her complete deliverance and faith in Jesus Christ, the officers were moved. They turned to the minister and said, "We refuse to stop this kind of work. Somebody else will have to arrest this man." And "somebody else" did. But an officer came to him in the middle of the night and said, "I find no fault with you. You can go." To this Smith replied, **"No, I'll only go on one condition; that every officer in this place gets down on his knees, and I'll pray for you."**[38]

PENTECOST!

Smith's ministry was flourishing by 1921. International ministry invitations flooded his home inviting him to embark on his longest itinerant journey of his life.

Though very popular in Europe and America, no one seemed to notice his arrival in Colombo, Ceylon (Sri Lanka). But within days, crowds packed the building trying to get a seat. Many had to remain outside. When the meeting was over, Smith passed through the thousands of people, touching them and believing God with them. Reports claimed that scores of people were healed as "his shadow" passed by them.[39]

In 1922, Smith traveled to New Zealand and Australia. Some believe that Smith's meetings birthed the Pentecostal churches in New Zealand and Australia. Though he spent only a few months there, thousands were saved, healed, and filled with the Holy Spirit with the evidence of speaking in tongues. Australia and New Zealand experienced the greatest spiritual revival they had ever seen.

CAN YOU BLESS A PIG?

Dr. Lester Sumrall from South Bend, Indiana, once shared a humorous incident that occurred during his travels with Smith. A dinner had been prepared for them while they were together in Wales. And just as it so happened, the main entree was roasted pig! Smith was asked to bless the food, so with a loud voice, he said, **"Lord, if You can bless what You have cursed, then bless this pig!"** Smith's humor along with his boldness made a great impression on Sumrall. Dr. Sumrall often laughed when he shared that story with me.

...Smith Wigglesworth prefered to be unattached to any denomination throughout his ministry. It was in his heart to preach all people...

AN UNPUBLISHED CONTROVERSY

Though many churches assembled as a result of his meetings, Smith Wigglesworth preferred to be unattached to any denomination throughout his ministry. It was in his heart to reach all people, regardless of their doctrine. He never wanted to be swayed by any particular denomination.

There is a little known controversy that surfaced in the life of Smith Wigglesworth that deepened his belief in independent ministry. In 1915, he had become a member of the Pentecostal Missionary Union. The union's governing council wasn't a denomination, nor did it offer ministerial licenses or ordinations. It was simply designed to be a covering for ministries of like faith. Smith served with the PMU until his forced resignation in 1920.

At the time he was forced to resign, Smith had been a widower for seven years and had developed a friendship with a woman named Miss Amphlett. Smith told her that he felt he had a **"spiritual affinity"** with her. But Amphlett rejected the idea, and she and another woman wrote a letter of complaint to the PMU. It was directed to the attention of Cecil Polhill, who notified the other council members along with the council's secretary, Mr. Mundell.

Though the PMU had very strict views concerning relationships between men and women, Smith Wigglesworth was sure the PMU would stand by him in spite of the accusations. But when the PMU received Amphlett's letter, Mr. Polhill promptly wrote Wigglesworth requesting his resignation from his council position. He went on to say that the council felt he should "abstain for a prolonged season from participation in the Lord's public work, and seek to retrieve your position before God and man, by a fairly long period of godly, quiet living, so showing works meet for repentance."[40]

Smith honored the request for resignation, though he felt the two women in question had joined together to ruin his work. In fact, Smith was so disappointed in Polhill for allowing the situation to be blown so out of proportion, that he wrote directly to the council's secretary, Mr. Mundell. Smith wrote:

"I think that Mr. Polhill has stepped over the boundary this time [they are] making things to appear as if I had committed fornication or adultery and I am innocent of those things. I have done and acted foolishly and God has forgiven me. This thing was settled in the spiritual way and after this at the church and with Mr. Polhill and he ought to of have seen the thing through."[41]

In a separate letter to Mr. Polhill, Smith wrote:

"...God will settle all. The good hand of God is upon me, and I will live it all down. This week, God has rebuked the oppressor through his servant. I shall go forward, dear brother, and ask you to be careful that the Gospel is not hindered through you and ought at this time to do unto me as you would wish one to do unto you. Do not trouble to send anything to sign. I signed my letter to you, that (is) all."[42]

From that point on Smith Wigglesworth was continually on the go answering invitations to minister all over the world. And to guard against any more false accusations of this nature, Smith always traveled with his daughter, Alice. The controversy resulting in his resignation never slowed Smith down. In fact, it seemed to speed him up.

This is often the case when people come out from under the direction of denominationalism. I know the PMU wasn't a denomination. But these kinds of governing committees can sometimes develop an element of control even after they start out in the right spirit. The control can be so slight, but it still affects the flow of ministry. It was better for Smith to branch out on his own. He didn't need the reputation nor the association with the PMU. He had power with God.

BETTER LIVE READY

Wigglesworth loved the Word of God and was very disciplined in his study of it. He never considered himself fully dressed unless he had his Bible with him. While others read novels or newspapers, he read the Bible. He would never leave a friend's table without reading, as he would say, **"a bit from the Book."**

AFFLICTION HAD TO BOW

Though the eyes of Wigglesworth had seen many miraculous and instant healings, he himself didn't receive such miracles. In 1930, as Smith was entering his seventies, he was experiencing tremendous pain. He prayed but wasn't relieved. So he went to a physician who, after X-rays, diagnosed his condition as a very serious case of kidney stones in the advanced stage. An operation was his only hope, since according to the doctor, if Smith continued in this painful condition, he would die. Smith responded:

"Doctor, the God Who made this body is the One Who can cure it. No knife shall ever cut it so long as I live."[43]

The physician was concerned and dismayed at his response, but Smith left, assuring the physician he would hear of his healing. The pain increased daily, now accompanied by irritation. All night, Smith was in and out of bed, rolling on the floor in agony as he struggled to emit the stones. One by one, the ragged stones passed. Smith thought his ordeal would be short-lived, but it lasted six long and painful years.

> *One by one, the ragged stones passed. Smith thought his ordeal would be short-lived, but it lasted six long and painful years.*

During this time, Smith never failed to appear at scheduled services, many times ministering twice a day. At some meetings, he would pray for as many as eight hundred people while in tremendous pain himself. Sometimes he would leave the pulpit when the pain became unbearable, to struggle in the restroom with passing another stone. Then he would return to the platform and continue with the service.

Frequently, he would arise from his own bed to go to others to pray for their healing. Very few ever knew he was going through the biggest test of his life. Sometimes, he would lose so much blood that his face would be pale and he would have to be wrapped in blankets to give him warmth. After the six years had passed, over a hundred stones had been emitted into a glass bottle.

Smith's son-in-law, James Salter, gave this great tribute to Smith:

"Living with him, sharing his bedroom as we frequently did during those years, we marveled at the unquenched zeal in his fiery preaching and his compassionate ministry to the sick. He didn't just bear those agonies, he made them serve the purpose of God and glorified in and over them."[44]

"THEIR EYES ARE ON ME"

Two years into the battle with kidney stones, Smith didn't give up. Instead, in 1932, he asked God for fifteen more years in which to serve Him. God granted his request, and during those years, he visited most of Europe, South Africa, and America. His greatest joy was seeing the Word confirmed by signs and wonders, through the faith of the people. His greatest goal was for people to see Jesus, not Smith Wigglesworth. He was saddened in the last month of his life, as he commented:

> **"Today in my mail, I had an invitation to Australia, one to India and Ceylon, and one to America. People have their eye on me."**

Sadly, he began to weep:

> **"Poor Wigglesworth. What a failure to think that people have their eyes on me. God will never give His glory to another; He will take me from the scene."**[45]

AND HE WAS NOT...FOR GOD TOOK HIM

Seven days later, Smith Wigglesworth journeyed to a minister's funeral. Along the way, he commented to his friends how **"wonderful"** he felt. He pointed out the different landmarks where he and Polly had visited or preached, then would tell of the great miracles that had happened while there.

When he arrived at the church, his son-in-law, James, opened the door and helped him into the vestry where a warm fire was burning. As he entered, he was met by the father of a young girl he had prayed for days earlier. The girl had been given up to die, but Smith had great faith for her healing. When he saw the man, he asked, **"Well! And how is she?"**[46] He was expecting to hear that the girl was completely delivered, but the answer came hesitantly. "She is a little better, a bit easier; her pains have not been quite so bad during the past few days." Disappointed by what he heard,

> *Has the power that Smith Wigglesworth walked in left the earth? Did it go with him when he died? Of course not! The same power Wigglesworth operated in is here for us today, we don't need more power.*

Smith let out a deep, compassionate sigh. Then his head bowed, and without another word or experiencing any pain, Smith Wigglesworth went home to be with the Lord. He left on March 12, 1947.

FAITH + COMPASSION = MIRACLES

As I ministered in a prayer line years ago, a man came up to me with tears streaming down his face. He told me of the power he had experienced in the

Voice of Healing revival meetings. The power of God in those meetings set him free. Then he said something I will never forget as long as I live: "Isn't there anybody who walks in the power like they did back then? Isn't there anybody who can set me free? Is there anyone like that today?"

Has the power that Smith Wigglesworth walked in left the earth? Did it go with him when he died? Of course not! The same power Wigglesworth operated in is here for us today, we don't need *more* power. We just need to use our faith *and* compassion for that power to operate. Wigglesworth operated in the boldest faith I have ever seen since the book of Acts, but that faith was ignited by *compassion*. Smith took God at His Word and was moved by compassion for the people, and that combination produces miracles.

The challenge now comes to our generation. God has issued the call for men and women to invade cities and nations with the power of heaven. Will you answer the call of God? Will you dare to *only believe*? Is your heart so moved by compassion for the multitudes, that you will take God at His Word and step out? Let it be said of our generation, *"...through faith* [they] *subdued kingdoms, wrought righteousness, obtained promises, stopped the mouths of lions, Quenched the violence of fire, escaped the edge of the sword, out of weakness were made strong, waxed valiant in fight, turned to flight the armies of the aliens."* (Hebrews 11:33,34.) Stir up the gift within you, and invade your home, your community, and your nation with the power of God. Let the will of heaven be done on earth – through you!

CHAPTER SEVEN, SMITH WIGGLESWORTH
References

1 Stanley Howard Frodsham, *Smith Wigglesworth: Apostle of Faith* (Springfield, MO: Gospel Publishing House, 1948), 58-59.

2 W. E. Warner, *The Anointing of His Spirit* (Ann Arbor, MI: Vine Books, segment of Servant Publications), 1994), 237.

3 Frodsham, *Smith Wigglesworth: Apostle of Faith*, 12.

4 Ibid., 13.

5 Ibid., 15.

6 Ibid., 17.

7 Ibid., 18-19.

8 Ibid., 19.

9 Ibid., 22.

10 Ibid.

11 Ibid., 35-36.

12 Ibid., 21.

13 Ibid., 37-38.

14 Ibid., 42.

15 Ibid.

16 Ibid., 44.

17 Ibid., 46.

18 Ibid., 47.

19 Ibid., 48-49.

20 Ibid., 53.

21 Ibid.,

22 Ibid., 148.

23 Warner, *The Anointing of His Spirit*, 238.

24 Ibid.

25 Frodsham, *Smith Wigglesworth: Apostle of Faith*, 76.

26 Kenneth and Gloria Copeland, *John G. Lake: His Life, His Sermons, His Boldness of Faith*, (Forth Worth, TX: Kenneth Copeland Publications, 1994), 443.

27 Ibid., 432.

28 Ibid., 27.

29 Gordon Lindsay, *New John G. Lake Sermons*, (Dallas: Christ for the Nations, Inc., 1976), 19-20.

30 Lindsay, *John G. Lake: Apostle to Africa,* 9.

31 Ibid., 65-66.

32 Ibid., 55

33 Ibid., 56.

34 Ibid., 126.

35 George Stormont, *Wigglesworth: A Man Who Walked With God,* (Tulsa, OK: Harrison House, Inc., 1989), 53-54.

36 Frodsham, *Smith Wigglesworth: Apostle of Faith*, 114.

37 Ibid., 72.

38 Ibid., 102-103.

39 Ibid., 79.

40 Polhill to Wigglesworth, October 20, 1920, Polhill Letters 1910-1929.

41 Wigglesworth to T. H. Mundell, October 21, 1920, Letter.

42 Wigglesworth to Polhill Letters, October 21, 1920, Wigglesworth File.

43 Frodsham, *Smith Wigglesworth: Apostle of Faith*, 137.

44 Ibid., 139.

45 Albert Hibbert, *Smith Wigglesworth: The Secret of His Power,* (Tulsa, OK: Harrison House, Inc., 1982), 14-15.

47 Frodsham, *Smith Wigglesworth: Apostle of Faith,* 150-151.

CHAPTER EIGHT

Aimee Semple McPherson

"A Woman of Destiny"

"A WOMAN OF DESTINY"

"Somebody must have seen her marching up Main Street from the direction of the bank and the barbershop; she was a very young woman in a white dress, carrying a chair.

"Standing on the chair, she raised her long hands toward heaven as if calling for help.... And then she did nothing.... She closed her large, wide-set eyes and just stood there with her arms straight up, like a statue of marble...

"Even with her eyes closed Aimee could feel the critical mass of the crowd when it grew to be fifty spectators gaping and hooting...The young woman opened her eyes and looked around her.

"'People,' she shouted, leaping off the chair, 'come and follow me, quick.'

"Hooking her arm through the back of the chair, she pushed through the crowd and started running back down Main Street. The people chased her, boys first, then men and women.... They followed her right through the open door of the Victory Mission. There was just enough room for all to be seated.

"'Lock the door,' she whispered to the usher. 'Lock the door and keep it locked till I get through.'"[1]

Aimee Semple McPherson has been described as a woman born before her time. Actually, Aimee was the spiritual pioneer who paved the way for the rest of us and should be considered largely responsible for the way we demonstrate Christianity today.

Aimee defied all odds. Her life story portrays her as a woman alive and dramatic. There was nothing mellow about her. To her, a challenge was fair game to be taken and conquered. She rode on the wave of the media, and actually directed its course. If publicity seemed bad, she hyped it further, smiling all the way. If everyone warned her against doing something, she was apt to do the opposite, refusing to bow to fear. In fact, there was *nothing* too radical for Aimee Semple McPherson. Whatever it took to "get the people" – Aimee did it. She sat with the "publicans and prostitutes," showing up in places where the average Christian was afraid to go. The poor, the common, and the rich all loved her for it, and they showed up at her meetings by the thousands.

> *...there was nothing too radical for Aimee Semple McPherson. Whatever it took to "get the people" — Aimee did it.*

But of course the "religious" hated her. When denominational politics seemed to hinder and wound so many ministers, Aimee rarely gave them thought. She demolished religious seclusion and narrowness, seeming to almost pity those controlled by its grip. Aimee set about building a ministry so vast and so great, that even Hollywood came to take notes.

In a time when women were only recognized as an "accessory," to ministry, Aimee built Angelus Temple to include them. The Temple was built and dedicated during the Depression, and was an elaborate building that could seat five thousand people. When the building filled three times each Sunday, Aimee ventured even further. She built the very first Christian radio station in the world, and founded one of the fastest growing denominations today.

Aimee lived during the height of the Pentecostal Movement that was full of the *"dos"* and *"don'ts"* of religion, when women in general weren't accepted in the ministry. And to make matters worse to the religious mindset of the day, she was divorced.

A NEW GENERATION IS BORN

Her life began in controversy and scandal. Aimee was born to James Morgan and Mildred "Minnie" Kennedy on October 9, 1890, near Salford, Ontario, Canada. The only daughter of James and Mildred, Aimee Elizabeth Kennedy grew up in a town that roared with gossip because of those who took issue with the circumstances surrounding her birth. Her father, age fifty, married her mother, Minnie, when she was only fifteen years old.

Prior to their marriage, the orphaned Minnie had been a fervent laborer with the Salvation Army. Feeling the call to the ministry, she evangelized day and night in cities throughout Ontario. Then she read in the paper one day about the Kennedys' need for a live-in nurse to care for the ailing Mrs. Kennedy. So she accepted the position and moved in with the family, setting her ministry aside.

After Mrs. Kennedy's death, Minnie remained in the Kennedy home. Not long after, the older man asked Minnie to become his wife. The town roared with gossip, but James Kennedy simply let them talk.

The day after their marriage, Minnie got down on her knees and prayed. She confessed that she had failed in her call to the ministry, and asked God's forgiveness. Then she prayed:

> "If You will only hear my prayer, as You heard Hannah's prayer of old, and give me a little baby *girl*, I will give her unreservedly into Your service, that she may preach the Word I should have preached, fill the place I should have filled, and lived the life I should have lived in Thy service. O Lord, hear and answer me...."[2]

Soon Minnie was pregnant. She never doubted that she was carrying a girl, so everything she designed, bought, or received for the baby was pink. Then in answer to her prayers, a little girl was born on October 9 in the Kennedy's Canadian farmhouse near Salford.

The Salvationists came to visit the baby, and brought with them the sad news that Catherine Booth, wife of the great General William Booth, had died. Catherine had been the co-founder of the Salvation Army and one of the visitors suggested that Aimee could very well be her successor.[3]

Whatever plan God had for the child, it was especially clear to Minnie after hearing these words, that Aimee would certainly grow far beyond her expectations.

BULLFROGS AND SCHOOL SLATES

When Aimee was three weeks old, Minnie dedicated her to the Lord at a Salvation Army service. Her childhood was picture-perfect. She was raised as an only child on a large country farm in a rambling farmhouse with farm animals as playmates. She grew up with the stories of Daniel in the lion's den, Joseph and Pharaoh, and Moses leading the children of Israel out of Egypt. By the time Aimee was four, she could stand on a street corner, in the middle of a drumhead, and draw a huge crowd by reciting Bible stories.

Aimee was a spunky little girl. She was full of headstrong ideas. Nothing intimidated her, except the realization that no matter where she was, God could see everything she was doing.

Once, while sick in bed, a hired man poked his head through her door, asking if he could do anything for her. Aimee sighed in a spoiled way and said, "I would like to hear the frogs sing. Do go down to the swamp and bring me three or four frogs and put them in a pail of water by my bed."

So the man did as he was told, and about an hour later, he came back into her room with a large pail, complete with lilies and frogs. But as he left for work, he failed to hear Aimee screaming for him to retrieve the frogs which had jumped out of the bucket, and were now bouncing around the room! It was Aimee's mother Minnie who had to be the one to catch the slimy intruders![4]

As a young girl in school, Aimee was always in charge. When other children teased her, calling her a "Salvation Army child," Aimee got angry. But instead of fighting back, she would play along with them. In later years, it was just this sort of response that caused Aimee's popularity to soar.

> *As a young girl in school, Aimee was always in charge. When other children teased her, calling her a "Salvation Army child," Aimee got angry. But instead of fighting back, she would play along with them.*

Once when Aimee was made fun of, instead of retaliating against her classmates, she got a box, a ruler, and a red tablecloth. Then she appointed a boy to carry a "red flag," and marched around banging on her box like a drum while singing at the top of her lungs. At first, the boys fell in behind her, making fun of the march, but then they started to enjoy it. Soon, the girls stepped in and joined her lively parade. And from that day forward, no one teased Aimee about the Salvation Army. Her faith always embraced, never repelled.[5]

When Aimee was a young girl, she loved to watch her mother, who was the Sunday school superintendent at the Salvationists' meetings. As soon as Aimee came home from church, she would gather up chairs and set them in a circle in her room. Then she would imitate her mother by preaching to her imaginary crowd.

In her school picture, Aimee, then eight years old, is holding the class slate while sitting in the middle of the other students. The children on either side of the teacher look noticeably angry. They look upset because before the picture was taken, an argument had broken out over who was going to hold the slate sign. But as they bickered, Aimee suddenly jumped into the middle of the group and grabbed it! Then when the others tried to take it from her, the teacher corralled them all and seated them long enough to snap the photo.

The photo serves as somewhat of a prophetic snapshot of Aimee Semple McPherson's future ministry. The children surrounding her sit aggravated by her bold, determined action. And there in the middle, between the protective legs of her teacher sits Aimee – full of joy and confidence in triumphant victory!

GO FOR THE GOLD!

Throughout her youth, Aimee's dogmatic character began to surface. She had a sportive, playful attitude toward authority. If you were chosen to be a leader over her, you would have to impressively prove you could do it before expecting any submission from her!

Aimee wasn't completely disrespectful or rebellious, and she never truly meant to be a challenge to authority. It was just that her leadership ability was so great, that those around her were automatically challenged and left speechless. Even as a child, when Aimee walked into a room, she would capture everyone's attention without having to speak one word.

Some say Aimee was a spoiled child, and that it was her father, James Kennedy, who spoiled her. James took great delight in his spunky little girl. Others say Aimee simply wore her parents out with her high spirits and creativity. But to them, Aimee Elizabeth was an answer from God, and they treated her like a treasure.

Minnie Kennedy watched over Aimee like a hawk. She was a good mother to Aimee, but learning to stand up to Minnie was no small feat. Just holding her own around Minnie served to groom Aimee for answering the many hard questions that would come her way as a future Christian leader.

Because of her zeal for life and emotional strength, Aimee soon began to enjoy the applause. As a preteen, her dramatic personality became well-known in local village theater productions. And she was a popular orator while in grammar school.

At the age of twelve, Aimee won the silver medal for a speech that she presented at the Women's Christian Temperance Union in Ingersoll, Ontario, Canada. She would go on to compete in London, Ontario, to win the gold medal.

By the time she was thirteen, Aimee was a celebrated, outstanding public speaker. She was invited to entertain at church suppers, various organizations, Christmas auctions, festivals, and picnics. The communities of Ingersoll and Salford soon realized that people would come from miles around to be entertained by this specially gifted girl.[6]

DARWIN OR JESUS?

But Aimee's training in the Methodist church in Salford would soon cause her some confusion. Though the Methodists encouraged speech and entertainment within their building, they absolutely condemned movie theaters and plays outside of it. In fact, Minnie had been led to believe that "moving pictures" were the most sinful thing ever created. So Aimee grew up in a generation that believed in strict, religious rules. Church authorities and others had solemnly warned her that if she was ever to visit a movie theater, Aimee would end up in hell. Nevertheless, once when she was invited to a movie, she consented to go. And when she did, she recognized several other members from her church. One was a Sunday school teacher. The hypocrisy of it all touched her deeply.

When Aimee entered high school in 1905, the Darwin theory had just been popularized. Suddenly, every new textbook was filled with Darwin's theory that claimed life on earth began from an amoeba, and that man was cousin to the chimpanzee.

> *...in her reading, Aimee finally decided that Darwin's theory had to be true. After all, the church no longer practiced what the Bible said. It seemed the church was only a social gathering for plays and entertainment, and there were no miracles being worked like those she read about in the Bible.*

Aimee was shocked. Though she was not yet a born-again Christian, she had been raised on the Bible, and was truly insulted by Darwin's claims. So she approached her science professor and gallantly questioned him on the matter. As far as he was concerned, "biological research had superseded ancient superstition."[7] But Aimee cornered the poor man to such a degree that he finally had to side step her, then handed her a library list to study.

Aimee accepted the challenge. Not only would she read these secular authors and their theories, but when she was finished no one but those authors would know more on the subject of Darwin's theory than she did. This would become a pattern throughout her life. Aimee was diligent and unbeatable.

But in her reading, Aimee finally decided that Darwin's theory had to be true. After all, the church no longer practiced what the Bible said. It seemed the church was only a social gathering for plays and entertainment, and there were no miracles being worked like those she read about in the Bible. So she began debating with visiting ministers and questioned why they preached if there were no miracles today.

When questioned, one minister cleared his throat and explained how miracles had passed away, describing it as the "cessation of charisma." Then when

Aimee challenged him with other Scriptures, he finally told her that these matters were completely over her head. The man obviously didn't know of Aimee's determination.

Another night after an evening church service, Aimee challenged a visiting preacher in such a manner that her parents were mortified. **"If the Bible is true, why do our neighbors pay good tax money to tear down our faith?"** she asked the trembling minister.[8] Again, Aimee had the last word. But she was miserable, because no one seemed to have the spiritual ammunition to address her confusion.

Aimee finally came to the conclusion that according to her beliefs, if portions of the Bible were no longer true, then none of the Bible could be true. She further reasoned that if there was a leak in one place, the whole thing should be thrown out. So she decided to become an atheist.

Arriving home after this one last searing battle of words with the minister, Aimee sprinted into her room, opened the shutters, and peered out into the night. As she surveyed the magnificence of the stars, Aimee was moved within herself. Someone had to have made the heavens, and she longed to know what, or who. No more stories, and no more hearsay. She wanted facts.

So Aimee prayed, **"O God — if there be a God — reveal Yourself to me!"**[9] Two days later, God would answer her plea.

THE HOLY ROLLERS ARE HERE!

Aimee was a "study in relaxed determination." At seventeen, she was a beautiful girl who seemed to have everything she wanted. Unlike the other girls of the district, she never spoke of marriage and children. She was very intelligent and her family was financially comfortable. Her tailored clothes were stylish, and her parents adored her. She also had the ability to speak and capture an audience with a sentence or two, and had won every speaking competition she ever entered. She went around to dance halls, finding them full of church members. In fact, the first person who whirled her on the dance floor was a Presbyterian minister. But more than ever, Aimee needed the Lord. And soon she would find Him.

The day after Aimee had prayed for God to reveal Himself, she was driving home from school with her father. As they traveled down Main Street in Ingersoll she noticed a sign in a storefront window that read: HOLY GHOST REVIVAL: ROBERT SEMPLE, IRISH EVANGELIST.

Aimee had heard how these Pentecostal people fell on the floor and spoke in unknown languages. And she had heard the wild stories of their shouting and dancing. She was very curious, so the next evening before Aimee's Christmas program rehearsal, James Kennedy took his daughter to the mission. They sat on the back row.

EVEN THE BIRDS SMILED

At the meeting, Aimee was all eyes. She was amused as she saw certain townspeople singing and shouting, "Hallelujah" with their hands uplifted. *What a show!* she thought. Had she not been an atheist, Aimee thought she would shout herself! She was thoroughly enjoying this naive show from her intellectual tower. Then, Robert Semple walked into the room.

At that moment, everything changed for Aimee. Semple was about six feet two inches tall, blue eyed, with curly-brown hair, and had a wonderful sense of humor. Years later, Aimee would still affectionately go on about his blue eyes as, **"having the light of heaven."**

> *The young evangelist saw no middle ground between serving the world and serving God. If you loved one, then you couldn't love the other. You were either for, or against Him. It was as simple as that. Aimee hung on every word.*

An Irish Presbyterian, Semple left his homeland by boat to sail to New York. He then traveled over land to Toronto, Canada, and then to Chicago, Illinois. It was in 1901 that the Pentecostal manifestation of speaking in other tongues spread from Topeka, Kansas, to Chicago. And it was here in Chicago that Robert Semple first spoke in other tongues. While working as a clerk at Marshall Field's department store in the city, God called him to the ministry. He became a very successful evangelist who was known throughout the northern U.S. and Canada. And now, he had come to Aimee's hometown.

When Semple walked into the little mission, it seemed that Aimee's whole world stood still. Rev. Robert Semple strode up to the pulpit and opened his Bible to the second chapter of Acts. Then he repeated a simple command: "Repent...repent."

Aimee began to squirm uneasily. Every time Semple spoke, his words pierced her heart like an arrow. Later Aimee said, **"I had never heard such a sermon. Using the Bible as a sword, he cut the whole world in two."**

The young evangelist saw no middle ground between serving the world and serving God. If you loved one, then you couldn't love the other. You were either for, or against Him. It was as simple as that. Aimee hung on every word. Then the young evangelist turned his head toward heaven, and began to speak in tongues. As she watched, his face seemed to glow with an inner light.

As Semple spoke, Aimee could understand perfectly what was being said. It was the voice of God, showing Himself to her, answering her prayer:

> **"From the moment I heard that young man speak with tongues, to this day, I have never doubted for the shadow of a second that there was a God, and that he had shown me my true condition as a poor, lost, miserable, hell-serving sinner."**[10]

Three days later, Aimee stopped her carriage in the middle of a lonely road, lifted her hands toward heaven and cried out for God's mercy. Then, suddenly, as she writes it:

> **"The sky was filled with brightness. The trees, the fields, and the little snow birds flitting to and fro were praising the Lord and smiling upon me. So conscious was I of the pardoning blood of Jesus that I seemed to feel it flowing over me."**

Aimee had finally been born again.

SHAKING WITH THE POWER

Seeking direction for her life, Aimee prayed and received a vision. As she closed her eyes, she saw a black river rushing past with millions of men, women, and children being swept into it. They were being helplessly pushed along by the river's current and falling over a waterfall. Then she heard — "Become a winner of souls."[11]

Puzzled at how in the world *she* could accomplish this task, Aimee began to seek the Lord even further. Women couldn't preach. It was simply not allowed. But Aimee believed that if Peter, a fisherman, could preach, maybe a Canadian farm girl could too. So she searched the New Testament. And as she did, she came to the conclusion that the only requirement necessary for the one called to preach was the baptism of the Holy Spirit. So against her mother's wishes, Aimee started attending "tarrying" meetings that had gone on in Ingersoll, Ontario, for some time.

There were manifestations in abundance at Ingersoll's tarrying meetings. They had been instituted for the purposes of receiving the baptism of the Holy Spirit, and in 1908, were viewed by most as extremely radical. Even the Salvation Army approached Minnie to discuss her daughter's sudden, Pentecostal behavior.[12]

But Aimee never cared what anyone thought. All she really wanted to do, was to please God...and Robert Semple. It was Robert's love for God that caused Aimee to fervently pursue God. She fervently wanted to know Him as Robert did.

Aimee's school grades were now slipping because of spending so much time at the tarrying meetings. One morning, as Aimee passed the house of the woman who held the tarrying meetings, she felt she just couldn't go on to school – she wanted to speak in tongues! In fact, she wanted to speak in other tongues so much, that she turned back from the train and rang the woman's doorbell. Now she was skipping classes to tarry in prayer.

Once Aimee had been invited in and had explained her heart's cry, she and the tarrying group leader started to seek God and pray. Aimee even asked God to delay school so she could continue to tarry there to receive. And when she did, a blizzard hit Ingersoll. The icy blast not only prevented her from traveling to school, it also kept her from going home. Aimee was thrilled! She had been snowed in for an entire weekend to tarry for the Spirit.

Early the next Saturday morning while everyone else was asleep in the house, Aimee arose early to seek the Lord. As she lifted her voice in adoration, her praises came deeper from within her, until at last, there was a thunder that came out of her that vibrated from head to toe.

Aimee slipped to the floor, feeling as if she were caught up in billowy clouds of glory. Then, suddenly, words began flowing out of her mouth in another language – first in short phrases, then in full sentences. By now, the whole house had been awakened by her sounds, and the group came shouting and rejoicing down the stairs. Among them, was Robert Semple. It isn't known exactly how much time Robert Semple spent in Aimee's town. But he must have traveled back and forth because of his being there when Aimee was baptized in the Holy Spirit.

"ELECTRIC" DANCING

Robert traveled extensively, but corresponded regularly with Aimee throughout the winter. Then in the early spring of 1908, Robert returned to Ingersoll and proposed to her. In fact, he proposed to Aimee in the same house in which she received the baptism a few months earlier. Six months later on August 12, 1908, Aimee married Robert Semple in her family's farmhouse near Salford, Ontario.

Aimee would not finish high school because of her love for Semple. In fact, she left behind everything in order to love, honor, and obey her new husband. Robert was all she needed for a fulfilled and enriching life.

"He was my theological seminary," she would later write, **"my spiritual mentor, and my tender, patient, unfailing lover."**[13]

Before their marriage, Aimee and Robert had convinced her parents that speaking in other tongues was scriptural. But it took much more to convince Minnie of God's will concerning the couple's call to China.

In preparation for their trip, Robert worked in a factory by day and preached by night. Soon, his ministry took them to London, Ontario, where they ministered in homes. Robert would preach while Aimee played the piano, sang, and prayed with the converts. In just a few months, a hundred people had received the baptism of the Holy Spirit, with many more saved. They also saw many remarkable healings.[14]

In January of 1909, the Semples went to Chicago, Illinois, where Robert was ordained by Pastor William Durham. They ministered there for several months in an Italian neighborhood and were very content and happy.

Robert and Aimee Semple

Later in the year, the Semples traveled to Findlay, Ohio, with Pastor Durham to work in another mission. It was here that Aimee had her first experience with divine healing. It happened when Aimee broke her ankle after falling down some stairs. The physician who put the cast on Aimee told her that she would never have the use of four ligaments again. And she was told to stay off of her foot for at least one month. But Aimee continued to hobble to the prayer meetings, even though the slightest vibration on the floor would cause tremendous pain.

> *A feeling like a shot of electricity struck her leg, and immediately the blackness left her toes. She felt the ligaments pop into place as her bone mended together, then suddenly, she felt no pain.*

Finally at one meeting, the pain became so intense that she had to return to her room. As she sat and stared at her black and swollen toes, she heard a voice saying, "If you will go over to the (mission) and ask Brother Durham to lay hands on your foot, I will heal it." Recognizing it as the voice of the Lord, Aimee did as she was told.

At the mission, Brother Durham had been walking up and down the aisles, but stopped and placed his hand on Aimee's foot. A feeling like a shot of electricity struck her leg, and immediately the blackness left her toes. She felt the ligaments pop into place as her bone mended together, then suddenly, she felt no pain.

Aimee excitedly asked for someone to cut away the cast. After some debate, they finally agreed to do so. Once the cast was removed, they were shocked to see a perfectly healed foot. Then Aimee put on her shoes and danced all over the church![15]

DEMONS, CATERPILLARS & BURNING HINDUS

In early 1910, the Semples, who were now expecting a child, set sail for China. The couple visited Robert's parents in Ireland, then stopped over in London where he preached at several meetings. While he was away at one of these meetings, a Christian millionaire asked Aimee to preach in Victoria and Albert Hall. Aimee was just nineteen years old, and had never preached in public before, but she didn't want to turn down an opportunity to serve God. So she nervously accepted.

As Aimee stood before the people crowded in the hall, she opened her Bible to Joel 1:4. Then she began to prophetically teach on the restoration of the Church throughout the ages. In fact, she was so caught up in the moment of it, that after the meeting, she could only remember the tremendous anointing that had inspired the message. She couldn't remember what she said, but she could see the clapping and wiping of eyes of the many who had heard her.

In June of 1910, the Semples arrived in Hong Kong. But Aimee wasn't ready for what she saw. The Chinese diet of caterpillars, bugs, and rats revolted her, and their apartment was very noisy, so they got very little rest. They eventually discerned their little apartment was "haunted" by demon spirits that were making some of the noises heard day and night.

One day, the Hindus burned a man alive outside their kitchen window. This, along with everything else, had Aimee living on the edge of hysteria most of the time. She had grown to hate the mission. And soon, because of their poor living conditions, she and Robert both contracted malaria. Robert's case was worse than hers, and on August 17, only two months after they had arrived, Robert Semple was dead.

Aimee was now left alone to fend for herself in this strange and foreign land. Her grief was unbearable and she was pregnant with Robert's child. One month after Robert's death on September 17, 1910, she gave birth to a small, four pound baby girl, naming her Roberta Star.

But Robert's death had flooded Aimee's life with grief. Nothing could describe her misery as she laid in her hospital bed overcome with the horror of the reality of carrying on alone. At times she would turn toward the hospital walls and scream into them.[16]

Aimee's mother, Minnie, sent her the money to finally travel home. As the forlorn missionary widow steamed home across the Pacific, the tiny baby she was holding was the only thing that brought her any hope.

HOME SWEET HOME

Once home, Aimee mourned the loss of Robert for over a year, but she also continued to search for God's will in her life. She went to New York and then on to Chicago, hoping to minister in the churches Robert had left. Then the baby's health suffered, and she returned to her childhood home. But Aimee's grief wouldn't allow her to sit still for long, and she eventually returned to New York.

While in New York Aimee met Harold McPherson, who would soon become her second husband. McPherson was from Rhode Island, and was described as a solid, clear-thinking man, great in strength, and very kind.

On February 28, 1912, Aimee and Harold were married. Aimee nick-named Harold, "Mack." Roberta would call him Daddy Mack. They moved to Providence, Rhode Island, to settle into a small apartment where Harold got a job in a bank and Aimee stayed home as a housewife. And by July of 1912, Aimee was expecting her second child.

According to Aimee, the only real problem that she and Harold had to contend with in their marital relationship was in the area of their vastly different goals. She described the three years following their wedding as being much like the story of Jonah. Aimee had run from God, and as a result, was suffering from depression. She was plagued with illnesses, and finally experienced an emotional breakdown.

> *With hope almost gone, the interns moved Aimee from her room to a ward where they took the dying. It was then that Aimee began speaking out of the lifelessness of her coma. She was calling the people to repentance — and she was hearing the voice again: "WILL YOU GO?"*

"WILL YOU GO?"

Then Rolf, her only son, was born on March 23, 1913, and as a mother, she began to realize that an emotional maturity and stability was being built within her that would benefit her future. Not long after his birth, Aimee began to hear the voice of the Lord telling her, "Preach the Word! Will you go? Will you go?" She would hear the voice especially when she was cleaning the house.[17]

The sensitivity to the voice of God's Spirit that Aimee developed in those years would eventually shake a sleeping nation. It has been said that she tenderly spoke to the thousands in her ministry like a mother would speak to her children.

In 1914, Aimee worked around the community, preaching and teaching in Sunday schools, but this didn't satisfy the call that by now had begun to boom, "DO THE WORK OF AN EVANGELIST! WILL YOU GO?"

But it was also in 1914, that Aimee became gravely ill. After several surgeries, she grew no better and became despondent to the point of begging God to let her die.

The physicians called Harold's mother and Minnie to inform them of Aimee's approaching death. But as Minnie listened to their report, she vividly remembered praying to God for her little girl. And she remembered her vow – that Aimee would fulfill the call Minnie had rejected herself. She held on to God's promise, refusing to let Aimee die. The nurses wept as they watched Minnie standing over Aimee's body, crying and renewing her promise to God.

With hope almost gone, the interns moved Aimee from her room to a ward where they took the dying. It was then that Aimee began speaking out of the lifelessness of her coma. She was calling the people to repentance – and she was hearing the voice again: "WILL YOU GO?" She mustered up the energy to whisper that she would. Then she opened her eyes, and all the pain was gone. And within two weeks, she was up and well.

"I WAS ON MY BACK IN THE STRAW"

By now, Harold had a good job and wanted Aimee to be like other women – clean the house and cook in the kitchen. But Aimee felt she could not remain so confined and be able to fill the call to go. So in the spring of 1915, after Harold left for work, Aimee bundled up Roberta and Rolf, along with their belongings, and left for Toronto.[18]

She wired Harold before leaving to attend her first Pentecostal camp-meeting, **"I have tried to walk your way and have failed. Won't you come now and walk my way? I am sure we will be happy."**[19]

Minnie agreed to take care of the children so Aimee could start the ministry. Harold responded to Aimee's wire many months later. By then they were so far apart, Harold could not catch up to her. After months of trying to work out their differences, they faced up to the inevitable.

With her future now committed, Aimee was concerned she would never again operate in the power that she did while married to Robert. She feared God's anointing had left her. But her fears ended when she was welcomed by her friends at the campmeeting warmly. She was inspired when she heard all their hearty praise and sensed God's fire ignite within her.

Still, she felt the need to confess her laxity to the Lord, and at the camp meeting's first altar call, she was the first one down. When she knelt at the altar, she felt God's grace and acceptance.

"Such love," she recalled, **"was more than my heart could bear. Before I knew it I was on my back in the straw, under the power."**

Aimee would remain at this camp meeting for weeks. She washed dishes, waited tables, and prayed for people. It had been a long time since she had been this happy.[20]

A RIPPED TENT & SPIRITUAL POWER

Soon Aimee began preaching on her own. She would use any method to draw a crowd, and people would travel from all over the countryside to hear her. In 1915, one of her meetings drew more than five hundred people. She had become a novelty. Besides her dramatics, she was a woman, and women preachers were hard to find in those days. So everyone was curious to see and hear her.

The townspeople collected $65 for her at one of her meetings. With the offering she was able to purchase a much needed $500 tent. Thrilled at obtaining the bargain, Aimee unrolled the seasoned canvas to set it up. But unfortunately, it wasn't a bargain. The canvas had been ripped to shreds in some places. So Aimee quickly assembled her volunteers and sewed holes with them until their fingers were stiff and sore. By sunset, the patchwork tent was up.

Once, looking out over the crowd, Aimee saw Harold. He had traveled to one of her meetings to see her preach. Before the night was over, he was filled with the Holy Spirit and joined her briefly in the meetings.

There was a natural empathy in Aimee that accentuated her ministry mannerisms and drew huge crowds of people from every walk of life. People could relate to her, because after all, everyone had a mother. And those who came would experience the power of God through amazing manifestations. Many would come just to sense the presence of God, and thousands received the baptism.

THE ROLLING CHURCH

For the next seven years, Aimee crossed the United States six times. Between the years of 1917 and 1923, she preached in more than one hundred cities with meetings ranging in duration from two nights to a month.

Her first ministry experience with divine healing took place with a woman afflicted by rheumatoid arthritis. The woman's neck was so twisted that she was unable to look at the evangelist. But immediately following the prayer of faith, she turned her neck and looked into Aimee's face. God had healed her, and how Aimee knew it, as she looked at her eye to eye.

Aimee stated emphatically that she never sought a healing ministry, and hardly relished the idea of one.[21] But healing came with her evangelistic call, and after hearing of the unusually successful results in answer to her prayers, people came in droves for prayer.

In one meeting, the offerings were large enough to buy a 1912 Packard touring car. It would soon become her rolling church. Aimee would stand in the back seat and preach eight to ten meetings a day. Then between meetings, she would pass out tracts and handbills, inviting all to come.

Though Aimee conducted her meetings with grace, she was also very strong. She had developed a great deal of strength from hauling her tent, and from hammering its stakes into the ground during setup. In fact, she was louder and stronger than most men.

BURNS, BLISTERS, & MARDI GRAS

As discussed earlier, Aimee was noted for her affectionate preaching. She would often treat her audiences as a mother would her child. She was never condemning or threatening, always encouraging her listeners to fall in love with the grace and mercy of God.

> *"The lady who preaches divine healing has been hurt. She burned her face, so there will be no meeting tonight."*

But, like a strong mother, Aimee wasn't weak. Once, a lamp exploded in her face, covering her with flames. She quickly plunged her head into a bucket of water, but not before blisters developed on her neck and face. To make matters worse, all of this happened as hecklers were watching and jeering. The tent was full the night this occurred, so she exited behind it, being in great pain. One of the hecklers jumped on the platform and said, "The lady who preaches divine healing has been hurt. She burned her face, so there will be no meeting tonight."

But right after he said it, Aimee furiously rushed in through the tent flaps and leapt on the platform. She was in agony, but was able to draw enough strength to sit down at the piano and cry out, **"I praise the Lord who heals me and takes all the pain away!"** Then within two to three stanzas of the song, the crowd witnessed a miracle: Aimee's face went from lobster red to the color of normal flesh![22]

Aimee used every opportunity to draw a crowd, so while in a town during a Mardi Gras parade, she felt her efforts would be feeble if she didn't come up with a plan. She noticed the many parade floats being entered with the themes of different states and local businesses. So she quickly turned her 1912 Packard into a floating church! Her staff helped her quickly cover the top, making it appear to be a hill with a tent on its summit, then decorated it with green palms and Spanish moss. On the sides, she painted, "Jesus is coming soon," and "I am going to the Pentecostal camp meeting. R.U.?" Then inside, Aimee played her baby organ, while Harold drove the car into the parade line, unnoticed by the policeman. The crowd loved it and shouted their approval with raucous laughs and cheers! And that night, they packed the tent! **"The** very audacity of the thing which we had done," Aimee recalled, "seemed to appeal to them."[23]

FROM HAROLD TO MINNIE

It was around this same time that Aimee started publishing *The Bridal Call*. The publication began as a four-page newspaper, but within three months, had grown to a sixteen-page magazine complete with photos, sermons, poems, and a subscription price. Aimee's intentions in publishing it were to reshape the Church, by taking "away the damnation and sin to take on the tone of a celebration, a happy wedding."[24]

> *Minnie immediately took charge of the crowd phenomenon. ...She believed evangelism was more than faith — it required organization!*

Aimee's reputation for freedom in the Holy Spirit attracted people from many different backgrounds. Soon every sort of thrill seeker, rover, and thug in the area would show up at her tent. When the meetings were small, she could control them. But when they grew to over a thousand in attendance, the only way she could calm their emotional outbursts was to resort to music and singing, and she did it very masterfully. Before long, she was incorporating narrative and drama into her preaching.

Aimee found herself at ease among the black culture. She loved visiting in their homes, usually finding herself much poorer than any of them. They knew she loved them also. They thronged her in the South as she visited and worked with them in the cotton and tobacco fields.

Now the crowds were soaring in numbers. But Aimee's personal life began to suffer again as she and Harold disagreed about the ministry. He didn't like the vagabond life they were leading, nor did he understand her vision for the future. So finally, after an all-night confrontation, Harold packed his belongings and left.

Several years later, Harold filed for divorce, claiming that Aimee had deserted him. But she countered the suit, stating the opposite. Harold would go on to remarry and live a much more normal family life.

Minnie now joined Aimee's ministry and brought along with her Aimee's daughter, Roberta. Roberta was now seven and hadn't seen her mother in two years. But now that she was with her, she was quickly filled with the excitement of her mother's ministry and loved to watch her preach.

Minnie immediately took charge of the crowd phenomenon. Aimee had drawn multitudes of people. As the thousands thronged her meetings, Aimee desperately needed someone to help manage them. And Mother Kennedy was a natural for this. She believed evangelism was more than faith – it required organization! Minnie's meticulous detailing was up to the task of Aimee's anointing, and it would eventually take her daughter from tents to coliseums.

STRETCHED SHOES AND A BOTTLE OF CLOUDS

Amid all the frenzy and obsession of the ministry, Aimee's children said they always felt secure with their mother on the road. They loved traveling with her. Some accused Aimee of making life difficult for them. But the truth of the matter was, both were greatly disappointed when they couldn't go with her!

Rolf and Roberta both have wonderful memories of their mother. Roberta remembers the stories her mother told her as they drove down the highway. Once, Roberta wanted to catch a cloud after her mother had described one so beautifully. So Aimee promptly steered to the side of the road, grabbed an empty bottle, and got out of the car. Then she held the empty bottle up in the air until the mist and fog surrounding her formed tiny droplets on the bottle's inside. When she brought it back to the car, she presented it to Roberta with a genuine cloud.

Rolf remembers how badly he once needed shoes, and how he received a pair as a gift. When the box arrived, the family was excited. But when Rolf tried to put them on, they wouldn't fit. Disappointment set in until Roberta asked, "Mother, what did the Israelite children do for shoes in the wilderness?...their feet must have grown." Then without thinking Aimee quickly replied, **"God must have stretched their shoes."** Roberta then asked if God would do the same for Rolf's shoes, so Mother Aimee said, **"I don't know, but let us kneel and ask Him."** Then Rolf tried the shoes on again, and this time – they fit perfectly!

There was another time when Rolf was playing barefoot in the tall grass of a campground when he injured his foot by stepping on a hidden rake. His foot was deeply pierced and was bleeding dark red blood.

When Aimee learned of Rolf's accident she quickly rushed to his side and carried him to his cot in their little tent. Rolf fondly remembers how his mother held his foot while kneeling in prayer to ask God for his healing. After she prayed for God to heal her son, then almost immediately, Rolf fell asleep.

Many hours later Rolf was awakened by the distant roar of the masses in the tent meeting. When he sat up he saw the blood stains on his bed, and he grabbed his foot. When he did, he looked at the bottom where the rake had pierced him, but there was no sign of a wound. Thinking he had looked at the wrong foot, he grabbed the other, but it was also smooth. Elated by the sight, he realized his foot was completely healed!

DRESSING THE PART

The only early Pentecostal belief Aimee was ever known to have taken a stand against was the doctrine of sanctification as a second work of grace. She strongly felt that those who claimed or pursued "Christian perfection" often turned their backs on the people of the world, creating a religious isolationism.

Aimee wanted the Gospel to fit everyone. And she didn't want anyone to feel intimidated about coming to hear about God's Word. She was burdened by the eliteness she had seen in the Church that kept needy sinners away. She called sin, sin, inviting everyone to repentance:

On the way to the West Coast, Aimee drove into Indianapolis just as they had lifted the influenza ban. It was then that she met Maria Woodworth-Etter. It was the thrill of her life to finally meet this woman who had so inspired her — and to hear her preach!

"Whatever fancy name you give it, sin is sin....God looks on the heart and as for holiness, why, without holiness no man shall see the Lord. We must be saved, we must be sanctified, but 'tis all through the precious atoning blood of Jesus Christ."[25]

In 1918, when World War I was raging in Europe, and America was plagued with a deadly outbreak of influenza, Aimee was viewed as a ray of hope because of her doctrine. One of her major thrusts of ministry appreciated by everyone was that of servanthood. To demonstrate this, the Lord directed Aimee one day while she was out looking for a new dress to actually make a purchase:

"You are a servant of all, are you not? Go upstairs and ask to see the servants' dresses," the Lord said.

So Aimee obeyed and bought two servants dresses for $5. And from that time on she was always seen in her distinguishing white servant's dress and cape.[26]

I DID PROMISE YOU A ROSE GARDEN

One afternoon, when Roberta was suffering with influenza, she asked her mother why they didn't have a home like everyone else. As Aimee prayed for Roberta's healing, God spoke to her and proclaimed that He would not only raise up her daughter, but would also give them a home in sunny Southern California. She even received a vision of their new home, seeing a bungalow with a rose garden.

When Roberta recovered, the group set out for California. Roberta would later say they had no idea of how much of a miracle the house really was because, "When mother told us something would happen, it was like money in the bank."[27]

The trip was no small exploit. Road maps were few, towns were far apart, and the conditions of the roads were questionable. But none of this hindered Aimee.

On the way to the West Coast, Aimee drove into Indianapolis just as they had lifted the influenza ban. It was then that she met Maria Woodworth-Etter. It was the thrill of her life to finally meet this woman who had so inspired her – and to hear her preach!

When she finally arrived in Los Angeles in late 1918, Aimee's fame had preceded her. By now, the Azusa Street Mission was just a memory. Its members had scattered throughout the city, but they were waiting for the person whom God would use to pull them back together. And when Aimee arrived, they believed it was her.

Two days after she arrived, Aimee preached a message to seven hundred people entitled, "Shout! For the Lord Hath Given You the City." By early 1919 the aisles, floors, and window sills of the Philharmonic Auditorium were packed with people to hear her.

The people of Los Angeles couldn't do enough for Aimee and her family. Less than two weeks after she arrived, a woman stood up in one of her meetings, saying the Lord had impressed her to give the evangelist some land on which she could build a home. Others stood and pledged their labor and the material. Even the rose bushes in her vision would be donated, and by April, the house with gabled porches and a fireplace was a reality.

A COAT OF MANY COLORS

By now, Aimee could see that a permanent place to preach was a great need. So between the years of 1919-1923, she traveled across the U.S. nine times, preaching and raising money for the building of Angelus Temple. And everywhere she traveled, people loved her.

Aimee's preaching tone could change from "baby talk" and girlish stories, as she would often like to do in delighting older audiences, to the solemn, deep-toned demeanor of a dynamic, soulwinning prophetess. God gifted her in her delivery to accommodate many different situations.

The press discovered Aimee in 1919. And when they did, they were invited into what was to become in later years one of America's most celebrated media love/hate relationships ever on record. Aimee loved them, but they were never sure of what she was doing to them! They weren't accustomed to anyone taking advantage of their methods, and would try to trip her up with trick questions such as, "Aimee, are silk stockings evil?" In response, she would gracefully cross her legs and reply, **"It depends altogether on how much of them is shown."**[28] This sort of coverage lent itself to making Aimee a national phenomenon.

In Baltimore, Maryland, the first auditorium Aimee preached in seated three thousand people. But people were turned away for lack of seating space. So she rented another auditorium that seated sixteen thousand. It was here that Aimee

On the road

shocked the Baltimore masses through her pointing out of the demonic behavior in an overly-demonstrative worshipper. Up until then, it was considered unethical to confront someone who was "ecstatic" for God. But Aimee rebuked her and called for a choir member to retain her in a smaller room.

After prayerfully observing the woman, Aimee challenged the leadership ethics of her day and would call the Church to spiritual maturity:

> **"The woman proved to be a maniac who had been in an asylum....Yet this was the kind of woman many of the saints would have allowed to promenade the platform — fearing lest they quench the Spirit."**[29]

While Aimee was in Baltimore a national healing campaign began. Incredible and highly unusual miracles occurred. The headlines screamed the results of each meeting.

It has been said that when Aimee would enter the hall before a meeting, there were often throngs of desperately ill people seeking to touch her. And that when she saw them, she would run back overwhelmed into her dressing room to pray for God's help.

Everywhere Aimee went, crowds pressed in to touch her. She would watch in regret as the police were forced to bolt the doors in trying to protect her.

After a while, when she closed her eyes at night, all she could see was the seventeen hundred people who were packed into a place that was built to hold a thousand. She would see the altars and basements overflowing with the sick and would wake up thinking of how Jesus had dealt with all this:

> **"Wouldn't you just realize how Jesus had to get into a boat and push away from land, in order to preach to the people?"**[30]

In 1921 Aimee held a three-week meeting in Denver, Colorado, at which sixteen thousand people filled the Municipal Auditorium two and three times each day. One night, eight thousand people were turned away.

"MINNIE" — NOT A MOUSE

During these great days of ministry, Minnie aggressively guarded her daughter's health. She considered it the highest of priorities, because if Aimee's

health were to fail, so would the ministry. They were more like sisters than mother and daughter, but would never truly bond spiritually.

Minnie was an incredible organizer. She ran Aimee's ministry from the rafters to the basement, keeping their finances in the black. She was tough,

> *If anyone ever got too close to Aimee, Minnie would harass her daughter until that particular relationship was broken. Many employees quit or were fired because of Minnie.*

and sometimes only slept two hours a night. She screened every sick person before the service to weed the troublemakers out. And she spent long hours with the invalids before the service began.

Minnie would never sit down to a meal. She would grab food at the oddest of moments between registering invalids, greeting delegates, and organizing the ministry of helps. She worked diligently to establish a business foundation for the ministry. But she never grasped the fullness of Aimee's call. And she never really understood why Aimee did what she did.

If anyone ever got too close to Aimee, Minnie would harass her daughter until that particular relationship was broken. Many employees quit or were fired because of Minnie. Perhaps this was the one reason Aimee never had a close friend for very long. Their mother-daughter relationship had always involved much stress. And in the years to come, Aimee's feeling of being "owned" and "controlled" would eventually cause them to part.

In 1921, Aimee was weary from her time on the road and began searching for the land on which they could build Angelus Temple. She found it adjoining Los Angeles' prestigious Echo Park area that was surrounded by abundant grass, picnic grounds, and a beautiful lake.

A "FIRST" — FROM THE KKK TO HOLLYWOOD

Aimee was a "first" in many areas. While building the Temple, the Oakland Rockridge radio station invited her to be the first woman to ever preach on the air. This would ignite another fire within her, and in time she would build her own radio station. But first, she would build the Temple.

Everyone contributed to the building project. Mayors, governors, gypsies — even the Ku Klux Klan were quick to give. Though Aimee didn't agree with the KKK, they loved her. But it was this "love" for her, that caused them to commit a crime.

After another meeting in Denver in June of 1922, Aimee was in a side hall with a woman reporter when someone asked her to pray for an invalid outside. She took the reporter outside with her because she wanted her to witness the prayer. But when they walked out the door, the two were abducted, blindfolded, and driven to a meeting of the KKK.

As it turned out, all the KKK wanted was a private message from the evangelist. So she gave them a message out of Matthew 27 on "Barabbas, the man who thought he would never be found out." After she preached, Aimee listened politely as the Klan pledged their national and "silent" support for her. To them, this simply meant that wherever Aimee went in the U.S. she could depend on them to observe and protect her. Then they blindfolded the two once again and took them back to the hall in Denver.[31]

The reporter published a great story about the kidnapping that hurled Aimee to even greater heights and brought more money in for the Temple.

In late 1922, Aimee's five thousand seat temple was finally completed. Its dedication took place in an extravagant service on New Year's Day of 1923. Those who couldn't attend saw its likeness on a flower-covered float that was ridden by singing choir members in Pasadena's Tournament of Roses parade. This carried away the first prize of its division.[32]

The New York Times gave the dedication full coverage, and from then on, Angelus Temple's five thousand seats were filled four times each Sunday.

Angelus Temple, Los Angeles, California

The Temple had perfect acoustics. It was said that many Hollywood producers were hoping Aimee would fail so they could simply acquire the building to turn it into a theater. But Aimee wouldn't fail, and she would eventually have it transformed into a theater herself. It was a theater for God.

According to Aimee, the entire Bible was a sacred drama that was meant to be preached and illustrated dramatically. And it was here that she believed denominational churches had lost their cutting edge. Aimee truly believed the Church had grown too cold and formal, while the world's love for entertainment brought them encouragement, joy, and laughter. She also felt this to be the reason that so many Christians were hungry for entertainment.

Most of Los Angeles knew attending a service at Angelus Temple was quite a major event.

In July of 1922, Aimee named Angelus Temple, THE CHURCH OF THE FOURSQUARE GOSPEL because of a vision she received while preaching from the first chapter of Ezekiel. The first signing day of her new association produced one thousand pastors.

Two meetings were set aside each week at the Temple to pray for the sick. Though she had twenty-four elders on staff, Aimee would personally conduct most of these meetings until her passing in 1944.

The healing results in Los Angeles were astounding, but they were less observed by the general public than they had been in Aimee's national campaigns. In the Temple's larger services, the focus was on soulwinning, and on the training of soulwinners.

SOME TEMPLE TALES

Without question, Angelus Temple was a very busy place. Aimee had a prayer tower that was manned twenty-four hours a day. She also formulated a one-hundred-voice choir and a brass band of thirty-six people. The sanctuary was filled with music in every service. And she purchased costumes, props, and scenery to accent her sermons in Hollywood. Most of Los Angeles knew attending a service at Angelus Temple was quite a major event.

Aimee had a remarkable sense of humor, and though there were many flaws in her early illustrated sermons, she always made the best of them. Once, to give her Garden of Eden scene some life, she ordered a macaw from a visiting circus. But she didn't know of its coarse, vulgar language learned while working with the show. And in the middle of her oratory, the macaw turned to her and said, "Oh, go to hell."

The five thousand in attendance froze in disbelief. Then, as if the bird wanted to be sure that *everyone* had heard it, it repeated itself again! But Aimee was not to be outdone! She made the best of the mistake – as she did every blooper – by proceeding to "witness" to the bird, encouraging it to respond. Then when it did respond with the very same words, the audience was hysterical! She finally "persuaded" the rented bird of the true Christian way by promising it a bird perch in heaven for its part in her show.[33]

Of course, certain ministers persecuted Aimee for her methods. But she would respond to them publicly by saying:

> **"Show me a better way to persuade willing people to come to church and I'll be happy to try your method. But please...don't ask me to preach to empty seats. Let's not waste our time quarreling over methods. God has use for all of us. Remember the recipe in the old adage for rabbit stew? It began, *first catch your rabbit.*"**[34]

TWINKLING STARS, BIBLE SCHOOL & RADIO

Many Hollywood stars were interested in what Aimee had to say. Frequent attendees at the Temple were Mary Pickford, Jean Harlow, and Clara Bow. Charlie Chaplin was able to slip into a few of her services, and would later become good friends with the evangelist. In fact, Chaplin would later help Aimee with the Temple's staging for her illustrated sermons – and Aimee would show him the truth of life.

Also, Anthony Quinn played in Aimee's band. Quinn was with Aimee before his great debut as an actor. While Quinn was a teenager, Aimee took him as her translator on a Spanish crusade. The world renowned actor would later say that one of the greatest moments of his life was when Aimee noticed him. And, he would write:

> "Years later, when I saw the great actresses at work, I would compare them to her...Ingrid Bergman...Katharine Hepburn... Greta Garbo...they all fell short of that first electric shock Aimee Semple McPherson produced in me."[35]

In February of 1923, Aimee opened her school of ministry that would eventually become known as L.I.F.E. (Lighthouse of International Foursquare Evangelism) Bible College. Aimee was an avid instructor.

At the school, "Sister," as the movement called her, served as a teacher and openly revealed her weaknesses as well as her strengths to the student body. Her favorite Christian authors were Wesley, Booth, and a Canadian revivalist by the name of Albert Benjamin Simpson. Aimee often quoted these men and taught from their writings.

Sometimes she would test the students by leaving early and ask them to remain and pray. Then she would hide in a hallway. As the students left she would watch for those who left frivolously, and for those who were attentive enough to pick up a piece of planted, paper trash. The attentive ones would receive her praise because of her belief that attention to detail produced a valuable, sensitive minister.

In February of 1924, Aimee opened Radio KFSG (Kall Four Square Gospel), with the first FCC license ever issued to a woman. It was also the first Christian radio station ever operated.

IS AIMEE DEAD?

By 1926, Aimee was in need of a good vacation, so she traveled to Europe and the Holy Land. She ended up preaching during most of it. Then upon her return in 1926, the greatest scandal and controversy of her ministry took place. On May 18, while enjoying an afternoon at the beach with her secretary, Aimee made some final notes on a sermon to be given that night. She asked her secretary to call the information back to the Temple, but when her secretary returned, Aimee was gone. Thinking Aimee had gone for a swim, the secretary scanned the water, then notified the authorities.

The next thing she knew, someone was holding her head back, and the woman pushed a chloroform-soaked pad into her face.

Over the next thirty-two days, Aimee's disappearance became the hottest news story in the world. Los Angeles' beaches were combed, and its outlying waters were searched for any trace of her. But nothing was found.

In the meantime, a ransom letter for $25,000 was received at Angelus Temple. Minnie threw it away with the rest of the crazy mail that was now pouring in. Then another letter came from a different source demanding $500,000, and the press went wild. "Aimee sightings" were the order of the day. Once she was reportedly seen sixteen times on the same day, from coast to coast.

KIDNAPPED!

A memorial service was finally scheduled for Aimee at Angelus Temple on June 20. Then three days after the service, Aimee walked into Douglas, Arizona from the desert at Agua Prieta, Mexico.

When questioned about her whereabouts, Aimee told the world that a man and a woman approached her to pray for their dying child that day at the beach after her secretary left. She said the woman was crying, and that the man brought a cloak to cover her swimsuit in the hopes that she would consent. She then agreed to help the couple and followed them to their car. Aimee explained how she had done this many times in her ministry, and thought nothing much of it.

But when the three of them arrived at the car, Aimee noticed it was running. She said there was a man at the wheel, and that the woman posing as the mother stepped into the car before her. Then she was told by the supposed father to get inside as he roughly pushed her in. The next thing she knew, someone was holding her head back, and the woman pushed a chloroform-soaked pad into her face.

When Aimee awoke, she was being held in a shack by a woman and two men. She said they threatened her, cut off a piece of her hair, and burned her fingers with a cigar. She also said that when they moved her to another place, the two men left, and that she was able to make her escape when the woman went shopping. The woman had tied Aimee up with bed cloths before she left, but Aimee was able to cut through them with the jagged edge of a tin can. Once she was free, Aimee left through a window, then walked through the desert for hours until she came upon a cabin in Douglas, Arizona.

When she finally received cooperation from the police once they believed her "claimed" identity, Aimee phoned Minnie in Los Angeles. But even Minnie didn't believe her until she revealed a secret that only Aimee could have known about their private life.

WHAT DO YOU THINK?

Following a night in the hospital, some fifty thousand people welcomed Aimee back to Angelus Temple. But her ordeal had just begun.

Aimee had accused and described her kidnappers, but they were never to be found. And when the police accompanied her in an attempt to retrace her desert footsteps, there was no shack matching her description anywhere to be found.

Then Los Angeles District Attorney, Asa Keyes, accused Aimee of lying and went to great lengths to discredit her. She had been reportedly seen in a

Flying the Foursquare colors

Angelus Temple

Everyone say, "Praise the Lord!"

Los Angeles Times Photo

Five thousand seats

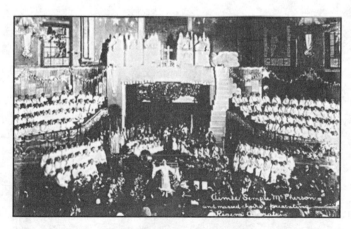

Aimee and choir presenting one of her many operas in Angeles Temple

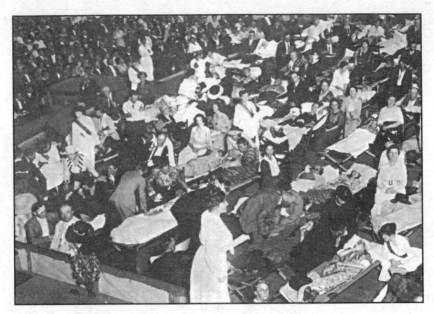

"Stretcher Day" at a revival

Thousands lined up at Aimee's funeral

Carmel bungalow with her radio producer, Kenneth Ormiston, and Keyes produced many witnesses in an attempt to confirm the fact.

So far as possible kidnappers were concerned, it is true that Aimee had made many enemies in the underworld. Gangsters had a huge network of prostitution, drug-trafficking, loan sharking, and bootlegging in the Los Angeles area. And Aimee had won several of their key people to the Lord.

It's also true that Aimee regularly opened the airwaves of her radio station to allow new converts to give salvation accounts. But when these former underworld converts broadcasted their testimonies, they would often give not only their salvation accounts – they would expose the criminal deeds of their former associates – many times calling them by name.

Aimee's kidnapping story never varied. In fact, her's was the only story that never changed. Reporters, detectives, and prosecutors all changed their accounts time and time again. Even the witnesses who testified against Aimee changed their testimony. And when they did, her charges of corruption of public morals, obstruction of justice, and conspiracy to manufacture evidence were finally dropped.

Some interesting side-notes concerning Aimee's scandal include the facts that District Attorney Keyes would eventually be sentenced to San Quentin. And Aimee's attorney would later be found dead. Incidences have suggested to many that the mob was really involved.[36]

DID SHE BREAK MINNIE'S NOSE?

Following her return to the ministry, Aimee would wear the robes of a true apostolic evangelist. She would show up at night clubs, dance halls, pool halls, and boxing matches to announce her meetings during intermissions. Managers liked the publicity, and their clientele adored her.

Aimee wasn't afraid of the world's sinners and now would seek with even greater fervor to bring Jesus to where they were. She thought it funny that so many Christians set boundaries as to where-or-where-not the Gospel should be preached.

But in the latter part of 1926, lawsuit after lawsuit was assaulting her, and her promoters were involving her in all kinds of business ventures. When their plans failed, the blame and unpaid bills always fell on Aimee. Attorneys only seemed to make matters worse. And now more than ever, Aimee desperately needed a friend. She needed someone she could trust. It seemed that everyone she had ever been close to was either betraying her or withering under the criticism.

Even Minnie, Aimee's mother, was now wavering back and forth in her support for her daughter. Minnie kept crossing back and forth between her role of the devoted, helping mother, and the malevolent overseer of a ministry that she didn't understand. She was always quick to criticize her daughter when she saw things differently. And soon she would do so publicly.

> *Minnie kept crossing back and forth between her role of the devoted, helping mother, and the malevolent overseer of a ministry that she didn't understand.*

Aimee had always honored her mother in public, but when Minnie went public with her antagonistic jabs, things reached a breaking point. Now that Aimee's own mother was fighting her in the public square, she felt totally betrayed. And the church started to split. Those serving under Minnie were torn in their loyalty, while the Temple's Board of Elders sided with Aimee. In fact, when the end came, the elders would help work out Minnie's "permanent retirement plan."

Miraculously, in the midst of all of this, Aimee would compose her first opera in 1931 and name it, *Regem Adoratge*, or, *Worship the King*. This was followed by another visit to the Holy Land. But she was reluctant to come home this time because of the growing difficulty with her mother. And her apprehensions proved to be well founded, because when she did get home, she and Minnie would finally have it out.

It was a well-known fact that when Minnie got angry at Aimee, her words were cruel and vicious. But following this final round of their famous disagreements, it was made known in the press that Minnie ended up with a bruised and bandaged nose. The headlines accompanying her front-page picture deceitfully read, "MA SAYS AIMEE BROKE HER NOSE!"

But things were not as they seemed. In fact, Minnie had just undergone plastic surgery on the eve of their argument, and would later deny the whole thing.[37] All the same, that was it. Minnie was finished. Now she was gone.

Following Minnie's forced "retirement," a series of managers would file through to take her place. Coupled with the expense of settling with her mother, the depression, and lawsuits, Aimee's debts quickly mounted up. In fact, it would take the next ten years to settle all the lawsuits and to pay her debtors off. And when it finally happened, there was a celebratory notice placed atop the Temple.

SHE'S NOT BIONIC

But the strain of it all had simply turned out to be more than Aimee could bear. And in 1930, she suffered a complete emotional/physical breakdown, and was confined to a Malibu beach cottage under a physician's constant care.

Following this ten-month ordeal, Aimee would return to Angelus Temple, and would recover to some extent. But she would never regain the vim and vigor that she formerly enjoyed. Aimee's physician explained her problem by simply stating she "could not get her needed rest."[38]

By the time 1931 arrived, Aimee was very lonely. The price of fame was high, she had no close friends, and she dearly wanted companionship.

Rolf would marry a Bible school student in the middle of that year, and Aimee was elated. Then on September 13, 1931, she would marry again. This time, to her third husband, a Mr. David Hutton. It has been said that because of Aimee's loneliness, and her desperate need for love and protection, that she imagined all sorts of virtues in this man. But in reality, they simply weren't there.

> *Aimee was sued by disgruntled employees, associate pastors, and whoever else thought they could make a dollar on her.*

Not long after they were married, Hutton was sued by another woman he had promised marriage to. The court proceedings lasted a year, and the ruling went against him.

But Aimee carried on in her calling around the nation. She experienced tremendous success in New England, as thousands came to hear her. Due to her health, on April 22, 1927, she offered to resign as pastor of Angelus Temple. This offer was refused. Then in January she set sail for Europe, in accordance with her doctor's advice. And again, thousands crowded her meetings. While she was away, Hutton, amid scandal, filed for divorce.

THE QUIET WAR QUEEN

The years between 1938 and 1944 were very quiet years for Aimee. There was very little said about her in the press.

Aimee was sued by disgruntled employees, associate pastors, and whoever else thought they could make a dollar on her. So she hired a new business manager, Giles Knight, who kept her out of the public eye. Every reporter had to go through him to see her, and everyone was refused. Aimee would keep

Knight informed of her whereabouts, then stay away to live a halfway anonymous life.

Rolf McPherson still speaks highly of Knight for the service rendered his mother that brought so much peace into their house.

Much of Aimee's efforts during these years was given to pastoring, training future ministers, establishing hundreds of churches, and sending missionaries around the world. But in 1942, she also led a brass band and color guard into downtown Los Angeles to sell war bonds. She sold $150,000 worth of the bonds in one hour, so the U.S. Treasury awarded her a special citation for her patriotic endeavor. She would also organize regular Friday night prayer meetings at Angelus Temple for the duration of World War II, gaining the expressed appreciation of President Roosevelt and California's governor for doing so.

A GREAT ONE IS RESTING

By 1944, Aimee's health was very poor. She was suffering from tropical infections that she had contracted during her missionary trips. So in February of that year, she named Rolf as the new vice president of the ministry. Rolf had proven his faithfulness and served his mother well over the years. In fact, he was the *only* person who stayed with her through both good times and bad.

Then in September of 1944, Rolf flew to Oakland with his mother to dedicate a new church. There was a blackout in the city because of the war, so Aimee and Rolf spent the evening together in her room for some ministry and family talk. Huge crowds and the work of the ministry always exhilarated Aimee, so she was in high spirits. When the evening drew to a close, Rolf kissed his mother goodnight and left the room.

Aimee had always been plagued with insomnia. She was taking sedatives from her physician, and she had obviously taken a couple on this night to sleep. She probably didn't know how many it would take, and she was scheduled to preach the next day. So she must have decided she needed more to fall off to sleep.

According to the physicians, it was about dawn when Aimee must have known something was wrong. But instead of calling Rolf, she placed a call to her physician in Los Angeles. He was in surgery and didn't respond. So she called another physician, who referred her to a Dr. Palmer in Oakland, California. But before she could make this third call, Aimee lost consciousness.

At 10:00 A.M. Rolf tried to wake his mother and found her in bed, breathing hoarsely. Unable to revive her, he called for medical assistance. But it was too late, and on September 27, 1944, Aimee Semple McPherson, went home to be with the Lord. She died at the age of fifty-three.

Aimee's body laid in Angelus Temple for three days and three nights as sixty thousand people filed by to pay their last respects. The stage on which her open casket rested, the orchestra pit, and most of the Temple's aisles were filled with flowers. Five car loads of them had to be turned away.

Then on Aimee's birthday, October 9, 1944, a motorcade of six hundred automobiles drove to Forest Lawn Memorial Park where this front-line General of God's Christian army was finally laid to rest. The cemetery admitted two thousand people, along with seventeen hundred Foursquare ministers whom Aimee had ordained.

The complete story of Aimee Semple McPherson could never be told in just one chapter. As with God's other great Generals, only heaven will reveal everything she accomplished. But for our purposes here, let me say that in her lifetime, Aimee composed 175 songs and hymns, several operas, and thirteen drama-oratorios. She also preached thousands of sermons and graduated over 8,000 ministers from L.I.F.E. Bible College. It is estimated that during the Depression, some one and a half million people received aid from her ministry. And today, the Foursquare denomination is continuing to expound the truths of God's Word as they were revealed to Sister McPherson, in her revealed Foursquare Gospel's original Declaration of Faith. The four squares are: "Jesus is Savior, Jesus is healer, Jesus is baptizer in the Holy Spirit, and Jesus is coming King."

What Aimee was literally telling us to do when she said to, "stay in the middle of the road" was this: Being excessive might sky-rocket you, but you will eventually explode and plummet to earth. The Christian faith is a way of life, so run it like a marathon — not a sprint.

DIRECT YOUR DESTINY

In conclusion, I want to focus on an important point that Aimee would always make with her Bible school students:

"Stay in the middle of the road."

From all you have now read about her, it should be clear that this statement is not referring to compromise. Sister Aimee was talking about the strength it takes to stand firm in one place. And the statement had a twofold meaning to her.

First, she would say, *be bold in the mainstream of life,* but don't allow the secular world to clone you in their mold. Be uninhibited and freely demonstrate the love and freedom that Jesus brought to the earth. And stand firm in the face of pressure, never flinching in the face of fear. Also, be bold to perform the plan of God for your life in the strength of what heaven has called *you* to do.

Second, be passionate in the gifts of the Spirit, *but never be excessive.* Don't intimidate the crowd just because you have the power. Aimee often used the example of an automobile and its power to make this point. Although it could easily go eighty miles an hour, one would have to be very foolish to rev it to that speed in the middle of a crowd. She would point out that such power from the Holy Spirit was always there, but that it was meant to be used over the long haul of ministering God's service to others.

What Aimee was literally telling us to do when she said to, "stay in the middle of the road" was this: Being excessive might skyrocket you, but you will eventually explode and plummet to earth. The Christian faith is a *way of life,* so run it like a marathon – not a sprint.

Now take the torch Aimee has passed to us, never settling for the mediocrity of a "religious" life. Shake your world for God with the freedom, boldness, and wisdom that God has given you. And stand strong in the "middle of the road," as you fulfill your personal destiny in the call of God.

CHAPTER EIGHT, AIMEE SEMPLE MCPHERSON
References

[1] Daniel Mark Epstein, *Sister Aimee: The Life of Aimee Semple McPherson* (Orlando, FL: Daniel Mark Epstein, reprinted by permission of Harcourt Brace and Company, 1993), 3, 80-81.

[2] Ibid., 10.

[3] Ibid., 11.

[4] Ibid., 21.

[5] Ibid., 22-23.

[6] Ibid., 28.

[7] Ibid., 30-31.

[8] Ibid., 36.

[9] Ibid., 39.

[10] Ibid., 41-47.

[11] Ibid., 48-49.

[12] Ibid., 50.

[13] Ibid., 55.

[14] Ibid., 57.

[15] Ibid., 57-59.

[16] Ibid., 67.

[17] Ibid., 73.

[18] Ibid., 75.

[19] Ibid., 76.

[20] Ibid., 77-78.

[21] Ibid., 111.

[22] Ibid, 119.

[23] Ibid., 120.

[24] Ibid., 122.

[25] Ibid., 134.

[26] Ibid., 144.

[27] Ibid., 145.

[28] Ibid., 159.

[29] Ibid., 172.

[30] Ibid., 201.

[31] Ibid., 241-243.

32 Ibid., 248.
33 Ibid., 256-257.
34 Ibid., 259.
35 Ibid., 378.
36 Ibid., 312.
37 Ibid., 340.
38 Ibid., 343.
39 Ibid., 417.

CHAPTER NINE

Kathryn Kuhlman

"The Woman Who Believed in Miracles"

"THE WOMAN WHO BELIEVED IN MIRACLES"

"Hundreds have been healed just sitting quietly in the audience without any demonstration whatsoever. None. Very often not even a sermon is preached. There have been times when not even a song has been sung.

"No loud demonstration, no loud calling on God as though He were deaf. No screaming, no shouting, within the very quietness of His presence. There were hundreds of times when the presence of the Holy Spirit was so real that one could almost hear the rhythm as thousands of hearts beat as one."[1]

In this rapt silence a voice speaks, "I–ah...belieeeeeeeve–ah – in–ah merrrrrrricals–ah!" Suddenly the applause is deafening as thousands watch a tall, slim figure emerge from the shadows in a white, frothy gown. She glides to center stage, and another Kathryn Kuhlman miracle service is underway.

In her international ministry, Miss Kuhlman laid a foundation for the workings of the Holy Spirit in the lives of countless thousands throughout the world. Her unique ministry shifted the focus of the body of Christ from the outward show of the supernatural gifts of the Holy Spirit back to the GIVER of the Gifts, the Holy Spirit.

A prophetic tone in her ministry set the pace for what the Church would be like in times to come. Her ministry was literally a forerunner for the Church of the future.

Though she called herself **"an ordinary person,"** Kathryn was unique. Many have tried to imitate her voice and her theatrical mannerisms, but to no avail. Others have tried to translate her special anointing into techniques and methods without success.

I thank God for Kathryn Kuhlman. She was an example of one who fearlessly paid the price to walk in the service of God. I am grateful for the lessons I have learned through her life. And in this chapter I want to share some of those lessons with you, many from her own words.

RED HAIR AND FRECKLES

Concordia, Missouri, was settled by German immigrants who began arriving in the late 1830s. Kathryn's mother, Emma Walkenhorst, married Joseph Kuhlman in 1891. According to her permanent high school record, Kathryn Johanna Kuhlman was born May 9, 1907, on the family farm about five miles from Concordia. Kathryn was named after both of her grandmothers. She never had a birth certificate since one was not required by Missouri law until 1910.

When Kathryn was two years old, her father sold their 160 acre farm and built a big house in town. This was the house that Kathryn always called "home."

A childhood friend described young Kathryn as having: "...Large features, red hair, and freckles. It couldn't be said of Kathryn that she was pretty. She wasn't dainty or appealingly feminine in any sense of the word. She was taller than the rest of 'our gang' (five feet eight), gangly and boyish in build, and her long strides kept the rest of us puffing to keep up with her."

As a young girl, Kathryn was also noted for her "independence, self-reliance and a desire to do things her way."[2] She managed to twist her "papa" around her little finger, getting almost anything she wanted from him. According to Kathryn,

Kathryn in front of childhood home

the discipline was always left to her mother, a harsh woman, who never praised Kathryn or gave her any affection. Yet Kathryn never once felt unloved or unwanted. Her papa gave her all the love and affection she ever needed. In fact, she so adored her papa that even thirty years after his death, tears would come to her eyes as she talked about him.

Once, when Kathryn was about nine years old, she wanted to do something nice for her mother's birthday. So she decided she would give her a surprise birthday party.

Well Kathryn never thought about her mother's birthday falling on a Monday. So she went around to all the neighbors, telling them *all* to show up with a cake.

Mondays were wash days at the Kuhlman household. Every other day of the week, Emma Kuhlman would dress from head to toe in her best clothes. One never knew when an unexpected guest might come by, and she dreaded the idea of anyone seeing her groomed poorly.

So Monday came and Emma Kuhlman was dressed for wash day. As she labored over a hot tub, her hair hung down wrung in the sweat, her clothes were damp and soiled, and she was bare-legged. There was a knock at the door, and when she opened it – there stood the neighbors all dressed up in their finest attire. And there stood Emma, totally wilted and fatigued from her wash day! Her pride ruined, Emma vowed to Kathryn under her breath that she would take care of her later.[3]

And take care of her she did! In fact, Emma Kuhlman made Kathryn stand and eat every one of the birthday cakes the neighbors brought!

Kathryn's father taught her the principles of business. He was a stable owner. She loved to go with him as he collected bills, and in later years would give him credit for everything she knew about organization and business.

> *As a young girl, Kathryn was also noted for her "independence, self-reliance and a desire to do things her way." She managed to twist her "papa" around her little finger, getting almost anything she wanted from him.*

"PAPA! JESUS CAME INTO MY HEART!"

Kathryn was fourteen years old when she was born again. She told the story many times during her life of how she answered what seemed to be a sovereign wooing directly from the Holy Spirit Himself, not from any person. She came from a "religious" background rather than a spiritual one, so the churches she attended never gave altar calls to receive salvation.

Of this, Kathryn would later write:

"I was standing beside Mama, and the hands of the church clock were pointed to five minutes before twelve o'clock. I can't remember the minister's name or even one word of his sermon, but something happened to me. It's as real to me right now as it was then — the most real thing that ever happened to me.

"As I stood there, I began shaking to the extent that I could no longer hold the hymnal, so I laid it on the pew...and sobbed. I was feeling the weight of (conviction) and I realized that I was a sinner. I felt like the meanest, lowest person in the whole world. Yet I was only a fourteen-year-old girl.

"...I did the only thing I knew to do: I slipped out from where I was standing and walked to the front pew and sat down in the corner of the pew and wept. Oh, how I wept!

"...I had become the happiest person in the whole world. The heavy weight had been lifted. I experienced something that has never left me. I had been born again, and the

The Kuhlman family — Kathryn wearing ribbon

Holy Spirit had done the very thing that Jesus said He would do (John 16:8)."[4]

Kathryn's father was standing in the kitchen when she came running home from church that day to share with him her good news. It was her custom to tell Papa everything.

In her words, she rushed up to him and said, **"Papa...Jesus has just come into my heart."**

Without any emotion, he just said "I'm glad."[5]

Kathryn recalls how she was never really sure whether or not her father understood what she meant. She would eventually choose to join her father's Baptist church rather than her mama's Methodist church. But even then, she had a mind of her own.

Kathryn says she was never sure if her father was born again. At times, she would speak convincingly that he was. But privately, she sometimes expressed frustration at not knowing for sure.

Kathryn did know, however, that her father had a strong aversion to preachers. Actually, she said that he despised preachers! If Joseph Kuhlman saw a preacher coming down the street, he would cross over to the other side to keep from speaking to him. He thought all preachers were "in it for the money." And the only time he attended church was on holidays or for special services at which Kathryn was giving a recitation. As far as she knew, he never prayed or read the Bible.

THEIR FIRST EMBRACE

According to Kathryn, church attendance was just as important as going to work. At first she attended the Methodist church with her mother. It was there, in 1921, that she was born again. But from 1922 on, the entire family was listed as members of the Baptist church. Though she came from a denominational background, her ministry in later years would become ecumenical as she freely moved through all churches from the Pentecostal to the Catholics. No denomination barred the ministry of Kathryn Kuhlman. She refused to be a part of a denomination and gave no organization any credit for her ministry. She gave credit only to God.

According to Kathryn, church attendance was just as important as going to work.

Throughout Kathryn's teenage years, her mother taught the Epworth League for young people in the Methodist church. A neighbor said Mrs.

Kuhlman was an "excellent Bible teacher, and Kathryn and her sisters and brother must have received some very fine teaching and training at home." The neighbor also talked of hearing someone in the Kuhlman family singing in the evening and someone else playing the piano.[6]

Even though her mother was called an excellent teacher in the Epworth League at church, she was not actually born again until 1935 during one of Kathryn's meetings in Denver.

Kathryn had invited her mother to the meeting. After the close of the first service, Kathryn went into the prayer room behind the pulpit to pray for those who answered the invitation to receive salvation. Later, her mother walked into the prayer room, saying she wanted to know Jesus as Kathryn knew Him.

Kathryn, now choked with tears, reached out and laid her hand on the back of her mama's head. The moment her fingers touched her mother, Mama began to shake, then cry. It was the same kind of shaking and crying that Kathryn remembered when she had stood beside Mama in that little Methodist church in Concordia. But this time, there was something new. Mama lifted her head and began to speak, slowly at first, then more rapidly. But the words weren't English, they were clear, bell-tone sounds of an unknown tongue.

"Kathryn fell to her knees beside her, weeping and laughing at the same time...when Emma opened her eyes, she reached out for Kathryn and held her tightly. It was the first time that Kathryn could ever remember being embraced by her mother."[7]

Her mother didn't sleep for three days and two nights after that. She was a new person, and for the rest of her life in Concordia, Emma Kuhlman had a wonderful, sweet communion with the Holy Spirit.

THE EVANGELISTIC MAID

One characteristic of those greatly used by God is their willingness to drop everything and follow His leading. In 1913, Kathryn's older sister Myrtle married a young, good-looking evangelist who was just finishing his course at Moody Bible Institute. So Myrtle and her new husband, Everett Parrott, began an evangelistic tent ministry. About ten years later, in 1924, she and Myrtle persuaded their parents that it was God's will for Kathryn to travel with them.

At that time, the Parrotts, whose headquarters were in Oregon, were acquainted with Dr. Charles S. Price, who had a healing ministry. He had introduced them to the baptism of the Holy Spirit. However, wonderful as this experience was, the Parrott's marriage had not been a happy one, and now financial strains were adding to the problems.

It would have been easy for Kathryn to slip into self-pity because of these circumstances. Instead, she busied herself around the Parrott house, taking over the washing on Monday and the ironing on Tuesday.

A PORTION OF HER CHARACTER

During this time, along with earning the lessons of patience in adversity, Kathryn also learned not to give way to self-pity. Later many of her messages flowed out of her personal spiritual growth in these areas. Self-pity and self-centeredness were the same to Kathryn. Obviously, she determined as a teenager not to allow either of these have a place in her life, regardless of what happened to her.

> "Be careful of the person, whether they're a member of your family, whether you work with them, whether they are an employee, be careful of a person who can't say, 'I am sorry.' You will find that person very self-centered.
>
> "That is the reason you have heard me say ten thousand times that the only person Jesus can't help, the only person for whom there is no forgiveness of sins is the person who will not say, 'I'm sorry for my sins.'...Such a self-centered person usually draws disease to themselves like a magnet."[8]

Kathryn learned early in life that self-centeredness, along with all the other "self" sins, such as self-pity, self-indulgence, or even self-hatred, causes a person to judge or condemn himself. And that this hinders the Holy Spirit's working in his or her life.

Kathryn learned early in life that self-centeredness, along with all the other "self" sins such as self-pity, self-indulgence, or even self-hatred, causes a person to judge or condemn himself. And that this hinders the Holy Spirit's working in his or her life.

Kathryn always said that anyone could experience the operation of the Holy Spirit in his life if he was willing to pay the price.

"Paying the price" is not a one-time experience. It begins with an initial commitment, a determination to follow God each day of your life.

There were many times and places where Kathryn could have chosen not to submit to the correction of the Holy Spirit. But, fortunately for the present-day body of Christ, she made the right choices and is an example for us to follow.

THERE'S NOTHING LEFT TO PREACH!

Kathryn spent five years with her sister and brother-in-law, preparing the foundation for her own ministry. She worked in the household to ease any burden her presence might have brought, and spent many hours reading and studying the Word.

In 1928, the Parrotts arrived in Boise, Idaho. By this time they had acquired a tent and a pianist by the name of Helen Gulliford. But their marital problems continued to grow. So they decided that Everett would go on to South Dakota while they would leave Myrtle, Kathryn, and Helen in Boise to conduct a meeting there.

After two weeks, the offerings collected weren't enough to pay the rent on the building, their small apartment, or to buy food. They lived meagerly on bread and tuna.[9]

Myrtle soon felt that her only recourse was to rejoin her husband. Kathryn and Helen couldn't see any hope for their future by continuing to travel with the Parrotts. So like Paul and Barnabas in the New Testament church, they decided to part company. A local pastor in Boise offered them a chance to preach in a small pool hall that had been converted into a mission – and that was the beginning of The Kathryn Kuhlman Ministry!

From the "pool hall" mission, they went to Pocatello, Idaho, where Kathryn preached in an old opera house. The building was filthy and had to be cleaned before they could use it. You can guess who did the cleaning – the evangelist, of course. From there, they went to Twin Falls, Idaho, in the dead of winter where Kathryn slipped on the ice and broke her leg. Though the doctor had told her to not put her foot down for two weeks, she immediately continued to preach with her foot in a cast. She never allowed her flesh to cause her to compromise the will of God.

Kathryn once said,:

"From that first sermon I preached in Idaho – Zacchaeus up a tree, and God knows if anyone was up a tree, I sure was

– one thing I knew, I was sold on the things of God. Jesus was real to me. My heart was fixed."[10]

After preaching four or five sermons, she would humorously say:

"...I wondered, 'What more can I preach about?' There isn't anything else in the Bible. I have absolutely exhausted the supply of sermons. For the life of me, I can't think of anything else to preach about."[11]

STABLE AND STRONG IN THE TURKEY HOUSE

Many times in those early years, their accommodations were meager, to say the least. On one occasion, the family with whom she was scheduled to stay didn't have a place for her – until they scrubbed out the turkey house. Kathryn often said she would have gladly slept on a straw stack, because her need to preach was so strong within her. Years later she would often laugh and tell how she would lock the doors and not let anyone out until she was sure they were all saved! That was her joke; however, she would also stay at the altar until the wee hours of the morning praying with anyone who lingered.

Other places Kathryn stayed might have been cleaner than the turkey house, but they weren't as warm. In those days guest rooms weren't heated. Later she would tell how she snuggled under great piles of covers until she got the place warm where she lay. Then she would turn over on her stomach and study the Word of God for hours at a time.

What keeps a person devoted to their call? Kathryn's answer was "loyalty."

Her heart was "sold out" to the Lord. That was the secret of her ministry. Her heart was *fixed* on Jesus. She determined to be loyal to Him and to avoid grieving the Holy Spirit.

In Kathryn's early years of ministry, two other characteristics were developed – dedication, and loyalty to God and His people. Kathryn expanded and developed her spiritual understanding from the foundation of character that she developed early in life.

KATHRYN'S "LOYALTY"

What keeps a person devoted to their call? Kathryn's answer was "loyalty."

"The word *loyalty* has little meaning in these days because there's so little of it being practiced...Loyalty is something that is intangible...It's like love. You can only understand it as you see it in action...*Love is something you do,* and that's also true of loyalty. It means faithfulness. It means allegiance. It means devotion.

"...My heart is fixed. I'll be loyal to Him at any cost, at any price. Loyalty is much more than a casual interest in someone or something. It's a personal commitment. In the final analysis, it means, 'Here I am. You can count on me. I won't fail you.'"[12]

In other words, true loyalty for those called into the ministry would be expressed by their decision never to deviate from God's call. Do not add to it or take from it – just do it. According to Kathryn, when people begin to do their own thing, their loyalty changes from God, to themselves.

I WANT IT B-I-G!

After preaching all over Idaho, Kathryn and Helen moved into Colorado. Following a six-month revival in Pueblo, they arrived in Denver. A businessman, Earl F. Hewitt, had joined her in Pueblo as her business manager. That year of 1933 the Depression was in full swing. Businesses were closed down, millions of people were out of work, and churches were struggling to stay open.

Kathryn was a traveling evangelist without the financial backing of any denomination, yet her belief was in a big God whose resources weren't limited. She believed if you were serving a God of *limited* finances, then you were serving the wrong god. She lived by the principle of faith and trusted in God.

She told Hewitt to go into Denver and act as if they had a million dollars. When he pointed out that in reality they had only $5, she said:

"He [God] is not limited to what we have or who we are. He can certainly use our five dollars and multiply it just as easily as He multiplied the loaves and fishes...Now go on up to Denver. Find me the biggest building you can. Get the finest piano available for Helen. Fill the place up with chairs. Take out a big ad in the *Denver Post* and get spot announcements on all the radio stations. This is God's business, and we're going to do it God's way – big!"[13]

Hewitt took her at her word and followed the instructions. The building had been a Montgomery Ward Company warehouse. The meeting lasted five months, during which time they moved to yet another warehouse. The first night, one hundred twenty-five people were present, the second night, over four hundred people attended. From then on, the warehouse filled to capacity every night. After five months, Kathryn announced that the meeting was over, but the people wouldn't hear of it. One man offered to make the down payment on a permanent building and erect a huge neon sign over it which would read, "Prayer Changes Things."

People were hungry for the Word of God. However, her main message in those years was salvation. From time to time, pastors were born again at her invitation to receive Jesus as Savior and Lord. Kathryn's was a ministry of hope and faith. During this time, Helen had developed a choir of one hundred voices and composed much of the music they sang.

Because the response to Kathryn's ministry was so great, she agreed to stay in Denver. Everything seemed to be flawless, so they began to search for a permanent building. Then suddenly, out of nowhere, tragedy struck.

Early ministry years

PAPA IS GONE

Kathryn experienced the first real trauma of her life in late December of 1934, when her beloved father was killed in an accident. She learned much later that he had fallen on an icy street and had been struck by a car that swerved to try to miss him in a snowstorm.

Because of the storm, it was hours before a friend could reach Kathryn in Colorado. Upon receiving the news that her father was near death, she started home, driving in blizzard conditions from Denver across Kansas toward Missouri. She said only God knew how fast she drove on icy roads and in near-zero visibility.

On December 30, Kathryn had made it to Kansas City. From there she called home to tell her father that she was almost home, only to find that he died early that morning.

She arrived home to find Papa laid out in his casket in the living room with the mourners keeping the traditional vigil. The trauma was almost more than Kathryn could bear. Hate welled up inside her toward the youth who drove the car that struck her father.

"I had always been a happy person, and Papa had helped to make me happy. Now he was gone, and in his place, I was battling unfamiliar strangers of fear and hate.

"I had the most perfect father a girl ever had. In my eyes, Papa could do no wrong. He was my ideal."

Kathryn had left home more than ten years earlier, visiting only a few times in between. Now her Papa would never be able to hear her preach. Later, she related that the hatred for the young man who killed her father seethed within her, and she spewed out this venom about the accident to everyone – until the day of the funeral.

"Sitting there in the front row of the little Baptist church, I still refused to accept my father's death. It couldn't be."

"Sitting there in the front row of the little Baptist church, I still refused to accept my father's death. It couldn't be ...One by one, my family rose from their seats and filed by the coffin. My two sisters. My brother. Only I was left in the pew.

"The funeral director walked over and said, 'Kathryn, would you like to see your father before I close the casket?'

"Suddenly I was standing at the front of the church, looking down — my eyes fixed not on Papa's face, but on his shoulder, that shoulder on which I had so often leaned ...I leaned over and gently put my hand on that shoulder in the casket. And as I did, something happened. All that my fingers caressed was a suit of clothes ...Everything that box contained was simply something discarded, loved once, laid aside now. Papa wasn't there.

"...This was the first time the power of the risen, resurrected Christ really came through to me. Suddenly, I was no longer afraid of death....as my fear disappeared, so did my hate. Papa wasn't dead. He was alive."[14]

RENEWED AND SMILIN'

Kathryn returned to Denver with a new understanding and compassion. Upon her return, a building was found and renovation began in February of 1935. On May 30 of that year, the Denver Revival Tabernacle opened with a huge neon sign over it, as promised — "PRAYER CHANGES THINGS." The auditorium held two thousand seats and the name of the Tabernacle could be seen from a great distance. Thousands of people from the surrounding areas attended Kathryn's meetings over the next four years. Services were conducted nightly except on Monday.

...the romantic involvement became publicly known between Kathryn and Waltrip, whom she nicknamed, "Mister."

The revival center soon developed into an organized church. There was no denominational affiliation. Ultimately a Sunday school was begun, and buses were in operation to bring people to the services. There were outreaches to prisons and nursing homes. Later on Kathryn began a radio program called, "Smiling Through."

In 1936, many musicians and preachers ministered at the Denver Revival Tabernacle. One of those was Raymond T. Richey, a prominent evangelist, who spent three weeks at the church. Richey had been a leading pioneer in America's earlier healing revivals.

Kathryn labeled the trauma of her father's death as her "deepest" valley experience, but there was another valley experience that would prove to be nearly as deep.

WHAT A "TRIP"

In 1935 an evangelist named Burroughs A. Waltrip from Austin, Texas, was invited to speak at the Tabernacle. He was an extremely handsome man and eight years older than Kathryn. Soon they found themselves attracted to each other.

The only problem was that he was married and had two little boys. Kathryn seemed to ignore the promptings of the Holy Spirit within her telling her that this relationship was a mistake. Shortly after his first visit to Denver, Waltrip divorced his wife and told everyone that his wife left him. However, his ex-wife, Jessie, said Waltrip believed that if you didn't love your spouse at the time of marriage, then there was no covenant, making a person free to divorce and remarry. After Waltrip left his wife, he never returned home to her, and his two little boys never saw their father again.[15]

MISTER IS SPELLED M-I-S-T-A-K-E

After leaving his family, Waltrip moved to Mason City, Iowa, representing himself as a single man, to begin a revival center called Radio Chapel. He was known to be a dramatic and sensational evangelist and began daily radio broadcasts from the Chapel. Kathryn and Helen came into town to help him raise funds for his ministry.

Soon, the romantic involvement became publicly known between Kathryn and Waltrip, whom she nicknamed, "Mister." Helen and other friends from Denver sincerely advised Kathryn not to marry the handsome evangelist, but she reasoned that his wife had left him, making him free to marry.

It should be noted that the details of Waltrip's separation from his wife and the timing of Kuhlman's involvement are not clear. Those who loved and appreciated her ministry kept these things quiet. Obviously, they felt that God had forgiven Kathryn of any mistakes in this relationship, so the details weren't important.

On October 16, 1938, Kathryn announced to her Denver congregation that she planned to join the ministry with "Mister" in Mason City, Iowa. Two days later on October 18th, almost sixteen months after Waltrip's uncontested divorce, Kathryn and Burroughs were secretly married in Mason City.

WHAT IS THE ISSUE, ANYWAY?

Let me make a point here. Divorce was not the issue. Of course, it is an issue with religious people and their self-righteous denominations, but it is not an issue to God. He lays it out very simply. According to the New Testament, there are two scriptural reasons for divorce. One spouse being involved in repeated immorality is one reason. And the other comes into play when one spouse leaves the marriage. If either one of these things happen to a person, that person is free before God and blessed to remarry. If you made a decision regarding divorce that didn't line up with the Word of God, there is forgiveness and restoration and a new and clean beginning waiting for you. Self-righteous people and certain denominations may not give you a new beginning, but God can help you if you seek Him.

Kathryn found herself in a situation where there were lying and deceiving spirits in operation. Waltrip left his wife in Texas and divorced her, which was his first mistake. Then, he tried to cover it by embracing a deceiving doctrine and lied about it to those around him. The Kuhlman-Waltrip marriage was *totally wrong* from the start!

SHE ALMOST DID IT...

Kathryn chose to believe this man's story that his wife left him. However, her heart was constantly troubled throughout their wedding plans. She found no peace in her spirit. Most people say that "Mister" didn't love Kathryn at all. Instead, he loved her ability to draw a crowd and raise money. He was well-known for his greed and extravagant lifestyle. When he married Kathryn, people in eight different states were "hounding" him for money.

Even "Mister's" mother begged Kathryn not to marry her son. She had hoped he would come to his senses and re-unite with his wife and sons. You may ask, then *why* did Kathryn go ahead with the marriage?

Before the scheduled marriage in Mason City, Kathryn discussed the issue with her friends, Lottie Anthony and Helen. Lottie remembers Kathryn saying, **"I just can't seem to find the will of God in this matter."** The women tried to convince Kathryn to wait and follow the peace of God. But she would not listen to them.

When the three women arrived in Des Moines on the way to Mason City, Helen announced to Kathryn that she wouldn't go through with it. She remained at their hotel. Lottie agreed with Helen and also refused to attend the wedding.

But Kathryn found another friend to witness the marriage between her and Waltrip. Kathryn fainted during the ceremony. Waltrip helped to revive her so that she could finish the vows. The deliberate decision to step out of the will of God obviously weighed heavily upon her.

As the newlyweds drove back to Des Moines from the ceremony, Kathryn did an odd thing. After the couple checked into their hotel, Kathryn refused to stay with her new husband. Her close friend Lottie Anthony states that Kathryn jumped in the car and drove to her and Helen's hotel.

Kathryn sat in their hotel room, weeping and admitting she had made a mistake with the marriage and would get an annulment. Lottie called Waltrip, informing him of Kathryn's plans. As Waltrip complained of losing his wife, Lottie snapped, "She was never yours in the first place!"

In spite of the looks, the whispers, and the wholesale rejection, it took great faith and dogged determination to restore Kathryn's ministry.

The three women left Des Moines, hoping to explain the situation away to the Denver congregation. But the congregation never gave her a chance. They were furious with her for taking the situation so lightly and for the secrecy of the marriage. Lottie said that the Denver congregation "drove her back into Waltrip's arms."[16]

THE SHATTERED DREAMS

The work Kathryn had so diligently built over the previous five years quickly disintegrated. Hewitt bought out Kathryn's share of the building, and Helen went to work for a smaller church in Denver. The "sheep" scattered. Because of this grievous mistake, Kathryn lost her church, her close friends, and her ministry. Even her relationship with God suffered because Kathryn put "Mister" and his desires over her passion for God.

Kathryn Kuhlman, the woman some had worshipped as a "perfect madonna," was actually a human being, subject to human temptations. She was a great woman of God, but *what made her great was her choice and action to recover from her mistake*. In spite of the looks, the whispers, and the wholesale rejection, it took great faith and dogged determination to restore Kathryn's ministry. It is said that her own mistakes produced the powerful revelation behind her sermons of temptation, forgiveness, and victory.

But this action and revelation didn't come overnight. Kathryn spent the next eight years in oblivion as far as major ministry was concerned. Six years were spent in the marriage and the next two she spent trying to find her way back to full-time ministry. Friends who traveled to Mason City the year Kathryn lived there said she would sit on the platform behind her husband and weep while he preached.

When the people of Mason City learned that Waltrip had lied about his first marriage, they stopped attending, and Radio Chapel soon closed. The few times Waltrip allowed Kathryn to minister alone were in places where no one knew she was married. At least once, a series of meetings were canceled at the last moment after the pastor who invited her was told by a member of his congregation of Kathryn's marriage to a divorced man.[17]

THE PAIN OF DYING

Kathryn left Waltrip in 1944 while they were living in Los Angeles, but he didn't get a divorce until 1947.

On one of the rare occasions when she would talk of those years and what happened, she said:

> "I had to make a choice. Would I serve the man I loved, or the God I loved? I knew I couldn't serve God and live with Mister. No one will ever know the pain of dying like I know it, for I loved him more than I loved life itself. And for a time, I loved him even more than God. I finally told him I had to leave, for God had never released me from my original call. Not only did I live with him, I had to live with my conscience, and the conviction of the Holy Spirit was almost unbearable. I was tired of trying to justify myself."[18]

In one of her final appearances, in a question and answer session, a young man asked her how she "met her death." He had heard her speak of this death several times.

She answered:

> "It came through a great disappointment, a great disappointment, and I felt like my whole world had come to an end. You know, it's not what happens to you, it's what you do with the things after it happens. And that goes back to the will of the Lord.
>
> "At that time, I felt that which had happened to me was the greatest tragedy of my life. I thought I would never rise again, never, never. No one will ever know — if you've never died — what I'm talking about ...Today, I feel it was a part of God's perfect will for my life."[19]

Kathryn commented several times how she suffered for the sake of the ministry. But actually, there were other people who suffered also. There was a wife who had been left in Texas with two small boys, needing an explanation of why they would never see their dad again. The ordeal brought great heartache to everyone who knew and loved the couple.

BOTH SIDES OF THE COIN

But from the moment she made her decision, Kathryn Kuhlman never wavered from answering the call on her life, never deviated from the path God had set for her, and never saw "Mister" again. She bought a one-way ticket to Franklin, Pennsylvania, and never turned back.

Kathryn was totally restored in her life with God. Though this was a difficult time for Kathryn, the blessings of God soon followed her. But the fate of Waltrip was uncertain. He simply dropped out of sight, not even contacting his family. According to his ex-wife Jessie, it was years later that his brother, James Waltrip, sadly discovered that Burroughs had eventually met his death in a California prison, convicted of stealing money from a woman.[20]

...Kathryn came out of her "wilderness" and moved into the "Promised Land" of her real ministry.

OUT OF THE CAVE

No one ever seemed to know why Kathryn picked Franklin, Pennsylvania, to begin her "comeback." Franklin was a coal-mining city, settled by German immigrants. Perhaps she felt at home there. Perhaps it was because they accepted her there. Whatever the reason, it worked!

From Pennsylvania she went through the midwestern states and the south into West Virginia, Virginia, and the Carolinas. In some places, she was quickly accepted, in others, her past surfaced quickly and the meetings were closed. In Georgia, a newspaper took hold of the story concerning her marriage to a divorced man and printed it. Kathryn then took a bus back to Franklin.

In 1946, Kathryn came out of her "wilderness" and moved into the "Promised Land" of her real ministry. After an unsuccessful tour of the South, she was invited to hold a series of meetings in the fifteen hundred seat Gospel Tabernacle located in Franklin, Pennsylvania. The Tabernacle had been famous in circles since Billy Sunday preached there. And Kathryn's meetings were so glorious in this building that it was as if the last eight years never existed.

THE MANY VOICES

Not too long after she opened her meetings at the Tabernacle, she began daily radio broadcasts from WKRZ Radio in Oil City, Pennsylvania. Response had been so great, that within a few months, she added a station in Pittsburgh.

Instead of being shunned, Kathryn was now being inundated with mail. The Oil City station finally had to bar visitors from the studio because they hindered the staff's work.

World War II had just ended, and many luxuries were still scarce. One day, Kathryn casually mentioned over the air that she had made a run in her last pair of stockings, and soon afterwards the station was deluged with packages of nylon stockings.

The Holy Spirit moved in the days surrounding the end of the war to restore the body of Christ through the gift of healing. The great healing revivals were in full swing, and great healings were manifested through the ministries of such men as Oral Roberts, William Branham, and the late Jack Coe. The late Gordon Lindsay, founder of *The Voice of Healing* magazine and Christ for the Nations Bible School, published the news of these great revivals in *The Voice of Healing* magazine.

At this time, Kathryn was still praying mainly for people to receive salvation. But she was beginning to pray and lay hands on people who came for healing. Though she despised the term "faith healer," she attended the meetings of these ministers hoping to find out more about this phenomenon of God. Kathryn didn't have the slightest idea that a "healing ministry" would bring her international fame.

As she observed various tent meetings, Kathryn walked away with greater understanding. Though she always had unanswered questions about divine healing, she did establish a standard for her ministry:

> **"In the early part of my ministry, I was greatly disturbed over much that I saw occurring in the field of divine healing. I was confused by the many methods that I saw employed. I was disgusted with the unwise performances that I witnessed, none of which I could associate in any way whatsoever with either the action of the Holy Spirit or the nature of God.**
>
> **"...To this very day, there is nothing more repulsive to me than the lack of wisdom.... There is one thing I can't**

stand, and that is fanaticism — the manifestations of the flesh that bring a reproach on something that is so marvelous, something that is so sacred."[21]

Kathryn went on to speak of her heartache while watching these meetings. For the rest of her life, she exhorted the people to focus and concentrate on Jesus, and nothing else. After attending a tent meeting in Erie, Pennsylvania, she said:

> "I began to weep. I couldn't stop. Those looks of despair and disappointment on the faces I had seen, when told that their lack of faith was keeping them from God, were to haunt me for weeks. Was this the God of all mercy and great compassion? I left the tent, and with hot tears streaming down my face, I looked up and cried, 'They have taken away my Lord, and I know not where they have laid Him.'"[22]

> *The moment Kathryn saw in God's Word that healing was provided for the believer at the same time as salvation, she began to understand the Christian's relationship with the Holy Spirit.*

It is interesting to note that Kathryn Kuhlman chose not to associate her ministry with Gordon Lindsay's *Voice of Healing* publication. The publication was the promotional outlet for the healing evangelists of that era, and Kuhlman chose not to be a part of it. Many of these evangelists were sincere and honest, but others turned to sensationalism and used questionable methods in their ministries.

HERE COME THE MIRACLES!

The moment Kathryn saw in God's Word that healing was provided for the believer at the same time as salvation, she began to understand the Christian's relationship with the Holy Spirit. In 1947 she began teaching a series on the Holy Spirit. Some of the things she said during the first night of her teaching were revelations even to her. Later she spoke of being awake all that night, praying and reading more in the Word.

The second night of her meeting was a momentous occasion. A unique testimony had been given by someone who was healed in a Kathryn Kuhlman meeting. A woman stood up and told of having been healed while Kathryn preached the night before. Without anyone laying hands on her and without

Kathryn even being aware of what was happening, this woman was healed of a tumor. The woman had gone to her doctor to confirm her healing before the evening service.

On the following Sunday, the second miracle occurred. A World War I veteran who had been declared legally blind from an industrial accident, had 85 percent of his vision restored in the permanently impaired eye, and perfect eyesight restored to his other eye.

SHARK, SHERIFF, AND GLORY

Once the healings and miracles began to take place, the crowds at the Tabernacle were even larger than those brought in by Billy Sunday. God began to prosper Kathryn's ministry greatly, but the devil's adversaries had now stepped in, attempting to undermine the working and flow of the Holy Spirit in Kathryn's ministry.

The attack came through M. J. Maloney and the Tabernacle trustees. Maloney insisted that he receive a certain percentage of all the ministry revenue, including that which came from the radio broadcast and mailouts. Kathryn balked and Maloney threatened to sue her.

The activities surrounding this "showdown" included Maloney's locking her out of the building. A fight ensued between Kathryn and her coal miner followers and Maloney's men, ending in Kathryn's partisans breaking off the padlocks so services could continue. It only ended when Kathryn's supporters raised $10,000 and purchased an old roller skating rink in nearby Sugar Creek. They named that roller rink Faith Temple. It was twice the size of Maloney's building and was packed from the first service.

Ironically, during this hectic and crucial time of 1947, another amazing thing happened. One night, Kathryn heard a knock on the door of her apartment. When she opened the door, there stood the sheriff dressed in street clothes. He proceeded to tell her that "Mister" had filed for divorce in Nevada and his office had received the papers that morning, naming her as the defendant.

Kathryn looked down and saw the papers in his hand. Her head remained bowed. Seeing her shame and disappointment, the sheriff reached out and touched her arm, for he had been attending Kathryn's services and knew she had been sent by God to their area. Knowing that names of famous persons on divorce papers were often given to the media for press release, the sheriff made sure the papers remained private by delivering them personally.

The sheriff went on to reassure Kathryn that no one but the two of them would ever know of this legal action. Kathryn told the sheriff she would be grateful to him for the rest of her life.

His goodness saved Kathryn from great heartache. Seven years later reporters did find out about it, but by that time, Kathryn's ministry had so advanced, it was not affected by old news.

> *...signs from heaven would urge Kathryn to move to Pittsburgh.*

Great healing services continued at the reno-vated roller rink, and additional services expanded into neighboring towns and to Stambaugh Audito-rium in Youngstown, Ohio. The Holy Spirit had found a ministry that wouldn't try to take the credit for His deeds, nor the glory from the results of His operations.

A former secretary remembered:

> "Miss Kuhlman was so tender toward God. I was standing in the Tabernacle after a service and could see into the radio room. There Miss Kuhlman, unaware that anyone could see her, was on her knees praising God for the service."[23]

As her ministry developed, she put less emphasis on faith, and more emphasis on the sovereignty of the Holy Spirit. In her meetings, there were no prayer cards, no invalid tents, and no long lines of sick people waiting for her to lay hands on them. She never accused people who failed to receive healing of being weak in their faith. It seemed that the healings took place anywhere throughout the auditorium while the people sat in their seats, looking toward Heaven and focusing on Jesus.

THE ROOF FELL IN!

At her first meeting in the Carnegie Hall in Pittsburgh, the custodian told her that even opera stars couldn't fill it, but she insisted that enough chairs be set up to fill the auditorium. It was a good thing she did, because every chair was filled.

The first service was in the afternoon, and the hall was packed. A second meeting was held that evening to accommodate the throng. Jimmy Miller and Charles Beebee ministered in music at these services, and remained in min-istry with Kathryn until the end.

The radio ministry continued to expand, and by November of 1950, the peo-ple began to urge Kathryn to relocate to Pittsburgh permanently. Even Maggie

Hartner, the woman who became her "right arm" agreed they should move. Kathryn was reluctant, feeling committed to the people in Franklin who had stood by her and supported her, and had taken her in and loved her when no one else would.

But signs from heaven would urge Kathryn to move to Pittsburgh.

In response to pleas that she move, Kathryn announced:

"No! The roof on Faith Temple literally would have to cave in before I'd believe God wanted me to move to Pittsburgh."

On Thanksgiving, 1950, the temple's roof fell in under the weight of the greatest snowfall in area history.[24]

Three weeks later, Kathryn moved to the Pittsburgh suburb of Fox Chapel, where she lived until her death.

"I WANT TO BE LIKE AIMEE"

In 1950, a worldwide ministry began to develop. In later years, Kathryn said that God didn't call her to build a church, maintaining that her ministry was not to be isolated to any one building. Some may be called to build buildings, but she wasn't one of those.

The fact that she did build churches was largely overshadowed by the publicity of the miracle services. The Kathryn Kuhlman Foundation, established in Pittsburgh, financed more than twenty churches in foreign mission fields with nationals as pastors.

Many call her "pastor" out of love and respect, but Kathryn was never ordained to the office of pastor. After her stay in Denver, she never pastored a church. Kathryn said she was not called to a five-fold office, i.e., Ephesians 4:11. She walked in the simplicity of being "a handmaiden" of the Lord.

It is said by those closest to her, that Kathryn announced at the very beginning of her ministry, that she would be the next Aimee Semple McPherson, founder of the Four Square denomination. Aimee was definitely Kathryn's role model. When the flamboyant "Sister" built Angelus Temple in Los Angeles, Kathryn was present during its highest popularity. It is said that Kathryn attended Aimee's Bible school, and sat in the balcony of her church, taking in every aspect of the anointed messages and theatrics of "Sister". Unlike the other L.I.F.E. Bible School students, Kathryn chose not to stay with the Four Square denomination. She chose an independent route. It is interesting to note that Rolf McPherson, Aimee's son, doesn't remember Kathryn being a student at the school.[25]

Though she never met Aimee personally, the effects of her ministry rubbed off on Kathryn. There was a major difference between the two: Aimee taught people to seek for the baptism in the Holy Spirit; Kathryn thought to "seek for it" was a devisive practice. Kathryn was Pentecostal but didn't make an issue of it. People had always compared Kathryn with Aimee, but it was six years after Aimee's premature death before Kathryn made the national headlines.[26]

A MEDIA CHURCH

Kathryn's messages were heard all over the United States and various places overseas, via short-wave radio broadcast. It seemed that America could hardly wait to hear that warm, pleasant voice ask listeners at the beginning of her program, **"Hello, there, and have you been waiting for me?"**

If it looked like she wouldn't have freedom, or if questionable people were present who might taint her ministry, she canceled. It has been said that even "those in charge were not in charge" when Kathryn was present.

Her radio program was not religious or stuffy. Instead, the program made a person feel as though Kathryn Kuhlman had just dropped by for coffee. She ministered to the needs, concerns, and hurts of her audience, and her encouragement changed lives. She frequently chuckled, making the listener feel as though they had just had a heart-to-heart talk with her. If she wanted to cry – she cried; if she wanted to sing – she sang. Kathryn had the ability to minister over radio just as she ministered in public. Not many could do that, but Kathryn did. By popular demand, the Kuhlman Foundation was requested to supply her old-recorded radio tapes to the radio stations for six years after her death!

For more than eight years before her death, her weekly television program was aired nationwide. At the time, her program was the longest running half-hour series produced in the CBS studios, though it didn't air on the CBS network.

IT HAD TO BE "KATHRYN'S" WAY

Her meetings were moved from Carnegie Hall to the First Presbyterian Church in Pittsburgh, and for years these sessions were attended by some of the most elite Bible scholars in Pittsburgh. For the last ten years of her life, she held monthly services at the Shrine Auditorium in Los Angeles, where she ministered to countless thousands, and hundreds were healed. She also spoke at large churches, conferences, and international meetings. She especially enjoyed ministering at the Full Gospel Business Men's Fellowship International, a laymen's organization founded by Demos Shakarian in Los Angeles.

It was several years before Kathryn would consent to integrate the miracle services with other conferences. She felt the confinements of a general conference, with schedules and time limits, might restrict the liberty of the Spirit that was so a part of her meetings.

If another group wanted Kathryn to speak for them, they had to adjust their program to fit her style. She knew that God had called her to minister a certain way, and there would be no changes. If it looked like she wouldn't have freedom, or if questionable people were present who might taint her ministry, she canceled. It has been said that even "those in charge were not in charge" when Kathryn was present.[27]

SHE DIED A THOUSAND TIMES

Kathryn never preached against smoking or drinking alcoholic beverages. She didn't advocate their use, but she refused to alienate people. Also, she didn't like the way that some of the healing evangelists ministered. Kathryn felt it was "rough," and she would not support that type of ministry.

She never taught that sickness was from the devil. She avoided the subject, pointing instead to how big God is. She felt if she could turn the eyes of the people toward God, then everything would fall into place. Early in her ministry, she encouraged people to leave their denomination. In her later years, Kathryn encouraged them to return and be a shining light and a healing force.[28]

It is said that Kathryn's life was a prayer. Traveling constantly, she didn't have conventional times of devotion, so she learned to make wherever she was her prayer closet. Before her meetings, Kathryn would be seen "pacing back and forth, head up, head down, arms flung into the air, hands clasped behind her back." Her face would be covered in tears. It seemed she was pleading with the Lord, saying, **"Gentle Jesus, take not Your Holy Spirit from me."**[29]

Though this depth of prayer would seem to be a personal thing, it wasn't so with Kathryn. Many times, she would be interrupted with a question, which she would answer, then she would resume the same depth of prayer at the point of interruption. Oral Roberts described her relationship with the Spirit this way:

"It was like they were talking back and forth to each other, and you couldn't tell where Kathryn started and the Holy Spirit left off. It was a oneness."[30]

> *Though there were thousands upon thousands of miracles, the greatest miracle to Kathryn was when a person became born again.*

People from all walks of life and denominations came to her meetings: Catholics, Episcopals, Baptists, Pentecostals, drunkards, the sick, the dying, the deeply spiritual and the unconverted. And Kathryn knew she was the vessel who would point them to God. In some way, she could cross every barrier and bring them all to the same level of understanding. How could she do this? I believe it was because she lived in such surrender to the Holy Spirit. She always said, **"I die a thousand deaths before every service."**[31]

Being an ecumenical evangelist, Kathryn never permitted the spiritual gifts of tongues, the gift of interpretation, or prophecy to operate in her services. If someone repeatedly spoke in tongues loudly enough to disturb, she discreetly had them removed from the service. Kathryn believed in all the gifts of the Spirit, but didn't want to do anything that would hinder or distract the uninitiated from a simple belief in God.

However, she did allow people to be "slain in the Spirit." Many came to believe in the awesome power of God from witnessing this manifestation alone. Kathryn offered this simple explanation:

> **"All I can believe is that our spiritual beings are not wired for God's full power, and when we plug in to that power, we just can't survive it. We are wired for low voltage, God is high voltage through the Holy Spirit."**[32]

She never left the platform, even when a musician or soloist ministered. She usually stepped to the side, but always remained in the view of the audience, standing, smiling, and lifting her hand to God.

Kathryn was always aware that she would, one day, stand before the Lord and give an account for her ministry. She never believed she had been God's first choice for the ministry. She believed a man had been called to do it, but was not willing to pay the price. She was never quite sure if she was even second choice or third choice, but she did know that she had answered **"yes"** to the Lord. Her ministry stands out as one of the leading ministries, if not *the* leading ministry, of the Charismatic Movement.

TOO MANY TO NAME...

What were some of the outstanding miracles? Though there were thousands upon thousands of miracles, the greatest miracle to Kathryn was when a person became born again. On one occasion a five-year-old boy, crippled from birth, walked to Kathryn's platform without assistance. On another, a woman, who had been crippled and confined to a wheelchair for twelve years, walked to the platform without aid from her husband. A man in Philadelphia, who had received a pacemaker eight months earlier, felt intense pain in his chest after Kathryn laid hands on him. Returning home, he found the scar gone from his chest where the pacemaker had been implanted, and he couldn't tell if the pacemaker was functioning. Later, when the doctor took X-rays, he discovered the pacemaker was gone and the man's heart healed!

It was common for tumors to dissolve, cancers to fall off, the blind to see and the deaf to hear. Migraine headaches were healed instantly. Even teeth were divinely filled. It would be impossible to list the miracles that the ministry of Kathryn Kuhlman witnessed! God alone knows.

Screen stars were coming to her meetings. Even comedienne Phyllis Diller recommended one of Kathryn's books to a dying fan.

Kathryn was known to weep for joy as she watched the thousands being healed through the power of God. Some even remember her teardrops falling on their hands.

It is also said that Kathryn would weep as she watched the people leave who remained sick or in wheelchairs. She never tried to explain why some received their healing and some did not. She believed the responsibility remained with God. She liked to refer to herself as in sales, not management. Whatever Management decided to do, she would have to oblige. But she did say it would be one of the first questions she would ask God when she got to heaven!

NORTHERN EXPOSURE

In August of 1952, Kathryn preached to over fifteen thousand under Rex Humbard's tent in Akron, Ohio. On the pre-dawn hours before Kathryn's first Sunday service, the Humbard's were awakened by a loud knock on their mobile home door. It was a policeman who said, "Reverend Humbard, you're gonna have to do something. There's nearly eighteen thousand people out at

Rushing for seats at a Kuhlman meeting

Seattle, Washington, 1974

Laying hands on the sick

Ministering to the lame

Emptying more wheel chairs

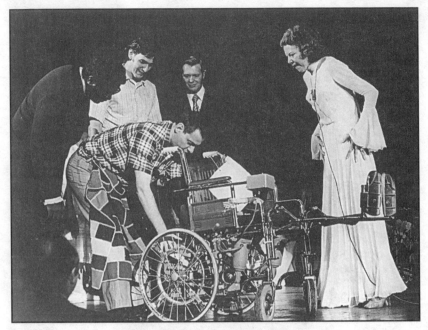

"Rise and push!"

Kathryn with Oral Roberts

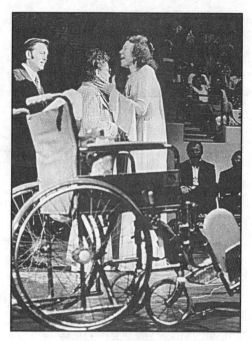

"Be set free in Jesus' name!"

"Don't you just love Him, honey?"

that tent." It was 4:00 A.M. in the morning, and the service was not scheduled to start until 11:00 A.M. that morning.

Kathryn, being used to crowds of people who couldn't all fit under one roof or into one tent, told Humbard there was only one thing to do, they would have to start the service at 8:00 A.M. And that's what they did! Maude Aimee, Rex's wife, remembered that Kathryn ministered until 2:30 P.M. that afternoon.

After these meetings, the Humbards parked their mobile home in Akron and subsequently built one of the largest churches and television ministries of that era – the 1960s and 1970s. Kathryn and the Humbards also built a life-long friendship as a result of their Akron experience.

Around this time, Kathryn was diagnosed with suffering from an enlarged heart and defective mitral valve. Yet, she kept going, remaining entirely dependent upon the Holy Spirit.

GLITTER AND THE FALLING STARS

By now, Kathryn had become a celebrity figure in the Christian as well as the secular world. Screen stars were coming to her meetings. Even comedienne Phyllis Diller recommended one of Kathryn's books to a dying fan.[33] The Pope granted Kathryn a private audience in the Vatican, and gave her a pendant engraved with a dove. The largest cities in America were presenting her with the "key" to their cities. Even the nation of Viet Nam gave her a Medal of Honor for her contributions to the hurting.

Of course, in the midst of honor came attacks. Some she was able to ignore. But there were others that wounded her deeply. Among those were the betrayals of her employees, Dino Kartsonakis and his brother-in-law, Paul Bartholomew.

In short, Dino and his brother-in-law demanded a high pay increase in their contracts after they discovered the Kuhlman Foundation had signed a multimedia contract.

Kathryn had greatly enjoyed Dino's company. No doubt many of her crusade audiences remember how she fondly introduced him, saying with a great sweep of her arms, **And now, heeere's DeeeeNo!** Kathryn had taken Kartsonakis out of obscurity and launched him into an international ministry. It was said that she dressed him in the finest of clothes and exalted his name constantly before the media.

But Dino seemed to have fallen under the influence of his brother-in-law, Paul Bartholomew. Though Bartholomew had been the highest paid person on staff, he wanted more, and eventually sued Kathryn for an outrageous sum of money. And when Kathryn didn't approve of Dino's publicized relationship with a secular show-girl, he became bitter and also demanded more money. As a result, Kathryn fired them both. But not before they made many public accusations concerning her character that were heard around the world.[34]

In her later years, Kathryn didn't spend much time analyzing the character of her staff members. Instead, she chose people she simply enjoyed, but often the enjoyment she received was short-lived and heartache followed. It is possible that her mistakes in hiring came from her physical and mental exhaustion. Her schedule was tremendously hectic. Though she was warned that the hiring of Bartholomew and Kartsonakis was a mistake, Kathryn hired them anyway, resulting in the foregoing fiasco.

Though there may have been mistakes made in judgment, lack of understanding, and mistakes made through the people around her, she never allowed flesh to participate in any of the movings of the Holy Spirit, and she never took any of the credit. Kathryn Kuhlman always gave the glory to God.

With the ministry continuing in full swing, major denominations gave Kathryn credit for having the purest ministry of the Holy Spirit in their time. Kathryn had no hidden agendas and no ulterior motives, what you saw was what you got. She never pretended to have answers that she didn't have, and she was always concerned that she might grieve the Holy Spirit. She remained committed, submitted, honest, and sincere as long as she lived.

HOW CAN YOU MISS THE BLEACHERS?

In 1968, Kathryn ministered for Pat Robertson and his associate, Jim Bakker, to a crowd of over three thousand people. Shortly after the meeting began, a row of bleachers broke loose and fell back against the wall. Many fell to the floor or were suspended in the air. The emergency squad arrived and carried some away on stretchers. Folding chairs replaced the bleachers, and the meeting finally returned to normal – yet, Miss Kuhlman oblivious to it all, was half-way through her sermon!

Was it possible that Kathryn knew she would never return to the platform? Was it possible that, at that moment, she said good-bye to her earthly ministry?

During 1968, Kathryn traveled internationally to Israel, Finland, and Sweden. She was guest on *The Johnny Carson Show*, *The Dinah Shore Show*, and many others. Though Kathryn was very diplomatic and accepted among all kinds of people, she still manifested the power of the Holy Spirit in her life on all of these media programs. It was said that the employees of the CBS studios always knew when Kathryn entered the building, because the whole atmosphere seemed to change.

In 1975, though now in her late sixties and weakened from her physical ailment, Kathryn made a ministry trip to Jerusalem to speak at the Second World Conference on the Holy Spirit. Despite her age and ailments, she was still spunky when it came to ministry.

Kathryn Kuhlman was a special treasure. Her ministry pioneered the way for us to know the Holy Spirit in our generation. She attempted to show us how to fellowship with Him and how to love Him. She truly had the ability to reveal the Holy Spirit to us as our Friend.

Kathryn had heard that Bob Mumford was going to be a featured speaker there, and threatened to cancel her appearance because of it. She said his teachings on discipleship were complete heresy and she wouldn't participate. In the end though, Kathryn went to Israel and helped many of the Middle Easterners experience the ministry of the Holy Spirit.

IT IS WELL WITH MY SOUL

The last miracle service of Kathryn Kuhlman's ministry was held at the Shrine Auditorium in Los Angeles, California, on November 16, 1975. As she left the building, an employee in Miss Kuhlman's Hollywood office saw something she would never forget.

As everyone left the auditorium, Kathryn walked quietly to the end of the stage. She raised her head and slowly scanned the balcony, as if she was gazing at every seat. It seemed like an eternity. Then, Kathryn dropped her gaze to the second balcony, following every row and every seat with her eyes. Then, she looked at the ground floor, studying every seat.[35]

We can only imagine what was going through Kathryn's mind, the memories, the victories, the healings, the laughter, and the tears. Was it possible that Kathryn knew she would never return to the platform? Was it possible that, at that moment, she said good-bye to her earthly ministry?

In just a little over three weeks from that November date, Kathryn lay dying in the Hillcrest Medical Center of Tulsa, Oklahoma, after open-heart surgery.

By now, Kathryn had given complete control of her ministry to Tink Wilkerson, formerly in the automobile business in Tulsa, Oklahoma. Wilkerson is the son of the late Jeannie Wilkerson, who was a true prophetess of the Lord.

Wilkerson was with Kathryn for only a short ten months. She trusted Wilkerson. He was the one who chose where she would have the heart surgery. After her death, she left the majority of her estate to him. When the former Kuhlman staff was questioned about him, there was division. Some felt Wilkerson deceived Kathryn, others felt he was sent by God for her final hour. However, the media ran rampant with questions of why Wilkerson received so much of Kathryn's estate, and Maggie Hartner, her associate for years, received so little.

In 1992, Wilkerson was convicted in two U.S. district courts in Oklahoma for fraud in a former auto business. He was scheduled for release from prison in the summer of 1993 at which time he planned to write a book on his and his wife's friendship with Kathryn.[36] Wilkerson has kept quiet for all these years, possibly out of respect. I believe he has a story that needs to be told.

"I WANT TO GO HOME"

Oral and Evelyn Roberts were among a few of the visitors permitted to see Kathryn in Hillcrest Medical Center. As they walked into her room and went to her bedside to pray for her healing, Oral remembers a significant occurrence. "When Kathryn recognized that we were there to pray for her recovery, she put her hands out like a barrier and then pointed toward heaven." Evelyn Roberts looked at Oral and said, "She doesn't want our prayers. She wants to go home."

Kathryn's sister Myrtle received the same message from Kathryn. She told Wilkerson, "Kathryn wants to go home."[37]

The wonderful red-headed lady who introduced the ministry of the Holy Spirit to our generation and thrilled the hearts of millions, finally received her heart's desire. It was said that the Holy Spirit descended upon her one more time and her face began to shine. The nurse in her room noticed a glow that enveloped her bed, creating an indescribable peace.[38] At 8:20 P.M. on Friday, February 20, 1976, Kathryn Kuhlman went home to be with Jesus. She was sixty-eight years old.

Oral Roberts presided over her funeral at Forest Lawn Memorial Park in Glendale, California. Kathryn was buried in the same cemetery a half mile from Aimee Semple McPherson's vault. Oral had a vision, at Kathryn's death, that God would raise up and spread similar ministries throughout the world, making the magnitude of God's power greater than He did through Kathryn's life.

Kathryn Kuhlman was a special treasure. Her ministry pioneered the way for us to know the Holy Spirit in our generation. She attempted to show us how to fellowship with Him and how to love Him. She truly had the ability to reveal the Holy Spirit to us as our Friend. So no one can close this chapter as well as she:

"The world called me a fool for having given my entire life to One whom I've never seen. I know exactly what I'm going to say when I stand in His presence. When I look upon that wonderful face of Jesus, I'll have just one thing to say: 'I tried.' I gave of myself the best I knew how. My redemption will have been perfected when I stand and see Him who made it all possible."[39]

CHAPTER NINE, KATHRYN KUHLMAN

References

[1] Roberts Liardon, *Kathryn Kuhlman: A Spiritual Biography of God's Miracle Working Power* (Laguna Hills, CA: Embassy Publishing Company, 1990), 68.

[2] Helen Hosier, *Kathryn Kuhlman: The Life She Led, the Legacy She Left* (Wheaton, IL: Tyndale House Publishers, 1971), 38.

[3] Jamie Buckingham, *Daughter of Destiny: Kathryn Kuhlman... Her Story* (Plainfield, NJ: Logos International, 1976), 17-18.

[4] Hosier, *Kathryn Kuhlman: The Life She Led*, 32-33.

[5] Buckingham, *Daughter of Destiny*, 23.

[6] Hosier, *Kathryn Kuhlman*, 44.

[7] Buckingham, *Daughter of Destiny*, 70-71.

[8] Sermon by Kuhlman, "Not Doing What We Like, But Liking What We Have To Do."

[9] Buckingham, *Daughter of Destiny*, Chapter 3.

[10] Sermon by Kuhlman, "Guidelines for Life's Greatest Virtue."

[11] The Kathryn Kuhlman Foundation, *Heart to Heart with Kathryn Kuhlman*, 58.

[12] See Footnote 10.

[13] Buckingham, *Daughter of Destiny*, 57.

[14] Hosier, *Kathryn Kuhlman*, 60-64.

[15] Wayne E. Warner, *Kathryn Kuhlman: The Woman Behind the Miracles* (Ann Arbor, MI: Vine Books, segment of Servant Publications, 1993), 84, Footnote 5, 263.

[16] Ibid., 93-94.

[17] Buckingham, *Daughter of Destiny*, Chapter 5.

[18] Ibid., 88.

[19] Sermon by Kuhlman, "The Ministry of Healing."

[20] Warner, *Kathryn Kuhlman*, 104.

[21] Sermon by Kuhlman, "The Secret of All Miracles in Jesus' Life."

[22] Buckingham, *Daughter of Destiny*, 101-102.

[23] Warner, *Kathryn Kuhlman*, 120.

[24] Buckingham, *Daughter of Destiny*, 118-119.

[25] Personal Interview with Rolf McPherson, February 1996.

26 Warner, *Kathryn Kuhlman,* 203-205, 276, Footnote 4.

27 Ibid., 210.

28 Ibid., 162.

29 Buckingham, *Daughter of Destiny*, 147.

30 Warner, *Kathryn Kuhlman*, 234.

31 Ibid., 212.

32 Ibid., 220.

33 Ibid., 164.

34 Ibid., 186-189.

35 Ibid., 236.

36 Ibid., 242.

37 Ibid., 240.

38 Buckingham, *Daughter of Destiny*, 305.

39 "A Tribute to the Lord's Handmaiden," quoted from the *Abundant Life Magazine* (Tulsa, OK: Oral Roberts Evangelistic Association, May 1976), cover.

CHAPTER TEN

William Branham

"A Man of Notable Signs and Wonders"

"A MAN OF NOTABLE SIGNS AND WONDERS"

'You are of the devil, and deceiving the people,' he shouted, 'an imposter, a snake in the grass, a fake, and I am going to show these people that you are!' It was a bold challenge and everyone in the audience could see that it was not an idle threat.... It appeared to be an evil moment for the little figure on the platform, and most of them must have felt exceedingly sorry for him. Certainly they could see there was no room for trickery. The man on the platform would have to have the goods or else take the consequences.

"The seconds passed.... Presently it appeared that something was hindering the challenger from carrying out his evil designs. Softly but determinedly the voice of the evangelist...could be heard only a short distance.... 'Satan, because you have challenged the servant of God before this great congregation, you must now bow before me. In the name of Jesus Christ, you shall fall at my feet.'

"Suddenly he who a few minutes before had so brazenly defied the man of God with his fearful threats and accusations, gave an awful groan and slumped to the floor sobbing hysterically. The evangelist calmly proceeded with the service as if nothing had happened as the man lay writhing in the dust."[1]

William Branham was a humble, soft-spoken man familiar with tragedy, heartbreak, and poverty. Semiliterate by worldly standards, Branham was educated through supernatural occurrences. Gordon Lindsay, founder of Christ For the Nations, was a personal friend of Branham's, and his official biographer. He said Branham's life was "so out of this world and beyond ordinary" that if it had not been for documented truths, a person could, under normal circumstances, consider the stories of his life and ministry "far-fetched and incredible."[2]

Simple in his reasonings and poor in his command of the English language, Branham became the leader in the Voice of Healing revival that originated in the late forties. There were many healing revivalists who came to the forefront during this era and each had his or her own uniqueness. But none were able to combine the prophetic office, the supernatural manifestations, and divine healing as William Branham did.

> *Simple in his reasonings and poor in his command of the English language, Branham became the leader in the Voice of Healing revival that originated in the late forties.*

Sadly though, the final phase of his ministry carries a shadow. As this Branham chapter progresses, what is written will be shocking to some, and sad to others. Understand that the details are for instruction. Branham's life is a tragically sad illustration of what happens when one does not follow the times and seasons of heaven. However, the beginning of Branham's life and ministry is a tribute to the supernatural influence of God in the earth. If there is any "religious" tradition in you, the early life and times of William Branham will, no doubt, send a shock wave through your system.

A WHIRL OF LIGHT

Just as morning dawned on April 6, 1909, a small, five-pound baby boy was born in the hills of Kentucky. Pacing the dirt floor of the old cabin, the eighteen-year-old father was dressed in his new overalls for the occasion. The baby's mother, barely fifteen years old, held her new son as they decided his name: William Marrion Branham.

With the light beginning to break through the early morning skies, the grandmother decided to open a window so the Branhams could better see their new son. It was here the first supernatural occurrence happened to young Branham. In his own words, he tells the story as it was described to him:

"Suddenly, a light come whirling through the window, about the size of a pillow, and circled around where I was, and went down on the bed."[3]

Neighbors who witnessed the scene were in awe, wondering what kind of child had been born to the Branhams. As she rubbed his tiny hands, Mrs. Branham had no idea those same hands would be used by God to heal multitudes, and lead one of the greatest healing revivals to date.

Two weeks later, little William Branham had his first visit to a Missionary Baptist church.

DIRT FLOORS AND PLANK CHAIRS

William Branham's family was the poorest of the poor. They lived in the back hills of Kentucky, with dirt as their floor and planks as their chairs. These people were totally uneducated, as far as worldly standards go. So reading the Bible, or any book, was nearly impossible.

Living conditions were poor and there was little emphasis on serving God. The Branham family had a general knowledge of God, and that was about it. Theirs was a rugged environment, and they gave all their effort to survival. The Branhams went to church mainly as a moral duty, or occasionally as a social event.

When you understand Branham's background, it is easier to see why God used sovereign and supernatural signs to speak to William Branham. He didn't know how to read or study the Bible for himself. Branham didn't know how to pray, and throughout his youth, he never heard anyone pray.

Branham's cabin/birthplace near Berksville, Kentucky

If you do not know how to read, then you can't hear from God through His Word.

If you do not pray, then you can't hear from your inner voice, or spirit.

God is not limited to the confines of educational theology. He is God — and sometimes, He will call a person like William Branham to come along and break our religious molds. Religion wants us to forget that the word "supernatural" describes God's presence. It makes some people nervous when God breaks through the confines of their "religiosity."

If no one around you knows God, then there is no one to teach you.

In these kinds of situations God is left to convey His message to a person through signs and wonders. It is rare, but God is not limited because of ignorance and poverty. It happened then, and it can happen today. God will get His message to an individual, one way or another.

In the Old Testament, a donkey spoke to Balaam. It was the only way Balaam would hear the Word of the Lord.

God spoke to Moses through a burning bush. In the book of Acts, signs and wonders empowered believers to turn a dark, "religious" world upside down.

God is not limited to the confines of educational theology. He is God – and sometimes, He will call a person like William Branham to come along and break our religious molds. Religion wants us to forget that the word "supernatural" describes God's presence. It makes some people nervous when God breaks through the confines of their "religiosity."

It was God working through signs and wonders that caused Branham to know God, to understand God's call on his life, and eventually to walk in it.

SAVED FROM A FREEZING DEATH

The providence of God was with Branham from his birth. His father, working as a logger, had to be away from home for long periods of time. When Branham was only six months old, a severe snowstorm blanketed the mountains, trapping the young child and his mother inside their cabin. With firewood and food supply gone, death seemed certain. So Branham's mother wrapped herself and her baby in ragged blankets, and then they laid hungry and shivering in the bed to face their fate.

But "fate" cannot change God's plan. He was watching over them through the eyes of a neighbor. This neighbor, concerned that smoke was not coming from their chimney, trudged through the heavy snow to their cabin and broke through their door. Quickly he gathered wood for a warm fire and waded through the heavy snow back to his own cabin to get food for the Branhams. This man's goodness and alertness saved their lives.

Soon after this ordeal, Branham's father moved his family from the backwoods of Kentucky to Utica, Indiana, where he went to work as a farmer. Later, the family moved to Jeffersonville, Indiana, which would become known as the hometown of William Branham.

Although the family had moved to Jeffersonville, a moderately sized city, they remained extremely poor. At age seven, young Branham didn't even have a shirt to wear to school, only a coat. Many times he sat sweltering in the heat of the small school, embarrassed to take his coat off because he had no shirt underneath. God never chooses between the rich and the poor. God looks upon the heart.

THE WIND FROM HEAVEN

School had just ended for the day, and Branham's friends were going to the pond to fish. Branham wanted to go with them, but his father told him to draw water for that evening.

Branham cried as he drew the water, upset that he had to work instead of going fishing. As he carried the heavy bucket of water from the barn to the house, he sat down under an old poplar tree to rest.

Suddenly, he heard the sound of wind blowing in the top of the tree. He jumped up to look, and he noticed that the wind was not blowing in any other place. Stepping back, he looked up into the tree, and a voice came saying, "Never drink, smoke, or defile your body in any way, for I have a work for you to do when you get older."

Startled by the voice and shaking, the little boy ran home crying into the arms of his mother. Wondering if he had been bitten by a snake, she tried to calm him. Failing to soothe him, she put him to bed and called the doctor, fearful that he was suffering from some strange sort of nervous disorder.

For the rest of his childhood, Branham did everything he could to avoid passing by that tree.[4]

As strange as that experience may have been to Branham, he found that he could never smoke, drink, or defile his body. Several times, as a result of peer pressure, he tried. But as soon as he would lift a cigarette or drink to his lips, he would again hear that sound of the wind blowing in the top of the tree. Immediately, he would look around to see, but everything else was calm and still as before. The same awesome fear would sweep over him and he would drop the cigarette or the bottle and run away.

As a result of his strange behavior, Branham had very few friends as he was growing up. Branham said of himself, **"It seemed all through my life I was just a black sheep knowing no one who understood me, and not even understanding myself."** He often commented that he had a peculiar feeling, **"like someone standing near me, trying to say something to me, especially when I was alone."**[5] So Branham spent the years of his youth searching and frustrated, unable to answer or understand the call of God upon his life.

NO PLACE TO RUN

Although Branham had received supernatural manifestations in his life, he was not yet born again. When he was fourteen, he was injured in a hunting accident that left him hospitalized for seven months. Still, he didn't receive the urgency of God's call that pressed upon him. He had no idea what was happening to him. His parents weren't familiar with God, so he had no encouragement from them. All he had was his own limited knowledge, so he resisted the call of God.

At the age of nineteen, Branham made a decision to move, hoping that a new location would relieve him of this pressure. Knowing that he would meet with disapproval from his mother, he told her he was going to a campground that was only fourteen miles away from his home, when actually he was going to Phoenix, Arizona.

With new surroundings and a different way of life, Branham secured a day job on a local ranch. At night, he pursued a professional boxing career, and even won a few medals. But try as he might, Branham couldn't run from God even in the desert. As he looked out upon the stars at night, he would again sense the call of God upon him.

One day, he received news that his brother, Edward, who was closest to him in age, was seriously ill. Branham felt that, in time, everything would be all right, so he continued working at the ranch. Just a few days later, Branham received the heartbreaking news that his brother had died.

The grief was nearly unbearable for Branham. **"The first thing I thought of was,"** Branham recalled, **"whether he was prepared to die....Then again God called me, but as usual I tried to fight it off."**[6]

As Branham traveled home, tears ran down his cheeks as he thought of their childhood together. Remembering how hard things were for them, he wondered if God had taken Edward to a better place.

The death was very hard on the family, because no one knew God, and it was impossible for them to find peace. As a matter of fact, it was at his brother's funeral where Branham remembered hearing his first prayer.[7] It was here that he decided to learn to pray. After the burial, Branham intended to return to Arizona, but his mother begged him to stay at home. Branham agreed and found a job at the Gas Works in New Albany.

IN THE FACE OF DEATH

About two years later, while testing gas meters, Branham was overcome with the gas. The entire lining of his stomach was coated with chemical acid, and he suffered for weeks before seeking medical help from specialists.

The doctor diagnosed Branham with appendicitis and placed him in the hospital for surgery. Because he wasn't experiencing pain, Branham asked for a local anesthetic only. Then he could remain conscious and watch the surgery. Even though he was not yet born again, Branham asked a Baptist minister to go into surgery with him.

After surgery, Branham was moved to his room, where he found himself growing weaker and weaker. As the beating of his heart became fainter, he felt death upon him.

Gradually, the hospital room grew dark to Branham, and in the distance he heard the sound of wind. It seemed as if it were blowing through a forest, rustling the leaves of the trees. Branham remembered thinking, **"Well, this is death coming to take me."**

The wind came closer – and the sound grew louder.

"All at once, I was gone," Branham said. **"I was back again a little barefoot boy standing in the same lane, under the same tree. And I heard that same voice, 'Never drink or smoke.' But this time the voice said, 'I called you and you would not go.' The words were repeated the third time.**

"Then I said, 'Lord, if that is You, let me go back again to earth and I will preach Your Gospel from the housetops and street corners. I'll tell everyone about it!'"

Suddenly Branham awoke and saw that he was in his hospital room. He was feeling better, but the surgeon thought him to be dead. When he came in and saw Branham, he said, "I'm not a church-going man,...but I know God visited this boy."[8]

A few days later, Branham was released from the hospital, and true to his vow, he immediately began to seek the Lord.

HEALED! AND PROUD OF IT!

Branham searched from church to church, trying in vain to find one that preached repentance. Finally, in desperation, he went out to the old shed in back of his house and tried to pray. He had no idea of what to say, so he simply started talking to God as he would talk to anyone.

Suddenly, a light came and shown on the wall of the shed, forming a cross. Branham believed it was the Lord, as it seemed "a thousand pounds were lifted off him." It was there by that old shed that Branham was born again.

The accident he had suffered with chemical acid left Branham with strange side effects, and when he looked at anything too long, his head would shake. Branham told the Lord that if he was to preach, he would have to be fully healed. So he found a small, independent Baptist church that believed in healing, went forward for prayer and was healed instantly. Seeing the power this

Branham in his early years

church exhibited, Branham began to pray and seek God for that kind of power in his life. Six months later, he received his answer.

After accepting the call to preach, Branham was ordained an independent Baptist minister. Securing a small tent, he immediately began to minister with great results.

THERE'S THAT LIGHT AGAIN!

In June, 1933, at the age of twenty-four, Branham held his first major tent revival in Jeffersonville. As many as three thousand people attended in one night.

He conducted a water baptism service on June 11, immersing one hundred thirty people in the Ohio River. As he baptized the seventeenth person, another supernatural occurrence took place. In Branham's own words he describes it:

> *That autumn, the people who had attended his meetings built a tabernacle, calling it "Branham Tabernacle."*

> **"A whirl came down from the heavens above, here come that light, shining down...it hung right over where I was at...and it liked to a-scared me to death."**

Many of the four thousand on the river bank who saw the light, ran in fear, some remained and fell in worship. Some claimed to hear an actual voice, others didn't.[9]

That autumn, the people who had attended his meetings built a tabernacle, calling it "Branham Tabernacle." From 1933 to 1946, Branham was the bivocational minister of the Tabernacle while he worked at a secular job.

HIS WONDERFUL "HOPE"

It was during this happy time of the 1930s that Branham met a wonderful Christian girl. Her name was Hope Brumback. She met Branham's requirements; she never smoked or drank, and he loved her greatly.

After several months, Branham decided to ask Hope to marry him. But being too shy to speak with her, he did the next best thing and wrote her a letter. Fearing her mother would get the letter first, he hesitatingly slipped the letter in her mailbox. But Hope got the letter first and promptly answered, "Yes!"

The two were married shortly afterward, and Branham recalled, **"I don't believe there was any place on earth that was any happier than our little home."** Two years later, a son, Billy Paul, was born to the Branhams. As he described that moment, Branham said, **"When I first heard him cry in the**

hospital I seemed to know that he was a boy, and I gave him to God before I even saw him."[10]

A NEW DOSE OF POWER

The Great Depression of the 1930s soon hit the Branham Tabernacle, and times became a little hard. Soon Branham began to preach without compensation. He continued to work in a secular job to support his family. After saving some money, he decided to take a fishing trip to Michigan. All too soon, he ran out of money and started back home.

On the return trip, he saw a great group of people gathering for a gospel meeting and wondered what kind of people they were, so he stopped and had his first experience with "Pentecostalism."

The gathering was a "Oneness" camp meeting. (The Oneness people were a denomination of people who believed, as they explained it, in "Jesus only.") Branham was impressed with their singing and clapping. The longer he stayed, the more he realized there was something to this power they talked about.

That night, Branham drove his Model "T" into a cornfield and slept in the car. He was eager to return the next day. He had introduced himself as a minister, and that very day the leader announced that the group would like to hear from the next to the youngest minister there, William Branham.

Branham was so shocked, that he ducked in embarrassment. He didn't want anyone to know he was there. He had used his good trousers for a pillow the night before and was wearing an old pair of seersuckers.

The speaker again asked for William Branham to come to the platform, but Branham sat still, too embarrassed to respond. After all, no one knew who he was anyway, so he thought he was safe.

Finally, a man leaned over to him and asked, "Do you know who William Branham is?" Branham replied, **"It's me,"** but explained that he couldn't preach before these people appearing as he did. The man said, "They care more about your heart than how you look." The man stood up and pointing to Branham, yelled, "Here he is!"

Branham reluctantly walked up and took the platform, and as he began to preach, the power of God engulfed him and the meeting lasted two hours. Afterwards, pastors from all over the country approached Branham, asking him to come to their churches to conduct a revival. When Branham left, his calendar was filled for the year. These Oneness people had no idea they had just asked a Baptist to conduct weeks of meetings in their churches!

"TRASH" AND TRAGEDY

Branham raced home. As he pulled into their driveway, Hope ran out to meet him. Branham, excited from his experience, told Hope of the camp meeting and the meetings he had scheduled. She seemed as excited as he, but family and friends were not as jubilant. The main opposition came from Branham's mother-in-law who was adamant in her opposition. She exclaimed, "Do you know that's a bunch of holy rollers?...Do you think you'd drag my daughter out amongst stuff like that?....Ridiculous! That's nothing but trash that the other churches has throwed out."[11]

> *The main opposition came from Branham's mother-in-law who was adamant in her opposition. She exclaimed, "Do you know that's a bunch of holy rollers?..Do you think you'd drag my daughter out amongst stuff like that?... Ridiculous! That's nothing but trash that the other churches has throwed out."*

Influenced by his mother-in-law, Branham cancelled his meetings for the Oneness Pentecostals. Later, he regretted it as the greatest mistake of his life. If he had gone on to hold those meetings, his family would not have been in the great Ohio flood of 1937.

The winter of 1937 was severe. As heavy masses of snow began to melt, it caused the Ohio River to swell over its natural boundaries. Even the dikes and levees couldn't hold back the great swell of water.

The flood couldn't have come at a worse time for the Branhams. Hope had just had another baby, and this time they were blessed with a baby girl, whom they named Sharon Rose. Because of childbirth, Hope's immune system had not been completely restored, and as a result, she contracted a serious lung disease.

It was during Hope's convalescence that the levee on the Ohio River gave way to the force of water, which quickly flooded the area. The sirens blared out the warning that all must evacuate for their own safety. Hope was in no condition to be moved, yet there was no choice. Despite the cold and the rain, she was transported to a makeshift hospital on higher ground. Also, during this great flood of 1937, both Branham babies became seriously ill with pneumonia.

"WHERE'S MY FAMILY?"

As much as he wanted to stay with his loved ones, Branham knew he must help the town fight the rising flood. So he joined the rescue squad, only to

return to the hospital four hours later and find that flood waters had broken down the walls, and his family was gone.

Frantically, Branham searched for his family throughout the night. Finally, he was told they were placed on a train and sent to another town. Feverishly, he attempted to make his way to them, but the floodwaters trapped him. For two weeks he was marooned and unable to leave or hear any word regarding his family.

As soon as the waters went down, he left in his truck to search for his family. He didn't know if they were dead or alive. When he arrived at the next town where he supposed they were sent, no one knew of a hospital, much less about his family.

Totally despondent, Branham walked the streets with his hat in his hands, walking, praying, and crying out for his family. Someone recognized him and told him where his family had been sent, but the flood waters had cut off any travel to that city. Branham thanked the man and continued his search.

Suddenly, as if it were an act of God, he ran into a friend who told him that he knew where his family was, and that Branham's wife was near death. The two men searched until they found a way to bypass the flood waters, and by evening Branham and his friend pulled into the town and found his family.

"I WAS ALMOST HOME..."

The Baptist church in this town had been turned into a makeshift hospital. When Branham found Hope, he knelt down beside her bed, only to learn that the X-rays had shown tuberculosis creeping deeper and deeper into her lungs. Branham spoke with Hope softly, and she told him the children were with her mother. When he found them, their health was deteriorating as well.

Branham determined he would work and make whatever amount was necessary to see Hope and the children recover. One day while working, he received a call from the hospital. The doctor told Branham that if he wanted to see his wife alive, he needed to come right away.

Racing to the hospital, Branham ran through the door, where the doctor met him and took him straight to his wife's room. The sheet was already pulled over her face. Nevertheless, Branham grabbed her and shook her, crying, **"Honey! Answer me!...God, please let her speak to me once more."** And suddenly, Hope opened her eyes. She tried to reach out to Branham, but she was too weak.

She looked at her husband and whispered, "I was almost home. Why did you call me?" Then in her weak, faltering voice, she began telling Branham about heaven. She said, "Honey, you've preached it, you've talked of it, but you can't know how glorious it is."

Tearfully, she thanked Branham for being a good husband, then she began to grow quieter....Branham finishes the story this way: **"She pulled me down to her and kissed me good-bye....Then she went to be with God."**

As Branham drove home, alone in the darkness, everything he saw reminded him of Hope. His grief seemed unbearable. At home, thinking of his motherless babies, he fell asleep, only to be awakened by a knock at the door.

THE SADDEST NIGHT ON EARTH

"Billy, your baby is dying now," were the words from the man at the door.

Feeling that his life was at its very end, Branham got into the man's pick-up truck, and they transported baby Sharon to the hospital, but to no avail. X-rays showed the baby had spinal meningitis.

The hospital moved Sharon into the basement where they kept isolated cases. The fatal disease had twisted her little leg out of normal position, and the pain caused her eyes to cross. Unable to see her in such agony, Branham laid his hands on Sharon and prayed, asking God to spare her life. Sadly, Branham thought God was punishing him for not going on the Oneness revivals. Shortly after his prayer, baby Sharon joined her mother in heaven.[12]

In just one night, Branham had lost two of the three most precious people on earth to him. Only Billy Paul was left.

> *The next five-year period was a "wilderness experience" for Branham. No one seemed to understand. His Baptist church seemed to grow impatient with him, calling his visions demonic.*

Two days later, a heartbroken man buried his daughter in the arms of her mother. It seemed his grief was too great to be endured. Yet, in the coming years, the remembrance of those feelings would cause the tears of compassion to flood his cheeks as William Branham prayed for the sick.

THE WIND RETURNED

The next five-year period was a "wilderness experience" for Branham. No one seemed to understand. His Baptist church seemed to grow impatient with him, calling his visions demonic. They even suggested that the light which appeared at his birth probably indicated the presence of a demon in his life. They went on to warn Branham to stop the visionary experiences, or his ministry "would fall into disrepute."[13]

During these years, Branham married again. He said many times that he would have never done so, but Hope had asked him to, for the children's sake.

He continued to preach at the Branham Tabernacle, working as a game warden on the side. On May 7, 1946, a very beautiful spring day, Branham came home for lunch, and a friend came over. The two men were outside under a large maple tree when, according to Branham, **"It seemed that the whole top of the tree let loose...it seemed like something came down from that tree like a great rushing wind."**

His wife came running out of the house to see if he was all right. Trying to get control of his emotions, Branham sat down and told her the story of the past twenty years. At that point, he made a decision that he was going to find out, once and for all, what was behind this "wind." He said, **"I told her (his wife) and my child good-bye and warned her that if I didn't come back in a few days, perhaps I might never return."**

THE ANGEL OF THE LORD CAME

Branham went to a secluded place to pray and read the Bible. So deep was his travail that it seemed his soul would tear out of his body. **"Will You speak to me some way, God? If You don't help me, I can't go on,"** he cried.

That same night about 11:00 P.M., he noticed a light flickering in the room. Thinking someone was coming with a flashlight, he looked out the window, but saw no one. Suddenly, the light began to spread across the floor. Startled, Branham jumped up from his chair when he saw a ball of fire shining on the floor. Then he heard someone walking. As he looked, he saw the feet of a man coming toward him. As he continued up from the feet, he saw a man that appeared to be about two hundred pounds in weight, clothed in a white robe.

As Branham trembled in fear, the man spoke, "Fear not. I am sent from the presence of Almighty God to tell you that your peculiar life and your misunderstood ways have been to indicate that God has sent you to take a gift of divine healing to the peoples of the world."

THE ANGEL CONTINUED...

"If you will be sincere, and can get the people to believe you, nothing shall stand before your prayer, not even cancer."

Branham's first response was like Gideon's, of old. He told the angel that he was poor and uneducated, thus, he felt no one would accept his ministry or listen to him.

But the angel went on to tell Branham that he would receive two gifts as signs to vindicate his ministry. First, Branham would be able to detect diseases by a physical vibration in his left hand.

When the unclean disease in the afflicted person met with the supernatural power of God through Branham, it would set off a physical reaction, or, a vibration.

Some have made fun of this physical manifestation, or labeled it demonic. To comprehend the Word of the Lord, we must grasp the law of righteousness and the law of the Spirit, then formulate the principle. It is possible that the "vibration" can be accurately explained this way: When the unclean disease in the afflicted person met with the supernatural power of God through Branham, it would set off a physical reaction, or, a vibration. When the unclean meets the clean, *there is going to be a reaction!*

In later years, Gordon Lindsay witnessed this supernatural phenomenon. He said that the "electric, current like" vibration was so strong at times, it would instantly stop Branham's wristwatch. Lindsay went on to say that after the spirit was cast out of the person, Branham's "red and swollen" hand would return to normal condition.

The angel continued to instruct Branham, that when he felt the vibration, he was to pray for the person. If the vibration leaves, the person is healed. If not he was to "just ask a blessing and walk away."

THERE WILL BE A SECOND SIGN

Branham responded to the angel, **"Sir, I'm afraid they won't receive me."** The angel responded: "Then it will come to pass that you'll know the very secret of their heart. This they will hear."[14]

In connection with this second sign, the angel made this statement: "The thoughts of men speak louder in heaven than do their words on earth." Any sin in a person's life that was under the blood was never revealed. But if the sin was unconfessed or covered, it would be brought to light through this spiritual gift, the word of knowledge. When this occurred in his prayer line, Branham would step away from the microphone and speak privately with the person, leading him to an immediate repentance.

Was this a true visitation from God? Yes. How do we know? Because angels are sent to minister to the heirs of salvation (see Hebrews 1:14). Angels announced the birth of Jesus and ministered to Him throughout His life on earth. Throughout the Bible angels ministered, proclaiming the Word of the Lord to mankind.

The angel of the Lord will never reveal anything that is contrary to Scripture. He never adds anything to or takes anything away from the Word of God. In other words, the angel of the Lord neither invents an additional Bible nor does he distort Scripture. The Word of God is always the standard.

During his visit, the angel of the Lord went on to tell Branham many other things concerning his ministry. First, he said that Branham, an unknown preacher, would soon stand before thousands in crowded arenas. Second, He told him if he would be faithful to his call, the results would reach the world and shake the nations. The visitation lasted about half an hour.[15]

NO TIME WASTED

After the visitation from the angel, Branham returned to his home. The following Sunday evening, he told the people in the tabernacle of his visitation. Ironically, they fully believed his revelation.

The word of the Lord came to pass quickly. While Branham was speaking, someone came in and handed him a telegram. It was from a Rev. Robert Daughtery, asking Branham to come to St. Louis and pray for his daughter to be healed. He had exhausted the aid of physicians and felt that prayer was the only answer.

Branham had no money to make the trip. So the congregation quickly took an offering, collecting enough money for a round-trip train fare. He borrowed a suit of clothes from one of his brothers, and a coat from another. At midnight, members of the congregation escorted him to the train bound for St. Louis.

THE FIRST MIRACLE

The little girl in St. Louis lay dying from some unknown malady. The church had fasted and prayed for her, but to no avail. The best physicians of the city had been called, but were unable to diagnose her case.

Tears rolled down the cheeks of Branham as he walked toward the little girl. She was skin and bones and lay in bed, clawing at her face like an animal. She had become hoarse from screaming in pain. She had been in torment this way for three months.

Branham joined his prayer with the rest of them, but to no avail. He finally asked for a quiet place to be alone and seek the Lord. This became his pattern in his early ministry. In seeking the Lord, he would often see the answer through a vision. He would wait until the conditions were exactly as he saw in the vision, then he would act on what he had seen. The results were always immediate when he followed this pattern.

After a while, Branham marched confidently back to the house. He asked the father and the others, **"Do you believe that I am God's servant?"** "Yes!" they cried. **"Then do as I tell you, doubting nothing."** Branham proceeded to ask for several things, then prayed for the child, according to the vision the Lord had given him. Immediately, the evil spirit left the girl and she was healed. She lived to see a normal, healthy childhood.

When news of the healing spread, the people flocked to see Branham, but he withdrew from them, promising he would return later. He did return within a few weeks.

THE DEAD ARE RAISED

In June of 1946, Branham returned to St. Louis and conducted a twelve-day meeting to preach and pray for the sick. The tent was packed with many people standing outside, even in the torrential rains. Tremendous manifestations took place as the lame walked, the blind saw, and the deaf heard. A minister who had been blind for twenty years received his sight, a woman who rejected the Spirit of God fell dead outside the tent from a heart attack. Branham went out to her and prayed. She arose and found salvation in Jesus Christ. The healings multiplied and grew beyond count. Branham often stayed until 2:00 A.M., praying for the sick.

From St. Louis, he was asked to hold a revival in Jonesboro, Arkansas, where some twenty-five thousand people attended the meetings.[16] During this meeting, Branham slipped out of the service to go inside an ambulance where an elderly woman had died. After praying a simple prayer, the woman sat up and hugged her husband. There were so many people standing against the back door of the ambulance that it

> *Branham proceeded to ask for several things, then prayed for the child, according to the vision the Lord had given him. Immediately, the evil spirit left the girl and she was healed.*

could not be opened for Branham to leave. So the ambulance driver held his coat over the front window so Branham could leave through the front door.[17]

One woman, who had driven hundreds of miles, made a tearful attempt to describe to others the humility, compassion, and meekness of Branham. When she looked at Branham, she said "all she saw was Jesus," adding that "You will never be the same after seeing him."[18]

LET'S SPREAD OUT

In Arkansas, Branham acquired his first campaign manager, W. E. Kidson, an editor for *The Apostolic Herald*. This was the newsletter that had published the results of Branham's ministry. Kidson, being a die-hard pioneer of the Oneness doctrine, had introduced Branham to that denomination, and took him around to several small churches.

The year 1947 is remembered as a high-profile time for the Branham ministry. *Time* magazine published the news of his campaigns, and his ministry team took their first tour of the western states.

T. L. and Daisy Osborn were greatly influenced by his meetings in Portland, Oregon. They had just returned from India, where they had served as missionaries. They were defeated in vision and purpose, and nearly ready to quit the ministry.

The story is told that T. L. was present as Branham turned a little cross-eyed girl around to face the audience. As Branham laid his hands on her, T. L. watched as her eyes gradually straightened. It is said that T. L. heard these words, "You can do that! You can do that!" After the Branham meeting, the Osborns were refreshed, rekindled, and focused. They finally found the answer for which they were searching. The result was an incredible international missionary and healing ministry through the Osborns to the nations of the world.

It was also in 1947 that Branham met and joined with Gordon Lindsay. Jack Moore was a Oneness minister who had been traveling with Branham when they joined with Lindsay. Although Lindsay was a Trinitarian, the two men formed a coalition that proved imperative to Branham's success.

When Lindsay realized that an unprecedented divine move of God had begun, he urged Branham to take his ministry beyond the boundaries of the Oneness circles and into the Full Gospel circles. Realizing that Lindsay was being used to fulfill the words that came during his angelic visitation, Branham agreed. Lindsay was a master in organization, an attribute that Branham lacked. So Branham gave Lindsay the liberty to organize and promote one of the greatest healing revivals to this day.

Moore and Lindsay formulated the first Union Campaign in the fall of 1947. These meetings were to bring the Oneness and Trinitarian believers together in one great meeting. Held in the northwestern states and parts of Canada, the Union Campaign was well received because Branham's messages avoided doctrinal differences. The people attending experienced "their greatest religious experiences ever." Oftentimes, according to reports, as many as fifteen hundred people were born again in a single service. W. J. Ern Baxter joined the healing team in Canada, and wrote that as many as thirty-five thousand healings were manifested during that year of ministry.[19]

"VOICE OF HEALING" IS BORN

In an effort to give voice to this message of healing throughout the land, the Branham team devised a new method of publicity. They decided that a new publication should be created, which would circulate outside of the isolated Oneness congregations and into every realm of Christianity. Realizing again that this fulfilled the word of the Lord concerning him, Branham agreed. However, Kidson, his editor, didn't agree, so Branham relieved Kidson of his duties and appointed Lindsay and Moore as editors, and himself as publisher. Together, the team conceived *The Voice of Healing* magazine.

Originally, only one magazine was to be published, introducing Branham. But the demand was so great, the pilot magazine was reprinted several times. The team finally decided to publish *The Voice of Healing* on a monthly basis.

From that point on, Branham made it a key issue never to discuss doctrinal issues. He said:

"God didn't put His endorsement upon one particular church, but He revealed that the pure in heart would see God," Branham often added: "Let the fellow believe whatever he wants to about it. These things don't amount to very much anyhow. Be brothers, have fellowship with one another."

Branham often said that believers should be able to "disagree a million miles on theology," but if they ever came to the place where they couldn't embrace one another as brothers, then they should feel "backslid."[20]

EARLY TROUBLE

In 1948, Branham's ministry came to an abrupt halt when he suffered a nervous breakdown. He was physically and mentally fatigued from overwork in the ministry. Before hiring Lindsay as his campaign manager, he would pray until the early morning hours for those in the healing lines, totally exhausting himself. He did not know when to stop. His weight dropped considerably, and rumors began to circulate that Branham was dying.

As a result, Lindsay, administrator of his campaigns, cut Branham's ministry time to one hour or less each evening, and visitors were no longer allowed in Branham's hotel room. Lindsay expanded Branham's meetings, but wisely cut down on the interruptions and excesses.

When Branham experienced his breakdown, he began to point fingers at those he blamed for the illness. He accused Lindsay of overextending him. Then he informed Lindsay and Moore that in the future *The Voice of Healing* magazine would be their sole responsibility.

Lindsay was shocked at Branham's accusations. He had just planned an extensive healing campaign for Branham, and felt deserted when *The Voice of Healing* magazine was dropped in his lap. But he continued to publish the magazine, expanding the articles to cover other healing ministries. Although they continued to work together, Lindsay and Branham's close relationship never quite recovered from that point on.

During this time, other healing evangelists began to surface. Oral Roberts, who had entered the ministry one year after Branham, requested that everyone pray for Branham's restoration. Six months later, Branham suddenly appeared back on the scene, claiming he was miraculously healed. His return was greeted by his followers with great excitement.

Branham held his first major crusade after his illness in 1950. It was at this time that F. F. Bosworth, the great healing evangelist from the 1920s, had now joined the Branham team. Crowds of over eight thousand people came to a single service.

It was here that the most famous photo of Branham's ministry was taken. It is known as the "halo" photo. A Baptist pastor had challenged Branham to a debate on healing. Branham accepted. The Baptist hired a photographer to capture the event. It was one of the pictures taken there that featured a halo of light resting over Branham's head. Lindsay immediately had the photo authorized and documented as an original, certifying that no make-overs or touch-ups were performed on either the photo or negative.

SHAKING NATIONS

In April of 1950, Branham traveled to Scandinavia, making him the first Voice of Healing evangelist to travel to Europe.

Before going to Europe, Branham had a vision of a little boy being hit by a car and being raised from the dead. He told this vision throughout America.

While in Finland, Branham's car was behind a car that had struck two small boys. Branham's party picked up one boy and proceeded to the hospital. Realizing his pulse and circulation had stopped, Branham knelt on the floor of the car and prayed for God's mercy. The boy came back to life and began to cry. He was released from the hospital three days later. The next day, Branham received a vision showing him that both boys would live.

Realizing his pulse and circulation had stopped, Branham knelt on the floor of the car and prayed for God's mercy. The boy came back to life and began to cry.

The associate who was traveling with him wrote Branham's first vision about the boy on a piece of paper at the time the vision occurred, and placed the piece of paper in his wallet. After the incident happened, it is said the associate pulled the paper out of his wallet and read it to Branham. It was the exact vision Branham had told throughout America.

He had also received many prayer requests from Africa, some of which were accompanied by a plane ticket. In the fall of 1951, Branham and his ministry team traveled to South Africa. They held campaigns through December. It is reported that the meetings were the greatest ever in South Africa, with crowds estimated to be fifty thousand in number, with thousands turned away.

The city of Durban had a population of well over two hundred thousand people. Every bus in the city was put to work, and still all the people could not be transported to the Branham meetings. The results were so incredible, that a book entitled, *A Prophet Visits South Africa*, was written to describe it.

HOW DID HE OPERATE?

Branham's personality was captivating. He didn't have a charismatic, exuberant personality, but was best remembered for his humility and humble origins. He often apologized for his lack of education and cultural abilities. Branham couldn't speak well before crowds. When he did speak, it was usually with a very quiet and stuttering voice. Branham usually left the preaching to Bosworth and others, then he ministered divine healing to the multitudes.

Everything about his ministry was geared toward the supernatural. He refuted any person who was led by intellectualism, and would not permit them to be on the platform with him. His entire ministry team focused on creating an atmosphere in which divine healing could manifest. Baxter and Bosworth preached in the morning and afternoon services. Baxter preached in his evangelistic role, while Bosworth gave special instructions for receiving and maintaining healing. Lindsay, the coordinator of the campaigns, would handle the altar calls. Though Branham insisted his primary role was praying for the sick, he always spoke in the evening services.

Since the demand for a Branham campaign was so great, his meetings became limited to a few nights in each city. To handle the flow of people, Lindsay devised and authored a small booklet, *Divine Healing in the Branham Meetings*, that was widely distributed in a city before the team came to town. Unlike the earlier healing evangelists, Branham couldn't spend weeks instructing the people on healing before he prayed for them. This booklet served as a teaching tool for those seeking healing. As a result, they came ready to receive and Branham was able to pray for them during the first night of his campaign.

Branham avoided all personal interviews prior to the night services. Most of the time, he spent three days of prayer and fasting before each campaign.

Branham would not pray for people until he sensed his angel standing at his right side.

"Without this consciousness," Bosworth said, "he seems to be perfectly helpless. When he is conscious of the angel's presence, he seems to break through the veil of the flesh into the world of the Spirit, to be struck through and through with a sense of the unseen."

A few witnesses claimed they had seen the angel standing beside Branham. However, the majority that noticed the presence, usually described it as a "heavenly light." Bosworth wrote that in the 1951 South African campaign, a light was seen over the heads of the people whose faith had reached the necessary level. While under the anointing, Branham would recognize that light.[21]

When Branham prayed for the people in a prayer line, he directed them to line up on his right side as well. This way, he felt the people received a double dose of power because they passed by the angel and Branham. The Branham team used the popular "prayer cards," where each person was given a card with a number on it, and the numbers were randomly called during the service. Branham also prayed over handkerchiefs to be carried to the afflicted (see Acts 19:12).

HIS DOCTRINE IN THE EARLY DAYS

Branham believed that healing was the finished work of Calvary. He also believed that all sickness and sin were caused by Satan. **"What doctors call 'cancer,' God calls it a devil,"** Branham preached.[22]

Branham also had a strong deliverance ministry. Along with sin and sickness, he identified insanity, temper tantrums, disbelief, and lustful habits as the work of demons. Branham didn't believe that deliverance healed a person, but he did believe it cleared a pathway for healing to have entrance.

Before Branham would cast out demons in his services, he would stop and tell the skeptics present that he couldn't be responsible for what "evil fate befell them."[23]

If a person desired healing in his meetings, the person must do two things: (1) believe and confess that Jesus died for his healing and (2) believe that Branham was the prophet of God sent to administer healing.

Branham believed that faith was a sixth sense. To him, faith was believing what God has revealed. People lost their healing because they quit believing what had been revealed to them. **"As faith kills it [disease], unbelief resurrects it,"** Branham reasoned.[24] A person didn't have to be a Christian to be healed, but they must become a Christian to remain healed, according to Branham.

While Branham supported the work of physicians, he also believed their work was limited. He felt that medicine merely "kept the body clean while God performed the healing." Branham asserted, **"There's not one speck of medicine ever did cure any sickness."** It is said that Branham would "bristle" when one described divine healing as fanaticism. He would respond by stating that **"medicine was never defined as fanaticism when a person died from incorrect medical treatment."**[25]

Branham was also against the prosperity of Christians, especially ministers. He often claimed that he could have been a millionaire from the revenue of his ministry, but chose not to be, refusing great gifts of wealth by stating, **"I want to be like the people who come to be prayed for."** When he finally accepted a Cadillac as a gift, he kept it in his garage for two years, out of embarrassment.[26]

HE BEGAN TO SLIP...

Branham remained very influential in the ministry of divine healing for nine years. During this time, healing evangelists began to surface all over the country, operating through great signs and wonders. In 1952, at one of the heights in the Voice of Healing revival, forty-nine prominent healing evangelists were featured in *The Voice of Healing* magazine. The revelation of divine healing had reached an all-time peak across the world. But from that year on, the healing revival fires began to dwindle. By 1955, Branham began to experience difficulties, and his ministry took on a radical change.

LOST LINDSAY

Gordon Lindsay was one of the greatest things that could have happened to the ministry of William Branham. Lindsay had the Word and Branham had the gift. Lindsay also had the organizational skills that would enhance Branham's gift and ministry. Obviously, they were a ministry team made in heaven.

But Branham refused to acknowledge the worth of Lindsay. Instead, he pointed fingers at him, accused him, and abandoned him to some degree. I firmly believe the Lord had ordained Lindsay to help Branham, because Branham couldn't make it by himself. Therefore, I also believe that Branham's disassociation with Lindsay was a great mistake, and that Branham plunged into doctrinal error because of it.

SURROUNDED BY "YES" MEN

Due to Branham's coolness toward him, added to the fact that his own ministry was growing, Lindsay left the Branham team after four years. The men who replaced Lindsay were far from his caliber in character and integrity.

Branham was unable to match the wits and sophistication of those who came to take subtle advantage of him. It was a widely publicized fact that Branham had no business sense and could really care less about it. With the hedge of protection that came with Lindsay's management gone, many felt that Branham's managers took advantage of him and his ministry funds by using them for themselves and their own wealth. During Lindsay's management, Branham's ministry had always excelled financially, but under new administration, the ministry was hurting for money. It became so bad, that Branham thought he would have to leave the ministry and go to work at a secular job.

Branham's crowds were down in number, and soon the ministry took on a $15,000 deficit. Branham's mail count had dropped from one thousand letters a day to approximately seventy-five.

In the height of the revival, Branham's carelessness in financial matters didn't seem to show. But now that things were tight, his carelessness brought the attention of the Internal Revenue Service. In 1956, a tax-evasion suit was brought against the evangelist. Despite his objections, Branham incurred a $40,000 out-of-court settlement, a debt he carried for the rest of his life.[27]

Eventually, Branham found that a cult had formed around his personality. As other healing evangelists began to come to the forefront, these men would pacify Branham's ego. They encouraged Branham in his weird visions, claiming him to be the new Elijah, the forerunner of Christ's return, and the head of the seventh Church age. They claimed that only Branham could carry this calling of the Laodicean messenger, no one else would be able to impersonate it.

By 1958, there were only about a dozen prominent healing evangelists. It was evident to everyone that the glory days of the Voice of Healing revival had come to a close. It was now time to seek the Lord and find the roles to be played in the next move of God.

HE DID NOT STAY IN HIS CALLING

Branham didn't take the change well, in fact, he never made the transition at all. Instead of seeking the Lord for his place of ministry in the next move of God, he turned to radical doctrine and sensationalism. Branham took on the office of the teacher by his own will, not by the command of God.

It is possible that through his prophetic gift, Branham saw the awakening of the teaching gift that would move on the earth through the Word of Faith Movement, which began in the late 1970s. He obviously jumped ahead of its timing, perhaps hoping to regain his status as the leader of it. Branham failed to realize that he was already an undeniable leader in the Church world, he just needed to get back into his calling.

God didn't call Branham to be a teacher, because he didn't know the Word. As a result, disturbing doctrines were taught and emphasized through his ministry. Everything he had stood for in the former days of ministry seemed to have escaped him.

Eventually, Branham found that a cult had formed around his personality. As other healing evangelists began to come to the forefront, these men would pacify Branham's ego. They encouraged Branham in his weird visions, claiming him to be the new Elijah, the forerunner of Christ's return, and the head of the seventh Church age.

Without a doubt, this great mistake caused his life to end early and continues to overshadow his ministry today.

Oral Roberts attended the Branham campaign in Kansas City in 1948. The above is a rare photograph showing, from left to right, Young Brown, Jack Moore, William Branham, Oral Roberts, and Gordon Lindsay

The Voice of Healing Convention of leading evangelists in December of 1949, which Brother Branham attended. Back row, left to right: Orrin Kingsriter, Clifton Erickson, Robert Bosworth, H. C. Noah, V. J. Gardner, H. T. Langley, Abraham Tannenbaum.... Middle Row: Raymond T. Richey, William Branham, Jack Moore, Dale Hanson, O. L. Jagger, Gayle Jackson, F. F. Bosworth, Gordon Lindsay....Front row: Mrs. Erickson, Mrs. Kingsriter, Mrs. Lindsay, Miss Anna Jeanne Moore, Mrs. Bosworth, Mrs. Jackson, and Mrs. Langley

Preaching the Word!

Branham in South Africa

Branham with F. F. Bosworth

Ministering in a Spanish church, Phoenix, Arizona, 1947

Gordon Lindsay, William Branham, and W. V. Grant in Dallas, Texas, 1964

The famous halo photo

HE DID IT HIS WAY

Branham claimed to have strange spiritual visions that seemed to make him ever-searching and driven for their fulfillment. Throughout the 1960s, he lamented his decline in popularity, noting that other evangelists had surpassed him.[28] It had become a competitive race to him.

Branham tried to push his popularity through doctrinal teaching, which, according to him, was given by prophetic revelation. By abusing his gift, the prophecies became warped. Instead of using his prophetic ability to call the hearts of men back to God, he tried to predict international events.

BRACE YOURSELF..

When you read a sample of these doctrines, you will understand why it was such a great mistake for Branham to allow Lindsay to leave. If Lindsay had remained, all the other mistakes would have been sorted out of Branham's life. Here is a sample of the shocking "prophetic" doctrines Branham taught until the end of his life.

NO ETERNAL HELL

Introduced as new revelation, Branham taught that there was no eternal hell. He said that hell was forever, but not for eternity. Forever, to him, meant a period of time. After this period of time, those in hell would be annihilated.[29]

SEED OF THE SERPENT

He also taught that women weren't a created product of God, but were merely a by-product of man. He even suggested that animals were a higher rank of species than women because they were created from nothing. Their secondary status, according to Branham, marked women as **the most easily deceived and deceitful beings on earth.**

Branham also taught that women carried the seed of the Serpent. This doctrine taught that Eve and the Serpent had sexual relations in the Garden and created Cain. Branham said that God had meant for multiplication to come from the dust of the earth, as occurred with Adam, but Eve's action with Satan altered that plan. Because of Eve and her sexual relationship with Satan, the inferior method of procreation came about. According to Branham, every woman carries the literal seed of the devil.

Branham once said:

"Everytime that a funeral goes down the street, a woman caused it...Everything that's wrong, a woman caused it. And then put her head of the church...shame on her."[30]

Because of this hereditary and disgraceful act with Satan, Branham argued that women weren't qualified to be preachers. He also taught that Eve's supernatural offspring, Cain, built great cities where scientists and intellectualism were born. Therefore, to Branham, every scientist and every intellectual person who rejects the supernatural nature of the Gospel, is from the seed of the Serpent.[31]

Branham taught that denominationalism was the mark of the beast, that the Protestants were the harlots and the Catholics were the Beast.

DIVORCE

According to Branham, since women introduced men to sex, polygamy was brought about. Women had to be punished. So men could have many wives, but women only one husband. Branham taught that when Jesus spoke on divorce, He was speaking to the woman, not the man. A woman couldn't remarry under any circumstances. But a man could divorce whenever he wanted to and remarry a virgin.[32]

MARK OF THE BEAST

Branham taught that denominationalism was the mark of the beast, that the Protestants were the harlots, and that the Catholics were the Beast. From a vision, he insinuated, (though never formally acknowledged) that he was THE end-time messenger, and THE Laodicean prophet, who could reveal the seventh seal in the book of Revelation. He predicted that the destruction of the United States would begin in 1977.[33]

HIS MOUTH HAD THE POWER

Branham felt that there would come a day in his ministry where the "spoken Word" from his mouth would change physical bodies into glorified bodies for the Rapture. This tremendous power would be unleashed because Branham's words would restore God's original name of JHVH. Previously, the name had never been pronounced correctly, however "Branham's mouth was specially formed to say it."[34]

ONENESS

Although he denied it at the beginning of his ministry, Branham now openly declared the Oneness doctrine. However, Branham criticized the "Jesus Only" churches, citing that **"there were many people named 'Jesus,' but there is only one Lord Jesus Christ."** He would teach one day that Trinitarians weren't born again, then on other days, he would declare that only some were. He even prophesied stating that **"Trinitarianism is of the devil,"** then commanded everyone listening to the tape of that message to be baptized in the name of Jesus Christ.[35]

He often changed in his salvation doctrine as well. At times, he would say that **"anyone could be saved."** Then, he would be heard speaking in line with Calvinistic doctrine. He would say, **"There was millions that would do it if they could, but they can't. It's not for them to have it."**[36]

A following was born out of this group of disciples. They called themselves "The Messengers." Today, they are also known as "The Branhamites." These churches are not affiliated with any denomination, since Branham detested that form of organization. They are followers of Branham, believing him to be the Laodicean messenger for this church age. To this day, a large portrait of Branham hangs in the church, introducing him as their "pastor."

The Messengers, or the Branhamites, are a worldwide movement. In fact, the fourth largest church in the nation of Zaire is of this group.[37]

THE STORY OF HIS DEATH

Branham preached his last message during Thanksgiving week of 1965 at Jack Moore's church. Though Moore disagreed with Branham's doctrine, he remained friends with him throughout his ministry.

On December 18, 1965, while traveling back to Indiana via Texas, Billy Paul Branham was driving the car in front of Branham and his wife. A drunk driver swerved and missed Billy Paul, but crossed the middle line and hit Branham's car head on.

Turning his car around, he headed to the scene of the accident. Jumping out of his car, he noticed that Branham had gone through the windshield and back again.

Checking his father, Billy Paul noticed that his bones were broken, but there was a pulse. In checking Mrs. Branham, there was no pulse. She was obviously dead.

Suddenly, Branham stirred. Upon seeing his son, he asked, **"Is Mom okay?"**

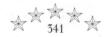

Billy Paul answered, "Dad, she's dead." Then Branham said, **"Just lay my hand on her."**

Billy Paul picked up Branham's bloodied hand and placed it on Mrs. Branham. Instantly, a pulse returned and she revived.[38]

William Branham remained in a coma for six days before dying December 24, 1965. Mrs. Branham lived.

Though saddened by his death, the Pentecostal world was not surprised. Gordon Lindsay wrote in his eulogy that Branham's death was the will of God. He said, **"God may see that a man's special ministry has reached its fruition and it is time to take him home."**[39]

I think it is interesting to note that Lindsay had accepted the interpretation of the young evangelist, Kenneth E. Hagin, from Tulsa, Oklahoma. God had told Hagin of Branham's death two years before it happened. In a prophetic word spoken through Hagin, the Lord said that He was "removing the prophet" from the scene. Branham died exactly when the Lord told Hagin he would.

Hagin was conducting a meeting when the news came of Branham's accident. Hagin called the saints to the front of the altar to pray. As Hagin himself knelt to pray, the Spirit of the Lord spoke to him saying, "What are you praying for? I've told you that I'm taking him." Hagin got up, unable to pray any further.

Because of Branham's disobedience to his call and the creation of doctrinal confusion, Hagin believed that God had to remove the "father" of the healing revival from the earth.

Four times the Holy Spirit had told Lindsay that Branham was going to die, and that he was to tell him. But Lindsay couldn't get through the barrier of "yes" men that surrounded Branham.

Finally, he got through the barrier, and slipped through to Branham unannounced. He attempted to reason with Branham. He asked Branham, "Why don't you function where God wants you and manifest the gift God's given you? Stay there! Don't try to get over into this other ministry."

Branham said simply, **"Yeah, but I want to teach."**[40]

Branham had an incredible healing gift. But having no Bible knowledge to match it, he turned into a doctrinal disaster. Ignorance is not bliss, especially

> *Branham had an incredible healing gift. But having no Bible knowledge to match it, he turned into a doctrinal disaster. Ignorance is not bliss, especially when you affect the multitudes with your words.*

when you affect the multitudes with your words. God had given Branham a great gift, He couldn't take it back. That gift was misleading people, causing them to follow Branham's doctrine, so God practiced His sovereign right in 1 Corinthians 5:5; "To deliver such an one unto Satan for the destruction of the flesh, that the spirit may be saved in the day of the Lord Jesus." Actually, it was an act of mercy on God's behalf. It is believed that He saved Branham from hell.

UNABLE TO RESURRECT

Although the funeral was held December 29, 1965, Branham's body was not buried until Easter of 1966. All sorts of rumors were circulating. One was that his body was being embalmed and refrigerated. Many of his followers were believing Branham would be raised from the dead. Whatever the reason, the official statement came from his son on January 26, 1966, at a Memorial Service.

It was said that Mrs. Branham had requested the delay in burial because she was trying to make a decision whether to move to Arizona or remain in Indiana. She wanted his body buried where she chose to live. Until she decided, Branham's body remained in the attic of the funeral home.

Still, there remained great hope among The Messengers that Branham would be raised on Easter Sunday. Branham's son affirmed that his father claimed Easter to be the time of the year that the Rapture would take place.

Reluctantly, and with great disappointment, William Branham was buried on April 11, 1966. His grave monument is a large pyramid with an eagle on top. (Unfortunately, the eagle keeps being stolen.) Branham is memorialized as being the only person to open the seventh seal, as the head of the seventh church age.

Branham's followers refuse to see him as a human being, and rumors of his return continued to circulate even through the 1980s. Each year, Branham Tabernacle continues to have a special Easter Service, in which the followers listen to Branham's taped sermons. Some of them still secretly hope for his return at that time. It is said that the current pastor does not encourage speculation of Branham's resurrection, however, the Branhamites have never accepted his death.[41]

LEARN THE LESSON

The story of William Marrion Branham was not written for criticism. I believe it contains a lesson more powerful than this one chapter can hold.

The lesson here is this: Do what God says to do, nothing more and nothing less. There is no game here. There is one move, and it belongs to God. Your job is to follow it.

In this generation, heaven must determine the timing of your life and your church as a whole. You are either in the will of God, or out of it. Your call must stay with the timing of heaven.

All Branham wanted was to be a voice. If he had remained in the plan of God, Branham could have been one of the greatest voices that had ever lived. His greatness in the ministry is never to be forgotten or discounted, his gift was legitimate. *But we must understand that great error comes from not having both the Word and the Spirit working together in our lives.*

Many of us weren't yet alive when these men and women of God had their great ministries. As a result, we didn't have the opportunity to watch and study their lives. And this is the reason I wrote this book. So study what you have read, and learn from it. Cry out to God to help you in the things you are unsure of. Ask Him to train you and teach you how to operate through His Spirit and within His timing. Follow His exact plan all the days of your life, and never deviate from it because of your own ideas, or pressure from others. Your anointing will only come when you follow the plan that God has outlined for you. So embrace that plan, and hold to it tightly. Then, run strong with it and do mighty exploits, in Jesus' Name.

CHAPTER TEN, WILLIAM BRANHAM
References

[1] Gordon Lindsay, *A Man Sent From God* (Jefferson, IN: William Branham, 1950), 23-25.

[2] Ibid., 11.

[3] C. Douglas Weaver, *The Healer-Prophet, William Marrion Branham: A Study of the Prophetic in American Pentecostalism* (Macon, GA: Mercer University Press, 1987), 22.

[4] Lindsay, *William Branham*, 30-31.

[5] Ibid., 31.

[6] Ibid., 38-39.

[7] Weaver, *The Healer-Prophet*, 25.

[8] Lindsay, *William Branham*, 39-41.

[9] Weaver, *The Healer-Prophet*, 27.

[10] Lindsay, *William Branham*, 46.

[11] Weaver, *The Healer-Prophet*, 33.

[12] Lindsay, *William Branham*, 52-63.

[13] Weaver, *The Healer-Prophet*, 34.

[14] Lindsay, *William Branham*, 76-80 and Weaver, *The Healer-Prophet*, 75.

[15] Lindsay, *William Branham*, 75-79.

[16] Ibid., 93.

[17] Ibid., 94.

[18] Ibid., 102.

[19] Weaver, *The Healer-Prophet*, 46-47.

[20] Ibid., 54.

[21] Ibid., 72, 74.

[22] Ibid., 62.

[23] Ibid., 63.

[24] Ibid., 65.

[25] Ibid., 66-67.

[26] Ibid., 109.

[27] Ibid., 94.

[28] Ibid., 96.

[29] Ibid., 118-119.

[30] Ibid., 110-113.

[31] Ibid., 113.

[32] Ibid., 112.

[33] Ibid., 116.

[34] Ibid., 138-139.

[35] Ibid., 120.

[36] Ibid., 121-122.

[37] Ibid., 152-153.

[38] Personal interview with Billy Paul Branham.

[39] Weaver, *The Healer-Prophet*, 105.

[40] Kenneth E. Hagin, *Understanding the Anointing* (Tulsa, OK: Faith Library Publications, 1983), 60-61.

[41] Weaver, *The Healer-Prophet*, 153-155.

Jack Coe

"The Man of Reckless Faith"

"THE MAN OF RECKLESS FAITH"

66 "I went before the judge and he asked me if I was guilty of disturbing the peace. I replied, 'Whose peace?'

'Well,' he replied, '...you folks clap your hands and shout, and other such things as that.' 'Judge, is it not true that people at the ball game make a lot of noise, and do I not hear them yell, shout, and clap their hands also?'

"He answered, 'Well, their hand clapping doesn't seem to bother anyone, but when you folks do it, people just can't sleep.'

"I asked, 'Judge, do you want to know what the difference is?' He answered, 'Yes, I'd like to know.'

"'The difference is that the Holy Ghost is in our shout, and it bothers the neighbors, keeping them awake...and it causes the beer joints to close their doors.'"[1]

Jack Coe was a large, domineering man with a tactless sense of humor in the healing tent. And he was a loving, compassionate "father" figure to the orphans in his children's home. As one of the main leaders in the Voice of Healing revival, Coe was either greatly loved, or greatly despised. He was raised without a father, so he learned as an adult to make God his Father. As a result, he had no problem putting men – no matter how high their denominational title – in their place, that is, if they tried to override the voice of God. The revivalist's dynamic personality left little room for a lukewarm response!

Coe was considered a radical evangelist because he, along with others, was doing much to combat racial prejudice in the Church. At a time when society was calling for segre-

Coe was considered a radical evangelist because he, along with others, was doing much to combat racial prejudice in the Church. At a time when society was calling for segregation, Coe strongly encouraged all races and cultures of the community to participate in his meetings.

gation, Coe strongly encouraged all races and cultures of the community to participate in his meetings.

A DESOLATE CHILDHOOD

Jack Coe was born on March 11, 1918, to Blanche and George Coe of Oklahoma City, Oklahoma. He was one of seven children. Blanche had been raised a Baptist, but when Jack was born it isn't certain that she was born again. It is believed that his father was born again at a Billy Sunday meeting, but George never attended church afterwards.

Coe's grandparents were Christians, so his father had been raised in a good home. Besides the positive atmosphere, his grandparents were also excellent providers, and left a considerable inheritance for Coe's father. But their solid principles of stewardship never seemed to rub off on his father, George. He had a bad habit of gambling and drinking. His mother tried to attend church for awhile, but since George wouldn't go with her, she stopped going too. Coe always believed things would have gone differently for his family if his mother would have continued in church and sought to pray for his father.

When Coe was five years old, a moving van backed up to their home. When he saw it, he got all excited, thinking something new was being delivered. He watched as the men approached his mother and spoke to her. Then he watched his mother turn pale and break out in tears. As he watched the men, young Coe realized that nothing new was coming out from that truck. Instead, these men were removing from their home what furniture they had! George had left them all after gambling away every possession in their home – and these men were coming to collect!

As the van pulled away, his mother was left to face the future with her seven children, having no one to turn to. So she knelt on the porch and began to pray. It was the first time Coe saw his mother pray!

Things got worse. The next day, a man came to see their house. Thinking he came to buy it, Blanche informed him that it wasn't for sale. "I didn't come to buy the house," the man said, "it's already mine! I'm very sorry, but you'll have to move out." It was unbelievable. His father had also gambled away their home.[2]

"NO DICE, MR. COE!"

Blanche Coe moved her children to Pennsylvania, where she tried to make a life for them. They lived in a basement. As Coe's older sister watched after the children, Mrs. Coe worked doing laundry by day and went to nursing school by night. It was a terrible struggle for all of them.

Then one day, Coe's father showed up at their door. He pleaded with Blanche to come back to him, and he promised to quit gambling. Feeling that life had been too difficult by herself, she reunited with him, and George took his family back to Oklahoma. The gambling started all over again, and this time, Blanche Coe left George for good. But she kept her daughter and left Jack and his brothers with their father.

NO ONE WANTED HIM

The young boys were often left alone as their father went to gamble. Many times they had nothing to eat. It wasn't long until Mrs. Coe returned for the boys and took them with her.

By the time Coe was nine years old, his mother felt overwhelmed by the responsibility of caring for her children alone. So she took Coe and his brother to a large home. Then after talking to the people and saying her good-byes, she turned and walked away, leaving young Coe and his brother standing on the steps of an orphanage.

Of this experience Coe would later write:

When he turned seventeen, he started to drink and carouse, and before long, he too, like George, had become an alcoholic.

"I thought to myself, dad didn't want me, and now mother...the only friend I've ever had...she's turned her back on me and left me. I thought my heart would break within me as I saw her going down that walk. For a long time I stood and cried."[3]

He didn't know that his mother also cried for days.

Coe's brother, who was three years older than him, would later run away from the orphanage. After hopping railroad cars and stealing a bicycle, he was hit by a car on the highway and was killed instantly. At the funeral, young Jack felt even more alone.

NO FRIEND IN THE BOTTLE

Coe remained at the orphanage for eight years. During this time, he knew very little about God. When he turned seventeen, he started to drink and carouse, and before long, he too, like his father, had become an alcoholic.

There were times during his alcoholic enslavement when Coe sought to know God. But everyone who went to the church he attended occasionally, lived uncommitted lives. They didn't have his answers. So, he sank more deeply into sin.

Soon, Coe's health began to suffer. He had developed ulcers in his stomach due to the alcohol, and his heart was beating twice as fast as the normal rate. He had nearly drank himself to death, and the doctor cautioned him that the next drink could kill him.

So Coe tried to make a new resolution to help himself. But still not knowing God, he wondered who could help him keep this commitment. This led him to move to California. His mother lived there, and if anyone could help him, she certainly could.

Upon his arrival, his sister invited him to a dance. But soon, Coe found himself at the bar while the others danced. He was brought home that night in a drunken stupor, without his mother knowing about it.

"GOD, GIVE ME UNTIL SUNDAY!"

The next evening, Coe thought he was dying. He was very weak, and could hardly walk. He was picked up in an ambulance, taken to a hospital, and examined. He sat in the chair and raised his hands pleading, **"Oh God, don't let me die, please give me one more chance. I don't want to go to hell."**[4] Then suddenly, Coe got better. His weakness left and so did his symptoms. He didn't know what happened to him at the time, but he was glad!

After this, Coe decided to leave California. So he took his mother with him, and the two left for Fort Worth, Texas. There, Coe obtained a job as a manager for the Singer Sewing Machine Agency. He soon forgot about the promises he had made to God and came home one evening in another alcoholic stupor. But this time, when he fell into his bed, he couldn't sleep, tossing to and fro over the conviction of God. Finally, he got up and drank another pint of whiskey just so he could pass out. Then in a few days a unique experience happened that changed Coe's life forever.

He had just returned home from drinking. It was about 3:00 A.M., and he was trying to go to sleep. But he couldn't, and as he reached for another pint of whiskey, he heard someone in the room!

Startled, Coe noticed that his heart was bothering him. It would start, then stop. Start, then stop. Then he heard a voice. "This is your last chance," the voice said. "I've called you several times, and I'm calling you now for the last time."

At this, Coe jumped out of his bed and fell to his knees, crying, **"Oh God, give me until Sunday. If You'll just give me until Sunday, I'll get right with You."**

"HOT DOG, I'VE GOT IT!"

Sunday came, and Coe had no idea of where to go. As a youth, he had been baptized in several places, but nothing had ever changed his life or answered his questions. Because church started much later in the evening in those days, it wasn't until later in the afternoon that he began to seriously wonder about where to go. He simply had no idea. So at 5:00 P.M., he finally went to his office to look at the telephone book. Coe had heard about people opening their Bible to whatever verse their thumb fell on, taking that to be a message from God. So he thought he would try it with the phone book.

Coe picked up the big book and let it fall, and when he opened his eyes, he saw the name and address of a Nazarene church. He arrived in the parking lot two hours before the service began. When the doors finally opened, he jumped from the car and found a seat at the back. Then after the sermon, when the preacher asked if there was anyone who wanted to go to heaven, saying, "We have a born-again experience for you," Coe ran to the altar, shouting, **"That's what I want! That's what I want!"** A little gray-haired lady prayed with him. Then suddenly, Coe felt something he had never felt before. Not knowing the "Christian lingo," he found himself running all over the church, shouting, **"Hot dog, I've got it! Hot dog, I've got it!"** Later, when Coe recalled the moment, he would say, **"I didn't know what 'Glory, Hallelujah' meant. I had to let something out — there was something within me!"**

...Coe ran to the altar, shouting, "That's what I want! That's what I want!" A little gray-haired lady prayed with him. Then suddenly, Coe felt something he had never felt before. Not knowing the "Christian lingo," he found himself running all over the church, shouting, "Hot dog, I've got it! Hot dog, I've got it!"

Coe returned to his home at 4:00 A.M. He had stayed at the church all that time, praying and praising God.

"WHAT HAVE THEY DONE TO YOU?"

For the next six months, Jack Coe was a "hungry" man. He went to church every night and would stay there into the early morning hours. He devoured his Bible, and often imagined himself in the place of certain Bible characters. His mother watched his behavior, and was quite concerned about it. Finally one night, she asked if he was going to church. Of course, he was. So his mother said, "We're going with you tonight to find out what they've done to you." At the end of the message, his mother made her way to the altar. She didn't know how to pray, so she just said, "Oh God, give me what Jack's got." Then suddenly, she came up with tears rolling down her cheeks, "Jack! I've got it! I've got it!" As they sat on the bench, Coe and his mother hugged each other, praising God.

On the way home, late that night they stopped at a grocery store to buy some food. Very few people were shopping and neither Coe nor his mother could contain their joy. So they ran up and down the aisles, shouting, laughing, and praising God. The store butcher said, "You must have just gotten saved." As they talked with the man, tears began to roll down his cheeks, and before long he too was down on his knees, asking God to save him![5]

"THEY'LL PUT A SPELL ON YOU!"

About a year and a half after he was saved, Coe learned of his first "holy roller" meeting. So out of curiosity, he and his sister went to check it out. He actually felt the meeting was a lot like his Nazarene church, except these people spoke in other tongues. And when people went to the altar, they would fall down under the power. At first he thought they were fainting.

Finally, the preacher spotted Coe. Pointing at him, he asked, "Are you a Christian?" After Coe answered positively, the preacher asked, "Have you received the baptism in the Holy Ghost? Did you speak in tongues?" Coe replied, **"No sir, I haven't, and I don't want to, either."**

Then the preacher asked Coe another question, "Will you go home and read everything there is on the baptism of the Holy Ghost? Then get down on your knees and pray that if it's for you, you'll get it, if not, there's nothing to it?"

Coe answered, **"Sure, I know there is nothing in the Bible about tongues."** To that the preacher said as he walked away, "That's fine, go home and read the Bible."

Every place Coe searched in Acts, he found the term, "other tongues." So the next evening, he went to the house of his Nazarene pastor. As Coe showed him the passages about tongues in Acts, the pastor replied, "If God ever wants you to speak in tongues, He'll let you do it after He calls you to be a missionary, so that natives can understand you." It made sense to Coe. And as he turned to leave, the pastor warned, "Stay away from those holy rollers, or they'll put a spell on you."

"I'LL DIE IF I DON'T GET IT!"

That night, Coe refused to go to the meeting with his sister. In fact, he told her the meetings were of the devil. To this she responded, "Then, why do they quit their lying and stealing, and other wrong things?" and went without him.

Coe tossed and turned in bed that night, then finally jumped out of bed, got dressed, and went to the meeting. When he arrived, the preacher pointed to Coe again. And again, Coe told him that he didn't want to speak in tongues. So the preacher said, "We'll make you a special case. If God wants to fill you without speaking in tongues, it will be all right with us."

"If that's the case, I'll come," Coe replied. Then he went to the front, but the people that gathered around him sounded like they were contradicting each other as they cried out – "Turn loose!" "Hold on!" "Empty him!" "Fill him!" After a few minutes of this, Jack jumped up from the altar and ran for the door.

Outside, he breathed deeply and managed to regain his composure. He straightened the wrinkles from his pants and managed a tight smile as he said to himself, *I sure proved there wasn't anything to it.* Then God immediately spoke to his heart, "You want it so bad you don't know what to do. You know it's for you; you know it's real." After that, Coe whined, **"God...if I don't get it, I'm going to die."** All the way home, he cried, **"Praise God for the glory!"**

> *The brighter the light became, the more Coe seemed to fade away. The more he praised God, the brighter the light. Finally, a hand reached out and took hold of his hand.*

The next night came and Coe made a run for the service. And when the altar call was given for the baptism of the Holy Spirit, he jumped to the front. The same people surrounded him, but this time he stayed. Suddenly, he saw a bright light. The brighter the light became, the more Coe seemed to fade away. The more he praised God, the brighter the light. Finally, a hand reached out and took hold of his hand. It was Jesus, and the two of them walked and talked together for quite some time.

When Coe came to, he was lying in sawdust. It was 4:00 A.M. and he found himself speaking in another tongue. In fact, all he could do for three days, was to speak in tongues! He had to write English words on paper. During those days, he lived in a heavenly atmosphere as all of creation seemed to praise God.[6]

BIBLE SCHOOL, JUANITA & THE ARMY

From 1939 to 1940, Coe attended Southwestern Bible Institute, an Assemblies of God Bible college. P. C. Nelson was college president at the time.

While there, he met a girl named Juanita Scott. Their meeting would prove to be more than mere coincidence.

In 1941, after Japan bombed Pearl Harbor, Coe joined the army. At first, he was a little embarrassed to pray and act like a Christian around his fellow soldiers. But once he realized these crude men had no shame with their behavior, he decided to behave like a believer. And he suffered great persecution for it. But the persecution didn't stop him. In fact, Coe could be as rough as these men. The only difference was, he would listen to the voice of God. So he continued to preach at every opportunity.

While stationed at the 130th Bomb Squadron in Walter Boro, South Carolina, Coe was able to receive a pass to go whenever he wanted. He was located, "in the middle of nowhere," and the closest church was forty-five miles away. So every night he would walk five miles, then hitchhike the rest of the way to attend church! He didn't care if it was raining. He never missed church. This went on for six months.

Then one day his sergeant told him to gather his belongings. He was being sent to the dispensary. From there he was sent to the hospital. Coe protested the whole affair, especially after he realized he had been sent to the psychiatric ward! After the psychiatrist interviewed him, Coe told him that anyone who disobeys the Bible is the one who is crazy, not the other way around. So they locked him up.

Private Coe

LIFE IN THE "PSYCH" WARD

Coe wanted to fast and pray, but in doing so, he simply convinced them even more of his "craziness." After he had been confined for nine days, Coe began to cry out to God. He opened his Bible to the book of Acts and read about how God sent an angel to rock Paul and Silas' prison cell, opening their jail doors when they sang their way out of prison. Feeling ashamed of his weak attitude after reading this, Coe began to lift his voice in song.

Suddenly, he heard a knock at his door. The ward boy walked in with tears in his eyes blubbering, "Preacher, I've stood it as long as I can. I come out here every night, and have to listen to you pray and cry and seek God all night long. I'm going to lose my mind if I don't get what you've got. My daddy was a Pentecostal preacher, but I never did get saved. Will you pray for God to save me?"

Coe knelt down with the boy, cried with him, and prayed, and the boy was gloriously saved. After the prayer they shouted so loud that the other inmates woke up and started yelling too!

Overcome with gratitude, the boy told Coe, "I don't know what I can do for you, but I'll try." The next morning, Coe was released. The doctor begrudgingly told him that he was suffering from a serious condition (psychoneurosis – or, religious fanaticism), but that he wasn't dangerous.

Coe changed companies seven times while in the army. And each time, sooner or later, they put him in the psychiatric ward for a while, because they didn't know how to handle him![7]

BE A...WHAT?

After serving in the army for fifteen months, Coe's heart burned to preach the Gospel. He would lie in his bed at night and imagine preaching to the multitudes. During the day, he would preach to himself.

Finally, he decided to visit the Church of God pastor in town hoping for an opportunity to preach. The pastor invited him to get involved with prayer at the altar and other altar work. This wasn't what Coe wanted to hear, so he turned to walk away. But as he started to leave the Lord spoke to Coe's heart to tell the pastor he would do anything he was asked to do.

"Well, I'm glad to hear that," the pastor said. "Our janitor recently left and I would appreciate it if you could take over and clean the church."

Coe felt insulted and informed the pastor that he was called to preach – not to be a janitor, then turned and walked out. But the Lord continued to deal with Coe, and after another sleepless night, he returned to the church to be their new janitor!

Coe felt insulted and informed the pastor that he was called to preach — not to be a janitor, then turned and walked out. But the Lord continued to deal with Jack, and after another sleepless night, he returned to the church to be their new janitor!

SPIRITUAL BOOT CAMP

Coe would later say that this pastor was the toughest inspector he had ever worked for. He would run his hands over the wood that had been polished, making sure it was clean. After a season of this the pastor invited Coe to begin teaching Sunday school. Coe was elated! He would finally get to preach. That is, until he found out he would be teaching the "beginners'" class. Coe was in shock. At first he resisted, then he reluctantly accepted. The class ranged from toddlers to three year olds.

After a while, Coe was promoted to song leader, then to youth minister, then to associate pastor. Then when the pastor was called to another church, the congregation asked Coe to fill in as pastor. Finally, he was ready to preach to someone![8]

MARRIAGE AND A VISION

While Coe was at this church he heard that Juanita Scott was traveling the country with a singing group. Coe and Juanita had written each other through the years, but their relationship had never swung toward the romantic. After the Church of God hired a new pastor, Coe decided to start a church of his own. He wrote to Juanita's singing group, the Southern Carolers, asking them to come to town to help him raise the new work. But by the time the group came to town, Coe's plans had fallen through. He had been restricted to his army post, and couldn't carry on with regular meetings.

Coe located other revival work for Juanita's singing group and would meet them after services. During these times, he and Juanita grew closer. Soon, they were married, and Coe found them government housing. Having no money, they slept on a concrete floor with army blankets and fasted for three days, until they could buy some food. But before long, the Coes had three rooms of furniture, a car, and a thousand dollars in the bank. He was good with his hands, so he fixed a broken radio and sold it for $60. He also tripled his investment on the sale of some hens. And he was blessed with a car for helping a friend.

Also during this time, Coe began to pray and seek for an understanding of divine healing. He had heard of people being healed, but knew nothing about it. One day while reading a book by P. C. Nelson on healing, Coe fell asleep. He dreamed that his sister was dying in a hospital room. Then suddenly, a bright light filled her room, as she jumped up and ran, shouting, "I'm healed! I'm healed!"

The next day, Coe found out that the dream was a reality. His sister had double pneumonia and was given up to die. He immediately got leave to see her.

As Coe entered her hospital room, he found the surroundings were identical to his dream. He also learned that after a series of critical events that were against all odds, God healed and saved his sister – at the last possible moment. It was a total miracle that powerfully affected his life.[9]

READY TO DIE

When Juanita was expecting their first child in 1944, Coe fell ill. He had contracted tropical malaria at the age of twenty-six and his weight had now dropped from 230 to 135 pounds. He was literally skin and bones. Once his fever shot up to 106 degrees, then remained there for fifty-four hours. His spleen and liver swelled to twice their normal size, producing pain so great that Coe would bite his tongue until it bled.

Finally, when the fever broke enough for Coe to understand conversation, the doctors told him of his condition. They saw there was nothing they could do for him, so after a few days, he was discharged and sent home to his family. **"Now, God, what shall I do?"** was his earnest prayer. The Lord's answer was, "I've called you to preach the Gospel. Go out and preach it!"

For a while, Coe would appear to be well, then another malaria attack would bring him down. Strong chills and a high fever brought the man to his knees. It was difficult for him to maintain a normal life. The intense pain in his spleen and liver was almost unbearable. Juanita would sit with him for hours, applying ice packs to comfort him.

Finally, Coe thought he could stand it no more. Feeling it was her husband's time to die, Juanita left their trailer in tears. It was then that Coe began to repent as the Lord showed him different things. This went on for some time, and Coe began to feel inwardly free. **"All right Lord, I'm ready to go now,"** were his words toward the end of this time. A voice spoke back to his heart, "You're ready to go, but you don't have to." Then suddenly, Coe felt as if he were covered with warm oil from head to toe as the Lord spoke, "You are healed now."

Coe jumped out of bed. He grabbed his wife, who by this time, was asleep near him and shouted, **"Honey! Honey! I'm healed! I'm healed!"**

The next night, despite harassing thoughts from the devil, Coe dressed and preached on the street. Three people were saved. Later that same year, the Assemblies of God ordained him into the ministry.[10] Coe would never have another attack of malaria – God had truly healed him!

OH NO! A BLIND PERSON?

In 1945, Coe went to Longview, Texas, where he continually studied and prayed on the subject of divine healing. He asked God for a special manifestation of His power, then decided to announce a healing meeting. **"God's going** to open the eyes of the blind and cause the lame to walk, and the deaf to hear. He's going to do it right here in this church tomorrow night," was his bold confession of faith.

> *Desperate, Coe prayed, "Lord, that woman is almost to me now. What am I going to do?" But the Lord quickly rebuked saying, "Son, whatever made you think that you could open the eyes of the blind, anyway? Do what you are supposed to do and I will do what I am supposed to do."*

The next night, the church was packed. After Coe preached, the people lined up. The ailments didn't seem too bad. There were a few stomachaches, headaches, and other minor ailments. But then suddenly Coe looked up – and there she stood – a blind woman. **"Oh Lord, what in the world am I going to do with her?"** he asked, then began worrying about what people would say if she didn't receive her sight.

When the blind woman stepped up for her turn to be prayed for, Coe sent her to the back of the line. He was hoping by the time she came to him again, he would have enough faith! And soon, she was nearing her turn again. Desperate, Coe prayed, **"Lord, that woman is almost to me now. What am I going to do?"** But the Lord quickly rebuked saying, "Son, whatever made you think that you could open the eyes of the blind, anyway? Do what you are supposed to do, and I will do what I am supposed to do."

Coe repented, then prayed and anointed the woman with oil. Her eyes were opened and she could see something moving in the back of the church, but not clearly. So remembering that Jesus had prayed for someone twice, Coe prayed again. And this time, she began to cry out, "I can see! I can see!"[11]

AWAY WE GO!

News of her healing saturated the town, and Coe's faith skyrocketed. A pastor from Oklahoma asked him to come and hold a three-day meeting. After the first night, they had to rent the high school gymnasium to hold the people because deaf ears and blind eyes were opened, and people got up from stretchers and walked.

At that time, Coe thought he had to stay and pray for everyone who came up. He would often be found still ministering to the people at 5:00 A.M. the next morning. As he began traveling throughout Oklahoma, praying for the sick, he got very little sleep.

In different towns, he would stay in private homes. When he did, people would come to that home for prayer. If he was asleep, they would wait until he woke up. If there were very many of them, they would wake him up to pray for their needs. Sometimes, this would happen four or five times a day.

Soon, Coe's body began to break down. He was only sleeping an hour or so each night. But the needs of the people were so great and demanding that he would always pray for them whenever they came. In those days, healing campaigns were still new and there were many practical ministry principles people didn't understand. Finally, God told Coe that he needed to use wisdom and get proper rest. So he obeyed and was revitalized to pursue a stronger ministry to the sick.

SAY GOOD-BYE TO THE HOUSE

In 1946, Coe merged his editorial efforts with Gordon Lindsay's *The Voice of Healing* publication, and was named a co-editor. Then in 1947, Coe and his wife made a dramatic decision that affected the rest of their lives. The couple had purchased a small home, and Juanita was very proud of it. She had furnished it nicely, and worked on the lawn to keep it immaculate.

But after returning home from a church service one day, Juanita began to cry. She knew God was speaking to them to sell all they had to enter into the ministry full time, so they decided to sell. Before Coe awoke the next morning, someone was at his door to buy it. A few days later, Coe purchased an old tent, a new truck and house trailer.

The Coes were ready to go, and the first place they would go to would be Chickasha, Oklahoma. The second night of this meeting, they experienced their first real ministry challenge. A storm blew in and tore the canvas off the top of the tent, leaving only its ropes. After the storm, their pastor challenged them to really know whether or not they were in the will of God. To this, Juanita responded, "If everything we have is gone, I still believe we are in the will of God." So as he turned to go, their pastor said, "If you've got that much faith in God, I've got enough faith to help you." Then he handed them $100.[12]

By the time this first meeting had closed, the Coes had enough money to re-canvas their tent and to buy a larger truck to carry it.

TENT TALES

In 1948, Coe headed for Redding, California, for his next meeting, having been specifically directed to this city. Before hearing God's Word of direction,

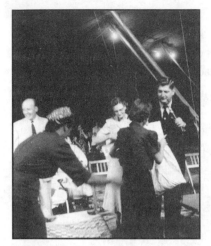

Healing the sick

Jack and Juanita Coe

The Big Top

Jack Coe

Behind bars

Under the Big Top

he had never even heard of Redding. Once there, the devil went about his business of blocking the meetings. The fire marshall told Coe that his tent wasn't fireproof and that he wouldn't allow him to set it up. The cost of fireproofing it was $1,700, and the tent only cost $400.

Coe bought the fireproofing solution himself, then dipped each part of the tent in it until the entire canvas was covered. But the make-shift solution failed the fire marshall's inspection. Utterly frustrated, Coe began to cry. And when he did, the fire marshall told him that if it meant that much to him, he could go ahead with his meetings and set the tent up.

> *Once there, the devil went about his business of blocking the meetings. The fire marshall told Coe that his tent wasn't fireproof and that he wouldn't allow him to set it up. The cost of fireproofing it was $1,700, and the tent only cost $400.*

The first few nights, crowds were small. But Coe was faithful to pray for the sick. One lady came wearing a brace and using crutches. She was totally healed. That night, for the first time in years, she knelt down to pray beside her bed. She prayed until the sun came up, then walked to the next meeting. Her testimony stirred the entire city. She shared that the doctors were preparing to amputate her leg.

Coe aired the testimony on radio and the lady who managed the radio station was saved. A prominent Catholic lady arrived at his meeting that night in a chauffeur-driven Cadillac. The lady was saved and immediately closed all the drinking establishments she owned. She would come into the meetings with her hands raised and leave the same way.

Up to this time, the offerings had been very small. Creditors had threatened to take his truck, so Coe stood up in front of the people and told them he needed $740 badly. When he did, one lady walked up to him and wrote out a check for the entire amount. Two nights later, he said, **"I sure would like to have a Hammond organ or some kind of music for this tent,"** and the same lady bought him an organ. Coe's revival team would stay in Redding for seven weeks, and would receive enough money to fund the next crusade.[13]

After a much needed vacation, the Coes continued ministering in California. In Fresno, he was arrested for disturbing the peace. Coe pleaded "not guilty," and the court case came to trial several months later. But it was thrown out due to lack of evidence and was never mentioned again.

THE MAN AND THE MINISTER

Coe was a very boisterous man who brilliantly played to the crowds. He was said to be saucy, angry, flippant, humble, and always nervy. It was also said that he loved controversy and attracted lots of it. He appeared to enjoy a good fight. Of him, Gordon Lindsay wrote, "In growing up it was root hog or die. For that reason, he tangled."[14]

Coe's faith was "reckless and challenging," but no one seemed to mind when they walked away healed! He was often seen hitting people, slapping them, or jerking them. But, again, they all walked away healed. Some didn't even feel it when he hit them. He was also the first evangelist to attract, and welcome, large numbers of the black community into his services. He preached bluntly, and called things as he saw them. He was a preacher with a sting. Once, a group of young people were standing on the chairs in the tent, and he shouted out at them, **"Those are my chairs! I wouldn't do that at your house!"**[15]

Another time the highway patrol approached Coe to tell him that his crowd was blocking the highway, and to get the people off of it. He responded by telling the highway patrol that he didn't have anything to do with the highway, and that it was up to them to arrest the people if they wanted them off. He then proceeded with his meeting, undisturbed by their demand.[16]

By 1950, Coe seemed to always be in competition with other preachers. He competed by ordering larger and larger tents. And still his team would have to turn away thousands every night.

In 1951 Coe visited an Oral Roberts meeting. He measured the length of Roberts' tent and ordered one slightly larger. Then in July of that year, he ran a notice in *The Voice of Healing* magazine that said:

> "A letter from the Smith Manufacturing Company, Dalton, Ga., declares that according to his measurements the Coe tent is by a slight margin, the largest gospel tent in the world. Since Oral Roberts has a prayer tent 90' x 130', Brother Roberts has the largest amount of tent equipment. Both the Coe and Roberts tents are larger than the Ringling Brothers [circus] big top."[17]

"THE FRECKLED FACE" VISION

One night in a Lubbock, Texas, meeting, a little freckled-face boy approached the revivalist. Locking his arms around Coe's legs, the boy said with a lisp, "Pleathe, mithter, let me go home with you." Then a woman dragged him away, as Coe stood watching. But the impression stayed with Coe the entire night. The next day, he looked for the boy, but couldn't find him.

Coe had always felt he would someday provide a home for other homeless children, as he had been a homeless child himself. But he also knew that if God was speaking to him that He would speak to Juanita as well. He couldn't escape the memory of this little boy's freckled face.

Finally, while driving home after a meeting, Coe asked his wife, **"Honey, what would you say if I told you that God had been speaking to me about starting a children's home?"** It looked financially impossible. But Juanita said, "I always thought that I should work in a children's home, so maybe this is it. You go ahead and obey God!"[18]

PIECE BY PEACE

In obedience, the Coes put a small down-payment on a lot in Dallas, and continued on with their healing crusades. In every meeting, Coe let the people know of his children's home plans, and soon, people began to donate lumber

> *Coe had always felt he would someday provide a home for other homeless children, as he had been a homeless child himself. But he also knew that if God was speaking to him that He would speak to Juanita as well.*

and supplies. The Coes put their own home up for sale. It sold the same week, and they used the proceeds to help pay the workers. Then they moved into a portion of the children's home still under construction and lived there until it was finished.

There was no running water and the heater couldn't sufficiently heat the room. As a result, their baby fell ill with pneumonia. They put the child's health in God's hands and left for their next meeting. After they had traveled about fifty miles, the baby's fever broke, and the baby was playing in the car – instantly healed!

Little by little, God made the finances available for the children's home. People began to donate draperies, blankets, and clothing, and before long, the Coes were able to hold their "Open House." The home was ready and children were received.

One day as Coe sat watching the children play, a little boy walked up to him and said, "You'll be my daddy now." Then several others locked their arms around him, wanting his love. Of this, Coe said, **"It seemed that my dream had at last, been fulfilled."**[19]

GOD SAID, "NO."

Bob Davidson was a young boy in the children's home. His own father had been crippled, and could not take care of his family. Although Coe was a national evangelist, Davidson said he was like a "compassionate father" when he was at the home. Coe was remembered by some as always being happy. He was a fun-loving man, who enjoyed playing jokes on people. Even so, Coe heard from God concerning the children, and knew when to draw the line.

Once, after being at the home for several years, Davidson had wanted to go to a State Fair with some of his friends. When he went to ask Coe for money to go, Coe told him that if he finished his chores, he could go.

Davidson worked hard to complete his duties in time to go. Running to meet Coe, he shouted that he had finished all his work. About that time, the guys he was going to the Fair with pulled in front of the home in a brand new Plymouth Fury. They waved to Davidson, telling him to hurry and get in the car so they could go.

Watching the scene, Coe gave Davidson money for his chores, but changed his mind about the boy going to the Fair. Coe told him, **"God said not to let you go."**

Of course, Davidson didn't understand. He cried and yelled at Coe, "You lied! You lied!" Then he ran to another part of the home.

After a while, Coe found Davidson and said, **"If you really want to go to the Fair, I'll take you myself. But God said you could not go with those boys. I didn't feel right about letting you leave."**[20]

So Davidson dried his face and left for the Fair with Coe. As they traveled down the road, an ambulance and a sheriff's car passed them at high speeds, heading straight ahead of them.

Driving up ahead, nothing could match the horror of what they saw. There in the ditch, was the brand new Plymouth Fury, crushed and mangled. Beside it, scattered along the ground, were the broken bodies of Davidson's friends – all of them dead. Coe and Davidson stood by the road, holding one another, and crying.

DRESSED LIKE ROYALTY

Davidson has never forgotten how Coe cared enough to hear God for him. He feels that he owes his life to the strict compassion of Jack Coe.

Sometimes, seventeen children would be in the home. Davidson remembers it reaching one hundred children at one point. Some of the children came so dirty, their hair would have to be washed four or five times just to see their scalp. Most of the children had been left alone, some starving. Neighbors of the abandoned children would report the condition to authorities. Then the children's home would take what it could hold.

Coe always told the donors, **"Don't send me worn out clothes for the kids in my home. My kids are going to be dressed as good as yours."** It was said that after Coe took the kids, that even the governor of the state would have been proud to claim them. They were all taught to pray, led to Christ, and taken to church regularly. Most all of them spoke in other tongues.

Eventually, Coe was able to purchase two hundred acres outside of Dallas for the home. This was enough room for a self-sustaining farm and four large dormitories. Coe targeted two hundred children as his goal. God honored his efforts, and abundantly supplied the needs of the children's home.

"Well, the 'holy rollers' are going. What's the matter? Where's your faith in God?" So Coe yelled back, "That's just the reason we're leaving. We've got faith in God, and God told us to go!"

THE BIG TOP

By now, Coe had purchased and sold several tents, working his way toward owning the largest tent in the nation. Finally, he succeeded. He now bragged that his new tent was "bigger than the big top." Storms had destroyed others, but Coe was believing for this one to be supernaturally sustained by the hand of God.

Coe didn't just have small, confined tent meetings. His meetings were huge! One of his largest meetings was held in Little Rock, Arkansas, where the governor estimated over twenty thousand people were in attendance! Deaf ears were unstopped, blind eyes were opened, and crippled persons walked as God miraculously healed them. Thousands were also born again.

Finally, another dreaded storm swirled around Coe's gospel tent. On this night, the wind blew so hard, the revivalist himself could hardly stand outside. There were thirty-five hundred people still inside the tent when the worst of the storm passed through, when lightning struck the electrical system and all the lights went out. When this happened, Coe ran into his trailer and began to pray. As he did, the wind suddenly subsided and the storm calmed.

Coe went back inside to see how the people were, and a woman was lying on the ground with an apparent heart attack. He could hear the rattle of death in her throat. Someone suggested they call an ambulance, but Coe said, **"We'll pray and believe God. God will heal her."** Within a few minutes, she was back to normal praising the Lord with the rest of the people![21]

A PRESENT-DAY FLOOD STORY

Coe was also present when the greatest flood in U. S. history struck Kansas City. Before he had arrived in the city, he dreamed of a great flood, closing in on every side. But it didn't keep him from coming. He had raised his big top on the Kansas side. And God was speaking judgment in the meetings through the gift of prophecy. But most of the people ignored the warnings. Some of them, laughing and jeering, even left the meetings. It rained every night, soaking the ground as thousands answered the altar calls. But Coe remained troubled in his spirit. For two nights, he was unable to sleep.

The next day, he turned to his wife and said, **"Would you think I were crazy if I took that tent down? Something tells me to take the tent down."** As he began putting action to his words, he walked out to find that his trucks were stuck in the mud, and that the dampness had affected the batteries – they wouldn't start. After working on them feverishly the crew was finally able to start the trucks late that afternoon.

As Coe moved to strike the big tent, people began to question his motives. "What are you doing?" "You're not having service tonight?" "I don't think you have anything to worry about." "The most the water would do if the river flooded, would run under your chairs." "There's no danger of the water coming over the dikes." "Don't let the devil defeat you." Nevertheless, God had spoken clearly to Coe: "Get the tent out of here."

But by 7:30 P.M. that night, the crew had made no progress. So he organized them, urging them to hurry. They were just getting ready to lower the top, when another minister approached Coe and said "Don't take the tent down. God can take care of this tent." To this Coe responded, **"I know God can take care of this tent, and that's the reason I'm moving. God told me to move it, and I'm going to move it."**

Finally, three hours later, as they were pulling out the last stake, the puller locked and refused to give another inch. At that very moment, every whistle and siren in town began to blast and shrill. "The dikes are breaking!" came the call.

Coe was ready to go, but he couldn't get all the canvas in the trucks, and the men were running off. So he stood on a large box and pleaded with them, **"Men, don't leave me now. The tent is rolled up, don't leave me!"** By this time, the bridge leading out of their area was snarled as panic-stricken people fought one another to cross. The men would look at the congestion, then look at Coe. Finally, one said, "We ought to be men enough to stay here and help him. If he isn't afraid of drowning, I'm surely not." With that, forty men came alongside of Coe to help him load the canvas. Once loaded, they headed out of town.

As Coe's trucks left Kansas City, some of the people who refused to leave sat on their porches and jeered at him. "Well, the 'holy rollers' are going. What's the matter? Where's your faith in God?" So Coe yelled back, **"That's just the reason we're leaving. We've got faith in God, and God told us to go!"** Others stood on their porches and laughed too. They never thought the flood would destroy everything they had, but for many it did.

On his way out of town, Coe stopped to help Pastor Barnett move his furniture and belongings to the church. (This was Tommy Barnett's father. Today, Tommy Barnett pastors one of America's largest churches located in Phoenix, Arizona.) But their moving party proved to be too little, too late as Barnett watched with Coe from the truck as the flood waters crashed through the windows of the church. Losing everything he had, Barnett made a fresh commitment to stay in Kansas City.

Barnett and Coe attempted to save many people from the disaster. But in the process they witnessed the drowning of many. After they had done everything possible, they started out over the bridge to safety, and as Coe looked behind them, he saw that the water level where the tent had stood was now standing at around twenty feet. The tent would have been completely destroyed, and only a small part of Barnett's church building still showed.[22]

Here the sick would be allowed to remain until they received their healing. Prayer and classes on healing would be offered daily.

The two men turned their backs, thanking God in their hearts for His absolute provision and deliverance.

EMBARRASSED? WHAT ELSE IS NEW?

In 1952, Coe went throughout the South holding massive healing crusades. Two years earlier he had started publishing, *The Herald of Healing*, and by 1951, its circulation had reached 35,000. The masthead boasted that it was one of the nation's fastest growing magazines, with 100 percent renewal each year. By 1956, the circulation had reached 250,000.[23]

In August of 1952, Coe went on the radio with the Gospel. His broadcasts eventually grew to one hundred different stations a week. Thousands were saved and healed as a result of his program. It was around that time that creative miracles – the miraculous appearance of missing body parts – also began taking place in his meetings.

When Coe finally held a meeting in Springfield, Missouri, the Assemblies of God began to oppose him. They weren't comfortable with divine healing and deliverance ministries. But Coe had a volcanic personality, especially when it came to someone trying to dictate or control his call. He tried to cooperate with their suggestions and criticisms, and even sponsored the *Pentecostal Evangel* (the official Assemblies of God publication) at one of his meetings, receiving one hundred twenty new subscriptions for it. He also took up a large offering for their missions program.

> *No medicine was ever offered or permitted in the building, and patients were taken nightly to the Dallas Revival Center.*

But Coe wasn't a denominational man. As much as he tried, he couldn't stand for all the restraints and regulations placed upon him. He felt the Assemblies of God leaders no longer believed in the miraculous. So he wrote a bold letter, suggesting they replace their present leadership with men who believed in the miraculous power of God. The General Council found his letter offensive.

Finally, in 1953, Coe was expelled from the Assemblies of God. They had become frustrated by his "extreme independence" and embarrassed by some of his methods. A bitter feud followed. It has been said that Coe even thought of establishing a split-off group called the Fundamental Assemblies of God, but decided to pursue his own call, instead.[24]

NEW CHURCH, NEW HOME, NEW UNDERSTANDING

Soon Coe began grasping the vision for his own independent church. It would be a revival center where evangelists could come and hold continuous campaigns. It would provide accommodations large enough to hold the people their ministries drew. And it would eventually be duplicated around the nation in every major city. Coe realized he would be highly criticized for this move, but he decided to pursue the dream regardless of persecution, and in 1953 he started the first one, the Dallas Revival Center.

In the spring, Coe began to ask God why people weren't healed. Though he had seen thousands healed, he had also seen thousands walk away without their healing. After a season of prayer, God revealed to Coe that many didn't understand how to receive healing and that they needed instruction in His Word concerning His will and His power. This was a tremendous revelation in that day! Up until then, most of the Voice of Healing evangelists depended upon the anointing of their healing gift, and many knew little about what the Word of God had to say on the subject.

So in an effort to strengthen the faith and dispel the doubts of those who were seeking healing, Coe built a faith home. Here the sick would be allowed to remain until they received their healing. Prayer and classes on healing would be offered daily. Finally, after months of struggling through the city's resistance to his building plans, Jack Coe's Faith Home opened next door to his Herald of Healing Children's Home in the summer of 1954. In September, Coe's Faith Home received its first full-time patient. From there, the numbers grew. No medicine was ever offered or permitted in the building, and patients were taken nightly to the Dallas Revival Center.

In July of that year, Coe experienced the greatest tent revival in the history of his ministry. He had taken the big top to Pittsburgh, Pennsylvania, where it is estimated that thirty thousand people were born again. One night was devoted to "stretcher cases" only. More than 75 percent of those on stretchers got up and walked. A local television station broadcast the revival meetings, drawing even greater crowds. Though great winds ripped the big top while he was in Pittsburgh, this month-long meeting was the high point in Coe's life.

Ironically, it seems that the Voice of Healing generation didn't understand the stewardship of the physical body as we do today.

Throughout 1953, his church, the Dallas Revival Center, continued to grow. Meetings were held in a large rented theater, which he and another pastor had renovated for nightly attendance. Coe's love for children moved him to develop a full Christian school at the Dallas Revival Center, where children were taught and loved by Spirit-filled teachers.

The church balcony and lower floor were packed every night, and by the fall of that year, the congregation had grown to the point where they were able to construct their own building.

In January of 1954, Coe opened the new Dallas Revival Center Church. It was beautifully and simply built, with a huge white cross gleaming across its front. The center provided a place to attend church every night of the week. Bus service picked up those who had no way to get there, and an ambulance provided free service to anyone who wished to come from the hospital, or home, for prayer.

SEVERAL TRIALS — MINISTRY & LIFE

Coe continued to evangelize around the nation, trying to raise money for a television program. But in 1956, he was arrested in Miami, Florida, for practicing medicine without a license.

Let me make a point here. At this time, the city of Miami was known for its persecution of ministers. Especially those who preached on divine healing. When the persecutions broke out, most evangelists would usually just pack up and leave town. But not Coe! He stayed to fight. Remember, Coe loved a good fight. As a result, the Miami police arrested him and threw him in jail. He was later released on a $5,000 bond.

Because of his incarceration, Coe began admonishing other healing evangelists to come to Miami and stand up for what they believed. And when his case came to trial, it was evident that his words had been heard. Many prominent healing evangelists came to testify on his behalf. In fact, it is recorded that these evangelists had healing miracles manifest – while they were on the stand! God turned the situation around for his good, and in the end the judge dismissed the case.

Coe's Miami incident had proven to be a great victory. But a turning point was soon to come in his ministry. In December, while preaching in Hot Springs, Arkansas, the healing evangelist became critically ill.

If we fail to be good stewards over our flesh, our bodies die early and our spirits have to leave.

It was a known fact that Coe had terribly neglected his health. Coe maintained an extremely rigorous schedule, holding three meetings a day, that lasted four to six weeks at a time. The overwork, the stress, and a lack of proper rest soon took its toll. Because of the tremendous wear and tear on his body, it was said that Coe inwardly possessed the body of a ninety-year-old man.

Today, the Coe family says the Lord told him of his death one year before the time, and that Coe accepted that he was soon to die. They also say he believed the coming of the Lord would follow shortly after his death. Because of these two things, Coe worked relentlessly to spread the Gospel – even to the extreme.

Besides Coe's brutal schedule, his eating habits were irregular and unhealthy. Many times after a crusade, Coe would eat a heavy meal at 3:00 A.M. As a result, he was extremely overweight.

Ironically, it seems that the Voice of Healing generation didn't understand the stewardship of the physical body as we do today. We must understand that the physical body is the only thing holding our spirit on the earth. We must practice a healthy maintenance of our eating habits, mental attitudes, and general well-being. Otherwise, our physical "house" – our bodies – will break down and die. Then our spirits will have to leave the earth and go to heaven.

I like to compare our physical bodies to a space suit. If you go to the moon, the only thing that will hold your body to the surface of the moon is your space suit. Such a suit contains an oxygen supply, a body shield, and is heavy enough to walk upright in the weightlessness of space. But if you were to harm that space suit, your oxygen supply would be cut off, your shield would be broken, and your body would float away from the surface of the moon. Why? Because you need such a space suit to remain on the moon.

The same is true with our physical bodies. If we fail to be good stewards over our flesh, our bodies die early and our spirits have to leave. Therefore, if you don't take care of your physical body, your life and your ministry will come to an end.

AN UNTIMELY DEATH

One of the great things about Jack Coe, is that he never allowed his past to hold him back. His past might have influenced his attitude, but it never stopped him or caused him to withdraw.

At first, Coe thought he was suffering from exhaustion, but soon he was diagnosed with polio. His wife wanted him admitted to the hospital, so Coe consented for her peace of mind.

In the hospital, Coe remained unconscious most of the time. There were a few times when he would regain his ability to speak and make his desires known. According to his wife, the Lord spoke to Coe and told him that He was going to take him home.[25] Then early in 1957, Jack Coe went home to be with the Lord.

Juanita Coe was scolded by many evangelists for not allowing them to pray for her husband. But Gordon Lindsay said his death must have been the will of God, or "providence would have allowed someone to pray for him. His ministry had simply been fulfilled."

There is a story that says Coe had been warned of his impending death, due to some health habits, personal habits, and his rigorous schedule. The story says that the Lord had spoken several times to one minister in particular. This prophetic man of the time is said to have heard the warning of the Lord for Jack Coe. And it is said that he obeyed God and went to Coe.

As the story goes, Coe was told to judge himself in three areas: (1) his love of the brethren; (2) his weight problem; and (3) the love of money. The prophet reportedly told Coe that if he would not judge himself in these areas, he would die early. And Coe did die early. He was only thirty-eight years old when he died.

It is important to note that the Coe family strongly refutes that this particular prophet ever spoke to Coe. The family maintains that a member of the Coe family approached the prophet to confront him about this widespread report. According to the Coe family, this prophet said that he never spoke to Coe directly, although he was told by God to do so.

THE MINISTRY CONTINUES

After Coe died, Juanita Coe announced that she and the department heads would continue her husband's ministry. She served as assistant pastor of the Dallas Revival Center, and for a time, continued to conduct healing campaigns. There were many that felt she could have gone on to have her own major revival ministry, but she chose to let that phase of the ministry end. More and more Juanita Coe directed her energies toward foreign missions and the Herald of Healing Children's Home. Even after Coe's death, the *Herald of Healing* had a circulation of 300,000 readers. It was only when Juanita decided to taper off that phase of ministry, that her husband's popularity dwindled.

Today, both of Coe's sons, Jack Jr. and Steve, are in the ministry, pastoring their own churches, and Mrs. Coe is still active in the church. The Coes are continuing to preach and teach Jesus Christ to this generation and to the next, carrying on the plan of God for their individual lives.

LIVE PAST YOUR PAST

One of the great things about Jack Coe, is that he never allowed his past to hold him back. His past might have influenced his attitude, but it never stopped him or caused him to withdraw.

As a child, he was terribly hurt by his home condition, but it never caused him to sit in a corner and feel sorry for himself. Instead of pushing him under, those hard times built an awareness in him of a need for deliverance. He knew that he couldn't depend on others to find it for him. He was a fighter. And it is true that he sometimes fought in the flesh. But he was determined to do something with the hunger in his heart! He was determined to take control of his horribly disadvantaged life instead of allowing it to continue controlling him.

As a result, Coe was hurled headfirst into his place as one of the leaders in the Voice of Healing revival. He had the kind of "independence" that it takes to keep you on the cutting edge. It is when we base our lives and faith on the words of men, or on the horrors of our past, that we are defeated. But when we pursue and run after the cry of our hearts, God will meet us every time and manifest His glory.

Another important lesson to be drawn upon from Coe's life is this: Understand that you don't have to exaggerate the facts or compete with someone else to show your worth. This is the only place where I can see that the ministry of Jack Coe bears reproach. Sometimes, if insecurity prevails in a ministry, the person will either withdraw or go overboard to prove his worth. When we go the way of the flesh, we have to rely on our own strength, and we wear out before our time.

Your past will never determine your future, that is, unless you give it the power to do so. There is a whole new future in faith. It is clean, untouched, waiting for you to pioneer with it by the dream in your heart. Keep God as your number one passion, and the desire of your heart will surely follow.

CHAPTER ELEVEN, JACK COE
References

[1] Jack Coe, *The Story of Jack Coe*, (Dallas, TX: Herald of Healing, Inc., 1955), 78-79.

[2] Ibid., 5-6.

[3] Ibid., 12.

[4] Ibid., 15.

[5] Ibid., 16-20.

[6] Ibid., 21-26.

[7] Ibid., 29-34.

[8] Ibid., 42-44.

[9] Ibid., 48-54.

[10] Ibid., 55-59.

[11] Ibid., 60-62.

[12] Ibid., 68-69.

[13] Ibid., 72-75.

[14] David Harrell Jr., *All Things Are Possible*, (Bloomington: Indiana University Press, 1975), 58-59.

[15] Interview with Pastor Gary Ladd who attended Coe meetings in Tyler, Texas, in 1949.

[16] Coe, *The Story of Jack Coe*, 79-80.

[17] Harrell, *All Things Are Possible*, 59-60.

[18] Coe, *The Story of Jack Coe*, 86.

[19] Ibid., 90.

[19] Ibid.

[20] Interview with Bob Davidson on July 25, 1995.

[21] Coe, *The Story of Jack Coe*, 98.

[22] Ibid., 99-106.

[23] Harrell, *All Things Are Possible*, 60.

[24] Ibid., 61.

[25] Personal comments from the Coe Family, April 1996.

A. A. Allen

"The Miracle Man"

"THE MIRACLE MAN"

Before we get into A. A. Allen's story, I would like to make a few comments that I feel will help your perspective in this story.

Everyone has a personal preference when it comes to ministry gifts. There are certain ministries that you enjoy more than others, but not every ministry gift is going to fit into your personal mold.

Some of us might be surprised to find that our idea of ministry, or how a ministry should operate, wasn't Jesus' idea at all. I like to describe "preference" as more of an idea in your mind than a revelation in your spirit.

Our personal preferences are just that – preferences. They are not rules. Therefore, we must be very careful not to judge the call or ministry gift of another according to our personal preferences. Surrounding yourself with ministries that satisfy your preferences only – could cause you to miss out on something important.

I have great compassion for A. A. Allen. Sure, he made mistakes. Every General did, and every future General will. Personally, I also feel there are things Allen did in the "flesh" that he called "Spirit."

But when you consider Allen's disastrous background, you must take note of how he triumphed over it all to affect the world for Jesus. Very few people, if any, have overcome what Allen did to successfully answer the call of God. His story should speak to every generation. Consider this as you read.

A LITTLE MILK, A LOT OF WHISKEY

Asa Alonzo Allen was born on a stormy Easter morning, March 27, 1911. His parents, Asa and Leona, decided to name him after his father and his

He was severely criticized for his dramatics and sensationalism...

father's uncle, a Presbyterian minister. His name was the only connection to God that his parents gave him, and they certainly didn't think he would end up a preacher. But Asa Alonzo would arise from out of their little known region of Sulphur Springs, Arkansas, to become one of the most sensational revivalists of modern time.

It is true that A. A. Allen drew more controversy than any other of the Voice of Healing evangelists. He was severely criticized for his dramatics and sensationalism, and he was totally denounced for his personal habits. The media scorned him to the fullest, and denominational leaders banished him while ordering others to distance themselves from him. Nevertheless, some consider him to have been one of the most important revivalists to emerge during the Voice of Healing revival.[1] It is also important to note that those who criticized Allen were far less productive in the ministry than was Allen.

> *Nevertheless, some consider him to have been one of the most important revivalists to emerge during the Voice of Healing revival.*

Allen was born into a troubled home in which "turmoil" was a household word. At the time of his birth, Allen had two brothers and four sisters. As a young boy, his sisters brought him the only joy he knew; they loved him, played with him, and treated him like a little prince. But his parents were drunkards and raised the children in total poverty. Even Allen's first pair of shoes were bought for him by a total stranger.

Allen's parents also made home brew liquor behind their shack. His mother drank heavily while she was pregnant with Allen, and being as poor as they were, a new baby was hardly anything to be joyful about.

A favorite pastime of his parents was to give Allen and his sisters some of their home brew liquor until they were drunk. Then they would sit back and laugh at their children's drunken antics until they would either fall down or pass out.[2] Allen's mother repeatedly filled his bottle with liquor to keep him from crying, and he would go to bed nightly with a baby bottle filled with the home brew.

Tobacco was also plentiful in the household. Being home grown, it was very strong, yet, Allen learned to smoke before he was old enough to go to school. He always took a few puffs of his mother's cigarettes when he lit them for her.[3]

His father was a talented musician, and though he wasn't a Christian, the local church asked him to lead their choir and perform with them. He usually did so while drunk. Young Allen caught hold of those talents and sometimes stood on the street corner singing to the crowd. It must have been a sight, hearing that baby voice sing hymns he had learned from his drunken father. Young Allen would sing the church hymns over and over because the crowd tossed pennies, nickels, and dimes to him. He stepped into the entertainment world at an early age, and it seemed he was born for it.

A BUCKET OF BEER 'N' TROUBLE

Allen's parents were always fighting, throwing furniture, and threatening one another with weapons. Finally, when he was four years old, his mother left his father. She took the children with her to Carthage, Missouri.

Soon after his mother left, she married again, but the turmoil was the same. In drunken rages, his mother and stepfather would fight to such an extreme that the young children would run out of the home in terror. By the time Allen was six years old, he was carrying tin buckets of beer home from the saloon to his stepfather.

Allen recalled:

> **"Every one of us grew up with a taste for liquor. I had only two brothers. One of them died when I was just a tiny lad. I hardly remember him at all. But my oldest brother died a drunkard. My father filled a drunkard's grave. My mother quit drinking before I was grown, but my four sisters and I were well started on the road to a drunkard's hell."[4]**

In addition to the drinking problem, his mother had fits of jealousy. She had married a younger man, and as Allen's stepfather would go to work, she would watch him with binoculars to see if he stopped to talk with any women. They lived very close to his work, so she watched everything he did and made him give account for it on payday. If the paycheck seemed less than usual, she accused him of spending it on another woman. His stepfather finally had all he could take and left, and so had young Allen.

At eleven years old, Allen ran away from home, determined to go back to Arkansas and find his father. But he wasn't sure of the way, and once he left the weather turned bad, so he returned home to his mother. Carefully plotting his next attempt, he decided that the next time he wouldn't fail.

When he was fourteen, Allen was as large as a grown man, so he ran away again. This time, he decided he would do whatever it took to make it, so he hitched rides in vehicles and empty freight cars and traveled over a large portion of the South. While traveling with several other vagabond friends, he picked cotton, worked in gins, and dug ditches; and he still ended up in jail for stealing corn.

"RUN HIM OUT OR KILL HIM!"

Everywhere he went, Allen was known as the life of the party. He had a beautiful tenor voice and a great sense of rhythm. He was always singing, dancing, drinking, and smoking. Though his energy seemed boundless, Allen said later that he was miserable. Many times, he would leave the party and go into the woods to weep bitterly.

By the time he was twenty-one years old, Allen was a nervous wreck. When he lit a cigarette, he had to hold his wrist with the other hand because he shook so badly. It was said that he couldn't even hold a cup of coffee without spilling it. His chest burned, he was racked with a deep hacking cough, and his memory was slipping. In short, by the early prime of his life, Asa Alanzo Allen was dying.

> *By the time he was twenty-one years old, Allen was a nervous wreck. When he lit a cigarette, he had to hold his wrist with the other hand because he shook so badly.*

With nowhere else to turn, Allen went home to his mother. Thinking that farm life and regular meals would be good for him, he hoped for the return of his health.

But once back home, he returned to his old ways. In their rugged, country setting, Allen and his mother built a bootleg still to make their own liquor. In addition to the still, they turned their place into a dance hall every Saturday night, and soon, attracted large groups of rowdy people who were eager for entertainment.

Just down the road, another man who was called Brother Hunter was opening his home for a different reason. Though unlearned, he was born again and filled with the Holy Spirit. So, he decided to form a church and become the pastor. But he was uneasy about the dance hall down the road.

Brother Hunter sought out the young people, but most of them were too mesmerized by the Allen "Dance Hall and Still" to be interested in church. So the preacher decided that if the community was ever going to see revival, the dance hall would have to be shut down. A group gathered together and began praying. They cried out:

"God, close up that Allen dance hall! Save him if you can. But if he won't yield to God, either run him out of the neighborhood or kill him. But close down that dance hall, one way or another!"[5]

Well, thank God, a portion of their prayer was graced!

THE LADY IN THE WHITE DRESS

In June of 1934, things began changing when one of Allen's rough friends asked him to accompany him on an errand. As they traveled, they passed by a country Methodist church. The lights were blazing, and inside there was a celebration of loud singing, clapping, and dancing.

Allen was amazed, these people were enjoying themselves! He thought church was to be solemn and mournful, so he asked his friend to stop.

When he went in to investigate, he found an even greater surprise. The preacher was a woman, dressed in white, and as she talked, Allen thought she must be an angel. He didn't want this woman to notice him because she seemed so pure. So every time she came near to him, he would hide behind the stove pipe. For the first time in his life, conviction seized him. But before the altar call was made, he and his friend quietly slipped out.

All through that night and the next day, he struggled with God and his heart. He longed for the joy and peace he had seen on the faces of those people at the country church. So deciding not to fight it any longer, he went back to the service the following night.

As the meeting started, Allen listened carefully to every song and testimony. The sermon was about the blood of Jesus and how it washed away every sin, and as soon as the call for salvation was given, his hand shot straight up!

The lady evangelist knew of him, and thought he was only there to cause trouble, so she asked those who were serious to stand. Without a second thought, he stood.

She became fearful because she felt he was there to cause a scene, but she decided to continue. She asked those standing to come down to the front if they were really serious, and Allen was the first one down the aisle. In fact, he was the only one who had stood to actually walk down to the front. Thinking he was still there for trouble, the lady asked him, "Do you *really* want to be saved?"

"Certainly, that's what I came down here for," Allen said.

To her great surprise, he fell to his knees and asked Jesus to be the Lord of his life. From that moment on, there was a new A. A. Allen. No more dances. No more bootlegging. His old friends laughed, but that didn't change Allen back to his old ways. He was a new creation.[6]

"THEY'RE OF THE DEVIL!"

In an old trunk in the attic, Allen found a Bible that his sister had won in a contest. It had never been read, so he took the little Bible and read it from cover to cover. He took it to the fields and read it, and would read it before every meal. According to Allen, it seemed he just couldn't read enough of the Bible.

In the meantime, there was great rejoicing in Brother Hunter's Pentecostal church down the road! "That Allen boy" was born again! Their prayers had been answered, and it even seemed that many of the young people who used to attend Allen's Dance Hall were now stopping by the church because they were curious about the singing and worshipping. The biggest surprise of all was when Allen himself slipped into one of their services. After he left, the congregation prayed that God would fill him with the Spirit and use him to win souls.

The morning after he attended the Pentecostal meeting, he visited with a Methodist pastor who warned him to stay away from the Pentecostals saying they were of the devil because they spoke in tongues.

"After that, I just couldn't wait to go back," Allen said. **"I was curious to hear them talk in tongues!"**[7]

> *The morning after he attended the Pentecostal meeting, he visited with a Methodist pastor who warned him to stay away from the Pentecostals saying they were of the devil because they spoke in tongues.*

A few services later, the gift of tongues and interpretation operated in one of the meetings, and as Allen sat and listened, he could tell that this was from God. Now he really wanted what these people had.

The next day, he met with the Methodist pastor again. He shared his experience with him and showed him Scripture to prove that speaking in tongues was for today. The pastor declared, "You can't have it! No one is getting that kind of an experience today!"

"Well, I'm going to have it," answered Allen. **"And Pastor, that is just what you need."**[8]

The pastor left in a rage, and Allen severed ties with the Methodist church.

Soon after this, one of Allen's sisters was born again. And not long after that, Allen would finally receive the baptism of the Holy Spirit. He received and spoke in tongues at a Pentecostal camp meeting in Oklahoma that he and his sister attended together.

Those days were like heaven on earth to him. The night he was filled with the Spirit, he wore his only change of clothes – a solid white shirt and solid white pants! He fell to the ground which was covered with saw dust, but he didn't care. All Allen wanted was God. Soon, he felt as though electricity was slowly inching its way down his fingertips, until it covered his entire body. Then it happened. Allen was aware of nothing but the presence of God. He stood up and shouted out in other tongues! His white suit had been ruined, but Allen had the desire of his heart!

COLORADO & LEXIE = LOVE

Drought hit Missouri hard in 1934, and there was no work anywhere. Then one day, Allen received a letter from an old friend who invited him to Colorado to work on a ranch.

So in September of 1934, Allen found himself walking through the Colorado plains, tired and thirsty and feeling a little alienated from the lack of Pentecostal fellowship. Though he was going to a new place to work, he was concerned there would be no Christians who shared his new belief. As he walked along, the wind blew a sheet of paper into his pathway. Bending down he picked it up. And seeing what it was, he smiled broadly. It was a page of the Foursquare publication, *Bridal Call*. He knew then that somewhere, someone on these plains believed in the power of God as he knew it.

As soon as he arrived at the ranch, he asked if anyone attended the Foursquare Church. His friends told him that a girl who lived up the road possibly did. They said: "She even thinks she's called to preach."[9]

Soon afterwards, Allen introduced himself to Lexie Scriven, who was called to preach and had just returned home from traveling with some evangelist friends. The two quickly became friends, studying the Bible together daily, searching Scripture and seeking answers to questions. Lexie was challenged and refreshed as she listened to Allen, who regularly challenged the religious tradition that she held to. He was never raised with tradition, so he felt he saw things more clearly than she did. She was soon persuaded to his way of seeing the Scriptures, and they began attending church together. They seemed inseparable, but it was nothing more than mutual friendship.

Soon, Allen returned to Missouri to help his mother move her belongings to her new home in Idaho. Lexie left to attend Central Bible Institute in Springfield, Missouri, but every day, the letters came from Allen. They both began to realize they were in love with each other. So he wrote to her, proposed, and the couple married on September 19, 1936, in Colorado. Their marriage was later blessed with three boys and one girl.

THE THANKSGIVING OPOSSUM

The Allens began their new life together with one hundred dollars, a few wedding gifts, and an old Model A Ford. They had no jobs and no promise of any, but they knew they were called of God to preach.

They saved what money they could to enroll at Central Bible Institute that September and then left Colorado, heading for Missouri, with plans to stop and visit his mother. But they found her very sick, with no income and no one to care for her. So immediately, the couple bought her food and necessities, cared for her home, and paid the bills. Soon, they found their money was gone and so was their hope to enter Bible college.

When his mother's health improved, the couple continued on their way, searching for jobs and a place to live. During this search, someone suggested

> *The Allens began their new life together with one hundred dollars, a few wedding gifts, and an old Model A Ford. They had no jobs and no promise of any, but they knew they were called of God to preach.*

they hold a church meeting in a local home. So God provided Allen's first chance to preach, and before the meeting was over, they left that home with plans made for the first A. A. Allen revival meetings.

But there was one problem – no money and none expected coming in, so the couple began chopping wood and selling it during the day. The money they made bought gasoline for their preaching trips. For two weeks, they chopped and hauled wood, stopping only to write down thoughts God would give them for preaching that evening.

Allen's heroes were Dwight L. Moody and Charles Finney. The first sermon he preached was based on the sermons of these men.

At their first Thanksgiving dinner, instead of turkey, they ate opossum, which they gladly accepted from the congregation. Lexie stuffed it and prepared it just as she would a turkey. The congregation took an offering at the end of two weeks to surprise the preacher, and collected thirty-five cents.

BEANS AND BACKWOODS

When the last meeting ended, they were given an invitation to conduct another one, but that posed a problem – the location was too far from their home to drive to in one day, so they would have to find another place to stay near their new meeting location. The only place vacant was a two-room cabin being used as a granary, but the kind old man who owned the building agreed to remove the grain and allow them to stay. There were huge cracks in the floor, the windows were broken out, and the back door had disappeared. However, they made the best of it by hanging a blanket in place of the door, draping cloth over the windows, and using cushions out of their car for a bed. Lexie used old orange crates covered with tea towels for chairs and a table, and for weeks, they lived on beans and cornbread, relying totally on the Lord to supply their needs. In their diary, they recorded special offerings with amounts like "five cents."

During these meetings, the Allens learned the power of prayer. After one prayer session, everyone who attended the following revival meetings was born again with a total of thirty people saved in two weeks, many of them having walked six miles just to attend the meeting. After holding a baptismal service, they set out on the road again.

If there had been jobs at this time, Allen would have taken secular employment, but there were none to be had, so he worked at studying the Bible and praying. The rest of his time was spent visiting people and praying for their needs.

"LIKE A WHIRLWIND, I HEARD HIS VOICE"

In the late 1930s, just weeks after their first son was born, Allen accepted a pastorate with the Tower Memorial Assembly of God, in Holly, Colorado. While there, Allen was licensed by the Assemblies of God.

Determined to find the secret of God's power, Allen began to fast and pray and seek the Lord. Fasting was new to him and so he encountered considerable trouble. Just as he would start to seek the Lord, he would smell the food his wife was cooking for her son and herself. But try as he might to be committed, the spirit was willing but the flesh was weak. He would finally give in, emerge from his prayer closet and join the family meal.

Then one day, just as he had taken a bite of food, he was immediately convicted. Dropping his fork, he announced to his wife that he wasn't coming out of his prayer closet until he heard from the Lord, and even instructed her to lock him in the closet. She laughed and told him that he would be pounding to get out within an hour.

But hours passed, and he didn't knock to get out. Wrestling with his flesh, he found the victory inside of his prayer closet, and in his own words, he tells of his experience with the Lord:

> "...I began to realize that the light that was filling my prayer closet was God's glory!...The presence of God was so real and powerful that I felt I would die right there on my knees....Then, like a whirlwind, I heard His voice. It was God! He was speaking to me! This was the glorious answer that I had sought so diligently and for which I had waited since my conversion at the age of twenty-three....It seemed faster than any human could possibly speak, faster than I could follow mentally, God was talking to me....God was giving me a list of the things

which stood between me and the power of God. After each new requirement was added to the list in my mind, there followed a brief explanation, or sermonette, explaining that requirement and its importance.... As God spoke to me, I wrote them down."

THE PRICE TAG FOR MIRACLES

"...It seemed faster than any human could possibly speak, faster than I could follow mentally, God was talking to me. ...God was giving me a list of the things which stood between me and the power of God."

"...When the last requirement was written down on the list, God spoke once again, and said: *'This is the answer. When you have placed on the altar of consecration and obedience the last thing on your list, you shall not only heal the sick, but in My Name shall you cast out devils, you shall see mighty miracles as in My Name you preach the Word, for behold, I give you power over all the power of the enemy.'*

"God revealed to me at the same time that the things that were hindrances to my ministry...were the very same things which were hindering so many thousands of others.

"At last, here was the price I must pay for the power of God in my life and ministry. THE PRICE TAG FOR THE MIRACLEWORKING POWER OF GOD!"[10]

Here are the thirteen things A. A. Allen said the Lord told him. He would see the miracle-working power of God, if he understood and did these things:

1. He must realize he couldn't do greater quality miracles than Jesus.
2. He could walk as Jesus walked.
3. He must be blameless like God Himself.
4. He must measure himself to Jesus alone.
5. He must deny his fleshly desires with fasting.
6. After self-denial, he must follow Jesus seven days a week.
7. Without God, he could do nothing!
8. He must do away with sin in his body.

9. He must not continue in shallow, pointless discussions.

10. He must give his body wholly to God forever.

11. He must believe all of God's promises.

The remaining two guidelines were "pet sins" that God had pointed out by name. Allen never felt he could share them with anyone.[11]

HEAVEN'S VISIT — THE FIRST MIRACLE

Finally, Allen began pounding on the closet door for his wife to let him out, and as soon as she saw his face she said, "You've got the answer!"

"Yes...God has paid me a visit from heaven, and here is the answer."

Written on a piece of cardboard were the thirteen requirements from the Lord. The couple sat at their old kitchen table. They both wept as he told her the story and went over the list.

Shortly after that visitation from God, the Allens resigned from their church, feeling called to the evangelistic field and so, by invitation, set out for Missouri. It was there that the Allens saw their first miracle service.

An old coal miner who was totally blind as a result of a mine explosion years earlier began attending the services. Night after night, he sat and listened to the Word of God, and finally, in response to an altar call, came forward for healing.

The Allens were shocked by his faith, and both admitted later that it would take more faith than they had for this man to receive his healing! They prayed for everyone who came forward and placed the blind man at the end of the line. People who had headaches, colds, and deaf ears were healed and went on their way rejoicing, but the blind man remained.

Suddenly, Allen called for everyone who had faith for the healing of this blind man to come up and pray with them. Then he said, **"There is unbelief in this room. I can feel it!"** And with that, a man got up and stomped out the door.

A. A. Allen

God answered their prayer. When the prayer was finished, the blind man could name the color of Allen's tie and point to objects around the room![12]

WOMAN — THE COAT OF MANY COLORS

For the next four and a half years, Allen traveled as an Assemblies of God revivalist. Though he held a prestigious position, his pay was very low, and financially, life remained hard during the first half of the 1940s, especially now that they had four children. Lexie stayed at home to care for the young babies. Allen was away sometimes for three consecutive months at a time.

> *Lexie had to cope with the frustrations of not seeing her husband regularly, while having to deal with her own call.*

Lexie had to cope with the frustrations of not seeing her husband regularly, while having to deal with her own call.

Though she longed for the stability of a normal home life, she learned a valuable ministry lesson. She was called into the ministry, but her ministry also consisted of being a mother. She realized there was a timing to all things. Motherhood and a stable home were to never be sacrificed for the other half of her ministry call, because those days would come again for her, and then she would have fulfillment, knowing that every facet of her call had been completed.

Years later, as the children grew older, Allen continued to evangelize alone. Lexie looked around her community and found a section without a Full Gospel church. So she started a church and became the pastor! When Allen was financially able to take her and the children on his trips, she eventually resigned the church and turned it over to another pastor![13]

HEAVEN ON EARTH — TEXAS!

Then, in 1947, Lexie received a phone call from Allen, telling her to get ready to move to Corpus Christi, Texas. He had been asked to pastor one of the largest Assemblies of God churches in the area, and was very excited, thinking of the stability this would provide his family. He told Lexie that they would probably stay there until Jesus came again.

The Allen family loved Corpus Christi and the church there, but in a city of over one hundred thousand people, there were only a handful of Full Gospel churches.

The Allens came at the time of the church's building program, and where some would have been overwhelmed, Allen's spiritual appetite was only whetted. He threw himself into this new phase of work, dreaming of a church that would operate in the gifts of the Spirit, evangelize, and progressively move forward in the things of heaven. This church seemed to be his answer. The church members heard him preach for two weeks before asking him to be their pastor. He preached hard, holding nothing back from what he believed, and they still wanted him!

He gave every area of that ministry his utmost attention, with each worker being selected and given special training. The attendance grew, and they soon ran out of space.

A DEADLY BLOW

Now, the church was reaching a few hundred people, but Allen was considering how to reach the city through radio. So he began to lay plans for an effective radio ministry and even attended a radio seminar in Springfield, Missouri.

He returned home, thrilled and filled with energy, so he called a special board meeting and carefully explained his radio plans to reach the city, knowing the men of the board would catch his vision.

Allen had tried to compromise his heavenly call for earthly security, which is understandable, because he wanted to be a dad to his children.

But one of the men proceeded to inform him that the board didn't approve of what he was doing, and that he was wearing them out! The board member went on to say that Allen had helped them build one of the finest churches in Texas, but they needed time to recover from that, and that they couldn't keep up the pace.

Then another stood and called attention to the tremendous cost and burden it would be on the church. The general opinion was that enough had been accomplished for the time being, and no further advances needed to be made for some time.[14]

Allen was absolutely crushed, and he quickly dismissed the meeting.

A point here: It was Allen's *call* that energized him to move forward. His call wasn't to the pastorate, but to evangelize the nations. Allen was spiritually built for this kind of thrust; it came with his call. Lay people are not automatically built that way, and there is nothing wrong with this. It is just a fact. God gave us the fivefold ministry gifts in order to step up the spiritual process so we can all keep the timing of heaven. We need lay people, and we definitely need pastors. But just as importantly, we *need* everyone to stand in the office of their calling and operate in the heavenly anointing.

Sadly though, Allen innocently tried to disguise and confine his call to that of a pastor. Can you imagine how it must have felt to try to restrict the call of an evangelistic revivalist? When the board vetoed Allen's thrust, they unknowingly killed a large portion of his being by bridling his life and snuffing out a portion of his destiny.

Allen had tried to compromise his heavenly call for earthly security, which is understandable, because he wanted to be a dad to his children. But soon, Allen would see that the price was too great. It would have been better, though possibly harder, to seek God and find another way of making it work.

BLACKNESS, TORMENT, HELL: THE BREAKDOWN

When Allen returned home, he said nothing to his wife, trying to act as if nothing had happened. He even discussed a vacation with her.

But during the night she awoke to hear Allen sobbing in the next room. She thought he was interceding for someone until he came into the bedroom, still sobbing deeply.

Startled, she questioned him. It was then that he told her what happened at the board meeting, and she saw he was more than disappointed, he was devastated. There was no bitterness, no anger, no blame – just a broken heart.

Allen offered his resignation and felt he could never preach again. But the church really loved him, and they offered him several months of vacation with full salary. They even insisted that additional offerings be given to him to take care of any expense he incurred on the trip.

It was apparent Allen was suffering from an emotional breakdown. The church thought he was overworked, but his wife aware of his strength and his zeal, knew that wasn't possible. She knew the breakdown came from a broken heart. A portion of his being was held captive, and he thought he had lost it forever.

Lexie took him on an extended vacation, but he was so tormented, he could find only a partial rest as they traveled, and as his condition grew worse, it became impossible for either of them to rest. After only a week in the mountains with no relief, he wanted to go home, thinking he would never return to normal.

"COME OUT OF HIM!"

Lexie began to seek the Lord desperately. Suddenly, it came to her! They had not failed...God wasn't through with them! The call and purpose of God for A. A. Allen was just as it had always been! When she finally realized that Satan had taken advantage of his deep hurt, she began to pray against the attack. Soon Allen also saw that he was being tormented by a demon that was taking advantage of his emotional hurt. He realized he was being attacked by a tormenting spirit.

While driving back to Texas, Allen pulled the car to the side of the road and asked his wife to lay hands on him. According to Allen, the second Lexie said, "Come out of him, I command you to GO," the evil spirit left him, and they rejoiced together as he actually felt a physical release and lightness replace the heaviness he had felt. Then suddenly, he began to get sleepy, and before Lexie could pull onto the road, he was asleep, never remembering getting home, nor getting into his own bed. He slept like a baby for three days straight, and when he woke up, he was fully recovered.

"YOU FAILED TO PAY THE PRICE"

By fall of 1949, the Allens began to hear stories about miraculous healing meetings that were taking place. The evangelists conducting the meetings weren't necessarily outstanding preachers. In fact, many preachers were more eloquent in their sermon delivery than these evangelists, but when these healing evangelists prayed for the sick, miracles happened so quickly, no one could count them. The Allens refused to believe half of the stories they were told, but their curiosity was aroused.

> *...when these healing evangelists prayed for the sick, miracles happened so quickly, no one could count them.*

One day, a friend gave Allen a copy of *The Voice of Healing* publication. After reading it, Allen said, **"As I read its pages, I laughed in ridicule. *Fanatics*, I thought, as I closed the magazine and laid it away in my study."**[15] Some of his church members came from these tent meetings with glowing reports, but Allen discounted them and felt they were drifting into fanaticism.

Personally, I don't believe that was his true heart in the matter. He might have spoken those words, but I believe he was incredibly stirred inside, because he knew this was his own call being manifested before his very eyes.

However, you can become so backslidden in your calling that the things you once held as precious and attainable, are now a distant memory.

Not long after this, some minister friends persuaded Allen to go to Dallas and attend an Oral Roberts tent revival. Along the way, he remembered the experience he had with God in his prayer closet many years ago, recalling the thirteen things that stood in his way of walking into the miraculous. Being out of his spiritual office and trying, instead, to be a pastor had caused him to shelve the vision God gave him.

As he approached Dallas, he became more and more aware that there he would witness the very thing God had called him to do. **"But I had never paid the price for God's miracle-working power in my life,"** he added.[16]

He was captivated by the tent meeting and by the power of God being displayed through Roberts, feeling as though he was living in the book of Acts. Miracle after miracle took place as he watched, but it wasn't fanaticism; it was God's miracle working power.

As he sat watching the prayer line, he again heard the voice of God say:

"My son, eleven years ago you sought My face.... Eleven years ago I called you into the same ministry.... But you failed to pay the price and to make the consecration. Therefore, you have failed to do this thing which I have called you to do." With tears streaming down his face, Allen lifted his hands and cried out, **"Lord, I'll do it!"**[17]

GOING, GOING...GONE!

Two Sundays later, he resigned his pastorate. He would have left the first Sunday after his return, but his wife asked him to wait and make sure he was doing the right thing.

Immediately, pastors from all over the nation called for his services as an evangelist, and in less than a month, a new pastor occupied the pulpit. The Allens kept the Corpus Christi church as their home base and traveled out from there.

They moved all their possessions into a house trailer, and in less than three months after his "breakdown," A. A. Allen was on the revival trail.

Allen began studying the list of thirteen requirements the Lord had given him eleven years earlier. He couldn't believe all the time that had been lost. Eleven years! As he studied the list, he noticed that numbers twelve and thirteen had not been accomplished in his life, but that every other item had been marked through. Finally, with great determination, he was able to mark through the last two. After that, noticeable miracles began to take place through his ministry.

In May of 1950, Allen sent his first report to *The Voice of Healing* magazine, the result of a great campaign in Oakland, California. Of the meeting he writes:

> **"Many say this is the greatest revival in the history of Oakland.... Night after night, the waves of Divine Glory so sweep over the congregation that many testify of being healed while sitting in their seats."**[18]

In 1951, Allen made a great leap. He decided to purchase a tent and advertise himself as a "healing" revivalist. He heard of a tent for sale, equipped with lighting, seats, a platform, and a public address system, all for $8,500!

But he only had $1,500, so he called the minister and made the offer of $1,500 as a downpayment. The owner told him that another preacher had just called and offered the full price, but he would pray about the matter and call him the next day.

The next day when Allen called the man, he wasn't surprised to learn that the owner decided to give the tent to him with a $1,500 downpayment. The rest was to be paid in $100 payments, as Allen could afford, so the tent was his!

On July 4, 1951, the A. A. Allen Revival Tent went up for the first campaign in Yakima, Washington.[19]

FINALLY — RADIO!

In November of 1953, Allen finally saw his dream come true, when he began the nationally known radio broadcast, *Allen Revival Hour*, on nine stations and two superpowered stations. By 1955, Allen was on seventeen Latin American stations and eighteen American ones.[20] Soon, he had to set up a permanent office to take care of the flood of mail coming in. He began conducting yearly services in Cuba and Mexico. Many responded to the altar calls by denouncing witchcraft and destroying their idols on the platform. These revivals continued from 1955 until 1959 when Castro took power.

Allen seemed to thrive on persecution and pressure. Described as a short, "jowly" man, his face would contort into a scowl as he loudly roared one minute and whispered the next.

Allen seemed to thrive on persecution and pressure. Described as a short, "jowly" man, his face would contort into a scowl as he loudly roared one minute and whispered the next. He was an "old-time religion" preacher, complete with foot-stomping, shrieks, sobs, cries of **"Glory to God!"**, loud tongues, and wild, dramatic dancing. He would sometimes hop up and down while pounding on a tambourine, and during his meetings you were likely to see someone turning cartwheels down the aisle, "jerking" across the front of the platform, and several people dancing ballet style throughout the crowd.

Allen was never influenced by the changing fads, but he felt it was his job to preach this way. He didn't mince words when he preached, and he seemed to always turn adversity into his advantage. He said what he thought, and that is what the people came to hear.

> *...Allen told his friends that he had been kidnapped and knocked unconscious. When Allen awoke, one friend said he was in a "smoke-filled room, and somebody was pouring liquor down his throat."*

HARD KNOCKS IN KNOXVILLE

In 1955, accusations began surfacing, each one more serious than the previous one, each affecting Allen greatly.

The charge that Allen drank abusively always seemed to follow his ministry. Whether people believed the charges or not depended on whether people listened to his enemies or his friends.[21] Some never believed that he was able to overcome the excessive abuse of alcohol that was so much a part of his youth.

But his greatest crisis came in the fall of 1955 while conducting a revival in Knoxville, Tennessee. Allen was arrested for drunken driving, but the case never came to trial because Allen failed to appear in court, so he forfeited his $1,000 bail and left the state.[22]

The entire incident is hazy. But Allen maintained that the Knoxville media was notorious in their slander of evangelists, and he stated that he was even shown a list of preachers who paid certain newspapers to slander him. According to one close associate, Allen told his friends that he had been kidnapped and knocked unconscious. When Allen awoke, one friend said he was in a "smoke-filled room, and somebody was pouring liquor down his throat." However, word had already spread that Allen had confessed the charge to prominent ministers of Knoxville.[23]

WITHDRAW? NO WAY!

In 1956, upon hearing of the charges and the controversy, Ralph M. Riggs, superintendent of the General Council of the Assemblies of God, sent Allen a letter asking him to withdraw from public meetings until things cleared up. Allen felt this request was impossible, and felt his organization had deserted him when he needed them the most, in order to save their reputation. He sent Riggs a searing letter reminding him how he had ministered with him for **"eighteen years with no question being raised at any time concerning my integrity,"** and then turned in his ministerial credentials to the Assemblies of God, stating that in doing so there was **"no great loss."** He told Riggs that **"a withdrawal from public ministry at this time would ruin my ministry, for it would have the appearance of an admission of guilt."**[24]

The accusation also caused great problems in the Voice of Healing association. Though Lexie assured the leadership of the Voice of Healing association that the charges weren't true, Gordon Lindsay felt that those who belonged to the group must make a strong stand on ethics, so Allen resigned from that group as well.

Allen's daughter felt that the Voice of Healing was really an Assemblies of God organization of evangelists, stating that they were trying "real hard to work within the framework of the Assemblies." If the rules weren't obeyed within the general denomination, a minister could possibly have trouble with the Voice of Healing network.[25]

R. W. SCHAMBACH SPEAKS

One of the greatest evangelistic ministries in our generation is that of R. W. Schambach from Tyler, Texas. When Schambach was just starting out in ministry, he joined Allen's revival team and soon became his right-hand man. Being a man of character and integrity, he knew what it meant to pay the price for revival.

Recently, Schambach and I were in the same town, attending the same meeting, when I shared my views with him concerning the importance of preserving history for the generations to come.

He agreed to tell me his side of the A. A. Allen story, so as we spoke, he shared with me some very interesting things. Schambach told me how he joined the A. A. Allen revival team the night before the Knoxville incident. Then, he made a startling statement, contrary to every other written account of A. A. Allen.

Schambach said that Allen *wasn't* drunk. "I know," he stated, "because I was with him in the car!" He said the entire incident was a conspiracy to ruin Allen's ministry, and after the Knoxville trouble, he saw the extreme persecution that Allen suffered. It was here that Schambach began to learn how to pay the price for revival. No matter what kind of accusation was hurled at Allen, Schambach knew the man's innocence, because he was with him all the time. So, Schambach remained faithful to serve Allen in his ministry. For the six years that Schambach was his associate, he went on every crusade with the evangelist.

> *"There was not a jealous bone in his body," Schambach smiled. "If I would get started on a point, he'd yell out, 'Go ahead Schambach, you've got it!'"*

"He was a man of God," Schambach remembered. "I was with him all the time, like a hand in [a] glove. When we had to travel together, I even slept in the same room with him! He never did one thing contrary to the Word. He was a man of prayer and a man of miracles. That's how I knew him."

Schambach also described Allen as a "very touchable" man, accessible to the people at all times. "There was not a jealous bone in his body," Schambach smiled. "If I would get started on a point, he'd yell out **'Go, ahead Schambach, you've got it!'** Then he would sit back and let me preach, no matter where we were." Schambach humorously compared Allen's clothes and personality to a "cross between James Cagney and Spike Jones."

As Schambach and I walked outside of the hotel to continue our discussion, we noticed a fire truck in the parking lot.

"Oh, that reminds me of another story, Roberts."

Schambach said that the story about the fire on top of the tent during the Los Angeles meeting really happened! It seemed that the fire trucks went rushing up and down the streets searching for the fire but could never find it. They knew that a fire was coming from somewhere because they could see the smoke. Finally, the fire trucks went in the direction of the tent, but once they arrived, no fire was to be found.

"God wanted everyone to know that we were in town," he smiled. "So He put His holy fire on the top of that tent just to let the folks know we were there."

What about the "miracle oil" that appeared in the palms of people's hands?

"That was real, too. I even had an element of it on my own hands," Schambach answered.

In Los Angeles, at one of the Allen meetings, "Everyone got the oil on their hands but Allen," Schambach smiled. "I believe God allowed that just to prove that it was true and not a hoax."[26]

Schambach left A. A. Allen to begin his own ministry in 1961. But Schambach stood faithfully by Allen for the rest of his life. If there is anyone who operates similar to the ministry of A. A. Allen, it is the great evangelist, R. W. Schambach.

FORWARD! FOR A WHILE

So, Allen had turned in his license with the Assemblies of God and broken his ties with the Voice of Healing association, and became an independent evangelist. Many said it suited him well, and history books note the same.

Most evangelists do work well independently, as long as they stay "hooked up" with those who understand their call and can scripturally speak into their lives. They can call a church their "home church," but that local church must give them the freedom to pursue their individual call. It is sometimes difficult for their methods to meet with the approval of an organized establishment because the two are so different. Evangelistic revivalists are fast, wild, dramatic, and have the strength of an ox. If a pastor understands the call of an evangelist, the two can work well together, but if the pastor tries to control an evangelist to fit within needs of the local church, there will be trouble.

The year of 1956 seemed to be a time when ministries were changing. But Allen found a way to thrust forward when many were pulling back. He had a great ability to raise money, and at this time, was still attempting to stay within his call.

So Allen progressed forward by starting his own publication, *Miracle Magazine*. It consisted of his messages on healing and deliverance and featured many healing testimonies. By the end of 1956, it had a paid subscription list of over two hundred thousand people.

By the fall, Allen had started the Miracle Revival Fellowship, an independent organization to license ministers and to support missions. He firmly denied any charges that it was "denominationally minded." Allen reported five hundred ministers in its first ordination.[27]

SENSATIONALISM, CONTROVERSY, AND MIRACLES

After the Knoxville incident, Allen became an extremely controversial figure, and the media followed him everywhere hoping for a story. Wild and sensational occurrences were reported to have happened at the Allen revivals, but much of these reports were aimed at discrediting his ministry. Lexie said that during this time, Allen's enemies did all they could to destroy him. It did seem that whenever persecution would attack him, he would retaliate with some unusual miracle or occurrence, going to the extreme in an attempt to prove his call.

In Los Angeles, it was reported that a cross appeared on Allen's forehead, and a flaming fire appeared over his tent...

In Los Angeles, it was reported that a cross appeared on Allen's forehead, and a flaming fire appeared over his tent, as R. W. Schambach mentioned earlier in the chapter. According to Allen, this was a sign. As proof, he cited Ezekiel 9:4, which says an angel was sent from heaven to place a mark on the foreheads of all the people who cry out for the Lord because of evil in the earth. The sighting on Allen's forehead and the flame over the tent were reported by the media.

Allen's cameraman, R. E. Kemery, took a picture of a man who had nail scars appear in his hands. At another meeting, "miracle oil" reportedly began to flow from the heads and hands of those attending the Allen revivals. Allen answered those who questioned this occurrence by referring to Hebrews 1:9 that stated, the reward for hating evil and loving righteousness was to be anointed with the oil of gladness.

He was also criticized for selling a recording that captured the sounds of a demon-possessed woman, and he also sold a booklet that contained eighteen drawings of demons, drawn by a demon-possessed, insane person.

Some of the healings were sensational, and in one meeting near Los Angeles, a five hundred pound woman lost two hundred pounds instantly when Allen laid hands on her. People testified to seeing her body shrink.

A Full Gospel pastor who had "alligator scales" on his arms for nearly fifty years, was healed as he sat on stage behind Allen. The scales dried up, fell off, new skin appeared, and the pastor was able to wear short sleeve shirts for the first time.

Another man was driving down the highway, and as he listened to the *Allen Radio Hour* he was moved in his heart. So he pulled the car over, laid his hands on the radio, and prayed with Allen asking God to "put all the parts back." He had his right lung, three ribs, and a chest bone removed by surgeons, plus he was missing his second toe on the left foot because of disease. That night, the man's toe grew in complete with the toenail, and his physician was amazed when the X-rays showed that what he had removed had returned in its proper place.

When Allen submitted an advertisement to the *Akron Journal* in 1957, he was refused. Instead, the paper published a front page "slander account" of this ministry warning the city of his revival. Allen announced that he had received $25,000 worth of front-page advertising, absolutely free.[28]

In the mid-fifties, he unleashed an all out attack on denominationalism and "man-formed religion." While many things he said and wrote concerning denominationalism were true, it was apparent he was speaking from hurt and frustration. When he tried to open lines of communication again with the Assemblies of God headquarters, according to Allen, they banished him and urged others to ignore him as well. While the General Council denied his charge, they did state that his ministry "threw a shadow."[29] In other words, if someone associated with Allen, that person's own character would be in question.

MIRACLES FROM THE VALLEY

Even with all the controversy, Allen's ministry continued to grow, and he began the International Miracle Revival Training Camp for ministers. Here, he taught ministers the principles of prosperity, healing, casting out demons, and various other topics.

And in January of 1958, while holding a revival in Phoenix, Arizona, God impressed him to build a Bible school there. That same morning, twelve hundred fifty acres of land a few miles from Tombstone, Arizona, were given to him. He called the land "Miracle Valley," and began building his headquarters and training center. He doubled the acreage, and many Native American tribe members were born again as a result of his ministry. Christians in the area were fervently revived, and the area became a thriving city by the 1960s.

> *He preached the same message with the same fervency to each audience, and never changed the text to fit the class of people.*

The year of 1958 became a time of crisis for the Voice of Healing revival, but it didn't seem so for Allen. That year, he announced a five-pronged program for his ministry in Miracle Valley – tent revivals, the *Allen Revival Hour* radio program, overseas mission programs, the Miracle Valley Training Center, and a publications department.[30] It was dur-

Anatomy of a miracle

"The Lord is here to set you free!"

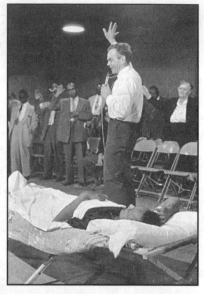

"We ask you now God to heal!"

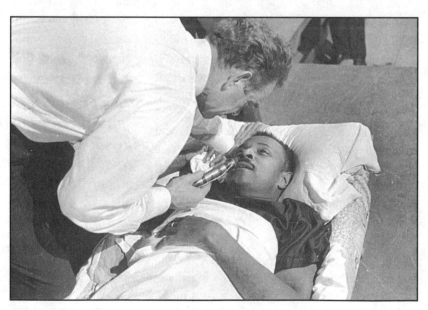

"What would you like Jesus to do for you?"

"If you believe God is healing you, rise up now in faith."

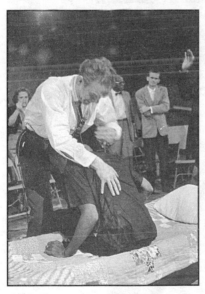

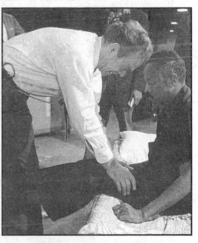

"Now do something with those legs you couldn't do before."

"That's it..."

"Healed in Jesus' name!"

"Let's walk a while."

ing this time that he began teaching prosperity according to the Bible. In fact, most everything he taught connected in some way with financial prosperity.

People from every social strata attended his meetings. He preached the same message with the same fervency to each audience, and never changed the text to fit the class of people. Everything from mink coats and pearls, to bare feet and overalls could be seen at his meetings. When people walked through the parking lot, they would see everything from polished Cadillacs, to car hoods tied down with rusted wire.

But in 1960, during the heat of racial tension, the Ku Klux Klan threatened to disrupt an Allen meeting where white and black people were present. They succeeded in blowing up a nearby bridge with dynamite hoping to scare Allen and his group, but both the worship service and the baptismal service continued without a hint of fear.

It was also in 1960 that Allen built a church in Miracle Valley that seated four thousand people. He had great plans for this city and wanted to build private homes, recreational facilities, and media centers.

A TRAGIC ENDING

Something happened during the last few years of Allen's life and ministry. Though the details are sketchy, Allen was sued for $300,000 in back taxes. And in 1967, Allen and his wife, Lexie, separated. Details about this incident are unclear, but close friends of the family state the couple never divorced.

The few details available report that before their separation, each were totally engulfed in serving the Lord until their deaths, with Lexie, a journalist, spending her time at home and Allen traveling extensively, rarely at home. Some believe if Allen had not died a short time after the separation, that he and Lexie would have reunited. Upon their deaths, they were buried side by side, sharing the same gravestone, on the grounds of Miracle Valley.

In 1969, Allen was a sick man suffering from a severe arthritic condition in his knee. He spent much time recalling his humble beginnings. According to him, that year the *Miracle Magazine* had a circulation of 340,000, with mail received from ninety nations.

But the arthritic condition soon worsened, so Allen submitted to surgery on his left knee. He suffered from so much pain that Don Stewart, a young man, full of zeal, began to fill in during the crusades.

On June 11, 1970, Allen traveled to San Francisco and checked into the Jack Tar Hotel (now named the Cathedral Hills Quality Hotel). He checked in at

12:56 P.M. He was scheduled the next day for a 9:00 A.M. doctor's appointment at the University of California Medical Center in San Francisco, to discuss whether a second surgery needed to be performed on his knees.

Sometime before 9:00 P.M. the same evening, Allen made a phone call to his close friend, Bernard Schwartz. The exact conversation is unknown, but Schwartz was alarmed and proceeded to the hotel. When Schwartz arrived at Allen's room, the door was locked and he didn't answer. Schwartz told the assistant manager of the problem and Allen's door was opened with a pass key.

At 9:15 P.M., Allen was found dead by Schwartz and the assistant manager. The Coroner's Report states Allen was sitting in a chair in front of his television. He was officially pronounced dead at 11:23 P.M. on June 11, 1970. A. A. Allen was fifty-nine years old.

> *...when Schwartz arrived at Allen's room, the door was locked and he didn't answer.*

WHAT HAPPENED? THE CORONER'S REPORT

There are some details about A. A. Allen and his death that are very important. Though not widely known, he was suffering from a severe arthritic condition. In fact, it is documented that his personal physician, Dr. Seymour Farber, prescribed Percodan, Seconal, and Valium to ease the pain and for insomnia brought on by the severity of the pain.

Here are the facts: The Coroner's Report, Case #1151 for Asa Alonzo Allen recorded the blood alcohol concentration in Allen's body measured .036 percent – a very high and concentrated level of alcohol in the blood system. The cause of death on the coroner's report was stated as "acute alcoholism and fatty infiltration of the liver."

At first, it would seem that Allen died a chronic alcoholic, but upon further investigation, I believe the opposite. Here is my opinion of what I believe happened.

HOLD ON! LET'S INVESTIGATE

First of all, his personal physician knew Allen very well. Though chronic alcoholics can deceive a novice, they cannot deceive their personal physician; especially if their personal physician sees them as many times as Dr. Farber saw Allen and tested him. Dr. Farber wouldn't have prescribed such highly addictive drugs as Percodan, Valium, and Seconal to a chronic alcoholic. It would have been a death sentence, because the mixture of alcohol and prescribed barbiturates and narcotics could lead to death. When Allen's blood scan was performed and reported by a laboratory toxiology department, there was no trace of drugs found in his system, though there were plenty of prescribed pills at the death scene.

His closest personal friends say that Allen detested, even hated prescribed medications. He continually stated that he wouldn't take the medications and preach, as the drug effects lingered with him and he couldn't think clearly.

Understanding how Allen was raised, I believe we are dealing with a position of attitude. Allen was in severe, arthritic pain – in fact, so much pain he could barely move.

Medical personnel who work with arthritic patients say it isn't unusual for the patients to use alcohol in a medicinal sense. Many turn to it instead of developing an addiction to prescribed drugs. I am not offering an excuse, but I am presenting a reality.

It should be recognized that the coroner's report stated Allen died of "acute" alcoholism, not "chronic" alcoholism. There is a distinct difference in the medical verbiage.

"Acute" means rapid onset or sudden, but "chronic " means ongoing; or in other words, an alcoholic. The coroner's report said Allen died of a sudden onset of alcohol, *not* of alcoholism.

Here is another fact. According to the autopsy report, fatty tissue found within the liver is consistent with alcoholic binge drinking.

We must also understand that there is a medical difference between chronic and habitual drinkers. Chronic drinkers have drunk for a long period of time, staying drunk most of the time whether you can tell it or not. A habitual drinker could have only been drinking for a few weeks, or, they are also called social drinkers.

...there is no evidence whatsoever that Allen was an alcoholic, as the condition of his liver proved.

In discussing this autopsy diagnosis with several prominent physicians and specialists throughout the country, they explained to me that this liver condition *was not* cirrhosis. Cirrhosis of the liver comes from chronic alcoholism and is a death of the liver tissue that spreads gradually over a period of time. If the fatty tissue throughout the liver remains intact from habitual drinking, it could lead to cirrhosis.

Habitual drinking of alcohol produces fatty tissue. After several days, if no further alcohol is ingested, the tissue dissolves and returns to normal. Allen had the liver of someone who, for a period of weeks or months, had been binge drinking, which means simply he was drinking to the point of drunkenness.

Throughout the coroner's report, the majority of the discussion centers around Allen's arthritic condition; not the alcoholic content found in his blood. In fact, there is no evidence whatsoever that Allen was an alcoholic, as the condition of his liver proved. Instead, there is much more evidence that the alcohol was taken medicinally.

That is what I believe as well. Allen wasn't an alcoholic, but I think he periodically binged on alcohol for medicinal relief, and to be honest, I really don't believe Allen saw much of a difference between alcohol and prescribed drugs. He hated prescribed drugs and their lingering effects. Alcohol can dissipate quickly and the effects were probably less severe with him. He might not have always chosen the alcohol over the drugs; but we medically know that at least for a few weeks, he did.

It is easy to think clearly if your body is free from pain, but attitudes are sometimes different in someone who is experiencing constant and excruciating pain.

It is my opinion that on the night of his death, Allen was in excruciating pain. This seems especially clear because he had flown to San Francisco for a doctor's appointment the next day.

From the facts that I have researched, it is my opinion that on this particular evening of June 11, 1970, in a desperate attempt to stop the pain, Allen literally drank himself to death.

THE VALLEY OF SHADOWS

Though some of the ministerial details at the end of his life are vague, his former banking department head, Mrs. Helen McMaines, has a great love and respect for Allen, saying he was "one of a kind." According to Mrs. McMaines, he was up front and honest with all the financial gain his ministry received, and she remembered how he would bring the love offerings to her and plop the heavy bags down on the counter. **"Put it all back into the ministry, Helen,"** she remembers Allen saying, **"This all belongs to God."** McMaines said that he worked day and night for the people, never seeming to tire.

"Nothing was put in his name; not the house or anything in Miracle Valley," Mrs. McMaines stated. "According to him, when he died, all of the property should go to God." Mrs. McMaines sadly reiterated that she believed there has never been another minister like A. A. Allen. "He was not afraid to fight the devil," she proclaimed, "and when you are not afraid to fight the devil, all kinds of persecution will rise up against you." The McMaines are a charming couple, and still maintain a close relationship with Allen's son, James. According to them, James Allen highly respects the ministry of his father and mother.[31]

In spite of Allen's fervency, it does seem that his charismatic personality and ministry direction did change in the later years, by publishing violent renunciations of certain churches, and focusing heavily on vows and financial prosperity. Did the extreme hurts, betrayals and denominational conspiracies against him push him into this type of ministry? Did God remove Allen's focus on the miracle ministry of divine healing? Whatever the reasons, I feel that the ministry of A. A. Allen ended sadly, much like the ministry of John Alexander Dowie.

Just like Dowie's Zion City, there is no longer a spiritual purpose for Allen's Miracle Valley.

Today, Miracle Valley is just twelve hundred fifty acres of land. Recently, I was informed that a farmer had purchased the acreage with plans to cultivate it. The buildings have all been torn down or rented.

I sponsored a group to go to Miracle Valley and search for memorabilia on Allen. What they found was shocking.

In a huge pile outside of a building, the group found hundreds of testimony letters, personal notebooks, letters, financial diaries, ministry photos, original text of the *Miracle Magazine*, film footage, undeveloped negatives, and a priceless notebook of healing testimonies with photos. The testimonies consisted of hundreds of healings: deafness, allergies, migraines, lung disease, ulcers, cancer, arthritis, bone deficiencies, blindness. It was all there, and whoever threw these things in the dumpster had obviously made one final attempt to destroy all traces of A. A. Allen's ministry.

But God had other plans.

Today, these items are registered in the historical museum of the Reformers and Revivalists Library, in Irvine, California. They will be safely preserved for this generation and the generations to follow. Here, not only can you study spiritual history, but you can see it and witness it as well.

LET'S GO FURTHER

I know Allen made mistakes. I have no problem with that. But in spite of the mistakes, he made an attempt to show how to pay the price for spiritual power. In fact, R. W. Schambach learned how to pay the price by observing him.

Allen overcame a horrendous background to pursue the call of God, and that is a great credit to him and his ministry, because he almost succeeded. But he didn't go far enough. We must go further than Allen did to succeed.

What does it take? It seems like a broken record, but I will say it again: *Stay in your call.* Don't venture out to satisfy a suggestion of someone else or the personal desire of your own and don't allow persecution and criticism to push you into a corner.

> *What does it take? It seems like a broken record, but I will say it again:* **Stay in your call.**

What else does it take? Begin to build an immunity to the things that affect you negatively. How? Guard your heart; let God lead you with His Word until there is no trace of withdrawal *or* self-propulsion within you, and soon, the persecution in that area of your life will not even affect you. Then if you begin to feel another "hit," or something begins to bother you, start building the immunity in that particular area as well. Find Scriptures that pertain to that area, according to your call. Then, speak them over your heart *until it saturates your being and becomes a part of you;* that's how you develop an immunity. Then, when that thing tries to capture you, you will walk right through it, and the Word will guard your heart. You will have built a spiritual strength in that area.

Be daily filled with the ministry of the Holy Spirit. Allow Him to impart the oil of joy and gladness into your life. His joy is what gives you the strength to succeed.

Don't try to stand alone, but keep yourself surrounded with people who know your call and are filled with the strength of the Word and the Spirit. If you don't have this operating in your life and ministry, then ask God to bring you those *divine* connections and relationships. These aren't "yes men" who pamper and encourage you in every decision you make, right or wrong, but are *divine relationships* with people who know how to stand strong in the Spirit because of their personal experience. If they keep themselves clean, they will be equipped to speak into your life and help you when a crisis comes your way.

Don't search the Scriptures to find retaliation against your accusers. If you do that, you will have a harsh and embittered ministry. At times, it is tempting, but God is the One who vindicates His own! So let God do His thing, and you do yours. Search the Scriptures for yourself *first.* And when God's Word heals you, you build an immunity through the Word, and are daily filled with the Holy Spirit, then you can take on the next level of ministry. But if you stop to point fingers, you will remain there. If you remain in one level too long, you will grow stagnant and search for other avenues of ministry. Or, you may search for other "highlights" within your current ministry. Some have remained in a position of stagnancy for so long they can't find their way back.

There is nothing new under the sun. What happened to these great men and women of the past, could happen again, so learn from their lives, and build strength in your inner man. It takes spiritual strength to fulfill the will of God. *Determine* that your life and ministry will be a spiritual success in heaven and in the earth, to the glory of God!

CHAPTER TWELVE, A. A. ALLEN
References

[1] David Harrell Jr., *All Things Are Possible* (Bloomington, IN: Indiana University Press, 1975), 66.
[2] Lexie E. Allen, *God's Man of Faith and Power* (Hereford, AZ: A. A. Allen Publications, 1954), 55.
[3] Ibid.
[4] Ibid., 56.
[5] Ibid., 17.
[6] Ibid., 18-20.
[7] Ibid., 22.
[8] Ibid., 25.
[9] Ibid., 29.
[10] Ibid., 98-104.
[11] A. A. Allen, *Price of God's Miracle-Working Power* (Miracle Valley, AZ: A. A. Allen Revivals Inc., 1950).
[12] L. Allen, *God's Man of Faith and Power*, 106-108.
[13] Ibid., 167-169.
[14] Ibid., 143-144.
[15] Ibid., 155.
[16] Ibid., 159.
[17] Ibid., 161-162.
[18] Ibid., 165.
[19] Ibid., 173-175.
[20] Harrell, *All Things Are Possible*, 68.
[21] Ibid., 70.
[22] Allen Spragget, *Kathryn Kuhlman: A Woman Who Believed in Miracles,* segment on Allen according to Knox County Criminal Court (New York: Signet Classics, published by the New American Library Inc., 1970), 32-33.
[23] Harrell, *All Things Are Possible,* 70.
[24] Ibid., 71.
[25] Ibid., 70-71.
[26] Personal interview with R. W. Schambach on March 22, 1996, El Paso, Texas.
[27] Harrell, *All Things Are Possible,* 74.
[28] Ibid., 72.
[29] Ibid., 71.
[30] Ibid., 74.
[31] Personal interview with Helen McMaines on April 29, 1996.

Books by Roberts Liardon

Breaking Controlling Powers

Smith Wigglesworth Speaks to Students of the Bible

Sharpen Your Discernment

Smith Wigglesworth:
The Complete Collection of His Life Teachings

God's Generals

God's Generals Workbook

A Call to Action

Cry of the Spirit:
Unpublished Sermons by Smith Wigglesworth

Forget Not His Benefits

Haunted Houses, Ghosts & Demons

Holding to the Word of the Lord

I Saw Heaven

Kathryn Kuhlman:
A Spiritual Biography of God's Miracle-Working Power

Religious Politics

Run to the Battle

School of the Spirit

Spiritual Timing

The Invading Force

The Price of Spiritual Power

The Quest for Spiritual Hunger

Also Available:

God's Generals Video Collection
(12 Video Tapes)

CHURCH HISTORY IS VALUABLE TO US

If you have any materials pertaining to Church history, we would like to know about them. Roberts Liardon Ministries is committed to preserving Christian archives in our Reformers and Revivalists Historical Museum. Memorabilia from our past is very valuable and vital to future Church growth.

We are looking for magazines, letters, books, manuscripts, photographs, audio and videotapes, movies, diaries, scrapbooks, and any other personal items that would portray our Church history. Thank you for desiring to bless the world with your historical treasures. Please contact our research department in California.

Roberts Liardon Ministries — Europe
P.O. Box 2043
Hove, Bringhton
East Sussex, BN3 6JU England
Phone and Fax: 44 1273 777427

Roberts Liardon Ministries — Australia
P. O. Box 439
Buderim QLD 4556
Australia
Phone: 011 61 754 422108

Roberts Liardon Ministries — South Africa
P.O. Box 3155
Kimberly 8300, South Africa
Phone and Fax: 27 531 82 1207

Roberts Liardon Ministries — USA
P.O. Box 30710
Laguna Hills, California 92654
Phone: (949) 833-3555
Fax: (949) 833-9555
or www.robertsliardon.org

Additional copies of this book and other book titles from ALBURY PUBLISHING are available at your local bookstore.

ALBURY PUBLISHING
P.O. Box 470406
Tulsa, Oklahoma 74147-0406

In Canada books are available from:
Word Alive
P. O. Box 670
Niverville, Manitoba
CANADA R0A 1E0

Bill,

"Check six!"

Robert Lawrence
Holt

GOOD FRIDAY

A NOVEL BY

ROBERT LAWRENCE HOLT

GOOD FRIDAY

A NOVEL BY

ROBERT LAWRENCE HOLT

AERO
A division of TAB BOOKS Inc.
Blue Ridge Summit, PA 17214

FIRST EDITION

FIRST PRINTING

Copyright © 1987 by Robert Lawrence Holt

Printed in the United States of America

Library of Congress Cataloging in Publication Data

Holt, Robert Lawrence.
   Good Friday.

   I. Title.
PS3562.A18G6 1987   813'.54   86-32182
ISBN 0-8306-8399-2

Questions regarding the content of this book
should be addressed to:

   Reader Inquiry Branch
   Editorial Department
   TAB BOOKS Inc.
   P.O. Box 40
   Blue Ridge Summit, PA 17214

Dedicated

to the young men and women of Saudi Arabia who are striving to bring their kingdom peacefully into the twentieth century. For their sake, I pray none of the cataclysmic events described herein become reality.

Foreword

Together with the late General Keith McCutcheon (the first four-star general in U.S. Marine aviation), I was one of the principal American generals during the period of 1970-1972 to push through the procurement of the AV-8A Harrier—one of the most remarkable weapons in the arsenal of the United States.

This is the first novel, of which I am aware, that reveals the great versatility of this marvelous piece of technology. As the reader will learn, the AV-8B (the most recent version) can outmaneuver any fighter in the world within its altitude. This is due to its superior turning capability, coupled with the dexterity to attain a near-instant hover in midair.

Detractors of this aircraft said the Harrier would operate under too many restrictions, such as limited airspeed, range, altitude, and payload. They were proved wrong in the air war over the Falklands, when only a V-STOL aircraft proved capable of landing on the primitive land conditions offered by those remote islands. More important, the British Harriers demonstrated they could operate off a small assault carrier at sea in the worst weather—under conditions which would normally ground all other naval aircraft. It is a fact that the Harrier can operate from any ship, including an *oil tanker*, which offers a small landing platform.

We are all aware of the volatile situation in the Persian Gulf today. While GOOD FRIDAY is an entertaining novel, I believe one of its important messages is how we and our Arab allies can defuse some of the explosiveness in this strategic, oil-rich region.

Major General Homer S. Hill, USMC (Ret.)
Deputy Chief of Staff, Marine Corps Aviation
and
Vice Chief of Naval Operations (Op-O5M) 1970-1972

Preface

Too much of this novel is already true:

- the oilfields of Russia have produced decreasing amounts of oil since the early 1980s.
- Russian military forces are stationed in South Yemen, 500 miles south of the major oilfields of Saudi Arabia.
- within the Persian Gulf (adjacent to the Saudi oilfields), the U.S. Navy has maintained a small assault carrier whose complement consists of 1800 Marines, 36 Sea Stallion helicopters, and 9 Harrier attack jets, plus a few accompanying small ships.
- mistrustful of its own security forces, the royal family in Saudi Arabia has hired three brigades of Pakistanis to guard their palaces.
- Cuban soldiers were flown into South Yemen in 1979 from Ethiopia to suppress South Yemen soldiers who remained loyal to their assassinated president.
- East Germans have managed concentration camps in South Yemen in recent years.
- in December 1979, three Soviet airborne divisions stormed into Afghanistan, murdering the Marxist leader then in power

and installing Babrak Karmal, who promptly issued a call to Moscow for Soviet troops who were already in his country.

- since the first Marxist government took office in Kabul (1978), more than 27,000 Afghani have been executed in a concentration camp (Poli Charki) outside Kabul.
- among the 18 Arab nations, only South Yemen has a lower literacy rate (12 percent) than that of Saudi Arabia (15 percent).

While serving as the Saudi minister of petroleum, Sheik Ahmed Yamani cautioned, "The Soviets may someday, when they become net oil importers, think our oil is in their strategic interests." Most Americans probably share my general feelings that we should not *overly* involve ourselves with the affairs of other nations; however, at times this generalization may prove a bit shortsighted.

In his book, *ARABIA, The Gulf and the West,* John B. Kelly aptly states, " . . . the temptation for the Russians to acquire by political or military means what they cannot afford to purchase must be a strong one. It can only be made stronger by the consideration that the acquisition of preferential access to the Gulf's oil would enable the Soviet Union to dictate the terms upon which oil would thereafter be supplied to the West."

I extend my gratitude to the men and women who permitted me to interview them concerning their experiences working and living in Saudi Arabia. Prudence dictates that their names not be listed herein. I would also like to express my appreciation to the men in uniform who gave generously of their time during the writing of the military action described in the book. And thank you, Gigi, for your able assistance in the editing and juxtaposition of events in this embroiled story.

RLH

List of Main Characters

King ASAD—Saudi monarch
Captain CARTER—air wing commander, *Constellation*
Emory CLARK—American ambassador to Riyadh
Premier DEREVENKO—Soviet premier
Senator FARRELL—U.S. Senate majority leader
Louis FRICKE—military attaché, Riyadh embassy
Colonel HABIB—Saudi national guard officer
Prince HAMUD—Saudi prince
Lt. Colonel HEMINGWAY—Marine air group commander
Lisa HILL—ham radio operator
General HUERING—Commandant, U.S. Marine Corps
Jim HOOLIHAN—special assistant to the President
IRENE—American woman from French Riveria
Sheik MANSUR—Grand Imam of Riyadh
General MORRISON—Chief of staff, U.S. Air Force
Dori NORLIN—American girl in ARAMCO compound
Kevin NORLIN—Dori's twin brother
Prince RAHMAN—Saudi defense minister
Edward ROLLE—CIA director
Colonel ROMANOV—Russian commander, South Yemen flight
Prince SALEEM—Crown Prince of Saudi Arabia
Edward SNELL—Speaker of the House
General STEEL—Chairman, Joint Chiefs of Staff
Allan STEINER—the President of the United States
Colonel TUPOLOV—Russian commander, Afghanistan flight
Clayton WALTERS—Secretary of State
Senator WINSLOW—Senate minority leader

After the pointless slaughter of 1.2 million soldiers (a fifth of whom were 14- to 16-year-old boys of Khomeini's Revolutionary Guards) in a twelve-year war of attrition with Iran, the army of Iraq abandons their strategic port of Basra in disorganized retreat northward.

Two weeks later, the Iranians invade the oil-rich state of Kuwait; and by mid-April, the Iranian army is massed along the Kuwait/Saudi Arabia border . . . their southern advance temporarily halted by an influenza epidemic.

To oppose the 300,000-man Iranian army in Kuwait, the Saudis have moved 45,000 men (three-quarters of their ground forces) to their northern border. The Saudi army is reinforced by the Peninsular Shield—9,000 men in a loosely-organized band of military units from neighboring Persian Gulf states.

Friday—4:15 A.M.
Riyadh, Saudi Arabia

"Kee-rist! They must be doing at least *a hundred*."

"Or more," responded the Corporal of the Guard. Both Marines stared at the fast-approaching headlights of the four-vehicle procession. The corporal spoke into the embassy intercom.

"Here come the maniacs!"

The lead vehicle—a jeep 100 yards in front of the others—

contained four, white-uniformed men with Uzi machine guns. Its driver braked hard and locked his wheels . . . laying 80 feet of rubber before releasing his foot and twisting the jeep sharply toward the compound gate.

The vehicle, its scorched wheels smoking, slid to a halt barely a foot from the barrier. Its sullen occupants wore the cocked red berets of the Saudi Royal Guard. The jeep's driver gave a perfunctory salute as the man beside him casually swung his Uzi around in the general direction of the Marines. The Corporal of the Guard whipped back an immaculate salute and pressed a button to open the iron gate.

At three-second intervals, the other vehicles roared up in similar fashion . . . each displaying a small green-and-white flag on its bumper. A dark green Buick careened through the gate on two left wheels, followed by a heavily-armored, white Cadillac limousine whose wheels squealed in protest at the high-speed, 90-degree turn.

The driver of the last vehicle, a jeep with a mounted machine gun, misjudged his speed and sideswiped the heavy stone pillar anchoring the iron gate. The man standing at the mounted gun tumbled off the jeep, amid whoops of laughter and jeers from his companions. Rolling on the concrete, the hapless man scrambled to his feet and limped after the procession.

Ambassador Emory Clark met the limousine as it jerked to a stop before the vestibule of the American embassy. A slim, tall New Englander with thinning blonde hair above a high forehead, Clark didn't feel the calm his reserved style suggested. The austere demeanor was carefully cultivated to mask his genuine feelings toward his early morning guest. Years of Middle East duty had taught him to dislike and distrust both the Arabs and Israelis—a general bias making him ideally-suited to his post in Riyadh.

An officer of the Royal Guard emerged from the front of the white limousine and opened one of its right rear doors.

Speaking as he pulled his portly, six-foot frame through the door, King Asad sternly inquired, "What is your President going to do?"

Clark was taken aback by the imperative tone, as the round-faced Saudi king normally displayed a docile and amenable nature. The American recognized both anger and fear on the king's face as the two men stood opposite each other, the eyes of the ambassador on the same level as those of Asad. As one of the shorter sons of Abdul Aziz Al Saud, the founder of the kingdom, Asad always wore elevator shoes in public.

"I don't know, Your Majesty." Clark replied. "President Steiner requested you come here in order to maintain direct communication with the White House." The ambassador checked his watch. It was exactly 45 minutes since the violation of Pakistani airspace had been reported.

They both hurried into the embassy, followed closely by the Royal Guard officer.

After berating their bruised comrade for his fall, the other white-uniformed members of the Royal Guard nervously smoked on the steps of the vestibule . . . making a point to direct the muzzles of their Israeli-made weapons at the two Marines guarding the embassy's entrance.

The two Americans stiffly maintained their brace on either side of the embassy door and traded an air of utter contempt for the ill manners of their guests.

Thursday—8:20 P.M.
The White House

The muted fluorescent light in the subterranean chamber cast an unhealthy pallor over its denizens . . . who, subdued by the atmosphere, seldom spoke in more than hushed tones. Electronic grid maps covered most of the pale yellow walls of the tennis court-sized, cavernous communications center of the White House. Eight stories directly beneath the Oval Office, it was officially termed the Situation Room for the benefit of the press and public. The twenty-odd men who manned its consoles preferred the more accurate single-syllable and referred to their workplace as the War Room.

"Tell *the professor* to make a decision quick!" crackled over the wall-mounted VCR-110 transceiver. General W. J. Morrison winced as he glanced toward the President and his chief assistant entering the room.

The radio's message abruptly halted the medium-height, paunchy frame of President Allan Steiner. His heavily jowled face, dominated by deceptively soft blue eyes, was topped by a shaggy mane of white hair. Peering over small, rectangular Ben Franklin glasses, he studied Morrison a moment.

"Who the hell was *that*?" the President demanded.

"Admiral Johnston on the Constellation, sir," replied the short, square-faced general. He spoke rapidly in a clipped cadence and wore the intense glare of a small man affirming his authority. A former fighter pilot, Morrison was accustomed to establishing dominance early over others; and he bridled before the President—a person he considered more an adversary than a superior.

"What's going on now?" the President inquired.

"Sir, the flight from Afghanistan left Pakistan airspace 11 minutes ago and turned due west over the Indian Ocean," answered Morrison, pointing to a cluster of flashing red dots on the 14-foot wide grid map of the Middle East. "The Constellation reported the aircraft carry the insignia of the Afghan Air Force."

"Clever bastards," muttered the President.

"They're definitely Russian," continued Morrison. "After turning west, their fighter escort was observed refueling from Soviet tankers tracked out of South Yemen."

"They must be crazy." President Steiner gaped at the imperceptively-moving, flashing dots on the wall map. "What the hell are they up to?"

You know damn well what they're up to thought Morrison with a piercing scowl.

Allan Steiner pivoted away from the wall map and shook his head, as if to deny the obvious. Recalling the trial Nikita Khrushchev had given the young Kennedy 30 years earlier, he raised a hand to knead his forehead and prayed . . . imploring that this too would prove but a test.

"Sir, I apologize for the fleet commander's choice of words," offered Morrison hollowly for the admiral's use of the presidential nickname, "but he *does* require orders. The Soviet flight is now entering the Gulf of Oman, and they could reach the coast of Saudi Arabia within two hours." He paused and boldly added, "I've taken the precaution of ordering the F-18s aboard the Constellation and Enterprise into the air."

In his dual role as Commander-in-Chief of the Air Force and a member of the Joint Chiefs of Staff, W. J. Morrison was the "military duty officer" in the capital on the eve of this holiday. The President's nominee for secretary of defense had not yet been confirmed by the Senate, and the undersecretary of defense was already on holiday.

In an undertone, the President dryly commented, "Why are you generals always so anxious to start World War III?"

Morrison locked eyes with President Steiner, refusing to be stared down. He wondered *how in the world did we elect a history professor to the White House?*

The bantam general raised his voice so it would be heard easily by others in the War Room. "Mr. President, are you prepared to hand over Saudi Arabia to the communists? Our stated mission in this sector is to safeguard their oil fields."

"You needn't lecture me, General." President Steiner cloaked his fury with a tight smile. The briefings before his inauguration had included the prediction that the Soviet Union would become a net importer of oil during the current presidential term. He had received this news with considerable optimism . . . believing the competition for the Free World's excess oil supplies would cause his Russian counterpart to bring a more cooperative attitude to the peace table. Allan Steiner spoke in a disgruntled tone.

"What is the total number of Russian planes involved?"

"The Puzzle Factory"—Morrison reconsidered his choice of words—"Fort Meade reports 40 Ilyushin Il-76Ms and 54 MiG-29 Fulcrums left Kandahar in southern Afghanistan shortly after 0200 hours, Saudi Arabia time."

"What are Ilyushins?"

"The Ilyushin Il-76M is a troop transport," Morrison explained with a note of disdain, "designed to carry two medium tanks and 140 fully-equipped infantrymen."

The presidential assistant, Jim Hoolihan, injected, "That means they could be carrying 5600 men."

"Jim, relay that information to our ambassador in Riyadh," directed the President. "And check to see if the king has joined him." As President Steiner moved closer to the Middle East wall-map, he told Morrison, "Describe the MiG-29 Fulcrum to me."

The general was mildly surprised the President could repeat the full name of the newest Soviet fighter. Allan Steiner had occupied the Oval Office only three months, after serving four terms in the Senate. He had been elected to the White

House with a promise to reduce defense spending and pursue serious peace negotiations with Russia. His knowledge of military matters was limited . . . as was his popularity among the military.

"Those are fighter aircraft, sir. They're faster than our F-18s, but not as maneuverable. We believe their weaponry to be comparable to our own."

Morrison received a teletyped message and, after scanning it, handed the note to the President who read it aloud.

"Pakistani military transmissions indicate flight out of Afghanistan intercepted by their F-15s. They report 12 F-15s lost and claim one Fulcrum destroyed."

"That's good news, Mr. President!" exclaimed the elated general. "If Pakistan's F-15s can shoot them down, we *certainly* can."

The President frowned. "General, this is *not* good news. If the Soviets are willing to fight their way through Pakistani airspace, they are likely to do the same over Saudi Arabia."

The blank expression of incomprehension on Morrison's face only served to further annoy the President, who addressed his assistant.

"Jim, where is General Steel? I want the JCS Chairman down here immediately!"

"He's on his way," Hoolihan replied. "He should arrive any minute."

"And where's Clayton Walters?" the President demanded.

"I'll check on his arrival," Hoolihan responded. He hurried to the telephones on the circular conference table that dominated the center of the War Room as the President returned his attention to Morrison.

"What do we have in the Persian Gulf to oppose the Soviets, General?"

"Our Middle East Force—one helicopter assault carrier, three destroyers, and two frigates—lying 35 miles off the coast of Saudi Arabia directly east of Dhahran." For the President's benefit, he added, "Dhahran Air Base controls the Saudi oil fields."

"That's not much of a force," grimaced President Steiner. "It sounds more like a *patrol.*"

Morrison spoke with emphasis. "The assault carrier is the Puller, sir. She carries a complement of 1800 Marines, 36 Sea Stallion helicopters, plus 9 Harrier fighter/attack aircraft."

After a thoughtful pause, the President unwillingly asked, "How effective would our Harriers be against the Fulcrums?"

Having considered the question already, Morrison lamely offered: "I'm not sure, sir."

"Well . . . *goddamn it,*" the President exploded. He deliberately raised his voice to even the score. "If *you* can't answer my questions"—he looked expansively about the room—"who in the hell around here can?"

"The Harriers on the Puller," Morrison testily replied, "are primarily ground-support aircraft and are not designed to optimally engage fighters such as the Fulcrums." He lowered his voice. "If we give the Puller orders soon enough, they could be outfitted with Sidewinders."

"What would that accomplish, General?"

This time Morrison weighed his answer carefully. "We might be able to delay the Soviet flight but not stop it."

"How long a delay?"

Morrison knew the Sidewinders of the Harriers would be no match for the longer-range missiles certainly carried by the Fulcrums . . . if the Soviets played it conservative. With little conviction, he answered, "Maybe ten . . . fifteen minutes."

"What *good* is ten or fifteen minutes?"

Morrison opened his mouth to reply, but was cut off by the President. "Why isn't the Constellation or Enterprise in the Persian Gulf?"

"You can't operate conventional aircraft carriers in a body of water that small," Morrison replied condescendingly. "Their flight operations require more room. Plus, the entire eastern shoreline of the Gulf is Iranian." *Dammit,* thought Morrison, *we're wasting precious time while I teach military basics to a president.*

"Then why's the Puller in the Persian Gulf?" queried the President.

"The Harriers on the Puller are V/STOLs, sir. They can take off and land vertically, permitting the Puller to remain stationary on the western side of the Gulf."

"Didn't we sell the Saudis some modern fighters five or six years ago?"

"Yes, sir. They've bought F-15s from us . . . and Tornados from our Nato allies, but Congress wouldn't approve the sale of long-range missiles to go with them so they'd probably be outgunned."

Recalling his repeated votes against the selling of Sparrow missiles to the Arabs, the President tugged at his ear. "I suppose we'd better tell the Puller to prepare for the Soviets."

"Sir, what will be their rules of engagement?"

President Steiner studied Morrison skeptically.

"Who fires first?" explained the general. "The commander of the Harriers should be told this before his planes are launched." Morrison paused. "Or does it matter?"

Of course it matters thought the President. Dropping his head pensively, he walked back to the conference table and sat down. Allan Steiner was a president often described as "a man of circumstance." He hadn't sought the Oval Office with the fervor of his predecessors; in fact, intimates knew he had been downright reluctant to accept the candidacy of his party, preferring to remain in the relative comfort of his Senate seat. When he had protested his lack of training for the job, it was quickly pointed out how little preparation most of the contemporary occupants of the White House had received.

His election campaign had stressed a "breath of fresh air" for the nation, a welcome change from the politician image of other candidates. His boosters also sensed the voters were ready for a change for the sake of change—that intuitive trait voters in democracies exhibit whenever they feel their country has simply had enough of one bent.

The President looked up at General Morrison and wearily said, "I need time to think this through."

"With due respect, sir . . . there *is* no more time."

President Steiner stared straight ahead, acting as if he hadn't heard the remonstrance.

"The Joint Chiefs have discussed possible options," Morrison calmly continued, "in the event of these confrontations, sir. We've concluded the best solutions are *limited reactions.*"

"What do you mean?" the President responded after a pause.

"Rather than engage the entire Soviet flight, we call their bluff by downing only a single aircraft. While doing this, we make it obvious to them that our action is limited . . . that we do not wish an expanded conflict."

President Steiner leaned back and crossed his arms. "Have we or anyone else *ever tried* such a strategem with the Soviets?"

Not wishing to reply in the negative, Morrison said, "We haven't had the opportunity yet."

"What if the Soviets aren't bluffing, General?"

Morrison looked aside momentarily.

"I may have been elected on a peace platform, General, but I'm no stranger to the Soviets. They've *overreacted* to provocations throughout their history, particularly during this century." The President's tone turned incredulous. "*Now,* you want me to believe they won't overreact this time also?"

The Chairman of the Joint Chiefs of Staff strode into the War Room. In his three-piece civilian suit, General J. Robert Steel looked more the statesman than a military professional for 41 years. A dark-bristled mustache gave his patrician face a youthful appearance. The only replacement on the JCS since the new administration had taken office, he had been selected due to his open support of the President's peace initiatives.

General Steel went directly to the Middle East grid map after greeting the President. Morrison and President Steiner followed, the latter explaining, "Bob, there are about 5600 Soviet troops less than two hours from the border of Saudi Arabia. Their transports are protected by 53 MiGs. General Morrison tells me neither the Saudi Air Force nor our Harriers in the Gulf can stop them."

Steel directed his first question to Morrison. "Have the F-18s on the Enterprise and Constellation been launched?"

"Yes, sir. They're approximately twenty eight minutes behind the Soviet flight."

"Raise them on the board," Steel ordered. A short moment after Morrison spoke to a console technician, a cluster of flashing blue dots appeared approximately one foot behind the red dots. When Morrison returned to his side, the JCS Chairman asked him, "Can they overtake the Soviet flight before it arrives over Saudi Arabia?"

"They could," offered Morrison, "but the fuel expended would severely limit their engagement time." The Air Force general correctly assumed Admiral Johnston in the Indian Ocean had ordered his fighters in immediate pursuit after launching, skipping the routine aerial refueling following their catapult shots.

"Order the F-18s to catch up," commanded Steel. "We need their option."

Gratified the JCS Chairman hadn't bothered to consult the President on the matter, Morrison swiftly wrote out a message on his clipboard. After handing it to a communications officer, Morrison reminded Steel, "Sir, both the F-18s and Harriers need their rules of engagement."

General Steel faced the President. "We can direct our fighters to harass the Soviet flight in an attempt to stop them or alter their course. If that doesn't work, do we have your permission to intercept them? Can we open fire first?"

Apprehension clouded the face of Allan Steiner. After a moment, he shook his head firmly. "No, we will *not* initiate a hostile act. We will harass them only."

Both generals stiffened. Morrison blurted out, "Sir, we *must* intercept the Russians! There's no other way to stop them."

"Yes, there is," the former professor half-smiled at his generals. "We're going to invade Saudi Arabia *first.*"

4:17 A.M.
Beach at ARAMCO

With the dim light of dawn, the air was already uncomfortably warm, and it assaulted the nostrils with a foul odor of processed petroleum. The salty waves lapping at the coarse sand of the beach were too tepid to enter comfortably, though some beachgoers—who didn't mind the greasy water—would splash it on themselves for its evaporative cooling effect. The ARAMCO beach was one of the least attractive in Saudi Arabia, yet Americans and other Westerners considered it one of the best. The beach was the *only* one in the country where a woman could safely wear an ordinary bathing suit . . . providing she kept a long robe handy in case a Saudi showed up.

Spreading their blanket, the Swedish brunette spoke in a slight British accent. "Can we rest a while before jogging, Tom? I've been on my feet the last eight hours."

"I thought nurses read books during night shifts."

"That's at ordinary hospitals." She dropped to her knees on the blanket, stretched out face down, and sighed. "Believe me, *no* hospital in this country is ordinary."

Tom sat beside her and began massaging her back. "What kept you busy?"

"*Thirty-nine* emergency trauma victims."

"What from?"

"Arab drivers," she replied. "Wrecking their cars is about the only form of entertainment they have."

Sandi lay silently on the blanket. She lazily closed her eyes. As the shimmering sphere of the sun lifted above the horizon, its blinding reflection off the dark green Persian Gulf forced Tom to look aside.

He bent over to whisper in her ear. "Sandi, you're missing the sunrise."

She smiled. "I can feel it." The air was suddenly warmer by five degrees.

Lightly tugging at the ties of her string bikini, he asked: "May I?"

"Are you a gentleman?" she teased.

"An officer *and* a gentleman."

"Did you see the movie?"

"Nope."

"Well, he wasn't a gentleman anymore than you are."

"Fine," Tom goodnaturedly replied, "you can *have* an oily suit."

"Oh, go ahead." Her voice was genial. She knew what was coming.

He shifted to a kneeling position at the head of her body and unhooked the bikini top. After brushing the long dark brown hair off her shoulders and pouring lotion into his palms, Tom leaned over to nuzzle the nape of her neck. His heavy hands slid effortlessly down each side of her backbone. Though her five-foot-nine frame carried an extra ten pounds, Sandi's statuesque figure normally halted conversation among members of the opposite sex when she entered a room—especially when riding on high heels. Tom's hands parted at her waist and curled around her full hips. He pulled at the sides of her body as his hands returned toward her shoulders.

"Tom," said Sandi wistfully, "when are you leaving?"

"When you've had all you can handle?"

She paused. "Isn't it the other way around?"

"What does that mean?"

"You Marines always retreat after taking your pleasure."

He ignored the jibe. "I thought you were talking about right now. I don't intend to leave off massaging you until you're *in pure ecstasy.*"

"I think you're getting more pleasure out of this than I am," she countered, enjoying his strong hands immensely but determined to keep the fact from him.

"Patience, my lady," he soothed. "Give it time."

Tom Hemingway was known by his military superiors as meticulous, hard-working, and brilliant—a natural leader by his own example. The Marine in him also knew the unreasonable demands an active military career could place on a family, which explained his consistent bachelorhood since being commissioned. The lack of one woman in his life had greatly enhanced his knowledge of all women, given the variety his lifestyle permitted.

He'd become particularly adept at giving small pleasures to the ladies of his life, and they invariably reacted in the same manner—by falling in love. Hence, he'd also become an expert in watering the flames. Usually, the women were left confused if not unhappy . . . always with a hint of more to come, but never the full measure.

His standards for women were the same he used to appraise the men he led. The Marine pilots of his command were highly-disciplined and carefully selected men, inherently blessed with unique physical and mental capacities. Few women he met compared.

Squirming into the blanket, Sandi asked, "How come a talented, 36-year-old like you isn't married?"

"There's a saying in the Corps," he recited pragmatically, "if the Marines wanted you to have a wife, they'd issue you one."

"We nurses have a saying, too," Sandi replied after a moment. "If a Marine's your date, a bed's your fate."

She twisted around to watch the little-boy smirk emerge on Tom's face. Her gaze was drawn to the broken pug-nose above his twisted smile, both the result of injuries received years earlier as a blocking fullback at The Citadel. His lips were too thick and the jaws too wide, yet this ruggedness attracted her, as it did most women. Her eyes dropped to take in the well-defined musculature beneath the thick hair of his upper body. Noticing her eyes, Tom sucked in his gut a bit more, rippling his shoulder and arm muscles as he did so. She smiled and replaced her head on the blanket. "So when are you leaving for the States?"

Damn, I hate that question, he mused, *even this time.* He considered asking his own question, but was uncertain how to phrase it.

"In three weeks."

"Well, easy come, easy go," she returned nonchalantly.

He placed Sandi's arms tightly against her sides and crossed her legs. "Ready?" he asked. Without waiting for a reply, Tom twisted her feet at the ankles, neatly flipping Sandi onto her back.

"*Hey, bozo,*" she protested goodnaturedly. "The smorgasbord is uncovered."

It was his favorite sobriquet for her exposed anatomy. Grinning at the splendid sight, Tom poured a liberal portion of lotion across each breast and asked, "How's that?"

"You're crazy!" Sandi exclaimed in mock anger. She raised up on her elbows to stare at her glossy bosom.

Tom feigned innocence. "I thought you didn't want any oil on your suit."

She reclined again, actually relishing the freedom of her unfettered chest. "You're still crazy, Marine," Sandi repeated in a friendlier tone.

"Over you, babe," Tom replied softly. He began tracing her ribs, discreetly moving around the curves of her firm breasts, grazing them lightly only when necessary to obtain more lotion.

She arched herself, as if reaching for his hands. "Are you crazy over me or my *body*, Tom?"

"What do you think?" he replied in a sardonic tone, then added, "It beats wrecking cars."

A slow grin crossed Sandi's face. "Are there any cars in the parking lot?"

Tom looked up and saw only her yellow Mustang convertible. "Nope, we're all alone."

She closed her eyes and Tom poured a circle of lotion around her navel, creating a small pool in its cleft. With one finger, he leisurely spread the lotion in ever-widening circles.

"Ummm, " purred Sandi as he repeated the movement over and over until she was totally relaxed.

The woman now reclined before him had a taunting way. She appeared fond enough of Tom, but at the same time, Sandi kept her distance. She was sufficiently clever to restrict her display of affection for him—to maintain a mystery of her feelings , which only motivated a greater display of his feelings toward her in an effort to solicit the same.

It had become confusing for the Marine officer, accustomed as he was to working with the more straightforward minds of men. He knew, however, one thing for sure of this woman. Sandi possessed a trait he valued highly in his men. She had a head on her shoulders.

"Tree time," he announced. Lifting her right leg and hooking its heel to his shoulder, he dripped oil along its length, and eased both his hands down the leg . . . pausing to ruffle her thigh muscles. The second time Tom did this, she told him:

"You Marines know *all the right moves.*"

Stroking the leg several more times, he unhooked it and moved to the other one. As he finished the second leg, Sandi reached up to him with glazed eyes.

"*Please,* Tom."

Taking her hands, he resisted their downward pull. When she opened pouting eyes, he falteringly spoke. "What . . . what do you think of marriage?"

Her eyes widened. Tom felt the tension release in her hands and added, "These last four months with you have been fantastic."

She paused to consider his meaning. "If that's a proposal"— she stopped for a negative reaction and, receiving none, continued—"my god, Tom . . . you haven't even said you loved me."

"Of course, I love you," he instantly declared.

Sandi looked askance. "*Of course, I love you,*" she repeated, mimicking his unemotional tone and rolling her eyes.

"When I get back to the States," he firmly stated, "I want you there waiting for me."

"Tom," she mildly remonstrated, "I'm not some corporal you can order around."

Confused by the direction his overture had taken, Tom selected what he considered a more direct approach. "Sandi, if I asked you to marry me, what would you say?"

Sandi smiled broadly. "I'd say that is the most bass-ackwards proposal I've ever heard of!" Seeing immediate hurt on his face, she gently added, "Why don't you ask and find out if you really want to know the answer?"

Realizing the folly in his plan to obtain her commitment first, Tom was even more uncertain of her reply. A noise from above blotted out his confused thoughts.

"Hey, we've got company!" yelled Sandi, searching for her bikini top.

Twelve-hundred feet above, an AV-8B from Tom's squadron floated down toward the two of them. Misnamed the "Harrier" by its British designers, the stout AV-8B's appearance was anything but that of its namesake—the slender, long-tailed English hawk. The aircraft's designers might have more aptly borrowed the name of their premier dogfighting breed—the bulky, square-jawed, pugnacious *bulldog*.

Like the canine, the AV-8B was a deadly opponent in close quarters. This superiority came from the four exhaust nozzles of its massive engine. Their direction could be adjusted inflight by the pilot. Normally, the nozzles were vectored (directed) aft as in conventional aircraft; however, within one second they could be vectored 98 degrees downward and forward to bring the plane to a near-instant hover. The nozzles could also be vectored to intermediate angles during air-to-air combat to increase turn rate and for rapid pitch/speed change. Experienced professionals often said the only plane that could outmaneuver a Harrier in a restricted airspace was another Harrier.

Cutting its power slightly, the Marine jump-jet began dropping in a near vertical descent. As it came closer, the roar of its powerful engine equalled that of a large passenger jet at takeoff.

Tom stood and defiantly waved the pilot away. Instead, the Harrier continued its descent. At 200 feet, the downward-deflected exhaust of the plane churned up a virtual sandstorm around the couple, and—having identified his commanding officer—the pilot increased power and ascended back over 1000 feet.

Tom glanced down at Sandi, who was sitting up with her hands over her eyes in the settling powder. The well-oiled body was no longer visible. It now wore a thick coat of gritty, yellow sand.

Shaking his fist at the Harrier, Tom shouted, "You dumb sonofabitch!" He tried to make out the serial number on the aircraft's fuselage as its pilot hit his flare/chaff dispenser button. A gray canister jettisoned from a pod attached to the rear of the plane and tumbled to the beach.

Running to where the canister hit the sand, Tom opened it and found a small notebook. After reading its message, he jammed it into his waistband and bolted to the wet sand at the water's edge. With his foot, he spelled out:

SEND HELO ARAMCO HOSP

The Harrier pilot acknowledged by nodding his aircraft. The jet climbed away at a 45-degree angle.

Tom ran back to the blanket where Sandi now stood, hands on hips. "Look at me!" she stammered helplessly.

He attempted humor. "You're sandy."

"You're . . . you're. . ."she sputtered in frustrated rage.

"Come on, let's go," Tom told her as he grabbed up their blanket and ice bucket. "I've got an Alert Three."

Sandi scoffed, "You have alerts twice a week."

"This is a *three*," he emphasized. Tom grabbed her hand and pulled her toward the parking lot.

"Wait a minute!" she protested. "Let me wash the sand off first."

Tom paused all of two seconds. "We haven't got time," he snapped. At the car, he draped a blanket around Sandi and pushed her inside.

Fuming all the way to the hospital, Sandi finally exclaimed: "Colonel, you want to know what I'd say if you asked me to marry you?"

He didn't invite the answer.

"I wouldn't marry a jarhead if he was the last man on earth!"

4:28 A.M.
Over the Gulf of Oman

Captain Ken Carter, USN, wiped the sweaty palm of his right hand on his flightsuit, aggravated that he was freely perspiring in the coolness of the F-18 cockpit. A few minutes earlier, Carter had received instructions from the Constellation to overtake the Soviet flight, but when he'd requested his rules of engagement, Admiral Johnston had told him to standby. As senior CAG (commander, carrier air group) of the airwings off the Constellation and Enterprise, Carter had overall command on the 48 F-18 Hornets chasing the Soviets.

"Falcon 101, this is Homeplate," came over his headset.

Recognizing the admiral's voice again, Carter replied, "I have you, Homeplate."

"Instructions for Red Dog flight are to harass and attempt to divert from Saudi Arabia. Do not open fire unless fired upon. Repeat: harass and attempt to divert, but do *not* initiate fire."

Carter tersely responded. "Clarify words: harass and divert."

Admiral Johnston knew the Soviets could be monitoring their transmissions and debated how to answer his flight commander. There had been no time to discuss these options before the F-18s were launched.

"Request clarification of instructions," repeated Carter.

"Buzz them. Thump them," offered the admiral. "Place

your aircraft between the transports and runways if they try
to land. Fly underneath if they prepare to drop paratroopers.
Do anything you can. Just do not initiate fire."

"Anything we *do*," Carter suggested with obvious dissatis-
faction, "could result in a firefight."

Admiral Johnston wanted to tell his CAG that he too was
frustrated by the inadequacy of the orders from Washington.
After a lengthy pause, he gave his final instructions. "Exer-
cise your best judgment."

"Roger, Homeplate."

Carter remembered the last time he'd thumped another aircraft. It had been 23 years earlier, shortly after flight school.
Coming from behind at high speed, he'd slipped beneath the
other plane and swooped up directly in front of it. The resulting turbulence caused the other pilot to temporarily lose control of his aircraft. It was a game occasionally played by rookie
pilots.

Due to a few isolated accidents, such aerobatics had been
outlawed back in the early seventies. Knowing many of his younger pilots had never tried thumping another aircraft, Carter wondered if they could safely execute this maneuver now. He also
knew an unplanned collision might appear deliberate to the
Soviets.

Admiral Johnston's suggestion to have the F-18s position
themselves beneath the Russian transports as they attempted
to land didn't sound any better. Carter didn't relish ordering
his fighter pilots to permit themselves to be sandwiched between
the transports and runways. *That would be pure suicide,* he
decided.

8:29 P.M.
The White House

Wearing his perpetually pained expression, the slightly-stooped figure of Secretary of State Clayton Walters hurried into the War Room. He was followed by Admiral Frank Sparks (Chief of Naval Operations) and General Edward Huering (Commandant of the Marine Corps). The President acknowledged their arrival by motioning them to the conference table where he was already seated with Steel, Morrison, and Hoolihan. After the JCS Chairman had provided a brief synopsis, the President spoke.

"From what I've been told so far, it's unlikely our military units in or near the Persian Gulf are sufficient to stop the Russian flight. Is that correct, Bob?"

"Basically," the JCS Chairman hesitated, "under—"

Cutting off the general, President Steiner continued. "Therefore, I recommend we invade Saudi Arabia . . . before the Soviets. If they think we've beat them to it, we may head them off. I doubt if they'll seek a direct confrontation with us."

"How?" Clayton Walters direly began, "can we invade Saudi Arabia within the next two hours?"

"Using 1800 Marines from one of our ships already in the Gulf," answered the President.

"Begging your pardon, sir," General Morrison dubiously commented. "We'll need a lot more than 1,800 men to invade and hold Saudi Arabia."

"Mr. President," interjected General Huering, "my Marines on the Puller are not your average soldiers. They're a Force Recon battalion—the elite of the elite, highly-skilled in high-explosives, underwater tactics, guerrilla warfare, and airborne operations. They also possess our latest weaponry. The eyes of the bald-shaven Marine general challenged those of the other military men at the table as he added, "With their training and firepower, they can seize and effectively hold a substantial amount of territory."

"I hope you're correct, Commandant," said President Steiner gratefully, "but I don't intend to *hold* Saudi territory. We only have to temporarily appear to do so in the eyes of the Soviets. Now, does anyone have a better suggestion?"

The men at the table exchanged glances. When no one spoke up, General Steel said, "Mr. President, I concur with your idea. I'll draw up plans for your approval."

"You've got five minutes to draw them up," stated the President, who shifted his attention to Hoolihan. "Jim, get Derevenko on the hot-line."

Hoolihan picked up the red phone at the center of the table and offered a skeptical hello. "Hello." Getting an immediate response, he said, "The President of the United States would like to speak to Premier Derevenko."

At the other end of the hot-line, he heard words spoken in an undertone and a second Russian came on the line. "This is the interpreter for Premier Derevenko. What do you wish to say?"

Hoolihan faced Allan Steiner. "Mr. President, his interpreter has asked for your message."

President Steiner frowned. "He doesn't *need* an interpreter." Before speaking into the phone, the President reached over to activate the speaker box on the conference table to enable others to hear the full conversation.

"This is the President of the United States. Tell Premier Derevenko only an ill-advised and foolish man could believe the United States would permit the invasion of Saudi Arabia."

The interpreter repeated the message in Russian, and

President Steiner made a taut grin as he heard laughter and loud voices in the background . . . even before the interpreter had time to repeat his words. This told him the English-speaking Derevenko was also using a speaker box, and more important, his call had been expected.

"President Steiner," offered the interpreter, "we know nothing of an invasion of Saudi Arabia. It must—"

"Don't give me *that*!" interrupted the President. "Your flight from Afghanistan is with Soviet aircraft and Soviet pilots. We've observed them refueling."

After another background in Russian, the interpreter said, "Premier Derevenko asks me to tell you perhaps the Afghans are on a training mission."

"Only an idiot would expect me to accept that!" snapped the President. "We know your flight fought its way across Pakistani airspace." Allan Steiner stopped abruptly, awaiting a reaction to his remarks.

There was no laughter this time. Following a lengthy pause, the interpreter came back on the line. "The Premier of the Soviet Union suggests you have nothing to worry about. He wishes you a pleasant Good Friday."

"What's your name?" demanded the President of the interpreter.

"My name is Nikolai Vishinsky."

"Nikolai, give this message to your Premier with great care. The United States of America has *already invaded* Saudi Arabia. Within the hour, we will control the airport at Dhahran *and* the oil fields!" The President slammed the phone into its cradle.

When Hoolihan and Walters met eyes with Allan Steiner, they could see his fury was genuine, though it was also at himself. Still fuming, the President muttered, "Derevenko thought I'd just roll over and play dead, didn't he? Just because I wanted to cut the fat out of the defense budget."

For a moment he recalled his election platform of the previous year. After the Central American disasters, the voters had swung to their periodic anti-military stance, and he'd ridden it into the White House. Now, he wondered if his campaign rhetoric should have been more subtle? Had the Soviets taken his positions as signs of weakness to be exploited? He shook his head despairingly at the answers.

"Come on," the President nodded his head toward the Middle East wall grid where the Joint Chiefs were congregated, indicating that Walters and Hoolihan should accompany him there.

"Gentlemen," the President told the military officers, "I've just told the Soviets we've invaded Saudi Arabia. Now, how quickly can we do it?"

"We've reduced it to three options," Steel replied. "Our forces can be split between Dhahran Air Base and the major oil fields lying directly to the south, or we can concentrate them at either the air base or the center of the oil fields."

"Which you do recommend, Bob?"

"I'd gamble the Soviet flight is headed for Dhahran," replied Steel without hesitation. "Whoever holds that air base will also control access to the major oil fields."

"What if you're wrong," suggested Clayton Walters, "and the Russian transports land or drop their 5000 men in the oil fields?"

"That's possible," nodded General Steel, "but they wouldn't last more than three to four days in the oil fields without logistical support, which would be nigh impossible unless they also controlled Dhahran Air Base. I might add it would be spreading our 1800 Marines rather thin if we were to distribute half or even all of them in the oil fields. To place the Marines in the oil fields effectively, we would have to accurately guess *precisely* where the Russians planned to concentrate their 5000-plus men . . . and I'm positive they'll be concentrated, wherever they're landed."

"What about Riyadh?" ventured Walters.

"The Saudi capital is two hundred miles into the interior," Steel promptly replied, "and of little tactical value."

A communications officer in the War Room handed Steel a memo which he read before repeating its message aloud.

"Satellite surveillance suggests two Soviet airborne divisions are poised at air base in Kandahar, Afghanistan for immediate deployment."

Steel handed the memo to the President. "Sir, *these* are the Russians who'll be headed for the oil fields."

President Steiner watched the flashing red dots on the wall-grid a moment. Then he locked eyes with Steel. "Issue stand-by orders to send the Marines into Dhahran."

"Mr. President," began General Huering, "to quickly prove our intentions to Moscow, I'd suggest we precede the Marines with an aerial attack by the Harriers. The Soviets probably have people in there already who'll report our military actions back to Moscow."

"We could restrict the bombing to runways," Steel offered, to which the President readily nodded.

"In addition to a mock invasion," said the secretary of state, "may I suggest we call a press conference to announce our actions?"

General Morrison sourly injected, "That's not—"

"Excellent idea," cut in the President. "If we reveal our invasion to the world, Derevenko may *believe* us." He pivoted to Hoolihan. "Jim, call a press conference in ten minutes."

As the presidential assistant hurried out, General Steel exchanged glances with Morrison before speaking. "Mr. President, in 1985 the Saudis agreed to let us use their military bases in case of Soviet aggression, but *if you announce we're invading them*, we may have problems with their military."

The President smiled, "That's why I gave you standby orders, Bob. First, I've got to talk to King Asad and tell him to sit tight when we come in. While I'm doing that, why don't you notify the Puller of our plan." As the military men left the conference table, the secretary of state handed the President the receiver to a white telephone.

"We've had Ambassador Clark standing by," explained Clayton Walters. President Steiner took the phone and indicated Walters should switch the call to the speaker box.

"Ambassador Clark?"

"Yes, Mr. President."

"Is the king with you?"

"Yes, sir. He's in the communications center of the embassy with me."

"Good, I want my conversation with him taped."

"That's routine, Mr. President."

"I'd also like you to listen in."

"Just a moment sir." After a brief pause, Clark said, "We're both on the line."

"Asad, this is Allan. Has Ambassador Clark filled you in on the situation?"

"Yes," answered the king. "My air and land forces are on full alert. What are your plans?"

"We don't want to start World War III over this, Asad. So we've decided the best way to stop the Soviets is for U.S. military units to invade your country first."

For an instant the Saudi king froze. Dropping the phone, he barked an order to his Royal Guard officer who drew a pistol.

Clark saw the muzzle of the gun aimed directly at his head. He heard the hammer click back. "Mr. President! You *can't invade* Saudi Arabia!"

"Asad, you—" began the President.

"He's not listening anymore!" Clark blurted out.

"Tell him it's a *mock* invasion," said the President, "to throw the Soviets off."

"Your Majesty," implored Clark in a wavering voice, "it is *not* a real invasion!" He glanced at the leveled pistol and shivered as he added, "President Steiner only wants to fool the Russians."

Asad hissed another order and the red-bereted officer lowered his pistol. Recovering the phone, the Saudi king angrily declared, "Allan, you *cannot invade my country!* You must stop the Russians before they reach Saudi Arabia."

"That is not possible, Asad," began the President patiently. "The Soviets are over international waters, and they've taken no hostile actions toward military units of your country or mine."

"Then the Saudi air force will stop them, " snapped the king.

"Asad, they may be bluffing . . . or testing us. If you attack them, you may give them the excuse they're looking for to invade your country."

The king's tone grew harsher. "If the United States declines to stop the Russians, then the Saudis will!"

Clayton Walters interjected, "Sir, may I speak to him?"

"Asad, my secretary of state wishes to speak to you." The President surrendered the phone.

"Your Majesty, I regret telling you this, but the aircraft in the Royal Saudi Air Force are no match for the Soviet planes."

The king paused a moment. "Then the land-based Hawk and Stinger missiles you have sold us for one billion dollars will stop the Russians, yes?"

"No, Your Majesty. These missiles will stop the Iranians, the Syrians, even the Israelis . . . but not the Russians. Their technology is superior to yours. It may even be better than our own."

The king fell silent as President Steiner took back the phone. "Asad, I have just been handed a communique from one of our AWACs over the Red Sea. I will read it to you.

A formation of 27 large aircraft have rendezvoused with 42 fighter-size aircraft at a point in South Yemen, 45 miles below the Saudi Arabia border. They have turned north, in the direction of Riyadh."

The President went on. "Do you remember who suppressed the South Yemen soldiers who remained loyal to their assassinated president in 1979?"

"Yes, I remember," replied Asad reluctantly. "Cubans . . . from Ethiopia."

"That's right, Asad. *Who* do you think are in those aircraft headed for Riyadh?"

The Saudi king groaned. "If my defenses are worthless against the Russians, what can I do?"

"Cooperate with me, Asad."

The king spoke in a subdued tone. "But you are a Jew, Allan. You are a Jew."

"That's ridiculous, Asad!" exploded the President after a stunned moment. "I'm only half—"

Allan Steiner knew it was useless to protest further. Though he had followed his father in becoming an elder of the Presbyterian church, it was far better known that his mother was born a Jew. And if bigots in his own country could hold it against him, certainly an Arab could. Now it was better to simply change the subject.

"Asad, do you *realize* your position at this moment? You are only one hour's flight-time from the concentration camps in South Yemen. The planes heading for Riyadh could take you and the 5000 other princes of your family back to those camps."

The king gave no response.

"Do you know who runs those camps, Asad? *East Germans.* How long do you think your family would survive?"

Still no response.

The President went on. "After the Marxists took over in Kabul, do you know how many Afghan civilians were listed by their regime as executed in the Poli Charki concentration camp? *Twenty-seven thousand!* Think of it—in a country with fewer people than yours."

President Steiner paused a few seconds. "Make your choice, Asad. And quickly!"

The king wearily replied, "You give me little choice."

"Not I," the President changed to a tight undertone. "It is *Derevenko* who gives you little choice. Listen to what I tell you now. Ambassador Clark, take notes. Aircraft from our assault carrier, the Puller, in the Gulf will simulate bombing attacks on Dhahran Air Base within thirty minutes. We'll also drop a few bombs on open runways of Riyadh's airport in case the Soviets have agents observing these airports. Then Marines off the Puller will land at Dhahran."

"I have a brigade of Pakistani commandos in the eastern oil fields," countered Asad. "*They* will come to Dhahran instead of your Marines."

"The Soviets would not hesitate to engage the Pakistanis, Asad, but they'll think twice before taking on American Marines. And there is too little time to transfer your men. My Marines are only minutes away."

"How soon will your Marines leave my country?" Asad asked stiffly.

"As soon as the Soviet threat is gone."

"I do not like your answer."

President Steiner felt his position weakening. "Asad, if we make a show of force, I believe the Soviet threat will be discouraged . . . and the Marines will be back on their ship by nightfall."

"That, I would like," affirmed the Saudi king.

"Then we have your permission, Asad?" Hearing no reply, the President continued. "And will you notify your military commanders not to interfere or respond to our actions?"

The American president waited for a reply this time. It came falteringly and with obvious reluctance.

"Yes, I will warn them . . . but I think you must do more to stop the Russians."

Allan Steiner was aware his predecessors had tried for two decades to obtain Saudi permission to permit American military units on their soil. He considered whether to remind the king that American air force units, in fact, had been stationed at Dhahran Air Base at one time, but they had been asked to leave over a minor dispute. There was too little time for such discussion now, so he said instead, "We are. In a few minutes, I will hold a press conference to announce our invasion of your country. And I've already called Premier Derevenko to tell him the same. If these measures do not work, we will try to turn them back at Dhahran . . . without starting a war in which we would all lose."

"What of the planes coming from the south?" asked Asad.

Temporarily at a loss, the President looked to General Steel before speaking. "Deploy your troops at the Riyadh airport." The JCS Chairman nodded in approval.

"We will do that."

"And Asad. Can you remain at the embassy? We may have to communicate again soon. I must leave now for the press conference. Good luck."

"Inshallah," the Saudi replied.

Replacing the receiver, President Steiner told General Steel, "Notify the Puller to execute their orders." As the President turned to leave, Clayton Walters stopped him.

"Sir, there are 40,000 American civilians in Saudi Arabia.

Shouldn't we try to warn them what's happening?"

"Yes, of course. Instruct Ambassador Clark to do that."

"It won't be easy," Walters allowed.

"Why not?"

"No one's at work today, sir. It's Good Friday, and this is the Muslim holy day of the week."

"Tell Clark to do the best he can," the President ordered, "then join me at the press conference."

The President shook his head in disgust, recalling the first members of three Soviet airborne divisions had chosen *Christmas Eve* of 1979 to invade Afghanistan in order to install Babrak Karmal—who promptly issued a call to Moscow for troops which were already there.

"Before you leave, sir," said General Steel, "I'd like authorization to mobilize our Rapid Deployment Force in Europe, plus the Marine battalion with the Nimitz in the Mediterranean."

"You've got it."

4:31 A.M.
Over the Red Sea

The Lear Jet was a private flight, one of hundreds flown each month from southern Europe. It cruised southward over the Red Sea at 31,000 feet, following an ancient trade route of smugglers from the Mediterranean to the population centers bordering the Red Sea. Modern day runners of contraband called the route *the Riviera-Red Express* and used it primarily to transport highly-prized but illicit items into Saudi Arabia. These included premium whiskeys and scotch, the highest-grade cocaine, adult video cassettes, and expensive Western women—preferably blondes.

The cargo of the Lear Jet differed in several respects from its usual contents. The American woman it carried was a redhead . . . and she was not bought.

Pulling herself upright on the sofa, she tossed her head to shake her sunstreaked auburn hair aside. A small, exquisite face gave her the appearance of a teenager, though she was nearing twenty-six. Her face was contorted with concern at the empty cockpit.

"Hamud . . . are you sure it's safe?"

"I've—" he smoothed his thick mustache while debating whether Irene would prefer to believe she was the first.

"I'm sure it's been done many times," he assured her.

"Have *you* ever done it?"

He grinned impishly. "Never!"

"Liar," snickered Irene, pushing the Saudi prince back down onto the luxuriantly-cushioned sofa.

Without rising again, Hamud reached a hand up and cautiously undid the lowest button of her blouse. She didn't move away or even notice the hand.

After checking the night sky through a window, Irene again shifted her attention to the empty cockpit of the Lear Jet, studying whether the aircraft was still level. Turning her head back to Hamud, she found his hand posed in mid-air . . . within the folds of her fully opened blouse.

The woman's eyes narrowed on his fingertips as they inched closer. She neither spoke nor moved—concentrating on the coming touch.

Noting her attentiveness, Hamud paused to let his fingers spread . . . suspending them over the pert breast.

As Irene took a deep breath, Hamud's bronzed face— dominated by the broad hook nose of the Saud family—took a raffish bent. His usually melancholy eyes sparkled at the game. One of the more westernized of the Saudi princes, he was known to expend prodigious sums gambling on the Riveria and entertaining beautiful women. But this one had remained unimpressed . . . even refusing the jewels other women eagerly sought. Therefore, she *amused* the Saudi prince, and now he chose to respond in kind.

"Never . . . never . . . have I seen such a magnificent rosebud."

In a trance-like state, Irene continued to gaze downward.

His tone became official and mocking. "I, Hamud Abdul Aziz Al Saud pronounce you . . . my Nipple Queen."

"You turkey!" Irene cried out, the precious spell broken. Her long nails dug deep into his ribs as they rolled, giggling like children on the soft carpeted aisle.

4:54 A.M.
Riyadh

The two Saudi military leaders stormed into the private office of Ambassador Clark in the American embassy. The haughty face of the six-foot-four Crown Prince displayed a neatly-sculptured black mustache and pointed beard. When excited, Saleem had a tendency to suck air between his brown, coffee-stained teeth, in addition to bouncing on the balls of his feet—an inherited mannerism accounting for his nickname: *the Royal Yoyo*. As commander of the Saudi national guard, Crown Prince Saleem led the 10,000-man private army of the ruling Saud family. His half-brother, Prince Rahman, followed him into Clark's office.

Rahman, 15 years younger and a few inches shorter than the 70-year-old Saleem, held the more powerful position of Minister of Defense and Aviation, because he was the first of King Abdul's 44 sons to pilot a jet. Rahman's bushy eyebrows arched delicately over soft, baleful eyes which furtively scanned the office's furnishings.

The king ordered his Royal Guard officer to close the door of the office as he stood to speak. "My brothers, a flight of Russian jets carrying 5000 men will arrive at our eastern border within two hours. And from South Yemen, another flight comes toward Riyadh. The Americans believe the planes from Yemen contain Cuban soldiers."

"*We must shoot the dogs down!*" shrieked Saleem, bouncing already.

Accustomed to the outbursts of his half-brother, Asad

waited a moment before continuing. "We cannot do that," he calmly said.

"WE CAN!" retorted Saleem, inhaling moistly through his teeth. "WE MUST!"

"If we try," Asad looked to Rahman as he spoke, "the Americans have said we will fail. They say our planes and missiles cannot stop the Russians."

"Then why," Prince Rahman dourly asked, "don't the Americans shoot them down?"

Asad made a hopeless shrug. "The Americans refuse to attack first. They and the Russians are like two scorpions in a bottle. If one attacks, the second will strike back . . . and both will die. But if neither attacks, both live."

"And then *we* shall die," sputtered Saleem.

Rahman pursed his lips in anguish. "How shall we stop the planes from the south?"

"*You're* the defense minister," Asad reminded him. As this failed to solicit a response, the king continued. "The Americans suggest we place our soldiers and missiles at the airport."

"What of the oil fields?" demanded Saleem.

The king shot a nervous glance at Saleem and continued to direct his words to Rahman. "To discourage the Russians from landing in the east, the Americans propose to carry out fake attacks at the airports of Dhahran and Riyadh." Asad delicately cleared his throat. "Then the Americans will pretend to invade Dhahran before the Russians. If they are first to occupy the air base, they believe the Russians will turn back."

"The Americans are *no better* than the Russians!" Saleem spit out. "Do you forget how they plundered our oil before 1973?"

"My brother," Asad said solemnly, "they have asked that we not oppose them."

The Crown Prince sneered. "My men will *never* lay down their arms."

"I cannot stop the Americans now," replied Asad faintly.

"*All* infidels must be opposed!" declared Saleem. He glared a challenge at Prince Rahman.

"I shall send our planes east and south," asserted Rahman reluctantly, "to intercept the infidels."

The king eyed his two brothers in acquiescence. "So be it."

Hissing inwardly, Saleem said, "Let us kill Clark now and be done with him."

Asad exchanged a brief, knowing glance with Rahman. They both knew the easily-excited Saleem was ninety-nine percent bluster; nevertheless, it was an often-expressed wish of the king that he would outlive his appointed successor . . . for the sake of the kingdom.

"No," Rahman quickly countered, "now is not the time for that."

"Our brother is right, Saleem," seconded Asad. "I must stay here to learn more of the American plans. Go now. Allah be with you."

The two Saudi princes moved swiftly from the embassy as Asad left the office and entered an elevator to return to the communications center on the top floor of the embassy. At a console in this room, a stocky, 54-year-old man wearing the uniform of an Air Force major switched off the television monitor to the ambassador's office and looked up at Ambassador Clark. The lopsided grin and bright eyes of the uniformed man's face were the complete opposite of the somber image projected by most embassy operatives of the Central Intelligence Agency. Louis Fricke quipped, "So much for our Saudi *partners.*"

Clark spoke calmly and deliberately. "Send a message to Washington informing them the Saudi leaders may not fully cooperate with our mock invasions. Include the fact that we're unable to contact American compounds because all telephone and telex lines are down. Then request permission to evacuate the embassy."

Just before the Saudi king entered, the first secretary of the embassy rushed in and approached the ambassador. He whispered to Clark, "The Royal Guard won't let me leave to warn our compounds."

"Why don't we send him in our helicopter?" Fricke suggested.

The ambassador considered the proposal and shook his head. "There's too little time now. We'll have to warn the compounds after we evacuate."

9:00 P.M.
The White House

When the President entered the press room, it was not necessary to request those present to rise. At three hours before midnight in Washington, most members of the White House press corps were home with their families. Only eleven reporters were in the room, and they stood in front of the podium waiting.

At the rostrum, President Steiner made a brief smile. "Gentlemen and ladies of the press, I have but two minutes to announce what is likely to be the most important news of my presidency." He methodically enunciated his next words.

"Military units of the United States have intervened in Saudi Arabia."

Hands shot up among the reporters. "Mr. President! Mr. President!"

He extended a hand over the rostrum for silence. "Let me continue. We have intervened in Saudi Arabia to protect its strategic oil fields from the Iranian army . . . poised 300 miles to the north. According to our intelligence sources, the Iranians have orders to invade within 96 hours. The oil reserves of Saudi Arabia are vital not only to the United States, but also to our allies in Western Europe and the Far East. We will not permit Saudi Arabia to suffer the same fate as Kuwait. Consequently, at the invitation of King Asad, within the last hour we have occupied the major military and oil installations in eastern Saudi Arabia."

The President pointed to an upraised hand.

"Mr. President, how long will the United States maintain its forces in Saudi Arabia?" asked Harry Kramer of the *New York Times*.

"Until that country is secure from external threats," replied the President.

UPI's George Epsen waved a hand. "Mr. President, which units have you sent to Saudi Arabia?"

"Our Rapid Deployment Force in Europe and two Marine battalions."

The President pointed to an unfamiliar reporter.

"Mr. President, Betty Dodds of the *Post*. Is this related to the violation of Pakistani airspace by planes out of Afghanistan just reported by Karachi?"

The President's inexperience at news conferences was as transparent as his deceptive reply. After too long a pause, he painfully offered, "At this time, we know of no relationship between those aircraft and the Iranians."

Hoolihan caught the eye of his embarrassed boss and motioned to his wristwatch.

"That's all for now," announced the President. He exited the room almost as quickly as the reporters, who raced down the double aisles to their phones. As the presidential party entered the elevator to return to the War Room, Hoolihan inquired, "Mr. President, why didn't you tell them we were invading to head off the Russians?"

President Steiner knowingly looked to his secretary of state, who answered for him. "Jim, the reason the Soviets weren't mentioned is we don't want them to lose face in turning around."

"And the first rule of diplomacy," added the President, "is never challenge a fool any more than you have to."

Hoolihan debated whether the expression on the President's face was a smile or grimace. He decided the latter.

"Perhaps," continued the President, "it will give the Iranians something to think about, too."

When they re-entered the War Room, an aide offered a phone to the President. "Sir, Prime Minister Weimann of Israel wishes to speak with you."

President Steiner took the phone and sat at the conference table. "Hello, Mort."

"Greetings, Allan."

"Why are you calling?"

"We're curious why your Sixth Fleet gave us notice several of its helicopter squadrons would be flying over our airspace.

Admiral Colby referred us to you."

"Mort, the Saudi king has requested that our military units enter his country to checkmate the Iranians in Kuwait."

Friendly sarcasm colored Weimann's reply. "The Iranians are *no* threat, Allan. Ninety percent of them are sick as a dog right now. Let us not play games. We know of the flights from South Yemen and Afghanistan. Do you need assistance?"

It occurred to Allan Steiner that the arsenal of the Israelis—the most powerful war machine in the Middle East—was the only military force in the area which *could* stop a serious Soviet thrust. Yet, he also knew the Israelis were the *only* people in the Middle East who could not be called upon. He stonily replied, "We have everything under control."

"Are you sure?" Weimann drew out.

Goddam . . . I wish I was mused the President, wrinkling an ear with a closed fist. "We'll let you know if we need anything."

"I've placed our National Defense Force on full alert just in case," offered Weimann.

"Thank you, Mort." After hanging up, the President addressed General Steel. "How soon can the Marines in the Mediterranean reach Dhahran?"

"If their choppers don't run into any problems refueling in northern Saudi Arabia," Steel replied, recalling the debacle experienced by the rescue helicopters in the aborted 1979 raid on Tehran, "they'll reach Dhahran in four to five hours."

"How quickly can they be on their way?"

"They're airborne, sir."

"Excellent," the President smiled. "Soviet satellites should have picked them up by now. How about the Rapid Deployment Force?"

Steel matter-of-factly replied, "It'll take four days to bring the RDF in."

"*Four* days?" President Steiner's tone was incredulous. "You've got to be kidding."

"No, sir. That's their time-frame. A light division requires four days to move that distance.

"Well," declared the President encouragingly, "let's bring in more transportation then."

"That's using every available aircraft, sir."

The President paused. "Does it include British military transports?"

Steel reluctantly admitted, "No, sir."

"French military transports?"

"No, sir."

"How about the planes Pan Am and TWA have in Europe?"

General Steel again replied in the negative.

"Then you're not utilizing *all available planes*, Bob."

"No, sir," responded Steel, "but—"

"No time for 'buts' now," interrupted President Steiner. He turned to Hoolihan. "Tom, get on the phone to Pan Am and TWA and alert them to our needs. Any problems . . . give me the phone."

Hoolihan inquired, "Where should I have them send their planes?" The President looked to the JCS Chairman.

"Rhein Main Air Force Base in Germany," replied Steel.

"Clayton," directed the President, "you get Paris and London on the phone. Explain the situation and tell them we need every military transport they can lend us."

General Morrison broke in. "Sir, this is highly irregular. We *can't* use those planes."

Thinking *that's your third strike, General,* President Steiner brusquely inquired, "Why not?"

The general raised his hands futilely. "It would break our security. It would tip off the Russians."

"That's exactly what we want to see happen, General," the President angrily retorted.

Morrison shook his head and half-turned away, then came back around and spoke with renewed urgency. "Mr. President, *we haven't even alerted Omaha yet.*"

President Steiner studied Morrison dispassionately. "Why do you want to alert Omaha?"

Morrison stared at his commander-in-chief as if the President was a complete idiot. "We've got to get the bombers in the air," the general exclaimed. "Before it's too late!"

"And what would that accomplish?" The President remained as placid as his tone.

Morrison paused in further disbelief. After glancing at the

other JCS members, who had chosen to remain spectators to the exchange, the general forcefully replied, "It'll let the Soviets know *we mean business!*"

"Then," began the President impassively, "they'll put their strategic bombers in the air . . . right, General?"

"Yes, sir!" Morrison's face split into a wide grin, relieved he'd finally got his point across. "That's what is done in this type of situation."

President Steiner raised his voice. "General Morrison, I've told you before that's precisely what we *don't* want to see happen at this time."

Morrison gawked at the President. "Sir, you're violating *too many* military rules."

President Steiner waited a moment to calmly observe his antagonist. "I would prefer to violate your military rules, General . . . than violate world peace."

The general glared in repudiation.

Glowering back, the President harshly asked, "How long have you been on duty, General Morrison?"

It took a moment to register. "Since 0600 this morning," he replied.

The icy edge to President Steiner's voice halted all movement and talk in the War Room. "*Then it's time you went home, General.*"

Morrison's blank expression went to bewilderment.

"Go home, General," repeated the President firmly. When the perplexed officer still did not move, President Steiner addressed the JCS Chairman. "Bob, have the Air Force Deputy Commander report to the War Room immediately . . . to relieve General Morrison."

Steel went to the speechless general, took his arm, and eased him from the room as a civilian rushed into the War Room and handed Clayton Walters an envelope. Before he'd completed the first sentence of the message inside, Walters began reading aloud.

"After observing Asad meet with Crown Prince Saleem and Prince Rahman at embassy, we are uncertain of their cooperation. Some opposition may be encountered. Unable to warn American compounds, as telephone and telex lines down. Request approval for embassy evacuation."

"That doesn't make sense!" the President exclaimed. "*Why* would Asad change his mind?"

"Mr. President," began Walters gravely, "the Arabs are masters of prevarication. They often say what they believe others wish to hear, and then do the exact opposite."

Allan Steiner nodded as he smirked, thinking the prevarication label might be aptly applied also to a few members of Congress. Clayton Walters interrupted his thoughts.

"I suggest we evacuate the embassy . . . before we lose control of the situation."

"Is that possible?" the President questioned. "With the king there?"

Walters nodded his head. "Most of Asad's guards are probably waiting outside the building. And this being a holiday, there should be fewer than 15 of our own people in the embassy. The embassy helicopter could do it in one trip."

"I didn't know we kept helicopters with that capacity at embassies," commented the President.

"Larger helicopters are at all Arab embassies, sir. They could go to the Lockheed compound or one of the other large enclaves of Westerners outside of Riyadh."

"Okay, order the evacuation," agreed the President. After a pause, he quickly added, "Tell Clark I'd like Asad to accompany them . . . for the king's own safety."

Walters was taken aback. "Shouldn't we let the Saudis protect him, sir?"

"That's who I was thinking of protecting him *from*, Clayton. I wouldn't put it past the Soviets to have a Quisling waiting in the wings."

Clayton Walters doubtfully eyed the President, who continued, "When you tell them to evacuate, instruct Clark to bring out a tape of the conversation I had with Asad, plus the one with his brothers if it exists." President Steiner turned to the JCS Chairman. "Bob, if there's sufficient time, have the Marines on the Puller notify all nearby American compounds of the Soviet flight and our response."

4:54 A.M.
Riyadh

In his Defense Ministry office, Prince Rahman paused at the wide window overlooking the largest public square in the capital of Saudi Arabia. He frowned at the sight of scattered men in Western-style clothes, as their stilted movements broke the symmetry of the scores of Saudis gracefully gliding in their thobes (cotton shifts) across the plaza for early morning prayers. It also annoyed the prince when foreigners referred to this plaza as "Chop Square" instead of its proper name: the Dira.

Rahman sat at his desk and tapped out a code on a console built into the desk-top. Swiveling around, he watched a panel in the cabinet behind his desk silently slide sideways, revealing a medium-frequency two-way radio. After tuning it to 2485 kilohertz, Rahman spoke into its microphone.

"Come in, Fox One."

A computer voice instantly responded, *"Call being routed."* A few seconds later, a man's voice came up. "This is Fox One."

"This is the Lion," responded Rahman. "I have sent my planes to intercept the Russian flights. My land forces will continue to guard the northern frontier and the oil fields. They will not oppose your Marines at Dhahran."

Fox One urgently asked, "Can you control the national guard in the Eastern Province?"

"Maybe," Rahman cautiously replied, "in some areas."

"You must control *all* Saudi military forces in the east."

"That is not possible," Rahman insisted. He knew even the Crown Prince could not fully control some of the Bedouin chieftains among the national guard units.

The voice on the radio became harsh. "Then *make it possible!* This could be the opportunity you've been waiting for."

Rahman paused to consider the prospects and quietly replied, "I will try."

"Why don't you tell The Yoyo to stay in Riyadh where his men can protect the royal family?"

"I will try," repeated Rahman with only slightly more fervor.

"Good. Contact me with any news, and remember," stated Fox One firmly, "do not make mistakes . . . like your brothers."

4:55 A.M.
Over the Persian Gulf

As his fighters passed over the Strait of Hormuz, Captain Carter watched the gray morning haze below take on a reddish-brown hue as they entered the befouled air of the Persian Gulf.

Two-hundred-thirty miles to the northwest, Jim Toomey, the air control officer of a U.S. Navy E-2C out of Oman, grinned in relief. The F-18s finally had come in range of the revolving radome (a 24-foot-wide disc) mounted on a pylon above the fuselage of his twin-prop electronic surveillance aircraft.

The display panel of Commander Toomey's microcomputer printed out:

Red Dog flight is on 310 radial of Hornets. Hornets will overtake in 6 minutes. Red Dog in tight formation at 22K.

Toomey hit the orange button on his console and the printout on the display panel was instantly garbled, relayed to the air-data computer of Captain Carter's F-18, and degarbled. Carter's display panel lit up and the printout appeared in its original form. The entire transmission had required less than two seconds.

Captain Carter scanned the message twice before electronically acknowledging its receipt. *What the hell am I going to do?*

pondered Carter. No further directions had come from the
Constellation. It had been 18 years since he'd taken a fighter
aircraft into combat; and even then, the restrictions hadn't been
this bad. A glimpse at his fuel gauge told him the F-18s wouldn't
make Dhahran at the rate they were burning fuel. It occurred
to Carter that he might not return from the mission. For a second, he thought of Anita . . . his parents . . . playing ball in
college . . . making it through flight school. The solution came.

Carter punched his UHF button. "Strike Force, this is
Falcon 101. Descend to 21K."

As the F-18 formation descended, Carter partially described
his plan. "We close in five minutes. When Ilyushins are sighted,
I will designate sectors to squadron commanders who will assign
an F-18 escort to each transport. Confirm to me when matchups
complete. On my command, we will then assume the same flight
formation as the Ilyushins. When both formations coincide, again
on my command, escorts will move behind and under the bellies
of Ilyushins, maintaining a 500-foot interval. Further instructions
to follow."

A few seconds later, Carter decided what to do with the
two extra F-18s in each squadron and punched his UHF button.
"Strike Force, this is Falcon 101. The following modifies
previous. Each squadron commander will assign his two least-
experienced pilots to fly CAP with me at 24K. Their mission
will be to respond to any hostile fire."

One of his squadron commanders promptly came up on the
UHF radio. "Falcon 101, did you say 'least-experienced' pilots?"

"Affirmative," replied Carter. "The *two least-experienced
pilots* in each squadron will fly CAP."

Carter mused, I hope Ivan is listening. This in mind, he hit
his UHF button. "Strike Force, this is Falcon 101. Under no
circumstance do we fire at Red Dog flight . . . unless they fire
first. I repeat, *do not* fire unless fired upon. Squadron
commanders, acknowledge my last."

"Roger 101," repeated four times.

Checking his fuel gauge again, Carter calculated he had less
than 19 minutes of remaining fuel. His display panel lit up with
a second message from the E-2C.

38 F-15s—Saudi Royal Air Force—approaching head-on intercept with Red Dog. Close three minutes.

Captain Carter swore to himself. He knew the Saudi fighter jockeys would be ineffective against the Fulcrums, but they might be effective in delaying his own plan—beyond the ability of his flight's remaining fuel.

Ten seconds later (after the radome of the E-2C had completed another full revolution), more data appeared on Carter's display panel.

10 Fulcrums from Red Dog moving out to intercept F-15s. Mach II speed. Close 70 seconds.

———

After electronically confirming the identity of the hostile aircraft headed in his direction, Colonel Tupolov spoke into his headset. "Assume file formation . . . with 100-meter stepdown at 200-meter intervals."

The ten Fulcrums neatly tucked themselves in a slanted file behind their commander, who then barked his next order. "Prepare program fire-control computers for tandem execution." A few seconds later, Tupolov ordered, "Count off," starting with himself. This permitted his pilots to combine their computers into a single unit which would select separate targets among the oncoming aircraft. The count reached ten, and Tupolov completed his instructions.

"Execute Immelman after release. I will commence fire in six seconds. Five, four, three, two, one." Releasing four missiles, Tupolov jammed his throttle forward, forcing his aircraft into a steep, backward-curling climb. As his Fulcrum began to assume an upside-down position, he smoothly righted it and headed back to rejoin the Ilyushins.

Each of the other Soviet fighters duplicated the actions of their leader.

———

Commander Toomey punched the orange button to relay the latest computer message to the flight leader of the F-18s.

Fulcrums released missiles. Missile speed indicates Sparrow class. Fulcrums returning to Red Dog flight.

Toomey impatiently waited ten seconds for the radome to revolve 360 degrees and register the results of the missile release. He started to count and looked down at his display panel after the required time had elapsed. No message appeared. *Did they miss?* he thought. *They couldn't have.* He counted out the interminable seconds of another revolution of the radome.

In his F-18, Carter wondered if the Saudis were close enough and smart enough to release their own missiles.

"Damn," Toomey exclaimed in an extended breath as he read his display panel.

Two F-15s remain of Saudi flight. They have made 180-degree turn.

After receiving this last message from the E-2C, Carter began having serious doubts whether his plan would work. And his fuel gauge showed only 14 minutes of remaining fuel.

4:55 A.M.
U.S.S. Puller in
the Persian Gulf

Having received his orders from Colonel Moore, the overall commander of the Marine Amphibious Unit (MAU) on the Puller, Lieutenant Colonel Thomas E. Hemingway now stood before his pilots.

"Listen up!" he snapped.

The strident words silenced the wardroom chatter and the seated men focused their attention on the five-foot-ten, broadshouldered commander of the Puller's composite air squadron. Hemingway tensed as he spoke, and the bulging biceps of his black-haired arms strained at the rolled-up sleeves of his flightsuit. His build and dense body hair had led to the running name of *Gorilla* among his peers. As was his habit when initially speaking, Hemingway spoke in a low voice, forcing his listeners to strain forward in order to make out his words. It was his way of getting complete attention.

"Recon's loading up in our Stallions because there's a flight of Commies coming up the Gulf from the Indian Ocean. It's codenamed 'Red Dog' and includes 40 Ilyushins and 53 MiG-29s. Higher-up says their objective could be the air base at Dhahran. If so, they'll be passing over our position in 85 minutes. Another Soviet flight from South Yemen is headed toward Riyadh."

Hemingway surveyed the immobile faces before him. They were frozen, as if in a still photograph. He continued.

"Our mission comes directly from JCS. We're to simulate aerial attacks on Riyadh's airport and Dhahran Air Base. Then we're to support Recon in defending Dhahran. JCS thinks the Commies will turn around if we already occupy it. Harriers will drop two loads of MK-81s on open runways of Dhahran and return to saddle up Sidewinders. The Saudi military units on the base have been briefed. Stallions will commence immediate transfer of Recon to the air base. The second wave of Stallions will offload as much combat gear as possible from the ship, then go under the tactical control of the ground commander, Colonel Banks. Recon's immediate objectives are the Control Tower and fuel dumps in the northeastern sector of the base. Any questions from the Stallion pilots?"

There were none. Hemingway checked his watch.

"I want the first Stallions and support helos airborne in five minutes," he growled. "Move out!"

The helicopter pilots cleared out of the wardroom, leaving only the Harrier pilots in the high-backed easy chairs. Each of them feigned a nonchalance that none of them felt. As Hemingway exchanged glances with his pilots, a flicker of a smile played on some of their faces.

"Don't get your hopes up," he told them. "I don't know if we're going duckshooting this morning or not. The Hornets on the Connie and Big E were ordered to harass and divert the Russians . . . whatever that means. If the F-18s don't stop them, we're to meet them with Sidewinders, but we're not to open fire unless they fire first."

Seeing grimaces coming up, Hemingway added, "Yeah, I know these are mucked-up orders."

Captain "Potato Joe" Graybeal flashed his hand. "Colonel, are we going to *have time* to deliver two loads of MK-81s?"

"What're you getting at?"

"Even with two loads, we're not going to crater more than three miles of runway. There's still nine more miles at Dhahran."

Hemingway stroked his chin. "You're right. . . the bombs

are for show anyway. We'll drop one load and pick up Sidewinders."

"Dammit, I almost forgot," continued Hemingway, shaking his head, "We're supposed to warn American compounds
what's happening, too." He looked to Graybeal.

"Joe, you're going to Riyadh. Have your plane fitted with
two MK-81s and four Sidewinders, plus fuel pods. Drop the
bombs on the Riyadh runways within sight of their Control Tower. Before you launch, get the locations of the American compounds in Riyadh from CIC and do what you can to alert them."

"Want me to mess with the planes from South Yemen?"
Graybeal eagerly asked.

"No! They'll be well-escorted. Stick to the American compounds." Hemingway jerked a thumb toward the hatch of the
wardroom. "Get going! You're going to need full throttle to get
there in time."

Hemingway addressed the remaining pilots. "When you return for Sidewinders, CIC will give you assignments to warn
the compounds. I'm going directly to ARAMCO after unload-
ing my bombs. At 0530 hours, we'll marshall at 15K over the
Dhahran Control Tower. Let's go!"

4:58 A.M.
Riyadh

A phalanx of 60 Bedouin, each man over six-feet tall and wearing the distinctive red-and-white checkered gutra (headdress) of the Saudi national guard, bustled into the white, unimposing two-story building of the only television station in Riyadh. The humble edifice of Riyadh TV was in marked contrast to the grand architecture of the city's other public buildings—perhaps testimony to the omnipotence of the Saudi religious leaders, who had vehemently fought the late King Faisal for years before tolerating the introduction of the "infidel's" television to Saudi Arabia.

Following closely behind the guardsmen was their commander, Crown Prince Saleem. The Bedouin muddled menacingly in the hallways until Saleem led them into the small room which served as the studio of the station. One of the guard officers brought a short, bespectacled Egyptian before Saleem.

"Your Highness, this is the station manager."

The Crown Prince scowled at the timid Egyptian before exclaiming in his high-pitched voice, "I shall make an announcement at once on the television."

"Your Highness," the manager meekly offered, "that is not possible."

"*Seize him!*" shrieked the affronted prince.

Two Bedouin flanked the Egyptian and grabbed his arms,

raising him off his feet. As the terrified man gaped at Saleem's khanjar (dagger) sliding from its sheath, he struggled to make his voice audible.

"The prayers . . . Your Highness, the morning prayers." The Egyptian's eyes pointed to the clock on the studio wall. The long narrow secondhand of the clock was on the upswing, 15 seconds from 5 a.m.

The two guardsmen instantly released their grip and the Egyptian collapsed to the floor. Glaring at the clock, Saleem snapped, "Let us *pray*, then!"

A wizened imam who had silently observed the proceedings from a corner of the studio came forward. Getting to his feet, the station manager joined the imam before the standing microphone on a short dais. Raising his hand as he watched the clock, the manager signaled his director in the control room. The imam began to recite from the Koran as the Egyptian moved out of camera range and dropped to his knees.

A few guardsmen kneeled with the manager, and within seconds all in the room were on their knees.

Concluding five minutes of prayer, the imam hastened from the studio and the station manager cautiously approached Saleem.

"Your Highness, we—"

The Crown Prince silenced the Egyptian with a wave of his hand and strode to the microphone where he pointed to the control room. "Let them begin," he ordered.

The station manager nodded to his director.

The still-smoldering prince shouted into the microphone as he would before a multitude, forcing rapid adjustments in the control room. "In the name of Allah, the Compassionate, the Merciful, heed my words! The kingdom is being attacked by infidels. As I speak, their airplanes are crossing our sacred borders. We must oppose the foreigners . . . *wherever we find them!* In the name of Allah, *death to the infidels!"*

Saleem drew his khanjar and with each chant—"Death to the infidels!"—he thrust the curved tip of the blade higher until he was joined by his guardsmen and the building reverberated with their fervor. When he'd howled himself hoarse, the Crown

Prince stepped down from the dais and beckoned the Egyptian before him.

"You will repeat my words *every ten minutes!* Do you understand?"

The station manager bowed low. "It will be done, Your Highness."

Saleem and his men stalked from the building.

A short while later, an agitated mob of several thousand Saudi men surrounded the Riyadh TV building. They were held back by members of the national guard, left there by Saleem to ensure the station followed his instructions.

4:59 A.M.
Over the Persian Gulf

Finishing the message on the computer display, Captain Carter consciously loosened his grip on the Hornet's throttle. *Lighten up* he told himself *for the fine touch.* The thought took him back to his last dogfight over Haiphong. He scanned the display again.

> *24 Fulcrums separated from Red Dog flight. Headed toward Hornets. Coming in at three o'clock.*

He relayed this data to his squadron commanders and spotted the Russian fighters forty seconds later swinging around in a wide arc to take up positions directly behind his F-18s at a half-mile interval. Carter was much relieved a few minutes later when he made visual contact with the main Soviet flight and no fireworks had broken out. The Ilyushins offered *safety*, at least from the Fulcrums' missiles. Now the Russians would be foolish to release any missiles at the F-18s, as the Hornet pilots could easily dodge most of them, leaving the Ilyushin engines to suck up the errant rockets. The American commander spread his F-18 squadrons to generally conform with the Ilyushin formation before telling them, "Strike Force, commence matchup."

Carter repeatedly checked his chronometer as his squadron commanders matched their pilots to the Russian transports. When the formations finally coincided, the F-18s started moving into stepdown positions to their respective Ilyushins. As they did so, Colonel Tupolov ordered a Fulcrum into a shorter stepdown to each of the threatening Hornets.

Seeing no interference to his plan yet, Carter hit his UHF button. "Strike Force—on my command—climb and take up position thirty yards to left-front of your Ilyushins. Accomplish this in *twenty seconds*. Execute!"

As the forty American fighters ascended in unison, the computer voice of Carter's F-18 announced, "*Bingo! Bingo!*" His fuel was now critically low.

Tupolov warned his transports, "Comrades, the Americans approach you from below. Maintain your speed and direction. *Do not* let them alter your course!" To himself, the Russian commander thought *whatever you Americans do, you will do it only once.*

At the relatively slow speed of the F-18s, the air turbulence experienced by the transports was minimal. Carter prayed he was guessing the right distance as his thumb depressed the UHF button. If it was too far, there wouldn't be fuel for a second try; if too close, each of the transports would break up in a terrifying conflagration.

"Strike Force—on my command—close to fifteen yards directly in front of their canopies. You have ten seconds. Execute!"

A communications technician in one of the Russian transports told his superior, "Lieutenant, the American fighters are to close within fifteen meters of our cockpits!" This was relayed to Tupolov who quickly repeated his previous orders to the Ilyushin pilots as Carter issued his final command.

"*Strike Force*"—the American commander took a deep breath—"*hit your afterburners!*"

From the side-by-side twin exhausts of each Hornet, a six-foot-wide mass of white-hot flame emerged as their powerful engines went to maximum throttle. The effect on the Ilyushin cockpits was immediate. The thermal-shock cracked and crazed the surface of the canopies into a fine spiderweb network that obliterated the vision of the pilots within. From a distance, the canopies appeared to have frosted over.

Within seconds, the F-18 Hornets rocketed a mile in front of the Russian formation. The trailing MiGs also shot forward in pursuit, a few of them having to dodge Ilyushins that were drifting as their pilots could no longer see to maintain their flight formations.

"Come back, you idiots!" shrieked the enraged Tupolov at the pursuing MiGs. "Forget the Americans!"

By hastily instructing the squadron commanders of his MiGs in a sequence similar to that used by the American flight leader, Tupolov re-established control of his transports. Using visual communication through the tail-gunners of the Ilyushins, the MiG pilots guided their respective transport pilots until separate radio frequencies could be assigned to each pair of aircraft.

"Those whoring bastards," swore Tupolov, realizing he now had unrestricted use of only twelve Fulcrums, not including his own. Having no alternate instructions, he maintained his formation on course, intending to follow his orders explicitly.

Carter keyed his mike. "Homeplate, this is Falcon 101. Have used afterburners to roast canopies of Ilyushins. They are now flying blind. Our fuel levels too low to continue. Request instructions."

Johnston's response from the Constellation came instantly.

"This is Homeplate. We have approval to land in Oman . . . at Misirah Air Base. Look for long wide valley near tip Musandam Peninsula. Great flying! Repeat: Great flying!"

Carter punched his UHF button. "Strike Force, this is Falcon 101. Follow me on bearing 174. We will try to make air base at northern tip of land mass to south. If you cannot make it, eject over land as close as possible to coast."

5:12 A.M.
ARAMCO Compound

"Come on, Dori. Pitch!" yelled Kevin.

The softball was suspended in midswing as his twin sister froze. She looked over her right shoulder. The muffled thunder of explosions in the direction of Dhahran Air Base had diverted her attention.

"Let's play ball!" implored Kevin. "That's just another Saudi hot dog bailing out."

It was not unusual for residents of ARAMCO (the largest compound for Westerners and non-Saudi Arabs in the country) to hear fighters of the Royal Saudi Air Force slamming into the terrain of the air base. Few of the pilots lost their lives in these crashes, as they were quick to yank their ejection handles—a far easier maneuver than attempting to regain control of their planes. The air base was littered with the charred remains of these aircraft, many of them tail up with their noses embedded deep in sand.

Dori flung the ball, and her 12-year-old brother swung hard. Missing completely, his body contorted in a twist.

"Hey, Elmer Fudd!" taunted his sister, using the nickname he hated. "You swing like an old cow."

On the next pitch, Kevin controlled his swing and smacked a line drive directly at his tormentor. She ducked, pushing her glove out at the projectile. When ball and glove both fell to the ground, Dori snapped up the ball and threw out her brother.

As Kevin rounded first on his way to the outfield, his attention was drawn to a noisy, gray and olive-green camouflaged aircraft overhead. He slowed to a walk, then stood still, craning his neck upward. The Harrier maintained a near-level flight position as it descended in a deep slant to the ground, much like a bird preparing to alight.

"What kind of plane is that?" shouted Kevin. "It looks like it's going to crash."

The boy got no reply as the screaming whine of the dropping aircraft drowned out his voice. Its exhaust nozzles were almost vertical at 70 degrees as Colonel Hemingway aligned his slightly nose-up plane with the street bordering the playing field. At 15 feet, the Harrier made a familiar wobble when he increased power, slowing the plane considerably for touch down. His wheels hit the concrete with a jolt and the plane landed at a speed of 38 knots. The roar of his engine fell away as Hemingway brought it to idle and rotated his nozzles aft. Applying his brakes, he gently brought the plane to a rolling stop within ninety yards.

After letting his engine whine down, Hemingway popped his canopy and climbed out of the cockpit. The children, having recognized the stars-and-bars insignia on the side of the fuse-lage, ran to greet him. As they crowded around the pilot, he forced a smile. "What're you kids doing playing softball this early?"

"We have to play now," Kevin answered. "By seven, it's too hot."

Hemingway started to say, "The Russians are coming," and thought better. He pointed to a cluster of ranch-style homes several hundred yards away. "You kids live over there?"

"I do," nodded one of the children.

"Me, too," responded Kevin and Dori simultaneously—a trait the redheaded twins often displayed.

"You kids come with me," ordered the pilot as he began running toward the homes. Most of the children hopped on bikes, easily keeping pace with the pilot. At the first home, Hemingway paused to knock loudly at its open door before rushing inside.

"What's he doing?" asked Kevin of no one in particular.

"I think *I know*," responded Dori in a low voice.

"What?" inquired one of the children.

"What do you *think* he's doing?" Dori said with a knowing smile. The others looked at her quizzically.

"Dummies!" she finally exclaimed. "He's going to the bathroom."

A few giggled at the suggestion as the frowning pilot came out the door. "No one's home," he gruffly remarked. "*Who* has some parents who are at home?"

Surprised and frightened by the pilot's new tone, no one responded.

"Come on, kids, Hemingway pleaded forcefully. "I've got to talk to an adult."

Dori hesitantly spoke. "They're at the services."

"Services?" queried the pilot.

"You know. . .church," Dori replied.

"How far is it from here?"

Kevin pointed up a street. "Two blocks that way and to the left." It was considerably farther than the first house had been from the ball diamond.

"Well, take me there *quick*!" Hemingway demanded. He studied Kevin's dirtbike a moment. "Son, can I borrow your bike?"

The boy pushed his bike forward, and Hemingway straddled it as Kevin hitched a ride on another one. A few of the kids raced ahead of the pilot who at first awkwardly peddled the small bicycle. When they reached the end of the left-hand street, Hemingway stopped at the house where some of the children were already waiting. Except for its color, the home resembled the others on the street.

"This isn't a church," Hemingway stated as he dismounted.

"They don't allow churches," replied Dori breathlessly beside him. Hemingway looked down at the slender, heavily-freckled girl.

"The Saudis," she explained.

As the door was also open to this house, Hemingway hurried

inside without knocking. Entering a hallway, he found adults seated in a broad living room and adjoining veranda. Coming into the room, the Marine pilot stood silently among bowed heads as a short, middle-aged woman in a white, flowered dress read from a small Bible.

". . . are those who mourn, for they shall be comforted. Blessed are the meek, for they shall inherit the earth. Blessed are those who hunger and thirst for righteousness, for they shall—"

"Excuse me!" Hemingway interrupted.

The woman stopped reading and everyone turned to stare at the intruder, behind whom the children had gathered.

"You're being"—Hemingway hesitated, searching for the right words—"*invaded.*"

"Yes," smiled the woman, "we can see that. Would you like to join us?" Hemingway darkly frowned at the light laughter and the kind faces. His voice was dead serious.

"The *Russians* are invading Saudi Arabia. I'm Colonel Hemingway, with the Marines on the U.S.S. Puller in the Persian Gulf. My forces have already occupied Dhahran Air Base."

The Marine took scant satisfaction as his words wiped the smiles off the friendly faces. "I have instructions to warn as many of the American compounds in this area as possible. I suggest you remain inside ARAMCO until you hear otherwise."

Most of the adults were now standing. One of them asked, "Where've the Russians landed?"

"They haven't yet. We're expecting them to come into Dhahran. That's all I can tell you. I have to go now." Hemingway abruptly pivoted and was halfway down the hallway before he paused. Turning around, he spoke to the nearest adult. "Tell everyone to start phoning their friends in ARAMCO and other compounds. . . to warn them also."

"We can't" replied the man. "The phones are down."

"Damn," said Hemingway under his breath.

"I've got a ham radio," offered a girl's voice behind them.

The two men scrutinized the slim girl, who unfalteringly returned their gaze. "A lot of other compounds have hams, too," said Dori. "I know most of their call signs."

"What's your name, young lady?" asked Hemingway.

"Dori . . . Dori Norlin."

"And yours?" Hemingway inquired of the man.

"I'm her father. Name's John."

"Great," said Hemingway. "Use your radio then." Rushing from the house, he ran to the dirtbikes in the driveway and picked out the one he'd ridden earlier. The pilot looked back to the door of the house, but Kevin was already beside him.

"I need your bike again, son."

"Sure, mister. I'll run beside you."

This time, Hemingway arrived at their destination first, slightly ahead of the boy. Placing the bike behind the backstop, he sprinted to the Harrier and climbed into its cockpit. Before closing his canopy, he checked the clearance of his aircraft and saw Kevin standing no more than 50 feet away. Hemingway motioned the boy over to him.

"Get behind the backstop," yelled the pilot. "My exhaust is going to kick up a lot of dirt and rocks."

As the boy ran to the backstop, Hemingway slid his canopy shut and hit the start button. At first there was a low whining noise from behind the cockpit. The whine retarded a moment and then exploded in a deafening roar as the engine fired. Conducting his instrument check during the minute it took to bring up his engine, Hemingway hurriedly connected his oxygen supply, pressure system to inflate his G-suit in tight turns, and a survival pack (dinghy and life vest). After fastening leg restraints in case he needed to eject, Hemingway strapped himself to four more pairs of harnesses before attaching oxygen and radio leads to his flight helmet.

Adjusting the exhaust nozzles of the Harrier ten degrees from the horizontal, Hemingway glanced at the backstop. Kevin stood behind it, hands tightly covering his ears.

The pilot applied his brakes and brought the throttle to 55 percent. After scanning his gauges, Hemingway simultaneously released his brakes and jammed the throttle to full power. He sank back into his seat as the plane snapped forward.

During the 1.6 seconds the Harrier engine took coming to full power, he kept his eyes on his speed dial and at 40 knots pushed the exhaust nozzles to 60 degrees. In almost the same instant, the plane came free of the ground, having traveled little more than 200 feet.

Kevin squinted through the debris and dust thrown up by the plane, feeling both fright and exhilaration as the echoing howl of the Harrier brought pain to his ears. The slingshot take-off was almost comparable to being catapulted off the deck of a carrier and explained why the Marines called their plane the *jump-jet.*

———————

9:15 P.M.
The White House

The red and blue clusters of flashing dots had disappeared mysteriously off the Middle East wall grid, causing irate generals and harassed communication technicians in the War Room. The technicians were also unable to make contact with the Puller or AWACs planes over the Persian Gulf.

When the VCR-110 announced, "Standby, Connie," indicating an incoming from the carrier, the President and generals hastily gathered before the wall radio.

"Admiral Johnston reporting. We have received word from the flight commander of our F-18s that they've used their exhausts to cloud up the cockpit canopies of the Ilyushins. The Russian transports are now flying blind."

The JCS Chairman moved nearer to the transmitter and spoke into its wall mike. "Have they reversed course?"

"We're not sure," came the reply. "Following this contact with the F-18s, further communications are being jammed out of the Persian Gulf. We've sent the Puller the same message I've just given you, but they've failed to acknowledge it."

"Thank you, Admiral," said Steel. "When you can, pass my congratulations to your flight commander." When he turned around, the somber expression on the face of the JCS Chairman didn't match those of the civilians in the War Room.

"Well," grinned the President, "if the Russians can't see,

they can't land. They'll have to turn around."

"Not necessarily, sir," countered General Huering. He watched the grin fade and continued. "Most certainly, the soldiers in those transports are outfitted with parachutes. And the planes *could* still land if the MiG pilots talked them down. We do that ourselves in emergencies."

President Steiner nodded thoughtfully. "We'll prepare for either contingency. How do we stop them if they use parachutes?"

When the JCS Chairman hesitated, Huering volunteered, "Sir, it's possible to stop the Russians cold, regardless of how they come into Dhahran."

"Explain yourself," said the President when the Marine general paused himself, long enough to glance at Steel who did not discourage him.

"It would involve the use of weapons which the United States disavowed back in the early eighties." Huering paused to get the President's reaction.

"Stop beating around the bush!" snapped Allan Steiner.

"In addition to standard-issue rifles," continued Huering, "our Force Recon units have recently acquired light-weight lasers. For security purposes, they're code-named CCWs, or crowd-control weapons. They have the capability of crippling nearby combat vehicles, including low-flying aircraft, or inflicting injuries of a debilitating nature on enemy soldiers."

"What do you mean by *debilitating?*"

"One of our laser weapons is called a PBL, sir. At low intensity, it projects a hot particle beam that can cause sufficient burns to incapacitate an enemy soldier. Higher intensities can melt internal controls of a nearby aircraft, or even sever a wing."

"What other types of laser weapons do we have?"

"Just one, sir," replied Huering. "The XRL—or X-ray laser. It's radar-guided and designed to counter missiles by causing violent vibrations of its target. It can also be applied to ground targets."

Clayton Walters broke in. "May I raise a point, Mr. President? We're discussing the initiation of hostile actions against the Soviet Union, which, in the case of an in-flight aircraft, could undoubtedly result in heavy casualties. Are there other solutions we should be considering—solutions that won't give the Kremlin cause to retaliate in kind . . . or worse?"

The secretary of state sensed hostility in the War Room, or at least impatience on the faces of those around him. "I'm only reiterating, Mr. President, the words of caution you spoke to the Saudi king."

President Steiner frowned. There was too little time to discuss further alternatives and he knew Gorbachev wouldn't be interested in listening to them. Wiping his face with his hands in a hopeless gesture, the President looked up at his generals.

"I don't intend to give the Russians an excuse to escalate this affair any further than necessary. General Steel, order the Marines at Dhahran to utilize these laser weapons to discourage the landing of transports, *without* shooting the planes down."

General Huering interjected: "Mr. President, this discussion may be academic . . . if we can't communicate with the Puller."

The President looked to Steel. "I thought only *outgoing* communication from the Gulf was down?"

"That's confirmed, sir. Both the AWACs and our satellites are being jammed in that sector. We don't know if they can receive our messages."

"Send my order to use lasers, then. If they don't receive it, let's hope they follow the guidelines we've already given them for their Harriers."

"Sir," began General Steel, "what if the Soviet troops get on the ground and—"

The President interrupted. "If they get on the ground, we'll use the laser weapons to *disable only*." To no one in particular, he added: "I'd rather share the Saudi oil fields with the Russians than start a war over them."

While the face of the JCS Chairman remained stoic, the other military men turned aside to conceal their expressions of disgust. General Steel thought to ask the President if he was certain the Russians would *share* the oil, but kept his counsel.

5:16 A.M.
Over Western Saudi Arabia

Trying to warm her toes within the too-short blanket, Irene cuddled closer to Hamud's back as the early sun sent slivers of silver into the lingering shadows of the Lear Jet cabin. She watched the play of light with half-open eyes.

The first week of vacation in Cannes had become tedious, spending days with her sister on the gusty beach where windswept sand stung the skin of sunbathers . . . and nights in the discotheques dancing with men too short for her five-foot-eleven frame. Running into Hamud at a casino had been a stroke of luck. They'd met formally several months earlier at an embassy reception in Riyadh. Away from his native country, Hamud was the complete opposite of the quiet, dignified image he exuded in Riyadh. In the course of Irene's second week of vacation, the young man and woman had acquired an intimacy that would never have been possible in Saudi Arabia.

Much of their affinity came from a shared aimlessness, not an uncommon trait of the many youths (and those not so young) who flocked to the Riviera in search of sybaritic pleasures.

Both Hamud and Irene led lives without challenge after many years spent gathering extensive and expensive educations. Now the search for known pleasures to fill their days seemed far more natural than a search for unknown goals. And in fulfilling their mutual gratifications, they temporarily dissipated the shared guilt of their wasted lives.

When Hamud had offered to return Irene to Riyadh in his private jet, she wasn't surprised to learn it would be just the two of them, though she did become mildly concerned when Hamud directed her to occupy the copilot seat and monitor a considerable number of gauges for him during the takeoff of the two-pilot aircraft.

Unable to fall back asleep, Irene eased away from Hamud, carefully replacing the blanket against his back. Catching a glimpse of crimson through a window, she paused at the circular view. A deep red on the curved eastern rim of the earth gradually gave way to an intense orange-yellow glow that began to fill the interior of the cabin. Mesmerized, Irene jumped at the hand that cupped the nape of her neck.

"Sorry," apologized Hamud, gently caressing where he touched. "Have you never witnessed the rising sun at 25,000 feet?"

"Not until now," she replied softly, still gazing at the blossoming sunrise.

"Only a desert dawn in the Rub Al Khali is more beautiful."

Irene leaned back slightly and half-turned her head to nuzzle against Hamud. She rolled her cheek along his.

"Someday, I will show it to you," he said softly.

Irene matched her lips to his. "I would like that." She pointed to a door at the rear of the small cabin and discreetly inquired, "Is that what I think it is?"

He nodded with a smile. "There is a shower . . . but no tub, so I shall *not* accompany you," he winked. Recalling the games in the massive tub of his condo in Cannes, she grabbed for the hook of his nose and missed. Laughing as he twisted away, Hamud checked his watch. "We should arrive at Riyadh within the hour."

Emerging from the bathroom in a conservative green dress and heels, Irene joined Hamud in the cockpit. He motioned her into the copilot's seat without speaking. Letting the plane slowly descend to afford Irene a better view of the deep-shadowed mountainous desert below, Hamud leveled off and wove through occasional opalescent wisps of clouds.

Flipping the switch to his radio, Hamud broke the long silence. "Riyadh Control, this is flight XK9. Request permission to land in approximately 15 minutes. Over."

The response was immediate. "Flight XK9, this is Riyadh Control. Permission denied. Suggest alternate landing at Al Hafuf. Over."

"Riyadh Control. Flight XK9 has insufficient fuel to reach Al Hafuf," Hamud lied.

"I'm sorry, Flight XK9," said a new, British-accented voice. "We cannot clear you to land here."

"Why not?" demanded Hamud.

"We're not at liberty to explain," responded the Briton.

Hamud clicked off his radio and jovially told Irene, "We shall have to find out for ourselves why they do not wish us to land."

From a mile up, the massive arches bounding each of the ultra-modern passenger terminals of King Khalid International Airport gave the appearance of a Bedouin tent billowing in the wind. Between two of the arches at one end of the structure sat a plump mosque with its rounded dome. The 3.4 billion dollar airport was the second largest in the world, surpassed only by a newer one in western Saudi Arabia. Its size was half-again as large as the combined runways of LAX, Kennedy, LaGuardia, and O'Hare in the United States. It had been built to the precise specifications of King Khalid to the dismay of its French architects and considerable profit of its British contractors.

Banking to the south, Hamud turned on the radio again and this time spoke in a deeper tone. "Riyadh Control. Is runway 14 clear?"

"Yes," responded the British accent, "but—"

"I have an emergency," interrupted Hamud in his new voice. "I'm coming in from the west on runway 14." He flipped off the radio before the controller could react.

As the sleek, two-engine Lear Jet screamed nearer the high-wire fence surrounding the airport's western runways, a Saudi army sergeant tracked its approach with a shoulder-mounted Stinger missile, rushing through the last of the 18 steps required to activate his weapon. His orders were to fire on any aircraft attempting to land at the airport. When the plane passed directly to his front, the sergeant sighted and pulled the trigger mechanism.

Getting no response, he squeezed harder. Still nothing.

Taking the mounted missile off his shoulder, the sergeant studied its controls. A furious Saudi officer ran up and also checked the controls.

Touching the red switch in front of the trigger mechanism with his swagger stick, the lieutenant shouted, "Imbecile! You have the brains of *a flea in a goat's ass!*"

The sergeant had remembered each of the first 17 steps to release the Stinger, but had omitted the last. The safety switch still engaged the trigger, and he humbly absorbed the officer's abuse. By the time the lieutenant had exhausted his deprecations, Hamud was braking the aircraft beside his car.

"Did you see the tanks and soldiers to our left just before we landed?" asked Irene.

Hamud nodded. "There were national guardsmen as well. They must be waiting for an important visitor," he explained as he flipped switches to cut the engine.

When Hamud jerked open the cabin's door, a military jeep slid to a halt before his plane. Using a hand to caution Irene away from the door, Hamud pressed a button to lower the plane's folding ladder. He stepped out onto the first step, half-closing the door behind him. The jeep contained three armed soldiers and an officer.

"*You are under arrest!*" blurted the officer excitedly, standing in his vehicle.

Hamud snorted. "And you are a fool," calmly stated the Saudi prince as he pointed to his white convertible. "That is my car."

The men in the jeep gaped at the car. To the left and below the silver *Corniche* signature on the lid of the trunk was a gold-rimmed, green license plate identifying the owner as a member of the royal family.

Hopping out of his vehicle, the officer smartly clicked his heels before saluting. "Praise to Allah . . . a thousand pardons.

We did not know who you were. Our orders are to kill any foreigners landing at the airport."

"Praise to Allah, I am no foreigner," smiled Hamud, adding, "You may go."

After another salute, the officer jumped into the jeep, and Hamud stepped back inside his plane. Irene spoke in a frightened voice.

"*Why* do they have orders to kill foreigners?"

"I didn't ask. For your sake, I wanted them to leave as soon as possible." Hamud completed dressing by placing a white thobe trimmed in gold over his western-style suit. Before snapping his suitcase shut, he removed an elaborately-decorated khanjar and tucked the curved dagger and sheath in his belt.

Though Irene knew the crescent-shaped blade of the khanjar made it an ill-suited weapon, she asked with new alarm, "Do you expect trouble?"

"No," replied Hamud, patting the jewel-encrusted sheath. "This is only symbolic."

She squinted. "Of what?"

"My virility." He gave his raffish smile and let fingers run along the uplifted curve of the khanjar.

"You're kidding?" she scoffed at the sexual metaphor.

"It's an old belief in my country," Hamud explained in complete seriousness. "Come, let us go now."

After throwing their luggage in the trunk of the convertible, they headed for the exit of the private aircraft section. At the gate, Hamud waved the Pakistani guard to his car window and asked, "Why are the army and national guard on the runways?"

"You have not heard?"

"No, I just arrived."

The sentry's eyes opened wide. "There is to be an invasion. Only a short while ago, many bombs were dropped."

"Open the gate," ordered Hamud, concluding the conversation. Instead of taking the highway toward Riyadh, he turned into the lane leading to the passenger terminals. It was clogged with both military and civilian vehicles. In the slowed traffic, Hamud lowered the top of the convertible.

"Why are we going this way?" asked Irene.

Hamud gave her a broad grin. "I want to see the *invasion.*"

"I'd like to get into Riyadh," said Irene anxiously.

"*After* the invasion," he joked. Their car moved sluggishly past parking lots filled with military vehicles. Irene was amazed that none of the civilian vehicles appeared to be leaving. They outnumbered the military vehicles as they neared the terminals.

"It looks like an invasion of sightseers," she commented derisively.

Pounding his horn now like most of the other drivers, Hamud switched lanes with abandon in an effort to get closer to the terminals. After working his way into a lane near the first terminal (normally reserved for members of the royal family and exalted guests of the kingdom), Hamud threw his gearshift into "park" before bringing the Rolls to a full stop. As the transmission ground the car to a halt, he jumped out and called, "Let's go!"

Looking back at the furious drivers blasting their horns in the now blocked lane, Irene shouted to Hamud, "You can't park here!"

Oblivious to the protesting drivers, Hamud opened the passenger door to the convertible and grabbed her hand. "We'll be just a minute," he promised and rushed her into the terminal.

The chaos inside the terminal reminded Irene of minor riots she'd seen on television. Saudi men, mostly in military uniforms, rushed to and fro. Scattered groups of officers loudly argued among themselves. Scores of Saudi civilians crowded around the floor-to-ceiling windows offering views of the runways. Irene saw no other women in the terminal.

"Upstairs," directed Hamud when he realized the downstairs windows were congested already. He pulled her by the sleeve instead of her hand as they pushed their way onto an escalator.

The mezzanine was also jammed with humanity, and a larger proportion were in military uniforms. Hamud resolutely pressed into one of the throngs around a window, still gripping Irene's sleeve. There were no planes in view, either on the

runways or near the terminal loading areas. After standing
several minutes in the crush of the noisy men around the
window, Irene jerked Hamud's arm and whispered, "If you
won't take me into Riyadh, I'll—"

He shook his head. "I cannot hear you."

"I'm going to call for a car!" she shouted over the din.

Hamud released her and watched for a moment as Irene
marched stiffly in high heels across the marble-floored
mezzanine. She ignored the leers and taunts of some of the Saudi
men, a few of whom deliberately jostled her as she passed.
Knowing Saudi men often treated unescorted women in this
manner, she felt no particular danger.

When Irene found a pillar containing telephones, she rapidly
punched out the number of the American embassy. Getting no
ring, she pressed the receiver to her ear. She shook her head
and decided she'd misdialed. Irene started to dial again and
gasped as a soldier locked her arms in a vise-like grip.

Twisting to scream at her assailant, Irene lost her voice.
The dusky faces of two heavily-armed soldiers glowered at her,
and their red-and-white checkered gutras told her protest was
useless. The two national guardsmen dragged her away from
the telephones, in the opposite direction from which she'd come.
She shouted over her shoulder for Hamud, causing one of the
guardsmen to jerk her arm violently and growl, "Quiet, woman!"

Thinking Hamud either could not hear her shouts or chose
to ignore them, Irene decided to remain silent. She was pulled
into a uniformed group gathered around another window and
Irene relaxed somewhat at the sight of the highly-decorated
chests of the uniforms, thinking the men must be senior officers.
Her guards spoke to one of the officers, who in turn addressed
a tall Saudi wearing a gold-trimmed thobe.

Irene immediately recognized Crown Prince Saleem and
blurted out, "Your Highness, I'm accompanied by—"

"I have not spoken to you," Saleem interrupted in English.
He glared at her a moment before flicking his wrist. "Take her
to the trucks!"

"*I* will take her," countered a hard voice to the rear of Irene,
who closed her eyes in relief at the sound of Hamud's words.

Saleem bellowed, "*Who speaks so?*"

"A brother, Your Highness." A path instantly parted between the two equally obstinate royal princes. Hamud, fully as tall as his older half-brother, smiled as he came forward to the side of Irene. Recognizing the youngest of his 44 brothers, Saleem smirked as he spoke.

"And what would you want with such a foreigner?"

"Praise to Allah, I do not want her," Hamud said with scorn, "but she is my guest."

"You are not in your home, my brother," Saleem reminded Hamud. "Here she is *my guest.*"

When Hamud did not challenge the Crown Prince further, Saleem again ordered his guards to remove Irene and turned back to the window. Placing a hand in front of the guards, Hamud signified they should wait a moment. He pushed his way up behind his half-brother and whispered into Saleem's ear.

The Crown Prince wearily came around. Showing great contempt on his face, he waved his hand and hissed, "I do not want her."

Hamud grabbed Irene's arm and roughly pulled her away from Saleem's group.

"You're *hurting* me," Irene protested. He lightened his grip, but did not slow their pace until they were on the escalator back to the ground floor. Coming off the escalator, he asked, "Do you have tennis shoes in your baggage?"

Irene nodded, and he pulled her outside to his car. When they returned inside the terminal, Irene had exchanged tennis shoes for the heels and wore Hamud's thobe (turned inside-out) over her dress. Hamud had fashioned a chador about her head with a blue shirt and it shielded all but her eyes from the staring men. This time they remained on the lower level, well away from the escalators.

5:30 A.M.
Dhahran Airbase

As his Harrier orbited the Control Tower at Dhahran, Hemingway keyed his mike. "Hammer, this is Gorilla 101. Come in."

"Hammer, here," responded Lt. Colonel Banks promptly.

"What's your progress?"

"Both objectives secured."

"Any problems?"

"None. Right after we went into the tower, the Saudi area commander showed up . . . a General Lakar. He's been cooperative, so I've positioned his men in the southern sector of the base. We've also borrowed jeeps and armored vehicles from them."

"Excellent," said Hemingway. "Where are their F-15s?"

"They tangled with the Russians, and according to Lakar only two F-15s survived."

"Saudis do any damage?"

"None claimed."

Poor bastards, mused Hemingway, *all they know how to do is point and pray.* And he wondered how his Harrier squadron would fare against the Fulcrums. "How many men do you still have undeployed?"

"Half."

"Any ideas on how to keep the Commies out of here?"

"PBLs," suggested Banks. "Give 'em a warm welcome."

Hemingway considered the last message from the Puller. It had stressed not to initiate any form of deadly fire on the Soviets . . . yet he was supposed to discourage their landing.

"That might work too well," allowed Hemingway. "If someone hit one of their fuel-lines, it'd look like a missile hit and all hell'd break loose."

"That reminds me," Banks said. "We talked Lakar into giving us control of all their Stinger and Hawk missiles."

"How'd you do that?"

"I explained to him the Commies can track them back to their sources and retaliate instantly . . . then I told him we'd assume the risk for them."

"Good work, Hammer," stated Hemingway. "I'd suggest you use your XRLs instead of the PBLs. That way, the Commies won't even know what's hitting—"

"Gorilla 101, this is 103," interrupted one of the other Harrier pilots. "Want another idea?"

"What's on your mind, 103?"

"Why not litter some of this A-Rab oil on the runways? That way the Commies'll have a helluva time coming in. If the first ones smash up, it oughta discourage the rest of 'em."

"I like it," said Banks instantly.

"So do I," agreed Hemingway. "My Stallions could haul drums from the fuel dump and spread oil on the runways. Your men could commandeer all the aviation refuelers on the base and do the same."

"Consider it done," concluded Banks.

"Hammer, have you heard from Pounder in the last five minutes?" asked Hemingway. Pounder was the radio designation for their commander, Colonel Moore, who was still on the Puller.

"Negative."

"I can't raise him on the radio," revealed Hemingway, "so I'm going back to Truckstop to check it out."

"Before you go," said Banks, "do you mind if I park a dozen of your Stallions around the Control Tower. . .to make our presence known?"

"Good idea, Hammer. Just don't leave any men in them."
Hemingway checked his watch. "Our friends are due in 55
minutes. I'll check back with you after seeing Pounder."

9:40 P.M.
The White House

After the President's brief summary for the seated three-member congressional delegation, Speaker of the House Edward Snell asked, "Can the Russians still land?"

President Steiner fiddled with his ear. After three months in office, he was still uncomfortable when forced to formulate replies to questions he had no idea how to answer. It wasn't the slight misinformation he occasionally provided that bothered him. What stung his conscience was when he found himself attempting to portray an overly optimistic view which he knew to be unrealistic.

"It's unlikely," Allan Steiner frowned at himself, "for reasons we've already outlined."

Snell switched his attention to the JCS Chairman. "General, if the Russians *do* manage to land at Dhahran, what do we do then?"

"We haven't had time to develop a detailed plan other than to instruct our field commanders to use measures which minimize potential casualties."

Hoolihan whispered into the ear of the President, who nodded and added, "We also called Derevenko to tell him our Marines have already invaded Saudi Arabia." Becoming increasingly conscious of his overuse of 'we' as if he sought a shared responsibility for his actions, the President made a mental note to avoid this posturing.

Senator Winslow, Senate minority leader and a member of the President's party, asked, "What was Derevenko's reaction?"

"He said the Afghan flight was a training mission . . . that we should not be concerned about it." The President added, "This was before the AWACs notified us of the flight coming from South Yemen."

"Pardon me for saying so, Mr. President," commented Snell, "but this is a goddamn mess."

President Steiner started to openly agree when the Senate majority leader, Joe Farrell, spoke up in a sour tone. "I find this all quite hard to believe, Mr. President. You were elected on a peace platform . . . and now you're authorizing actions which could lead to global war."

"On the contrary," the President promptly rejoined, "the actions I've authorized are geared to prevent that possibility."

"How can you say that," pressed Farrell, "considering what the F-18s have done already to the Soviet planes? For God's sake, do you realize *the risks* you're taking?"

Farrell went on. "We're now in a position to start a major conflict over a semi-friendly, Arab country that supplies us with less than five percent of our oil imports. If Asad had wanted to avoid a foreign takeover, he should have requested our military presence long before this."

Allan Steiner inwardly smiled, thinking *I had enough trouble getting the perfidious fool to accept our assistance now.*

Snell leaned forward, pointing his finger at the Middle East wall grid. "How can you be certain the destination of the Soviet flights are, in fact, Saudi Arabia? It could be Iraq . . . or even Kuwait. Have we contacted people in those countries to determine their involvement? With the Iranians on the warpath, either of those countries might have invited the Russians into the Persian Gulf area."

Though of the same party as the President, Snell had developed his speakership in a curmudgeon style. He considered himself above party lines and displayed a smug superiority to those who were mere members of partisan parties.

"Mr. Speaker," the President coyly remarked, "I find your

suggestion highly improbable. If Derevenko had no designs on the Saudi oil fields, it would be in his interests to tell us openly . . . and thereby avoid the possibility of confrontation with us. He would certainly have stated his planes were simply utilizing Saudi airspace to reach Iraq or Kuwait, if that were the case."

President Steiner switched to Farrell. "As for the F-18s, we gave them explicit orders not to fire unless fired upon."

Farrell threw up his hands. "What difference does it make *who* fires first?" he contended. "Either way, it could expand into World War III! We don't need that . . . not over Saudi Arabia, or any other *fickle-minded Arab country.*"

The President stood and spoke with a trace of irritability. "Gentlemen, I've called you down here to inform you of the current situation in the Persian Gulf. If you have positive suggestions how this crisis can be resolved, please offer them." He paused to look each politician in the eye. "I'm acting in what I believe to be the best interests of the United States. So far, we *are not* in a global conflict . . . or even a limited conflict with the Soviets."

"Mr. President," began the Speaker, "may I remind you of the War Powers Act of 1973? The President is required to report to Congress within 48 hours of ordering American troops into hostile situations."

"I'm quite aware of my responsibilities, Mr. Speaker," replied the President evenly. Wishing to keep the politicians away from the media, he added, "In order to keep you informed of the latest developments, may I suggest you remain in the White House?"

Receiving no objections, the President addressed his assistant. "Jim, escort these gentlemen to the Oval Office." As they filed out of the War Room, Farrell muttered to his small group, "This is a fine time to have *a rookie* in the White House!"

A uniformed aide approached President Steiner. "Sir, the director of the CIA is on line 8. He says it's urgent."

The President reluctantly picked up the phone. "What is it, Mr. Rolle?"

"We've just received a message from Riyadh that I wanted to relay to you personally."

"What is it?"

"The Saudi Land and Air Forces *will* cooperate with us," revealed Rolle matter-of-factly.

"How do you know that?" asked the President. "Only thirty minutes ago, the king and his brothers said they wouldn't."

Rolle's voice was friendly. "Sir, the Saudis seldom say what they mean, even among themselves."

Thinking *I've heard that before,* Allan Steiner asked, "What's your source?"

The CIA director paused significantly. "I'd rather not say over the phone, sir. Perhaps, I should come over."

Having intentionally kept Rolle—a holdover of the previous administration—out of the War Room, President Steiner debated his reply. He had found approval of the earlier CIA participation in Kuwait distasteful, even though the placement of the flu-compound in the Kuwait water supply had been disguised as an act of the Iraqi army. He was anxious to minimize Rolle's subsequent role in the crisis. And personally, the self-confident, almost contemptuous manner of the man aggravated him.

Still awaiting the President's reply, Rolle asked, "May I pose a question, sir?"

"Go ahead."

Fully aware of the presidential coolness, Rolle spoke cautiously. "Why hasn't Admiral Johnston ordered our F-18s to proceed to Dhahran after refueling in Oman?"

In the silence that followed, the CIA director considered how he might rephrase his words.

President Steiner responded with his own question. "How the hell do you know they're in Oman?"

"That's my job, sir."

"Get yourself over here," ordered Allan Steiner, who immediately implemented Rolle's suggestion.

6:11 A.M.
Dhahran Airbase

Joining up with the other Harriers, Hemingway ordered five of his aircraft to hide on the base, going under tactical control of Colonel Banks. The other two Harriers were directed to assume positions off his starboard wing.

"We're headed east," explained Hemingway, "to see why Truckstop's not talking."

At the shoreline of the Gulf, Hemingway snapped, "Move it up to 500 knots!"

A moment later, one of his wingmen exclaimed, "There's smoke coming—"

"I know," interrupted Hemingway. He'd already seen the black column of smoke rising from the water north of the island of Bahrain. At three miles, the pilots recognized the Puller— fire and smoke curling up its port side. A destroyer escort was beside the crippled ship.

"Circle at 3K," ordered Hemingway. "I'm going in."

After setting his Harrier down roughly, Hemingway jumped to the deck and raised a fist with his thumb out at a purple-shirt (fueler). He jerked the fist to his mouth like a Coke bottle, signaling he wanted fuel, and then sprinted to Flight Deck Control. Finding it deserted, he ran back onto the flight deck and grabbed the nearest seaman.

"What happened here?" Hemingway demanded.

"Two hits!" blurted the seaman, wide-eyed and near panic. "We took two hits from a gunboat."

Hemingway raced up the outside ladders to the bridge and found the Puller's skipper barking orders to several men. Seeing the Harrier commander, the skipper stared at him a moment. "Why're you back?"

Without answering, Hemingway asked his own question. "How'd you get it?"

"A Saudi gunboat, patrolling 200 yards to port, dropped two torpedoes on us." The ship's commander winced. "Wasn't a damn thing we could do."

"Where's Colonel Moore?" inquired Hemingway.

The skipper winced again. "Dead. His helo took a missile from the gunboat right after he lifted off. The torpedoes followed. They must have been waiting for him."

"Where's the gunboat?"

"In a couple thousand pieces," explained the skipper. "The destroyer blew it out of the water."

Hemingway jerked his head toward Bahrain. "Can you make the beach over there?"

Gawking at the flames licking over the edge of his flight deck, the skipper shook his head. "It may not be worth trying . . . if we can't get those fires under control. They'll reach our forward magazines in another twenty minutes."

"You'd better get your men onto the destroyer," suggested Hemingway.

The skipper nodded. "You'd do well to get off quick, too."

"Good luck!" called Hemingway, stepping off the bridge. Rejoining the two other Harriers, he headed back toward Dhahran. Before they reached the coast, one of his wingman broke radio silence.

"Gorilla 101, this is 103. Six bogeys coming up fast at seven o'clock."

"103 and 105, this is 101. Take a 1500-foot stepup, reduce speed to 325 knots, and standby to viff."

Three MiGs came up tight on Hemingway's aircraft—one on each wingtip at 20 yards and the third behind and below him.

Each of the other Harriers picked up a similar trio. Hemingway glanced to his port side and, for the first time in his life, saw a Fulcrum up close. The AV-8B was dwarfed by the MiG-29, which was a full third larger. Each of the MiG's twin engines had the same thrust as the Harrier's single power plant, giving the Soviet pilot a top speed more than double his counterpart. In addition, the Fulcrum had been designed as an air superiority fighter. Hemingway was not particularly concerned.

He gradually maneuvered nearer the port Fulcrum, placing the tip of his wing within five yards of the Russian's wingtip. Getting the Soviet's attention, the American raised his right hand and displayed three fingers. As the Fulcrum pilot stared back, Hemingway successively flashed one finger, four fingers, and two fingers . . . then pointed to his ear.

The Russian nodded.

Setting his UHF radio at 314.2 and keying his mike, the American pilot asked, "Do you read me?"

Hemingway heard guttural tones of several Russian voices over the signaled frequency. A voice asked him in crude English, "Who are you?"

"I'm with the American military forces at Dhahran air base," said Hemingway. "I want to speak to your flight commander."

More jabbering filled his headset.

The English-speaking pilot replied, "Commander not speak your language."

"Tell him," Hemingway stated succinctly, "United States Marines . . . occupy . . . Dhahran air base."

The MiG pilot came right back. "My commander say Marines leave Dhahran *at once!*"

The eastern shoreline of Saudi Arabia passed below. In a matter of a few minutes, they'd be over the air base. Hemingway's tone became severe. "I repeat. United States Marines hold Dhahran. You *cannot* land there. It will be—"

"How you say it, American?" interrupted the Soviet pilot. "Piss off!"

Hitting the UHF button, Hemingway growled, "Slide!"

Yanking their exhaust nozzles into breaking positions, the American pilots strained forward in their straps as their engines made a furious racket. The instant deceleration matched an arrested landing on a carrier deck as each of the Harriers squatted nearly motionless in midair. In less than three seconds, the hunted became the hunters—the Americans had neatly slid into deadly positions behind the MiGs.

A half-mile directly to his front, Hemingway now observed the tight formation of Fulcrums which moments before had been his escorts. "Goddamn," he muttered forlornly at the golden and forbidden opportunity. Within a few more seconds, he knew his Harriers could effortlessly slip Sidewinders up the exhausts of the MiGs.

The Fulcrums, realizing they'd been pole-whacked, briskly broke into erratic turns and dives to reduce the American advantage. Hemingway kept his wingmen in their stepups as they came over Dhahran.

Due to his warning, Hemingway correctly surmised the Soviet commander would first do a flyby at the air base to assess the American presence. When Hemingway observed a second group of MiGs coming over the base, he keyed his mike.

"Hammer, this is Gorilla 101. Hold your fire. We are escorting MiGs over your positions." Hemingway's message was meaningless, and Banks responded accordingly.

"This is Hammer, Gorilla 101. Roger your last."

These words were also received and interpreted for the perplexed Colonel Tupolov. As he flew over Dhahran at 2500 feet, he clearly observed the circle of Sea Stallions gathered around the Control Tower. Tupolov also detected small numbers of Marines atop the buildings overlooking the runways. On a second flyby at lower altitude, Tupolov was reassured to find the Americans on the rooftops were not armed with missiles. Noting a wetness on the runways at the lower height, he wondered why a heavy morning dew had not been included in the briefings back in Kandahar.

"Are all personnel on this floor?" asked Ambassador Clark.

"Yes, sir," replied Fricke in a hushed tone. "We're ready to roll."

"Let's talk to Asad now." Clark walked across the communications room to where the Saudi king sat. Picking up a memo pad, Fricke followed and casually stationed himself near the Royal Guard officer leaning against the wall behind Asad.

"Your Majesty," began Clark, "we have been ordered by President Steiner to evacuate the embassy."

Asad froze in his chair.

Clark tried to smile. "We'd like you to go with us, Your Majesty."

The Royal guard officer came off the wall, his hand going to his holster. As the astounded king groped for a reply, Clark encouragingly added, "It's for your own protection, Your Majesty."

Drawing his gun, the Saudi officer pointed it once more at Clark. "*I* will protect my king!" he declared.

Watching the eyes of the officer, Fricke in a deliberately slow motion flipped his memo pad toward the ceiling. In the split second the officer glanced up, Fricke gripped the muzzle of the gun and forced it down.

When the officer moved his other hand to the pistol, Fricke

buried the edge of his free hand in the soft plexus of the Saudi's neck. Doubling over, the bug-eyed Saudi released his gun and grasped his neck.

Fricke calmly emptied the gun's cylinder of its bullets and, placing the ammunition in his pocket, offered it back to its owner. Shaking his head in mock disapproval, Fricke said, "It's bad manners to point a gun at someone."

As the Saudi officer made no attempt to retrieve his pistol, Fricke reached over and jammed it back in its holster. The still-baffled king looked to Ambassador Clark, who smiled apologetically.

"Your Majesty, should the invasions succeed, you can take sanctuary with the Americans. We'll hide you until it is safe to leave the country."

"I do not wish to leave," Asad weakly protested.

Clark continued. "President Steiner asked me to remind you of the fate the Afghan leader met after the Soviets invaded his country in 1979. You must remember how Hafizullah Amin was hunted down like a dog and shot within 72 hours . . . and *he* was a Marxist."

"But my people"—Asad glanced at his Royal Guard officer—"will protect me."

"If that is true," Clark argued, "why are the many palaces of the Saud family guarded by Pakistani troops instead of *your people*?"

The frightened king was too disconcerted to reply.

Clark nodded to Fricke, who summoned a Marine sergeant to his side. "Sergeant Hoctor, notify everyone we leave in one minute. And assign two men to escort the Royal Guard officer. He's coming with us, too."

The sergeant returned to the door of the communications room in less than a minute and gave a thumbs-up signal.

"Hit the seals!" snapped Fricke.

Hoctor began breaking the plastic seals protecting a bank of locks by the door. As he inserted a key into each lock, tear gas hissed from fire extinguisher nozzles in the ceilings of the floors below.

"Let's go!" said Fricke, leading the way up a narrow

staircase. Emerging on the roof, the Americans and their reluctant guests climbed into the waiting helicopter, its blades already churning. After conferring with Clark, Fricke informed the pilot to take them first to the nearby Lockheed compound. As they lifted off, the ambassador's eyes met those of Asad. Clark looked away hastily, wishing to avoid the accusing eyes of the Saudi king.

When they arrived over the Lockheed compound, a small international conclave of the firm's employees, Fricke shouted to the ambassador, "There's not much activity down there."

The streets were deserted within the walled compound of some three dozen western-style homes. After the pilot landed at its center, Sergeant Hoctor placed four Marines in defensive positions around the helicopter before running to the door of the nearest house. When no one responded to his knocking, he cautiously entered the home.

When the Marine sergeant came out, he appeared pale and shaken. Hoctor stepped off the sidewalk by the front door and leaned against the wall of the home to retch.

"Dammit!" exclaimed Fricke, jumping from the helicopter and sprinting toward the house.

Hoctor held up his hand to halt Fricke. "Major, you *don't* want to go in there."

Fricke pointed to an adjacent house. "Check that home, too." Entering the first house, Fricke emerged a few moments later with a stony face and walked stiffly to the helicopter.

Sergeant Hoctor shouted, "It's the same over here, sir."

Fricke continued toward the helicopter. At its open hatch, he leaned in and stared hard at Asad. "Mr. Ambassador, I think you and our *Saudi friends* should come take a look."

Clark stood and, with a motion of his arm, invited the king and his officer to precede him. Fricke waved the two Marine guards away from the Saudi officer and then followed behind the three men as they approached the house. At the open door, Asad could see enough and halted.

"I do not wish to enter," the king announced.

The ambassador stood to Asad's right, and the Saudi officer stood on his left. Fricke broke the stalemate. He violently shoved the officer from behind, and the Saudi staggered through the front door, struggling to keep his balance. Placing his hands on the backs of both Clark and Asad, Fricke applied minimal pressure as he said, "It gets worse."

The king meekly followed his Royal Guard officer inside. Both Saudis shuddered at the carnage, as Clark and Fricke crowded in behind.

Except for what clothes remained on them, mutilations made it difficult to distinguish the sex or ages of the bodies which hung on the furniture and strewed the floor. A small dog had been gutted, it entrails spilling from its twisted body.

"MY GOD," Clark gulped to the Saudi king. "Are *these* the 'infidels' your brother spoke of this morning in my office?"

Asad stared at the far wall of the living room, unable to view the bloodbath any longer.

Stepping forward, Fricke knelt down and picked up the limp body of a child—a boy of two or three. Cradling the body in his arms, Fricke faced the Saudi king and spoke hoarsely. "*Take this child!*"

Asad neither moved nor acknowledged the American's words.

With a fury burning in his eyes, Fricke came nearer and repeated his words in a low, clipped growl.

As the king gradually lifted his arms to accept the child, Fricke gently pushed the bloody body to Asad's chest. "If you drop this child," Fricke cautioned, "so help me, I'll—"

"It's time we left, Major," Clark interjected. As they walked from the home, Fricke instructed Sergeant Hoctor to have the Marines check for survivors in the rest of the compound. A few minutes later, Hoctor reported a body count of 117. One of his Marines had returned with a slight, middle-aged Oriental man. Fricke asked his Marine escort, "Where'd you find *him*?"

"He was kneeling outside one of the houses, sir. Praying or something."

Fricke addressed the man. "Who are you?"

The dismal eyes of the man were swollen and red. "My name Lee Chun. I am Korean."

"What're you doing here?"

Nodding in the direction of his escort, Chun said, "As I tell this one, I pray for spirits of my friends."

"Friends?" queried Fricke.

"Today my day off," the Korean said. "I come to visit friends—Jim Agnew and family."

"Were you here when this happened?"

The Korean stared sadly at his interrogator. "I think I not be talking now . . . if I be here then. When my bus come compound gate, I see many, many truck going out. Many soldier, making much noise."

"Mr. Chun," the American ambassador solemnly inquired, "what color were their headdresses?"

The Korean paused. "I think white and red."

Clark pivoted to Asad. "The United States will hold *you personally responsible* for the people murdered here by your national guardsmen."

"Ambassador," Asad weakly replied, "the United States attacked my country. Your planes dropped bombs at Riyadh airport."

"Ours was a mock attack," Clark stated bitterly. "Before this day ends, your own children may suffer the same fate as the child in your arms . . . from a *real* attack!"

Asad dropped his eyes to the body in his arms.

"Mr. Chun," Clark said, "I'd like you to come with us. We're going to the ARAMCO compound for safety."

The Saudi king looked up in alarm. "We cannot go there!" he exclaimed. "The Russians will be at Dhahran."

"They may be," Clark replied, "but I think they'll leave ARAMCO alone. There're too many Westerners there . . . and it's big enough to hide you."

"Mr. Ambassador," said Fricke, "do you plan to try and warn the other Western compounds here in Riyadh?"

Clark grimaced as he looked back at the house he'd entered. He shook his head. "We'd be powerless to keep this from happening . . . or too late. Let's try to make ARAMCO."

They re-entered the helicopter and before its rotor drowned out his voice, Clark turned to the Saudi king. "Your Majesty, do you realize at least half the families in the Lockheed compound were French and British?"

As the helicopter passed over the outskirts of the Riyadh, its pilot sent word back to Clark that company was coming. Two F-15s with markings of the Royal Saudi Air Force closed at high speed, overshooting the helicopter by a mile. Circling back, the fighters took up positions on either side of the helicopter and indicated they wished to communicate with its pilot. Receiving no response, the nearest F-15 came closer, attempting to alter the helicopter's course. When this too proved ineffective, the F-15 backed off and fired a burst of 20mm rounds in front of the helicopter.

The American pilot called the ambassador to his cockpit. "We're in trouble, sir. These boys mean business!"

"Can they force us to land?" asked Clark.

"They can do worse," replied the pilot. "May I make a suggestion?"

Clark nodded.

"Let's slide the hatch open back there and hold the king where they can see him. If they recognize Asad, they won't fire on us again."

Clark asked, "Can we do that safely?"

"We'll tie a harness to him."

"Okay, let's try it," Clark said.

"Send Major Fricke up here," requested the pilot, "and I'll tell him what to do."

The scheme worked. The Saudi fighter pilots backed off as expected and escorted the embassy helicopter for the balance of its flight.

6:20 A.M.
Dhahran Air Base

For those at ground level, the vapors from various jet fuels created steamy mirages on the runways of Dhahran Air Base. High above, Hemingway squinted into the morning sun in search of the main flight of Soviet planes as Colonel Tupolov issued his final instructions.

"Comrades, there are no military targets on the runways other than small barriers of barrels. We will land according to plan. A pair of Fulcrums will precede each transport of the first wave to clear its runways."

After Tupolov assigned pairs of Fulcrums to clear the four preselected runways and three more MiGs to knock out the helicopters gathered at the Control Tower, he told them, "You will coordinate your attacks immediately prior to touchdown of the first wave. We must not give the enemy time to react before the Ilyushins are on the ground."

The well-rehearsed plan Tupolov intended to execute consisted of an initial wave of four Ilyushins landing simultaneously on separate runways near each side of the Control Tower. This accomplished, the remaining transports would land in successive waves around the strategic center of the air base.

What seemed like specks on the canopy of Hemingway's Harrier soon became a swarm of enemy aircraft . . . approaching at 3500 feet. For an instant, he thought of the long-bodied brunette reaching up for him a scant two hours earlier. As his mind switched back to the approaching danger, he regretted he had no children by her . . . or any other woman.

The first four Ilyushins, each with an escorting MiG, lumbered over the airfield from the east at a height of 500 feet. A mile from the Control Tower, the transports were at 300 feet when they separated for their respective runways.

The Fulcrums assigned to destroy the barriers and helicopters came screaming in ahead of the Ilyushins. Their 20mm cannon fire scattered the stacks of barrels like bowling pins, and tracers kicked up pockets of flames where they came in contact with the soaked runways. Where other tracers found the fuel tanks of the Sea Stallions, brilliant fireballs erupted.

The smile on Colonel Tupolov's face at these initial explosions turned to bewilderment—then alarm—as sheets of flames raced along the runways, enveloping his transports just as they neared touchdown.

"*Pull up!*" shrieked Tupolov, echoing the instructions the Ilyushin pilots were already receiving from their escorting MiGs.

Orange flames licked at the undercarriages of the four planes as their engines struggled against the heat and smoke created by the oxygen-sucking inferno. As the flames flashed ahead of the transports, turning the entire airfield into a sea of fire, the crackling roar of the blaze obliterated the howl of the straining Ilyushins.

Tips of flames scorched the bellies of the transports, and the paratroopers within tore at their seatbelts to get off their super-heated metal benches. Standing in the pitching transports provided only temporary relief, as the floor grating soon seared their feet as well.

The four Ilyushins gained little altitude until reaching the perimeter of the blazing airfield, at which point the men inside two of the planes opened doors to dissipate the heat within. This had little immediate effect, so a few men opted to jump from the transports, triggering a stampede by the others. Most of the Russians jumped from heights less than 500 feet, well under the 700 feet required to hit the ground safely. While Colonel Tupolov watched the action below in horror, Hemingway spoke into his mike.

"Hammer, this is Gorilla 101. Commies have jumped from planes at east and west ends of air base. Suggest you send two helos of men to each location. Use your Harriers for east. I will cover the west."

"Gorilla 101, this is Hammer. Helos on the way."

Hemingway hit his UHF button. "Gorillas 103 and 105, this is 101. Fly cap for me. I'm heading to west end of field." Out of respect for any SAMs (surface-to-air missiles), Hemingway kept a half-mile distance from the western Russians until the Sea Stallions approached.

When the helicopters touched down and discharged their men, Hemingway watched the Marines cautiously come up on the ragged line of Soviet paratroopers still stretched out over a distance of 600 yards. Instead of training their weapons on the Marines, it appeared most of the Russians were struggling with their feet. Establishing contact with the American ground commander, Hemingway asked:

"What the hell's going on down there?"

"This is Hammer Three. These suckers are in pretty bad shape, sir. The rubber of their footgear has melted onto their feet. The ones who've gotten their boots off have removed half their skin as well. Most of them appear to have fractured legs or serious back injuries, too."

"Hammer Three, move the Russians into a tighter group and keep your men close to them. If the MIGs come down, you may need them for cover."

Thinking of his helos, the ground commander came back. "Sir, why don't we gather the Commies around the two Stallions?"

"Make it happen!" agreed Hemingway, turning his Harrier to the east.

At the eastern edge of the airfield, elements of the Saudi army had reached the planeload of Russian paratroopers first. By the time the Marines arrived, the Saudis were expending the last of their ammunition into the inert bodies of the Russians.

As the Americans approached, the Saudi soldiers began prancing among the grotesquely-turned bodies, loudly proclaiming their "victory." A few busily looted the corpses.

Seeing no casualties among the Saudis, the American commander commented to a Marine NCO: "Doesn't look like much of a firefight."

The NCO studied the contorted positions of the bodies. "The Commies didn't put up much resistance," he concurred. "Only a few were holding weapons when they bought it."

A nearby Marine, removing a small camera from his pack, began taking pictures of the dancing Saudis.

"Put that away, you moron!" barked a sergeant.

The American commander wheeled around and eyed the Marine with the camera. "That's all right," countermanded the officer. "Take some more . . . just keep *the Saudis* in the background. And when you're finished, give me the roll of film." To the Marine sergeant, he explained: "I want proof who did this."

At one end of the line of bodies, a looting soldier jumped up and placed an object on the tip of his rifle's bayonet. Screaming: "Allah Akbar! Allah Akbar!" he strutted among the other Saudis who quickly joined in his cry.

As this crazed procession approached the Americans, a tall Marine raised the butt of his rifle and clipped the chin of the Saudi holding the bloody object aloft on his bayonet.

The Saudi collapsed, dropping his rifle. The blonde head of a young Russian hit the ground with a thud . . . still fixed to the bayonet.

The stunned Saudis fell silent, some lowering their rifles menacingly at the Marines and muttering muffled threats. The Americans leveled their weapons, awaiting an order from their commander.

The Saudi soldiers began backing off.

"You . . . Marine!" thundered the American commander.

Everyone froze and looked to the officer, who was pointing at the tall Marine standing over the still-prone Saudi.

"You!" repeated the officer to the tall Marine. "Pick up his rifle and return it to him."

The Marine gawked at his commander.

"That's an order!" bellowed the officer.

As the Marine stooped to pick up the Saudi rifle holding

the head of the Russian, the American officer called out: "Where's the camera?"

Its owner swiftly came forward.

Indicating the head, the officer told him: "Get some more pictures."

The flattened Saudi staggered to his feet and warily accepted the rifle. When it was in his hands again, another Saudi howled:

"Allah Akbar!"

As the Saudis resumed their celebration, the Marine commander shook his head and commented to his NCO: "You know, Sergeant . . . I thought I'd seen it all in Nam, but these Arabs take the cake."

"They're having more fun," the NCO drawled disgustingly, "than pigs in shit."

"When the camera's out of film," stated the officer, "disarm the bastards. Kick ass, if you have to."

"With pleasure," the NCO replied. "What about the head?"

The officer watched the blonde head bouncing above the Arabs a moment. "Put it back where it belongs."

Hemingway, appearing overhead, keyed his mike. "This is Gorilla 101. Give me a report."

"This is Hammer Four," replied the ground commander. "The Russians were slaughtered by the Saudis before we arrived. We've taken photos of it."

Hemingway glanced overhead for MiGs. "Check for survivors."

An NCO ordered two squads of Marines down each end of the line of fallen Russians.

"We don't want word to get out what's happened here," Hemingway cautioned. "I suggest you secure the nearest building and place the bodies inside."

"What about the Saudis, sir?"

"Keep them in the building, too. Isolate the Saudis until we decide what to do with them."

The NCO returned and reported to the ground commander, who relayed his words to Hemingway. "We have two survivors, but they've got more holes in them than a piece of Swiss cheese."

"Put them in a helo," ordered Hemingway, "and get them back to"—he paused, remembering the Puller had been hit—"Tell the helo to head southeast toward the ARAMCO compound. There's a small hospital there . . . a light yellow, four-story building."

Listening to the interpretation of Hemingway's exchange with his ground commander, Colonel Tupolov trembled as he switched his radio to its home base frequency. "Hilltop, this is Cossack."

"We read you, Cossack," came through the static. "This is Hilltop."

The Russian flight commander chose his words with great care. "Have attempted four landings without success. Airfield is burning, and Americans occupy objective."

"*How* does an airfield burn, Cossack?"

"It is burning," Tupolov repeated. "The flames reach to 100 feet."

"Can the Ilyushins land next to *your* burning airfield?"

Tupolov debated. "I cannot be certain. Terrain is sandy and irregular." Hoping to discourage the idea, he added, "The Ilyushins may be unable to takeoff after landing."

"That is of no consequence, Cossack. How many Americans have you observed?"

Tupolov's answer was given hesitantly. "Eight fighter aircraft and 200 men on the ground with helicopters."

"Don't waste our time! *Land your planes*, Cossack."

"It would be better to use parachutes," suggested Tupolov.

"We must have the tanks. Follow your orders immediately!"

Tupolov blurted out: "But the Ilyushin pilots cannot see to land!"

"Then land farther from the smoke, imbecile!" came the furious reply.

"It is not the smoke," replied Tupolov, knowing his next words would seal his fate. "The transport pilots cannot see out their cockpits."

The raging voice was clear over the static. "*Why? Why* can our pilots not see out their cockpits?"

"Americans scorched their canopies with the afterburners

of their F-18s," admitted Tupolov. In the ensuing silence, he added: "I have assigned a Fulcrum to escort each transport."

The radio was still as his superiors conferred. Their orders came within the minute. "Cossack, land a transport immediately on the best terrain available near the airfield. We await your report."

The Russian flight commander dropped to 800 feet and circled the air base. The uneven ground of the perimeter contained a haphazard array of abandoned aircraft, fuel trucks, and other vehicles—disguised in varying degrees by the sand.

Tupolov rejoined his transports and maneuvered to the side of an Ilyushin, relieved its MiG escort and closed to twenty meters of the transport's port wingtip.

"Comrade," began Tupolov calmly, "I will guide you to a safe landing outside the airfield. Do exactly as I say."

Concern was evident in the Ilyushin pilot's voice. "Cossack, I require a minimum of 200 meters to land on rough terrain . . . and that is with a touchdown speed of 140 kilometers."

Both men knew the MiG-29 stalled at no less than 155 kilometers per hour and therefore could not properly escort the Ilyushin to touchdown. Tupolov made the only choice available.

"Comrade," he said, "you will land at a speed of 160 kilometers. Commence descent now, and I will control your direction."

Tupolov halted the descent at 150 meters and guided the transport to the west side of the runways where he'd seen a suitable site. Slowing their airspeed to 165 kilometers, the Russian commander felt fear for the first time this day. One-hundred-and-fifty meters was insufficient altitude to regain control of his Fulcrum if it stalled.

"I do not like this," whined the Ilyushin pilot. "By the time you give me corrections, it may be too late to respond."

"Just do as I say. Everything is fine," assured his commander. Approaching the optimal terrain, Tupolov eased the transport down below twenty five meters.

"You are now ten meters off the ground," announced Tupolov. "Lower your speed and land."

The Ilyushin pilot hesitated in lowering his speed; and Tupolov, realizing the transport would touchdown past the ideal terrain, veered away and shouted a last instruction.

"Get your nose up!"

The pilot of the Ilyushin—unable to visually correct his error—compounded it. The overcompensation brought the tail of his plane into the ground where it rebounded, causing the front of the fuselage to seesaw downward. The nose of the transport dug deep into the soft sand, plowing into the carcass of a half-buried truck.

As the tail of the aircraft lifted high in the air, a tank within ripped from its moorings and tipped the plane onto its port wing. The Ilyushin stood suspended in air a moment . . . before pancaking upside-down. A large cloud of sand enshrouded its position.

Twisting his MiG around, Tupolov winced as a knot of red flames and smoke replaced the suspended sand about the transport. He keyed his mike.

"Hilltop, this is Cossack. Landing attempted on best terrain. Aircraft destroyed."

The reply was quick. "Cossack, this is Hilltop. Abort. Repeat . . . abort. Tankers will refuel over Strait of Hormuz."

After the Soviet commander regrouped his flight and gave it a bearing to the southeast, he considered his options: A single bullet from his pistol . . . the strychnine tablet in his emergency packet . . . or . . .

He was too loyal a party member to seriously consider the third option.

6:52 A.M.
ARAMCO

Following the withdrawing Ilyushin flight, Hemingway continued over the Persian Gulf to the spot where he'd left the Puller. He found the assault carrier's destroyer escort steaming near a large oil slick filled with debris. Unable to get anything but white noise in his attempts to talk with the destroyer, he turned back to Dhahran. Over the air base again, he keyed his mike.

"Hammer, this is Gorilla 101. Red Dog flight's over the Gulf now. I'm heading for ARAMCO to try and raise JCS." Hemingway dispatched his wingmen to fly cap over the air base and turned south. As he passed over the giant ARAMCO compound this time, he picked out the movie theater, radio and TV station, hospital, schools, stores, office buildings, and other facilities of the self-contained township. The 15,000 Westerners and non-Saudi Arabs within were isolated from the surrounding local population by an eight-foot wall with gates controlled by Lebanese and Yemeni guards.

The compound had been built for the American employees of the Arabia American Oil Company, commonly known as ARAMCO; and even after the Saudis assumed control of the company, the Westerners who provided management and technical assistance to the country's oil industry had continued to grow in number.

The purpose of the wall was not to keep the Westerners

inside as much as it was to keep the Saudis outside, away from the "contaminated" way of life in Little America. Bacon, a forbidden item to Muslims, was readily available inside the walls under the label, *Breakfast Beef*. And more than a few of the ranch-style homes within had their own stills. As Hemingway viewed these homes, he contemplated with pleasure his report to JCS that the largest oil reserves in the world and its ARAMCO custodians were again secure.

Beginning his descent over the softball diamond, Hemingway spotted smoke and sucked in his breath . . . "Damn!" he exclaimed. "What a fool I am. *God . . . damn!*"

Jamming his throttle forward and throwing his exhaust nozzles out of the vertical, he sped toward the source of the smoke. Four homes were burning close to a gate of the compound, and in the middle of the street between the houses was an empty jeep with a mounted machine gun.

He spotted two Saudi soldiers emerging from one of the homes with a blonde woman in tow. For a moment, Hemingway thought the soldiers had rescued her until they began ripping her robe off as she struggled. A man, obviously hurt, lurched from the same house before Hemingway could react. Flinging the nude woman aside, the soldiers leveled their Uzis at the man. Hemingway watched the submachine guns jerk in the hands of the Saudis as the man staggered backward into the house from the force of their bullets. The blonde jumped up and ran toward the man.

Observing the woman a moment, the soldiers pointed their weapons at her back. Hemingway knew the crackling of the fires masked his engine noise from the soldiers, and he squeezed off a short volley of 25mm rounds to get their attention.

The heavy staccato of the Harrier's guns ripped the air above the soldiers, drawing their muzzles to the aircraft. After emptying their Uzis at the hovering plane, they ran to the jeep. The Saudis charged their vehicle toward the gate.

"Keep going . . . you yellow, sucking bastards," muttered Hemingway, easing the nose of his aircraft downward in pursuit.

When the jeep was clear of the burning homes, Hemingway flipped the HEAT switch on his weapons panel—activating a heat-seeking sensor on the tip of one of his Sidewinders. The sensor promptly registered the hot exhaust of the jeep by emitting an aural tone through the earphones of the Harrier's pilot. He squeezed his trigger.

White-hot flames shot from the tail of the five-inch-wide, 86-pound, nine-and-a-half-foot-long missile. It separated from Hemingway's wingtip and dropped toward the street as it homed in on its target.

The rocket's initial impact gave off a bright, white flash followed by an orange-red explosion that enveloped the jeep. Fragments flew out of the fireball, twisting in the air; and Hemingway saw the still intact front axle, its wheels aflame, sliding through the gate of the compound.

Keying his mike, Hemingway yelled, "Hammer, this is Gorilla 101! *Come in! Come in!*"

"Gorilla, this is—"

"Hemingway cut in. "Have the Russians returned?"

"Negative," replied Banks, "but F-18s from the Connie and Big E have—"

Interrupting again, Hemingway half-shouted, "The Saudis are murdering our people! Send a platoon of Marines into every American compound on the coast . . . *on the double*! My Harriers know where they are."

"On their way," responded Banks.

"And drop off a squad of Marines at the ARAMCO hospital," added Hemingway, thinking of Sandi, "to guard the Russian wounded." He pivoted in his hover and landed helicopter fashion beside the burning houses. Cutting his engine, Hemingway jumped to the street and sprinted to the home the blonde woman had re-entered.

Smoke poured from its door now, forcing him to crouch low in order to see inside. A few feet within the door, the naked woman was bent over her dead husband, arms locked around his torn, bloodied body. Flames ate at a rug beside the couple.

Hemingway crawled to them under the smoke. "Lady, is there anyone else in the house?"

She turned terror-stricken eyes to him and shook her head once. Over the roar of the flames, Hemingway cried out,

"You've got to get out of here!"

The blonde fell upon her husband, fiercely renewing her grip. Reaching for her arm to ease the woman away from the body, Hemingway's hand slipped from her hot skin. A gust of smoke enveloped them as he placed his hands at her waist. He pulled gently, then harder when she still wouldn't let go. In the thickening smoke, Hemingway braced himself as he felt for her hipbones and yanked both the woman and her husband from the flames.

Their progress was halted at the door when the man's body became wedged in its opening. Hemingway attempted to loosen the woman's hands from her husband. Unable to break her death grip, he raised his fist to knock her unconscious but could no longer see the blonde's head through the swirling smoke.

In frustration and hopelessness, Hemingway opened his mouth to yell at her and got a lung full of acrid fumes instead. The blind and coughing Marine felt hands pulling him away from the house. He reached for the woman, but she was no longer there.

Halfway to the street where he could breathe again, Hemingway rasped, "The woman! Get the woman!"

As he struggled to his feet again, one of the men restraining him pointed down the sidewalk. "We got her, too!" shouted the man. At the curb, the soot-darkened woman still clutched her husband.

Recovering his senses, Hemingway told the men, "Get your cars out and barricade the gate!" As the three men ran to their garages, he climbed back into his cockpit and started his engine. This time, bringing the engine up as rapidly as possible, Hemingway was fully strapped in and had his exhaust nozzles at 10 degrees within 45 seconds. Stabilizing his engine at 55 percent, he moved his nozzles to 50 degrees and checked duct pressure—the pressure in tubes running to vents in his wingtips, nose, and tail through which engine air would be bled in order to stabilize the aircraft in vertical takeoff. A moment later, Hemingway moved the nozzles vertical and pushed his throttle to full power. In three seconds, the Harrier was thirty feet above the street.

Hemingway was barely over the housetops when he saw two open-bed, camouflaged trucks barreling down the highway parallel to the compound's wall. They were crammed with frenzied Saudi soldiers firing their weapons randomly into the air. Lowering his hover, Hemingway flipped on the HEAT switch again and moved forward. He saw the three American men who had blocked the compound gate with their cars walking down the street in his direction.

"Damn it!" swore Hemingway. "Get out of my way!" He released a burst of 25mm rounds over their heads and watched them scramble aside.

The first truck pulled into the entrance at high speed and bowled through the cars. The Harrier pilot again heard the aural tone in his earphones and pressed the trigger.

"Get in there, baby," he urged as another Sidewinder squirted off his wing and leaped forward.

The image of the truck disappeared a short moment in the blast of the rocket's impact, to be revealed again in a tangled mass of orange flames and fiery metal. Bringing his hover higher to pump 25mm rounds into the second truck, Hemingway recognized a flash from its rear.

"God, no!" he exclaimed.

Reacting instantly to the Stinger fired from the truck, Hemingway pushed his throttle to full power and with the thumb of the same hand selected his flare dispenser button. A canister dropped off the fuselage as the Harrier moved sluggishly higher.

He watched the heat-seeking missile surge toward him. It appeared to slow down by the force of his own concentration. At the last moment, the Stinger curved lower to seek out the white-hot ball of the magnesium flare, but this gave little comfort to the Marine pilot.

He waited for the buffet of the missile's detonation below him. It occurred at street level, little more than thirty feet from the belly of his Harrier. The slight thump it provided caused a temporary loss of stabilization as the plane yawed to port. This was followed by a low-pitched tone in this headset and flashing red gauges on the warning panel of his cockpit, telling

Hemingway what he could already feel.

The decoy of the flare had only been a temporary escape. Shrapnel from the missile had penetrated and ignited fuel cells in his fuselage, in addition to damaging hydraulic and electrical lines. The engine ran rough, and his controls gave poor response as Hemingway fought to keep his aircraft near level. He knew he had only seconds to get out of the plane.

Cutting power, he put the Harrier into a controlled fall—the worst of learned options. There were no others. Ejection from the tilted aircraft had the potential of throwing him onto one of the burning homes to his rear. Better to ride it in and pray.

What're the soldiers going to do to these people? he thought. *I'll miss you, Sandi. Is my landing gear still down?* There was no time to pray.

5:46 A.M.
King Khalid International Airport
Riyadh

"Your Highness," reported the Saudi general, "all units are in place."

Standing on the viewing platform atop the arch of the *royal* terminal at King Khalid International Airport, Prince Rahman and Crown Prince Saleem could see the tanks, mechanized vehicles, and soldiers clustered at the four corners of the airfield.

"How many Hawk and Stinger missiles are in each corner?" Rahman inquired of his general.

"Three truck-mounted Hawks and 20 Stingers, Your Highness. I have also placed 35 more Stingers on the roofs of hangars."

"Praise to Allah," replied Rahman. "And how many men at each corner of the runways?"

"A mobilized Land Force battalion, Your Highness." The officer added, "And units of the national guard are in reserve."

"My men have tasted blood," growled Prince Saleem, "and they want more."

This comment made little sense to Rahman, who had withheld the news that his men had also tasted blood—their own. The 32 Mirage-V fighters he'd sent to intercept the flight from South Yemen had fared worse than the F-15s over the Gulf. Officially, Rahman had reported half the Yemeni flight destroyed . . . with no losses among the Mirage-Vs. In fact, Rahman was uncertain *if any* of the planes from South Yemen had even been hit. He was certain of the fate of his Mirage-Vs. None had returned.

Two-hundred-fifty miles to the south, the Soviet flight commander issued instructions to Lieutenant Ivanoff. "Weasel 88, this is Drifter. I have received word the Saudis are defending the runways as expected. Wind-direction from the west. It is time for you to go."

"*Spasibo,* Drifter!" acknowledged Ivanoff buoyantly. He and seven other Fulcrums dove for ground level—stepping their speed up to Mach One—to avoid radar detection.

Colonel Romanov grinned at the lieutenant's reply. Ivanoff was a good choice. Few of the other fighter pilots in his command would have expressed gratitude for such a mission. Romanov did not report the earlier bombing of the runways, because his superiors had decided against informing their flight commanders of the American attacks.

The Fulcrums whipped past the landscape at fifty feet, the ground on either side and in front to a distance of 600 feet appearing only as a blur. Their shockwaves echoed across the desert floor, fracturing the eardrums of those caught within 2100 yards of their path. As a precaution to further mask their approach, the MiG pilots switched on their radars. At ground level, the MiG-29 radar was powerful enough to kill any mammal lower than the rabbit species within 1000 yards. The brains of higher mammals would be scrambled. Nearing Riyadh, the advance unit circled west to make their run.

The airfield in sight, Lieutenant Ivanoff barked: "Execute strike!" The eight MiG-29s paired off, each duo heading for a corner of the field. The fighters assigned to the eastern corners skirted around the western perimeter of the runways and increased their speed to Mach 1.6, which was barely enough to temporarily outrun any missiles launched by the ground forces.

As their fire-control computers locked onto the heat of the Saudi tanks and trucks, the Fulcrum pilots released their laser-controlled binary missiles and began evasive maneuvers.

Atop the royal terminal, the first indication of an attack was light-blue, billowing gas in the western corners of the airfield. Pointing to the west, Prince Rahman yelled to his chief of staff: "What is that?"

The general snatched a military radio from the petrified soldier beside him and shouted the name of his commander in the northwest corner. "Colonel Hassan! Colonel Hassan!"

Even holding the radio receiver tightly to his ear, the general did not hear the choked rasp from Hassan's radioman as dual thunderclaps followed the first MiGs across the runways.

Alerted by the straining afterburners of the Soviet fighters, the Saudis frantically searched the skies for the source of the sound. As the MiGs were now covering a mile every three seconds (almost twice the speed of sound), only a few Saudis who looked far ahead of the ear-splitting roar and near ground level spotted the streaking MiG-29s. The Hawk missiles, pointed skyward, were useless against the low-flying planes.

Crown Prince Saleem peered at the western corners of the airfield through binoculars. "No one moves!" He thrust the glasses toward his half-brother.

Rahman watched through the magnifying lenses as the blue gas began to drift eastward. Except for a few motionless bodies on the ground, Colonel Hassan's command appeared deserted. Prince Rahman wheeled at Saleem's outcry.

"The eastern corners, *too*!"

The Saudi units in the east had disappeared in the same blue gas.

Glancing back over his target, Lieutenant Ivanoff shouted in alarm to his wingman. "Weasel 93! Missile on our six!"

The wingman veered sharp left and Ivanoff cut hard right. Viewing the corners of the airfield—each still wrapped in a bluish shroud—Ivanoff hit his UHF button to make his report. "Drifter, this is Wea—"

A tracking Stinger slipped up the exhaust of his MiG-29, splitting the fuselage. Knocked unconscious, Ivanoff felt nothing as a second missile exploded on the front half of his plane.

An Englishman wearing a mobile headset appeared at Rahman's side. "Your Highness, the Control Tower reports a large flight of unidentified aircraft approaching from the southwest."

"How soon do they arrive?" Rahman asked.

The Englishman checked his watch. "Fourteen minutes."

In seconds, the Englishman was the only one still standing on the viewing platform as Rahman, Saleem, and their staffs jammed the elevators and stairs leading from the arch. At the main floor of the terminal, they raced toward the exits. Scores of Saudi civilians who were at the broad windows facing the runways turned to watch the panicked soldiers.

"*Save yourselves!*" shrieked one of the Land Force officers. "The Russians come!"

The men at the windows stared after the officer as he pushed his way out a door. A few of the civilians started for the exits before the momentary silence was broken by a Saudi dressed in a cream-colored Western-style suit.

"Save Saudi Arabia!" he passionately cried out. Then even louder: "In the Name of Allah, SAVE SAUDI ARABIA!"

Most of the Saudis moving toward the exits paused as the young man in the light suit jumped onto a ticket counter and fiercely declared:

"I am *Hamud bin Abdul Aziz Al Saud!*"

The others recognized at once the youngest and most profligate son of the late founder of their kingdom. Prince Hamud glowered at those below as he snarled, "And I will not leave like a crawling dog."

The few Saudis still moving froze in their tracks at the taunt.

"Who will be the first," Hamud challenged, "to smash a Russian plane with his car?"

"In the Name of Allah," a young Saudi in traditional thobe shouted back, "*I will!*"

Hamud acknowledged his cousin with a raised fist. "Only if you are swifter than I, Prince Karrim! *To our cars!* We shall see who will be first!"

Hamud leaped from the counter, grabbed Irene's sleeve, and ran to an exit . . . followed by the young men in his audience. Outside, most of the military vehicles were now gone, as were many of the civilian cars. Releasing Irene at his convertible,

Hamud jumped over the driver's door and switched on the ignition. When he looked up, Irene still stood by her door.

"Let's go!" Hamud yelled.

She shook her head. "I'm not going with you."

"Don't worry," he smiled reassuringly. "The Russians won't land when they see cars blocking the runways."

"You're out of your mind," snapped Irene.

Hamud yelled back: "Do you want to stay *here*?"

Urgently glancing around, Irene saw no Westerners—only Saudi men, a few of whom eyed her as if waiting to see whether Hamud would leave her behind. Irene got into the car.

As they snaked in and out of the traffic, Hamud reached over to touch her arm. "I need your dress," he said.

Irene's eyes opened wide. "What?"

His expression was dead-serious. "I will give you ten-thousand dollars for it."

This solicited an even more bewildered look from Irene.

"Fifty-thousand!" Hamud impatiently offered.

"Why?"

"It is *green*," he declared. "The color of the Saudi flag."

She shook her head in disbelief.

"Please," he urged. "*One-hundred-thousand dollars*."

Still shaking her head, Irene reached under the thobe to remove the dress. When she handed it over, Hamud began waving it high over his head as he drove.

The cacophony of horns behind them trebled.

Agitated at his slow pace, Hamud abruptly pulled his car onto the long passenger island and blared his horn to clear off the pedestrians as he accelerated down his newly-created lane. He was followed by a tight line of Mercedes, Cadillacs, BMWs, assorted limousines, and several European sports cars. With his green standard held high in the air, Hamud led his procession from the terminal area and swung onto a transition road leading to the parking lot where he'd left his Lear Jet.

At its gate, Hamud slammed on his brakes. The iron-barred gate was locked and the Pakistani guard gone. Backing up, Hamud told Irene to buckle up her seatbelt as he aligned the white Rolls directly at the center of the barrier. Hamud didn't bother with his seatbelt.

He floored his gas pedal. On contact, his head pitched forward and bounced off the steering wheel as the gate halted the charging convertible. Bleeding slightly from his forehead, Hamud threw his car in reverse again and gunned it backward. Handing Irene the dress, he snapped on his seat belt and directed the two nearest Saudi drivers to charge with him. Hamud pointed a black Mercedes limo to the middle position. When they were aligned, Hamud screamed, "Allah Akbar!"

Out of unison, the cars leaped forward, failing to hit the barrier together. On the next try, they bowled over the pillar holding the gate and burst into the parking lot.

When the Saudis still in the terminal saw the madly weaving caravan led by a white convertible flying a green standard, many of them also ran to their vehicles to join the foray.

Prince Hamud halted in the middle of the airfield and stood atop the hood of his car. From this vantage point, he directed cars to patrol all of the runways as Irene worriedly scanned the skies.

———————

7:18 A.M.
ARAMCO

The blurred figure above Hemingway gradually became clearer. He recognized the distinctive earphones of a Sea Stallion pilot before the man's face fully registered.

"Coming to, Doc," announced the helicopter pilot.

The Navy corpsman kneeled at Hemingway's side.

"What happened?" asked Hemingway, his jaw movement dislodging the petrolatum gauze over his left cheek. The resulting pain kept him from saying more.

Repositioning the gauze, the medic placed Hemingway's hand over it. "Colonel, hold your bandage in place and don't try to talk."

When the searing agony of his cheek subsided, Hemingway's eyes opened again and scrutinized the corpsman who'd ordered him quiet. The corpsman scowled back.

"You've got third-degree burns over the entire left side of your face, Colonel. It'll hurt like hell again if you let the gauze fall off." The medic took a syringe from his packet and removed the cap covering its needle. He plunged the needle deep into the bicep muscle of the pilot.

Hemingway jerked his arm away, and most of the crystal-clear fluid in the syringe spurted into the air.

"No drugs!" snapped the Marine colonel.

"It's just morphine," protested the corpsman.

"No drugs," repeated Hemingway, feeling drowsy already

from the minor dosage he'd received. Grimacing as he spoke, Hemingway switched his attention to the Sea Stallion pilot.

"What happened?" he demanded again.

"After you crash-landed," replied the lieutenant, "the people here broke through your canopy with their tire irons and pulled you out."

"Where're the Saudis?"

The lieutenant grinned. "They turned tail when they saw my Stallion coming in." He added, "I spotted the flash of your 'Winder and came in fast."

Disapproval clouded Hemingway's face at the thought that the escaping Saudis might return with reinforcements.

"Relax, sir," said the lieutenant, reading the frown. "The Saudis won't be back. One of our PBLs accidentally sliced into the fuel tank of their truck."

The medic leaned over Hemingway. "I've got to get back to the others, Colonel. They're worse off than you."

"These people were sure determined to get you out of that Harrier," commented the lieutenant. "Two of them lost all their hair and most of their clothes."

Holding the petrolatum-saturated gauze to his cheek, Hemingway attempted to raise himself to his elbows and nearly passed out from the pain of his effort. He collapsed, squeezing his eyes shut and breathing heavily.

"What's wrong, sir?"

Hemingway whispered, "My back."

"Probably jammed it hitting the deck, Colonel. I'll tell the medic."

"Forget that," Hemingway told him sharply. "Take me to the Norlin house."

The lieutenant raised his brow in concern. "Sir, we've already called in another helo to take you to the hospital."

The Marine lieutenant colonel slowly repeated himself. "Take me to the Norlin house first."

"I don't think that's wise, sir," persisted the lieutenant. "Your back may be broken."

"Goddamn it!" blustered Hemingway, wincing at his aching face, "as long as I can breathe, *I'm* in command around here!"

The junior officer hesitated.

"Follow my orders, Marine!" Hemingway threatened, "Or I'll have your ass court-martialed!"

The lieutenant jumped to his feet. "I'll be right back, sir." He returned with a civilian, the two of them carrying a narrow plywood panel. Against the Navy corpsman's objections, they slid Hemingway onto it and placed him in the back of a station wagon.

At the Norlin house, Hemingway asked to be taken into the room with the ham radio. As they carried him through the hallway, he saw the horrified faces of Dori and Kevin gaping down at the large, raised blisters covering his reddened, hairless scalp. The two children followed Hemingway into Kevin's bedroom where the open-mouthed boy managed to speak.

"What happened to *you?*"

"A little accident," replied the pilot, looking away from the repulsive expression on the boy's face. "Kids, I need your help. Do you have any friends in the States with ham radios?"

The twins exchanged glances. "She has one in Florida," replied Kevin, "and I have one in Philadelphia."

"I want you to reach one of them. Whomever you get first, tell them to contact the White House in my name—Colonel Thomas Hemingway."

Dori sat down before the radio, put on the headset, hit several switches, and began working the dials.

"Kevin," said Hemingway, "is there a mirror around here?"

The boy brought a small vanity mirror to the bed.

After checking his scalp, the pilot lifted the protective gauze from a corner of his cheek. A section of beet-red skin came away with the gauze, exposing raw-meaty flesh, white tendons, and open blood vessels. A dime-sized portion of his left ear had melted away. Handing the mirror back to Kevin, Hemingway shut his eyes and listened as Dori repeated her call sign. After several fruitless minutes, she turned the radio over to her brother. Kevin had no better luck.

"There's no answer from either of our friends," declared Dori. "We usually write before calling them, so they'll know when to listen."

"Keep trying," Hemingway told her. "We've got to get

through to them." As she moved out of his line of vision, he added, "Try to reach anyone . . . as long as they're in the States."

Kevin surrendered the radio's headset back to his sister, who rotated the dials again and listened for English without a British accent. Hemingway had fallen asleep when she cried out, *"I've got someone!"* Hitting several switches to fine-tune, she pulled the mike before her and spoke excitedly.

"Break! This is SA8ADN . . . this is SA8ADN!"

Hearing the rare Middle East call sign, a ham operator in Bangor, Maine promptly broke off her Stateside call to respond.

"SA8ADN," responded the woman, "this is NA1DGH. Do you copy? Over."

"NA1DGH, this is SA8ADN. I read you loud and clear. I have emergency traffic. Can you handle it? Over."

"SA8ADN, what is the nature of your emergency traffic? Over."

Dori smiled at Hemingway. "NA1DGH, I have a military message for the White House. Over."

The voice of the woman from Maine turned shrill. "SA8ADN, *get off* this frequency! Go find someone else to play with, young lady?"

Hemingway called out, "Let me talk to her!" Dori extended the microphone to him.

He took the mike and set it on his chest. "This is Colonel Thomas Hemingway of the United States Marines speaking. I am in Saudi Arabia and it is imperative that I get a message to the White House as soon as possible. Will you help me?"

The woman's voice was still skeptical. "Why are you using a ham radio if you're in the military?"

"I'm at the ARAMCO compound in eastern Saudi Arabia," he replied, "and our normal communications have been knocked out or jammed. Who and where are you?"

"Lisa Hill," she answered hesitantly. "Bangor, Maine."

"Fine, Miss Hill. Now will you contact the White House for me?"

"It's *Mrs.* Hill," she corrected. After a pause, she replied, "Even if I believed you, I doubt if anyone at the White House would believe *me*."

"Just try," pleaded Hemingway. "Tell them Colonel Hemingway of the U.S.S. Puller wishes to speak with the President."

The woman replied without enthusiasm. "I'll try . . . once. Standby."

The long-distance operator surprised her by getting an immediate connection. Then again, it was late.

"Hello, this is the White House," announced a formal woman's voice.

Mrs. Hill swallowed. "Hello . . . I'm calling from Maine, and I have a Marine officer on my ham radio who wants to communicate with the President."

"I'm sorry, ma'am," came the quick and aloof reply, "we cannot connect you with the President. Would you care to leave a message?"

"Well . . . yes. A Colonel Hemingway in Saudi Arabia wishes to talk with the President. He has some communications problem."

"I have your message," the operator replied impatiently. "Thank you for calling."

"*Wait a minute!*" cried out Mrs. Hill. "You don't have my phone number yet."

The operator's tone became curt. "I'll take it if you wish, ma'am."

"It's 809-8593, area code 209."

"Very well, ma'am, *Goodbye.*"

Hearing the disconnect, Mrs. Hill muttered, "Goodbye to you, too . . . bitch."

6:22 A.M.
King Khalid International Airport
Riyadh

"There they are!" cried Irene, pointing to the northwest. Hamud slipped behind the steering wheel of the Rolls and hit his horn to alert the others . . . keeping an eye on the lone MiG preceding the Russian flight.

Making a high pass over the runways, the Soviet commander saw that Lieutenant Ivanoff's strike had been deadly accurate. No missiles or anti-aircraft fire climbed to greet him. The cars scampered like mice across the airfield but failed to impress Colonel Romanov until scores of them converged behind his flight path. Sensing their purpose, he hit his UHF button.

"Weasels, this is Drifter. Descend and clear the runways." Romanov then ordered his Ilyushins to circle at 3000 meters, an error he wouldn't realize until debriefed by superiors.

In their initial runs, the MiGs knocked out a quarter of the Saudi cars—most of whom foolishly tried to outrun the fighters in headlong sprints. When the cars began circling at high speed, the MiG pilots were less successful and had destroyed only a few more when the careless pilots of two planes collided. As the pair of MiGs exploded on the tarmac, Romanov depressed his UHF button.

"Weasels, this is Drifter. Enough of this play! Marshall at 4000 meters."

The Saudis blared their horns in triumph as Prince Hamud sped across the airfield in an attempt to evenly distribute the remaining cars.

Altering his original plan, Colonel Romanov issued instructions to his first Ilyushin. "Ghost 216, you will land at the east end of the northernmost runway. Weasels 72, 74, 76, and 78 will clear your path."

When the single transport with its fighter escort circled down to the field, most of the Saudi drivers left their assigned areas to charge the intruders, and the 20mm cannon of the MiGs tore a wide swath through those cars which accurately anticipated the touchdown point of the Ilyushin. Most of the drivers, however, drove directly at the in-flight transport and quickly trailed behind it, remaining relatively untouched by the MiGs and unseen by the transport pilot. Seeing the danger, Romanov barked another order. "Weasels, 62, 64, 66, and 68. Clean up the Ilyushin's rear!"

As the main wheel mounts of the transport made contact with the concrete, a brown Maserati swept under its tail and aimed for the eight-tire wheel mount beneath its left wing. Coming in at 140 miles per hour, the car bounced off the massive tires, yet the impact still blew the four rear tires of the mount. The reduced port traction caused the Ilyushin to veer right before its pilot added power to his starboard engine to maintain a semblance of direction.

Adjusting his port throttles to three-quarters, the Ilyushin pilot reversed the turbo-fans of his engines as a gray Jaguar angled in toward the already-damaged wheel mount. Traveling much faster than the slowing transport, the car sheered off the mount, causing the tip of the left wing to slam to the tarmac.

Trailing a hail of sparks, the plane spun sharply to the left and after three revolutions came to a halt. Dark-complexioned soldiers burst from the hatches of its fuselage, formed a tight circle around their plane, and began firing upon the cars. The Saudi drivers drove in irregular patterns about the Ilyushin and became easy prey for the diving Fulcrums . . . until they followed the lead of the white convertible flying a green standard from its antenna. Hamud and Irene were weaving a wide circle around the downed aircraft.

Four thousand feet above, Romanov waited anxiously for the ramp of the Ilyushin to drop and deliver its cargo. When no tank appeared within a reasonable time, he hit his UHF mike button.

"Ghost 216, this is Drifter. *Drop* your ramp!"

"It doesn't open," came the reply. "The landing jammed it." The transport pilot's attention was drawn elsewhere.

A blue-and-silver Porsche had broken inside the weaving circle and made a beeline for the nose wheel of his Ilyushin. The ring of soldiers at the front of the plane parted for the speeding car, which swerved from the nose wheel at the last moment, clipping the nose mount with its rearend. The weakened mount slowly bent from the vertical and collapsed, plopping the nose of the Ilyushin to the tarmac as the out-of-control Porsche rolled, throwing the driver into the air. The body twitched on the concrete as it was saturated by the bullets of the soldiers.

A cherry-red Ferrari turned in next from the circling cars and accelerated directly at the nose of the Ilyushin. As the soldiers peppered the Ferrari, the pilot and copilot of the plane tore at their seat belts. Twenty yards from the nose, the Ferrari driver opened his door and rolled out.

The fuselage shuddered slightly at the impact of the car, and its nose erupted in flames. A Bedouin sheik saw the driver of the Ferrari lying motionless in a face-down position and punched the intercom to his chauffeur. "Drive between the plane and the driver of the red car!" ordered the sheik.

The pink and chrome limousine instantly cut inside, and bullets whanged off its armored frame and windows as it screeched to a halt beside the prone body. When the Bedouin jumped from his door to rescue his countryman, the Ferrari driver popped up and dove inside the car. Stepping to the front door of his Continental, the sheik yanked his chauffeur out and pointed him into the rear seat.

The Bedouin tromped on his gas pedal. Instead of returning

to the circle of cars, he turned toward the plane. Paralleling the fuselage, the limousine plowed through its defenders. When it returned to the band of cars, one soldier's body partially blocked its windshield and two more hung from its grill.

A slew of Saudis promptly left the circle and darted for the other side of the fuselage. The first of the cars to attack received heavy fire, and few of the drivers succeeded in their quest. Other cars, as they neared the side of the plane, twisted in tight curves in an effort to pick off their own trophies.

The cordon of cars around the Ilyushin soon dissolved as all the Saudis charged the burning plane in the contest to drag off its defenders. Before the soldiers retreated under the fuselage and onto the downed wing, more than a few of the Saudi drivers carried off proof of their courage.

Losing their targets, the cars reformed in a tighter ring about the plane to avoid the MiGs. The Saudis were now content to let the fire complete their work.

Prince Karrim—having clipped several soldiers with his BMW, yet having no proof of his prowess—cut inside and sped toward the tip of the downed wing. Freezing his brakes just before the wingtip, he released them the instant before his front wheels made contact. The car jumped onto the wing and Karrim floored the accelerator. The soldiers who had sought refuge on the left wing scattered off as he raced toward the fuselage. Where both wings met at the top of the fuselage. Karrim continued his charge and crossed over to the starboard side. Completely surprising the soldiers on this wing, the BMW spilled them off like dominoes.

From far above, Colonel Romanov watched a small car sail off the upright wing of the downed Ilyushin before crashing on its side. The Russian flight commander swore to himself. "For every bastard we kill, five crazier bastards take his place!" Punching his UHF button, he announced, "Weasels, disengage and return to Marshall."

Later, there would be little dispute among the participants on the runways of King Khalid International Airport that the driver of the BMW had executed the finest charge of the day.

For a short time, the surviving soldiers huddled under the

fuselage and delivered an ineffective fire on the cars. When the heat from the burning plane became unbearable, the Ilyushin crew and soldiers dropped their weapons and tried to move away from the flames with raised hands. They were shown no mercy.

As the brief contest came to a close, Hamud and Irene extricated the injured Karrim from his crushed BMW. His proud grin beamed through a face streaming with blood.

"Praise to Allah," he said. "Only my arm is broken."

After staunching the flow of blood from his split scalp, they placed Karrim in their backseat and returned to the middle of the field with a few of the other cars. Most of the Saudis charged haphazardly about the runways, again blasting their horns in triumph.

"Another comes!" pointed Hamud to the same northern runway. As the Ilyushin glided down, Irene checked far above and behind the transport.

"Where're the MiGs?" she asked.

"Wait!" called Hamud to the Saudis who'd joined him at midfield. They watched the other drivers chase after the new prize.

"Ghost 222, this is Drifter," announced the Russian flight commander. "Commence touchdown."

The transport pilot gunned his engines to push ahead of the slower cars and descended to the tarmac. The trailing drivers frantically raced each other for the honor of being first to cripple the second plane. After touching the runway, the Ilyushin went to full throttle and became airborne. It touched down again at half-mile intervals farther down the runway. And each time, the Saudi drivers charged en masse.

"*They are fools!*" exclaimed Prince Karrim. With the hand of his good arm, he directed their attention to the southeast. "Look to the *smoke!*" At a height of thirty feet, an Ilyushin skimmed over the desert toward the airfield, trailed by twelve Fulcrums belching black smoke at their reduced speeds.

Colonel Romanov smiled at the seven cars speeding south. The Ilyushin's tank would make short work of any drivers who got through his Fulcrums. He pressed his UHF button. "Weasels in the south, this is Drifter. The mice come."

When the drivers of the seven cars spotted the ground-level MiGs coming directly at them in the distance, they spread wider, which only served to give the MiG pilots better target selection. The cars swerved from side to side as they increased speed.

The fighter pilots, approaching in three sections, had already selected the HEAT buttons of their fire-control computers. Getting aural tones, the first section of four MiGs released their missiles and watched the four nearest cars disintegrate moments later. Hamud thanked Allah his Rolls Royce was slower than the others as he dodged the burning pieces of fragmented vehicles.

The second section of MiGs released their missiles seconds after the first wave, and the third section followed in unison. Standard operating procedure for the pilots would have been to climb abruptly to avoid target debris, but their orders were to promptly regroup around the landing Ilyushin.

As the relatively slow-moving MiGs banked right and left low to the ground, the missiles fired by the second and third waves curved away from the surviving cars in pursuit of the greater sources of heat. By the time radar scans in the first two sections of MiGs reported tracking missiles, evasive action from the supersonic rockets was out of the question. A few of the pilots chose their first instinct and yanked ejection handles— another hopeless option. With their aircraft banking in tight turns, these pilots rode their seats out of their cockpits toward the horizon and cartwheeled along the concrete runways at speeds exceeding 80 miles per hour, separating from their seats in the process. Those pilots who took longer to think had their fate decided for them as the exhausts of their Fulcrums sucked up the missiles fired by the other MiGs. The stunned pilots in the third section circled after the Saudi drivers, reaching the cars as the Ilyushin touched down.

Hamud and Irene, accompanied by a Clenet and Lamborghini, were 150 yards from the transport's port side when 20mm cannon fire began ricocheting off the runway beside them. The Clenet burst into flames, and the Lamborghini suddenly swerved right, forcing Hamud to jerk his wheel away from the second vehicle. Regaining control of his car, Hamud felt a hot, stabbing pain in his left shoulder and saw pieces of blood-stained, cream-colored cloth splatter across the dashboard in front of him.

Hamud's left hand went limp, falling uselessly from the steering wheel. Feeling the strength ebbing from his right arm as well, he whirled to Irene. She stared in shock at the bone splinters, spongy body tissue, and blood dripping off the burled wood of the dash.

"*Steer!*" Hamud cried out.

Holding a scream, Irene seized the wheel.

"Under the plane!" howled Prince Karrim. "Under the plane! They cannot shoot us there!"

Irene pulled herself across the seat and maneuvered the car below a wing of the aircraft. Keeping pace with its shadow, she was uncertain what to do next. Thinking to alarm the transport's pilot, she repeatedly pounded the horn. With great effort, Hamud raised his right hand and pointed to the wheel mount at the nose of the jet.

"Hit it," he weakly commanded.

Controlled by her fear, Irene could not react.

"Steer!" Hamud cried again. He jammed his foot over hers and floored the gas pedal. Prepared to die, Hamud stiffened and closed his eyes.

Irene let go her scream as the car came up on the wheel mount.

Hamud felt no impact and wondered if he was in heaven. He mumbled, "Praise to Allah." He opened his eyes and watched the image of the Ilyushin grow smaller as he slipped into unconsciousness.

Colonel Romanov hit his UHF button. "Tikonov, *what are you doing?*" he shrieked. "Get back on the ground!"

For a long moment, the transport's pilot did not respond. When he did, it was in a low, tense voice.

"I cannot land, Drifter."

Romanov bellowed back, "*Why the hell not?*"

"I have no choice."

"Damn you, Tikonov!" bellowed Romanov in frustration. "Get back down!"

Observing the confusion below, the pilots and troop commanders in the circling Ilyushins listened intently to the strange exchange. The lone transport continued to climb and left the perimeter of the airfield with its remaining MiG escorts.

"If I attempt to land again," Tikonov explained, "I shall be shot, just—"

"I'll shoot you down myself," Romanov interrupted, "if you *do not!*"

"The Cubans have killed my copilot," Tikonov responded. "They now hold a gun to *my head.*"

"That is not possible!" howled the Russian flight commander.

A Cuban officer listening to the conversation through the headset of the dead copilot coolly replied, "Comrade Colonel, you promised our landings would be unopposed. This is not true. Therefore, I have ordered my plane to return to Yemen."

"*You yellow dog!*" screamed Romanov. "I'll have you shot if you return to Yemen."

"We will see *who* is to be shot, comrade," scoffed the Cuban.

"But your plane had a chance," Romanov desperately argued.

"For how long?" hissed the Cuban officer. "Your fighters could not even protect the first transport. They are better at shooting down their own. My men never had a chance."

On the airfield below, dozens of Saudi cars patrolled the southern runways, having realized the Soviet ploy. Colonel Romanov could say or do nothing to dissuade the Cubans in the other Ilyushins from also heading south to safety.

11:20 P.M.
The White House

After scribbling the message on a memo, the operator placed it in a dispatch box above her console. Fifteen minutes later, a clerk collected all the messages in the switchboard room and deposited them in the routing office.

Sorting through several hundred messages, the router pulled twenty-six of them for forwarding and discarded the balance. Three of the messages were marked "rush," including Hemingway's. The router then pressed a buzzer to summon a courier. In this manner the message from Bangor reached the presidential assistant in the War Room forty minutes after it arrived at the White House.

Upon examining the memo, Hoolihan offered it to the President. "Sir, would you like me to contact this lady?"

President Steiner scanned it and picked up the phone himself. "This is the President. Put me through to 209-555-8593." When the telephone started to ring, he transferred the call to the speaker box on the conference table and sat down.

Lisa Hill skeptically answered, "Hello."

"Are you the person who just called the White House?" asked the President.

"Yes," she hesitantly replied. "About an hour ago."

"This is President Steiner, Mrs. Hill. Can you tell me how you obtained the name of Colonel Hemingway?"

"Is this *actually the President?*" she queried.

He laughed good-naturedly. "Yes, Mrs. Hill. Now, please tell me how you heard from Colonel Hemingway?"

"He interrupted me on my ham radio."

"Is he still on it?"

"Hold on," she responded. "I'll check."

General Steel addressed the President. "Sir, if she'll tell us what frequency her radio's on, we may be able to establish direct communication with Hemingway."

The President nodded, waiting for the woman to return.

"He's still there," she finally replied.

"Thank you, Mrs. Hill. Would you mind telling me what frequency your ham radio's on?"

"Fourteen point one seven zero megahertz."

"Fine," said the President. "Did Colonel Hemingway have any messages for me?"

"He told me earlier that there was a war going on over in Saudi Arabia. Hold on while I check with him again."

After a lengthy interval, she returned. "President Steiner, I'm sorry it took so long. I had to make a list of what he told me. Here it is:

> *Landing from the east repulsed. Have 142 Soviet prisoners, and a body count of 289 more. 138 killed by Saudis and balance from plane crash. U.S.S. Puller sunk by Saudi gunboat. MAU commander and 7 others dead, 24 wounded. No Marine casualties at Dhahran. Request instructions for Russian POWs.*

That's his message," she concluded.

"*Thank you*, Mrs. Hill," gushed the President. "Thank you very much indeed. Please tell Colonel Hemingway we'll respond shortly."

"After I tell him that, I'm going next door to get some help."

The President paused. "Why do you need help?"

"I can't be two places at once. My ham radio's about sixty feet from this telephone."

President Steiner kept his tone cordial. "I'd prefer, for security purposes, to minimize the number of people on this line, Mrs. Hill."

"Oh, don't worry about that," she quickly added. "I was only going to get my sister . . . she doesn't gossip with anyone but me."

"Okay," the President half-smiled, "but hurry back, please." Hearing the phone contact a countertop, the President surveyed the faces around the conference table. "Well, gentlemen, we did it. We lost some men, but we did it."

Hoolihan nodded his head. "Congratulations, sir."

"Thanks, Jim. I'd like you to go upstairs and inform the congressmen that the Russians have been turned back at Dhahran, and we have 142 prisoners. Don't reveal more than that."

General Steel extended his hand. "My compliments, sir."

"Thank you, Bob," grinned the President. "Now, what do we do with the prisoners?" Before anyone could respond, he added quizzically, "And what happened to the Puller?"

The general pondered both questions a moment. "We'll find out soon enough about the Puller, I imagine. Concerning the prisoners, I'd suggest their immediate evacuation from Saudi Arabia . . . if we wish to maintain control over them."

As he listened to his general, the President was bemused that he'd requested a military opinion first. Without looking at his secretary of state, he said, "Clayton, what do you think?"

"Under international law, we have no jurisdiction over them. They belong to the Saudis." Walters paused a moment. "But leaving them in Saudi Arabia might encourage the Soviets to attempt a rescue mission . . . or another invasion under that guise. I would eliminate that risk and therefore concur with General Steel."

"The next question," the President stated, "is how to evacuate them and to where."

Steel offered, "Our helicopters at Dhahran could take them to Oman, and from there they could be transferred to our carriers."

"The helicopters would have to refuel on the way," injected the Marine Commandant.

"Where?" asked Clayton Walters pointedly.

Huering studied the Middle East wall grid. "Somewhere within the United Arab Emirates."

I'd advise against the helicopters then," asserted Walters. "The leaders in both the Emirates and Oman are even less predictable than the Saudis. If we lost control of the POWs in either country, the results could be grievous."

General Huering broke the resulting silence. "Why not bring the Connie into the Gulf?"

President Steiner watched frowns of disapproval light up among the other military men at the conference table.

"That's a two-billion dollar gamble," declared Steel.

"I agree," Huering nodded, "but I was also considering the deterrent effect a carrier battle group would pose. We don't know what's happening to the Soviet flight coming into Riyadh. If it succeeds in gaining a foothold, the Connie's presence might help us contain them."

Knowing what he intended to do, President Steiner addressed Admiral Sparks. "What's your position, Admiral?"

"Sir, I agree with General Steel." The President's expression hardened to a scowl as Sparks continued. "Pulling the Connie into the Gulf would be a brash move. However, at this moment, I don't know of a better option if we want to show the Russians we mean business."

The President's expression almost changed to one of relief . . . but the last words he'd heard jogged his memory. A scant two hours earlier, he had relieved a general who'd spoken the same words. Now, he himself *was considering them.*

"Then we do it," announced the President. "Bob, issue the necessary orders."

"It is vital," interjected Admiral Sparks firmly, "that the F-18s belonging to the Enterprise return to her, so she can provide cover for the Connie. The Enterprise can do so by taking up a station just south of the Strait of Hormuz."

"A relay of F-18s," added Huering, "could also keep us apprised of what's happening in the Gulf until the jamming stops."

President Steiner nodded affirmatively. "Instruct our communications people to resume coding messages, Bob. The Russians don't need to know what we're doing now."

Jim Hoolihan returned to the War Room and approached the President. "Sir, the congressmen asked me to convey their concern that the Soviet prisoners be repatriated without delay."

President Steiner made a grim smile. "They sound scared."

Hoolihan nodded.

"So am I," continued the President. "We're not out of this yet." He stood to pick up the open line to the ham radio in Bangor. "Hello? Mrs. Hill?"

"Hi!" came the shrill reply. It was a child's voice.

The President held his phone away for a moment to study it. "Who is this?" he hesitantly asked.

"Chris—ti—na," the girl proudly drew out.

"And who are you?" President Steiner inquired uncertainly.

"I'm a girl, silly?" The child giggled with delight, believing the man's words were a joke.

The man's words became serious. "Is this the Hill residence?"

The child paused. "What?"

"Is this Mrs. Hill's house?"

Another longer pause. "You mean Aunt Lee?" the girl asked.

"Yes . . . your Aunt Lee. May I speak to her?"

"Aunt Lee?" Her amplified voice carried throughout the War Room as the President pushed the phone out to arm's length to protect his ears.

"Hello," said the girl's aunt.

"There you are," sighed the President. "Would you give Colonel Hemingway this message? Prisoners are to be evacuated to the Constellation, but safeguard them for now. We'll send details soon."

The woman's voice went lower. "I was just talking to him, and he asked me to tell you that Saudi Arabian soldiers have killed Americans in the ARAMCO compound."

A sharp, electrical shock paralyzed the President's legs, and the constriction in his veins forced him to throw out a hand to the conference table to steady himself.

"How many, Mrs. Hill? Ask him how many."

"He's already told me. Five for sure, and maybe more in some houses they burnt down. He also said to tell you that Marines have been sent into all American compounds in eastern Saudi Arabia.''

Restored somewhat, President Steiner thanked her and thought to ask of the young girl. "By the way, who's Christina?''

"That's my five-year-old niece. Her mother had to stay with her sick baby, so she sent Christina over to watch the phone. No one believes I'm actually talking to you, sir . . . ah, Mr. President.''

"That's just fine, Mrs. Hill. For the time being, let's keep it that way. Now, could you ask Colonel Hemingway to tell us what he knows of the Puller's sinking?''

8:24 A.M.
Dhahran Airbase

Eighty miles west of Dhahran Air Base, the F-15 fighters escorting the Saudi king from Riyadh picked up approaching F-18 Hornets on their radarscans. The two Saudi fighters came up tighter on the embassy helicopter for their own protection. When the helicopter touched down beside the Control Tower at Dhahran, the F-15s landed closeby and taxied toward it.

Louis Fricke alighted from the helicopter as a jeep carrying three Marines pulled up. He addressed the officer in the jeep. "Where's your CO, Lieutenant?"

"Hop in, sir. I'll take you to him." The lieutenant slipped to the rear of the jeep. After Fricke settled into the front seat, the driver twisted the wheel and reversed direction.

"Wait!" shouted Fricke. He scrutinized the two Saudi F-15s now approaching the helicopter. "Lieutenant, can you blow their tires?"

"Now?"

"Now!" repeated Fricke.

"The PBL, Corporal."

The Marine in the rear seat aimed a suitcase-shaped weapon and pressed its activator. A silent and intense ray of red emitted from the short, squared muzzle of the weapon. Fricke's eyes followed the line of the laser to the nosewheel of the nearest Saudi fighter.

"How's that, sir?" inquired the lieutenant smugly.

The nosewheel became a soft mass of jellied rubber. The plane still managed to move forward, turning slowly in the direction of the jeep as the PBL melted its other tires.

"That's not stopping them!" Fricke shouted.

The Saudi pilot released a burst of 20mm rounds to the front of the jeep.

"On his flank!" howled the lieutenant, yanking the XRL off the driver's shoulder. The jeep swung around to a position thirty-five yards beside the aircraft as the lieutenant leveled the new weapon.

Fricke impatiently watched the muzzle of the XRL. Seeing a cobalt blue beam spurt from the weapon, he shifted his attention to the F-15. Its nose suddenly appeared out of focus. As the entire plane became an agitated blur, its left wing loosened and clattered to the tarmac, followed by a bright flash. The F-15 became engulfed in flames. A split second later, the men in the jeep observed the Saudi pilot and his seat rocketing out of the plane to a height of about one hundred feet above the ground. At the apex of the ejection, the seat separated from the pilot whose parachute blossomed above him. He yanked frantically on his shroud lines to keep from drifting toward the flaming remains of his aircraft.

"Damn," muttered Fricke.

The Marine officer aimed the weapon at the other fighter.

"Hold it!" yelled Fricke.

The cockpit canopy of the second F-15 had popped up. Its pilot stretched his hands high above his head where they remained until the Marines approached and removed him from his aircraft.

After receiving a brief description of the action at Dhahran and ARAMCO from Colonel Banks, the embassy party reboarded their helicopter and were escorted by a Sea Stallion to ARAMCO. Banks radioed ahead and they were met at the softball field by John Norlin. The Saudi king still carried the child, now wrapped in a field jacket provided by a Marine.

As they silently crowded into the bedroom—the one with the ham radio—Ambassador Clark studied the disfigured head of the sleeping pilot a moment. Dori sat on the edge of the bed holding the bandage to his face.

"Is that Colonel Hemingway?" whispered Clark.

John Norlin nodded. "His plane crash-landed defending us from two truck loads of Saudi national guard. He told me to wake him when you arrived." Norlin nudged the pilot's arm.

Hemingway opened his eyes and gazed at the newcomers.

"I'm Emory Clark," began the ambassador, stepping forward. He motioned behind him. "This is King Asad and my Air Force attache, Major Fricke." The Royal Guard officer and Korean waited by the door.

After his head cleared, Hemingway explained, "The morphine they gave me keeps knocking me out." Scrutinizing the Saudi king, he asked the ambassador. "Why'd you leave Riyadh?"

Clark described the events at the embassy and at the Lockheed compound. Taking it in, Hemingway bitterly glared at Asad before speaking.

"I wonder why Washington forgot to inform the Marines that the national guard decided not to cooperate? It cost us more lives here, too . . . plus our ship."

Clark shook his head. "I don't know, Colonel."

"Just before you landed at Dhahran," Hemingway began, "I reported to Washington the South Yemen flight was—"

"Colonel Hemingway!" Kevin Norlin cut in excitedly. "*The President's on our radio now.*"

———————◆———————

8:31 A.M.
Riyadh

The thirty-one young Saudis—most of them in Western-style clothes—pressed through the chanting crowd surrounding the compound of the Riyadh television station. Openly gripping khanjars in their waistbands, the young men maintained a protective ring around the tallest of their group. Prince Hamud held his head high to emphasize his advantage. His left arm hung in a sling below a heavily-bandaged shoulder, and his eyes blazed in anger at the crowd that jostled his entourage.

The young Saudis with Hamud boldly stared down those in the unruly horde who uttered slurs at the modern dress worn by his group. Reaching the entrance to the inner wall surrounding the television station, they found further progress barred by soldiers in the garb of the national guard.

"Let us through!" demanded Hamud.

A sneering sergeant retorted, "Who are you?"

The royal prince bristled at the insult. He enunciated his words with a waspish bitterness. *"Hamud bin Abdul Aziz Al Saud."*

The sergeant lowered his head in brief penitence. "Your Highness, permit me to summon my commander." He pivoted and hastily shoved his way through the cluster of soldiers behind him.

Noticing dried blood on the uniforms of the soldiers, Hamud spoke to the nearest. "Where did you fight the invaders?"

The soldier appeared perplexed by the question. Another soldier answered for him. "We killed the infidels."

"Yes, I can see," smirked Prince Hamud, indicating with his good hand the multiple blood-stained watches and rings worn by most of the guardsmen. "*Where else* did the infidels land?" he asked.

"They didn't land," offered the soldier. "We—"

The sergeant returned and roughly pushed the talkative soldier aside. An officer following the sergeant inquired, "Which of you is Prince Hamud?"

"I am," glared the prince.

"And I am Colonel Habib," haughtily responded the officer, saluting casually. "May I ask your purpose here?"

"I wish to make an announcement on the television."

"That is not possible."

"Why not?" snapped the prince.

"No unauthorized persons are permitted within the station."

"Who gives such orders?"

The colonel hesitated. "It is the Crown Prince."

"Then take me to him!" demanded Hamud. "I will speak with my brother."

Habib avoided the prince's eyes as he countered, "Prince Saleem is not here."

"Where is he?" prodded Hamud.

"I do not know," Habib dully replied. His lie was obvious.

Spinning around, Hamud led his followers through the crowd again. As they neared their cars, the congestion of people became even greater.

Hamud's compatriots who were too severely wounded to walk had remained with the vehicles. Now, they regaled the surrounding throng with the origins of the cargo carried by all of the cars except the white Rolls convertible. Secured by ropes to the hoods and trunks of the cars were inert bodies of Cuban soldiers.

Irene sat nervously in the driver's seat of the Corniche, as it was officially forbidden in Saudi Arabia for a woman to drive. The engine was still running, and her green dress fluttered on the antenna where Hamud had insisted it remain. Her escort in Hamud's absence, Prince Karrim, held court in the back seat. He had been the first to relate the events at King Khalid Airport to the throng . . . in response to a challenge issued from the crowd at Irene's position behind the steering wheel. Karrim was in the midst of his third and expanded version of the early morning fight when he spotted Hamud. Waving his eager listeners away, Karrim called out to his cousin, "What did you say?"

"Nothing," came the sullen reply. "The Crown Prince lets no one in the station."

"Let us go to the Al-Riyadh then," suggested Karrim. "The newspaper will print the truth."

Hamud shook his head. "They would not be open on this day . . . but we can go elsewhere." He walked to the driver's side of his car and motioned Irene to the passenger side for the first time since receiving his wound.

Prince Hamud placed the Rolls Royce in gear, applied full brakes, and gunned its engine full bore. After the Saudis in front of his car scattered, Hamud abruptly released his brakes. The convertible shot away from its parking spot, and his entourage followed in the same manner.

1:00 A.M.
The White House

Stunned, the President slumped into a chair, shaking his head slowly from side to side. "Those bastards . . . those *goddamned* bastards," he moaned. "How could they commit such an act?"

"Don't blame yourself, sir," Clayton Walters gently intoned.

Allan Steiner raised an eyebrow a moment to study his secretary of state. It hadn't occurred to him that he *should* blame himself for the deaths of the Americans in Riyadh . . . until Walters had suggested it.

"It's a terrible tragedy, sir," Edward Rolle offered. The CIA director pushed his chair away from the conference table and strolled over to the Middle East grid map. The oldest man in the room at seventy-three and of ample girth, he made a grandfatherly appearance. He'd come up through the ranks in *The Company* and had demonstrated a facility for avoiding the overly zealous errors of his politically appointed predecessors. When Rolle returned to the President's side, he spoke in a hushed, tentative tone.

"This *could* help solve the Saudi leadership problem."

Absorbed with his thoughts, Allan Steiner failed to respond. Comparing the fifty-odd deaths of the Americans in the compounds of Saudi Arabia with the tens of thousands who had finally broken Lyndon Johnson, he found little solace.

"What leadership problem?" asked Clayton Walters curiously.

The CIA director glanced at Walters but returned his attention to the silent, brooding President. "Mr. President?" Rolle said quietly. He repeated himself, a bit more loudly.

Snapped from his doleful reverie, the President searched the faces close by for the person who'd spoken. Rolle leaned over to discreetly inquire, "Sir, may I have a word with you by the map?"

The President nodded skeptically and asked Clayton Walters and General Steel to join them at the wall grid of the Middle East. Masking his disappointment at the invitation to the others, Rolle prefaced his question with a slight smile.

"Mr. President, at what percentile of the labor force does a middle class become threatening to a monarchy?"

Wondering what possible relevance it could have to the current situation, the President indulged the question. "Somewhere," he replied, "between eight and ten percent."

Though Rolle already knew the answer, he made his face register concern. "A recent British survey in *The Economist* stated the Saudi middle class now stands at 8.1 percent."

"What are you getting at?" asked the President. Rolle had paused to let the figure sink in.

"It's quite possible the monarchy in Saudi Arabia," stated Rolle matter-of-factly, "could be overthrown in a time of crisis . . . such as this."

The President turned to his secretary of state. "What do you think, Clayton?"

Walters shrugged. "Inasmuch as the Saud family has consistently taken strong measures to silence any opposition to their rule, I don't know of any instability in Riyadh at this time."

"If it's a stable regime," Rolle smiled, "then why do the Sauds find it necessary to silence their dissenters?"

Walters shook his head. "I don't see the relationship."

"I do," countered Rolle, "and if my assessment of the situation in Riyadh proves accurate, we have a responsibility to encourage a peaceful transition . . . and stable energy sources for our Western allies. On the other hand, if we sit on our hands, Saudi Arabia could easily become another Iran. And that might be little better than Soviet control over the Saudi oil fields . . . *and* reserves."

President Steiner led the three men back to the conference table and sat down. Looking askance at his CIA Director, he spoke in a caustic tone.

"I don't intend to help anyone overthrow the government in Riyadh, Mr. Rolle."

"Of course not, sir," Rolle hastily replied, "but we might encourage a more moderate, enlightened leadership to come forward."

The President rubbed his temple roughly. "Clayton, we need your input."

Walters frowned at Rolle. "I would have to admit that we—the free world for that matter—would benefit by a more enlightened rule in Saudi Arabia, but that doesn't mean we should cause it to happen."

Rolle quickly replied, "I agree with you, Clayton, completely. It would be foolhardy to commit any covert acts in this regard. I might also point out"—Rolle switched his attention to the President—"when our national press gets wind of the number of Americans killed by Saudis, there's going to be hell to pay . . . if you'll pardon the expression, Mr. President."

"And a change in the Saudi leadership," continued the President, "might appear as adequate atonement."

Rolle couldn't immediately tell whether Allan Steiner was being facetious or serious. "I'm not a politician, sir," Rolle too humbly offered.

"Both Saleem and Rahman appear to be involved in the deaths of Americans," stated the President. "Who else could assume the leadership, Mr. Rolle?"

The CIA director shook his head slightly. "I doubt if Prince Rahman had anything to do with the Puller, sir—directly or indirectly."

"Why do you think that?"

"He's ambitious *and* careful, sir. Rahman is next in line behind Saleem for the throne, but by the time Asad dies and Saleem reigns, Rahman may be an old man. Therefore, he would do nothing which might jeopardize a quicker route to the kingship."

"For the sake of discussion," said President Steiner, "how would we *encourage* Rahman forward?"

Rolle glanced purposefully at the Middle East wall grid to delay his reply. "By making him a hero, sir."

"And how do you intend we do that?" asked the President.

"With a little help from General Steel," replied Rolle. "In your press conference, sir, you announced our troops had moved into Dhahran to counter the threat of the Iranian army. Since that army is incapacitated at this time, why not move more Saudis northward and push the Iranians out of Kuwait. . .with Rahman as their field commander?"

"So he returns a hero," agreed the President, "but that doesn't solve the problem of shoving the king and Saleem aside."

"Saleem's disgraced himself," replied Rolle, "and Asad has a heart condition. If Rahman emerged from this crisis in a position of strength, his immediate future would be greatly enhanced."

"I still don't intend to help topple the current regime," reiterated the President.

"We wouldn't have to," Rolle insisted. "Prince Rahman can handle the situation himself, if and when the opportunity arises. And if it does, Saudi Arabia would be replacing a near-maniac and his subservient half-brother king for a man dedicated to bringing his country out of the Middle Ages."

The last statement was an exaggeration, but Allan Steiner chose not to dispute it. He gradually pivoted in his chair to the secretary of state. "Clayton, I won't approve helping Rahman without your concurrence."

Walters stroked his chin. "Mr. President, when I stop to think about the 40,000 Americans still in Saudi Arabia, I can become exceedingly concerned with the current leaders. I don't particularly like Rahman, but he's better than the alternatives as long as we have no role in what happens to the king and Saleem."

The President made a wry face. "General Steel, how would you implement the ouster of the Iranians from Kuwait?"

"The Saudis have 45,000 soldiers on their northern border already," replied Steel. Eleven thousand more could be shuttled from their oil fields. If necessary, our F-18s could neutralize the Iranian armor and air power.

Allan Steiner looked to Rolle. "How do we contact

Rahman?"

"He's in Riyadh awaiting our instructions, sir."

With the vague sense he'd been had, President Steiner spoke with a bitter quality. "I'd like to speak with Rahman personally before he heads north."

"He can be at ARAMCO within an hour, sir." Rolle picked up a phone and dialed. The men around the conference table listened intently to his subdued words.

"Bring the Lion to Dhahran."

———————◆———————

Dori ran into the bedroom. "Prince Saleem's on TV again!"

Carrying Hemingway on his board, the men moved into the living room. "Turn up the sound, Dori," requested her father.

"There's something wrong with it, Daddy." As she manipulated the set's controls, they watched the Crown Prince shoving at men who blocked the camera's view of him in the jammed studio of the Riyadh television station. Jostled from behind by other members of his staff, Saleem whirled about and summoned his bodyguards. Tall white-uniformed Bedouins used the stocks of their rifles to wedge their way through the crowd and formed a tight circle around Saleem.

The angry prince grasped the microphone and appeared to be shouting into it. His body noticeably bobbing up-and-down in excitation, Saleem accentuated his words with flailing arms.

Dori giggled. "He looks like a flying chicken."

"What a nerd," exclaimed Kevin.

Even Asad was inwardly amused at the spectacle of his brother making a fool of himself.

The Egyptian station manager squeezed past the circle of bodyguards and flipped the 'on' switch of the microphone—an act which instantly halted Saleem's delivery.

The Crown Prince glowered at the Egyptian and then at the microphone.

"It is on now," meekly explained the station manager.

"*You two-legged goat!*" exploded Saleem . . . now live on both camera and sound. Calming himself, the Saudi prince started over. His words, translated into English, appeared along the bottom of the TV screen in the ARAMCO living room.

"In the name of Allah, listen to my words. The brave men of my national guard have defeated the invaders at King Khalid airport!" Deafening acclaim at this announcement continued in the small studio until Saleem motioned for quiet.

"We have killed many infidels," Saleem went on, "yet they injured not one of us. The enemy who survived the wrath of my men have returned to the south. Riyadh is now safe . . . Praise to Allah."

Again, pandemonium erupted. Many clasped Saleem, kissing him on his cheeks and lips. Warmly receiving these embraces for a short time, Saleem again called for silence to resume his delivery.

"However, we are still in great danger. Our king is in the hands of the Americans who have invaded our Eastern Province. My brother, if you are still living, hear my words. We shall find and rescue you! And we shall *drive the infidels from our sacred soil!*"

With these exhortations, the Saudis in the studio repeatedly screamed, "Allah Akbar! Allah Akbar!"

Dori lowered the sound of the TV set.

"He's got to be lying," declared Hemingway. "Potato Joe— one of my Harrier pilots—reported civilian cars on the runways prevented the Yemen flight from landing."

Dori piped up, "Why doesn't someone go over to ARAMCO TV and tell the truth?"

"Honey," gently replied Ambassador Clark, "no one would believe us."

"They *will* believe me," came from the back of the room.

The Americans pivoted as one to face Asad, who repeated, "They will listen to me."

Clark's tone was dubious. "What would you say?"

"What is true," said the king sadly.

The ambassador studied Asad apprehensively. "Let's talk to Washington first." After Clark related the words of the Crown

Prince and Asad's offer over the ham radio, President Steiner asked to speak to the Saudi king, who took the chair before the radio.

"Asad, after what's happened in your country," began the President, "your statement could be critical to the future of Saudi Arabia. I think we should discuss what will be said."

"Your suggestions are welcome, Allan."

"First, you must state it was American Marines and planes which compelled the flight from Afghanistan to withdraw." The President paused to ask, "Is someone writing this down?"

"I will," volunteered Clark.

"The next point Asad must mention is crucial. It is the fact that *he* invited our Marines to enter Saudi Arabia. Is that clear, Asad?"

"I understand," replied the king.

"You must also," declared the President with emphasis, "call for the arrest of those responsible for the murder of Americans."

"Mr. President," interjected Clark, "I forgot to reveal earlier that half of the compound's residents in Riyadh were British and French."

"I think it would be helpful," continued the President, "if Asad personally requests his countrymen to safeguard the lives of all Westerners in Saudi Arabia."

"I will say all that you mention," agreed Asad.

There was silence on the ham radio before Allan Steiner resumed speaking in a lowered voice. "Asad, I am greatly bothered by what happened in Riyadh. Why were even the women and children killed?"

The Saudi king hesitated, knowing a non-Arab could never understand. "It is difficult to explain," he offered.

"Try me, Asad. I need an answer . . . for my people."

"It is a custom of the desert," Asad haltingly began. "In war, we either show great compassion . . . or none at all. When peace cannot be made by intermarriage, it is common to show mercy to no one. The women, especially the children, cannot live for they will seek to avenge the men who have died."

"That's crazy!" retorted the President. "Those Americans were not a desert tribe, and they were *not* at war with you!"

The king replied weakly. "Not all Saudi—"

President Steiner cut him off. "Ambassador, did you get everything down on paper?"

"Yes, sir."

"I would like to speak confidentially to you and your Air Force attache now."

Rather than carry the Marine colonel from the room again, Clark asked, "Colonel Hemingway's on the bed beside the radio. Can he remain here?"

"On the bed?"

"Yes, sir. I believe he has a serious back injury."

"Of course, he can stay. Is everyone else out?"

"It's just the three of us, sir."

"Were you able to bring out the tape of Asad's discussion with his brothers in the embassy?"

"We have that, sir. Plus his conversation with you this morning."

"Ambassador, on the way to the television station, I want you to remind the king we have evidence of his complicity in the massacre in Riyadh. And put a copy of the tapes on a plane to Washington immediately."

"Yes, sir."

"I have someone who wishes to speak with Major Fricke now," stated President Steiner.

Clark didn't recognize the voice.

"Major Fricke, are you still a bachelor?" inquired the CIA director.

"Confirmed," replied Fricke, acknowledging the coded question.

Rolle's voice was friendly. "Isn't it about time you *got* married?"

"When I do," Fricke genially responded, "you'll be the first to know."

The President came back on the radio. "Ambassador, Prince Rahman will be joining you soon in ARAMCO. When he arrives, bring him to this radio immediately."

"Yes, sir. May I inquire why he's coming."

The President hesitated. "I can't say over the air yet. After

Asad appears on TV, give me a report."

"We'll tape it for you, sir," replied Clark.

As Asad and his Royal Guard officer stepped from the helicopter at ARAMCO TV, Fricke extended both hands to the king. "I'll take the child now, Your Majesty."

Asad continued to cradle the body in his arms. "I must show my people what Prince Saleem's fools have done," he explained.

Fricke looked to Clark, who nodded in assent. The four men walked briskly to the entrance of the television station where they were met by its British manager. Clark told him, "The king wants to make an immediate statement on television. Can you hook up with the stations in Riyadh, Jeddah, Medina, and Damman?"

"If they're willing," replied the Briton.

"Tell them," Asad spoke sternly, "it is *my* will."

In the station studio, Clark gave the king the sheet of paper on which he'd taken notes from President Steiner. Asad looked it over and announced, "It would be best if I did not read from this. I shall remember everything without it."

Before the ambassador could protest, Asad spoke brusquely to the station manager. "I am ready to speak now." The king unwrapped the bundled child and handed the boy to his Royal Guard officer.

His presentation was in marked contrast to the heated harangue of his half-brother. Asad began in a weak voice, so low the control room increased it electronically.

"In the name of Allah, heed my words. My brother, Crown Prince Saleem, who spoke earlier to you, is poorly informed. That I am in the Eastern Province is true, but I am not a prisoner. I came here to direct the defense of our oil fields. And with the help of the Americans whom I invited into the kingdom, the invaders from Afghanistan have been repulsed."

Asad turned to his Royal Guard officer and took the child before continuing. "Do not be alarmed by the blood on my thobe. It is not my own. It comes from the body of this American child . . . and this child comes from a foreign compound in Riyadh where all were killed. Were it not for our American friends, this could be one of my children . . . or one of yours.

"Those who killed the Americans in this compound," Asad continued in a slightly-raised voice, "must be brought to justice. A witness observed trucks of the national guard leaving the compound. I call on Prince Saleem to arrest those responsible for this piteous crime. And I call on all Saudi citizens to protect those foreigners who have helped defend our kingdom on this day. Praise to Allah."

With that, Asad waved the camera away and slumped to a nearby sofa.

———————◆———————

1:15 A.M.
The White House

"Jim," began the President, "bring the congressmen down again. Don't say anything about the Lockeed compound yet."

Noting a quizzical expression from his secretary of state, Allan Steiner explained, "We've got to prepare an announcement for the press, and I want some political heads to bounce ideas off of."

Arriving in a jubilant mood, the congressmen congratulated the President on the Soviet defeat at Dhahran. After he'd invited them to be seated, Senator Farrell spoke first.

"What's happened to the flight coming up from Yemen?"

"Our latest communication indicates the Saudis managed to prevent its landing also," replied the President without emotion. "We have other news from Riyadh, though, which is why I've asked you to join me. Our ambassador has reported elements of the Saudi national guard massacred a compound of Westerners in the capital."

In the silence which followed, Speaker Snell asked, "How many Americans?"

"Approximately fifty . . . and as many more British and French citizens."

"That's incredible!" exclaimed Farrell. "Why?"

President Steiner briefly looked away from his questioner. "We don't know for certain . . . other than Crown Prince Saleem objected to our Marines entering his country."

"*For Christ's sake!*" exploded Farrell. "The Marines came in to protect his goddamn country."

"Saleem commands the Saudi national guard," offered Clayton Walters, "which is composed of desert Bedouins. They're noted for their vengefulness and unpredictability."

"That's an understatement," glared Farrell.

"Mr. President, what're we doing to protect other Americans in Saudi Arabia?" asked Snell.

"Marines have been sent into compounds of the Eastern Province, and King Asad is at ARAMCO TV right now, making a statement on our behalf."

"Why don't we seize the Saudi oil fields," suggested Farrell coldly, "to guarantee the safety of Americans?"

"That might endanger our citizens," injected Walters "more than it would safeguard them."

Senator Winslow calmly inquired, "Mr. President, how do you propose to explain the massacre to the American people?"

Allan Steiner eyed Winslow impassively for a moment. "What would you tell them, Senator?"

"It's not what the American people should be told," Speaker Snell broke in. "It's what they'll *accept*."

Clayton Walters' voice was speculative. "We could announce Arab radicals committed the massacre."

"That's without a doubt!" quipped Snell.

"Mr. President," said Farrell, "if the Saudis had slaughtered 50 civilians in a Russian compound, I can assure you what would happen. The Russians would come in and line up 500 Arabs!"

Allan Steiner visibly flinched.

"I was only making a comparison," added Farrell, "not suggesting anything."

"Last week," began Winslow, "I read that most of the Saudi foreign monetary reserves are here in the States . . . and they amount to 85 billion dollars. We could confiscate some of those assets as reparations and freeze the rest to guarantee the safety of Westerners in Saudi Arabia."

"Why not *keep* the rest?" suggested Senator Farrell. "Or dole it out to the banks stuck with defaulted loans from Third World nations who were squeezed when the Arabs jacked up their oil prices?"

"That might be difficult to justify," stated the President, actually looking for comments to support Winslow's proposal."

"Not to the American people," retorted Farrell.

Receiving no other opinions, Allan Steiner shifted his attention to the Middle East wall map. In view of the congressmen's earlier statements, he hadn't expected the drastic measures they now suggested. He stood up from the table.

"Gentlemen, thank you again for joining me. I'd prefer you not speak with the press until I've had an opportunity to issue a statement."

As the congressmen left, Walters commented to the President, "That Farrell's a real nut."

"Unfortunately," President Steiner nodded. "He's also a better barometer of the American public than the others."

"Sir," offered Hoolihan, "if you're considering the confiscation of Saudi reserves, I'd suggest a freeze order on their bank accounts immediately . . . before they can be wire-transferred."

The President nodded. "Notify the chairman of the Federal Reserve to do that." As Hoolihan picked up a phone, President Steiner addressed Clayton Walters. "While we're covering their assets here, why don't you contact the British and French embassies? Inform them of the massacre and suggest they take similar action."

When Hoolihan and Walters completed their calls, they joined the President and Edward Rolle before the Middle East wall grid. Walters asked, "Sir, did you intend to discuss the Russian POWs with the congressmen?"

"No, I already knew what they thought."

"They may be right, sir," said Walters. "And if Derevenko's anxious to get them back, we may be able to negotiate concessions."

"Such as?"

"For one, commitments to stop arming the Middle East."

The CIA director grinned broadly. "Come on, Clayton. They break their commitments as soon as it suits them."

"Even a short-term halt in arms shipments," insisted

Walters, "would be valuable."

"On the other hand," argued Rolle, "by delaying the return of the prisoners, we could embarrass Derevenko, and that could be a greater deterrent to his future meddling in the Middle East than a piece of pap—"

"Gentlemen," cut in the President, "I'd rather have Derevenko owe us. What's important now is the crisis be defused. Plus, I think world opinion will more favorably consider our actions against the Saudis if we act magnanimously toward the Soviets. Jim, get Derevenko on the line. Let's see how interested he is in getting his men back."

After picking up the red phone and making his request, Hoolihan appeared to be listening intently. Waiting a minute, President Steiner asked, "What're you listening to, Jim?"

Hoolihan covered the receiver. "There's quite a bit of shouting in the background."

"Repeat my request."

"*Hello.* President Steiner *is waiting* to speak to the Premier!"

The interpreter's reply was again, "One moment."

When Hoolihan relayed this, the President took the phone and loudly exclaimed, "This is President Steiner! I want to speak with Premier Derevenko. What is the delay?"

After several awkward starts, the interpreter managed to speak. "Our premier cannot come to the phone at this time, President Steiner. What would you like to say to him?"

"Tell him we're holding nearly 150 of his soldiers in Saudi Arabia and wish to make arrangements for their return."

The interpreter, following a lengthy pause, came back on the line. "How soon will you return them?"

"In one week. My secretary of state will make arrangements with your foreign office." When the President had hung up the phone, he commented, "That's not the same interpreter with whom I spoke earlier. Clayton, start making inquiries to our people in Moscow. Find out what's happening in the Kremlin."

"I'd imagine Derevenko is in the frying pan right now," offered the CIA director. "I'll have my people work on it, too."

Feeling a singe himself, Allan Steiner wondered if he was out of his own.

<hr>

9:49 A.M.
Riyadh

As a throng of thousands now milled and chanted before the compound of the Riyadh television station, gray-robed members of the mutawwa (religious police) gradually filled its front ranks.

At precisely the noon hour, the call of the muezzins blared from the loudspeakers of nearby minarets.

"God is great.
I testify that there is no God but one God.
I testify that Mohammed is His Prophet.
Come to prayers.
Come to success.
God is great.
No God but one God."

It was barely discernible over the clamor of the crowd, and when they failed to respond to the midday call to prayer, the mutawwa began beating on their shoulders with bamboo poles . . . ordering them to their knees.

As the crowd slowly began to kneel, a stout member of the mutawwa turned to the Bedouin national guardsmen blocking the inner entrance to the compound. Confronting the youngest of them, he shouted directly into the soldier's face.

"Face Mecca and kneel!"

The confused soldier glanced to his rear, and the mutawwa pointed to the southwest.

"Mecca is *that* way."

Stuttering, the young soldier said, "I cannot—"

"You *dare not* fail to serve Allah!" shrieked the mutawwa, who then passed through the entrance and repeated his call to prayer among the other Bedouins. More gray-thobed mutawwa immediately followed through the entrance.

Coming up behind the young soldier with whom he'd first spoken, the stout mutawwa used his knees to strike the back of the man's legs. As the soldier's own knees buckled, the mutawwa placed his hands on the man's shoulders and forced him to a kneeling position.

The other members of the mutawwa screamed at the standing soldiers, demanding they follow suit. Before the end of the five-minute prayer period, the entire company of national guardsmen within the inner compound was prostrate with the mutawwa. They were also outnumbered by Saudis wearing thobes of the religious police.

As the minarets called an end to the noon prayers, the driver of a black Lincoln limousine behind the throng opened a door of the car and offered his forearm to an elderly, bearded man. Three others wearing the distinctive gray-white thobes of imams also stepped from the limousine.

Whispers ran through the crowd as they recognized the 82-year-old Grand Imam of the Riyadh Mosque. They automatically parted for the passage of Sheik Muhammed ibn Abd Mansur and his three companions, who closely held their gutras to obscure their faces.

The Bedouin guards at the gate to the inner compound moved aside in obeisance as the sheik and his company passed. Seeing the Grand Imam, the mutawwa converged with him at the door of the television building. They pushed aside the soldiers at the door but stepped back when Colonel Habib appeared from within.

"Praise be to Allah," greeted Habib, seeing the thobes of imams.

"Praise be to Allah," Sheik Mansur intoned.

Only now noticing the Grand Imam, Habib sputtered, "Why . . . why are you here?"

"We are here," began the sheik in a raised voice, "to do the will of Allah."

"And what," Habib uneasily asked, "is the will of Allah?"

The deep-set eyes of the Grand Imam turned hostile. "We come to recite the Koran."

The national guard officer hastily calculated the relative risks to his life from denying the senior member of both the Riyadh clergy and judiciary *or* incurring the wrath of the Crown Prince.

"I am honored," Habib generously replied, "to escort you."

Most of the Saudis wearing the gray thobes of the mutawwa followed the sheik and crowded into the studio. When told he could begin, Sheik Mansur peered mournfully into the camera and spoke in a fatigued whine.

"In the Name of Allah, the Compassionate, the Merciful. There is no god but God. Muhammed is the Messenger of God. Praise be to the Lord of the Worlds, Master of the Day of Judgment. Thee do we worship, and Thine aid we entreat. Show us The way of those on whom Thou hast bestowed Grace, not of those with whom Thou are Wrathful, nor to those who go astray."

The Grand Imam paused to glance at Colonel Habib beside him. On the other side of the national guard officer were the three who had accompanied the sheik in his limousine.

"There are forces within our kingdom which threaten our sacred way of life. There is *no force* on this earth as great as the power of Allah. To fulfill our sacred duty in following His will, we must seek truth. Beside me now are those who fought bravely for Allah at our airport. *Heed their words!*"

Sheik Mansur beckoned the three in gray-white thobes to the camera. Two of them threw off their shifts, revealing Western clothes beneath.

Recognizing the taller of the two, Habib raised a hand in front of Prince Hamud. The Saudi prince leaned into the face of the national guard officer and spoke his words with menacing sweetness.

"Go fuck a camel."

Habib's hand was snatched by two gray-thobed men who

pinned his arms to his sides. Noting Western clothes under their thobes, Habib asked in alarm, "Who are you?"

"You shall learn soon enough," sneered one of them.

Sheik Mansur stepped aside for Hamud and Prince Karrim.

"Praise be to Allah!" began Prince Hamud. "You have heard *lies* from my half-brother, Saleem. He and his cowardly men fled the airport at the first sign of enemy planes! It is through a miracle of Allah and the bravery of Prince Karrim and many others that the invaders were turned back. If it pleases you, I give proof of our presence at King Khalid Airport."

Lifting a blood-darkened shirt from his shoulder, Hamud ripped the hospital dressing from its place. Fresh blood poured from the jagged wound at the top of his shoulder, reopened by the violence of his movement. With wild eyes, Hamud turned to his cousin. Karrim pulled off his gutra, exposing a reddened row of stitches across his forehead.

"I've been told," continued Hamud, "our king appeared on television and revealed members of the national guard attacked a Western compound in this city. Do you wish the *truth* of this, too?"

Hamud spun around, his eyes searching among the soldiers in the studio. Pointing at the two nearest, he commanded they be brought forward. Gray-thobed Saudis disarmed the soldiers before forcing them before the camera.

"Hold up your arms!" snapped the prince.

Hamud pointed to their bejeweled hands and forearms, one of which held six watches. "These hold jewelry and watches *torn* from bodies in the compound of Westerners," he loudly proclaimed.

"Arrest them!" continued Hamud. "And all others who wear *proof of their guilt!*

The mutawwa, with the help of Hamud's retinue who'd disguised themselves in gray thobes, speedily disarmed the other soldiers in the room and knocked them senseless with bamboo poles. This completed, many of the gray-thobed Saudis rushed from the studio to mete out similar treatment to the guardsmen outside the building.

Hamud stepped away from the camera and went to the side

of Irene who'd accompanied Karrim and him into the building. Removing her headdress, he took her firmly by the wrist and led her to the camera.

"This woman was at King Khalid airport," began Hamud in a low voice, "when we were attacked. Many cars fought the enemy planes, but it was my car which blocked their final attempt to land."

The Saudi prince lifted her hand high. "This is the *hand* which steered my car at that moment!" He paused before exclaiming, "It is the hand of an American!"

In the ARAMCO compound, the reception of this news was as enthusiastically received as it was by the Saudis in the studio of Riyadh TV.

Louis Fricke placed a hand on the shoulder of the dumbstruck American ambassador. "What was your daughter doing at Riyadh's airport?"

Clark shook his head, keeping his eyes on the television image of Irene among the cheering Saudis. "She's supposed to be on the Riviera with her sister," he finally responded.

"Thank God," Fricke uttered, "she isn't."

1:51 A.M.
The White House

"This call's for you, Ed," said Hoolihan.

The CIA director took the phone. "Rolle here."

"Sir, this is Kamsler. We've isolated the jamming source in the Persian Gulf. It's a Czech-registered freighter that delivered cargo to Kharg Island seventy-two hours ago."

"Where is it now?" Rolle inquired.

"Thirty miles north of Dhahran, just outside Saudi territorial waters."

"Good work, Len." Rolle put the phone down and announced the news.

General Steel responded with uncommon briskness. "We've got to blow that ship out of the water."

President Steiner raised an eyebrow.

"We have the Connie and 15,000 troops from Europe coming into that sector," explained Steel, "and right now, there's no way you or I can effectively control them. All we have is an unsecured, civilian ham radio."

"I'm aware of that, Bob," the President replied, "but I'm not sure we want to *blow* it out of the water."

"Why don't we simply borrow it?" suggested the Marine Commandant. "I, for one, would like to see their technology. Jamming satellite communications is something *we* haven't developed yet."

"How would you do that?" Steel asked.

Huering smiled. "It could be done with three Marines."

The JCS chairman squinted at the commandant. "Three Marines?"

"Three Recon Marines," Huering nodded. "Two to foul the props, and a third for the ship's fresh air funnel."

"Mr. President," began Rolle, "I agree with General Huering. I also have an idea how we could get the ship into a friendly port." The CIA director explained his plan, which was immediately approved and relayed to Louis Fricke in ARAMCO.

After an hour's further discussion, Allan Steiner arose from the conference table and scanned the faces of his military and civilian advisors. "That's settled. We stay in Saudi Arabia and confiscate their foreign monetary reserves. Jim, raise Ambassador Clark on the radio."

10:15 A.M.
ARAMCO

Ambassador Clark leaned into the microphone of the ham radio. "We received word ten minutes ago that Prince Rahman landed in his own jet at Dhahran, Mr. President."

"I want you to tell Rahman we have two conditions for helping him," the President stated. He outlined them.

"Rahman may welcome our continued military presence," Clark replied, "but I strongly doubt he'll cooperate if we tell him we're taking their foreign reserves."

Fricke added, "I believe the Ambassador's right, sir."

"Mr. President," Clark began, "it may be prudent to present our conditions as accomplished facts after Rahman returns." *And,* he mused, *after Irene's out of Riyadh.*

"You may be right," President Steiner conceded. "We'll wait."

John Norlin poked his head into the bedroom to report the arrival of Prince Rahman.

"He's here," Clark announced over the radio. "Do you wish to speak to him, sir?"

The President debated a moment. "No, not yet . . . but I'd like to listen to your discussions with him."

Rahman entered the bedroom and, after a short exchange, asked to see his brother privately. As Fricke lead Rahman to the bedroom where Asad rested, he hastily described the plan to clear the Iranians from Kuwait.

At the door of Asad's bedroom, Prince Rahman waved the Royal Guard officer outside before entering and closing the door. After awakening Asad, Prince Rahman offered to obtain coffee for the two of them.

At the ham radio, Ambassador Clark asked to speak to the President again. "Sir, I almost forgot. A young prince of the Saud family appeared on Riyadh TV and confirmed that the national guard was responsible for the Lockheed compound. The same prince led the civilians whose cars stopped the Yemen flight from landing at King Khalid airport. My oldest daughter, Irene, was with him at the time."

"*Your daughter?*"

"Yes, sir. Evidently, she helped them."

"Are you certain of this?"

"That's what the prince said . . . on national television."

"You should have told me this earlier."

"I'm sorry, sir. Considering the importance of the other matters we were discussing, it didn't occur to me until now."

"What's the name of this prince?"

"Hamud, sir."

"Try to establish contact with him," ordered the President.

Rahman, after requesting coffee of the Norlins, insisted on serving the cups himself. Before re-entering the king's bedroom, Rahman briefly visited an adjacent bathroom, where he emptied the contents of eight Sominex capsules into one of the cups.

As the Saudi king sipped the coffee, he shook his head in disgust at the fouled black liquid. Rahman smirked and commented, "Western coffee is hardly fit for a child." He watched his brother closely . . . and reached over to remove the cup from Asad's hand as the king slipped into unconsciousness. After arranging his brother comfortably on the bed again, Rahman rinsed Asad's cup with coffee from his own and threw the residue into a corner of a closet.

When Prince Rahman rejoined the Americans in the bedroom, Fricke explained the proposed invasion of Kuwait in greater detail. "On your return," he concluded to the Saudi prince, "you will be irresistible to your people."

Rahman remained straight-faced. "Can you send your Marines with me?"

Ambassador Clark shook his head. "I am certain the President would not approve the commitment of American soldiers against a Middle East army."

"Besides," Fricke added, "your men have all been protected by the flu vaccine. Ours have not."

Continuing his false show of indecision, Rahman asked, "How can I be assured of success in the north?"

"You will have total air superiority," replied Fricke.

"How can that be?" Rahman asked sourly. "I no longer have an air force."

"The Constellation is moving into the Gulf," revealed Fricke.

Rahman blinked in surprise.

"She's taking up a battle station on the other side of Qatar," continued Fricke, "and tonight we'll drop leaflets over Kuwait warning of a full-scale attack tomorrow by a joint Saudi-Iraqi force."

"I must have more than paper," Rahman muttered.

"You will," responded Fricke. "Our F-18s will provide air cover. The Saudi insignia is being painted over ours. They will be fully capable of providing any assistance you require, and I shall personally accompany you."

"Then let us begin," Rahman smiled for the first time. "We must act quickly before the effects of the flu wear off. I will say goodbye to my brother and we shall leave."

After checking Asad's pulse, Prince Rahman rushed back to the Americans. "Ambassador Clark, you must help me," pleaded Rahman. "The king is ill!"

"What's wrong with him?" asked Clark in equal alarm.

"I cannot wake him!" replied Rahman, casting a furtive glance at Fricke and adding, "It may be another heart attack."

"We'll get him to the ARAMCO hospital immediately," said Clark.

Rahman shook his head. "No, the king must see his British specialists."

"Where are they?" asked Clark.

"London," answered Rahman with a hopeful note.

Clark looked at the Saudi prince in consternation. "You want us to take Asad to London?"

"No," replied Rahman. "The royal hospital plane will do that."

"Ambassador," interjected Fricke, "they have a 707 with a fully-equipped emergency room for heart attack victims. I believe that's what Prince Rahman is speaking of."

"Well, where is it?" asked Clark in some confusion.

"It should be arriving at Dhahran in a short while," Rahman announced. "I took the precaution of ordering it to follow me."

"Precaution?" repeated Clark, looking to Fricke for more explanation. Fricke shrugged his shoulders.

"Yes," nodded Rahman. "It normally follows the king whenever he travels. It carries three doctors, including a cardiologist."

"We'll get Asad to the ARAMCO hospital for now," decided Clark, "and transfer him to his plane later." As they started to leave the bedroom, Hemingway broke his silence.

"Major Fricke, I've got a suggestion for that leaflet you're planning to drop over Kuwait." While the others carried the Saudi king to a helicopter, Hemingway described his idea to Fricke.

Later, after Clark had concluded his report to Washington, the President asked, "How did Colonel Hemingway injure his back?"

"I've been told," replied Clark, "that he was forced to crashland in the process of stopping two truckloads of marauding Saudi national guardsmen. Half his face is burnt to a crisp, too. And he's refused to go to the hospital."

"Colonel Hemingway," the President called out. "Can you hear me?"

"Yes, sir," the Marine replied.

Allan Steiner selected his words with care. "Is the situation well-in-hand, Colonel?"

"Yes, sir," Hemingway repeated. "I've turned over my command to Colonel Caliguiri who came in from the Med."

"Then it's my wish," stated President Steiner firmly, "that

you proceed immediately to the hospital, Colonel."

When the Marine officer didn't respond, Clark did. "I'll arrange transportation at once, Mr. President."

3:00 A.M.
The White House

Slamming his empty coffee cup on the conference table, General Huering nearly bowled over his chair in getting up. He hurried to General Steel's side.

"Bob, why haven't we involved the British assault carrier in the northern Gulf?"

The JCS Chairman clenched his eyes at the oversight. They both approached President Steiner in conference with Clayton Walters and Jim Hoolihan.

"Mr. President," interrupted Steel, "the Commandant just reminded me the British have a small carrier in the Persian Gulf . . . which could be decisive in the Kuwait operation."

Huering added, "It's similar to the Puller in capability."

"If the British are invited in," Clayton Walters cautiously offered, "they'll almost certainly ask for a political voice."

Allan Steiner looked directly at his secretary of state. "What's wrong with that? We're going to have a difficult enough time justifying our actions in Saudi Arabia, much less in Kuwait, too. Jim, get Prime Minister Colburn on the line."

"Mr. President," said Rolle, "assuming the Iranians are driven out of Kuwait, do we want the Saudis to retain a military presence there?"

"No, of course not."

"The British would solve that problem for us," continued Rolle.

"I have Colburn, sir," announced Hoolihan, as he switched on the table speaker and handed over the phone.

"Chet, this is Allan. How are you?"

"Very good, Allan. What's going on? We've frozen Saudi assets as Clayton Walters suggested."

After describing the aborted invasions and the Kuwait plan to his British counterpart, President Steiner said, "I've called to suggest your carrier in the Gulf assist in the Kuwait operation."

"Why don't your own forces handle the job?"

"A Saudi gunboat torpedoed our assault carrier."

"A Saudi gunboat?" queried Colburn. "How'd that happen?"

"We don't know yet, Chet. We don't know why they killed everyone in the Riyadh compound either."

"What do you intend to do about it?"

"We're still discussing the matter. Our main concern now is eliminating the Iranian threat."

"I see," Colburn broadly replied, deciding to prod for additional information. "Are you positive the Saudis require our assistance?"

"We're uncertain of Rahman's ability to confront the Iranians, however debilitated they may be." Sensing Colburn's reserve, the President posed his own question. "Do you think we should also ask the French to participate?"

"No," answered Colburn instantly. "I don't think that's quite necessary. The French can be difficult to deal with."

"Fine," concluded Allan Steiner. "Have your navy coordinate with Admiral Sparks on the Constellation. It's steaming into the Gulf right now."

"I'm not certain we can reach our people in the Gulf," replied Colburn. "Our communication has been out."

"Damn," muttered President Steiner, having forgotten his own communications problem.

Ed Rolle extended his hand to get the President's attention. "Can the British still communicate with their ambassador in Oman?"

The President nodded. "Chet, if you can get a message to Oman, we can fly it into your carrier."

"I suppose my people could do the same," replied Colburn. "We have ships south of Oman with whom we've been talking."

"That's settled then. For the time being, Chet, I'd like to see your military remain in Kuwait. We'll encourage the Saudis to leave as soon as possible."

"That should pose no problem. The Kuwait government invited us into their country during a similar crisis in 1961. I'm sure they would much prefer us over the Saudis."

Rolle placed a hand-written note before the President.

"Chet, your military people must be inoculated against the influenza. The necessary vaccine can be delivered to your consulate in Bahrain within the hour."

"This is all quite irregular, Allan. I suppose we've little choice, though. Kuwait holds a tenth of the world's oil reserves." Colburn paused for the American leader's response.

"Their oil's a powder keg . . . just like the Saudi oil, Chet. With you sitting on it, I'll be much relieved."

"Are you going to be *sitting* to the south, Allan?"

After a short pause, the President replied, "As long as there's a threat."

"That could be quite some time, Allan."

"That's what we've been thinking."

11:20 P.M.
In the Persian Gulf

The two Gulf Oil supertankers, moving sluggishly through the night water, passed one-half mile east of the anchored Czechoslovakian-registered freighter. Further to the east and screened by the tankers, an American submarine quickly surfaced and dispatched a rubber raft with three men. In their black wetsuits and hoods, the Marines blended well with the murky surface of the oil-slicked waters. As their sub slipped under the waves again, the men adjusted the water cylinders in their inflated raft. By the time the swells of the first tanker reached them, the raft had disappeared just below the surface.

"Line up!" ordered Lieutenant Hardie. The two other men positioned their hand-held waterfans on either side of the officer's fan.

"All right," Hardie announced, "move out!" Each of the fans was attached to the barely-submerged raft which now trailed behind the men.

The aft lookout on the freighter lit another cigarette with the smoldering butt of his first one and then flicked the butt into the water thirty feet below. He watched the red glow hit the water, taking little notice of the passing supertankers now turning sharply eastward, away from his ship.

The bow of the freighter was more active. Katrina, a tall, thick-thighed Ukrainian in her late thirties, checked the deck behind her to see if it was clear. That she was still unmarried was better explained by the bulk of her figure than its six-foot-two height. Her dark brown hair was worn long to better frame her two strongest assets, one of which was a moderately attractive face. The other asset occasionally interfered with the pleasure she sought at the bow of the ship.

"Frederic," she whispered.

An equally cautious voice called out, "Over here."

Watching her feet, Katrina stepped through piles of coiled ropes and moved toward the voice. A hand reached out to clutch the woman's broad skirt and roughly pulled her off-balance. Landing hard among the ropes, she coarsely mumbled, "*You pig!*"

"Yes, my pudding," Frederic agreed. "I am a hungry pig!"

Grabbing her loose blouse, he yanked it up. As she struggled to pull it the rest of the way over her head, he clutched a mountainous breast in his hands and feverishly buried his face in its warmth.

"Stop that, you fool!" protested Katrina, shaking her chest and jerking away. "I am not a *cow.*"

Frederic, a full foot shorter and considerably lighter than his lover, reconsidered his approach. Gazing at her full bosom in the moonlight, he placed his fingertips just below her shoulders and followed the flow of soft skin down to the rounded peaks of the breasts—each one larger than his head.

"My dear," he soothed, "you are a poor man's Sophia Loren."

Katrina snickered. "Compared to me, she is but a child."

Frederic kissed the tips of her other asset.

"Come, little man," she beckoned. "Tonight, it is your turn first."

She knew Frederic would not last long above, for he had little stamina. And there was no place he could comfortably prop his arms . . . as her shoulders were too wide, and the flesh of her immense bust overflowed into the space between her ribs and arms when she reclined on her back.

Three hundred yards from the freighter, Lieutenant Hardie split off from the two other Marines, who slipped on aqualungs before continuing with the raft.

When the lieutenant reached the bow, he attached a bear-claw (magnetic clamp-ring) as high as he could reach on the ship's side. After tying his fins and waterfan to the bearclaw, he pulled half his body out of the water and attached himself to its ring with a loop from his belt. From a watertight packet on his chest, he removed an arc-gun and four electronic suction cups, two of which he fitted onto his knees and the others to his hands. Buttons controlled by his thumbs and toes could release the suction of the cups.

Fifty yards from the stern, the two other Marines adjusted the raft to drop another ten feet below the surface before pulling it to the side of the freighter and securing it to the hull with a bearclaw. Removing tools and a coil of cable from the raft, they made their way down to the twin screws of the ship.

At the other end of the freighter, Hardie slowed his ascent as he approached the opening in the bow for the anchor chain. He poked his head into the opening and saw something move. Instantly dropping down, the Marine officer pulled his arc-gun from its holster and waited for the lookout to peer over the railing of the ship.

In the stillness, Hardie thought he heard the faint slapping of waves on the sides of the ship. Interspersed with these sounds, he also noticed deep animal-like noises coming from above. When the rhythmic grunting did not come nearer, the lieutenant inched his head above the rim of the anchor opening again.

Fifteen feet away, the moonlight illuminated what appeared to be a pair of great white balloons pumping up and down like giant pistons. Confused by the sight, Hardie wiped the salt water from his eyes and looked again. It was several seconds before he distinguished among the ropes a smaller second body under the heaving buttocks of the first one. Realizing what he was witnessing, Hardie stared a moment longer and dropped out of sight. *My gawd,* he grinned, *that gal's gonna pump a gusher*. He debated whether to wait or not. Having duly considered the question, the lieutenant raised himself and aimed his weapon.

A dark blue arc appeared for an instant between the muzzle of the weapon and Katrina's right buttock. The charge caused her to stiffen and jerk upright. She swayed unevenly.

"Katrina . . . oh, Katrina," moaned Frederic in ecstasy.

Hardie couldn't stifle a short chuckle before pulling his trigger again.

The woman's body shuddered and started to topple forward. Feeling part of the last charge himself, Frederic tried to twist away from the falling body. Katrina fell solidly over her lover.

Hardie hastily pulled himself over the railing, shifted his suction cups aside, and crawled to the struggling, semi-buried man.

"Sorry, Romeo," offered Hardie. He touched the arm of the trapped Russian with the muzzle of the arc-gun and squeezed again. Frederic quivered . . . then lay as still as the woman atop him. The lieutenant craned his neck down to locate the man's head. Not finding it, he checked the other side of the woman. Seeing nothing there either, he nudged Katrina's body sideways and located the man's face. Confirming he was also unconscious, Hardie let the woman's body settle over her lover again.

The American paused to check in the direction of the ship's bridge. Smiling to himself, he gathered the clothes of the couple and flung them overboard before moving away in a crouch.

Twenty feet from the couple, he stopped and quickly retraced his steps. Hardie found the lovers and lifted Katrina's right breast with one hand . . . searching for the man's head with his other hand. He grasped Frederic's hair and tugged at the head. When the man was in a position where he again could breathe, the American gently lowered the breast to the side of his face.

The funnel intake for the ship's fresh air was on the bow, as expected. Hardie easily identified it by feeling its inflow of air. Attaching a length of cord to the pins of two gas canisters, he securely taped the containers inside the funnel. After moving a safe distance away, Hardie pulled the cords and heard the hiss of escaping gas.

His descent from the bow was accomplished at twice the speed of his ascent. Recovering his gear, Hardie swam along the starboard waterline of the freighter until he met the other two Marines at midship. They silently moved away from the freighter, keeping the raft underwater until they'd traversed 150 yards.

At that distance, the officer removed a flasher from his chest packet and—shielding it with his head from the freighter—flickered its red beacon twice.

Within seconds, he saw a responding double-flash, and the three men commenced moving further from the ship.

Several minutes later, the rear lookout on the freighter spotted the two Gulf Oil supertankers again. Nine hundred yards directly behind his ship, they were moving at seven knots and precisely side-by-side with an interval of seventy-five yards. When their distance from the freighter had closed to 500 yards, the tankers had slowed to three knots. The lookout, deciding it was too late for the tankers to veer away, notified his bridge.

The commands from the bridge to the engine room went unheeded. Had they been acted upon, the result would have been the same. The ship's screws were hopelessly fouled.

The aft lookout failed to see the double line of anchor chain stretched between the sterns of the supertankers. The weight of the chains kept them well below the surface until the Gulf Oil ships approached on opposite sides of the freighter's stern. At that point, the chains were winched up until they hung between the supertankers . . . just above the surface.

When the American ships passed the position where the freighter had been, a Saudi fisherman near the shore remarked to his partner, "Where did the little ship go?"

The other fisherman peered out over the moonlit water. "Big fish eat little fish," he lamely offered. "Maybe big ships eat little ships."

Throwing a handful of octopus bait at his half-witted partner, the first fisherman cried out, "You son of a camel turd."

By dawn most of the military equipment aboard the freighter had been removed, its entire hull had been repainted, and the name on its bow had been sandblasted and replaced with a new one.

In the drydock of the Saudi Arabian port of Qatif, a weary group of British shipfitters trudged down the freighter's gangplank.

"Hey, Harve!" yelled a man behind him. "What happened to your shirt?"

The other men sniggered. The story of the embracing lovers at the ship's bow had passed quickly among the **workers.**

Adjusting the sandblaster on his shoulders, the bare-chested Briton replied, "I gave it to a lady."

"A *ladee—*, you say?" bellowed his taunter. "What's a lady doing stark-naked atop a bloke half her size?"

"Maybe she warn't no lady, mate," recanted Harve, "but I'm still a gentleman."

His laughing friends nearly shoved him off the gangplank.

The Second Day—10:30 A.M.
ARAMCO

Their presence no longer being required at the Saudi/Kuwait border, Prince Rahman and Louis Fricke returned to Dhahran by mid-morning of the next day. As the Saudi prince described his "triumph" in the Norlin living room, Fricke briefed the White House over the ham radio.

"We fired leaflets at them, Mr. President," explained Fricke.

"The Iranians fled because of a *leaflet?*" asked the President incredulously. "What'd it say?"

"It wasn't what it said as much as what it pictured. Most of the leaflet was a blow-up of a photograph taken of an atrocity committed by Saudi soldiers on the Russians at Dhahran."

"I remember Colonel Hemingway mentioning that."

"We doctored the photo a bit," confided Fricke, "so the Russians appeared to be Iranian soldiers."

"Was there any opposition at all?"

"No, sir. The leaflets were dropped late yesterday. By this morning when the Saudi and British units moved in, the only Iranians left were those too sick to move. Almost every car and truck in Kuwait was expropriated by the Iranian army last night."

"How many men did they leave behind?"

"Almost four thousand, sir. Most of whom we transferred onto ships and sent back to Iran."

"I didn't expect such a rapid resolution."

"Wait until you see the leaflet, sir."

"I think I'll pass on that," remarked the President. "Send Rahman in now."

The Saudi prince strode pretentiously into the bedroom and was motioned to sit on the chair near the ham radio by Ambassador Clark, who spoke into the mike. "Mr. President, this is Emory Clark. Prince Rahman and I are both here now."

"Prince Rahman," greeted the President, "I'm pleased your army was able to drive the Iranians from Kuwait so quickly."

Rahman replied in a grave tone "It was the will of Allah."

It was the lack of will of the Iranians, Allan Steiner thought, who paused a long moment and spoke in an even graver tone. "I have a matter I'd like to discuss with you, Rahman. What your people have done at the Lockheed compound in Riyadh is of extreme consequence."

The Saudi prince lowered his voice. "It is to be regretted."

"Is that all you can say?" the President demanded.

Rahman's eyes narrowed and he made no reply.

"You don't even want to offer an apology?" President Steiner scolded, his voice rising.

Rahman nervously glanced at Fricke and saw no support. The CIA man kept his eyes intently on the ham radio.

"Answer me!" Allan Steiner demanded.

Rahman was nearly inaudible. "It is an unfortunate—"

"*Unfortunate,* you say!" exploded the President. "Your people have murdered more than 50 citizens of the United States, and you call it unfortunate!"

A desperate silence pervaded the bedroom.

"I shall see," said Rahman softly, "that those responsible are punished."

Allan Steiner stated, "I understand that includes the king, Saleem, and yourself. What punishment do you have in mind?"

Rahman replied, "I cannot be held responsible for the acts of those who follow Prince Saleem. The men under my command have not harmed Americans."

"Who ordered the attack on the Puller?" the President asked abruptly.

"I do not believe the gunboat was Saudi," Rahman nervously offered.

"It flew your flag."

"Anyone could do that. Iranians . . . South Yemenis . . . even the Russians."

Partially conceding the point, President Steiner continued, "A videotape of the meeting you had with your brothers yesterday at the American embassy has already been delivered to the White House. We know what you told them."

Rahman flashed his eyes at Clark, trying to recall what he'd said with his brothers.

"Where's your brother, Saleem?" the President asked.

"I do not know. My *half-brother* committed a terrible error."

"You are not without guilt yourself, Rahman."

Beginning to grasp the American's intent, the Saudi prince asked his own question. "What is it you want?"

"Rational co-action." The words were spoken with great care.

After a moment, Rahman said; "I do not understand."

Allan Steiner paced his words in short phrases as if addressing a large rally. "To prevent aggression in the future against your country, we believe it would be prudent for Saudi Arabia to re-establish the partnership you had with the American oil companies who originally formed ARAMCO. Such an arrangement would permit us to safely remove most of our military units from your country."

After a significant pause, the President asked, "Do you understand me now?"

By remaining silent, the Saudi prince signified his rebuff of the American's proposal. Each man waited for his opponent to speak . . . and thereby concede. Having played the game longer, President Steiner closed his eyes and patiently began to count. After a full minute, Rahman could hear himself breathe in the stone quiet of the bedroom where every eye seemed to bore into him. When he could stand it no longer, the prince coughed, and started to speak.

"I understand, but—"

"There's more," interrupted President Steiner. "After adequate reparations are made to the families of Westerners slain in your country, we believe the balance of your foreign monetary assets should be utilized to transfer the nonperforming loans of Third World nations to the Saudi national bank."

Rahman's voice became unsteady. "What you ask is—"

"I *ask* nothing!" Allan Steiner asserted. "We're telling you what is going to happen. It was the foolishness of your leaders which left your oil fields open to foreign seizure . . . *and* your greed that indirectly led to the necessity for those Third World loans. The loans are *yours* now."

"I cannot explain this to my people," the Saudi prince whined.

The President turned friendly. "Rahman, as a precaution, the ARAMCO hospital pumped your brother's stomach. We asked them not to tell Asad what they found." He added, "It's fortunate for you that it was *our* doctors who discovered this rather than those on your 707."

The Saudi prince sat motionless before the radio, slowly comprehending how thoroughly he'd been tricked.

"Mr. President," interjected Clark, "I think it would be prudent to also disband the Saudi national guard."

Knowing that this of all the American demands was the most impossible, Rahman quickly protested. "That cannot be done! *They* would not permit it. These men are the direct descendents of the Bedouins who established Saudi Arabia."

"Yes," agreed Allan Steiner, "and later they nearly destroyed your new nation during the Ikhwan revolt. Have you forgotten why your father chose the palm tree of the settled, rather than the camel of the wandering Bedouin, for your national flag?"

Rahman was taken aback by the American's knowledge.

The former history professor answered his own question. "Because the Bedouin could not be trusted, Rahman. They fought for whoever offered the most money or bounty . . . and to this day they have not changed. You must rid your country of this scourge."

"I do not dispute your words," replied Rahman, "but to disband the Bedouins would only make them more uncontrollable. It would be better to spread them among my land forces."

Clark glanced to Louis Fricke who nodded in agreement. The Ambassador leaned over the mike. "Mr. President, I would concur with Rahman's suggestion."

"Tomorrow," concluded President Steiner, "we will both hold press conferences to announce these actions."

Rahman muttered, "I will have difficulty explaining this to my family."

"It will not be as difficult as the explanation I must give my people," countered the President, "for what your national guard has done."

When the prince made no further response, Allan Steiner told him, "Rahman, you were lucky this time. Tell that to your family."

10:42 A.M.
ARAMCO Hospital

"Tom, why'd you wait so long to come here?"

Still doped by the drugs they'd given him prior to surgery the previous night, Tom Hemingway repeated Sandi's question to himself, trying to get it clearer in his mind. When he'd awakened, she had been there—sleeping in a chair, her head and arms resting on his bed. He'd gazed at her dark brown hair for some time before realizing who she was. Through the eye holes of his head bandages, he studied her plaintive expression and shook his head slightly.

"I couldn't come earlier."

When she accepted the reply, he was relieved. He didn't want to talk . . . to think anymore. Tom turned away from her eyes and, after a long silence, asked, "Were you there?"

"Where?"

"Last night," he said, "when they worked me over."

"Yes."

He turned further away, again visualizing the hideousness he'd seen in the mirror at the Norlin home.

"I want to rest," sighed Tom.

Sandi stood slowly, understanding the despondency which affected nearly all patients with facial burns. "I'll tell the doctors you're awake," she told him. At the door Sandi hesitated and looked back to see whether his eyes had followed her. They hadn't. Walking silently back to the bed, she gently placed a hand on his arm and spoke softly, "I love you, Tom."

It was the first time she'd said the words to him, but he made no reply. Sandi hadn't expected a response, or needed one before she left. The need was his.

A few minutes later, a surgeon entered the room and cheerfully inquired, "How's the warrior this morning?"

Hemingway paused to contemplate the intruder. "Not so hot," he uttered.

"You're lucky not to be sore at the other end, too," smiled the surgeon. "In cases like yours, we normally carve a piece off the buttock."

The Marine colonel squeezed his buns together and sensed no pain. He gave the doctor a sideways glance.

Having piqued his patient's interest, the surgeon continued. "We usually transplant skin from the buttock to replace facial skin. But with your back injury, we decided to give you a break." The talkative doctor grinned broadly.

"Where'd you get it?" asked his patient.

"It's coming from Texas."

"Texas?" repeated Hemingway.

"That's right, Colonel. Last night, we put a square-inch of your facial skin on an F-18 to Houston. In five days, we'll get back a square foot."

"Of what?"

"Skin—an expanded autograft of your tissue culture," explained the doctor. "You'll probably look better after we've finished than you did before dodging that missile."

Hemingway settled easier in his bed. "Thanks, Doc."

"Don't thank me," said the doctor. "Thank the California pathologist who developed the expanded autograft."

"Who was he?"

"As I recall, it was A-something Freeman. Aaron Freeman, I believe."

Hemingway was reminded of the Saudi king. "How's Asad?"

The doctor shrugged. "He was fine when he left here. Except for an elevated blood pressure, Asad was in perfect health. He had no reason to go to London."

Sandi, carrying a tray of food, entered the room.

Winking at the nurse, the doctor addressed the Marine. "Do you know this lady, Colonel?"

The Marine nodded. "We've met."

"Well, I've got a few other patients this morning," said the doctor. "I'll check back later."

"Doc," Hemingway called out, "what's the word on my back?"

"X-rays were negative. Probably just a bad sprain." He waved and left. Without speaking, Sandi set the tray on the bed and began cutting the food into bite-sized pieces. After he'd begun to eat, she commented, "You're scheduled for a sponge bath after breakfast."

He continued chewing his food.

After a short while, Sandi half-smiled without looking up. "Would you like me to give it to you?"

Tom noticed she'd put on new lipstick and brushed her hair since she'd left. He swallowed and waited for the next bite.

"Suit yourself," Sandi remarked, a twinkle in her eyes. "The other nurse on duty in this wing is Pakistani. When you're finished eating, I'll send *him* in."

The initial alarm in the Marine's eyes was replaced by a brazen stare. "*You* can have the honors," he smiled.

1:00 P.M.
King Khalid International Airport Riyadh

Prince Rahman was reminded of the scenes he'd viewed as a child. Instead of Saudi horsemen racing across the desert astride their sleek Arabians though, his countrymen swept back-and-forth on the runways below in swift cars. His *victory* had been heralded on every radio and television station in the kingdom, and now it appeared every Saudi male with a vehicle had come to King Khalid airport to greet the "Liberator of Kuwait."

Each time Rahman made an approach in his F-15, hundreds of cars wildly converged in his landing pattern. Circling the airport after his sixth aborted approach, the fuel warning light on his console flashed red.

The Saudi prince pointed his fighter in the direction of the open desert and reached above his head to grasp the yellow handle attached to the seat. A sharp report followed his downward yank.

Choked with fear, Rahman rode his seat up the rails. Then everything became quiet. As he tumbled backward through space, the seat sailed away from him and Rahman glimpsed parachute lines racing past his head. A moment later, he felt a stiff jolt and his body whipped around. A full canopy blossomed above.

Able to breathe again, he gaped at the runways below. From every corner of the airfield, drivers scrambled toward the point where they expected him to land. Rahman was more concerned with avoiding the cars than the shock of hitting the tarmac. The closer he came to the ground, the more deafening was the blaring of the horns. His flight boots made contact with the hood of a Jaguar sedan and slipped beneath him, throwing Rahman's full weight onto the hood.

Before nightfall, the Jaguar owner would be offered three million riyals for his sedan . . . due to the near-perfect outline of Rahman's body on its hood. The owner took particular pride in pointing out the round indentation where the royal prince's helmet had slammed into the metal. Firmly refusing all offers, the car's driver repeated to all who would listen how his car had broken Rahman's fall from the sky.

As the Saudi prince regained consciousness, he found himself being carried above the clamoring crowd by countless hands. This directionless parade continued until the men below finally heard his shouted demands to be put down. Once on his feet, Rahman removed his helmet, unhooked his parachute harness, and began making his way from the center of hundreds of hopelessly-jammed cars.

Standing on the front seat of his white convertible, Prince Hamud viewed Rahman's procession slowly winding its way out of the massed cars and people. Hamud directed Irene to drive the Corniche close to the point where Rahman would eventually emerge. The other young men who had become national heroes with Hamud the previous day had also held back from the tangled charge to greet Rahman. Their vehicles followed alongside the Corniche in a column led by Prince Karrim's new BMW, and a file of jeeps containing members of the Royal Guard flanked Hamud's other side.

Prince Hamud yelled sharply to a Royal Guard officer in the lead jeep. The officer led a group of his men into the crowd's perimeter where they quickly extracted Prince Rahman from his admirers and led him to Hamud.

The two half-brothers embraced emotionally and sat on the convertible's back seat as Irene twirled the car away from the encroaching people. The twenty-eight miles of freeway into Riyadh were lined with more ecstatic Saudis who'd been unable to crowd into the airport. After winding through the capital, the procession ended at Rahman's palace.

Two hours before sundown, the governing body of the country was ushered into the receiving hall of Rahman's royal residence. The eleven eldest living sons of Abdul Aziz Al Saud entered the great hall in hushed silence, and some were shocked to see those already seated in the plush, rust-red armchairs along the perimeter of the barren, green room.

At the center of the high wall opposite the main entryway sat Prince Rahman, his chair slightly apart from those on either side. To his left the chairs were empty. On his right sat Hamud, Irene, Karrim, and the thirty-one other young men who'd survived the MiGs and Cubans at King Khalid airport. All those seated wore the traditional thobe and headdress, except for Irene, whose chador included a modest veil.

The eldest of Rahman's half-brothers, Prince Benhar, halted in the middle of the hall and waved an arm toward the seated young men whose thobes did not display gold braid. "Who are the non-blooded," he shrilly demanded, "who sit in my presence?"

Prince Rahman turned with casual aplomb to his right. "Of the men who faced the invaders of Riyadh," he boldly retorted, "these are the ones *whose blood still flows.*"

Benhar, unsatisfied with the explanation for the break in protocol, remained fixed in the center of the hall. When the rest of the Royal Council took chairs to Rahman's left, Hamud rose and approached Prince Benhar. Standing but a foot away from the elderly man, he exclaimed in a loud voice, "And *where* were you yesterday, my brave brother?"

Inflamed by the insinuation, Benhar reached inside his thobe and made a show of gripping his khanjar.

A high-pitched voice pierced the thickened atmosphere of the hall. "In the Name of Allah," intoned the Grand Imam of Riyadh, "we are honored in the presence of the warriors for Islam . . . whether they be sitting or standing."

Sheik Mansur, his entrance unnoticed till now, walked unhurriedly to the center of the hall, followed by several senior members of the Ulema. Bowing slightly to the seated young men, the Grand Imam prayed in a lowered voice.

"May Allah bring the warriors of Islam the same blessings which they have brought to this kingdom."

The Grand Imam shuffled toward Prince Rahman, taking the first chair to his left. All in the hall had found seats, except for Prince Benhar who made one last effort to save face. "The infidel woman," he spit out, "must *leave* before I sit!"

"Very well, my brother," Rahman smiled back. "You may remain standing . . . if you wish."

Doubly insulted, the old prince stalked from the hall.

"Bring in Habib!" Rahman promptly commanded.

At the same entrance from which the Grand Imam had emerged, two members of the mutawwa escorted Colonel Habib into the hall. One of them pulled the sleeve of the national guard officer, guiding him before the Royal Council. Those in the great room recognized Habib's gait and stiffened back as that of a man suffering the severe welts of the Syrian flail.

The second mutawwa carried a heavily-laden basket. When the trio halted, he spewed the contents of the basket before the feet of Habib.

Rings, necklaces, bracelets, watches, and other jewelry clattered angrily across the marble floor. The eyes of the ruling princes fixated on the sparkling array of silver and gold.

"*Colonel Habib!*" Rahman's voice boomed. "Who are the owners of the treasure at your feet?"

The officer mumbled his reply with bowed head. "It belongs to the foreigners of the Lockheed compound."

"Then *why* is this jewelry in my palace?" thundered Rahman in mock anger.

Habib slumped further. "Because it was taken from the foreigners."

Prince Rahman spoke in a half-whisper. "*Who* took it from the foreigners?"

"Members of the national guard," Habib slowly answered.

"Colonel Habib!" Rahman snapped. "Why were your men in the compound of the foreigners?"

Habib continued his well-rehearsed recitation. "We were in trucks on the way to the airport. As we passed the compound, we were ordered to stop and enter it."

"And *who* gave such an order?" demanded Rahman.

Habib's reply was barely audible. "Prince Saleem."

"In the Name of Allah!" shrieked Rahman. "Does this man lie?"

The mutawwa holding Habib's shirt sleeve loudly replied, "We have the same from three other officers. This one does not lie."

Rahman feigned genuine curiosity. "What were your men to do in the Westerner's compound, Colonel Habib?"

The national guard officer raised his head off his chest. "We were told to beat the foreigners. With our rifles, we struck the men, but when we also hit the women and children, their men protested and tried to seize our weapons. A shot was fired, and then more rifles were fired. In the end, it was necessary to kill everyone . . . that there be no survivors."

Prince Rahman delivered his last question after a lengthy pause and without anger. "And who gave this final order?"

Absolute silence in the hall amplified the dogged voice of the national guard officer. "I received this order from my commander, Prince Saleem."

Rahman flicked his wrist, indicating Habib's dismissal.

"Saleem is a madman!" exclaimed Prince Karrim.

In the spirited discussions which followed, neither Hamud nor Rahman could discern what was being said in the multiple arguments around them. This tumult continued for several minutes until Prince Rahman signalled with a glance to Sheik Mansur. As the Grand Imam stood and paced to the center of the hall, Rahman and Hamud shouted the others into silence.

"In the Name of Allah, the Compassionate, the Merciful," began the sheik, "there can be no doubt who is responsible for bringing shame to our kingdom. And there can be no hesitation for what we must do."

"We have *no* Crown Prince!" bellowed Prince Karrim. When the cries of affirmation had subsided, the Grand Imam inquired loudly, "Where is Prince Saleem now?"

"He boarded the Abdul Aziz," replied Rahman promptly, "in the Red Sea early this morning."

"So be it," announced the Grand Imam. "The royal yacht shall be his prison. He will not return to the soil of our kingdom."

Rahman stood on cue. "I shall inform the king." Sheik Mansur and Rahman left the hall together.

When Asad's hospital room in London was reached, Rahman described the confession of Colonel Habib and the decision concerning Prince Saleem before handing the phone to the Grand Imam.

For the next hour, Sheik Mansur spoke in hushed tones with Asad. When he finally placed the phone in its cradle, the sheik turned to Rahman. "The king will take full responsibility for inviting the Americans into the kingdom. He announces his abdication in the morning."

A short while later, after the Grand Imam revealed Asad's decision to those in the palace hall, the Royal Council reacted as Rahman, Hamud, and the Grand Imam had anticipated. The new leaders of Saudi Arabia spent the balance of the night preparing for the press conference the following morning.

There was little opposition by the ruling council to the plan they drew up . . . after it was explained how most of the foreign monetary reserves would be safeguarded and that production in the oil fields would be reduced by eighty percent during the presence of the oil companies.

The Third Day—4:45 A.M.
ARAMCO

"The phone's working!" declared Kevin, startled by its first ring in forty-eight hours.

"Well, answer it," instructed his mother.

Dori jumped up from the breakfast table first and grabbed the phone before her brother. After saying, "Hi," she listened for a moment and looked up. "Mom, a lady wants to talk to Ambassador Clark."

"You'd better wake him up."

Dori ran down the hallway and rapped on the door to Kevin's bedroom.

"Yes?" came a tired voice.

The girl spoke through the door. "There's a woman on the telephone for you."

"I'll be right out," replied Clark. Tucking a loose shirt into his trousers, Emory Clark came into the kitchen and took the phone. "This is Ambassador—"

"Hi, Dad," a cheery voice interrupted.

"*Irene* . . . where are you?" He quickly added, "Are you okay?"

"Sure, everything's fine," Irene responded. "I'm in Riyadh. At the television station."

"Can you get out of there?" asked her father with great concern.

"Out of where?"

"Riyadh," he pointedly replied.

"Why should I?" Irene blankly asked. "Aren't you coming back?"

"For the time being," he firmly told her, "it's better that you come to Dhahran."

"Dad, we'll talk about that in a minute. I called to tell you who the new king is."

"Prince Rahman," Clark irritably stated, instantly regretting his lapse. Thinking someone might be listening on the line, he asked, "Am I right?"

"Yes," she answered. "How'd you know?"

"I guessed. What's happened to Saleem?"

"He's banned from the country." Irene merrily added, "Guess who the *new* crown prince is?"

"Who?"

"Prince Hamud," she proudly told her father.

"You're kidding?"

"In a few minutes, it'll be announced on Riyadh TV. Hamud asked me to notify you."

"I'm glad you called, honey. And I'm also concerned for your safety. Is there any way you could get to Dhahran?"

"Now?"

"Yes, now."

Irene hesitated. "Dad, after Rahman's coronation tonight, there's going to be a celebration at his palace. I'm invited, and I don't want to miss it."

"*You* were invited?"

"I think I'm part of it. They're going to make me an honorary princess . . . or something like that. I've got to go now, Dad. Watch the TV."

"Honey, be careful."

"Don't worry about me. I've got a thirty-three-man bodyguard."

Clark was puzzled again. "Who are *they*?"

"Hamud and the thirty-two other Saudis who survived the

fight at King Khalid Airport."

After a thoughtful pause, Clark told his daughter, "Call me tomorrow, okay?"

"Sure, Dad. Love you."

"I love you, Irene." She had hung up before hearing him. The half-dazed father glanced at the Norlin family gathered around their breakfast table eagerly awaiting some explanation from him.

"That was my daughter," Clark stated vacantly. "She's in Riyadh and acts like she's going to a picnic." He pivoted and started down the hall to his room, then stopped . . . trying to remember something. Spinning around, he exclaimed, "Get everyone up! There's going to be an important announcement on television."

One minute before 5 a.m., the ARAMCO TV station came on the air and revealed they'd be transmitting for Riyadh TV. An imam commenced the recitation of morning prayers. By the end of the prayers, everyone in the Norlin household was gathered close to the TV screen in order to read the English translations.

The face of Sheik Mansur appeared on the screen. When he spoke, his painfully hesitant delivery gave viewers the impression each word had been fastidiously chosen.

"In the Name of Allah, the Compassionate, the Merciful . . . the message I give you is of profound sadness. King Asad has suffered yet another heart attack . . . of greater severity than the ones before. Due to his condition, he has asked to renounce his throne."

The sheik continued. "The Royal Council and the Ulema . . . refusing to accept his decision . . . devoted the hours of last night attempting to dissuade him. Only when the king's physicians pled with us to spare his life . . . did we agree to his renunciation. Saudi Arabia will never have another king . . . who will compare as well to his father—the great Abdul Aziz Al Saud." The Grand Imam paused.

"What a crock of—" Fricke caught himself in mid-sentence. "I've never heard such baloney."

"It is my duty," the sheik resumed, "to now reveal the

judicial report concerning the conduct of our national guard units at King Khalid Airport two days ago. While Saudi Land Forces fought to the death defending our kingdom, the national guard fled before the infidels arrived. Crown Prince Saleem, their commander, has decided to take full responsibility for the acts of his men. Therefore, he has chosen self-exile . . . and relinquished his succession to the throne of the kingdom. For twelve hours, the Royal Council delayed acceptance of his great sacrifice . . . in the hope he would return to Saudi Arabia. To our sorrow, Prince Saleem has not returned."

Sheik Mansur stopped to lower his head, as if in prayer.

In the Norlin living room, everyone stirred for the first time in several minutes.

"Yesterday," began Fricke, "Rahman told me he'd been unable to keep his men who survived the initial attack from running also."

John Norlin asked, "Is *any* of that true?"

"Most of what he said was to save face," explained Clark.

"Whose face?" inquired Norlin.

"Anyone," Clark said, "who's involved with Asad or Saleem."

Sheik Mansur resumed. "When King Asad was told of Saleem's sacrifice, he recommended to the Royal Council that Prince Rahman be appointed his successor. After much debate, the Royal Council and the Ulema have assented to Asad's choice. Praise to Allah . . . Saudi Arabia is ruled by a new king."

The camera panned to the rear of Sheik Mansur where a group of Saudi men began chanting "Allah Akbar" with moderate enthusiasm. After the chant was repeated precisely fifteen times, Rahman and Hamud appeared at the microphone hand-in-hand. Rahman, with exaggerated dignity, spoke first.

"In the Name of Allah, the Passionate, the. . ."

Redfaced, Rahman began again. "In the Name of Allah, the Compassionate, the Merciful, we must pray for the health of my brother, Asad. We also must pray for the return of Prince Saleem. And we must seek out and punish those who have brought discredit to my brother, Saleem, and thereby return him to a place of honor."

The new king drew Hamud closer to the microphone. "The true hero of King Khalid Airport stands beside me . . . where he shall remain as long as I am king of Saudi Arabia. Prince Hamud is the choice of the Royal Council to be our new crown prince."

Though it was repeated but ten times, the chanting of "Allah Akbar" was significantly louder than before.

Releasing Hamud's hand, Rahman continued. "Of greater importance than even the announcements you have now witnessed is the decision of the Royal Council concerning the oil fields of the kingdom. To safeguard the resources of Saudi Arabia, we have asked the United States to temporarily assist the military forces of Saudi Arabia in protecting the oil fields. To ensure the long-term security of this national resource, the Royal Council also has requested our former partners in ARAMCO to resume their previous participation in the management of the oil fields. Our American friends have reaffirmed their friendship by agreeing to this request."

In the ARAMCO compound, Fricke snickered and commented, "Nice job, Rahman."

The new king took a paper from inside his thobe. As he began to read, his voice lost its imperious edge. "It is said we are the chosen people of Allah . . . and this is true. Was not the Great Prophet born on our soil? And are we not the guardians of the centers of Islam—Mecca and Medina? For this, Allah has rewarded our kingdom with oil, and we have benefited bountifully from its sale. We have been engulfed by a sea of extravagances. It has also been said: 'One of the paradoxes of Arabian oil is that it lies thickest where it benefits the fewest.' My brothers, this imbalance *must end* . . . or our kingdom will not survive."

As Rahman paused to catch his breath, John Norlin declared, "I can't believe what I'm hearing."

"Don't," Fricke advised.

Rahman went on. "It is Allah's will that we use our immense wealth to solve the problems of our poor neighbors, many of which are Islamic. If we fail to help them, they will continue to fall under the influence of opportunists . . . and when that occurs, as we have seen in South Yemen, Afghanistan, and Ethiopia, their problems become *our* problems." The new king gazed intently into the camera to emphasize his point.

In the living room of the ARAMCO compound, Ambassador Clark softly observed, "If they only believed half of what they say."

Rahman continued. "Therefore, the Royal Council with my approval and that of Crown Prince Hamud has decided to loan our foreign reserves to the International Monetary Fund . . . with express instructions that our wealth be reloaned to the people of Third World nations. By this act of generosity, both they and we shall benefit."

"Those smart sonofabitches," muttered Fricke under his breath. He checked his watch. "Ambassador, the press conference in Washington is *already* in progress."

Clark shook his head. "It should have been scheduled before this one." He touched Dori's shoulder. "Young lady, we need your help with the radio again."

Confirming President Steiner was at his press conference, Ambassador Clark told the War Room, "This is an emergency! You've got to get this message to the President. Rahman has announced that Saudi foreign reserves will be loaned to the I.M.F. for the benefit of Third World nations. If necessary, *interrupt* President Steiner to give him my message."

Returning to the living room, Dori and the two men saw Crown Prince Hamud speaking on the TV screen.

". . .conflicts in the Middle East, without intervention by non-Islamic nations."

"I think he's cute!" exclaimed Dori. "He looks like a movie star."

Hamud smiled. "My next words directly concern all Saudi men over the age of thirty years. The Royal Council has decreed you shall elect representatives to a Provincial Council, and this council will advise the King and me on matters concerning *all citizens* of our kingdom. With this measure, Saudi Arabia shall take its position among the democratic nations of the world."

The Saudis in the studio, which included all of Hamud's retinue, repeated, "Állah Akbar!" with a renewed fury.

John Norlin asked of no one in particular, "Why didn't they say anything about the massacre?"

"They did," Fricke told him. "In the discussion of Saleem and his national guard at the airport. It was unsaid . . . but understood."

"It doesn't make sense to me," Norlin replied.

"If they're going to punish the soldiers who were at the Lockheed compound," explained Fricke, "it must appear they were cowards in battle."

"They're all lying scoundrels," concluded Norlin.

Emory Clark shook his head at the statement. He'd been a diplomat too long to let it pass. "I don't know as if I would say that," reflected Clark. "Actually, they're little different from our Italian, French, or—for that matter—Japanese *allies.* If anything, they're more clever."

No one disputed his words.

The messenger from the War Room handed the note to Jim Hoolihan, who stood behind President Steiner with the secretary of state. Skimming the message, the presidential assistant placed it on the speaker's rostrum and did not withdraw his hand until the President stopped speaking to read it. Displaying no change of expression, President Steiner resumed his press statement.

"It is my belief this will provide an enduring stability to the Persian Gulf region, much as we've seen prevail in Western Europe due to the continued presence of our military units. American Air Force and Army units have been garrisoned in Western Germany since the end of World War II, and it has been a small price to pay for nearly a half-century of prolonged peace in Europe." The unsmiling President looked up from his rostrum. "This concludes my prepared statement."

A third of the reporters in the packed auditorium broke for the doors. Those remaining, crowded closer to the podium. Allan Steiner pointed among the waving hands to a familiar face.

"Mr. President, Fred Swegles of *The Dallas Times*. Your statement was somewhat unclear concerning the responsibility for the massacre of Westerners in Riyadh. Could you elaborate?"

The President inhaled deeply. "We're attempting to obtain additional information concerning that subject. So far, we only

know what the Saudis have told us. . .that it was a senseless
act by a maverick group of private Bedouin soldiers."

Before another member of the press could be selected, the
same correspondent spoke again. "Mr. President, a source at
the Saudi Arabian embassy suggested the massacre could have
been related to bombs dropped by an American plane on units
of the Saudi army at the capital's airport. Is this true?"

Studying his questioner a moment, President Steiner replied, "Why didn't you ask that question in the first place, Mr.
Swegles?"

Allan Steiner addressed everyone in the press room. "In
fact, we did have one aircraft drop a few bombs in an open area
of Riyadh's airport for the purpose of staging a mock attack.
This was necessary to confirm our military commitment to any
advance agents of the invading force from South Yemen. The
bombs damaged nothing other than the surface of a runway,
and the Saudi military were fully aware of our mission before-
hand. In addition, the Marine pilot of our aircraft reported no
military units on the airfield at the time he placed the bombs,
so there can be no causal relationship between the two events
mentioned by Mr. Swegles. One of them never occurred."

President Steiner returned his attention to the Texan.
"That's not the answer you were looking for, is it, Mr. Swegles?" The reporter didn't respond.

"Let's try it from another angle," grimaced the President.
"If my decision to deter the flight from Afghanistan had *not*
been made, it's unlikely that those Americans would have died.
Therefore, I could—conceivably—be blamed for their deaths.
Whether the results of the last two days will be worth the high
price we've paid is a question I shall silently debate every day
for as long as I live."

After a short delay, President Steiner pointed to another
hand.

"Mr. President, Bob Morrison of *The New York Times*. Why
did a Saudi gunboat attack the Puller in the Persian Gulf?"

"Mr. Morrison, when we were invited to occupy Dhahran
Air Base, we received assurances our forces would not be opposed by the Saudi military. In all likelihood, the attack on the

Puller was due to a failure in communication. This assumes, of course, that the gunboat was manned by Saudis. Before destroying it, we didn't stop to confirm the nationality of those aboard."

The President chose another reporter.

"Mr. President, Mary Shiffren of the *Los Angeles Times*. Will the freeze of Saudi foreign reserves be lifted eventually, as was the 1979 freeze on Iranian assets?"

"I'm glad you asked that question, Ms. Shiffren. We have already informed the new leaders of Saudi Arabia that, after adequate restitution is made to the families of American victims, we'd like to see the balance of these assets go to the International Monetary Fund. Lifting the freeze depends on how the Saudis respond."

"Mr. President, Jim Christensen of the *Philadelphia Inquirer*. Does the freeze on Saudi assets include investments such as Suliman Olayan's minority ownership in the Chase Manhattan Bank?"

"This will depend on the needs of Third World nations," the President replied, selecting another reporter in front.

"Mr. President, Irwin Zucker of the *Miami Herald*. Did our military assist the Saudis in driving the Iranians from Kuwait?"

"We did offer protection of their oil fields when they transferred army units north," the President answered rapidly and just as quickly pointed to another correspondent.

"Mr. President, Ted Miller of the *Atlanta Constitution*. Many military experts were amazed by the lightning speed in which the unseasoned Saudi army routed the vastly more-experienced Iranian army. Can you explain how this happened, and what role other representatives of the United States might have played?"

No, I can't tell you, thought Allan Steiner, *and you know it.* He hesitated too long, signaling his search for a valid subterfuge and thereby revealing more by his delay than he would in subsequent words.

"Of course, we offered the Saudis encouragement and other minor forms of assistance. To say what was the pivotal influence would be speculative at this time."

Miller's tone was friendly and inquisitive. "Mr. President, did you just answer my question?"

After scattered laughter, the auditorium fell silent as the press corps waited to see if more would be revealed.

"All too soon," lectured the former professor, "you will get the details of that operation, from many divergent sources—all of whom will represent themselves as being unquestionably reliable. I'm not unfamiliar with the making of history, including the role which the press can play, and I would advise you to carefully sift your findings. Frequently, there is no infallibly identifiable cause for a historical event. It just happened."

Another hand shot up. "Mr. President, Greg Hill of the *Des Moines Register*. "Do you expect Congress to endorse our military presence in Saudi Arabia?"

The President made a tired smile. "Over the next sixty days, I'm sure we'll have a lively debate in the halls of Congress on the subject. I also believe my actions are a valid extension of the Eisenhower Doctrine—that the United States is committed to provide military assistance to any Middle Eastern country requesting such aid against overt aggression from any nation controlled by international communism." Pausing for the reporters to write down his last remark, the President then asked, "How many of you recall President Eisenhower's statement in 1957 when he declared, "The existing vacuum in the Middle East must be filled by the United States before it is filled by the Russians?" A few heads nodded.

"While I am President of the United States, the vacuum in Saudi Arabia *will not* reappear."

Applause for his words—an unusual response among the press—gradually filled the entire room. Briefly acknowledging the ovation, President Steiner gathered his notes and exited the auditorium.

After entering the Oval Office with his secretary of state, the President stood looking out the tall windows behind his desk. Turning wearily, he caught the eye of Clayton Walters. Each man contemplated the other.

For something to say, President Steiner asked, "Who do you think will replace Derevenko?"

Walters shrugged. "Rolle only knows he's out. We don't have any idea who his successor will be yet."

Considering for a moment the disastrous consequences of the Soviet leader's decisions, the President shook his head at the thought of his own decisions. Derevenko was gone. Asad was gone. How many people were dead? He was beginning to feel the awesome and dreadful power of his office.

"Clayton . . . you know why Jimmy Carter didn't get re-elected?"

His secretary of state knew to wait for the answer.

The President sneered. "The American people don't want a decent, God-fearing, honest man in this office." He paused to sit at his desk and calmly surveyed its broad expanse before continuing.

"They want an arrogant, fearless leader . . . hard-nosed in negotiations . . . unscrupulous when necessary . . ." his voice trailed off, and he thought, *everything I don't want to be.*

Walters nodded sagely. "With the exceptions of Ford and Carter, our Presidents since 1960 have been bona fide rascals . . . everyone of them. That's what this office demands."

And I'm supposed to be a professor of history, reflected Allan Steiner.

The Fourth Day—3:00 P.M.
ARAMCO

"Prince Hamud, you cannot do that."

The Saudi prince smiled apologetically. "It is not I, Ambassador Clark, who determines it."

"In the eyes of the Western world," Clark tersely stated, "such an act will set your country back a hundred years!"

The smile on Hamud's face altered to one of self-amusement. He had expected the American to say a *thousand*. "It is out of my hands," Hamud replied.

"Then you must speak to those who do control it," Clark admonished.

"These are judicial matters, to be governed by the Ulema," Hamud patiently explained. "No one can tell them how to conduct such affairs."

"Hamud," interjected Irene, "why can't you go directly to the Grand Imam, as you did to gain entrance to Riyadh TV?"

"That was not a legal matter," Hamud told her.

Clark shook his head vigorously. "There *must* be another way."

"You are wrong, Ambassador. For my people, there can be no other way. All the citizens of Saudi Arabia must experience it . . . or the act will have no meaning."

"That's preposterous!" The American's words were uttered more in frustration than anger.

Hamud's voice remained calm. "Ambassador Clark, you have been in my country more than three years, yet you still do not know my people."

"Prince Hamud, it is not the end result which we dispute. It's *the uncivilized manner* of reaching that result!"

"There are many—maybe even a majority—in Saudi Arabia who think as I do . . . and we agree with Westerners that it is barbaric." Hamud frowned with his admission. "But we are controlled too often by a minority that is more vocal . . . more violent . . . more prone to follow their emotions than that which is logical."

"Why is that so?" Clark asked mildly.

"I do not know," offered Hamud. He bowed his head to avoid the American's stare and debated whether to reveal his thoughts. "Perhaps," began the Saudi, "it is due to the ancient custom which encourages the Arab to intermarry with cousins. As many as one-third of marriages in traditional Arab societies are between first cousins."

Irene stiffened in her chair. "That's unbelievable."

"Yes," nodded Hamud without looking up. "They account for an unbelievable number of hereditary diseases. Saleem comes from such a union. Two of his full-brothers are so high-strung they've been under care since childhood."

Clark spoke solemnly. "You must work to change such practices."

"We are," Hamud looked up eagerly. "Only a generation ago, more than half the marriages in my country were between first cousins."

The ambassador dropped his jaw in awe.

Hamud looked to Irene for her response and found downcast eyes. Standing to conclude the interview, the Saudi prince spoke with studied patience.

"Ambassador Clark, one of my reasons for coming here is to escort you back to Riyadh. I will take you before the king, and you may protest to him if you wish."

"After what happened to the embassy," Clark said, "I'm

not sure I should return so soon."

Hamud gave a small shrug. "It was only the first floor which was damaged. You shall be my personal guest and under my protection."

"I'll let you know tomorrow if I can return to Riyadh." Clark contemplated the Saudi prince a moment. "I understand you're going over to Bahrain this evening."

"Yes," smiled Hamud, "the rulers of the Persian Gulf states are honoring your daughter and me with a lavish banquet. You may accompany us if you wish."

Clark shook his head. "No, I have too much work to do here. I shall see you tomorrow."

———

It was one o'clock in the morning as Irene lingered with Hamud in the candlelit palace gardens of Bahrain's king. After they'd sat silently for some time on a bench before a pool of giant goldfish, Hamud reached within his thobe. When his hand came out, it held an object wrapped in black silk. He held it before her.

"This is for you."

Irene placed her palms together to receive the gift and was surprised at its heaviness.

Hamud took a corner of the black silk and gently lifted it, revealing a wide-band platinum bracelet. Inlaid around the band were 33 pear-shaped, one-carat diamonds in alternating clear and green colors. The glittering sight took away Irene's breath.

"It is fit for a queen," he whispered into her ear.

She could only voice one thought. "How much did this cost?"

He laughed at her frankness and said, "One hundred thousand of your dollars." It had cost considerably more.

Irene shook her head in disbelief.

"I want you to stay with me," Hamud told her.

"How can that be?" She looked directly at her lover. "A crown prince must take a Saudi woman as his wife."

"I need not marry," he quickly responded, taking her hands. "Do you love me?"

She made a grim smile and nodded. "You know the answer."

"Then it's settled!" Hamud ardently exclaimed.

Irene remained expressionless.

He raised an eyebrow and asked, "What is wrong?"

"Hamud, I'm not anxious to get married and have children like most women. So it isn't the fact we can't marry which bothers me."

"What bothers you then?"

She concentrated on the goldfish. "In your country, I would be as one of them."

"Them?" Hamud looked at her quizzically.

"I could not live in a society where I would be so restricted . . . even to what I wear. No movies, no theatre, no restaurants, no sports we could openly share together."

"We are trying to change much of that," he insisted. "It will be much better in the future."

Irene looked up with forlorn eyes. "I will be an old woman before that time. Saudi Arabia would be a prison to me."

"Okay," Hamud soothed, "you shall not live in Saudi Arabia. You can live in Europe . . . on the Riviera. We'll have a villa in Cannes."

"And what will you do when you're not in Cannes?"

"What do you mean?"

"Who will share your bed in Riyadh?"

"I love only you," he insisted playfully.

"I want to believe you," Irene reflected. She paused to yawn. "But I've never heard of a Saudi man who had only one woman when he could afford more . . . especially in your family."

Hamud made a short, derisive laugh. "I do not follow all the customs of my country."

"I remember reading only a few months ago," Irene said, "the words of a religious authority in Medina. He actually favored polygamy over monogamy."

Hamud's wan smile gradually disappeared.

Irene stood and wrinkled her eyes at him. "Because of what we've experienced, we have a stronger bond than just love."

Hesitantly, Hamud cupped her knees with his hands. The

hands moved up the sides of her slim body, stopping at her high ribs. "This is true, my fire goddess," he murmured.

Irene gently pulled his head to her breasts . . . then turned his face to hers and kissed him lightly.

"I shall leave in the morning." She offered the bracelet back to Hamud.

Irene would never forget the shadow of sadness which for a long moment darkened his face.

He nodded to the diamond-encrusted bracelet. "It is yours," Hamud quietly told her, "for the green dress."

When her face brightened, his rakish smile came round again, and he suggested an even greater exchange.

"And let this be a night we shall always remember."

———————◆———————

The Friday Following—11:00 A.M.
Riyadh

A liveried servant held the door of the gray limousine for the Crown Prince and Ambassador Clark. When the two men were seated, Hamud spoke the only words of their journey to his driver.

"The big square."

The *friends of Hamud*, as they were now known, also entered limousines at the foot of the broad marble steps leading from Hamud's palace. Two dozen jeeps of the Royal Guard brought up the rear.

By the time this procession was within a mile of the largest square in Riyadh, their progress was slowed by the throngs of Saudi men also moving toward the Dira. After a minute of watching the people afoot moving more quickly than his vehicle, Hamud snapped, "Stop the car! We must walk."

The Royal Guard hastily abandoned their jeeps to form a vanguard and began repeating, "Make way for the Crown Prince!" The white-uniformed soldiers reinforced their exhortations by brusquely shoving those who were slow to move aside.

When Hamud was a block from the Dira, he directed his group down a side street toward the rear of the Palace of Justice. Once inside the building which was normally closed to foreigners, Emory Clark noted the contrast between the whitethobed crowd within and the green-tiled ceilings, walls, and floor of the massive lobby. Most of the Saudis milling about wore gold-trimmed thobes of the royal family, and with the entrance of Hamud, a momentary hush fell over them. While older members of the Saud family glared at the new Crown Prince, most of the men looked aside in respect as Hamud spearheaded a path through the lobby for his retinue. They hurried up a staircase and entered the inner sanctum of the minister of justice. Hamud presented the American ambassador to Sheik Mansur, but there was no conversation. Clark had been warned earlier the sheik neither spoke nor understood English. The three men and Hamud's friends stepped out onto a second-floor balcony overlooking the square.

The Dira was packed shoulder-to-shoulder with Saudi men in white thobes. Mingling with the buzz of their voices were blaring loudspeakers from which a muezzin recited the Koran in a steady monotone. Obliquely to his left at a distance of seventy-five yards, Clark recognized the Great Friday Mosque—the largest in Riyadh—where religious services were still in session. Two-hundred-and-fifty yards directly across the square was the relatively modest three-story palace from which the Saudi king would observe the noon proceedings. The other fortress-like buildings fringing the quadrangle held various government ministries.

The attention of the American ambassador was drawn to the center of the northern half of the square where a fifty-by-fifty-foot wooden platform had been constructed under a watch tower—the site where public floggings and other punishments were meted out at noon on the Muslim holy day of the week. Standing seven feet above the ground, the platform was barren except for the placement of thirty-six white towels . . . laid out in symmetrical rows of six each. The surface of the platform appeared slightly lower on the side nearest the Great Mosque, as if it had been built too hastily. Parked along this side of the platform was a line of black ambulances—their rear doors backed up to the wooden structure. Clark turned to speak with Hamud, but the Crown Prince had moved away to converse with others.

It was near noon in eastern Saudi Arabia. The streets of ARAMCO were empty—its residents driven inside by the oppressive heat. Many of them had crowded into the meeting room of the compound's recreation center. The fortunate sat in closely arranged rows of chairs, while others stood at the sides and back of the large room. The weekly nondenominational services had been relocated due to an anticipated increase in attendance on this Friday.

The leader of the services, dressed in her customary white dress brightly embroidered with flowers, sat in the middle of a double row of chairs facing the gathered people. Someone from behind tapped her shoulder, and Diana Lindsay turned her head.

Hadn't we better get started?" suggested the choir member. "It's getting muggy in here."

Checking her watch, Diana whispered back, "Another three minutes."

Her gaze wandered from the five vacant chairs directly in front of her to the statuesque brunette sitting to the immediate right of the reserved chairs. Diana didn't recall seeing the young woman before, and she wondered how many others in the room had come simply to catch a glimpse of their specially invited guest.

When Diana checked her watch again, she was surprised that ten more minutes had elapsed. As she surveyed the waiting people, she noticed a few parents trying to calm their restless children. Closing her eyes a moment to compose herself, Diana stood and stepped to the head of the center aisle.

She raised her Bible and spoke in a clear, serene voice. "We will begin today where we were interrupted one week ago— *Matthew, Chapter 5, Verse 10.*" After pausing for others with Bibles to find the passage, Diana began to read.

"Blessed are those who hunger and thirst for righteousness, for they shall be satisfied. Blessed are the merciful, for they shall obtain mercy. Blessed are the pure in heart, for they shall see God. Blessed are the peacemakers, for they shall be called the sons of God."

Noting a small commotion at the far end of the aisle, Diana glanced up.

Her eyes were instantly drawn to a brilliant hue of blue—the uniform of a man standing between a boy and girl. Colonel Hemingway, in borrowed Marine Corps dress blues, stood motionless and erect with his hands braced on the shoulders of Dori and Kevin. The twins' parents waited behind.

Diana Lindsay smiled. "I think," she genially announced, "we're being invaded again."

The others in the room quickly shifted their attention to the Marine's resplendent blue uniform. The radiance of his regalia nearly distracted them from the white bandages covering the left half of his head and his right hand.

"This time," Diana beckoned the new arrivals forward, "please join us."

Pacing slowly with shortened steps, Hemingway started down the aisle, half-supporting himself on Dori and Kevin. A couple in the back of the room began to lightly clap their hands. They continued their rhythmic applause until, with restraint, a few others joined in.

When the Marine recognized a man sitting on the aisle who had helped pull him from the burning Harrier, he paused. The civilian wore bandages over both arms. Lifting his uninjured hand off Dori's shoulder, Hemingway extended it to the man before realizing the civilian's hands were too heavily wrapped in burn dressings to be touched. The man stood as applause built in the room . . . and for the first time in his life, the Marine pilot embraced another man. After grasping the shoulder of his rescuer, Hemingway instinctively pulled the man to him in an awkward hug.

As they parted, their eyes met, and Hemingway attempted to speak his gratitude. His throat tightened instead. He offered an embarrassed smile and experienced another first.

Other faces had crowded around . . . and they too fought back tears with broad grins. *Hey*, Hemingway told himself, *cut that out*. Hands appeared to move in slow motion around him, making repeated soft impressions on his arms and shoulders. He tried to turn his misting eyes from the blurred faces, but could not. They were everywhere.

Moving down the aisle, Hemingway spotted another of his rescuers attempting to applaud with bandaged hands. The pilot stopped the twins again and gradually made his way between rows to the second rescuer.

The two men reached out to another, gripping forearm to forearm. Any words they might have spoken would have been lost in outburst of acclaim now filling the room.

Returning to the aisle, Hemingway raised his chin, no longer trying to fight his natural emotions. A salty tear stung the still raw flesh of his left cheek. He and the twins made their way to the front of the room as the ovation began to abate. Arriving at the reserved chairs, Hemingway shuffled his escorts to gain the seat beside Sandi. He avoided her eyes, trying to gain control of his own.

The release of sentiment in the room provided a peculiar cleansing effect for those present, followed by an uneasy silence—a short moment forever etched in their memories.

Diana Lindsay said with a struggle, "Let us pray silently."

In the absolute stillness which followed, Hemingway reached into a pocket of his uniform and withdrew a small box. When it was open, he turned to Sandi. Her head was bowed with closed eyes. Melted mascara streaked her cheeks.

He leaned nearer and whispered. "I pray . . . you'll marry me."

Blinking her eyes, Sandi slowly looked up and followed his gaze down to the ring. She remained thoughtful a few seconds, tried a skittish grin, and whispered back, "Is it Marine Corps issue?"

He nodded seriously. It was. Or nearly so, as a friend had purchased it from the exchange on the Constellation.

When Diana Lindsay raised her bowed head, she saw the brunette lightly brush the Marine's lips with her own.

In a voice that faltered at first, the woman in the flowered-white dress resumed the *Sermon on the Mount:*

"You have heard it said, 'You shall love your neighbor and hate your enemy.' But I say to you, love your enemies and pray for those who persecute you, so that you may be sons

of your Father who is in Heaven. For if you love only those
who love you, what reward have you?"

"Judge not, that you be not judged. For with the
judgment you pronounce, you will be judged. And the
measure you give will be the measure you get."

"Ask, and it will be given you. Seek, and you will find.
Knock, and it will be opened to you. For every one who asks
receives, and he who seeks finds, and to him who knocks,
it will be opened."

"And in praying, do not heap up empty phrases, thinking
they will be heard for their many words. Your Father knows
what you need before you ask Him. Pray then like this. . ."

The voices in the room joined in a resounding recitation of *The
Lord's Prayer*.

Hamud returned to the side of Emory Clark and glanced at his
watch. "It will be soon," he announced. "Watch the doors of
the Great Mosque."

After concentrating on the multiple fifteen-foot high doors
of the mosque for some time, Clark's attention wandered over
the motionless mass of people before him. He guessed the Dira
now held between fifteen thousand and twenty thousand men.
A murmur rose above the din of the crowd, drawing his attention
back to the mosque. The doors had opened, and the harangue
of the loudspeakers abruptly halted. Clark watched as several
thousand more men exited the mosque and added to the crush
of the crowd.

Directly under his balcony, Clark heard harsh voices
shouting orders and two columns of soldiers carrying Uzi
submachine guns formed a path from the Palace of Justice to
the raised platform. When they reached it, a Saudi army officer climbed its steps and paced across the platform several times
before facing the Palace of Justice and saluting.

Through the pathway between the double column of
soldiers, additional armed soldiers passed and took up a perime-

ter around the sides of the wooden platform. Clark heard more orders barked from below and saw the first of a line of six prisoners wearing sparkling white thobes hobble from the Palace of Justice. The first man was flanked by two guards, neither of whom touched their charge.

Clark noted the first captive was missing his right hand and was surprised no bandage covered the stump. His arms were tightly bound to his sides by rope at elbow height. The man shuffled forward slowly in leg irons, as if in a daze.

The American quickly examined the forearms of the other prisoners as they came in sight. Each man was also missing the right hand, and one lacked his left hand as well. Reaching into his jacket, Clark pulled out his glasses and leaned over the balcony to see better. None of the men wore dressings over their mutilations. Having heard the account of Hamud's exposure of the guilty national guardsmen at the Riyadh television building, he also knew the mandatory punishment for Arabs caught stealing was the removal of a hand. Clark was perplexed now, as the wrist-stumps failed to display any redness from their amputation wounds.

Noticing Clark's close scrutiny of the six captives, Hamud leaned closer. "What is it, Mr. Ambassador?"

Clark considered whether to ask his own question. After a lengthy pause, he commented, "They appear to be drugged."

"Yes," nodded Hamud benevolently. "As a kindness, we give them something to calm their nerves."

When the first of the shuffling prisoners reached the platform, Clark saw why each of them had a two-guard escort. The square stilled as the soldiers gripped the arms of the first shackled captive and half-lifted him up the steps.

The six prisoners were led to the line of white towels alongside the lower edge of the platform. Each of them faced the Great Mosque and voluntarily fell to a kneeling position on a towel.

A soldier then stood over each kneeling man and removed the prisoner's gutra, setting it beside the towel. Using both hands to grip the collars of their charges, the soldiers jerked at the cotton shifts until they'd torn the material halfway down the back of each captive. With this act, the massed throng surged forward and began repeating, "ALLAH AKBAR! ALLAH AKBAR!"

The kneeling men lowered themselves even more, coming as near to the position of Muslim prayer as their bound arms would permit. To Clark's amazement, the escorting soldiers stepped back from their prisoners and marched off the platform. The American did not realize the hypnotic effect of the crowd's chanting on the prostrate men. The six captives *of the crowd* tucked their chins to their chests and would not move again.

The next six men to leave the Palace of Justice were tall, broad-shouldered Saudis who also wore the traditional white thobe . . . with three accouterments. Across their left shoulders was a wide black sash, and strapped to each waist was a large caliber pistol. Swinging from their left hips were the long crescent-shaped scabbards of their profession.

The tempo of the crowd's chanting increased slightly as the black-sashed men mounted the platform and unsheathed their great curved blades as they strode toward the kneeling men. The finely-polished swords glistened in the sun as the tall Saudis took up positions to the right of each prisoner. After spreading their legs for balance, the tall men slowly lowered the long blades to a position about eight inches above the necks of their respective victims.

Emory Clark considered whether to step off the balcony rather than witness more of the spectacle. Deciding instead to close his eyes at the last moment, he glanced toward Hamud.

The Crown Prince visibly shook as he imitated the other Saudis on the balcony. As if in a trance, Hamud feverishly repeated the Arab words for, "God is great! God is great!"

Returning his eyes to the wooden platform, it was too late for Clark to avert them.

Flashes of steel slashed downward. He clearly heard the sickening thump of metal on flesh. Four heads rolled away. The other two dangled at grotesque angles. Clark clamped his eyes shut as thick spumes of crimson fluid spurted from the stumps. The solid arcs of red blood hung in the air for a brief moment before the six bodies collapsed in lifeless heaps.

The roar of the satisfied crowd died . . . to be replaced by vigorous applause. The American reopened his eyes and watched as the executioners knelt beside their victims and spat upon their dripping blades before wiping them clean on the sleeves of the executed.

When the executioners withdrew, a doctor came up the steps to complete the medieval drama. He was followed by the guard escorts of the six captives. Each pair of guards carried a crude wooden stretcher. The doctor went through the motions of examining the bodies with a stethoscope.

After wrapping the heads of the captives in their gutras, the soldiers dumped the remains onto the wooden stretchers and handed them down to the waiting ambulance attendants. The white towels upon which the six men had knelt were used to hastily mop up the blood that had not already poured off the platform.

When the stage was again bare of men, Emory Clark stared, transfixed at the blood dripping off its edge. Six more prisoners emerged from the Palace of Justice and began to shuffle to their fate. After examining the healed wrist-stumps of their amputated hands, the American ambassador finally asked his question of Hamud.

"Were those prisoners members of your National Guard?"

The Crown Prince stiffened. He did not reply . . . or even turn his head.

It didn't matter.

The dogmas of the quiet past are inadequate to the stormy present. The occasion is piled high with difficulty. And we must rise with the occasion. As our case is new, so we must think anew, and act anew. We must disenthrall ourselves.

Abraham Lincoln, 1861